Barron's Regents Exams and Answers
English

CAROL CHAITKIN, M.S.
Former Director of American Studies, Lycée Français de New York
Former English Department Head, Great Neck North High School,
Great Neck, New York

BARRON'S

Barron's Educational Series, Inc.

All inquiries should be addressed to:
Barron's Educational Series, Inc.
250 Wireless Boulevard
Hauppauge, New York 11788
www.barronseduc.com

ISBN-13: 978-0-8120-3191-1
ISSN 1069-2924

10%
**POST-CONSUMER
WASTE**
Paper contains a minimum
of 10% post-consumer
waste (PCW). Paper used
in this book was derived
from certified, sustainable
forestlands.

PRINTED IN THE UNITED STATES OF AMERICA
9 8 7 6 5 4 3 2 1

Contents

A Guide to Proofreading for Common Errors   69

Appendices: 73
The New York State Common Core Learning Standards for English Language Arts

Regents ELA (Common Core) Examinations and Answers   85

Introduction

THE NY STATE ELA STANDARDS AND THE READING AND WRITING WE DO IN HIGH SCHOOL ENGLISH COURSES

Most middle school and high school students in NY State should be familiar with the guidelines for curriculum and instruction in their English courses. These guidelines include the following:

- Students will read both informational texts and literary texts in their English courses. Alignment with the common core requires a balancing of the two.
- In all academic subjects, students will be expected to build their knowledge primarily through engaging directly with text.
- Throughout secondary school, students will read texts of increasing complexity and will be expected to develop skills in close reading in all academic subjects.
- Students will be expected to engage in rich and rigorous **evidence-based** conversations/class discussions about text.
- Student writing will emphasize **use of evidence** from sources to express their understanding and to form and develop an argument.
- Students will acquire the academic vocabulary they need to comprehend and respond to grade-level complex texts. This vocabulary is often relevant to more than one subject.

HOW CAN THIS BOOK HELP YOU?

This book provides a detailed guide to the Regents ELA (Common Core) Exam, showing you exactly what each part of the exam looks like. Actual passages and multiple-choice questions, with analysis of the multiple-choice questions and guidelines for composing written responses, are included. The rubrics for the scoring of each section are fully explained. For your review, you will find a chapter on "Reviewing Literary Elements and Techniques" and detailed "Glossaries of Terms" that review structure and language in prose and poetry. There is also "A Guide to Proofreading for Common Errors." In the Appendix, you will find the New York State Common Core Standards for Reading, Writing, and Language. Actual ELA Regents (Common Core) Exams, all with sample essays and answers explained, are also included.

TERMS TO HELP YOU UNDERSTAND THE ENGLISH LANGUAGE ARTS LEARNING STANDARDS AND THE REGENTS ELA (COMMON CORE) EXAM

These are the learning standards in ELA and math, also known as **CCSS** (Common Core State Standards) developed and adopted by a consortium of over 40 states. New York State first adopted the CCLS in 2010 and will implement a revised set of standards in 2017. These revisions will not represent significant changes in the expectations for grades 11/12 expressed in the guidelines above.*

CCR—The phrase "**college and career ready**" is widely used in discussion of the curriculum and assessments. This refers to the fundamental principle of the Common Core Standards: to reflect the knowledge and skills that all students need for success in college and careers.

ELA/Literacy—English Language Arts (ELA) refers to skills in reading, writing, speaking, and listening. Courses and exams once identified as "English" may also be identified as ELA. Literacy refers to the ability to read and write and to use language proficiently. The term also identifies the quality of being knowledgeable in a particular subject or field. For example, we often refer to "digital" or "computer literacy."

Assessment—You may hear teachers and other educators using the term **assessment** instead of test or examination. An **assessment** is more than a simple test (in vocabulary, say) because it seeks to measure a number of skills at one time. Although we continue to refer to the English Regents as an exam or a test, its goal is to be a valid **assessment** of a broad range of the reading, thinking, language, and writing skills outlined in the Standards.

Text—Broadly, the term text refers to any written material. The Common Core standards uses the term to refer to the great variety of material

---

*See the NY State Education Department's website *www.engageNY.org* for details on all the changes in Standards and Regents Examinations.

students are expected to be able to read, understand, analyze, and write about. Texts may include **literary** works of fiction, drama, and poetry; and **informational**, or nonfiction, including essays, memoirs, speeches, and scientific and historical documents. The Common Core also emphasizes the use of **authentic texts**; that is, students will read actual historical documents or scientific essays rather than articles about them.

Close Reading—Skill in close, analytic reading is fundamental to the CCLS and to the ELA Regents exam. The Common Core curriculum focuses student attention on the text itself in order to understand not only what the text says and means, but also how that meaning is constructed and revealed. Close reading enables students to understand central ideas and key supporting details. It also enables students to reflect on the meanings of individual words and sentences, the order in which sentences unfold, and the development of ideas over the course of the text, which ultimately leads students to arrive at an understanding of the text as a whole.

Argument—What is an argument? In academic writing, an argument is usually a central idea, often called a **claim** or **thesis statement**, which is backed up with evidence that supports the idea. Much of the writing high school students do in their English courses constitutes essays of argument, in contrast to personal essays, descriptive pieces, or works of imagination.

Source-Based/Evidence-Based—The ability to compose sound arguments using relevant and specific evidence from a given text is central to the expectations of the Common Core Standards.

Writing Strategy—This is the general term for a literary element, literary technique, or rhetorical device. Examples include: characterization, conflict, denotation/connotation, metaphor, simile, irony, language use, point-of-view, setting, structure, symbolism, theme, tone, etc. (See the Glossaries in this book for definitions and examples of the most widely used terms.)

THE REGENTS ELA (COMMON CORE) EXAM— AN OVERVIEW

This 3-hour examination requires students to read, analyze, and write about both literary and informational texts.

PART 1—READING COMPREHENSION

This part of the exam requires close reading of three texts and will contain a literature passage (prose), a poem, and an informational text, followed by a total of 24 multiple-choice questions.

PART 2—WRITING FROM SOURCES: ARGUMENT

This part of the exam includes close reading of four or five informational texts. Students will compose an essay of argument with a claim based on the sources.

PART 3—TEXT ANALYSIS

Students will do a close reading of one informational or literature text and write a two to three paragraph response that identifies a central idea in the text and analyzes how the author's use of one writing strategy develops that central idea.

Strategy and Review for Part 1 of the Regents ELA (Common Core) Exam

CHAPTER 1
Reading Comprehension

WHAT DOES THIS PART OF THE EXAM REQUIRE?

This part of the exam requires close reading of three texts and will contain at least one prose literature passage, usually from a work of fiction; a poem; and one informational text, which may include a personal narrative, a speech, an account of historical significance, or a discussion of a scientific concept. The prose passages and the poems are sometimes works in translation. These passages are followed by a total of 24 multiple-choice questions. The questions require analysis of different aspects of a text, including: elements of character and plot development, comprehension of a central idea and how it is supported, elements of style, and understanding vocabulary in context. Most of the questions include more than one plausible answer; choosing the correct answer often requires comprehension of the text as a whole.

WHAT DOES THIS PART OF THE EXAM LOOK LIKE?

Sample Passage A and Multiple-Choice Questions

Passage A

It was eleven o'clock that night when Mr. Pontellier returned from Klein's hotel. He was in an excellent humor, in high spirits, and very talkative. His entrance awoke his wife, who was in bed and fast asleep when he

came in. He talked to her while he undressed, telling her anecdotes and bits
(5) of news and gossip that he had gathered during the day. From his trousers
pockets he took a fistful of crumpled bank notes and a good deal of silver
coin, which he piled on the bureau indiscriminately with keys, knife, handkerchief, and whatever else happened to be in his pockets. She was overcome
with sleep, and answered him with little half utterances.

(10)   He thought it very discouraging that his wife, who was the sole object of
his existence, evinced[1] so little interest in things which concerned him, and
valued so little his conversation.

          Mr. Pontellier had forgotten the bonbons and peanuts for the boys. Not-
withstanding he loved them very much, and went into the adjoining room
(15) where they slept to take a look at them and make sure that they were resting
comfortably. The result of his investigation was far from satisfactory. He
turned and shifted the youngsters about in bed. One of them began to kick
and talk about a basket full of crabs.

          Mr. Pontellier returned to his wife with information that Raoul had a
(20) high fever and needed looking after. Then he lit a cigar and went and sat near
the open door to smoke it.

          Mrs. Pontellier was quite sure Raoul had no fever. He had gone to bed
perfectly well, she said, and nothing had ailed him all day. Mr. Pontellier
was too well acquainted with fever symptoms to be mistaken. He assured her
(25) the child was consuming[2] at that moment in the next room.

          He reproached his wife with her inattention, her habitual neglect of the
children. If it was not a mother's place to look after children, whose on earth
was it? He himself had his hands full with his brokerage business. He could
not be in two places at once; making a living for his family on the street, and
(30) staying at home to see that no harm befell them. He talked in a monotonous,
insistent way.

          Mrs. Pontellier sprang out of bed and went into the next room. She
soon came back and sat on the edge of the bed, leaning her head down on
the pillow. She said nothing, and refused to answer her husband when he
(35) questioned her. When his cigar was smoked out he went to bed, and in half
a minute he was fast asleep.

          Mrs. Pontellier was by that time thoroughly awake. She began to cry
a little, and wiped her eyes on the sleeve of her peignoir.[3] Blowing out
the candle, which her husband had left burning, she slipped her bare feet

---

[1]evinced—clearly showed   [2]consuming—wasting away   [3]peignoir—dressing gown

(40) into a pair of satin mules at the foot of the bed and went out on the porch, where she sat down in the wicker chair and began to rock gently to and fro.

It was then past midnight. The cottages were all dark. A single faint light gleamed out from the hallway of the house. There was no sound abroad except the hooting of an old owl in the top of a water oak, and the everlast-
(45) ing voice of the sea, that was not uplifted at that soft hour. It broke like a mournful lullaby upon the night.

The tears came so fast to Mrs. Pontellier's eyes that the damp sleeve of her peignoir no longer served to dry them. She was holding the back of her chair with one hand; her loose sleeve had slipped almost to the shoulder of
(50) her uplifted arm. Turning, she thrust her face, steaming and wet, into the bend of her arm, and she went on crying there, not caring any longer to dry her face, her eyes, her arms. She could not have told why she was crying. Such experiences as the foregoing were not uncommon in her married life. They seemed never before to have weighed much against the abundance of
(55) her husband's kindness and a uniform devotion which had come to be tacit[4] and self-understood.

An indescribable oppression, which seemed to generate in some unfamil-iar part of her consciousness, filled her whole being with a vague anguish. It was like a shadow, like a mist passing across her soul's summer day. It
(60) was strange and unfamiliar; it was a mood. She did not sit there inwardly upbraiding[5] her husband, lamenting at Fate, which had directed her foot-steps to the path which they had taken. She was just having a good cry all to herself. The mosquitoes made merry over her, biting her firm, round arms and nipping at her bare insteps.

(65) The little stinging, buzzing imps succeeded in dispelling a mood which might have held her there in the darkness half a night longer.

The following morning Mr. Pontellier was up in good time to take the rockaway which was to convey him to the steamer at the wharf. He was returning to the city to his business, and they would not see him again at
(70) the Island till the coming Saturday. He had regained his composure, which seemed to have been somewhat impaired the night before. He was eager to be gone, as he looked forward to a lively week in Carondelet Street.

Mr. Pontellier gave his wife half of the money which he had brought away from Klein's hotel the evening before. She liked money as well as most
(75) women, and accepted it with no little satisfaction. . . .

---

[4]tacit—not actually stated   [5]upbraiding—severely scolding

A few days later a box arrived for Mrs. Pontellier from New Orleans. It was from her husband. It was filled with friandises[6], with luscious and tooth-some[7] bits—the finest of fruits, pates, a rare bottle or two, delicious syrups, and bonbons in abundance.

(80)   Mrs. Pontellier was always very generous with the contents of such a box; she was quite used to receiving them when away from home. The pates and fruit were brought to the dining-room; the bonbons were passed around. And the ladies, selecting with dainty and discriminating fingers and a little greedily, all declared that Mr. Pontellier was the best husband

(85)   in the world. Mrs. Pontellier was forced to admit that she knew of none better.

—Kate Chopin

excerpted from *The Awakening*, 1899

---

[6]friandises—dainty cakes   [7]toothsome—delicious

Multiple-Choice Questions

1 The primary purpose of the first paragraph is to

(1) create a metaphor
(2) foreshadow an event
(3) establish a contrast
(4) present a flashback   1 _____

2 Placed in the context of the rest of the text, Mr. and Mrs. Pontellier's disagreement about Raoul's fever (lines 19–31) reflects

(1) Mrs. Pontellier's resentment of her husband's night out
(2) Mr. Pontellier's belief in his authority over his wife
(3) Mrs. Pontellier's need for her husband's approval
(4) Mr. Pontellier's concern for his wife's well-being   2 _____

3 In lines 26–31, the author presents Mr. Pontellier as a man who feels

  (1) defeated
  (2) anxious
  (3) distracted
  (4) arrogant   3 _____

4 The author's choice of language in lines 38–46 serves to emphasize Mrs. Pontellier's sense of

  (1) isolation
  (2) boredom
  (3) disbelief
  (4) inferiority   4 _____

5 One major effect of the simile used in lines 45–46 is to emphasize Mrs. Pontellier's

  (1) anger
  (2) distress
  (3) defiance
  (4) exhaustion   5 _____

6 Lines 52–56 demonstrate Mrs. Pontellier's desire to

  (1) protect her reputation
  (2) question her situation
  (3) abandon her dreams
  (4) disguise her sorrow   6 _____

7 Lines 73–79 contradict a central idea in the text by describing Mr. Pontellier's

  (1) generosity
  (2) honesty
  (3) sympathy
  (4) humility   7 _____

8 Based on events in the text, which quotation best reveals the irony of the statement that Mr. Pontellier's wife "was the sole object of his existence" (lines 10–11)?

(1) "From his trousers pockets he took a fistful of crumpled bank notes" (lines 5–6)

(2) "Then he lit a cigar and went and sat near the open door to smoke it" (lines 20–21)

(3) "He assured her the child was consuming at that moment in the next room" (lines 24–25)

(4) "He was eager to be gone, as he looked forward to a lively week in Carondelet Street" (lines 71–72)   8 ____

Answers

(1) **3**   (2) **2**   (3) **4**   (4) **1**   (5) **2**   (6) **2**   (7) **1**   (8) **4**

Looking at the Questions

1. *The primary purpose of the first paragraph...*

   This question asks you to analyze the introduction of characters, their interaction and its significance to the development of plot and theme.

2. *Placed in the context, lines 19–31 reflect...*

   This question asks you to understand how the interaction of the two characters develops over the course of the text.

3. *The author presents Mr. Pontellier as a man...*

   This question requires further analysis of how characters are introduced and developed.

4. *The author's choice of language... serves to emphasize*

   Here you must determine the meaning of words and phrases in context and the role of word choice in the passage.

5. *One major effect of the simile...*

   Here you should sense in the metaphor the feelings of both calm and sorrow in the character.

6. *Lines 52–56 demonstrate…*

   This question asks for analysis of what the text says explicitly as well as what can be inferred about the character's feelings.

7. *Lines 73–79 contradict…*

   Here you are asked to determine a central idea and understand its development over the course of the text.

8. *Which quotation best reveals the irony…*

   Here you are expected to recognize the incongruity between what the character says he feels and what he is actually looking forward to.

Sample Passage B
Poem

View with a Grain of Sand

We call it a grain of sand
but it calls itself neither grain nor sand.
It does just fine without a name,
whether general, particular,
(5)   permanent, passing,
incorrect or apt.

Our glance, our touch mean nothing to it.
It doesn't feel itself seen and touched.
And that it fell on the windowsill
(10)   is only our experience, not its.
For it it's no different than falling on anything else
with no assurance that it's finished falling
or that it's falling still.

The window has a wonderful view of a lake
(15)   but the view doesn't view itself.
It exists in this world
colorless, shapeless,
soundless, odorless, and painless.

The lake's floor exists floorlessly
(20)   and its shore exists shorelessly.
Its water feels itself neither wet nor dry
and its waves to themselves are neither singular nor plural.
They splash deaf to their own noise
on pebbles neither large nor small.

(25)   And all this beneath a sky by nature skyless
in which the sun sets without setting at all
and hides without hiding behind an unminding cloud.
The wind ruffles it, its only reason being
that it blows.

(30)   A second passes.
A second second.
A third.
But they're three seconds only for us.

Time has passed like a courier with urgent news.
(35)   But that's just our simile.
The character's invented, his haste is make-believe,
his news inhuman.

—Wislawa Szymborska from Polish Poetry of the
Last Two Decades of Communist Rule,
translated by Stanislaw Barańczak and Clare Cavanagh
Northwestern University Press, 1991

Multiple-Choice Questions

1 The statement "Our glance, our touch mean nothing to it" (line 7) helps to establish the concept of

    (1) human resentment of the natural order
    (2) nature's superiority
    (3) human control over the environment
    (4) nature's indifference   1 ____

2 The purpose of lines 14 through 18 is to present

    (1) a contrast with human reliance on the senses
    (2) a focus on the complexity of natural events
    (3) an emphasis on human need for physical beauty
    (4) an appreciation for the role of nature in everyday life   2 ____

3 Lines 30 through 33 contribute to the poem's meaning by

    (1) questioning the finality of death
    (2) commenting on human perception
    (3) revealing the power of anticipation
    (4) describing an unusual phenomenon   3 ____

4 The inclusion of the figurative language in the final stanza serves to

    (1) modify an argument
    (2) stress a value
    (3) reinforce a central idea
    (4) resolve a conflict   4 ____

5 The poem is developed primarily through the use of

    (1) examples
    (2) exaggerations
    (3) cause and effect
    (4) question and answer   5 ____

Answers

(1) **4**   (2) **1**   (3) **2**   (4) **3**   (5) **1**

Looking at the Questions

1. *The statement... helps to establish the concept of*

   Reading the entire poem before answering the question helps you to recognize the central theme of the poem in this statement.

2. *The purpose of lines 14 through 18 is to present...*

   Here you are expected to see how specific details and imagery contribute to the development of the central theme.

3. *Lines 30 through 33 contribute to the poem's meaning by...*

   This question asks you to identify the tone of the passage and to hear the last line of the stanza as a comment on how humans perceive time.

4. *The inclusion of figurative language in the final stanza serves to...*

   Here you are expected to see how figurative language contributes to the meaning of a poem. In this case, the poet concludes with images of human perception of time as only a simile.

5. *The poem is developed primarily through the use of...*

   This question asks you to recognize in the sequence of stanzas the overall structure of the poem as a series of examples.

Sample Passage C
Informational Text

In this excerpt, Andrew Carnegie presents his philosophy regarding how the excess wealth of the rich should be used. Carnegie himself had risen from being an impoverished immigrant to one of the most successful industrialists of the 19th century.

The growing disposition to tax more and more heavily large estates left at death is a cheering indication of the growth of a salutary[1] change in public opinion. The State of Pennsylvania now takes—subject to some exceptions—one-tenth of the property left by its citizens. The budget
(5) presented inthe British Parliament the other day proposes to increase the death-duties; and, most significant of all, the new tax is to be a graduated one. Of all forms of taxation, this seems the wisest. Men who continue hoarding great sums all their lives, the proper use of which for public ends would work goodto the community, should be made to feel that the
(10) community, in the form ofthe state, cannot thus be deprived of its proper share. By taxing estates heavily at death the state marks its condemnation of the selfish millionaire's unworthy life. . . .

This policy would work powerfully to induce the rich man to attend to the administration of wealth during his life, which is the end that society
(15) should always have in view, as being that by far most fruitful for the people. Nor need it be feared that this policy would sap the root of enterprise and render men less anxious to accumulate, for to the class whose ambition it is to leave great fortunes and be talked about after their death, it will attract even more attention, and, indeed, be a somewhat nobler ambition to have
(20) enormous sums paid over to the state from their fortunes.

There remains, then, only one mode of using great fortunes; but in this we have the true antidote for the temporary unequal distribution of wealth, the reconciliation of the rich and the poor—a reign of harmony—another ideal, differing, indeed, from that of the Communist in requiring only the
(25) further evolution of existing conditions, not the total overthrow of our civilization. It is founded upon the present most intense individualism, and the race is prepared to put it in practice by degrees whenever it pleases. Under its sway we shall have an ideal state, in which the surplus wealth of the few will

---

[1]salutary—beneficial

(30) become, in the best sense, the property of the many, because administered for the common good, and this wealth, passing through the hands of the few, can be made a much more potent force for the elevation of our race than if it had been distributed in small sums to the people themselves. Even the poorest can be made to see this, and to agree that great sums gathered by some of their fellow-citizens and spent for public purposes, from which the masses reap the

(35) principal benefit, are more valuable to them than if scattered among them through the course of many years in trifling amounts. . . .

Poor and restricted are our opportunities in this life; narrow our horizon; our best work most imperfect; but rich men should be thankful for one inestimable boon.[2] They have it in their power during their lives to busy

(40) themselves in organizing benefactions from which the masses of their fellows will derive lasting advantage, and thus dignify their own lives. The highest life is probably to be reached, not by such imitation of the life of Christ as Count Tolstoi gives us, but, while animated by Christ's spirit, by recognizing the changed conditions of this age, and adopting modes of expressing

(45) this spirit suitable to the changed conditions under which we live; still laboring for the good of our fellows, which was the essence of his life and teaching, but laboring in a different manner.

This, then, is held to be the duty of the man of Wealth: First, to set an example of modest, unostentatious[3] living, shunning display or extrava-

(50) gance; to provide moderately for the legitimate wants of those dependent upon him; and after doing so to consider all surplus revenues which come to him simply as trust funds, which he is called upon to administer, and strictly bound as a matter of duty to administer in the manner which, in his judgment, is best calculated to produce the most beneficial results for the com-

(55) munity—the man of wealth thus becoming the mere agent and trustee for his poorer brethren, bringing to their service his superior wisdom, experience and ability to administer, doing for them better than they would or could do for themselves. . . .

Thus is the problem of Rich and Poor to be solved. The laws of accu-

(60) mulation will be left free; the laws of distribution free. Individualism will continue, but the millionaire will be but a trustee for the poor; intrusted for a season with a great part of the increased wealth of the community, but administering it for the community far better than it could or would have done for itself. The best minds will thus have reached a stage in the develop-

---

[2]boon—benefit   [3]unostentatious—not showy

(65)   ment of the race in which it is clearly seen that there is no mode of disposing
of surplus wealth creditable to thoughtful and earnest men into whose hands
it flows save by using it year by year for the general good. This day already
dawns. But a little while, and although, without incurring the pity of their
fellows, men may die sharers in great business enterprises from which their
(70)   capital cannot be or has not been withdrawn, and is left chiefly at death for
public uses, yet the man who dies leaving behind many millions of available
wealth, which was his to administer during life, will pass away "unwept,
unhonored, and unsung," no matter to what uses he leaves the dross[4] which
he cannot take with him. Of such as these the public verdict will then be:
(75)   "The man who dies thus rich dies disgraced."

Such, in my opinion, is the true Gospel concerning Wealth, obedience to
which is destined some day to solve the problem of the Rich and the Poor,
and to bring "Peace on earth, among men Good-Will."

—Andrew Carnegie
excerpted from "Wealth," 1889

---
[4]dross—waste

Note on the text: This text represents the philosophy of an important
American industrialist and philanthropist. One of the Common Core Standards
for informational text includes the following: "[Students should be able to]
analyze seventeenth-, eighteenth-, and nineteenth-century foundational U.S.
documents of historical and literary significance…for their themes, purposes,
and rhetorical features (RI.9)" See page 75 of the Appendix.

Multiple-Choice Questions

1 The first paragraph (lines 1–12) serves the author's
purpose by

  (1) providing examples of alternative tax policies
  (2) contrasting the current taxation system with his proposal
  (3) comparing equal taxation with graduated taxation
  (4) distinguishing estate taxes from income taxes   1 _____

2 The expression "sap the root of enterprise" (line 16)
refers to the

  (1) decline in consumer confidence
  (2) reduction in government funding
  (3) discouragement of private business
  (4) harm to international trade   2 _____

3 What evidence from the text best clarifies the author's
claim in lines 32–36 ("Even the poorest … amounts")?

  (1) lines 37–39 ("Poor and restricted … inestimable boon")
  (2) lines 48–50 ("This, then, … or extravagance")
  (3) lines 59–60 ("The laws … distribution free")
  (4) lines 60–64 ("Individualism … for itself")   3 _____

4 The author's tone in lines 48–58 can best be described as

  (1) confident
  (2) indifferent
  (3) humble
  (4) sarcastic   4 _____

5 A central idea in the text advocates that the wealthy should

  (1) be rewarded for their generosity to the public
  (2) contribute to the public during their lifetime
  (3) entrust their estates to charitable institutions
  (4) be focused on increasing their institutional worth   5 _____

6 Which statement best reflects a central argument used by the author?

  (1) There is no way to insure fair distribution of earnings.
  (2) People should only be paid what they actually earn.
  (3) Sharing wealth among all would limit large gifts from benefactors.
  (4) Equaling wealth among all would restrict the national tax base.   6 ____

Answers

(1) **1**   (2) **3**   (3) **4**   (4) **1**   (5) **2**   (6) **3**

Looking at the Questions

1. *The first paragraph (lines 1–12) serves the author's purpose by…*

  This question asks you to analyze how an author's ideas are developed in a particular paragraph and to recognize how an author effectively structures an argument.

2. *The expression "sap the root of enterprise" (line 16) refers to the…*

  Here you must recognize the use of figurative language and how it expresses a central claim of the argument.

3. *What evidence from the text best clarifies the author's claim in lines 32–36…?*

  This question requires analysis of a complex set of ideas and how they develop over the course of the text.

4. *The author's tone in lines 48–58 can best be described as…*

  Here you must recognize tone as it is determined in the connotation of words and phrases.

5. *A central idea in the text advocates that the wealthy should…*

  Determining the central idea of a text is a fundamental skill in the Common Core Standards.

6. *Which statement best reflects a central argument used by the author?*

  This question complements the one above because it asks you to identify the author's central argument of the passage as it is developed over the course of the text.

You can see that the questions in this part of the exam are primarily about:

> **identifying** themes and central ideas and **analyzing** their development
>
> **recognizing** the significance of tone and point of view
>
> **describing** the author's use of structure, rhetorical and literary elements
>
> **determining** the meaning of words and phrases as they are used in the text
>
> **understanding** figurative language, connotation, and nuances in word meanings

STRATEGIES AND REVIEW

- Remember, close reading means reading to understand <u>what</u> the text says and means as well as to recognize <u>how</u> the meaning is constructed and revealed.
- Be sure to first read through to the end of the passage before trying to answer any of the questions.
- Make your choice of the <u>best</u> answer based on the meaning of the entire passage; there may be more than one plausible choice.
- Recognize the key terms commonly used in the multiple-choice questions.
- Review the Glossaries to support your knowledge and use of literary terms and writing strategies.
- Be confident that the reading, discussion, and writing in your high school courses have prepared you for the exam.
- Review the actual Regents ELA/Common Core Exams and the Answers Explained.
- Review the tasks based on a poem in the Regents ELA/Common Core exams in the Answers Explained.

Strategy and Review for Part 2 of the Regents ELA (Common Core) Exam

CHAPTER 2
Argument

WHAT DOES THIS PART OF THE EXAM REQUIRE?

First, you must read and comprehend four informational texts. Depending on the topic, these may be examples of literary non-fiction, journalism, scientific publications meant for the general reader, or historical documents. There are no multiple-choice questions in this part of the exam. As in Part 1 of the exam, you must:

- Determine the central ideas of texts, including how ideas within and across texts interact and build on one another.
- Analyze a complex set of ideas and events.
- Determine the meanings of words and phrases as they are used in texts, including figurative, connotative, and technical meanings.

Then, you must take a position on the question and compose an evidence-based argument supported by your analysis of the texts, using valid reasoning and relevant and sufficient evidence from at least three of the texts. An effective essay of argument must clearly establish a claim that can be sufficiently supported with reliable evidence. The organization must be clear and coherent, and the writing is expected to demonstrate command of standard written English. These are reading, research, thinking, and writing skills that high school students are expected to demonstrate across the curriculum.

WHAT DOES THIS PART OF THE EXAM LOOK LIKE?

The topic is often based on a controversial issue of recent or current interest. Here is an example from the January 2016 Regents ELA exam.

SAMPLE TASK – EVIDENCE-BASED WRITING

Directions: Closely read each of the *four* texts provided on pages 23 through 31 and write a source-based argument on the topic below. You may use the margins to take notes as you read and scrap paper to plan your response.

> **Topic:** Should food be genetically modified?

> **Your Task:** Carefully read each of the *four* texts provided. Then, using evidence from at least *three* of the texts, write a well-developed argument regarding the genetic modification of food. Clearly establish your claim, distinguish your claim from alternate or opposing claims, and use specific, relevant, and sufficient evidence from at least *three* of the texts to develop your argument. Do *not* simply summarize each text.

Guidelines:

Be sure to:

- Establish your claim regarding the genetic modification of food.
- Distinguish your claim from alternate or opposing claims.
- Use specific, relevant, and sufficient evidence from at least three of the texts to develop your argument.
- Identify each source that you reference by text number and line number(s) or graphic (for example: Text 1, line 4 or Text 2, graphic).
- Organize your ideas in a cohesive and coherent manner.
- Maintain a formal style of writing.
- Follow the conventions of standard written English.

Texts:

Text 1—GMOs 101

Text 2—GMO Reality Check

Text 3—GMO Foods: Key Points in the Genetically Modified Debate

Text 4—The Truth about Genetically Modified Food

Text 1

GMOs 101

The six questions on every shopper's mind about the new biotech foods. ...

1 What are GMOs [Genetically Modified Organism], and what are they used for?

A GMO is created by injecting genetic material from plants, animals, or bacteria into a crop in hopes of creating a new and beneficial trait. For example, one of the most popular genetically modified (GM) crops is a corn plant that's capable of producing its own pesticide, called Bt, which is also
(5) used in spray form by some organic farmers. The idea is to make the plant resistant to insect damage and to limit the amount of harmful pesticides farmers have to spray. Other GM plants, such as Roundup Ready corn, were created to survive the spraying of the herbicide Roundup, which kills weeds and would normally kill the plant, too, says Stephen H. Howell, Ph.D.,
(10) director of the Plant Sciences Institute at Iowa State University.

Researchers are also using the technology experimentally as a way to nutritionally enhance fruits and vegetables.

Some GMO supporters say that both applications are necessary to help feed a growing world population, especially in poor countries where drought
(15) and famine are common. But there is very little agreement on whether bio-technology offers a uniform way to address world hunger. "We have plenty of food for the world right now. It's not the deficiency of technology that's a problem for developing countries," says Jane Rissler, Ph.D., a senior staff scientist with the Union of Concerned Scientists, a nonprofit watchdog
(20) group that partners with 80,000 researchers. The international hunger problem, she says, stems from "poverty, corruption, and poor distribution."

2 What kinds of foods contain GMOs?

About 80 percent of the food on grocery-store shelves already contains at least some ingredients made from altered genes. This means that almost any processed food, from salad dressing to snack crackers, could contain
(25) GMOs, unless it has been certified organic (federal regulations explicitly restrict food manufacturers from using the organic seal on products made with GMOs). That's because corn, soy, and canola are the top three GM food

crops in the United States, so anything that is produced with corn syrup, high-fructose corn syrup, or soybean or corn oil might include GMOs.

(30)   Very little fresh produce on the market, though, is genetically engineered, with the exceptions of most papaya, some squash, and a few strains of sweet corn. Meanwhile, we're not the only ones consuming GMOs—animals do, too. GM corn and soybeans are often used in livestock feed, though there's no evidence that GMOs show up in your steak or chops.

3 Should I be concerned about the safety of GM foods?

(35)   Federal agencies like the U.S. Food and Drug Administration (FDA) and the U.S. Department of Agriculture (USDA) say that they are safe, and there have been no documented cases of illness due to consumption of GMOs. The American Medical Association agrees at this point and has encouraged ongoing research in the field. ...

4 What do GM crops mean for the environment?

(40)   "I think a lot of scientists agree that there are no known environmental problems with the crops that are out there now," says Allison Snow, Ph.D., who studies environmental risk and genetically modified crops as a professor of ecology at Ohio State University. But organic farmers are becoming increasingly concerned about maintaining the integrity of their crops. For

(45) example, if Bt corn is planted too close to a neighboring organic-corn crop, crosspollination could occur and contaminate the latter.

         Scientists on both sides of the debate also widely agree that insects will eventually become resistant to the Bt crops, Snow says. "It could happen any year now. Then we would be back where we started, and we would have lost

(50) a valuable tool for managing insects," Snow says. ...

5 Is it possible to live completely GMO-free?

         Probably not. A study commissioned by the Union of Concerned Scientists and released in February already suggests that seeds that are supposedly non-GMO may be unintentionally tainted. Genetically engineered DNA was found in at least half of the small sample of tested corn and soy-

(55) bean seeds, and about 83 percent of the canola seeds. Even if you buy only certified-organic products, you probably can't avoid GMOs completely. That's because it is also possible for organic food crops to become inadvertently contaminated. ...

6 What will we see next from the biotech-food market?

Here are some GM foods that might end up on store shelves:

(60)
- The FDA and USDA are currently reviewing safety data on a variety of genetically engineered wheat that would tolerate the herbicide Roundup.
- Researchers are also working on wheat varieties that would resist drought, be less allergenic to those with gluten intolerance, and be
(65)   more nutritious.

Consumers may also start seeing major nutritional benefits in the future:

- Scientists at the University of California, Riverside, announced last year [2003] that they genetically engineered a corn plant to produce up to four times the normal amount of vitamin C by inserting a gene
(70)   from wheat plants. The researchers have filed a patent application and are soliciting companies that might be interested in commercializing the product. ...
- Other biotech foods that are currently in development include a vitamin A–enhanced rice and a tomato with increased amounts of the
(75)   cancer-fighting antioxidant lycopene.
- Monsanto Co., which is the largest producer of GM seeds, is continuing to tinker with soybeans in hopes of developing a variety that could produce an oil containing few or no saturated and trans fats.

—Alisa Blackwood excerpted and adapted from
"GMOs 101" *Health*, May 2004

Text 2

GMO Reality Check

... GMO Basics

So what are GMOs? To put it simply, they're plants and seeds created in laboratories. Genetic engineers insert genes from bacteria, viruses, animals, or humans into the DNA of a food crop or animal to create an organism that would never occur in nature. Biotech companies do this for two main
(5) reasons: to make crops that are tolerant to herbicides such as RoundUp that kill other plants, and to make crops that produce their own insecticides.

The FDA's own scientists actually warned that these never-before-seen foods could create new toxins and new allergens and needed to be more

thoroughly tested, but their concerns were largely ignored. Instead, the US
(10) government took the official position that GM foods were "substantially
equivalent" to conventional foods and didn't require safety testing or
labeling—in sharp contrast to 40 other countries that require such foods
be clearly labeled. Commercial planting of genetically modified seeds in
the United States began in 1996, and soon after, food products containing
(15) GMOs began appearing on store shelves, mostly without our knowledge.

By 2011, 94 percent of all soybeans and 88 percent of all corn grown in
the United States was genetically modified. Soy and corn, along with other
common GM foods (including canola oil. [sic] cottonseed oil, and sugar from
sugar beets), are used as ingredients in countless other products, so many
(20) Americans—including health food shoppers—likely have been eating GM
foods without realizing it.

No Benefits, Just Risks

What we didn't know about what we were eating may already be harm-
ing us. Based on animal research with GM foods, the American Academy of
Environmental Medicine (AAEM) says that there are serious health risks
(25) associated with eating GM foods, including infertility, immune system problems, accelerated aging, disruption of insulin and cholesterol regulation,
gastrointestinal issues, and changes in organs. In 2009, the AAEM urged
doctors to prescribe non-GMO diets for all Americans, saying that doctors
are probably seeing negative health effects in their patients right now with-
(30) out realizing that GM foods are major contributing factors.

Genetically modified crops pose risks to the environment, too, including
the serious threat of GM seeds spreading to and contaminating both organic
and conventional crop fields. Plus, the biotech industry claims that genetic
engineering reduces the use of pesticides, but research shows otherwise.
(35) According to a 2009 report by the Organic Center, overall pesticide use
dramatically increased—about 318 million pounds—in the first thirteen
years after GM crops were introduced.

Herbicides sprayed in high amounts on GM herbicide-resistant crops
have led to the development and spread of so-called "superweeds"—weeds
(40) that are able to adapt to and withstand typical herbicides. And the biotech
companies' proposed solution to this problem? Create new GM crops that
are resistant to ever more toxic chemicals, including 2, 4-D—a major com-

ponent of Agent Orange.[1] It's a "crazy" idea because weeds would eventually adapt to that herbicide and any others, says Andrew Kimbrell, executive
(45) director of the Center for Food Safety and author of *Your Right to Know: Genetic Engineering and the Secret Changes in Your Food.*

The most important thing to know about GM foods is that they benefit only the chemical companies that produce them, says Kimbrell. "[The biotech companies] have yet to produce anything that benefits the consumer.
(50) There's no better taste, no better nutrition, no lower price. That's the dirty little secret that's hardly ever reported. That's why those companies don't want GM foods labeled. They don't want the consumer to be able to have the choice to say, 'I want the same price, less risky version.'"...

—Melissa Diane Smith excerpted from "GMO Reality Check"
Better Nutrition, August 2012

---

[1]Agent Orange—chemical used as part of herbicidal warfare programs

Text 3
GMO Foods: Key Points in
the Genetically Modified Debate

... Safe or Unsafe?

Most studies show genetically modified foods are safe for human consumption, though it is widely acknowledged that the long-term health effects are unknown. The Food and Drug Administration generally recognized these foods as safe, and the World Health Organization has said no ill
(5) health effects have resulted on the international market.

Opponents on both sides of the Atlantic say there has been inadequate testing and regulation. They worry that people who eat genetically modified foods may be more prone to allergies or diseases resistant to antibiotics. But they have been hard pressed to show scientific studies to back up those fears.
(10) GM foods have been a mainstay in the U.S. for more than a decade. Most of the crops are used for animal feed or in common processed foods such as cookies, cereal, potato chips and salad dressing.

Europe largely bans genetically engineered foods and has strict requirements on labeling them. They do allow the import of a number of GM crops

(15)   such as soy, mostly for animal feed, and individual European countries have
opted to plant these types of crops. Genetically engineered corn is grown in
Spain, though it amounts to only a fraction of European farmland. ...

Can GM Food Help Combat World Hunger?

By 2050, the world's population is projected to rise to 9 billion from just
over 7 billion currently. Proponents of genetically modified foods say they
(20)   are safe and can boost harvests even in bad conditions by protecting against
pests, weeds and drought. This, they argue, will be essential to meeting the
needs of a booming population in decades to come and avoiding starvation.

However Doug Gurian-Sherman, senior scientist for the food and environment program at the Union of Concerned Scientists, an advocacy group,
(25)   said genetic engineering for insect resistance has provided only a modest
increase in yields since the 1990s and drought-resistant strains have only
modestly reduced losses from drought.

Moreover, he said conventional crossbreeding or cross-pollinating of
different varieties for desirable traits, along with improved farming, are get-
(30)   ting better results boosting yields at a lower cost. In fact, much of the food
Americans eat has been genetically modified by those conventional methods
over thousands of years, before genetic engineering came into practice. ...

Andrea Roberto Sonnino, chief of research at the U.N. food agency, said
total food production at present is enough to feed the entire global popula-
(35)   tion. The problem is uneven distribution, leaving 870 million suffering from
hunger. He said world food production will need to increase by 60 percent to
meet the demands of 9 billion by 2050. This must be achieved by increasing
yields, he added, because there is little room to expand cultivated land used
for agriculture.

(40)   Genetically modified foods, in some instances, can help if the individual
product has been assessed as safe, he said. "It's an opportunity that we cannot just miss."

To Label or Not to Label?

Europe requires all GM food to be labeled unless GM ingredients amount
to 0.9 percent or less of the total. The U.S. does not require labels on the
(45)   view that genetically modified food is not materially different than non-
modified food. Opponents of labeling say it would scare consumers away

from safe foods, giving the appearance that there is something wrong with them.

(50) U.S. activists insist consumers should have the right to choose whether to eat genetically modified foods and that labeling would offer them that choice, whether the foods are safe or not. They are pushing for labeling at the state and federal level. California voters last year rejected a ballot initiative that would have required GM food labeling. The legislatures of Connecticut and Maine have passed laws to label genetically modified foods, and more

(55) than 20 other states are contemplating labeling. ...

—Marjorie Olster excerpted from "GMO Foods:
Key Points in the Genetically Modified Debate"
http://www.huffingtonpost.com, August 2, 2013

Text 4
The Truth about Genetically Modified Food

... Benefits and Worries

The bulk of the science on GM safety points in one direction. Take it from David Zilberman, a U.C. Berkeley agricultural and environmental economist and one of the few researchers considered credible by both agricultural chemical companies and their critics. He argues that the benefits of GM crops

(5) greatly outweigh the health risks, which so far remain theoretical. The use of GM crops "has lowered the price of food," Zilberman says. "It has increased farmer safety by allowing them to use less pesticide. It has raised the output of corn, cotton and soy by 20 to 30 percent, allowing some people to survive who would not have without it. If it were more widely adopted around the

(10) world, the price [of food] would go lower, and fewer people would die of hunger." ...

Despite such promise, much of the world has been busy banning, restricting and otherwise shunning GM foods. Nearly all the corn and soybeans grown in the U.S. are genetically modified, but only two GM crops,

(15) Monsanto's $MON8_{10}$ maize and BASF's Amflora potato, are accepted in the European Union. Eight E.U. nations have banned GM crops outright. Throughout Asia, including in India and China, governments have yet to approve most GM crops, including an insect-resistant rice that produces higher yields with less pesticide. In Africa, where millions go hungry, several

(20)   nations have refused to import GM foods in spite of their lower costs (the
result of higher yields and a reduced need for water and pesticides). Kenya
has banned them altogether amid widespread malnutrition. No country has
definite plans to grow Golden Rice, a crop engineered to deliver more vitamin A than spinach (rice normally has no vitamin A), even though vitamin
(25)   A deficiency causes more than one million deaths annually and half a million
cases of irreversible blindness in the developing world. ...

A Clean Record
... Could eating plants with altered genes allow new DNA to work
its way into our own? It is theoretically possible but hugely improbable. Scientists have never found genetic material that could survive a trip
(30)   through the human gut and make it into cells. Besides, we are routinely
exposed to—we even consume—the viruses and bacteria whose genes end
up in GM foods. The bacterium *B. thuringiensis*, for example, which produces proteins fatal to insects, is sometimes enlisted as a natural pesticide
in organic farming. "We've been eating this stuff for thousands of years,"
(35)   [Robert] Goldberg [a plant molecular biologist] says.
In any case, proponents say, people have consumed as many as trillions of
meals containing genetically modified ingredients over the past few decades.
Not a single verified case of illness has ever been attributed to the genetic
alterations. Mark Lynas, a prominent anti-GM activist who last year pub-
(40)   licly switched to strongly supporting the technology, has pointed out that
every single news-making food disaster on record has been attributed to
non-GM crops, such as the *Escherichia coli*—infected organic bean sprouts
that killed 53 people in Europe in 2011. ...
Plenty of other credible groups have arrived at the same conclusion.
(45)   Gregory Jaffe, director of biotechnology at the Center for Science in the
Public Interest, a science-based consumer-watchdog group in Washington,
D.C., takes pains to note that the center has no official stance, pro or
con, with regard to genetically modifying food plants. Yet Jaffe insists
the scientific record is clear. "Current GM crops are safe to eat and can
(50)   be grown safely in the environment," he says. The American Association
for the Advancement of Science, the American Medical Association and
the National Academy of Sciences have all unreservedly backed GM crops.
The U.S. Food and Drug Administration, along with its counterparts in

several other countries, has repeatedly reviewed large bodies of research and
(55) concluded that GM crops pose no unique health threats. Dozens of review
studies carried out by academic researchers have backed that view. ...

—David H. Freedman excerpted and adapted
from "The Truth about Genetically Modified Food"
http://www.scientificamerican.com, August 20, 2013

LOOKING AT THE TEXTS

Text 1—GMOs 101: The Six Questions on Every Shoppers Mind About the Bew Biotech Foods...

—Alisa Blackwood, excerpted and adapted from "GMOs 101," *Health*, May 2004

This is an article from a popular, generally well-regarded magazine. The question and answer format serves as a good introduction to the topic. The article is rich in information, and details and opinions are documented, which suggests that the sources are reliable. The tone and purpose seem to be objective.

Text 2—GMO Reality Check

—Melissa Diane Smith, excerpted from "GMO Reality Check," *Better Nutrition*, August 2012

This is a good example of a document in which one side of the issue is forcefully expressed. The writer cites sources for much of the information used to support her opposition to the use of GMO foods. This would be an excellent source for the student writer who establishes a claim opposed to the use of GMO foods.

Text 3—GMO Foods: Key Points in the Genetically Modified Debate

—Marjorie Olster, excerpted from "GMO Foods: Key Points in the Genetically Modified Debate," *http://www.huffingtonpost.com*, August 2, 2013

Here is an example of a document that outlines the key points in the debate and offers detailed information both on the development of GMO foods and on how governments in the United States and Europe regulate them. This article acknowledges competing points of view and offers information that could be used to support a variety of arguments.

Text 4—The Truth About Genetically Modified Food

—David H. Freedman, excerpted and adapted from "The Truth about Genetically Modified Food," *http://www.scientificamerican.com*, August 20, 2013

This article presents a very clear opinion on one side of the argument. It is well documented and offers strong evidence for the student writer who establishes a claim for the use of GMO foods.

Note that two of the texts are rich in background information and acknowledge opposing points of view. They can be helpful to the student writer when determining which argument to make. The other two texts offer forceful arguments for one side or the other. All texts include useful information and are documented with reliable sources.

KNOW THE RUBRIC

Here is the information from the chart on pages 80 and 81. The key terms for this part of the exam have been highlighted.

SCORING RUBRIC FOR PART 2

> **Content and Analysis**: The extent to which the essay conveys complex ideas and information clearly and accurately in order to support claims in an analysis of the texts.

High Scores

6   Essays introduce **a precise and insightful claim**, as directed by the task and demonstrate **in-depth and insightful analysis** of the texts, as necessary to support the claim and to distinguish the claim from alternate or opposing claims.

5   Essays introduce **a precise and thoughtful** claim, as directed by the task and demonstrate **thorough analysis** of the texts, as necessary to support the claim and to distinguish the claim from alternate or opposing claims.

Middle Scores

4   Essays introduce **a precise claim**, as directed by the task and demonstrate **appropriate and accurate analysis** of the texts, as necessary to support the claim and to distinguish the claim from alternate or opposing claims.

3　Essays introduce **a reasonable claim**, as directed by the task and demonstrate **some analysis** of the texts, but **insufficiently distinguish** the claim from alternate or opposing claims.

Low Scores

2　Essays introduce a claim and demonstrate **confused or unclear analysis** of the texts, **failing to distinguish the claim** from alternate or opposing claims.

1　Essays **do not introduce a claim**; do not demonstrate analysis of the texts.

Command of Evidence: The extent to which the essay presents evidence from the provided texts to support analysis.

High Scores

6　Essays **present ideas fully and thoughtfully**, making highly effective use of a **wide range of specific and relevant evidence** to support analysis and demonstrate **proper citation of sources** to avoid plagiarism when dealing with direct quotes and paraphrased material.

5　Essays **present ideas clearly and accurately**, making **effective use of specific and relevant evidence** to support analysis and **demonstrate proper citation** of sources to avoid plagiarism when dealing with direct quotes and paraphrased material.

Middle Scores

4　Essays **present ideas sufficiently**, making **adequate use of specific and relevant evidence** to support analysis and **demonstrate proper citation** of sources to avoid plagiarism when dealing with direct quotes and paraphrased material.

3　Essays **present ideas briefly**, making use of **some specific and relevant evidence** to support analysis and demonstrate **inconsistent citation of sources** to avoid plagiarism when dealing with direct quotes and paraphrased material.

Low Scores

2 Essays **present ideas inconsistently and/or inaccurately**, in an attempt to support analysis, making use of **some evidence that may be irrelevant** and demonstrate **little use of citations** to avoid plagiarism when dealing with direct quotes and paraphrased material.

1 Essays present **little or no evidence** from the texts; do not make use of citations.

Coherence, Organization, and Style: The extent to which the essay logically organizes complex ideas, concepts, and information using formal style and precise language.

High Scores

6 Essays exhibit **skillful organization** of ideas and information to create a **cohesive and coherent essay** and establish and maintain a **formal style**, using **sophisticated language and structure**.

5 Essays exhibit **logical organization** of ideas and information to create a **cohesive and coherent** essay and establish and maintain **a formal style**, using **fluent and precise language and sound structure**.

Middle Scores

4 Essays exhibit **acceptable organization** of ideas and information to create a **coherent essay** and establish and maintain a **formal style**, using **precise and appropriate language and structure**.

3 Essays exhibit **some organization** of ideas and information to create a **mostly coherent essay** and establish but **fail to maintain a formal style**, using primarily **basic language and structure**.

Low Scores

2 Essays exhibit **inconsistent organization** of ideas and information, **failing to create a coherent essay** and **lack a formal style**, using some **language that is inappropriate or imprecise**.

1 Essays exhibit **little organization** of ideas and information, making assessment unreliable; use language that is **predominantly incoherent, inappropriate, or copied directly** from the task or texts.

Control of Conventions: The extent to which the essay demonstrates command of conventions of standard English grammar, usage, capitalization, punctuation, and spelling.

High Scores

6 Essays demonstrate control of conventions with **essentially no errors, even with sophisticated language**.

5 Essays demonstrate control of the conventions, exhibiting **occasional errors only when using sophisticated language**.

Middle Scores

4 Essays demonstrate **partial control**, exhibiting **occasional errors** that do not hinder comprehension.

3 Essays demonstrate **emerging control**, exhibiting **occasional errors that hinder comprehension**.

Low Scores

2 Essays demonstrate a **lack of control**, exhibiting **frequent errors** that make comprehension difficult.

1 Essays are **minimal**, making assessment of conventions unreliable.

STRATEGIES AND REVIEW

- The reading, writing, and discussion you do in English, social studies, and science classes form the basis of your preparation for this part of the exam.
- There is no "right answer." The topic and the texts provide for a variety of legitimate claims. Your task is to compose a relevant and defensible argument.
- Plan your response. This need not be a formal outline, but take time to articulate clearly what your claim (argument) will be. Then number and underline in the texts three or four passages that you can cite to support your argument. Decide on the most effective order for the examples.
- Review the Glossaries in the chapters that follow in order to recognize literary and rhetorical elements.
- Review the actual ELA/Common Core Exams and the Answers Explained for additional examples with essays for Part 2 of the exam.

Strategy and Review for Part 3 of the Regents ELA (Common Core) Exam

CHAPTER 3
Text-Analysis Response

WHAT DOES THIS PART OF THE EXAM REQUIRE?

The Part 3 question is designed to assess Common Core reading, writing, and language Standards. You will be required to do a close reading of a text (approximately 1,000 words). You will then write a two to three paragraph response that identifies a central idea in the text and analyzes how the author's use of one writing strategy (literary element, literary technique, or rhetorical device) develops this central idea.

There are no multiple-choice questions in this part of the exam.

WHAT DOES THIS PART OF THE EXAM LOOK LIKE?

Your Task: Closely read the text provided and write a well-developed, text-based response of two to three paragraphs. In your response, identify a central idea in the text and analyze how the author's use of one writing strategy (literary element, literary technique, or rhetorical device) develops this central idea. Use strong and thorough evidence from the text to support your analysis. Do *not* simply summarize the text. You may use the margins and scrap paper to take notes as you read and plan your response.

LOOKING AT THE TEXT

The following excerpt is from a speech delivered by suffragette Anna Howard Shaw in 1915.

...Now one of two things is true: either a Republic is a desirable form of government, or else it is not. If it is, then we should have it, if it is not then we ought not to pretend that we have it. We ought at least be true to our ideals, and the men of New York have for the first time in their lives, the rare
(5) opportunity on the second day of next November, of making the state truly a part of the Republic. It is the greatest opportunity which has ever come to the men of the state. They have never had so serious a problem to solve before, they will never have a more serious problem to solve in any future of our nation's life, and the thing that disturbs me more than anything else
(10) in connection with it is that so few people realize what a profound problem they have to solve on November 2. It is not merely a trifling matter; it is not a little thing that does not concern the state, it is the most vital problem we could have, and any man who goes to the polls on the second day of next November without thoroughly informing himself in regard to this subject is
(15) unworthy to be a citizen of this state, and unfit to cast a ballot.

    If woman's suffrage[1] is wrong, it is a great wrong; if it is right, it is a profound and fundamental principle, and we all know, if we know what a Republic is, that it is the fundamental principle upon which a Republic must rise. Let us see where we are as a people; how we act here and what
(20) we think we are. The difficulty with the men of this country is that they are so consistent in their inconsistency that they are not aware of having been inconsistent; because their consistency has been so continuous and their inconsistency so consecutive that it has never been broken, from the beginning of our Nation's life to the present time. If we trace our history back
(25) we will find that from the very dawn of our existence as a people, men have been imbued[2] with a spirit and a vision more lofty than they have been able to live; they have been led by visions of the sublimest[3] truth, both in regard to religion and in regard to government that ever inspired the souls of men from the time the Puritans left the old world to come to this country, led by
(30) the Divine ideal which is the sublimest and the supremest ideal in religious freedom which men have ever known, the theory that a man has a right to worship God according to the dictates of his own conscience, without the

intervention[4] of any other man or any other group of men. And it was this
theory, this vision of the right of the human soul which led men first to the
(35) shores of this country. ...

Now what is a Republic? Take your dictionary, encyclopedia lexicon or
anything else you like and look up the definition and you will find that a
Republic is a form of government in which the laws are enacted by representatives elected by the people. Now when did the people of New York ever
(40) elect their own representatives? Never in the world. The men of New York
have, and I grant you that men are people, admirable people, as far as they
go, but they only go half way. There is still another half of the people who
have not elected representatives, and you never read a definition of a Republic in which half of the people elect representatives to govern the whole of
(45) the people. That is an aristocracy and that is just what we are. We have been
many kinds of aristocracies. We have been a hierarchy[5] of church members,
than an oligarchy[6] of sex. ...

Now I want to make this proposition, and I believe every man will accept
it. Of course he will if he is intelligent. Whenever a Republic prescribes the
(50) qualifications as applying equally to all the citizens of the Republic, when the
Republic says in order to vote, a citizen must be twenty-one years of age, it
applies to all alike, there is no discrimination against any race or sex. When
the government says that a citizen must be a native-born citizen or a naturalized citizen that applies to all; we are either born or naturalized, somehow or
(55) other we are here. Whenever the government says that a citizen, in order to
vote, must be a resident of a community a certain length of time, and of the
state a certain length of time and of the nation a certain length of time, that
applies to all equally. There is no discrimination. We might go further and
we might say that in order to vote the citizen must be able to read his ballot.
(60) We have not gone that far yet. We have been very careful of male ignorance
in these United States. I was much interested, as perhaps many of you, in
reading the Congressional Record this last winter over the debate over the
immigration bill, and when that illiteracy clause was introduced into the
immigration bill, what fear there was in the souls of men for fear we would
(65) do injustice to some of the people who might want to come to our shores,
and I was much interested in the language in which the President vetoed
the bill, when he declared that by inserting the clause we would keep out of
our shores a large body of very excellent people. I could not help wonder-

(70) ing then how it happens that male ignorance is so much less ignorant than female ignorance. When I hear people say that if women were permitted to vote a large body of ignorant people would vote, and therefore because an ignorant woman would vote, no intelligent women should be allowed to vote, I wonder why we have made it so easy for male ignorance and so hard for female ignorance. ...

—Anna Howard Shaw
excerpted from "The Fundamental Principle of a Republic"
delivered at Ogdensburg, New York, June 21, 1915
http://www.emersonkent.com

---

[1]suffrage—right to vote   [2]imbued—inspired
[3]sublimest—noblest   [4]intervention—interference
[5]hierarchy—order of authority   [6]oligarchy—rule by a few

In this excerpted speech, suffragette Anna Howard Shaw uses several techniques to argue for the case of women's right to vote. She employs **repetition** and **rhetorical questioning** while discussing the **definition** of a Republic throughout her speech and a **sarcastic [ironic] tone** when referring to the consistent inconsistencies of men (paragraph 2) and the various requirements to vote in the U.S. (paragraph 3). Shaw's speech is also an excellent example of the use of **logical structure**, leading to her thinking "how it happens that male ignorance is so much less ignorant than female ignorance" (lines 69 and 70)

—Analysis from "Questions with Annotations," NYSED, June 2014

KNOW THE RUBRIC

Here is the information from the chart on pages 82 and 83. The key terms for this part of the exam have been highlighted.

SCORING RUBRIC FOR PART 3

> **Content and Analysis:** The extent to which the response conveys complex ideas and information clearly and accurately in order to respond to the task and support an analysis of the text.

4 Essays introduce a **well-reasoned central idea and a writing strategy** that clearly establish the criteria for analysis and demonstrate a **thoughtful analysis** of the author's use of the writing strategy to develop the central idea.

3 Essays introduce a **clear central idea and a writing strategy** that establish the criteria for analysis and demonstrate an **appropriate analysis** of the author's use of the writing strategy to develop the central idea.

2 Essays introduce a **central idea and/or a writing strategy** and demonstrate a **superficial analysis** of the author's use of the writing strategy to develop the central idea.

1 Essays introduce a **confused or incomplete central idea or writing strategy** and/or demonstrate a **minimal analysis** of the author's use of the writing strategy to develop the central idea.

> **Command of Evidence:** The extent to which the response presents evidence from the provided text to support analysis.

4 Essays present ideas **clearly and consistently**, making effective use of **specific and relevant evidence** to support analysis.

3 Essays present ideas **sufficiently**, making **adequate use of relevant evidence** to support analysis.

2 Essays present ideas **inconsistently, inadequately, and/or inaccurately** in an attempt to support analysis, making use of **some evidence that may be irrelevant**.

1 Essays present **little or no evidence** from the text.

> **Coherence, Organization, and Style:** The extent to which the response logically organizes complex ideas, concepts, and information using formal style and precise language.

4   Essays exhibit **logical organization** of ideas and information to create a **cohesive and coherent** response and establish and maintain a **formal style**, using **precise language and sound structure**.

3   Essays exhibit **acceptable organization** of ideas and information to create a **coherent response** and establish and maintain a **formal style**, using **appropriate language and structure**.

2   Essays exhibit **inconsistent organization** of ideas and information, failing to create a coherent response; lack a formal style, using language that is **basic, inappropriate, or imprecise**.

1   Essays exhibit **little organization** of ideas and information; use language that is predominantly **incoherent**, inappropriate, or copied directly from the task or text; or are **minimal**, making assessment unreliable.

> **Control of Conventions:** The extent to which the response demonstrates command of conventions of standard English grammar, usage, capitalization, punctuation, and spelling.

4   Essays demonstrate **control** of the conventions with **infrequent errors**.

3   Essays demonstrate **partial control** of conventions with **occasional errors** that do not hinder comprehension.

2   Essays demonstrate **emerging control** of conventions with **some errors** that **hinder comprehension**.

1   Essays demonstrate a **lack of control** of conventions with **frequent errors** that make comprehension difficult; are **minimal**, making assessment of conventions unreliable.

Note:
• A response that is a personal response and makes little or no reference to the task or text can be scored no higher than a 1.
• A response that is totally copied from the text with no original writing must be given a 0.
• A response that is totally unrelated to the task, illegible, incoherent, blank, or unrecognizable as English must be scored as a 0.

STRATEGIES AND REVIEW

- Plan your response. This need not be a formal outline, but be sure to articulate clearly which literary element or rhetorical device you choose. List on the blank page provided, and underline in the text itself, three or four passages that convincingly support your topic. Decide on the most effective order for the examples.
- Recognize that the texts for this part are primary sources, often narratives or speeches. They will have distinctive voices and may be of a particular historical context.
- There is no "right answer." The texts will be rich in information and are likely to employ several rhetorical strategies for effect. Choose the one you can discuss most confidently.
- Review the chapter in this book on literary elements and the Glossaries to help you recognize and write about writing strategies.
- Review this part of the exam in the Answers Explained for actual ELA/Common Core exams.

Reading and Writing About Literature

CHAPTER 4
Reviewing Literary Elements and Techniques

ELEMENTS OF FICTION AND DRAMA

When we speak of fiction, we are generally speaking of narrative works—
works in which events are recounted, are *told*, and which have been imagined
and structured by the author. Although not narrative in form, drama shares
many of the essential characteristics of fiction.

Plot and Story

The primary pleasure for most readers of narrative fiction is the story. If
we become involved in a novel or short story, it is because we want to know
how it turns out; we want to know what is going to happen to those characters. An author creates a plot when he or she gives order and structure to the
action: in a plot, the **incidents** or **episodes** of the story have a meaningful
relationship to one another. A story becomes a plot when we not only understand *what happened* but also *why*. In good fiction we are *convinced* of the
causal relationship among incidents and we are convinced by the relationship
of characters' motives and feelings to the action.

Plot and Conflict

At the end of any meaningful story, something has *happened*; something
is significantly different in the world and lives of the characters from what it
was at the beginning. **Conflict** in the most general sense refers to the **forces**

that move the action in a plot. Conflict in plot may be generated from a search or pursuit, from a discovery, from a deception or misunderstanding, from opportunities to make significant choices, or from unexpected consequences of an action. Although the term conflict connotes an active struggle between opposing or hostile forces, conflict in fiction may refer to any progression, change, or discovery. The **resolution** of conflict in a plot may be subtle and confined to the inner life of a character or it may be dramatic and involve irreversible change, violent destruction, or death.

Conflict may identify an actual struggle between characters, for anything from dominance or revenge to simple recognition or understanding. A plot may also focus on conflict between characters and the forces of nature or society. These are essentially *external conflicts*. A work may center on *internal conflict*: characters' struggle to know or change themselves and their lives. Most works of fiction and drama contain more than one aspect of conflict.

In Shakespeare's *Romeo and Juliet*, the most dramatic conflicts are external, vivid, and literal: the street brawls between followers of the rival Capulets and Montagues and the fatal fight with Tybalt that leads to Romeo's banishment and the tragic deaths of the young lovers. In *Macbeth*, the primary interest is in the internal conflict between Macbeth's ambitious desires and his understanding of the moral consequences of the actions he takes to achieve those desires.

The action in Edith Wharton's most famous story, "Roman Fever," is ironically serene and pleasant: two middle-age women, long-time friends now both widowed, sit on a terrace overlooking the splendors of Rome and reflect on their common experiences and lifelong friendship. At the end of the conversation—and the story—their actual feelings of rivalry have come to the surface, and one of the two learns something that reveals how little she truly knew her husband or understood her marriage or the life of her friend. The conflict between the two women emerges almost imperceptibly and its meaning is only fully understood in the completely unexpected revelation of the last line.

Structure/Plot and Chronology

Narrative is not necessarily presented in chronological order, but it does have chronology. That is, incidents may be presented out of the order in which they actually occurred, but by the end of the work the reader does understand their order and relationship and appreciates why the story was structured as it was. Plots that are narrated in flashback or from different points of view are common examples.

The Great Gatsby by F. Scott Fitzgerald and *Ethan Frome* by Edith Wharton are novels in which the narrator first introduces himself and his interest in the story, then tells it in a narrative flashback whose full significance to the narrator (and reader) is revealed only at the end. Tennessee Williams's play *The Glass Menagerie* has a similar structure, in which the character of Tom serves both as a narrator in the present and as a principal character in the series of memory scenes that make up the drama. The memory scenes in Arthur Miller's play *Death of a Salesman*, however, are not flashbacks in the same way. Willy Loman relives incidents from the past while the other characters and action of the play continue in the present. As the play progresses, the shifts in time occur only within Willy's mind.

Shakespeare's tragedies are dramas in which normal chronology is preserved, as it is in such familiar novels as William Golding's *Lord of the Flies* and Mark Twain's *Huckleberry Finn*.

Narrative Point of View

The narrator of a work is the character or author's *persona* that tells a story. Point of view is the standpoint, perspective, and degree of understanding from which the narrator speaks. For many students and scholars, the question of how a story is told is one of the most interesting questions. What is the narrative point of view? Is the narration *omniscient,* essentially the point of view of the author? Or, who is the narrator? What is the narrator's relationship to the story? What is the narrator's understanding of the story? How much does the narrator really know? Appreciating how, or by whom, a story is told is often essential to understanding its meaning.

One of the most easily discerned narrative points of view is the **first person** (*I*) in which either the central character or another directly involved in the action tells the story. J. D. Salinger's novel *Catcher in the Rye* is a vivid and popular example of such narration. Fitzgerald's *The Great Gatsby* is also told in the first person. In each of these works, the fundamental meaning of the novel becomes apparent only when the reader understands the character of the narrator. In each of these works, what the narrator experiences and what he learns about himself and the world are the novel's most important themes.

In **first-person narration**, the incidents of the plot are limited to those that the narrator himself experiences. First-person narrators can, however, report what they learn from others. In Wharton's *Ethan Frome*, the engineer who narrates tells us that he has "pieced together the story" from the little he has been able to learn in the town of Starkfield, from his limited conversations with Frome himself, and from his brief visit to the Frome house. Wharton's method, of course, dramatizes Frome's inability to express or fulfill the desires of his heart and reveals the reluctance of the people of Starkfield to fully understand the lives of those around them.

Authors may also use first-person narration to achieve an ironic or satiric effect. In Ring Lardner's story "Haircut," a barber in a small midwestern town narrates a story about a local fellow who kept the town entertained with his practical jokes on people. As the story progresses, the reader understands how cruel and destructive the fellow's pranks were, but the barber does not. The narrative method in this story reveals, indirectly, a story of painful ignorance and insensitivity in the "decent" citizens of a small town. Mark Twain's masterpiece, *Huckleberry Finn*, is told by Huck himself. Through the morally naive observations of Huck, Twain satirizes the evils of slavery, fraud, hypocrisy, and nearly every other kind of corrupt human behavior. Edgar Allan Poe's story "The Tell-Tale Heart" is the confession of a cunning madman.

In **third-person** narration (*he, she, it, they*), a story is reported. The narrative voice may be *omniscient* and, therefore, able to report everything from everywhere in the story and also report on the innermost thoughts and feelings of the characters themselves. In many novels of the eighteenth and nineteenth centuries, the omniscient narrator even speaks directly to the reader, as if taking him or her into the storyteller's confidence. In Nathaniel Hawthorne's *The Scarlet Letter*, the narrator pauses from time to time to share personal feelings with the reader. Nick Carraway, the narrator of *The Great Gatsby* also does this, but the method is not common in contemporary fiction.

A widely used narrative method is the *limited omniscient* point of view. The narrative is in the third person but is focused on and even may represent the point of view of a central character. The actions and feelings of other characters are presented from the perspective of that character. Hawthorne's short story "Young Goodman Brown" is an excellent example.

Some third-person narration is dramatically **objective** and detached; it simply reports the incidents of the plot as they unfold. This narrative method, too, can be used for intensely **ironic** effect. Jackson's "The Lottery" is one of the best examples. The real horror of the story is achieved through the utterly detached, nonjudgmental telling of it.

In some plays, too, there is a character who serves a narrative role: the Chorus in Shakespeare's *Henry V*, the character of Tom in Williams's *The Glass Menagerie*, and the Stage Manager in Thornton Wilder's *Our Town* are familiar examples.

In each of the works discussed here, narrative method is not simply a literary device; it is an intrinsic part of the meaning of the work.

Setting

The setting of a work includes the time and places in which the action is played out; setting may also include significant historical context. In drama, setting may be presented directly in the set, costumes, and lighting. In narrative fiction, setting is usually presented directly through description. In some works, the physical setting is central to the plot and developed in great detail; in other works, only those details necessary to anchor the plot in a time or place will be developed. Regardless of detail, responsive readers re-create images of setting as they read.

In addition to the physical and natural details of the fictional world, setting also includes mood and **atmosphere**. In some works, social or political realities constitute part of the setting. *The Scarlet Letter* is not only set in Puritan Boston, it is also *about* that society; and *The Great Gatsby* presents a vivid picture of life in New York during Prohibition and the roaring twenties.

For some works, the author may create specific details of setting to highlight a theme. In Golding's novel *Lord of the Flies*, the island on which the story takes place has everything essential for basic survival: there is food and water, and the climate is temperate. In order to explore the moral questions of the boys' regression into savagery, Golding carefully establishes a setting in which survival itself is not a primary issue. In *Ethan Frome*, details of the harsh winter and of the isolation of a town "bypassed by the railroad" intensify the story of a man's desperately cold and isolated life.

Character and Characterization

We understand characters in fiction and drama as we do the people in our own lives, by what they say and do, and by what others say about them. Because characters are imagined and created by an author, we can even understand them more reliably and fully than we can many of the people around us. Many students find their greatest satisfaction in reading works about characters to whom they can relate, characters whose struggles are recognizable and whose feelings are familiar.

Understanding character in fiction means understanding a person's values and **motivation,** beliefs and principles, moral qualities, strengths and weaknesses, and degree of self-knowledge and understanding. To fully appreciate a work, the reader must understand what characters are searching for and devoting their lives to.

Literature also seeks to account for the forces outside individuals that influence the direction and outcome of their lives. These "forces" range from those of nature and history to the demands of family, community, and society. The response of characters to inner and outer forces is what literature depicts and makes comprehensible.

In literature courses and on examinations, discussions of character are the most common. That is because any meaningful or convincing plot stems from human thought, motive, and action. Depending on the narrative point of view (see page 47) a character's thoughts and feelings may be presented directly through **omniscient** narrative or first-person commentary. In "Young Goodman Brown," the narrator tells us directly what the title character is thinking and feeling; in "Roman Fever," the most important revelations of character are discovered by the reader simultaneously with the two central characters. Character in drama is revealed directly in dialogue and action, but it may be expanded through soliloquies and asides. In Shakespeare's

Othello, for example, the full extent of Iago's evil is revealed through the variety of methods he uses to manipulate different characters and through the soliloquies.

In some works, the author's primary purpose is to reveal character gradually through plot; in others, the author establishes understanding of character from the beginning in order to account for what happens. In the opening pages of *The Great Gatsby*, the narrator, Nick, who is also a character in the novel, introduces himself and declares his judgment of the moral quality of the people and events he is about to narrate. With Nick's own character and motives clearly established, the reader then shares his gradual discovery of the truth about Gatsby and his life.

Theme

The subjects of literature may come from any aspect of human experience: love, friendship, growing up, ambition, family relationships, conflicts with society, survival, war, evil, death, and so on. **Theme** in a work of literature is the understanding, insight, observation, and presentation of such subjects. Theme is what a work *says about* a subject. Themes are the central ideas of literary works.

One way to think about theme is to consider it roughly analogous to the topic or thesis of an expository essay. If the author of a novel, story, or play had chosen to examine the subjects of the work in an essay, what might be the topic assertions of such an essay? The student is cautioned, however, not to overinterpret the analogy. Themes in literature are rarely "morals," such as those found at the end of a fable, but neither are they "hidden meanings." Although scholars and critics often express thematic ideas in phrases, students are often required to express themes in full statements. In the next paragraph are some examples of statements about theme.

Macbeth is a play about the temptation to embrace evil forces and about the power of ambition to corrupt; Macbeth himself makes one of the most important statements of theme in the play when he says, "I do all that becomes a man/who does more is none." *Ethan Frome* and Lardner's "Haircut" both illustrate that people in small towns do not truly understand the innermost needs and desires of people they think they know. William Golding's novel *Lord of the Flies* illustrates the bleak view that human beings' savage nature will prevail without external forces of authority, that human beings are not civilized in their fundamental natures. In contrast, in *Adventures of Huckleberry Finn*, Twain presents civilization as the source of corruption and finds truly moral behavior only in the runaway slave, Jim, and the ignorant boy, Huck.

ELEMENTS OF NONFICTION

Fiction and nonfiction share many common elements; they also make similar demands and offer comparable rewards to the thoughtful reader. In broad contrast to fiction, where characters and plot are imaginative creations of the author, nonfiction is about actual persons, experiences, and phenomena. Nonfiction also speculates on abstract and philosophical questions of history and politics, ethics and religion, culture and society, as well as the natural world. In biography and autobiography, the writer focuses on what is meaningful and interesting in the life of an individual.

On the Regents ELA exam you will read several examples of nonfiction. In Part 1 Reading Comprehension, you can expect to read one informational text, often on a historical or scientific topic. Part 2 requires reading at least four texts of informed argument and evidence to support a claim; and Part 3 Text Analysis often includes works of nonfiction, personal **narrative**. Authors of literary nonfiction often make imaginative use of **structure**, **chronology**, and **characterization**.

ELEMENTS OF POETRY

Part 1 of the Regents ELA exam will include one poem for close reading. The multiple-choice questions are designed to measure your skill at reading for the meaning. You are also expected to recognize and identify elements of poetry.

Poetry and Experience

In poetry, we are meant to sense a structure and to feel the rhythm (see **meter and rhythm**, page 64). The structure and rhythm of poetry may be formal, informal, even "free." Poetry is also characterized by its directness of effect and by its concentration—ideas and feelings are expressed in relatively few words. Karl Shapiro says, "Poems are what ideas feel like." Where the writer of prose may seek immediate clarity of meaning above all, the poet often seeks **ambiguity**, not to create "confusion," but to offer multiplicity of meaning: in single words, in images, in the meaning of the poem itself.

The experience of poetry is conveyed in vivid **imagery**, which appeals to the mind and to the senses. It is often expressed in **figurative language**; that is, through imaginative use of words and comparisons that are not literal but which create original, vivid, and often unexpected images and associations. (See **metaphor**, page 64, and **simile**, page 65.) Finally, in poetry there is particular significance in the way words and lines sound. The story or experience is enhanced through musical effects. A poem must be felt and heard!

Theme in Poetry

Some poems may assert a belief. Others may be a comment on the nature of human experience—love, death, loss or triumph, mystery and confusion, conflict and peace, on the humorous and the ironic, on the imagined and the unexpected in all its forms. Some poems reflect on the nature of time, of existence. Many poems are about poetry itself. These aspects of human experience are what we refer to as the **themes** of poetry.

Tone

Tone in poetry, as in prose and all forms of human communication, expresses the *attitude* of the speaker toward the reader or listener and toward the subject. Tone in literature is as varied as the range of human experience and feeling it reflects. When we speak of the *mood* of a piece of writing, we are also speaking of tone, of an overall feeling generated by the work.

Here are some terms to help you recognize and articulate **tone** or **mood** (see also Structure and Language in Poetry, beginning on page 61):

ambiguous	insistent	reconciled
amused	**ironic**	reflective
angry	melancholy	regretful
bitter	mournful	reminiscent
celebratory	mysterious	satiric
elegiac	nostalgic	sorrowful
grateful	optimistic	thoughtful
harsh	**paradoxical**	**understated**
humorous	questioning	

Note: Terms in bold are included in the glossary.

Reading and Writing About Literature

CHAPTER 5

Glossaries of Terms

STRUCTURE AND LANGUAGE IN PROSE

abstract In contrast to the *concrete*, abstract language expresses general ideas and concepts apart from specific examples or instances. Very formal writing is characterized by abstract expression. As a noun, *abstract* denotes a brief summary of the key ideas in a scientific, legal, or scholarly piece of writing.

analogy An expression of the similarities between things that are not wholly alike or related. (See *metaphor* in Structure and Language in Poetry, page 64.)

anecdote A very brief, usually vivid story or episode. Often humorous, anecdotes offer examples of typical behavior or illustrate the personality of a character. Writers of biography and autobiography make extensive use of anecdote to reveal the lives of their subjects.

antithesis In formal argument, a statement that opposes or contrasts a *thesis* statement. Informally, we use the term to refer to any expression or point of view completely opposed to another. In literature, even an experience or a feeling may be expressed as the *antithesis* of another. (See also *thesis*.)

argument In persuasive writing or speaking, the development of reasons to support the writer's position; it is the method of reasoning used to persuade. Informally, we may use the term to describe the development of a topic in any piece of expository writing. Historically, it has also denoted a summary of a literary work's plot or main ideas.

atmosphere Closely related to *tone* or mood, it refers to a pervasive feeling in a work. Atmosphere often stems from setting and from distinctive characters or actions. The atmosphere in many of Poe's stories is mysterious, troubling, even sinister. Hawthorne's "Young Goodman Brown" reflects the threatening and morally ambiguous world of its Puritan setting.

autobiography A formally composed account of a person's life, written by that person. Although we must trust, or be skeptical of, the reliability of the account, we often appreciate the firsthand narration of experience. Autobiography is also a rich source of information and insight into a historical period or into literary or artistic worlds. Autobiography, like the novel, has *narrative* and chronology. (See also *journal, memoir*.) We describe literary works that are closely based on the author's life as **autobiographical.** Eugene O'Neill's *Long Day's Journey into Night* and Tennessee Williams's *The Glass Menagerie* are plays that reflect many details of their authors' lives.

biography A narrative, historical account of the life, character, and significance of its subject. Contemporary biography is usually researched in detail and may not always be admiring of its subject. A critical biography of a literary figure includes discussion of the writer's works to show the writer's artistic development and career. Biographies of figures significant in history or public affairs also offer commentary on periods and events of historical importance.

character The imagined persons, created figures, who inhabit the worlds of fiction and drama. E. M. Forster distinguished between *flat* and *round* characters. Flat are those, like stereotypes, who represent a single and exaggerated human characteristic. Round are those whose aspects are complex and convincing, and who change or develop in the course of a work. In good fiction, plot must develop out of character. It is the desires, values, and motives of characters that account for the action and conflict in a plot.

characterization The method by which an author establishes character; the means by which personality, manner, and appearance are created. It is achieved directly through description and dialogue and indirectly through observations and reactions of other characters.

concrete The particular, the specific, in expression and imagery. That which is concrete can be perceived by the senses. Concrete also refers to that which is tangible, real, or actual, in contrast to *abstract*, which is intangible and conceptual.

conflict In the most general sense, it identifies the forces that give rise to a plot. This term may identify an actual struggle between characters, for anything from revenge to simple recognition or understanding. A plot may focus on conflict between characters and the forces of nature or society.

These are essentially external conflicts. A work may also center on internal conflicts: characters' struggles to know or change themselves and their lives. Most works of fiction and drama contain more than one aspect of conflict. (See Plot and Conflict, page 45.)

denouement A French term meaning "untying a knot," it refers to the way the complications or conflict of a plot are finally resolved. It also refers to what is called the "falling action" in a drama: that part of the play that follows the dramatic climax and reveals the consequences of the main action for minor characters; it also accounts briefly for what happens in the world of the play after the principal drama is resolved. In Arthur Miller's *Death of a Salesman*, the "Requiem" may be considered a denouement: it accounts for the response to Willy's death of his wife, sons, and only friend. In Shakespeare's *Macbeth*, the climax is in the scene following the death of Lady Macbeth in which Macbeth understands that he has destroyed all capacity for feeling and has rendered his life meaningless; the denouement occurs in the battle scene in which Macbeth comprehends the treachery of the witches and is killed by Macduff, thus restoring the throne to the rightful heir, Malcolm.

determinism The philosophical view that human existence is determined by forces over which humans have little or no control. The concept that fate predestines the course of a character's life or a tragic figure's downfall is a form of determinism.

episode A series of actions or incidents that make up a self-contained part of a larger narrative. Some novels are structured so that each chapter is a significant episode. Fitzgerald's *The Great Gatsby* and Mark Twain's *Huckleberry Finn* are good examples. A *scene* in a play is often analogous to an episode in a narrative. Many television series are presented in weekly episodes.

essay Denotes an extended composition, usually expository, devoted to a single topic. Essays may be composed to persuade, to reflect on philosophical questions, to analyze a subject, to express an opinion, or to entertain. As a literary form, the essay dates from the sixteenth century and remains a popular and widely practiced form. The origin of the term is the French word *essai*, which means an attempt, a trying out of something. (See *formal/informal essay*.)

exposition Writing whose purpose is to inform, illustrate, and explain. In literature, exposition refers to those passages or speeches in which setting, offstage or prior action, or a character's background is revealed. In *The Great Gatsby*, Nick Carraway pauses in the narrative to give the reader additional information about Gatsby's background. The prologue to Shakespeare's *Romeo and Juliet* is an example of exposition.

flashback A presentation of incidents or episodes that occurred prior to the beginning of a narrative itself. When an author or filmmaker uses flashback, the "present" or forward motion of the plot is suspended. Flashback may be introduced through the device of a character's memory, or through the narrative voice itself. William Faulkner's "Barn Burning" and *Light in August* include vivid passages of memory and narrative flashback. Jack Burden's recounting of the Cass Mastern story in Robert Penn Warren's *All the King's Men* is also a form of flashback.

foreshadowing Establishing details or mood in a work that will become more significant as the plot progresses. Thoughtful readers usually sense such details and accumulate them in their memories. In one of the opening scenes of *Ethan Frome*, Ethan and Mattie talk about the dangers of sledding down Starkfield's steepest hill. In the second paragraph of Shirley Jackson's well-known story "The Lottery," the boys stuff their pockets with stones and make piles of them on the edge of the square.

form The organization, shape, and structure of a work. Concretely, form may refer to *genre* (see below); for example, the sonnet form, the tragic form. More abstractly, form also refers to the way we sense inherent structure and shape.

formal/informal essay In contrast to the formal essay, which emphasizes organization, logic, and explication of ideas, the informal essay emphasizes the voice and perspective of the writer. In the informal essay, also called a *personal essay*, the reader is aware of the author's *persona* and is asked to share the author's interest in the subject. Examples of a personal essay might be included in Part 1 Reading Comprehension, among the texts in Part 2 Argument, or in the Part 3 Text Analysis.

genre A type or form of literature. Examples include *novel, short story, epic poem, essay, sonnet,* and *tragedy*.

image Although suggesting something that is visualized, an image is an expression or recreation through language of *any* experience perceived directly through the senses. (See also Structure and Language in Poetry, page 64.)

irony In general, a tone or figure of speech in which there is a discrepancy—a striking difference or contradiction—between what is expressed and what is meant or expected. Irony achieves its powerful effect indirectly: in satire, for example, to ridicule or criticize. We also speak of dramatic irony when the narrator or reader understands more than the characters do.

journal A diary or notebook of personal observations. Many writers use journals to compose personal reflection and to collect ideas for their works. The journals of many writers have been published. Students are often urged to keep journals as a way to reflect on their reading, compose personal pieces, and practice writing free of concern for evaluation.

melodrama A plot in which incidents are sensational and designed to provoke immediate emotional responses. In melodrama, the "good" characters are pure and innocent and victims of the "bad" ones, who are thoroughly evil. The term refers to a particular kind of drama popular in the late nineteenth century and, later, in silent films and early Westerns. A work becomes melodramatic when it relies on improbable incidents and unconvincing characters for strong emotional effect.

memoir A form of autobiographical writing that reflects on the significant events the writer has observed and on the interesting and important personalities the writer has known. The Regents ELA Exam often includes examples of memoir among the texts for comprehension or analysis.

monologue In a play, an extended expression or speech by a single speaker that is uninterrupted by response from other characters. A monologue is addressed to a particular person or persons, who may or may not actually hear it. In Ring Lardner's short story "Haircut," a barber tells (narrates) the story to a customer (the reader) who is present but does not respond. (See also **dramatic monologue** in Structure and Language in Poetry, page 62.)

motivation The desires, values, needs, or impulses that move characters to act as they do. In good fiction, the reader understands, appreciates, and is convinced that a character's motivation accounts for the significant incidents and the outcome of a plot.

narrative point of view The standpoint, perspective, and degree of understanding from which a work of narrative fiction is told. (See *omniscient point of view, objective point of view*.)

narrator The character or author's *persona* that tells a story. It is through the perspective and understanding of the narrator that the reader experiences the work. In some works, the narrator may inhabit the world of the story or be a character in it. In other works, the narrator is a detached but knowledgeable observer.

naturalism Closely related to *determinism*, naturalism depicts characters who are driven not by personal will or moral principles but by natural forces that they do not fully understand or control. In contrast to other views of human experience, the naturalistic view makes no moral judgments on the lives of the characters. Their lives, often bleak or defeating, simply *are* as they are, determined by social, environmental, instinctive, and hereditary forces. Naturalism was in part a reaction by writers against the nineteenth-century Romantic view of man as master of his own fate. It is important to note, however, that none of the Naturalistic writers in America (Crane, Dreiser, London, Anderson, and Norris chief among them) presented a genuinely deterministic vision. Several of these authors began their careers in journalism and were drawn to the Naturalistic view of life as a result of their own experience and observation of life in America. (See also *realism*.)

objective point of view In fiction or nonfiction, this voice presents a story or information without expressed judgment or qualification. A fundamental principle of journalism is that news *reports* should be objective. Ernest Hemingway's short story "The Killers" is an example of fiction rendered in a completely detached, objective point of view.

omniscient point of view Spoken in third person (*she, he, they*), this is the broadest narrative perspective. The omniscient narrator speaks from outside the story and sees and knows everything about the characters and incidents. Omniscient narration is not limited by time or place. In *limited omniscient* point of view, the author may choose to reveal the story through full understanding of only one character and limit the action to those incidents in which this character is present.

persona A term from the Greek meaning "mask," it refers in literature to a narrative voice created by an author and through which the author speaks. A narrative persona usually has a perceptible, even distinctive, personality that contributes to our understanding of the story. In Nathaniel Hawthorne's *The Scarlet Letter,* the omniscient narrator has a distinctive persona whose attitudes toward Puritan society and the characters' lives are revealed throughout the novel.

plot The incidents and experiences of characters selected and arranged by the author to create a meaningful story. A good plot is convincing in terms of what happens and why.

poetic justice The concept that life's rewards and punishments should be perfectly appropriate and distributed in just proportions. In Ring Lardner's short story "Haircut," Jim Kendall's ironic fate is an example of poetic justice: he is a victim of one of his own crude and insensitive practical jokes. The short story "They Grind Exceeding Small," by Ben Ames Williams, is also a vivid example of what is meant by poetic justice.

point of view In nonfiction, this denotes the attitudes or opinions of the writer. In narrative fiction, it refers to how and by whom a story is told: the perspective of the narrator and the narrator's relationship to the story. Point of view may be *omniscient,* where the narrator knows everything about the characters and their lives; or, it may be *limited* to the understanding of a particular character or speaker. Point of view may also be described as *objective* or *subjective*. *Third-person* narrative refers to characters as "he, she, they;" *First-person* narrative is from the "I" point of view. J. D. Salinger's *Catcher in the Rye* and Mark Twain's *Huckleberry Finn* are told in the first person. *Second person*, the "you" form, is rare but is found in sermons addressed to a congregation or in essays of opinion addressed directly to a leader or public figure: "You, Mr. Mayor (Madame President), should do the following . . ." Political columnists occasionally write pieces in the second-person voice for the Op-Ed pages of newspapers.

prologue An introductory statement of the dramatic situation of a play. Shakespeare's *Romeo and Juliet* begins with a brief prologue. The first two pages of Fitzgerald's *The Great Gatsby* are a prologue to the story Nick Carraway will tell.

prose Most of what we write is prose, the expression in sentences and phrases that reflect the natural rhythms of speech. Prose is organized by paragraphs and is characterized by variety in sentence length and rhythm.

protagonist A term from ancient Greek drama, it refers to the central character, the hero or heroine, in a literary work.

realism The literary period in America following the Civil War is usually called the Age of Realism. Realism depicts the directly observable in everyday life. Realistic writers seek to *present* characters and situations as they would appear to a careful observer, not as they are imagined or created by the author. After 1865, American writers became increasingly interested in the sources of power and force, and in the means to survival and success, in an increasingly materialistic society. For writers of this period, realism was a literary mode to express a *naturalistic* philosophy. (See also *naturalism, verisimilitude*.)

rhetoric From Ancient Greece, the art of persuasion in speech or writing achieved through logical thought and skillful use of language.

rhetorical question A question posed in the course of an *argument* to provoke thought or to introduce a line of reasoning.

romance A novel or tale that includes elements of the supernatural, heroic adventure, or romantic passion. Hawthorne's *The Scarlet Letter* is a romance, not because it is a love story but because it goes beyond *verisimilitude* in dramatizing elements of demonic and mystical forces in the characters and their lives.

satire A form or style that uses elements of irony, ridicule, exaggeration, understatement, sarcasm, humor, or absurdity to criticize human behavior or a society. All satire is **ironic** (see *irony*) in that meaning or theme is conveyed in the discrepancy between what is said and what is meant, between what is and what should be, and between what appears and what truly is. Although satire is often entertaining, its purpose is serious and meant to provoke thought or judgment. The verses of Alexander Pope and many poems by e. e. cummings are satiric. In prose, much of the writing of Mark Twain is satire; *Huckleberry Finn* is the most striking example. Other American writers of satire include Sinclair Lewis, Edith Wharton, Aldous Huxley, Joseph Heller, Kurt Vonnegut, and Tom Wolfe. Popular television programs such as *The Daily Show*, *South Park*, and *The Simpsons* are also good examples of satire.

short story This form is distinguished from most novels not simply by length but by its focus on few characters and a central, revealing incident. In stories, however, there is as much variety in narrative point of view, subject, and technique as there is in novels. Edgar Allan Poe characterized the short story as "a short prose narrative, requiring from a half-hour to one or two hours in its perusal."

soliloquy A form of *monologue* in which a character expresses thoughts and feelings aloud but does not address them to anyone else or intend other characters in the work to hear them. In essence, the audience for a play is secretly listening in on a character's innermost thoughts. Macbeth's reflection on "Tomorrow, and tomorrow, and tomorrow . . ." is the best-known soliloquy in the play.

speaker The narrative voice in a literary work (see *persona*). Also, the character who speaks in a *dramatic monologue*.

symbol Most generally, anything that stands for or suggests something else. Language itself is symbolic: sounds and abstract written forms may be arranged to stand for virtually any human thought or experience. In literature, symbols are not Easter eggs, or mushrooms—they are not "hidden meanings." Symbols are real objects and *concrete* images that lead us to *think about* what is suggested. They organize a wide variety of ideas into single acts of understanding. They embody not single "meanings" but suggest whole areas of meaning.

theme Roughly analogous to *thesis* in an essay, this is an observation about human experience or an idea central to a work of literature. The *subject* of a work is in the specific setting, characters, and plot. Theme in a work of fiction is what is meaningful and significant to human experience generally. Themes are the ideas and truths that transcend the specific characters and plot. Shakespeare's *Macbeth* is about an ambitious nobleman who, encouraged by his equally ambitious wife, murders the king of Scotland in order to become king himself. The themes in *Macbeth* include the power of ambition to corrupt even those who are worthy and the mortal consequences of denying what is fundamental to one's nature.

thesis The central point, a statement of position in a formal or logical argument. Also used to refer to the topic or controlling idea of an essay. Use of the term *thesis* implies elaboration by reasons and examples.

tone The attitude of the writer toward the subject and toward the reader. (See the discussion in Chapter 4, page 52, and a glossary of Terms for Writing, page 68.)

transition A link between ideas or sections in a work. In prose arguments, single words such as *first, second, moreover,* and *therefore* or phrases such as *in addition, on the other hand,* and *in conclusion* serve as transitions. In fiction, a brief passage or chapter may serve as a transition. In *The Great Gatsby,* the narrator pauses from time to time to "fill in" the reader and to account for the passage of time between the dramatic episodes that make up the novel's main plot.

turning point In drama and fiction, the moment or episode in a plot when the action is moved toward its inevitable conclusion.

verisimilitude A literal quality in fiction and drama of being "true to life," of representing that which is real or actual. Verisimilitude in fiction is often achieved through specific, vivid description and dialogue; first-person narration also creates the effect of verisimilitude. In drama, it may be achieved through means of set, costumes, and lighting that are realistic in all their details.

STRUCTURE AND LANGUAGE IN POETRY

allegory A narrative, in prose or verse, in which abstract ideas, principles, human values, or states of mind are **personified**. The purpose of the allegory is to illustrate the significance of the ideas by dramatizing them. *Parable* and *fable* are particular kinds of allegory, in which a moral is illustrated in the form of a story.

alliteration The repetition of initial consonant sounds in words and syllables is one of the first patterns of sound a child creates; for example, "ma-ma; pa-pa." The stories of Dr. Seuss are told in alliteration and **assonance**. Poets use alliteration for its rich musical effect: "Fish, flesh, and fowl commend all summer long/Whatever is begotten, born, and dies" (Yeats); for humor: "Where at, with blade, with bloody, blameful blade/He bravely broached his boiling bloody breast" (Shakespeare); and to echo the sense of the lines: "The iron tongue of midnight hath told twelve" (Shakespeare).

allusion A reference to a historical event, to Biblical, mythological, or literary characters and incidents with which the reader is assumed to be familiar. Allusion may, with few words, enrich or extend the meaning of a phrase, idea, or image. Allusion may also be used for ironic effect. In his poem "Out, out . . ." Robert Frost expects the reader to recall from Macbeth's final soliloquy the line, "Out, out brief candle!" Such expressions as "a Herculean task" or "Achilles heel," are also forms of allusion.

ambiguity Denotes uncertainty of meaning. In literature and especially in poetry, we speak of intentional ambiguity, the use of language and images to suggest more than one meaning at the same time.

assonance The repetition of vowel sounds among words that begin or end with different consonants.

ballads Narrative poems, sometimes sung, that tell dramatic stories of individual episodes and characters.

blank verse Unrhymed *iambic pentameter*, usually in "paragraphs" of verse instead of stanzas. Shakespeare's plays are composed primarily in blank verse. For example, from *Macbeth* (Act I, Scene 5):

> Your face, my Thane, is as a book where men
> May read strange matters. To beguile the time,
> Look like the time; bear welcome in your eye,
> Your hand, your tongue; look like the innocent flower,
> But be the serpent under't . . .

connotation The feelings, attitudes, images, and associations of a word or expression. Connotations are usually said to be "positive" or "negative."

couplet Two lines of verse with similar meter and end ryhme. Couplets generally have self-contained ideas as well, so they may function as stanzas within a poem. In the English (Shakespearean) *sonnet,* the couplet serves as a conclusion. You will also discover that many scenes in Shakespeare's plays end with rhymed couplets: "Away, and mock the time with fairest show/False face must hide what the false heart doth know." (*Macbeth* Act I, Scene 7)

denotation That which a word actually names, identifies, or "points to." Denotation is sometimes referred to as "the dictionary definition" of a word.

dramatic monologue A poem in which a fictional character, at a critical or dramatic point in life, addresses a particular "audience," which is identifiable but silent. In the course of the monologue, we learn a great deal, often ironically, about the character who is speaking and the circumstances that have led to the speech. Robert Browning is the best-known 19th-century poet to compose dramatic monologues; "My Last Duchess" is a famous example. In the 20th century, such poets as

Kenneth Fearing, E. A. Robinson, T. S. Eliot ("The Love Song of J. Alfred Prufrock"), Robert Frost, and Amy Lowell composed well-known dramatic monologues.

elegy A meditative poem mourning the death of an individual.

epic A long narrative poem often centering on a heroic figure who represents the fate of a great nation or people. *The Iliad* and *The Odyssey* of Homer, *The Aeneid* of Vergil, and the Anglo-Saxon *Beowulf* are well-known epics. Milton's *Paradise Lost* and Dante's *Divine Comedy* are examples of epic narratives in which subjects of great human significance are dramatized. *Omeros*, by Derek Walcott, is a contemporary example of an epic poem.

figurative language The intentional and imaginative use of words and comparisons that are not literal but that create original, vivid, and often unexpected images and associations. Figurative language is also called *metaphorical language*. (See *metaphor* and *simile*.)

free verse A poem written in free verse develops images and ideas in patterns of lines without specific metrical arrangements or formal rhyme. Free verse is distinguished from prose, however, because it retains such poetic elements as assonance, alliteration, and figurative language. The poetry of Walt Whitman and e. e. cummings offers striking examples. The poem "View with a Grain of Sand" on page 11 is also an example of free verse.

hyperbole An exaggerated expression (also called overstatement) for a particular effect, which may be humorous, satirical, or intensely emotional. Hyperbole is the expression of folktales and legends and, of course, of lovers: Romeo says to Juliet, "there lies more peril in thine eye/Than twenty of their swords." Hyperbole is often the expression of any overwhelming feeling. After he murders King Duncan, Macbeth looks with horror at his bloody hands: "Will all great Neptune's ocean wash this blood/Clean from my hand . . . ?" In her sleepwalking scene, Lady Macbeth despairs that "All the perfumes of Arabia will not sweeten this little hand." And everyone of us has felt, "I have mountains of work to do!"

iambic pentameter The basic meter of English speech: "I think I know exactly what you need/and yet at times I know that I do not." Formally, it identifies verse of ten syllables to the line, with the second, fourth, sixth, eighth, and tenth accented. There is, however, variation in the stresses within lines to reflect natural speech—and to avoid a "sing-song" or nursery rhyme effect. It is the meter in which most of the dialogue in Shakespeare's plays is composed (see *blank verse*).

image Images and imagery are the heart of poetry. Although the term suggests only something that is visualized, an image is the re-creation through language of *any* experience perceived directly through the senses.

internal rhyme A pattern in which a word or words within a line rhyme with the word that ends it. Poets may also employ internal rhyme at irregular intervals over many lines.

irony In general, a tone or figure of speech in which there is a discrepancy— a striking difference or contradiction—between what is expressed and what is meant or expected. Irony may be used to achieve a powerful effect indirectly. In satire, for example, it may be used to ridicule or criticize.

metaphor A form of analogy. Metaphorical expression is the heart of poetry. Through metaphor, a poet discovers and expresses a similarity between dissimilar things. The poet uses metaphor to imaginatively find common qualities between things we would not normally or literally compare. As a figure of speech, metaphor is said to be implicit or indirect, in contrast to simile where the comparison is expressed directly. In his final soliloquy, which begins "Tomorrow, and tomorrow, and tomorrow . . ." Macbeth creates a series of metaphors to express the meaninglessness of his own life: "Life's but a walking shadow, a poor player . . . it is a tale told by an idiot . . ." When we say, "the trip was a nightmare . . . .," or that "the meeting turned into a circus . . .," we are speaking in metaphor.

meter and rhythm Rhythm refers to the pattern of movement in a poem. As music has rhythm, so does poetry. Meter refers to specific patterns of stressed and unstressed syllables. (See *imabic pentameter*.)

ode A meditation or celebration of a specific subject. Traditional odes addressed "elevated" ideas and were composed in elaborate stanza forms. Keats's "Ode to a Nightingale" and "Ode to Autumn" are particularly fine examples. Modern odes may address subjects either serious or personal. One well-known contemporary ode is Pablo Neruda's "Ode to My Socks."

onomatopoeia The use of words whose sound reflects their sense. "Buzz," "hiss," and "moan" are common examples.

oxymoron Closely related to *paradox*, oxymoron is a figure of speech in which two contradictory or sharply contrasting terms are paired for emphasis or ironic effect. Students' favorite examples include "jumbo shrimp" and "army intelligence." Poets have written of the "wise fool," a "joyful sadness," or an "eloquent silence."

paradox An expression, concept, or situation whose literal statement is contradictory, yet which makes a truthful and meaningful observation. Consider the widely used expression, "less is more," for example.

Shakespeare's play *Macbeth* opens with a series of paradoxes to establish the moral atmosphere in which "foul is fair." John Donne's famous poem "Death Be Not Proud" ends with the paradox "Death thou shalt die."

personification A form of metaphor or simile in which nonhuman things— objects, plants and animals, forces of nature, abstract ideas—are given human qualities. Examples include "Pale flakes . . . come feeling for our faces . . ." (Owen); "Time . . . the thief of youth," (Milton); and "Blow winds, and crack your cheeks! Blow! Rage!" (Shakespeare).

prose poem This form appears on the page in the sentences and paragraphs of prose yet its effect is achieved through rhythm, images, and patterns of sound associated with poetry. The poetry of Karl Shapiro offers many excellent examples.

quatrain A stanza of four lines. The quatrain is the most commonly used stanza form in English poetry. Quatrains may be rhymed, *abab, aabb, abba,* for example, or they may be unrhymed.

rhyme In general, any repetition of identical or similar sounds among words that are close enough together to form an audible pattern. Rhyme is most evident when it occurs at the ends of lines of metrical verse.

rhyme scheme A regular pattern of end rhyme in a poem. The rhyme scheme in Shakespeare's sonnets, for example, is *abab/cdcd/efef/gg.*

satire A form or style that uses elements of irony, ridicule, exaggeration, understatement, sarcasm, humor, or absurdity to criticize human behavior or a society. All satire is **ironic** in that meaning or theme·is conveyed in the discrepancy between what is said and what is meant, between what is and what should be, between what appears and what truly is. Although satire is often entertaining, its purpose is serious and meant to provoke thought or judgment. The verse of Alexander Pope is often extended satire, and many poems by e. e. cummings are satiric.

simile An expression that is a direct comparison of two things. It uses such words as *like, as, as if, seems, appears.* For example, "A line of elms plunging and tossing like horses" (Theodore Roethke); "Mind in its purest play is like some bat" (Richard Wilbur); "I wandered lonely as a cloud" (William Wordsworth).

soliloquy A form of monologue found most often in drama. It differs from a dramatic monologue in that the speaker is alone, revealing thoughts and feelings to or for oneself that are intentionally unheard by other characters. In Shakespeare's plays, for example, the principal characters' reflections on how to act or questions of conscience are revealed in their soliloquies. Hamlet's "To be, or not to be . . ." is probably the most famous of dramatic soliloquies.

sonnet A poem of fourteen lines in *iambic pentameter* that may be composed of different patterns of stanzas and rhyme schemes. The most common forms are the English, or Shakespearean sonnet, which consists of three quatrains and a closing couplet, and the Italian sonnet, which consists of an *octave* of eight lines and a *sestet* of six lines.

speaker The narrative voice in a poem. Also, the character who speaks in a *dramatic monologue*.

stanza The grouping of lines within a poem. A stanza reflects the basic organization and development of ideas, much as paragraphs do in an essay. Many stanza patterns may have a fixed number of lines and a regular pattern of rhyme. Poets, however, often create stanzas of varying length and form within a single poem. A stanza that ends with a period, completing an idea or image, is considered "closed," whereas a stanza that ends with a comma or with no punctuation is called "open," indicating that there should be very little pause in the movement from one stanza to another.

symbol Most generally, anything that stands for or suggests something else. Language itself is symbolic: sounds and abstract written forms may stand for virtually any human thought or experience. Symbols are real objects and *concrete* images that lead us to *think about* what is suggested. Symbols organize a wide variety of ideas into single acts of understanding. They embody not single "meanings" but suggest whole areas of meaning.

understatement Expression in which something is presented as less important or significant than it really is. Understatement is often used for humorous, satiric, or *ironic* effect. Much of the satire in *Huckleberry Finn* stems from Huck's naive and understated observations. One particular form of understatement, actually a double negative, includes such expressions as "I was not uninterested," which really means "I was interested"; or "He was not without imagination," which really means "He had some imagination."

TERMS FOR WRITING

anecdote A brief story or account of a single experience, often biographical, that illustrates something typical or striking about a person. Anecdotes, like parables, are effective as vivid, specific examples of a general observation or quality.

argument The development of reasons and examples to support a thesis; narrowly, to outline a position on an issue or problem with the intent to clarify or persuade. Argument is also used in a broad sense to refer to the way a writer develops any topic. See Chapter 2, page 22 for an explanation and examples of Argument, Part 2 of the Regents ELA Exam.

audience For the writer, this term refers to the intended reader. Awareness of an audience determines, for example, what the writer may assume a reader already knows, the level of diction, and the tone.

coherence A piece of writing has coherence when the logical relationship of ideas is evident and convincing. In a coherent discussion, statements and sections follow one another in a natural, even inevitable way. A coherent discussion hangs together; an incoherent one is scattered and disorganized.

description The expression in words of what is experienced by the senses. Good description recreates what is felt, seen, heard—sensed in any way. We also use the term describe to mean *identify*, *classify*, *characterize*, even for abstract ideas. Description permits readers to re-create the subject in their own imaginations.

diction Refers to word choice. Diction may be formal or informal, complex or simple, or elegant or modest, depending on the occasion and the audience. The language used in casual conversation is different from the language used in formal writing. The good writer uses language that is varied, precise, and vivid. The good writer has resources of language to suit a wide range of purposes. In the rubrics for the ELA Exam, diction is evaluated as use of "formal style and precise language."

exposition The development of a topic through examples, reasons, and details that explain, clarify, show, and instruct—the primary purpose of exposition is to convey information. Much of the writing assigned to students is referred to as expository writing. Through exposition, you can demonstrate what you have learned, discovered, understood, appreciated. The task for Part 3 of the Regents ELA Exam is a good example of what is meant by expository writing.

focus Refers to the way a writer concentrates and directs all the information, examples, ideas, and reasons in an essay on the specific topic.

narrative Because it tells a story, a narrative has chronological order. The narrative method is commonly used in exposition when examples are offered in a chronological development.

prompt A set of directions for a writing task; may also be a quote or passage meant to stimulate a piece of writing.

tone Refers to the attitude of the writer toward the subject and/or toward the reader. Tone may range from *harsh and insistent* to *gentle and reflective*. There is as much variety of tone in writing as there is in human feeling. Some pieces, essays of opinion for example, usually have a very distinct tone. Other works, especially in fiction or personal expression, may be more subtle and indirect in tone.

transition Words or phrases used to link ideas and sections in a piece of writing. Common transitions include *first, second . . . in addition . . . finally; on the other hand, moreover, consequently, therefore*. Transitions make the development of an argument clear.

unity In the narrowest sense, unity refers to focus: the ideas and examples are clearly related to the topic and to one another. In the largest sense, unity refers to a feature of our best writing. All elements—ideas, form, language, and tone—work together to achieve the effect of a complete and well-made piece.

A Guide to Proofreading for Common Errors

THE BASICS

Review your essays to make sure that you have begun sentences with capital letters and ended them with a period! Carelessness in this basic use of the conventions could lower your score if the test raters feel that you have not mastered this aspect of formal writing.

PUNCTUATION

COMMA USE

There is one general guideline to keep in mind for comma use: The primary function of the comma is to prevent confusion for your reader. The comma shows how separate parts of sentences are related to one another.

Introductory clauses and phrases need a comma. This makes it clear where the introduction ends and the main clause begins. Note the following examples:

> *"Though I have traveled all over the world, it is the smell of the tides and marshes of Beaufort County that identifies and shapes me."*

> *"Because I came to Beaufort County when I was a boy, my novels all smell of seawater."*
>
> —Pat Conroy

Use the comma in compound sentences with coordinating conjunctions *and, but, yet, so, or, for*. A compound sentence joins two or more independent clauses that could be expressed separately as simple sentences. *Note that the comma precedes the conjunction:*

> *"I walked slowly,* for *the detail on the beach was infinite."*
> —Ernie Pyle

> *"The luncheon hour was long past,* and *the two had their end of the vast terrace to themselves."*
> —Edith Wharton

A final suggestion: Use a comma only where you *hear* a clear need for one.

THE APOSTROPHE

Remember, the most common use of the apostrophe is to show possession.

The *novel's* major themes = The major themes **of the novel**
Fiction reveals *characters'* motives and actions = The motives **of the characters**
Shakespeare dramatizes *Macbeth's* struggle with his conscience and ambition.

Avoid the increasingly common error of using the apostrophe to show the plural.

Mark Twain wrote several **novels;** he did not write "novel's."
Holden Caulfield spends several **days** (not day's) in New York before going home.
Students in New York State are expected to read at least 25 **books** (not book's) per year.

GRAMMAR

SUBJECT/VERB AGREEMENT

Be sure to match subjects and verbs. Agreement is a form of consistency and is one of the most basic elements of grammar. When you learn to conjugate verbs, for example, you are applying the concept of agreement. Singular subjects take singular verbs; plural subjects take plural verbs.

He speaks/they speak; One is/many are

PRONOUN/ANTECEDENT AGREEMENT

Because pronouns replace nouns or other pronouns, they must agree with their singular or plural antecedents.

Evelyn is very grateful to *her parents* for *their* constant support and encouragement.

Most pronoun/antecedent errors arise when we use the indefinite pronouns *anyone, anybody, everyone, everybody, someone, somebody, no one,* and so on. These pronouns are singular because they refer to *individuals:*

Everybody is responsible for *his* own work.
Someone has left *her* books on the floor.
If *anyone* calls while I am out, please tell *him* or *her* that I will call back after lunch.

The common practice of replacing *him/her* with *them,* or *her/his* with *their,* solves the problem of choosing gender, but it is ungrammatical and illogical. The careful writer (and speaker) avoids these errors, or rewrites:

Please tell *anyone who calls* that I will return at noon.
Someone's books have been left on the floor.
Everyone has individual responsibility for the assignments.

SPELLING

You are, of course, expected to spell correctly common words, the key terms of your essay, and the names of authors, titles, and characters. An occasional misspelling in an on-demand piece of writing should not lower your score if all other elements are good.

Be especially careful to proofread for these very common errors—they mar the overall impression that your essay makes on the reader.

accept/except

To *accept* is to receive, take willingly, agree to:
I *accept* your offer, apology, invitation
To *except* is to exclude, to separate out:
I will *except* you from the requirement.
Except is also a preposition:
Everyone *except* him will be leaving on Tuesday.

affect/effect

To *affect* (v.) means to move, influence, or change.
To *affect* also means to put on an artificial quality of personality or character; an exaggerated or artificial person may be called *affected.*
The *effects* (n.) are the consequences or results.
To *effect* (v.) means to put into action, to complete—a plan or a change, for example.

could of/should of

You mean *could have/should have*.

Do not make this unfortunate confusion in the way words sound!

hear/here

You may put your things *here* on the table.

I cannot *hear* you with all the noise outside.

its/it's

it's = a contraction for *it is*

its = a possessive form; do not add an apostrophe

loose/lose

Be careful not to *lose* your ticket; it cannot be replaced.

The dog ran *loose* when the leash broke.

principal/principle

Lack of effort is often the *principal* reason for failure.

Many consider honesty a fundamental *principle* in their lives.

than/then

My sister is several years younger *than* I am.

You will answer multiple-choice questions, *then* complete your essays.

there/their/they're

There he goes! It is over *there*.

Students should bring *their* books to class everyday.

They're = *they are*

to/too/two

You will have *two* weeks *to* complete the reading assignment; do not put it off until it is *too* late.

who's/whose

Who's (who is) that coming down the hall?

Whose books are these lying on the floor?

See Barron's *Let's Review: English, Fifth Edition* for a comprehensive review of punctuation, grammar, and usage.

Appendices

The New York State Common Core Learning Standards for English Language Arts

The following 11/12 grade-specific standards define end-of-year expectations and a cumulative progression designed to enable students to meet college and career readiness (CCR) expectations no later than the end of high school. The ELA/Common Core Regents Exam is designed to assess many (but not all) of the standards in each of the categories: Reading Literature, Reading Informational Texts, Writing, and Language.

READING STANDARDS FOR LITERATURE GRADES 11/12 (RL)

1. Cite strong and thorough textual evidence to support analysis of what the text says explicitly as well as inferences drawn from the text, including determining where the text leaves matters uncertain.

2. Determine two or more themes or central ideas of a text and analyze their development over the course of the text, including how they interact and build on one another to produce a complex account; provide an objective summary of the text.

3. Analyze the impact of the author's choices regarding how to develop and relate elements of a story or drama (e.g., where a story is set, how the action is ordered, how the characters are introduced and developed).

4. Determine the meaning of words and phrases as they are used in the text, including figurative and connotative meanings; analyze the impact of specific word choices on meaning and tone, including words with multiple meanings or language that is particularly fresh, engaging, or beautiful. (Include Shakespeare as well as other authors.)

5. Analyze how an author's choices concerning how to structure specific parts of a text (e.g., the choice of where to begin or end a story, the choice to provide a comedic or tragic resolution) contribute to its overall structure and meaning as well as its aesthetic impact.

6. Analyze a case in which grasping a point of view requires distinguishing what is directly stated in a text from what is really meant (e.g., satire, sarcasm, irony, or understatement).

7. Analyze multiple interpretations of a story, drama, or poem (e.g., recorded or live production of a play or recorded novel or poetry), evaluating how each version interprets the source text. (Include at least one play by Shakespeare and one play by an American dramatist.)

*8. Delineate and evaluate the argument and specific claims in a text, including the validity of the reasoning as well as the relevance and sufficiency of the evidence.

9. Demonstrate knowledge of eighteenth-, nineteenth-, and early-twentieth-century foundational works of American literature, including how two or more texts from the same period treat similar themes or topics.

10. By the end of grade 11, read and comprehend literature, including stories, dramas, and poems, in the grades 11–CCR text complexity band proficiently, with scaffolding as needed at the high end of the range.

11. By the end of grade 12, read and comprehend literature, including stories, dramas, and poems, at the high end of the grades 11–CCR text complexity band independently and proficiently.

*This anchor standard does not apply to literature.

READING STANDARDS FOR INFORMATIONAL TEXT GRADES 11/12 (RI)

1. Cite strong and thorough textual evidence to support analysis of what the text says explicitly as well as inferences drawn from the text, including determining where the text leaves matters uncertain.

2. Determine two or more central ideas of a text and analyze their development over the course of the text, including how they interact and build on one another to provide a complex analysis; provide an objective summary of the text.

3. Analyze a complex set of ideas or sequence of events and explain how specific individuals, ideas, or events interact and develop over the course of the text.

4. Determine the meaning of words and phrases as they are used in a text, including figurative, connotative, and technical meanings; analyze how an author uses and refines the meaning of a key term or terms over the course of a text.

5. Analyze and evaluate the effectiveness of the structure an author uses in his or her exposition or argument, including whether the structure makes points clear, convincing, and engaging.

6. Determine an author's point of view or purpose in a text in which the rhetoric is particularly effective, analyzing how style and content contribute to the power, persuasiveness, or beauty of the text.

7. Integrate and evaluate multiple sources of information presented in different media or formats (e.g., visually, quantitatively) as well as in words in order to address a question or solve a problem.

8. Delineate and evaluate the reasoning in seminal U.S. texts, including the application of constitutional principles and use of legal reasoning (e.g., in U.S. Supreme Court majority opinions and dissents) and the premises, purposes, and arguments in works of public advocacy (e.g., The Federalist, presidential addresses).

9. Analyze seventeenth-, eighteenth-, and nineteenth-century foundational U.S. documents of historical and literary significance (including The Declaration of Independence, the Preamble to the Constitution, the Bill of Rights, and Lincoln's Second Inaugural Address) for their themes, purposes, and rhetorical features.

10. By the end of grade 11, read and comprehend literary nonfiction in the grade 11–CCR text complexity band proficiently, with scaffolding as needed at the high end of the range. By the end of grade 12, read and comprehend literary nonfiction at the high end of the grade 11–CCR text complexity band independently and proficiently.

WRITING STANDARDS GRADES 11/12 (W)

1. Write arguments to support claims in an analysis of substantive topics or texts, using valid reasoning and relevant and sufficient evidence.

2. Write informative/explanatory texts to examine and convey complex ideas and information clearly and accurately through the effective selection, organization, and analysis of content.

3. Write narratives to develop real or imagined experiences or events using effective technique, well-chosen details, and well-structured event sequences.

4. Produce clear and coherent writing in which the development, organization, and style are appropriate to task, purpose, and audience.

5. Develop and strengthen writing as needed by planning, revising, editing, rewriting, or trying a new approach.

6. Use technology, including the Internet, to produce and publish writing and to interact and collaborate with others.

7. Conduct short as well as more sustained research projects based on focused questions, demonstrating understanding of the subject under investigation.

8. Gather relevant information from multiple print and digital sources, assess the credibility and accuracy of each source, and integrate the information while avoiding plagiarism.

9. Draw evidence from literary or informational texts to support analysis, reflection, and research.

10. Write routinely over extended time frames (time for research, reflection, and revision) and shorter time frames (a single sitting or a day or two) for a range of tasks, purposes, and audiences.

11. Develop personal, cultural, textual, and thematic connections within and across genres as they respond to texts through written, digital, and oral presentations, employing a variety of media and genres.

LANGUAGE STANDARDS GRADES 11/12 (L)

Conventions of Standard English

1. Demonstrate command of the conventions of standard English grammar and usage when writing or speaking.

2. Demonstrate command of the conventions of standard English capitalization, punctuation, and spelling when writing.

Knowledge of Language

3. Apply knowledge of language to understand how language functions in different contexts, to make effective choices for meaning or style, and to comprehend more fully when reading or listening.

Vocabulary Acquisition and Use

4. Determine or clarify the meaning of unknown and multiple meaning words and phrases by using context clues, analyzing meaningful word parts, and consulting general and specialized reference materials, as appropriate.

5. Demonstrate understanding of figurative language, word relationships, and nuances in word meanings.

6. Acquire and use accurately a range of general academic and domain-specific words and phrases sufficient for reading, writing, speaking, and listening at the college and career readiness level; demonstrate independence in gathering vocabulary knowledge when considering a word or phrase important to comprehension or expression.

HOW IS THE REGENTS ELA (COMMON CORE) EXAM SCORED?

WEIGHTING OF PARTS

Each of the three parts of the Regents Examination in English Language Arts (Common Core) has a number of raw score credits associated with the questions/tasks within that part. In order to ensure an appropriate distribution of credits across the test, each part is weighted.

For Part 1, each multiple-choice question is worth one point. The Part 2 essay is scored on a 6-point rubric then weighted $\times$ 4. The Part 3 Text Analysis is scored on a 4-point rubric and then weighted $\times$ 2.

As you can see, the Part 2 Argument Essay is the most heavily weighted section.

The table below shows the raw score credits, weighting factor, and weighted score credits for each part of the test.

Part	Maximum Raw Score Credits	Weighting Factor	Maximum Weighted Score Credits
Part 1	24	1	24
Part 2	6	4	24
Part 3	4	2	8
			Total 56

A student's final exam score is then determined in the conversion of the weighted score (of up to 56 points) on a scale of 0–100. Here is an example from a recent ELA exam:

SCORING RUBRICS FOR THE REGENTS ELA (COMMON CORE) EXAM

Parts 2 and 3 of the Regents Examination in English Language Arts (Common Core) is scored using holistic rubrics. Part 2 is scored using a 6-credit rubric, and Part 3 is scored using a 4-credit rubric. Both rubrics reflect the demands called for by the Common Core Learning Standards for English Language Arts and Literacy through the end of Grade 11.

Regents Examination in English Language Arts
(Common Core)—January 2017

Chart for Converting Total Weighted Raw Scores to Final Exam Scores
(Scale Scores) (Use for the January 2017 examination only.)

Weighted Raw Score*	Scale Score	Performance Level	Weighted Raw Score*	Scale Score	Performance Level
56	100	5	27	55	2
55	99	5	26	52	1
54	99	5	25	48	1
53	98	5	24	45	1
52	97	5	23	42	1
51	96	5	22	38	1
50	95	5	21	35	1
49	95	5	20	31	1
48	94	5	19	27	1
47	92	5	18	24	1
46	91	5	17	20	1
45	90	5	16	17	1
44	89	5	15	14	1
43	88	5	14	11	1
42	87	5	13	9	1
41	86	5	12	8	1
40	85	5	11	7	1
39	83	4	10	6	1
38	81	4	9	5	1
37	80	4	8	4	1
36	79	4	7	4	1
35	76	3	6	3	1
34	74	3	5	2	1
33	71	3	4	2	1
32	69	3	3	1	1
31	66	3	2	1	1
30	65	3	1	1	1
29	61	2	0	0	1
28	58	2			

The conversion table is determined independently for each administration of the exam. You will find the conversion tables for each exam in the Answers Explained.

New York State Regents Examination in English Language Arts (Common Core)
Part 2 Rubric
Writing from Sources: Argument

Criteria	6 Essays at this Level	5 Essays at this Level	4 Essays at this Level	3 Essays at this Level	2 Essays at this Level	1 Essays at this Level
Content and Analysis: the extent to which the essay conveys complex ideas and information clearly and accurately in order to support claims in an analysis of the texts	-introduce a precise and insightful claim, as directed by the task -demonstrate in-depth and insightful analysis of the texts, as necessary to support the claim and to distinguish the claim from alternate or opposing claims	-introduce a precise and thoughtful claim, as directed by the task -demonstrate thorough analysis of the texts, as necessary to support the claim and to distinguish the claim from alternate or opposing claims	-introduce a precise claim, as directed by the task -demonstrate appropriate and accurate analysis of the texts, as necessary to support the claim and to distinguish the claim from alternate or opposing claims	-introduce a reasonable claim, as directed by the task -demonstrate some analysis of the texts, but insufficiently distinguish the claim from alternate or opposing claims	-introduce a claim -demonstrate confused or unclear analysis of the texts, failing to distinguish the claim from alternate or opposing claims	-do not introduce a claim -do not demonstrate analysis of the texts
Command of Evidence: the extent to which the essay presents evidence from the provided texts to support analysis	-present ideas fully and thoughtfully, making highly effective use of a wide range of specific and relevant evidence to support analysis -demonstrate proper citation of sources to avoid plagiarism when dealing with direct quotes and paraphrased material	-present ideas clearly and accurately, making effective use of specific and relevant evidence to support analysis -demonstrate proper citation of sources to avoid plagiarism when dealing with direct quotes and paraphrased material	-present ideas sufficiently, making adequate use of specific and relevant evidence to support analysis -demonstrate proper citation of sources to avoid plagiarism when dealing with direct quotes and paraphrased material	-present ideas briefly, making use of some specific and relevant evidence to support analysis -demonstrate inconsistent citation of sources to avoid plagiarism when dealing with direct quotes and paraphrased material	-present ideas inconsistently and/or inaccurately, in an attempt to support analysis, making use of some evidence that may be irrelevant -demonstrate little use of citations to avoid plagiarism when dealing with direct quotes and paraphrased material	-present little or no evidence from the texts -do not make use of citations

Coherence, Organization, and Style: the extent to which the essay logically organizes complex ideas, concepts, and information using formal style and precise language	Control of Conventions: the extent to which the essay demonstrates command of conventions of standard English grammar, usage, capitalization, punctuation, and spelling
-exhibit skillful organization of ideas and information to create a cohesive and coherent essay -establish and maintain a formal style, using sophisticated language and structure	-demonstrate control of conventions with essentially no errors, even with sophisticated language
-exhibit logical organization of ideas and information to create a cohesive and coherent essay -establish and maintain a formal style, using fluent and precise language and sound structure	-demonstrate control of the conventions, exhibiting occasional errors only when using sophisticated language
-exhibit acceptable organization of ideas and information to create a coherent essay -establish and maintain a formal style, using precise and appropriate language and structure	-demonstrate partial control, exhibiting occasional errors that do not hinder comprehension
-exhibit some organization of ideas and information to create a mostly coherent essay -establish but fail to maintain a formal style, using primarily basic language and structure	-demonstrate emerging control, exhibiting occasional errors that hinder comprehension
-exhibit inconsistent organization of ideas and information, failing to create a coherent essay -lack a formal style, using some language that is inappropriate or imprecise	-demonstrate a lack of control, exhibiting frequent errors that make comprehension difficult
-exhibit little organization of ideas and information -are minimal, making assessment unreliable -use language that is predominantly incoherent, inappropriate, or copied directly from the task or texts	-are minimal, making assessment of conventions unreliable

- An essay that addresses fewer texts than required by the task can be scored no higher than a 3.
- An essay that is a personal response and makes little or no reference to the task or texts can be scored no higher than a 1.
- An essay that is totally copied from the task and/or texts with no original student writing must be scored a 0.
- An essay that is totally unrelated to the task, illegible, incoherent, blank, or unrecognizable as English must be scored as a 0.

New York State Regents Examination in English Language Arts (Common Core)

Part 3 Rubric

Text Analysis: Exposition

Criteria	4 Responses at this Level	3 Responses at this Level	2 Responses at this Level	1 Responses at this Level
Content and Analysis: the extent to which the response conveys complex ideas and information clearly and accurately in order to respond to the task and support an analysis of the text	-introduce a well-reasoned central idea and a writing strategy that clearly establish the criteria for analysis -demonstrate a thoughtful analysis of the author's use of the writing strategy to develop the central idea	-introduce a clear central idea and a writing strategy that establish the criteria for analysis -demonstrate an appropriate analysis of the author's use of the writing strategy to develop the central idea	-introduce a central idea and/or a writing strategy -demonstrate a superficial analysis of the author's use of the writing strategy to develop the central idea	-introduce a confused or incomplete central idea or writing strategy and/or -demonstrate a minimal analysis of the author's use of the writing strategy to develop the central idea
Command of Evidence: the extent to which the response presents evidence from the provided text to support analysis	-present ideas clearly and consistently, making effective use of specific and relevant evidence to support analysis	-present ideas sufficiently, making adequate use of relevant evidence to support analysis	-present ideas inconsistently, inadequately, and/or inaccurately in an attempt to support analysis, making use of some evidence that may be irrelevant	-present little or no evidence from the text
Coherence, Organization, and Style: the extent to which the response logically organizes complex ideas, concepts, and information using formal style and precise language	-exhibit logical organization of ideas and information to create a cohesive and coherent response -establish and maintain a formal style, using precise language and sound structure	-exhibit acceptable organization of ideas and information to create a coherent response -establish and maintain a formal style, using appropriate language and structure	-exhibit inconsistent organization of ideas and information, failing to create a coherent response -lack a formal style, using language that is basic, inappropriate, or imprecise	-exhibit little organization of ideas and information -use language that is predominantly incoherent, inappropriate, or copied directly from the task or text -are minimal, making assessment unreliable

| Control of Conventions: the extent to which the response demonstrates command of conventions of standard English grammar, usage, capitalization, punctuation, and spelling | -demonstrate control of the conventions with infrequent errors | -demonstrate partial control of conventions with occasional errors that do not hinder comprehension | -demonstrate emerging control of conventions with some errors that hinder comprehension | -demonstrate a lack of control of conventions with frequent errors that make comprehension difficult -are minimal, making assessment of conventions unreliable |

- A response that is a personal response and makes little or no reference to the task or text can be scored no higher than a 1.
- A response that is totally copied from the text with no original writing must be given a 0.
- A response that is totally unrelated to the task, illegible, incoherent, blank, or unrecognizable as English must be scored as a 0.

Regents ELA (Common Core) Examinations and Answers

Regents ELA (Common Core) Examination June 2014
English Language Arts

PART 1—Reading Comprehension

Directions (1–24): Closely read each of the three passages below. After each passage, there are several multiple-choice questions. Select the best suggested answer to each question and write its number in the space provided. You may use the margins to take notes as you read.

Reading Comprehension Passage A

It was upon the 4th of March, as I have good reason to remember, that I rose somewhat earlier than usual, and found that Sherlock Holmes had not yet finished his breakfast. The landlady had become so accustomed to my late habits that my place had not been laid nor my coffee prepared.
(5) With the unreasonable petulance[1] of mankind I rang the bell and gave a curt intimation that I was ready. Then I picked up a magazine from the table and attempted to while away the time with it, while my companion munched silently at his toast. One of the articles had a pencil-mark at the heading, and I naturally began to run my eye through it. ...
(10) "From a drop of water," said the writer, "a logician could infer the possibility of an Atlantic or a Niagara without having seen or heard of one or the other. So all life is a great chain, the nature of which is known whenever we are shown a single link of it. Like all other arts, the Science of Deduction and Analysis is one which can only be acquired by long and

---
[1]petulance—a quality or state of being rude

(15)   patient study, nor is life long enough to allow any mortal to attain the highest possible perfection in it. Before turning to those moral and mental aspects of the matter which present the greatest difficulties, let the inquirer begin by mastering more elementary problems. Let him, on meeting a fellow-mortal, learn at a glance to distinguish the history of the man and

(20)   the trade or profession to which he belongs. Puerile[2] as such an exercise may seem, it sharpens the faculties of observation and teaches one where to look and what to look for. By a man's fingernails, by his coat-sleeve, by his boot, by his trouser-knees, by the callosities of his forefinger and thumb, by his expression, by his shirt-cuffs—by each of these things a man's call-

(25)   ing is plainly revealed. That all united should fail to enlighten the competent inquirer in any case is almost inconceivable."

     "What ineffable twaddle!" I cried, slapping the magazine down on the table; "I never read such rubbish in my life."

     "What is it?" asked Sherlock Holmes.

(30)   "Why, this article," I said, pointing at it with my egg-spoon as I sat down to my breakfast. "I see that you have read it, since you have marked it. I don't deny that it is smartly written. It irritates me, though. It is evidently the theory of some arm-chair lounger who evolves all these neat little paradoxes in the seclusion of his own study. It is not practical. I should

(35)   like to see him clapped down in a third-class carriage on the Underground and asked to give the trades of all his fellow-travellers. I would lay a thousand to one against him."

     "You would lose your money," Sherlock Holmes remarked, calmly. "As for the article, I wrote it myself."

(40)   "You?"

     "Yes, I have a turn both for observation and for deduction. The theories which I have expressed there, and which appear to you to be so chimerical, are really extremely practical—so practical that I depend upon them for my bread-and-cheese."

(45)   "And how?" I asked, involuntarily.

     "Well, I have a trade of my own. I suppose I am the only one in the world. I'm a consulting detective, if you can understand what that is. Here in London we have lots of government detectives and lots of private ones.

---

[2]puerile—childish

(50) When these fellows are at fault they come to me, and I manage to put them on the right scent. They lay all the evidence before me, and I am generally able, by the help of my knowledge of the history of crime, to set them straight. There is a strong family resemblance about misdeeds, and if you have all the details of a thousand at your finger-ends, it is odd if you can't unravel the thousand and first. Lestrade is a well-known detective. He got

(55) himself into a fog recently over a forgery case, and that was what brought him here."

"And these other people?"

"They are mostly sent out by private inquiry agencies. They are all people who are in trouble about something, and want a little enlightening. I lis-

(60) ten to their story, they listen to my comments, and then I pocket my fee."

"But do you mean to say," I said, "that without leaving your room you can unravel some knot which other men can make nothing of, although they have seen every detail for themselves?"

"Quite so. I have a kind of intuition that way. Now and again a case

(65) turns up which is a little more complex. Then I have to bustle about and see things with my own eyes. You see, I have a lot of special knowledge which I apply to the problem, and which facilitates matters wonderfully. Those rules of deduction laid down in that article which aroused your scorn are invaluable to me in practical work. Observation with me is sec-

(70) ond nature. You appeared to be surprised when I told you, on our first meeting, that you had come from Afghanistan."

"You were told, no doubt."

"Nothing of the sort. I *knew* you came from Afghanistan. From long habit the train of thought ran so swiftly through my mind that I arrived at

(75) the conclusion without being conscious of intermediate steps. There were such steps, however. The train of reasoning ran: 'Here is a gentleman of a medical type, but with the air of a military man. Clearly an army doctor, then. He has just come from the tropics, for his face is dark, and that is not the natural tint of his skin, for his wrists are fair. He has undergone hard-

(80) ship and sickness, as his haggard face says clearly. His left arm has been injured. He holds it in a stiff and unnatural manner. Where in the tropics could an English army doctor have seen much hardship and got his arm wounded? Clearly in Afghanistan.' The whole train of thought did not occupy a second. I then remarked that you came from Afghanistan, and

(85) you were astonished." ...

I was still annoyed at his bumptious style of conversation. I thought it best to change the topic.

"I wonder what that fellow is looking for?" I asked, pointing to a stalwart, plainly dressed individual who was walking slowly down the other (90) side of the street, looking anxiously at the numbers. He had a large, blue envelope in his hand, and was evidently the bearer of a message.

"You mean the retired sergeant of marines," said Sherlock Holmes.

"Brag and bounce!" thought I to myself. "He knows that I cannot verify his guess." The thought had hardly passed through my mind when (95) the man whom we were watching caught sight of the number on our door, and ran rapidly across the roadway. We heard a loud knock, a deep voice below, and heavy steps ascending the stair.

"For Mr. Sherlock Holmes," he said, stepping into the room and handing my friend the letter.

(100) Here was an opportunity of taking the conceit out of him. He little thought of this when he made that random shot. "May I ask, my lad," I said, blandly, "what your trade may be?"

"Commissionnaire, sir," he said, gruffly. "Uniform away for repairs."

"And you were?" I asked, with a slightly malicious glance at my com-
(105) panion. "A sergeant, sir, Royal Marine Light Infantry, sir. No answer? Right, sir." He clicked his heels together, raised his hand in a salute, and was gone.

—A. Conan Doyle
excerpted from *A Study in Scarlet*, 1904
Harper & Brothers Publishers

1 The phrase "with the unreasonable petulance of mankind" (line 5) emphasizes the narrator's

   (1) frustration with himself for missing sleep
   (2) irritation about not finding his breakfast ready
   (3) concern regarding the pencil-mark on the newspaper
   (4) impatience with Sherlock Holmes's silence   1_____

2 How do the words "logician" (line 10), "deduction" (lines 14, 41, and 68), and "analysis" (line 14) advance the author's purpose?

   (1) by indicating the relationship between science and art
   (2) by suggesting the reasons why private inquiry agencies seek outside help
   (3) by highlighting the complexity of the crimes encountered by Sherlock Holmes
   (4) by emphasizing the systematic nature of Sherlock Holmes's approach to solving crimes   2_____

3 What is the effect of withholding the identity of Sherlock Holmes as the author of the article (lines 10 through 39)?

   (1) It creates a somber mood.
   (2) It foreshadows an unwelcome turn of events.
   (3) It allows the reader to learn the narrator's true feelings.
   (4) It leads the reader to misunderstand who the writer is.   3_____

4 In this passage, the conversation between Holmes
  and the narrator (lines 27 through 44) serves to

  (1) reinforce the narrator's appreciation for deduction
  (2) establish a friendship between the narrator and Holmes
  (3) reveal how Holmes makes his living
  (4) expose some of Holmes's misdeeds   4____

5 As used in lines 42–43, the word "chimerical"
  most nearly means

  (1) unfair   (3) aggravating
  (2) unrealistic   (4) contradictory   5____

6 Which analysis is best supported by the details in
  lines 50 through 63 of the text?

  (1) Private detectives base their analyses on an
      understanding of human nature.
  (2) Sherlock Holmes's association with other well-
      known detectives improves his crime-solving
      abilities.
  (3) Government detectives are mostly ineffective at
      solving complicated crimes.
  (4) Sherlock Holmes's intuition relies on his ability
      to detect similarities among various crimes.   6____

7 Which quotation best reflects a central theme in the text?

  (1) "So all life is a great chain, the nature of which is known whenever we are shown a single link of it" (lines 12 and 13)

  (2) "What ineffable twaddle ... I never read such rubbish in my life" (lines 27 and 28)

  (3) "They are all people who are in trouble about something, and want a little enlightening" (lines 58 and 59)

  (4) "Now and again a case turns up which is a little more complex" (lines 64 and 65)   7_____

8 The narrator views the arrival of the messenger as "an opportunity of taking the conceit out of him" (line 100) because the narrator wishes to

  (1) challenge Holmes's theories of deduction

  (2) stress the importance of self-confidence

  (3) reveal Holmes's true intentions

  (4) practice his own deductive abilities   8_____

9 The author's description of the conversation between the narrator and the retired sergeant in lines 101 through 107 serves mostly to

  (1) develop a character

  (2) create a flashback

  (3) establish a comparison

  (4) resolve a conflict   9_____

10 The conversation with the retired sergeant (lines 104 through 107) leaves the narrator with a sense of

  (1) astonishment   (3) pleasure

  (2) confusion   (4) distrust   10_____

Reading Comprehension Passage B

Give Us Our Peace

Give us a peace equal to the war
Or else our souls will be unsatisfied,
And we will wonder what we have fought for
And why the many died.

(5) Give us a peace accepting every challenge—
The challenge of the poor, the black, of all denied,
The challenge of the vast colonial world
That long has had so little justice by its side.

Give us a peace that dares us to be wise.
(10) Give us a peace that dares us to be strong.
Give us a peace that dares us still uphold
Throughout the peace our battle against wrong.

Give us a peace that is not cheaply used,
A peace that is no clever scheme,
(15) A people's peace for which men can enthuse,
A peace that brings reality to our dream.

Give us a peace that will produce great schools —
As the war produced great armament,
A peace that will wipe out our slums—
(20) As war wiped out our foes on evil bent.

Give us a peace that will enlist
A mighty army serving human kind,
Not just an army geared to kill,
But trained to help the living mind—

(25)   An army trained to shape our common good
        And bring about a world of brotherhood.

—Langston Hughes
from *The Chicago Defender*, August 25, 1945

11 The prevailing tone of the poem is

    (1) demanding   (3) celebratory

    (2) angry   (4) proud   11_____

12 What is most likely not a purpose of the repetition
   of the phrase "Give us a peace" throughout the
   poem?

    (1) to provide a unified structure

    (2) to emphasize a central idea

    (3) to solicit the people's loyalty

    (4) to introduce the poet's requests   12_____

13 The military references throughout the poem
   serve to

    (1) recall the heroic cause of war

    (2) stress the destructive nature of war

    (3) rally the people for a new form of war

    (4) warn the people of an impending war   13_____

14 The poet's purpose in the poem can best be
   described as

    (1) a condemnation of war

    (2) an appeal for justice

    (3) an argument for colonial values

    (4) a criticism of education   14_____

Reading Comprehension Passage C

Science is a way of thinking much more than it is a body of knowledge.
Its goal is to find out how the world works, to seek what regularities there
may be, to penetrate to the connections of things—from subnuclear par-
ticles, which may be the constituents of all matter, to living organisms, the
(5)   human social community, and thence to the cosmos as a whole. Our intuition is by no means an infallible guide. Our perceptions may be distorted
by training and prejudice or merely because of the limitations of our sense
organs, which, of course, perceive directly but a small fraction of the phenomena of the world. Even so straightforward a question as whether in
(10) the absence of friction a pound of lead falls faster than a gram of fluff was
answered incorrectly by Aristotle and almost everyone else before the time
of Galileo. Science is based on experiment, on a willingness to challenge
old dogma, on an openness to see the universe as it really is. Accordingly,
science sometimes requires courage—at the very least the courage to ques-
(15) tion the conventional wisdom.

Beyond this the main trick of science is to really think of something:
the shape of clouds and their occasional sharp bottom edges at the same
altitude everywhere in the sky; the formation of a dewdrop on a leaf; the
origin of a name or a word—Shakespeare, say, or "philanthropic"; the
(20) reason for human social customs—the incest taboo, for example; how it
is that a lens in sunlight can make paper burn; how a "walking stick" got
to look so much like a twig; why the Moon seems to follow us as we walk;
what prevents us from digging a hole down to the center of the Earth;
what the definition is of "down" on a spherical Earth; how it is possible
(25) for the body to convert yesterday's lunch into today's muscle and sinew;
or how far is up—does the universe go on forever, or if it does not, is
there any meaning to the question of what lies on the other side? Some of
these questions are pretty easy. Others, especially the last, are mysteries to
which no one even today knows the answer. They are natural questions
(30) to ask. Every culture has posed such questions in one way or another.
Almost always the proposed answers are in the nature of "Just So Stories,"
attempted explanations divorced from experiment, or even from careful
comparative observations.

But the scientific cast of mind examines the world critically as if many
(35) alternative worlds might exist, as if other things might be here which

are not. Then we are forced to ask why what we see is present and not
something else. Why are the Sun and the Moon and the planets spheres?
Why not pyramids, or cubes, or dodecahedra? Why not irregular, jum-
bly shapes? Why so symmetrical, worlds? If you spend any time spinning
(40) hypotheses, checking to see whether they make sense, whether they conform to what else we know, thinking of tests you can pose to substantiate
or deflate your hypotheses, you will find yourself doing science. And as
you come to practice this habit of thought more and more you will get
better and better at it. To penetrate into the heart of the thing—even a
(45) little thing, a blade of grass, as Walt Whitman said—is to experience a
kind of exhilaration that, it may be, only human beings of all the beings
on this planet can feel. We are an intelligent species and the use of our
intelligence quite properly gives us pleasure. In this respect the brain is
like a muscle. When we think well, we feel good. Understanding is a kind
(50) of ecstasy. ...

Let us approach a much more modest question: not whether we can
know the universe or the Milky Way Galaxy or a star or a world. Can we
know, ultimately and in detail, a grain of salt? Consider one microgram of
table salt, a speck just barely large enough for someone with keen eyesight
(55) to make out without a microscope. In that grain of salt there are about
10^{16} sodium and chlorine atoms. This is a 1 followed by 16 zeros, 10 million billion atoms. If we wish to know a grain of salt, we must know at
least the three-dimensional positions of each of these atoms. (In fact, there
is much more to be known—for example, the nature of the forces between
(60) the atoms—but we are making only a modest calculation.) Now, is this
number more or less than the number of things which the brain can know?

How much can the brain know? There are perhaps 1011 neurons in
the brain, the circuit elements and switches that are responsible in their
electrical and chemical activity for the functioning of our minds. A typical
(65) brain neuron has perhaps a thousand little wires, called dendrites, which
connect it with its fellows. If, as seems likely, every bit of information in
the brain corresponds to one of these connections, the total number of
things knowable by the brain is no more than 10^{14}, one hundred trillion.
But this number is only one percent of the number of atoms in our speck of
(70) salt.

So in this sense the universe is intractable,[1] astonishingly immune to any human attempt at full knowledge. We cannot on this level understand a grain of salt, much less the universe.

(75) But let us look a little more deeply at our microgram of salt. Salt happens to be a crystal in which, except for defects in the structure of the crystal lattice, the position of every sodium and chlorine atom is predetermined. If we could shrink ourselves into this crystalline world, we would see rank upon rank of atoms in an ordered array, a regularly alternating structure—sodium, chlorine, sodium, chlorine specifying the sheet of (80) atoms we are standing on and all the sheets above us and below us. An absolutely pure crystal of salt could have the position of every atom specified by something like 10 bits of information.[2] This would not strain the information-carrying capacity of the brain.

If the universe had natural laws that governed its behavior to the same (85) degree of regularity that determines a crystal of salt, then, of course, the universe would be knowable. Even if there were many such laws, each of considerable complexity, human beings might have the capability to understand them all. Even if such knowledge exceeded the information-carrying capacity of the brain, we might store the additional information (90) outside our bodies—in books, for example, or in computer memories—and still, in some sense, know the universe. . . .

—Carl Sagan
excerpted from *Broca's Brain*, 1979
Random House

---

[1]intractable—stubborn
[2]Chlorine is a deadly poison gas employed on European battlefields in World War I. Sodium is a corrosive metal which burns upon contact with water. Together they make a placid and unpoisonous material, table salt. Why each of these substances has the properties it does is a subject called chemistry, which requires more than 10 bits of information to understand.

15 The central idea of the first paragraph focuses on the

   (1) nature of scientific investigation
   (2) unknowable nature of the universe
   (3) growth of our understanding over time
   (4) benefits of formal education   15____

16 Which phrase from the text clarifies the meaning of "dogma" as used in line 13?

   (1) "constituents of all matter" (line 4)
   (2) "infallible guide" (line 6)
   (3) "phenomena of the world" (lines 8–9)
   (4) "conventional wisdom" (line 15)   16____

17 Which statement from the text best summarizes the central idea of paragraph 2?

   (1) "Its goal is to find out how the world works, to seek what regularities there may be, to penetrate to the connections of things" (lines 2 through 3)
   (2) "But the scientific cast of mind examines the world critically as if many alternative worlds might exist, as if other things might be here which are not" (lines 34–36)
   (3) "We are an intelligent species and the use of our intelligence quite properly gives us pleasure" (lines 47 and 48)
   (4) "Even if there were many such laws, each of considerable complexity, human beings might have the capability to understand them all" (lines 86–88)   17____

18 According to the text, the "main trick" (line 16) of science is to

(1) follow one's intuition
(2) observe and develop questions
(3) experiment and create laws
(4) accept one's limitations   18____

19 The examples presented in lines 34 through 39 help the reader understand

(1) how scientific inquiry differs from ordinary questioning
(2) why multiple worlds could potentially exist
(3) how cultural stories influence scientific observation
(4) why popular explanations rarely rely on experimentation   19____

20 Which statement best summarizes the central claim made in lines 34 through 50?

(1) Science is based on human criticism of the world.
(2) Science is based on the accuracy of human perceptions.
(3) Humans have a capacity to experience joy through their intelligence.
(4) Humans consider themselves superior to all other species on the planet.   20____

21 The purpose of the figurative language in lines 48 and 49 is to

(1) question the function of the human brain
(2) contrast the human brain with the brains of other beings
(3) indicate the shape and composition of one's brain
(4) illustrate the effect of using one's brain   21____

22 The description of salt in lines 52 through 60 emphasizes the idea of

(1) interconnectedness
(2) complexity
(3) predictability
(4) uniqueness   22_____

23 What effect is created by the use of irony in line 60 and lines 67 through 71?

(1) humor   (3) scorn
(2) doubt   (4) awe   23_____

24 With which statement would the author of this text most likely agree?

(1) Understanding the world is essential to our well being.
(2) The human brain has an unlimited capacity to store knowledge.
(3) Scientific inquiry should only focus on objective reality.
(4) Technology allows us to have complete knowledge of the universe.   24_____

PART 2—Argument Response

Directions: Closely read each of the four texts on pages 104 through 111 and write a source-based argument on the topic below. You may use the margins to take notes as you read and scrap paper to plan your response. Write your argument on a separate sheet of paper.

Topic: Should companies be allowed to track consumers' shopping or other preferences without their permission?

Your Task: Carefully read each of the *four* texts provided. Then, using evidence from at least *three* of the texts, write a well-developed argument regarding companies being allowed to track consumers' shopping or other preferences without their permission. Clearly establish your claim, distinguish your claim from alternate or opposing claims, and use specific, relevant, and sufficient evidence from at least *three* of the texts to develop your argument. Do *not* simply summarize each text.

Guidelines:

Be sure to

- Establish your claim regarding companies being allowed to track consumers' shopping or other preferences without their permission.
- Distinguish your claim from alternate or opposing claims.
- Use specific, relevant, and sufficient evidence from at least *three* of the texts to develop your argument.
- Identify each source that you reference by text number and line number(s) or graphic (for example: Text 1, line 4 or Text 2, graphic).
- Organize your ideas in a cohesive and coherent manner.
- Maintain a formal style of writing.
- Follow the conventions of standard written English.

Texts:

Text 1—Cell Phone Carrier Marketing Techniques An Invasion of Privacy?

Text 2—EyeSee You and the Internet of Things: Watching You While You Shop

Text 3—Where Will Consumers Find Privacy Protection from RFIDs?: A Case for Federal Legislation

Text 4—RFID Consumer Applications and Benefits

Text 1

Cell Phone Carrier Marketing Techniques
An Invasion of Privacy?

BOSTON (CBS) – Your cell phone may be spying on you.

Every time you download an app, search for a website, send a text, snap a QR code or drive by a store with your GPS on, you are being tracked by your cell phone company.

(5)   "They know you were playing Angry Birds. They know that you drove by Sears. They know you drove by Domino's Pizza. They can take that and take a very unique algorithm[1] that can focus on your behavior," explained marketing expert Mark Johnson. "It's very impactful."

According to Johnson, your data trail is worth big money to the cell (10)   phone companies.

Details about your habits, your age and gender are compiled and can be sold to third parties. The information is predominantly used as a marketing tool so advertisers can target you with products or services that you are more likely to use or want.

(15)   The idea does not sit well with smartphone user Harrine Freeman. "It does seem creepy that companies are collecting all this information about consumers," she said.

Freeman is so uneasy; she turns off her GPS when she is not using it. She also clears her browser history.

(20)   "I think it is an invasion of privacy," she said.

All of the major cell phone carriers admit to collecting information about its customers. Some in the industry argue it benefits consumers because they get ads that are relevant to them. Cell phone companies do notify customers about the data they collect, but critics say the notices are (25)   often hard to understand and written in fine print.

Rainey Reitman of the Electronic Frontier Foundation doesn't like the fact that those who don't want to be tracked have to go out of their way to get the company to stop.

"This is something that consumers are automatically opted into," (30)   Reitman said.

---

[1]algorithm—process or set of rules followed in calculations

To find out how your cell phone company might be monitoring you, be sure to carefully read the privacy policy.

Also, make sure you read all of the updates your carrier might send you because this tracking technology keeps changing.

—Paula Ebben
http://boston.cbslocal.com, January 16, 2012

Text 2

EyeSee You and the Internet of Things: Watching You While You Shop

...Even the store mannequins have gotten in on the gig. According to the *Washington Post*, mannequins in some high-end boutiques are now being outfitted with cameras that utilize facial recognition technology. A small camera embedded in the eye of an otherwise normal looking man-
(5) nequin allows storekeepers to keep track of the age, gender and race of all their customers. This information is then used to personally tailor the shopping experience to those coming in and out of their stores. As the *Washington Post* report notes, "a clothier introduced a children's line after the dummy showed that kids made up more than half its mid-after-
(10) noon traffic... Another store found that a third of visitors using one of its doors after 4 p.m. were Asian, prompting it to place Chinese-speaking staff members by the entrance."

At $5,072 a pop, these EyeSee mannequins come with a steep price tag, but for store owners who want to know more—*a lot more*—about their
(15) customers, they're the perfect tool, able to sit innocently at store entrances and windows, leaving shoppers oblivious to their hidden cameras. Italian mannequin maker Almax SpA, manufacturer of the EyeSee mannequins, is currently working on adding ears to the mannequins, allowing them to record people's comments in order to further tailor the shopping
(20) experience. ...

It's astounding the amount of information—from the trivial to the highly personal— about individual consumers being passed around from corporation to corporation, all in an effort to market and corral potential customers. Data mining companies collect this wealth of information and

(25)   sell it to retailers who use it to gauge your interests and tailor marketing to your perceived desires.

All of the websites you visit collect some amount of information about you, whether it is your name or what other sites you have visited recently. Most of the time, we're being tracked without knowing it. For example,
(30)   most websites now include Facebook and Twitter buttons so you can "like" the page you are viewing or "Tweet" about it. Whether or not you click the buttons, however, the companies can still determine which pages you've visited and file that information away for later use. ...

As the EyeSee mannequins show, you no longer even have to be in
(35)   front of your computer to have your consumer data accessed, uploaded, stored and tracked. In August 2012, for example, data mining agency Redpepper began testing a service known as Facedeals in the Nashville, Tennessee area. Facial recognition cameras set at the entrances of businesses snap photos of people walking in, and if you've signed up to have a
(40)   Facedeals account via your Facebook, you receive instant coupons sent to your smartphone. Similarly, a small coffee chain in San Francisco, Philz Coffee, has installed sensors at the front door of their stores in order to capture the Wi-Fi signal of any smartphone within 60 yards. Jacob Jaber, president of Philz Coffee, uses the information gleaned from these sensors
(45)   to structure his stores according to the in-store behavior of customers. ...

Not even politicians are immune to the lure of data mining. In the run-up to the 2012 presidential election, the Romney and Obama campaigns followed voters across the web by installing cookies on their computers and observing the websites they visited in an attempt to gather informa-
(50)   tion on their personal views. CampaignGrid, a Republican affiliated firm, and Precision Network, a Democratic affiliated firm, both worked to collect data on 150 million American Internet users, or 80% of the registered voting population. ...

—John W. Whitehead
excerpted *https://www.rutherford.org*, December 17, 2012

Text 3

Where Will Consumers Find Privacy Protection from RFIDs?: A Case for Federal Legislation

What Are RFIDs? How Do RFIDs Work?

...RFID [Radio Frequency Information Device] technology is an automatic identification system that identifies objects, collects data, and transmits information about the object through a "tag." A device called a reader extracts and processes the information on the tag. Experts character-
(5)   ize RFIDs as devices "that can be sensed at a distance by radio frequencies with few problems of obstruction or misorientation."[1] In essence, RFIDs are wireless barcodes. However, unlike typical barcodes, which are identical for all common products, each RFID has a unique identification. Therefore, every individually tagged item has a different barcode sequence. Typical
(10) barcodes also require unobstructed paths for scanning, whereas RFIDs can be scanned through solid objects.[2] RFIDs have communication signals that facilitate data storage on RFID tags and enable the stored information to be gathered electronically—hypothetically permitting, for example, Coca-Cola to have a database storing information about the life cycle of a Coke
(15) can. The database would contain tracking details from the moment the can is manufactured through its processing at a garbage dump—since RFID readers can be attached to garbage trucks. Between the birth and death of a customer's Coke can, the RFID tags would tell the Coca-Cola Company where and when the Coke was purchased, what credit card the Coke was
(20) purchased with, and, in turn, the identity of the purchaser. Even if the customer did not purchase the Coke with a credit card, state issued ID cards equipped with RFID technology could relay the customer's identity to RFID readers as he or she leaves the store. Coca-Cola's final product of the RFIDs' communications is a database of the life cycles of individual cans of
(25) Coke and personal information about their purchasers. With this myriad of information, Coca-Cola has the ability to individually market to each of the 1.3 billion daily Coca-Cola consumers. ...

---

[1]KATHERINE ALBRECHT & LIZ MCINTRYE, SPYCHIPS 13 (Nelson Current 2005) quoting Raghu Das, *RFID Explained: An Introduction to RFID and Tagging Technologies*, ID TECHEX (2003).
[2]*Id.*

How Are RFIDs Used?

RFIDs are currently used in many ways, including, "livestock management[,] 24 hour patient monitoring[,] authentication of pharmaceuti-
(30) cals[,] tracking consignments in a supply chain[,] remote monitoring of
critical components in aircraft [, and] monitoring the safety of perishable
food."[3] Advocates of RFID technology, including retailers and manufacturers, praise the increased functionality and efficiency that will likely
ensue from using RFIDs. Once all products are individually tagged, shop-
(35) pers are expected to be able to purchase items without checking-out. This
should be possible since RFID readers will be able to scan every item as the
customer exits the store and charge an RFID credit card, thereby simultaneously increasing efficiency and possibly reducing shoplifting. Other
RFID uses include easy monitoring of product recalls, tracking lobsters
(40) for conservation purposes, and purchasing products with transaction-
free payment systems.[4] Additionally, in October 2003, the Department
of Defense set standards mandating suppliers to place RFID tags on all
packaging for the Department of Defense.[5] Thus, RFIDs can be used to
increase efficiency and safety. ...

Do Consumers Have a Right to Privacy
from RFIDs under Tort Law?[6]

(45)   ...In the context of RFIDs, there are some situations where gathering
information from RFID tags violates consumers' privacy expectations.
For example, a consumer does not have a reasonable expectation of privacy when carrying RFID equipped items in a transparent shopping cart.
However, once the items are placed in an opaque bag, a right to privacy
(50) immediately arises. If a business or third-party gathers data about the

---

[3]Viviane Reding, Member of the European Commission responsible for Information
Society and Media, Address at EU RFID 2006 Conference: Heading for the Future, RFID:
WHY WE NEED A EUROPEAN POLICY, 1,3 (Oct. 16, 2006).
[4]David Flint, *Everything with Chips!*, BUS. L. REV., Mar. 2006, 73, 73.
[5]PRESS RELEASE, US DEP. OF DEFENSE, DOD ANNOUNCES RADIO FREQUENCY IDENTIFICATION
POLICY, UNITED STATES DEPARTMENT OF DEFENSE NEWS RELEASE (Oct. 23, 2003).
[6]Tort Law—covers civil wrongs resulting in an injury or harm constituting the basis for
a claim by the injured person

items once the items are no longer visible to the naked eye, there is an objective invasion of privacy. Gathering information stored in the RFID tag in a winter jacket worn in public is also not an invasion of privacy, yet pulling data off undergarments is intrusive. However, since the home
(55) is always considered a private place, once an active RFID tag enters the home, any information gathered, including information from the winter jacket, immediately offends the principles of privacy. Protecting consumers from unreasonably intrusive actions of businesses requires that RFID tags become unreadable once they enter private places. However, the fun-
(60) damental nature of the technology does not harmonize with this privacy goal because RFID readers do not scrutinize whether the information is considered private before it gathers data from the tag. ...

With new technologies come new methods of consumer tracking and changing parameters for what may be considered highly offensive. These
(65) new methods of tracking are not considered intrusive simply because the nature of the technology requires consumer purchases to be recorded. If individuals make active decisions to use a credit card instead of cash—a voluntary act—their purchases can be tracked. Similarly, the gathering of information stored on RFID technology in consumer goods may not be
(70) deemed highly offensive depending on changing consumer expectations. ...

—Serena G. Stein excerpted and adapted
Duke Law & Technology Review, 2007, No.3

Text 4

RFID Consumer Applications and Benefits

...One of the first consumer applications of RFID was automated toll collection systems, which were introduced in the late 1980s and caught on in the 1990s. An active transponder is typically placed on a car's or truck's windshield. When the car reaches the tollbooth, a reader at the
(5) booth sends out a signal that wakes up the transponder on the windshield, which then reflects back a unique ID to the reader at the booth. The ID is associated with an account opened by the car owner, who is billed by the toll authority. Consumers spend less time fumbling for change or waiting on lines to pay their toll fee.

(10) In the late 1990s, ExxonMobil (then just Mobil) introduced Speedpass, an RFID system that allows drivers who have opened an account to pay for gas automatically. Drivers are given a small, passive 13.56 MHz transponder in a small wand or fob that can be put on a key chain. To pay for gas, they just wave the key fob by a reader built into the gas pump. Seven
(15) million people in the United States use the system, and it has increased the number of cars each gas station can serve during rush periods. ...

RFID has other consumer applications, besides being a convenient payment system. One is the recovery of lost or stolen items. A company called Snagg in Palo Alto, Calif., has created an electronic registry for musical
(20) instruments. It provides an RFID tag that can be affixed to a classic guitar or priceless violin and keeps a record of the serial number in the tag. If the instrument is recovered by the police after being lost or stolen, they can call Snagg, which can look up the rightful owner. ...

Merloni Elettrodomestici, an Italian appliance maker, has created
(25) a smart washing machine. When you drop your clothes in the machine, an RFID reader in the appliance can read the tags in the clothes (if your clothes have tags) and wash the clothes based on instructions written to the tag.

Whether smart appliances with RFID readers catch on depends on how
(30) long it takes for RFID tags to become cheap enough to be put into packaging for items. It also depends on whether consumers find RFID-enabled products convenient enough to accept the potential invasion of privacy

that comes with having RFID tags in products. But RFID will certainly have a positive impact on people's lives in less direct ways.

(35)   One area of importance is product recalls. Today, companies often need to recall all tires, meat or drugs if there is a problem to ensure people's safety. But they can never be sure they recovered all the bad goods that were released into the supply chain. With RFID, companies will be able to know exactly which items are bad and trace those through to stores.

(40)   Customers that register their products could be contacted individually to ensure they know something they bought has been recalled. ...

And RFID should enable consumers to get more information about the products they want to purchase, such as when the items were made, where, whether they are under warrantee and so on. When RFID tags are eventu-

(45)   ally put on the packaging of individual products, consumers will be able to read the tag with a reader embedded in a cell phone or connected to a computer and download data from a Web site. They'll be able to learn, for example, whether the steak they are about to buy is from an animal that was raised organically in the United States. Some companies will be reluc-

(50)   tant to share this information, but smart companies will provide it to their customers to build trust and loyalty.

RFID could also have an [sic] positive impact on our environment by greatly reducing waste. The main reason many companies want to use RFID is to better match supply and demand and to make sure that prod-

(55)   ucts are where they are supposed to be. If successful, there should be fewer products that are thrown away because no one wants to buy them or they pass their sell-by date (it's estimated that 50 percent of all food harvested in the United States is never eaten).

RFID tags could also help improve our environment by identifying

(60)   hazardous materials that should not be dumped in landfills. One day, robots at landfills might be equipped with RFID tags, and they might be able to quickly sort through garbage to locate batteries and other items that contain toxic materials. ...

—Bob Violino
excerpted *http://www.rfidjournal.com*, January 16, 2005

PART 3—Text-Analysis Response

Your Task: Closely read the text on pages 113 through 115 and write a well-developed, text-based response of two to three paragraphs. In your response, identify a central idea in the text and analyze how the author's use of *one* writing strategy (literary element or literary technique or rhetorical device) develops this central idea. Use strong and thorough evidence from the text to support your analysis. Do *not* simply summarize the text. You may use the margins to take notes as you read and scrap paper to plan your response. Write your response on a separate sheet of paper.

Guidelines:

Be sure to

- Identify a central idea in the text.
- Analyze how the author's use of *one* writing strategy (literary element or literary technique or rhetorical device) develops this central idea. Examples include: characterization, conflict, denotation/connotation, metaphor, simile, irony, language use, point-of-view, setting, structure, symbolism, theme, tone, etc.
- Use strong and thorough evidence from the text to support your analysis.
- Organize your ideas in a cohesive and coherent manner.
- Maintain a formal style of writing.
- Follow the conventions of standard written English.

Text

The following excerpt is from a speech delivered by suffragette Anna Howard Shaw in 1915.

...Now one of two things is true: either a Republic is a desirable form of government, or else it is not. If it is, then we should have it, if it is not then we ought not to pretend that we have it. We ought at least be true to our ideals, and the men of New York have for the first time in their lives,
(5)   the rare opportunity on the second day of next November, of making the state truly a part of the Republic. It is the greatest opportunity which has ever come to the men of the state. They have never had so serious a problem to solve before, they will never have a more serious problem to solve in any future of our nation's life, and the thing that disturbs me more than
(10) anything else in connection with it is that so few people realize what a profound problem they have to solve on November 2. It is not merely a trifling matter; it is not a little thing that does not concern the state, it is the most vital problem we could have, and any man who goes to the polls on the second day of next November without thoroughly informing himself in
(15) regard to this subject is unworthy to be a citizen of this state, and unfit to cast a ballot.
      If woman's suffrage[1] is wrong, it is a great wrong; if it is right, it is a profound and fundamental principle, and we all know, if we know what a Republic is, that it is the fundamental principle upon which a Republic
(20) must rise. Let us see where we are as a people; how we act here and what we think we are. The difficulty with the men of this country is that they are so consistent in their inconsistency that they are not aware of having been inconsistent; because their consistency has been so continuous and their inconsistency so consecutive that it has never been broken, from the begin-
(25) ning of our Nation's life to the present time. If we trace our history back we will find that from the very dawn of our existence as a people, men have been imbued[2] with a spirit and a vision more lofty than they have been able to live; they have been led by visions of the sublimest[3] truth, both

---

[1]suffrage—right to vote
[2]imbued—inspired
[3]sublimest—noblest

in regard to religion and in regard to government that ever inspired the
(30) souls of men from the time the Puritans left the old world to come to this
country, led by the Divine ideal which is the sublimest and the supremest
ideal in religious freedom which men have ever known, the theory that
a man has a right to worship God according to the dictates of his own
conscience, without the intervention[4] of any other man or any other group
(35) of men. And it was this theory, this vision of the right of the human soul
which led men first to the shores of this country. ...

Now what is a Republic? Take your dictionary, encyclopedia lexicon
or anything else you like and look up the definition and you will find
that a Republic is a form of government in which the laws are enacted by
(40) representatives elected by the people. Now when did the people of New
York ever elect their own representatives? Never in the world. The men of
New York have, and I grant you that men are people, admirable people, as
far as they go, but they only go half way. There is still another half of the
people who have not elected representatives, and you never read a defini-
(45) tion of a Republic in which half of the people elect representatives to govern the whole of the people. That is an aristocracy and that is just what we
are. We have been many kinds of aristocracies. We have been a hierarchy[5]
of church members, than an oligarchy[6] of sex. ...

Now I want to make this proposition, and I believe every man will
(50) accept it. Of course he will if he is intelligent. Whenever a Republic prescribes the qualifications as applying equally to all the citizens of the
Republic, when the Republic says in order to vote, a citizen must be twenty-
one years of age, it applies to all alike, there is no discrimination against
any race or sex. When the government says that a citizen must be a native-
(55) born citizen or a naturalized citizen that applies to all; we are either born or
naturalized, somehow or other we are here. Whenever the government says
that a citizen, in order to vote, must be a resident of a community a certain
length of time, and of the state a certain length of time and of the nation a
certain length of time, that applies to all equally. There is no discrimina-
(60) tion. We might go further and we might say that in order to vote the citizen
must be able to read his ballot. We have not gone that far yet. We have been

---

[4]intervention—interference
[5]hierarchy—order of authority
[6]oligarchy—rule by a few

very careful of male ignorance in these United States. I was much interested, as perhaps many of you, in reading the Congressional Record this last winter over the debate over the immigration bill, and when that illiteracy
(65) clause was introduced into the immigration bill, what fear there was in the souls of men for fear we would do injustice to some of the people who might want to come to our shores, and I was much interested in the language in which the President vetoed the bill, when he declared that by inserting the clause we would keep out of our shores a large body of very excellent peo-
(70) ple. I could not help wondering then how it happens that male ignorance is so much less ignorant than female ignorance. When I hear people say that if women were permitted to vote a large body of ignorant people would vote, and therefore because an ignorant woman would vote, no intelligent women should be allowed to vote, I wonder why we have made it so easy for
(75) male ignorance and so hard for female ignorance. ...

—Anna Howard Shaw
excerpted from "The Fundamental Principle of a Republic"
delivered at Ogdensburg, New York, June 21, 1915
http://www.emersonkent.com

Regents ELA (Common Core) Answers June 2014
English Language Arts

Answer Key

Part 1

1. **2**	9. **4**	17. **1**
2. **4**	10. **1**	18. **2**
3. **3**	11. **1**	19. **1**
4. **3**	12. **3**	20. **3**
5. **2**	13. **3**	21. **4**
6. **4**	14. **2**	22. **2**
7. **1**	15. **1**	23. **4**
8. **1**	16. **4**	24. **1**

Regents Examination in English Language Arts (Common Core)—June 2014

Chart for Converting Total Weighted Raw Scores to Final Exam Scores (Scale Scores) (Use for the June 2014 examination only.)

Weighted Raw Score*	Scale Score	Performance Level	Weighted Raw Score*	Scale Score	Performance Level
56	100	5	27	60	2
55	98	5	26	58	2
54	96	5	25	55	2
53	95	5	24	52	1
52	93	5	23	49	1
51	92	5	22	46	1
50	91	5	21	43	1
49	90	5	20	40	1
48	89	5	19	37	1
47	88	5	18	34	1
46	87	5	17	31	1
45	87	5	16	28	1
44	86	5	15	25	1
43	85	5	14	22	1
42	84	4	13	19	1
41	83	4	12	16	1
40	82	4	11	13	1
39	81	4	10	10	1
38	80	4	9	9	1
37	79	4	8	8	1
36	78	3	7	7	1
35	76	3	6	6	1
34	75	3	5	5	1
33	73	3	4	4	1
32	71	3	3	3	1
31	69	3	2	2	1
30	67	3	1	1	1
29	65	3	0	0	1
28	63	2			

The conversion table is determined independently for each administration of the exam.

Answers Explained

PART 1—Reading Comprenehsion

Multiple-Choice Questions

Passage A

(1) **2** "irritation about not finding his breakfast ready." The opening sentences reveal that the narrator has awoken earlier than usual and that his landlady is accustomed to setting his place at the table and preparing his coffee later. Although the narrator may express frustration and impatience later in the story, "unreasonable petulance" best expresses the narrator's grumpy mood at the beginning. This phrase helps establish the tone of the story as well. (RL.4)

(2) **4** "by emphasizing the systematic nature of Sherlock Holmes's approach to solving crimes." The author's purpose (that of A. Conan Doyle) is to illustrate Sherlock Holmes's skill in logical deduction: the ability to arrive at sound conclusions based on careful observation. The author's use of the terms "logician," "deduction," and "analysis" reinforce the characterization of Holmes as a systematic thinker. The author's purpose here is to help further the reader's understanding of how Holmes works. None of the other choices is about Holmes. (RL.4)

(3) **3** "It allows the reader to learn the narrator's true feelings." Readers already familiar with the character of Sherlock Holmes can anticipate that Holmes himself wrote the article to which the narrator is objecting. Because he is unaware of the article's author, the (grumpy) narrator's outburst reveals his view that using observation and deduction to know the occupations of strangers is "twaddle . . . rubbish . . . and not practical." By withholding authorship and letting the narrator fully express his skepticism, the author gives Holmes the opportunity to explain his work. By the end of the passage, the skeptical narrator will see how wrong he is. This incident prepares the reader for the rest of the story. However, the mood is not somber, and the events that follow cannot be described as unwelcome. (RL.5)

(4) **3** "reveal how Holmes makes his living." While defending the practicality of the theories expressed in the article, Holmes reveals that "I depend upon them for my bread-and-cheese." In other words, he depends on these skills to earn his living. These skills are his bread and butter. Holmes goes on to give the narrator a detailed description of his work as a consulting detective. This passage does not reveal any misdeeds, nor does it establish a friendship. The narrator remains unconvinced of Holmes's gifts for deduction. (RL.3)

(5) **2** "unrealistic." In this context, "chimerical" means unrealistic in the sense of impractical. Holmes asserts that, in fact, his theories "are really extremely practical." In this context, Holmes is using the term "chimerical" to describe the narrator's reaction to the article, which is summed up when the narrator says,"It is not practical," in line 34. The word unrealistic best describes the narrator's attitude toward Holmes's article. (L.4)

(6) **4** "Sherlock Holmes's intuition relies on his ability to detect similarities among various crimes." Holmes explains that his ability to put other detectives "on the right scent" is in his "knowledge of the history of crime." He also asserts, "There is a strong family resemblance about misdeeds." Choices (1) and (2) may be true, but they are not supported by any details in this passage. Holmes does not say government detectives are ineffective, as listed in choice (3), just that he helps them when they are "at fault," meaning mistaken or on the wrong track. (RL.3)

(7) **1** "So all life is a great chain, the nature of which is known whenever we are shown a single link of it." This sentence appears as the central theme of the article Holmes has written about the "Science of Deduction and Analysis." That article and the incident at the end of the passage give the narrator, and the reader, an example of how Holmes can deduce so much from a single detail, how he can know the nature of life when he is "shown a single link of it." This is the only statement among the four choices that is expressed as a general theme. The other three are important details from the narrative but are not expressions of a central idea. (RL.2)

(8) **1** "challenge Holmes's theories of deduction." The narrator reveals at line 86 that he "was still annoyed at [Holmes's] bumptious style of conversation." The word "bumptious" means boastful, self-satisfied. We know that the narrator still rejects Holmes's theories and has become annoyed by his arrogance. The arrival of the stranger first viewed across the street gives the narrator an opportunity to show that Holmes cannot really deduce anything about this man and thereby an opportunity to debunk Holmes's theories. This passage has no details to support the ideas in the other three choices. (RL.4)

(9) **4** "resolve a conflict." The conflict here is between Holmes's confidence in his powers of deduction and the narrator's skepticism. Note that the narrator gave a "slightly malicious glance at [his] companion," believing that he has finally caught Holmes in a faulty deduction about the man's occupation. The character of the retired sergeant is introduced only as a way to resolve the conflict in the story. This section occurs in the actual sequence of time, not as a flashback. The fact that the narrator also served in the military is an incidental detail, not an important comparison. (RL.3)

(10) **1** "astonishment." The narrator can only be astonished when the messenger reveals the truth of what Holmes intuited—that the messenger is a retired sergeant of marines. The messenger is plainly dressed; he is not even wearing a uniform! The narrator is left speechless. There is no confusion in the sergeant's answer, and the narrator's distrust of Holmes's skills has been dispelled. If anyone feels pleasure, it would be Holmes, not the narrator. (RL.3)

Passage B

(11) **1** "demanding." Each stanza begins with an earnest request, a demand, to "Give us a peace. . . ." The speaker's demands are urgent and intense but do not convey anger. Although the poem was published in the week the war in the Pacific and WWII ended, the poet withholds expressions of pride and celebration. The tone established by repetition of the phrase "Give us a peace" is best described as demanding in this context. (RL.4)

(12) **3** "to solicit the people's loyalty." No specific details appear in the poem to suggest an appeal for loyalty. Note that each of the other choices accurately identifies a purpose of the repetition of "Give us a peace." The repetition at the beginning of each stanza creates a unified structure and emphasizes the central idea; each stanza then elaborates on the poet's requests. (RL.5)

(13) **3** "rally the people for a new form of war." Several images in the poem illustrate what the poet means by a "peace equal to the war." These include, "Our battle against wrong . . . a mighty army serving human kind . . . an army trained to shape our common good." Some images in the poem inevitably remind us of the destructive nature of war. However, the images are meant to urge or rally the readers to convert the destructive power of war into a force for social progress. (RL.3)

(14) **2** "an appeal for justice." In the second stanza, the poet makes clear what he believes this new war must fight, "The challenge of the poor, the black, of all denied, The challenge of the vast colonial world." The poem is the appeal of an African-American to bring "reality to our dream . . . and bring about a world of brotherhood." With regard to the other choices, no details in the poem argue for colonial values or even imply a criticism of education. The poet actually acknowledges that the "war wiped out our foes on evil bent." (RL.6)

Passage C

(15) **1** "the nature of scientific investigation." The first paragraph focuses on how science "is a way of thinking . . . based on experiment . . . on an openness to see the universe as it really is." The entire passage is about how science pursues knowledge of the universe. Growth of understanding and formal education are only indirectly referenced. Choice (1) is correct because it expresses the central idea of the paragraph and of the entire passage. (RI.2)

(16) **4** "conventional wisdom." Sagan expands on what he means by "challenge old dogma" when he asserts that science sometimes requires the "courage to question the conventional wisdom (lines 14–15)." A common rhetorical strategy defines a term through elaboration in the sentence that follows. (L.4)

(17) **1** "Its goal is to find out how the world works, to seek what regularities there may be, to penetrate to the connections of things" In the second

paragraph, Sagan offers a series of questions about how the world works to illustrate what he means in the opening sentences of the passage (lines 1–3). The purpose of the second paragraph is to support the central idea established in the opening statement with specific details. Readers should recognize this as a common pattern of organization for informational texts. (RI.2)

(18) **2** "observe and develop questions." In lines 16–27, the author illustrates what he means by the "main trick" of science with a series of questions generated by what can be observed. Posing such questions and then seeking answers through careful observation and experiment constitutes scientific thinking. This question represents a continuation in the thread of items related to understanding Sagan's main theme and how it is developed throughout the passage. Careful reading shows that the "main trick" of science relies on developing questions, not on intuition or limitations. Experiments and laws come only after the questions have been asked. (RI.4)

(19) **1** "how scientific inquiry differs from ordinary questioning." In this passage, Sagan offers different ways of asking questions. He says that science "examines the world critically . . . spinning hypotheses." The reference to "alternative worlds" is to show how the scientific imagination works; Sagan is not explaining how these worlds could exist. Choice (1) is the best answer here because these lines 34 through 39 represent continued development of the central idea found in the first two paragraphs. (RI.3)

(20) **3** "Humans have a capacity to experience joy through their intelligence." The author expresses this idea in several phrases. He states that knowledge is a "kind of exhilaration. . . the use of our intelligence quite properly gives us pleasure . . . [u]nderstanding is a kind of ecstasy." These lines are focused on the idea that the intellectual challenge of science is enjoyable, even thrilling. None of the other choices is clearly supported in the passage. (RI.2)

(21) **4** "illustrate the effect of using one's brain." The figurative language further develops the claims discussed in question 20. The images in these lines illustrate Sagan's assertion, "When we think well, we feel good." Sagan's image of the brain as a muscle leads to the idea that exercising our brains is not only good for us but also brings pleasure. Close reading will show that the other choices do not reflect the purpose of these lines. (L.5)

(22) **2** "complexity." Here the word complexity means the condition of having many parts. The author begins with a description of a tiny grain of salt as tens of billions of atoms. He goes on to offer an image, a "modest calculation," of the brain's capacity to know. Out of context, interconnectedness, predictability, and uniqueness might apply to a grain of salt. However, the cumulative effect of Sagan's description is an image of something made up of more atoms than the brain could comprehend. (RI.2)

(23) **4** "awe." The irony is in the fact that the brain can "know" up to 100 trillion things, "only one percent of the number of atoms in our speck of salt." In this passage, Sagan's exploration of how much the brain can know

suggests feelings of astonishment, wonder, and admiration. Awe, not humor, doubt, or scorn, best captures the feeling of the passage. (RI.4)

(24) **1** "Understanding the world is essential to our well being." This commonsense statement reflects the ideas expressed in the third paragraph of the passage and in questions 20 and 21. The other choices are either unsupported or refuted by the text. (RI.2)

PART 2—Argument Response

Sample Essay Response

In most situations, data from consumer activity should not be tracked for the sole benefit of companies without permission. However, if the consumer does authorize its use by way of a contract, companies may have every right to track them. Companies should be allowed to track consumer shopping and other preferences only if the companies' practices are revealed and if consumers have the right to opt out.

When people walk into stores to buy things they need, they do not expect to be watched in order for those stores to gather information about the things they may just look at or be interested in. People have known about security cameras for years, but those are high in the air and primarily focused on monitoring shoplifting. With new technology such as the EyeSee camera and with the widespread use of RFIDs and barcodes, information about consumers is now passed directly to companies and advertisers without consumer permission or knowledge (Text 2, lines 3–7). For example, a camera installed in the eyes of mannequins allows companies to see exactly what kind of people enter a store and at what times. This technology, combined with RFID readers at entrances or at check-out counters, which have the ability to read state-issued ID cards, credit cards, and most product labels, allows companies to build databases about who buys their products most often. Consequently, companies attempt to appeal to those consumers (Text 3, lines 34–38). This complete invasion of privacy is instituted in a very public environment. Many people, including myself, are uneasy about this. In other places, like the Internet, tracking technology like cookies combined with social networking allows many kinds of businesses and groups to build consumer and participant databases without authorization. Even political campaigns make use of data collection. During the 2012 election, the Democratic and Republican Parties found ways to gather information about the personal views of nearly 80% of registered voters (Text 2, lines 50–53). Privacy is becoming more of an issue, even in the supposed seclusion of one's own home. On the other hand, RFID readers make some check-out processes more efficient. Tags on cars allow drivers to save valuable time when paying tolls (Text 4, lines 1–9). In those instances, consumers understand how and why they are tracked. Businesses need to practice consumer authorization of some sort.

Those businesses that do practice consumer authorization still get flak for tracking consumers, cell phone companies in particular. Businesses like Verizon and T-Mobile actually do tell customers what they are monitoring—data usage, GPS usage, and apps—because the companies sell these products and want to make the products more efficient and convenient. However, customers still complain about data monitoring. After all, the cell phone companies give marketers and advertisers details about what sites cell phone users visit, what games they play, and even where they have been. Consumers may know that their data is monitored, but they also need to know exactly what privacy protections they can expect (Text 1, lines 5–14).

Many businesses rely on data monitoring. If they give consumers accurate information about how their technology works, then these businesses should be able to use the information they collect. The consumer has voluntarily given permission and should not complain about invasion of privacy. In the much more common situations, where consumers do not authorize data tracking, the technology should not be used. In fact, the government should prohibit it.

Analysis

This is an excellent response to the task—composing a source-based argument.

The writer introduces a precise and thoughtful claim in the opening paragraph, "Companies should be allowed to track consumer shopping and other preferences only if their practices are revealed and consumers have the right to opt out." By rejecting an either/or position, the writer's claim acknowledges the complexity of the issue by recognizing that there are arguments for the rights of both businesses and consumers. This writer supports the claim with relevant evidence, accurately cited from all four texts. The essay is strengthened by the writer's use of specific examples that show both the benefits and risks to personal privacy in data collection and tracking of consumer preferences.

The essay is well organized. It includes a series of examples in which egregious invasion of privacy occurs as well as examples where "consumers understand how and why they are tracked." Coherence is achieved through reassertions of the main idea at the end of several paragraphs, "Businesses need to practice consumer authorization of some sort. . . . Consumers may know that their data is monitored, but they also need to know exactly what privacy protections they can expect." The conclusion is especially effective in outlining the responsibilities of both businesses and consumers.

This writer maintains an appropriately formal style of writing, while occasionally using an informal expression such as, "including myself" and "businesses still get flak."

The essay also demonstrates the writer's command of standard written English and skill in expressing ideas in varied and complex sentence structures. This response would merit a high score.

(See pages 80–81 to review the scoring guidelines.)

PART 3—Text-Analysis Response

Sample Essay Response

The central idea of Shaw's 1915 speech is that women deserve the right to vote. She constructs her argument around the definition of a Republic, "a form of government . . . [with] representatives elected by the people." Shaw's strategy is to lead her audience with logical reasoning to see the irony and hypocrisy in denying women the right to vote. She insists that since half the population, women, do not have the right to vote, then the United States is definitely not a Republic! She reminds her audience that "you never read a definition of a Republic in which [only] half of the people elect representatives . . . to govern the whole of the people." Shaw then challenges her audience with the assertion, "That is an aristocracy and that is just what we are."

In the last section of the speech, Shaw examines step by step the existing qualifications to vote: age, citizenship, and residence. She agrees that there is no discrimination (other than by sex!) in these requirements. Skillfully, she reminds her audience that under current law, an illiterate man may immigrate to America and receive the vote. The President even vetoed an illiteracy clause because such a clause "would keep out of our shores a large body of very excellent people." This gives Shaw the opportunity to examine the faulty logic behind denying women the right to vote: a large body of ignorant people would be able to vote. Shaw forces her audience to see the conclusion that an illiterate man is worthy of the vote but no woman, even an excellent or intelligent one, is worthy. She says she is confident that intelligent men will see the hypocrisy and irony in such logic.

Analysis

Shaw's central idea is clear to most readers. Many of the successful responses to this task focused on the use of irony in Shaw's speech. Others pointed out Shaw's technique of rhetorical question and answer and of provocative assertions. This writer offered a particularly thoughtful analysis of how Shaw used the strategy and language of logical reasoning to "lead her audience with logical reasoning to see the irony and hypocrisy in denying women the right to vote." The writer establishes the central idea with Shaw's harsh statement, "Since **[if]** half the population, women, do not have the right to vote, **then** the United States is definitely not a Republic!" The rest of the essay remains focused on how Shaw obliged her audience to follow her logic as she examines the realities and implications of denying women's suffrage. This response is brief but insightful; it is also coherent and well written. It would merit a high score.

(See pages 82–83 to review the scoring guidelines.)

Regents ELA (Common Core) Examination August 2014

English Language Arts

PART 1—Reading Comprehension

Directions (1–24): Closely read each of the three passages below. After each passage, there are several multiple-choice questions. Select the best suggested answer to each question and write its number in the space provided. You may use the margins to take notes as you read.

Reading Comprehension Passage A

Against the clamor of the city, who could hear the prayers being uttered in Peace Lane? Who would notice people whose dearest wish in life is not to be praised for merit but only to avoid making mistakes? Here a lean-to shed has been added on to the terrace and the courtyard roofed
(5)   over to make a kitchen. If you were to look down upon the rooftops of the city, you would find them in utter disarray, worn and dilapidated, structures built on top of structures, taking up every bit of free space. This was especially true of the older *longtang*,[1] like Peace Lane—it's a miracle that they haven't collapsed yet. About a third of the tiles were broken,
(10) patched over in places with bits of felt, the wooden frames on the doors and windows were blackened and rotting, with everything in view a uniform ash gray.

But though it was falling apart on the outside, the spirit of the place remained; its inner voice, though stifled, was still audible. But amid all

---

[1]*longtang*—vast neighborhoods inside enclosed alleys

(15) the noises of this city, just what did this voice amount to? There was never a moment of peace and quiet in the city; the day had its sounds, as did the night, and between them they drowned that voice out. But it was still there—it couldn't be silenced because it was the foundation upon which the hubbub and commotion fed; without it all of those noises

(20) would have been nothing but an empty echo. But what did this voice say? Two words: *to live*. No matter how loud the noise became, no matter what a rumpus it made, or how long it carried on, it could never find those two words. Those two little words weighed a ton, so they sank, and sank—all the way down, to the very bottom; only immaterial things

(25) like smoke and mist could float up to the surface. It was impossible to listen to this voice without crying. The prayers whispered in Peace Lane went on day and night, like an ever-burning alter [*sic*] lamp, but they weren't burning on oil: inch by inch, they were burning thoughts. In contrast, the chaotic noises echoing in the city's air were nothing but

(30) the scraps and leftovers of life, which is why they could be so liberally strewn about. The prayers concealed throughout those thousands of Shanghai *longtang* rang out louder and clearer than all the church bells in Europe: they created a rumbling thunder that seemed to emerge from the earth itself, the sound of mountains crumbling. A shame we

(35) had no way of participating in this ourselves, but just looking at the abyss they created was enough to make the heart grow cold. See what they have done to this place! It is hard to say whether this was a form of construction or destruction, but whatever it was, it was massive.

What Peace Lane prayed for was peace itself. You could hear it even

(40) from the bell that was rung every night to warn people to mind their kitchen fires. Peace is not something ordinary, but Peace Lane had an ordinary heart and its prayers were quite humble as well; these modest requests, however, were not easily granted. No major disaster had befallen Peace Lane in many years, but little things kept coming up,

(45) such as someone falling off the balcony while bringing in their laundry, another getting electrocuted when he turned off a light switch with a wet hand, pressure cooker explosions, rat poison accidentally ingested. If all these, who died wrongful deaths, had cried out, their howls would have been deafening. So how could one not pray for peace and security?

(50)   In the early evening, when the lights came on, you could see in all the windows the watchful eyes of frightened people looking out for signs of trouble. But whenever something bad did happen, no one ever saw it coming. This was where Peace Lane had gone numb and where it displayed its pragmatism. The residents were never prepared for the closest (55) dangers. Yes, they understood the dangers of fire and electricity, but beyond that they had no imagination. And so if you were to see the people of Peace Lane praying, they would be like idiots reciting a book from memory, chanting with their lips but not their minds, repeating the same incantations over and over again. Meanwhile the flowerpot (60) sitting on the windowsill was just an inch away from falling down, but no one ever bothered to move it; the termites had already done their work on the floors, but no one ever seemed to care; illegal structures kept being added one on top of the other, causing the foundation to sink, yet another one was about to be built. During the typhoon season, when Peace (65) Lane shook and rattled and it appeared as if the entire neighborhood was going to pieces, people curled up in their rooms, complacently enjoying the cool breeze brought by the storm. What people in Peace Lane prayed for was to be able to live in a fool's paradise—they would rather turn a blind eye and never ask questions. The pigeon whistles sounding in (70) the morning sang of peace, announcing the good but never the bad; but even if they had, would that have made a difference? You might be able to escape it in the first round, but would you escape in the second? Put that way, those prayers must imply an acceptance, a sort of Daoist resignation to reality. For want of anything else to pray for, night after night (75) they pray for peace, but that was just wishful thinking. ...

But now the story seems to be coming to an end. Even those who attempt brazen acts with a smiling façade are met with sober, straight faces: the time for equivocation[2] was over. The tide was receding and the rocks would soon be exposed. Counting on one's fingers, one finds that (80) the Shanghai *longtang* have quite a few years on them—a few more and they'll be treading on thin ice. Going up again to the highest point in the city and looking down, one sees that the crisscrossing *longtang* neighborhoods are already beginning to look desolate. If these had been large imposing building[s], that desolation might be mitigated by (85) their grand proportions. But *longtang* buildings all have low walls and nar-

---

[2]equivocation—avoiding the truth

row courtyards, filled with ordinary people carrying out their mundane tasks: could places like these be thought of as desolate? Desolation takes on a comical aspect in such places, and that only makes the people living there all the more dejected. Putting it in harsher terms: the whole place
(90) bore a certain resemblance to a heap of rubble. With the leaves falling in early winter, all we see are broken bricks and shattered tiles. Like an aging beauty who retains her alluring profile, it can no longer bear scrutiny. Should you insist on searching for a trace of her former charm—after all, not everything is erased—you would have to look
(95) for it in the turn of the alley. Left here, right there, as if glancing coquettishly[3] from side to side, but the eyes that are so flirtatious are also getting on in years, they have lost their luster and are incapable of grabbing hold of your attention. Soon, sleet began to come down—that was the frigid past accumulated over generations—turning to water before it even hit the
(100) ground. ...

—Wang Anyi
excerpted and adapted from *The Song of Everlasting Sorrow:
A Novel of Shanghai*, 1995
Columbia University Press

---

[3]coquettishly—flirtatiously

1 The sentence, "But it was still there ... an empty
   echo" (lines 17 through 20) contributes to a central theme by

   (1) connecting the people's inner feelings and outer
       lives
   (2) suggesting a reason for the *longtang*'s crumbling
       structure
   (3) emphasizing the people's quiet and calming
       activities
   (4) reflecting a shift in the *longtang*'s character   1____

2 The author's use of figurative language in lines 23
   through 25 serves to emphasize a sense of

   (1) community spirit   (3) emotional burden
   (2) societal unrest   (4) material value   2____

3 As used in line 24, the phrase "immaterial things"
   means that the things are

   (1) unimportant   (3) frightening
   (2) unforeseen   (4) difficult   3____

4 According to lines 39 through 49, a person living in
   the *longtang* would most probably pray for

   (1) protection from neighborhood conflict
   (2) a quiet and uneventful life
   (3) wealth and good fortune
   (4) an end to the current war   4____

5 Lines 50 through 67 suggest that the *longtang*
   people

   (1) make the best of their situation
   (2) survive difficult challenges
   (3) band together in times of need
   (4) ignore impending danger   5____

6 The comparison in lines 92 through 98 emphasizes the *longtang*'s

   (1) former vitality   (3) past importance

   (2) enduring strength   (4) lasting beauty   6_____

7 The reference to the seasons in the final paragraph conveys a sense of

   (1) anticipation   (3) hope

   (2) loss   (4) worthlessness   7_____

8 The author's description of the people's prayers and the *longtang* stresses the

   (1) futility of the people's situation

   (2) security of the people's future

   (3) importance of the people's traditions

   (4) complexity of the people's needs   8_____

9 Overall, the author's view of the people of the *longtang* could best be described as

   (1) intolerant   (3) sympathetic

   (2) objective   (4) ambiguous   9_____

Reading Comprehension Passage B

Money Musk

Listen, you upstate hillsides (nothing
Like the herb-strewn fields of Provence[1])
Which I have loved
So loyally, your wood lots
(5)   And trailers and old farmhouses,
Your satellite dishes—

Haven't I driven
Past the strip malls and country airports,
The National Guard armories and even
(10) That abandoned missile depot
Clutched in the lake's fingers
Past the tattered billboards.
The barns spray-painted with praise,

Past the farm tools, fiddles,
(15) And fishing lures, the sprung bellows
Of accordions on the tables of flea markets,
Just to catch a glimpse of you as you once were,
Like the brass showing, raw and dull,
Where the silver plate has worn off
(20) The frame around this mirror, and the silver
Gone too, the only reflection as faint

As light on dusty glass,
And beyond it, tarnished, dim, the rafters
And beams of the attic where I climbed
(25) To take out my grandmother's mandolin
And play on the three or four unbroken strings
With a penny for a pick.
                                        Listen,
Wasn't that offering enough, a life

---
[1]Provence—a region of southern France

(30) Of playing half-badly on an antique instrument,
      Trying to catch a tune you'd long ago
      Forgotten even the name of, *Money Musk*
      Or *Petronella*.[2] Wasn't it enough
      To take my vows of poverty of spirit
(35) Before the plain geometry of a 19th-century
      Farmhouse, and praise no other goods
      Than this rectitude,[3] this stillness,
      This clarity you have spurned now, oh
      Landscape I have sung
(40) Despite my voice, despite the stubborn
      Silence behind your tawdry,[4] best intentions.

—Jordan Smith
from *The Cortland Review*
Issue Eight, August 1999

---

[2]Money Musk or Petronella—classic old American dances
[3]rectitude—honesty
[4]tawdry—cheap

10 The details presented in lines 4 through 13 emphasize the landscape's

  (1) historical significance
  (2) beauty
  (3) economic possibilities
  (4) transformation   10_____

11 What shift in focus occurs from lines 7 through
27?

  (1) from social conflict to personal conflict
  (2) from external description to childhood memory
  (3) from the narrator's feelings to his family's feel-
     ings
  (4) from the narrator's thoughts to the narrator's
     actions   11_____

12 What is the effect of the simile used in lines 21
and 22?

  (1) It suggests how the narrator has changed.
  (2) It conveys the narrator's lack of awareness.
  (3) It indicates the darkness of the setting.
  (4) It emphasizes the diminishing of the past.   12_____

13 Which word best describes the narrator's tone in
lines 28 through 38 of the poem?

  (1) frustrated   (3) contentment
  (2) embarrassed   (4) respectful   13_____

14 Lines 33 through 37 contribute to a central theme
in the poem by describing the narrator's

  (1) wish to live in a suburban setting
  (2) obligation to continue a past tradition
  (2) commitment to the values of a past era
  (4) reluctance to accept different points of view   14_____

Reading Comprehension Passage C

This is an excerpt from a speech given by Red Jacket, Chief of the Seneca Nation, to the United States acting secretary of war in Washington, D.C., on February 10, 1801.

...Brother, the business on which we are now come is to restore the friendship that has existed between the United States and the Six Nations, agreeably to the direction of the commissioner from the fifteen fires[1] of the United States. He assured us that whensoever, by any griev-
(5) ances, the chain of friendship should become rusty, we might have it bright-ened by calling on you. We dispense with the usual formality of having your speech again read, as we fully comprehended it yesterday, and it would therefore be useless to waste time in a repetition of it.

Brother, yesterday you wiped the tears from our eyes, that we might
(10) see clearly; you unstopped our ears that we might hear; and removed the obstructions from our throats that we might speak distinctly. You offered to join with us in tearing up the largest pine-tree in our forests, and under it to bury the tomahawk. We gladly join with you, brother, in this work, and let us heap rocks and stones on the root of this tree that the
(15) tomahawk may never again be found. ...

Brother, we observe that the men now in office are new men, and, we fear, not fully informed of all that has befallen us. In 1791 a treaty was held by the commissioners of Congress with us at Tioga Point, on a sim-ilar occasion. We have lost seven of our warriors, murdered in cold blood
(20) by white men, since the conclusion of the war. We are tired of this mighty grievance and wish some general arrangement to prevent it in future. The first of these was murdered on the banks of the Ohio, near Fort Pitt. Shortly after two men belonging to our first families were mur-dered at Pine Creek; then one at Fort Franklin; another at Tioga Point;
(25) and now the two that occasion this visit, on the Big Beaver. These last two had families. The one was a Seneca; the other a Tuscarora. Their fami-lies are now destitute of support, and we think that the United States should do something toward their support, as it is to the United States they owe the loss of their heads.

---

[1]fires—fires refers to states

(30)   Brother, these offences are always committed in one place on the frontier of Pennsylvania. In the Genesee country we live happy and no one molests us. I must therefore beg that the President will exert all his influence with all officers, civil and military, in that quarter, to remedy this grievance, and trust that he will thus prevent
(35)   a repetition of it and save our blood from being spilled in future.

         Brother, let me call to mind the treaty between the United States and the Six Nations, concluded at Canandaigua. At that treaty Colonel Pickering, who was commissioner on behalf of the United States, agreed that the United States should pay to the Six Nations four thousand
(40)   five hundred dollars per annum, and that this should pass through the hands of the superintendent of the United States, to be appointed for that purpose. This treaty was made in the name of the President of the United States, who was then General Washington; and, as he is now no more, perhaps the present President would wish to renew the treaty. But
(45)   if he should think the old one valid and is willing to let it remain in force we are also willing. The sum above mentioned we wish to have part of in money, to expend in more agricultural tools and in purchasing a team, as we have some horses that will do for the purpose. We also wish to build a sawmill on the Buffalo creek. If the President, however,
(50)   thinks proper to have it continue as heretofore, we shall not be very uneasy. Whatever he may do we agree to; we only suggest this for his consideration.

         Brother, I hand you the above-mentioned treaty, made by Colonel Pickering, in the name of General Washington, and the belt that accom-
(55)   panied it; as he is now dead we know not if it is still valid. If not, we wish it renewed—if it is, we wish it copied on clean parchment. Our money got loose in our trunk and tore it. We also show you the belt which is the path of peace between our Six Nations and the United States. ...

         Brother, the business that has caused this our long journey was occa-
(60)   sioned by some of your bad men; the expense of it has been heavy on us. We beg that as so great a breach has been made on your part, the President will judge it proper that the United States should bear our expenses to and from home and whilst here.

         Brother, three horses belonging to the Tuscarora Nation were killed
(65)   by some men under the command of Major Rivardi, on the plains of

Niagara. They have made application to the superintendent and to Major Rivardi, but get no redress. You make us pay for our breaches of the peace, why should you not pay also? A white man has told us the horses were killed by Major Rivardi's orders, who said they should not be permitted
(70) to come there, although it was an open common on which they were killed. Mr. Chapin has the papers respecting these horses, which we request you to take into consideration.

—Red Jacket
excerpted from *Orations from Homer to William McKinley,*
Vol. VII, 1902
P.F. Collier and Son

15 The speaker's use of symbolism in lines 11 through 13 serves to represent the

(1) achievement of peace
(2) destruction of nature
(3) loss of cultural identity
(4) arrival of new leadership   15_____

16 The details in lines 19 and 20 contribute to the speaker's purpose by

(1) presenting a resolution to the conflict
(2) indicating the reason for the meeting
(3) emphasizing the need for caution
(4) explaining the terms of the treaty   16_____

17 Lines 26 through 29 establish a

(1) contrast between poverty and wealth
(2) comparison between family and government
(3) cause/effect relationship between power and crime
(4) connection between responsibility and accountability   17_____

18 In the speech, the Six Nations' uncertainty regarding the status of the Canandaigua Treaty in lines 30 and 31 is based on the

(1) loss of the Cayuga reservation
(2) conclusion of a major conflict
(3) recent changes in United States leadership
(4) new hostilities along the frontier   18____

19 Which statement best clarifies the sentence in lines 9 through 11?

(1) "We dispense with the usual formality of having your speech again read" (lines 6 and 7)
(2) "In the Genesee country we live happy and no one molests us" (lines 31 and 32)
(3) "But if he should think the old one valid ... we are also willing" (lines 44 through 46)
(4) "If the President ... thinks proper to have it continue as heretofore, we shall not be very uneasy" (lines 49 through 51)   19____

20 The speaker's attitude in lines 44 through 52 can best be described as

(1) uncertain   (3) sarcastic
(2) compassionate   (4) cooperative   20____

21 The speaker's request in lines 59 through 63 serves to emphasize the Six Nations'

(1) sense of growing confinement
(2) adoption of traditional lifestyle
(3) rejection of political influence
(4) desire for fair treatment   21____

22 Which words from the speech help the reader understand the meaning of "redress" as used in line 67?

(1) "judge it proper" (line 62)
(2) "They have made application" (line 66)
(3) "why should you not pay also" (line 68)
(4) "they should not be permitted to come" (lines 69 and 70)   22_____

23 Which purpose of the treaty between the United States and the Six Nations is not referenced in this 1801 speech?

(1) the need to prevent unlawful acts
(2) the preservation of the written agreement
(3) the method of fiscal payments
(4) the protection of Iroquois lands   23_____

24 The speaker repeats the word "Brother" throughout the speech in order to

(1) convey a sense of superiority
(2) establish a feeling of alliance
(3) emphasize a common greeting
(4) suggest a shared history   24_____

140   REGENTS ELA (COMMON CORE) EXAM August 2014

PART 2—Argument Response

Directions: Closely read each of the *four* texts on pages 142 through 153 and write a source-based argument on the topic below. You may use the margins to take notes as you read and scrap paper to plan your response. Write your argument on a separate sheet of paper.

Topic: Should the United States bid to host a future Olympic Games?

Your Task: Carefully read each of the *four* texts provided. Then, using evidence from at least *three* of the texts, write a well-developed argument regarding the United States bidding to host future Olympic Games. Clearly establish your claim, distinguish your claim from alternate or opposing claims, and use specific, relevant, and sufficient evidence from at least *three* of the texts to develop your argument. Do *not* simply summarize each text.

Guidelines:

Be sure to

- Establish your claim regarding the United States bidding to host a future Olympic Games.
- Distinguish your claim from alternate or opposing claims.
- Use specific, relevant, and sufficient evidence from at least *three* of the texts to develop your argument.
- Identify each source that you reference by text number and line number(s) or graphic (for example: Text 1, line 4 or Text 2, graphic).
- Organize your ideas in a cohesive and coherent manner.
- Maintain a formal style of writing.
- Follow the conventions of standard written English.

Texts:

    Text 1—Impact of the Games on Olympic Host Cities

    Text 2—When the Games Come to Town: Host Cities and the Local Impacts of the Olympics

    Text 3—3 Reasons Why Hosting the Olympics Is a Loser's Game

    Text 4—Factsheet: Legacies of the Games

Text 1

Impact of the Games on Olympic Host Cities

Introduction

...Staging an Olympic Games represents a long and expensive commitment of a city to this mega event. The impact can be divided into four separate periods:

1. the preparation of a bid and the winning of the right to host the
(5)   Games;
2. the seven year period of preparation for the staging of the Games;
3. the short period (16 days in 2000) when the Olympic Games are staged followed by the Paralympic Games;
4. the much longer post-Games era.

(10) There are also many types of impact to consider:
   - alterations in design of the city;
   - changes to the physical and the built environment;
   - the representation of a city and country and its culture;
   - improvements in air, road and rail transport;
(15) - increased costs and taxes;
   - changes in governance and public decision-making;
   - innovations in politics and political relationships;
   - potential increased tourism and business activity;
   - the creation of new sporting venues which have potential for post-
(20)   Games community use;
   - the potential of greater community consultation, involvement and even protest;
   - the involvement of the community as volunteers and torch-bearers.

Debates and controversies

The impact of an Olympic Games on host cities is a matter of con-
(25) tinuing debate and controversy. There are many continuing issues and questions and [sic] about the impact of the Games. Below are six areas of continuing debate.

1. The decision to bid for the games—does it represent 'manufactured consent'?

     While an Olympic bid is made on behalf of all the people of a city, the majority are only indirectly consulted as to whether they want their city to
(30) bid for an Olympic Games and what they want to achieve in the process. A bid is usually framed in terms of some community benefit—such as urban renewal, improved transport or better sporting facilities—which it is claimed will counter the potential costs and burdens to the community. Public opinion polls are usually cited by the bid proposers
(35) as proof of public support for a bid. ...

2. Community consultation about the impact of the games

     This is a related issue about the degree of community consultation during the preparations for the staging of an Olympic Games. Fast-tracking of venues and other Olympic projects are common practices because of the enormity of the task of preparing for the Games in a short
(40) time frame. As a result there is usually limited community consultation and the over-riding of local concerns are justified as being in the city and national interest. ...

3. Positive versus negative impacts on host cities—weighing the balance

     The costs and benefits of an Olympic Games are matters of continuing debate before, during and after the Games. It is virtually impossible
(45) to know the true cost to a city of hosting an Olympic Games because there is no accepted way of assessing expenditure. Olympic budgets are both political, contentious[1] and notoriously unreliable. To present Olympic expenditure in the best possible light host cities often hide certain items or shift them to other budgets. Olympic infrastructure[2] costs
(50) may appear in the government's public works budget rather than the Olympic budget. Presumably there is a fear that the disclosure of the full costs of staging an Olympic Games might diminish the degree of public support for this event. ...

---

[1]contentious—likely to cause arguments
[2]infrastructure—the basic facilities, services, and installations needed for the functioning of a community

4. Spreading the costs and benefits of the games

(55) There has been much discussion about who benefits most from the Games in the host city—and the host country for that matter—and whether the costs and burdens are shared equally. While it is clear that the Games can produce tangible benefits for government and business, and the tourism industry in particular, the non-tangible benefits for the community are less self-evident, other than the privilege of

(60) participating in the Games in one way or another. A lot depends, in this instance, on whether the promises to the community at the time of the bid—better sports facilities and urban infrastructure—are actually kept. ...

5. Community anti-Olympic lobbies

...While there has been a proliferation of community anti-Olympic

(65) and watchdog groups, there is very limited empirical[3] evidence of their support base. It is difficult to assess their significance and whether they speak for anyone other than radical fringe groups.

6. An erosion in human rights in the host city?

Because so much is at stake when an Olympic Games are held—the city and the country needs to look its best—the staging of an Olympic

(70) Games can lead to an erosion of human rights for the citizens of that city and country. The demands of tighter security also provide the justification for an organising committee or a government to introduce laws to restrict individual liberties particularly during the Games so as to eliminate any 'negativities' that might be seized upon by the international

(75) media. ...

There is the danger that this erosion of civil liberties, during an Olympic Games, may be extended and provide the excuse for 'temporary' measures to remain in place for the longer term. ...

—Richard Cashman
excerpted and adapted from "Impact of the Games on Olympic Host Cities"
Barcelona: Centre d'Estudis Olimpics (UAB), 2002

---

[3]empirical—based on experience

Text 2

When the Games Come to Town:
Host Cities and the Local Impacts of the Olympics

Employment and the Olympics

...Most of the employment growth related to the Olympics happens before the Games, in the preparation stage. As we might expect, there have been some steep losses in employment immediately after the Games, once construction is over and supporting services are not needed (LERI
(5)   2007:27). These losses almost stand against the intention to regenerate the locale or host city, as the ability to maintain the momentum of economic growth is important. ...

Employment opportunities?

Although the Olympics do create employment, the majority of Olympic-related work is **temporary** (Miguelez 1995:157). As a result
(10)   analysts suggest we should strongly question the 'value' of the employment created (Horne & Whitson 2006:79). It will mostly be short and sweet—and low-skilled.
- **LA Games 1984:**   16,520 people for 30 days
- **Seoul Games 1988:**   33,500 people for 30 days

(15)   The main form of job creation in the Olympics relates to the creation of infrastructure, what is built to accommodate the hosting of the Olympics. Here the major source of employment pre-event is in construction.

CONSTRUCTION Major work creation is in construction, where
(20)   jobs will broadly fit into two skill levels—highly skilled specialist labour and low skilled labour (Crookston 2004:57). As a result there is potential for polarisation in the job market (Poynter 2006:26), especially because the Olympics has to be built to a very tight schedule and it is unlikely contractors will train unskilled workers, instead recruiting more
(25)   widely (Evans 2007:315).

SERVICES & TOURISM Some of the indirect jobs provided will be in services and especially those related to tourists and visitors. This will refer to economic activities and roles in support of the Games. As above, we should question the value of this work, as much of it could be low-
(30) skilled, badly compensated and usually temporary.

The **services sector** will benefit from the Games, but for a limited amount of time (Crookston 2004:56). There will be temporary opportunities, pre-, during and after the event in:

- Catering, accommodation, retail, interpreting, security and gen-
(35)   eral administration (Poynter 2006).

For example, the media interest in the Games means that there will be additional visitors before the Games. Atlanta had an estimated extra 18,000 overnight stays as a result of the Olympics before the Games. Temporary work in this sector in the run up to the Sydney
(40) Games is estimated to have generated in the region of 100,000 jobs specific to the event itself. ...

Winners and losers?

It is unfortunate but generally agreed that each host city has its winners and losers. Middle classes, political elites and tourists may gain from infrastructural reforms, economic investment and social activities
(45) and interest in the city as a result of the Games. By comparison, the city's poor tend to suffer and sometimes become poorer as a result of the Olympics (Preuss 2004:23; Short 2004:107). ...

The following chart sets out some outcomes—both positive and negative—that might be expected amongst the host population, with
(50) particular attention to psychological and social outcomes:

Type of Impact	Positive	Negative
Social/Cultural	Increase in permanent level of local interest and participation in types of activity associated with event	Commercialization of activities which may be of a personal or private nature
	Strengthening of regional values and traditions	Modification of nature of event or activity to accommodate tourism
		Potential increase in crime
		Changes in community structure
		Social dislocation
Psychological	Increased local pride and community spirit	Tendency towards defensive attitudes concerning host region
	Increased awareness of non-local perceptions	Culture shock
	Festival atmosphere during event	Misunderstandings leading to varying degrees of host/visitor hostility
Tourism	Increased awareness of the region as a travel/tourism destination	Acquisition of poor reputation as a result of inadequate facilities, crime, improper practices or inflated prices
	Increased knowledge concerning the potential for investment and commercial activity in the region	Negative reactions from existing local enterprises due to possibility of new competition for local manpower and government assistance

(Preuss & Solberg 2006:398)

However, research also suggests that some of the community are more likely than others to take a 'socially altruistic' approach, coping with the changes positively believing that they are in the interests of the greater good. A social impacts study carried out in Sydney showed (55) that:

- Those more likely to accept any inconveniences with equanimity included: younger people, families and ethnic minorities who took up and enjoyed the sense of inclusion and community spirit the Games offered (Waitt 2003). ...

—Dr. Mary Smith
excerpted from *When the Games Come to Town: Host Cities and the Local Impacts of the Olympics*
London East Research Institute Working Papers, December 2008

References

Crookston, M. 2004. 'Making the Games Work: A Sustainable Employment Legacy' in *After the Gold Rush: A Sustainable Olympics for London*. London: IPPR & DEMOS. Pp. 51–68.

Evans, G. 2008 'London 2012' in *Olympic Cities: City Agendas, Planning, and the World's Games*. (Eds.) J. Gold & M. Gold. London & New York: Routledge: 298–318.

Horne, J. & Whitson, D. 2006 'Comparing the outcomes of Sports mega-events in Canada and Japan' in *Sports Mega Events: Social Scientific Analyses of Global Phenomenon*. W. Manzenreiter & J. Horne (eds.) London: Blackwell Publishing Ltd. Pp: 73–89.

LERI 2007 *A Lasting Legacy for London? Assessing the Legacy of the Olympic Games and Paralympic Games*. London East Research Institute & London Assembly.

Miguelez, F. & Pilar, C. 1995 'The Repercussion of the Olympic Games on Labour' in *The Keys to Success: The Social, Sporting, Economic and Communications Impact of Barcelona '92*. M de Moragas (ed.) Barcelona: Centre d'Estudis Olimpics i de l'Esport. Pp. 149–64.

Poynter, G. 2006 *'From Beijing to Bow Bells':* Working Papers in Urban Studies. London East Research Institute.

Preuss, H. 2004 *The Economics of Staging the Olympics: A Comparison of the Games 1972–2008*. UK & US: Edward Elgar.

Preuss, H. & Solberg, H. 2006 'Attracting Major Sporting Events: The Role of Local Residents' *European Sport Management Quarterly* 6(4): 391–411.

Short, J. 2004 *Global Metropolitan: Globalizing Cities in a Capitalist World*. London & New York: Routledge.

Waitt, G. 2003 'Social Impacts of the Sydney Olympics' *Annals of Tourism Research* 30 (1): 194–215.

Text 3

3 Reasons Why Hosting the Olympics Is a Loser's Game

THE OLYMPIC STIMULUS

(5)

These days the summer Games might generate $5-to-6 billion in total revenue (nearly half of which goes to the International Olympic Committee). In contrast, the costs of the games rose to an estimated $16 billion in Athens, $40 billion in Beijing, and reportedly nearly $20 billion in London. Only some of this investment is tied up in infrastructure projects that may be useful going forward.

The high costs are bound to make hosting the Olympics a bad deal in the short-run. Promoters, however, claim that there is a strong benefit that accrues over time connected to the advertising effect of hosting the games.

(10)

The idea is that the hundreds of hours of television exposure to hundreds of millions of viewers around the globe will generate increased tourism and business for the city. ...

It should be added that there is little evidence that tourism increases during the Games. Rather, Olympic tourists replace normal tourists who want

(15)

to stay away to avoid the congestion and greater expense during the Games.

Finally, it would appear that most of the positive developmental functions that could be associated with the Olympics, could also occur absent the Olympics. The needed infrastructural investments could be made, the national airline could offer reduced rates for stays of over one week, trade

(20)

missions could multiply their efforts, and so on. Of course, it is always possible that a proactive, efficient government in a potential-laden, burgeoning city could use the Olympics to boost its fortunes. Barcelona ran up a reported $6 billion debt to host the 1992 Games, but the city's image gained enormously and tourism has since flourished. The stars all aligned

(25)

and Barcelona is arguably a case in point for Olympics promoters. Whether or not Barcelona would have experienced its favorable development without the Games, we'll never know.

—Andrew Zimbalist
excerpted from "3 Reasons Why Hosting the Olympics
Is a Loser's Game"
http://www.theatlantic.com, July 23, 2012

Text 4

Factsheet: Legacies of the Games

IOC [International Olympic Committee] SUPPORT

As the Olympic Games have grown to become the world's foremost sporting event, their impact on a host city and country has also increased. This has meant that cities interested in hosting the Games are now placing increasing emphasis on the legacies that such an event
(5) can create for their citizens and, in many cases, they are using the Games as a catalyst for urban renewal. ...

GAMES OF THE OLYMPIAD

BEIJING 2008

Education: 400 million children in 400,000 Chinese schools were exposed to the Olympic values, and 550 Chinese schools partnered with schools in other countries to conduct cultural sports and educa-
(10) tional exchanges. ...

Transport Infrastructure: Beijing's Capital Airport saw its capacity increased by 24 million passengers; a new express way and high speed rail link was built to Tianjin; and three new subway lines were constructed, as well as a new ring road and airport express road. Public transport
(15) capacity was increased by 4.5 million people.

Venues: Twenty-three of the Beijing 2008 venues will be used as sports facilities, conference centres and public event facilities; six venues were located on university campuses for use by students after the Games; and the International Broadcast Centre and Main Press Centre will serve
(20) conventions and tourism. ...

Environment: Some 140 billion Yuan was invested in air quality improvements alone, with 60,000 coal-burning boilers being upgraded to reduce emissions; a number of public buses being converted to run on natural gas; and restrictions being put in place on private automobile
(25) use, a form of which is still in place today. There were also significant improvements in water treatment facilities.

ATHENS 2004

Transport Infrastructure: Athens 2004 saw a new and renovated urban and underground system capable of carrying 1,000,000 passengers a day (20 per cent of the population of Athens); 90km of new
(30) roads were built and a further 120km widened, with a new computerised traffic management system installed to help manage traffic. A new airport was also constructed. ...

Environment: Some 90 per cent of the Schinias rowing facility which is on reclaimed wetland was designated a wildlife preserve. Hundreds
(35) of thousands of trees and shrubs were planted. ...

Education: One hundred thousand Greeks received technical, managerial or other Games-related training. ...

Venues: Some Athens 2004 venues were converted for post-Games use, ranging from sports facilities to a local theatre, to shopping and con-
(40) vention centres, to Government offices and a new university campus. ...

SALT LAKE CITY 2002

Venues: The Utah Athletic Foundation was created to manage the Olympic Oval and Park, allowing the local community to use the facilities, as well as host major events. Both the Park and Oval are USOC Olympic training sites. Fourteen venues in total continue to be used for
(45) events, elite training and recreational purposes.

Education: The Salt Lake City Organising Committee provided Olympic-related experiences to 600,000 Utah school children and those experiences continue today with 5,000–10,000 students visiting Olympic facilities every year. Salt Lake also ran a "One School, One Country" pro-
(50) gramme partnering schools in Utah with schools in countries around the world, thus letting students learn about a variety of cultures, languages, customs, music and sport.

Environment: Thanks to energy efficient designs, water conservation efforts, aquatic habitat restoration projects, recycling of Games waste,
(55) a worldwide tree planting programme and the encouragement of transit use, Salt Lake 2002 was certified as climate neutral by the Climate Neutral Network. ...

LILLEHAMMER 1994

Environment: The Lillehammer Games were noteworthy for their focus on environmental conservation, which set the stage for the forma-
(60) tion of the "Green" Olympics.

Venues: Lillehammer Olympia Park AS was created to manage the legacy of five of the Olympic Venues. The Lillehammer Olympic venues are used for a host of purposes ranging from sporting to cultural and commercial events in both summer and winter. The venues are available for
(65) public use, as well as for elite athletes. In 2016, Lillehammer will host the Youth Olympic Games. ...

Infrastructure: The Games allowed improvements to be made to the roads, the railway to Oslo, the local telecommunications system, and the water and sewage systems that would otherwise have taken 20
(70) years. ...

Education: The International Broadcast Centre allowed the Lillehammer College to increase enrolment from 600 to 3,000 students, thanks to the extra space it created. The local authority also developed an educational programme for local primary and secondary school students. ...

—International Olympic Committee
excerpted and adapted from "Factsheet: Legacies of the Games"
July 17, 2012

PART 3—Text-Analysis Response

Your Task: Closely read the text on pages 155 through 157 and write a well-developed, text-based response of two to three paragraphs. In your response, identify a central idea in the text and analyze how the author's use of *one* writing strategy (literary element or literary technique or rhetorical device) develops this central idea. Use strong and thorough evidence from the text to support your analysis. Do *not* simply summarize the text. You may use the margins to take notes as you read and scrap paper to plan your response. Write your response on a separate sheet of paper.

  Guidelines:

    Be sure to

- Identify a central idea in the text.
- Analyze how the author's use of *one* writing strategy (literary element or literary technique or rhetorical device) develops this central idea. Examples include: characterization, conflict, denotation/connotation, metaphor, simile, irony, language use, point-of-view, setting, structure, symbolism, theme, tone, etc.
- Use strong and thorough evidence from the text to support your analysis.
- Organize your ideas in a cohesive and coherent manner.
- Maintain a formal style of writing.
- Follow the conventions of standard written English.

Text

   ...It turned out to be true. The face of the water [Mississippi River], in time, became a wonderful book—a book that was a dead language to the uneducated passenger, but which told its mind to me without reserve, delivering its most cherished secrets as clearly as if it uttered them with
(5) a voice. And it was not a book to be read once and thrown aside, for it had a new story to tell every day. Throughout the long twelve hundred miles there was never a page that was void of interest, never one that you could leave unread without loss, never one that you would want to skip, thinking you could find higher enjoyment in some other thing.
(10) There never was so wonderful a book written by man; never one whose interest was so absorbing, so unflagging, so sparklingly renewed with every reperusal. The passenger who could not read it was charmed with a peculiar sort of faint dimple on its surface (on the rare occasions when he did not overlook it altogether); but to the pilot that was an
(15) *italicized* passage; indeed, it was more than that, it was a legend of the largest capitals, with a string of shouting exclamation points at the end of it, for it meant that a wreck or a rock was buried there that could tear the life out of the strongest vessel that ever floated. It is the faintest and simplest expression the water ever makes, and the most hideous
(20) to a pilot's eye. In truth, the passenger who could not read this book saw nothing but all manner of pretty pictures in it, painted by the sun and shaded by the clouds, whereas to the trained eye these were not pictures at all, but the grimmest and most dead-earnest of reading matter.
   Now when I had mastered the language of this water, and had
(25) come to know every trifling feature that bordered the great river as familiarly as I knew the letters of the alphabet, I had made a valuable acquisition. But I had lost something, too. I had lost something which could never be restored to me while I lived. All the grace, the beauty, the poetry, had gone out of the majestic river! I still kept in mind a certain
(30) wonderful sunset which I witnessed when steamboating was new to me. A broad expanse of the river was turned to blood; in the middle distance the red hue brightened into gold, through which a solitary log came floating, black and conspicuous; one place a long, slanting mark lay sparkling upon the water; in another the surface was broken by boil-

(35) ing, tumbling rings, that were as many-tinted as an opal; where the
ruddy flush was faintest, was a smooth spot that was covered with graceful circles and radiating lines, ever so delicately traced; the shore on our
left was densely wooded, and the sombre shadow that fell from this forest
was broken in one place by a long, ruffled trail that shone like silver; and
(40) high above the forest wall a clean-stemmed dead tree waved a single leafy
bough that glowed like a flame in the unobstructed splendor that was
flowing from the sun. There were graceful curves, reflected images, woody
heights, soft distances; and over the whole scene, far and near, the dissolving lights drifted steadily, enriching it every passing moment with new
(45) marvels of coloring.

I stood like one bewitched. I drank it in, in a speechless rapture. The
world was new to me, and I had never seen any thing like this at home.
But as I have said, a day came when I began to cease from noting the
glories and the charms which the moon and the sun and the twilight
(50) wrought upon the river's face; another day came when I ceased altogether to note them. Then, if that sunset scene had been repeated,
I should have looked upon it without rapture, and should have commented upon it, inwardly, after this fashion: "This sun means that we are
going to have wind to-morrow; that floating log means that the river is
(55) rising, small thanks to it; that slanting mark on the water refers to a bluff
reef which is going to kill somebody's steamboat one of these nights, if it
keeps on stretching out like that; those tumbling 'boils' show a dissolving
bar and a changing channel there; the lines and circles in the slick water
over yonder are a warning that that troublesome place is shoaling
(60) up dangerously; that silver streak in the shadow of the forest is the 'break'
from a new snag, and he has located himself in the very best place he could
have found to fish for steamboats; that tall dead tree, with a single living
branch, is not going to last long, and then how is a body ever going to
get through this blind place at night without the friendly old landmark?"

(65) No, the romance and the beauty were all gone from the river. All the
value any feature of it had for me now was the amount of usefulness it
could furnish toward compassing the safe piloting of a steamboat. Since
those days, I have pitied doctors from my heart. What does the lovely flush
in a beauty's cheek mean to a doctor but a "break" that ripples above some
(70) deadly disease? Are not all her visible charms sown thick with what are to

him the signs and symbols of hidden decay? Does he ever see her beauty at all, or doesn't he simply view her professionally, and comment upon her unwholesome condition all to himself? And doesn't he sometimes wonder whether he has gained most or lost most by learning his trade?

—Mark Twain
excerpted and adapted from *Life on the Mississippi*, 1901
Harper & Brothers Publishers

Regents ELA (Common Core) Answers August 2014
English Language Arts

Answer Key

Part 1

1. 1	9. 3	17. 4
2. 3	10. 4	18. 3
3. 1	11. 2	19. 1
4. 2	12. 4	20. 4
5. 4	13. 1	21. 4
6. 1	14. 3	22. 3
7. 2	15. 1	23. 4
8. 1	16. 2	24. 2

Regents Examination in English Language Arts (Common Core)—August 2014

Chart for Converting Total Weighted Raw Scores to Final Exam Scores (Scale Scores) (Use for the August 2014 examination only.)

Weighted Raw Score*	Scale Score	Performance Level	Weighted Raw Score*	Scale Score	Performance Level
56	100	5	27	62	2
55	98	5	26	59	2
54	96	5	25	56	2
53	95	5	24	55	2
52	93	5	23	51	1
51	92	5	22	48	1
50	91	5	21	45	1
49	90	5	20	42	1
48	89	5	19	39	1
47	88	5	18	36	1
46	87	5	17	33	1
45	87	5	16	29	1
44	86	5	15	26	1
43	85	5	14	23	1
42	84	4	13	20	1
41	83	4	12	17	1
40	83	4	11	14	1
39	82	4	10	12	1
38	80	4	9	10	1
37	79	4	8	8	1
36	78	3	7	7	1
35	77	3	6	6	1
34	75	3	5	5	1
33	74	3	4	4	1
32	72	3	3	3	1
31	70	3	2	2	1
30	68	3	1	1	1
29	66	3	0	0	1
28	65	3			

The conversion table is determined independently for each administration of the exam.

Answers Explained

PART 1—Reading Comprehension

Multiple-Choice Questions

Passage A

(1) **1** "connecting the people's inner feelings and outer lives." These lines elaborate on the theme introduced at the beginning of the paragraph: the spirit of the place is heard in the inner voice—the prayers of the people in the *longtang* simply "to live." The entire passage develops the contrast between these prayers, which represent the inner lives of those whose voices are stifled, and the clamor (hubbub, commotion) of life in Peace Lane.

(2) **3** "emotional burden." The sense of burden is clear when the narrator tells us that "… the two little words *to live* weighed a ton." The desperation in simply hoping to survive weighs heavily on the *longtang*, even if the words themselves are too heavy to be heard.

(3) **1** "unimportant." The "immaterial things" represent the easily observed signs of life in the *longtang*; "smoke and mist" are only what rises to the surface, but the "inner voice" of the place remains unheard and the people unnoticed.

(4) **2** "a quiet and uneventful life." The narrator tells us that the people "had an ordinary heart and its prayers were quite humble…." They suffer no major disasters but "little things kept coming up:" death from a fall, accidental electrocution, or poisoning. Peace Lane prays for a life spared such "events," for a life of "peace and security." None of the other choices is suggested in this paragraph.

(5) **4** "ignore impending dangers." In these lines, the narrator offers several examples of how "The residents were never prepared for the closest [impending] dangers." They ignored the flowerpot ready to fall, the illegal structures, and the termites in the floor. Recognizing the meaning of *impending* in this passage is key to choosing the correct answer.

(6) **1** "former vitality." These lines (92–98) develop the simile of the *longtang* as "an aging beauty," a woman once lovely and charming, who has some of her former attraction if one does not look too closely.

(7) **2** "loss." The narrator tells us that "the story seems to be coming to an end." In the descriptions that follow, there is a sense of anticipation of how the *longtang* will end; but loss expresses more effectively the feelings of the narrator here. The simile described in the question above, images of broken bricks and shattered tiles and a receding tide, all suggest a powerful feeling of loss.

(8) **1** "futility of the people's situation." The narrator sums up the futility [uselessness, ineffectiveness] of the prayers and the longtang in the last few sentences of the fourth paragraph, which concludes: "The prayers... must imply resignation to reality...they pray for peace, but that was just wishful thinking."

(9) **3** "sympathetic." There are details in this passage to suggest each of the choices might be correct; there is certainly ambiguity in how the narrator seems to judge the *longtang*. Overall, however, the effect of the passage is sympathetic: the narrator wants us to see places that try to remain hidden, to understand the desolation of the lives there, and above all, to hear the voices, the prayers of the *longtang*.

Passage B

(10) **4** "transformation." The images in these lines are of modern transformations [changes, alterations, and additions] to what had been a landscape of 19th-century rural life. The narrator in the poem reveals that his purpose for driving past the strip malls and armories is "...Just to catch a glimpse of you as you once were." (line 17). The images of abandoned sites and tattered billboards do not suggest beauty or historical significance, and the economic possibilities have begun to fade.

(11) **2** "from external description to childhood memory." This phrase best describes the shift in the narrator's focus from description of what he sees as he drives to his "tarnished, dim" memory of climbing to the attic and playing his grandmother's mandolin.

(12) **4** "It emphasizes the diminishing of the past." The simile "... faint/As light on dusty glass" completes the narrator's description of how the "upstate hillsides" have so changed that they are "raw and dull" [diminished] like worn brass and like a mirror whose silver is gone and can give back only a faint reflection. None of the other choices expresses the meaning in these images of fading and loss.

(13) **1** "frustrated." From the opening line, "Listen, you upstate hillsides...," we sense the narrator's frustration with a landscape he has "loved so loyally" and whose values and traditions he has offered much of his life to. At the end of the poem, he tells us he has sung the virtues of this place, "despite [the landscape's] tawdry best intentions."

(14) **3** "commitment to the values of a past era." This phrase best describes the narrator's declaration that he has been devoted to the values of simplicity, honesty [rectitude], and clarity that life in this place once represented. Throughout the poem we hear the voice of someone who has "... loved/So loyally" these hillsides and the values the lives there once represented.

Passage C

(15) **1** "achievement of peace." Readers will recognize here the origin of the expression "to bury the hatchet," meaning to bring a peaceful end to an argument and, often, to restore a friendship.

The language here may be symbolic, but the expression is based on the custom of literally *burying a hatchet* [or tomahawk] as a symbol of peace between Native American tribes.

(16) **2** "indicating the reason for the meeting." The details at the beginning of the paragraph report the murders "by white men" of seven warriors since the end of the war. Chief Red Jacket observes that "men now in office" may not know "what has befallen us"; the purpose of the meeting is to present this "mighty grievance" and to seek a way to prevent [such acts] in the future.

(17) **4** "connection between responsibility and accountability." In these lines, Chief Red Jacket asserts that the United States is **responsible**— "it is to the United States they [the families of the dead warriors] owe the loss of their heads"—and is **accountable**—"the United States should do something toward their support."

(18) **3** "recent changes in United States leadership." Chief Red Jacket reminds his audience (the acting secretary of war) that the Canandaigua Treaty was concluded when George Washington was president. He goes on to say that , "…as he is now dead we know not if it is still valid." (line 55) None of the other choices accounts for the uncertainty.

(19) **1** "We dispense with the usual formality of having your speech again read." Lines 9–11 are a summary of what the Six Nations "fully comprehended…yesterday." The Chief assures his audience that the tribes have no need to hear the secretary of war's speech repeated.

(20) **4** "cooperative." In this part of the speech, the chief assures the secretary of war that if the new president "thinks it proper" to let the current treaty remain in force, "Whatever he may do we agree to…." None of the other choices describes the chief's attitude here.

(21) **4** "desire for fair treatment." In this passage the chief points out that because he has come to Washington to address a crime committed by some of "your bad men," the United States should bear the considerable expense of his long journey. Throughout the speech, the chief bases his claims on the need for justice and fairness.

(22) **3** "why should you not pay also." Here the chief points out that the Six Nations must "pay for our breaches [violations of the treaty]…." It is only right that the United States pay for comparable breaches on their side. This too is an example of the chief's insistence on fairness in relations between the United States and the Six Nations.

(23) **4** "the protection of Iroquois lands." The chief makes no reference to the Iroquois nation. Each of the other choices does identify a purpose of the Canandaigua Treaty.

(24) **2** "establish a feeling of alliance." The chief opens his speech with a desire to "restore the friendship that has existed between the United States and the Six Nations...." The chief's use of "Brother" to address the secretary emphasizes his belief that the parties are not only allied [joined, associated] by treaty but also have a mutual interest in maintaining goodwill. This feeling best describes the tone of the chief's speech.

PART 2—Argument Response

Sample Essay Response

The Olympic games have long been regarded as a positive event, drawing international attention to the host city and its people. It is often considered an honor to host the games, and many people regard it as benefit for all. However, we must look at actual statistics of hosting the games in order to find the truth. The Olympic games take their toll on the host cities; and though there certainly are benefits for being a host city, the cons far outweigh the pros. Past experience tells us the United States should not bid to host a future Olympic games.

Primarily, the exorbitant costs of the Olympics should be enough to deter most countries from bidding. Though one can never know the true costs of the games (Text 1, lines 45–47) they are often very high. It cost $16 billion in Athens, $20 billion in London, and $40 billion in Beijing. (Text 3, lines 3–5). The massive amounts of money needed to fund Olympic facilities often put countries into debt. For example, Barcelona slipped into a $6 billion debt after hosting the games. (Text 3, lines 23–25). Additionally, a government is often evasive when reporting the costs of preparing for the Olympic games. Infrastructure costs may be reported in a budget as public works, thereby hiding some of the true costs. (Text 1, lines 48–50). This is done to present the Olympics in the best possible light. The fact of the matter is that Olympic games cost way too much, a price that the United States cannot afford, especially considering the delicate economic state we are in today.

It can be argued that the Olympics actually do benefit the economy, by creating jobs in preparation and execution of the games. This argument, however, is not completely true. The Olympics create temporary jobs, which does not help an economy reach a stable employment rate. In the LA games of 1984, 16,250 people had Olympics-related jobs for only 30 days. In the Seoul games of 1988, 33,500 people had jobs for only 30 days as well. (Text 2, lines 13–14). The long-term value of the employment created was little because after 30 days, people were probably unemployed again. Much of the work is construction related and will require some very high-skilled workers and many unskilled workers, who will remain untrained for the future. Some analysts suggest this leads to a polarization in the labor market. (Text 2, lines 21–25). Thus, even the jobs created, the supposedly positive aspects of being a host city, are not so positive after all.

The United States definitely should not bid to host future Olympic games. It has little long-term benefit for the host city and the costs are simply unacceptable. Though it may promote benefits such as improved transportation infrastructure (Text 4, lines 27–32), or increased tourism and business for the city (Text 3, lines 8–12), the potential benefits do not stand up against the concrete, inevitable costs of hosting such an event.

Analysis

Many students who chose to develop arguments against hosting the Olympic games focused on the issue of costs, because there are many compelling details in the texts to support that view. This essay offers a good example of that argument. The opening paragraph establishes a claim: "Past experience tells us the United States should not bid to host a future Olympic games," and distinguishes it from alternate claims by acknowledging that,"…many people regard it as a benefit for all."

The essay is developed with several specific and relevant details from all four of the texts, and the writer correctly cites each reference. The focus on only one aspect of the arguments for and against hosting the games gives the essay coherence. The essay is written in clear, direct sentences and appropriately formal language. The writer's strong personal view is sensed throughout, and the tone of the essay makes it suitable for publication where opinion would be expected, such as on an op-ed page. Although this writer made somewhat limited use of all the ideas in the four texts, the essay presents a sound argument and would merit a high score.

(See pages 80–81 for the scoring guidelines.)

PART 3—Text-Analysis Response

Sample Essay Response

The author of this passage used vivid imagery to convey the beauty of the river and to convey how the acquisition of knowledge means losing that beauty. Before the author learned to see the signs of danger in navigating the river, he saw only beauty. When Twain was new to steam boating, he witnessed a particularly magnificent sunset. The sky was red, which reflected on the water and slowly transitioned to gold. He noticed delicate rings growing from a spot in the water. He noticed a dead tree rising above the wall of forest, with a bough of leaves that shone with brightness of flames. He was in a state of "speechless rapture."

Later on, the beauty faded as he learned the signals behind what he saw. Twain tells us that the river was a "wonderful book," but it was also "the grimmest and most dead-earnest of reading matter." That beautiful red hue in his surroundings would mean wind the next day. The growing ripples marked a dangerous obstacle that could kill a steamboat. The dead tree, whose leaves were like fire, was a "friendly landmark" and would be lost after it fell. In learning to read the book of the river, Twain loses forever the ability to see the beauty and grace of the Mississippi and regrets what he has lost in learning his trade.

Analysis

In the opening sentence, this writer expresses the central idea of the passage and identifies Twain's use of vivid imagery as key to understanding its meaning. The analysis is developed in two paragraphs, each of which cites several specific and relevant examples from the text. In the first paragraph, the images recall Twain's delight in the beauty of the river; in the second, these images become examples of how the knowledge Twain acquires destroys his ability to see beauty in them. This organization in parallel details is both sophisticated and effective. The incorporation of quoted phrases also enhances development of the central idea. The writing is clear and demonstrates control of the conventions. This response would merit a high score.

(See pages 82–83 for the scoring guidelines.)

Regents ELA (Common Core) Examination June 2015

English Language Arts

PART 1—Reading Comprehension

Directions (1–24): Closely read each of the three passages below. After each passage, there are several multiple-choice questions. Select the best suggested answer to each question and write its number in the space provided. You may use the margins to take notes as you read.

Reading Comprehension Passage A

Newland Archer is reacquainted with Ellen Mingott (now Countess Olenska) while attending a party with some of 1870s' New York aristocracy.

It was generally agreed in New York that the Countess Olenska had "lost her looks."

She had appeared there first, in Newland Archer's boyhood, as a brilliantly pretty little girl of nine or ten, of whom people said that she
(5) "ought to be painted." Her parents had been continental wanderers, and after a roaming babyhood she had lost them both, and been taken in charge by her aunt, Medora Manson, also a wanderer, who was herself returning to New York to "settle down." ...

Every one was disposed to be kind to little Ellen Mingott, though
(10) her dusky red cheeks and tight curls gave her an air of gaiety that seemed unsuitable in a child who should still have been in black for her parents. It was one of the misguided Medora's many peculiarities to flout the unalter-

able rules that regulated American mourning, and when she stepped from
the steamer her family were scandalised to see that the crape veil she wore
(15) for her own brother was seven inches shorter than those of her sisters-
in-law, while little Ellen was in crimson merino and amber beads, like a
gipsy foundling.[1]

But New York had so long resigned itself to Medora that only a few
old ladies shook their heads over Ellen's gaudy clothes, while her other
(20) relations fell under the charm of her high colour and high spirits. She
was a fearless and familiar little thing, who asked disconcerting questions, made precocious comments, and possessed outlandish arts, such
as dancing a Spanish shawl dance and singing Neapolitan love-songs
to a guitar. Under the direction of her aunt (whose real name was Mrs.
(25) Thorley Chivers, but who, having received a Papal title,[2] had resumed her
first husband's patronymic,[3] and called herself the Marchioness Manson,
because in Italy she could turn it into Manzoni) the little girl received an
expensive but incoherent education, which included "drawing from the
model," a thing never dreamed of before, and playing the piano in quin-
(30) tets with professional musicians. ...

These things passed through Newland Archer's mind a week later as he
watched the Countess Olenska enter the van der Luyden drawing-room on
the evening of the momentous dinner. The occasion was a solemn one, and
he wondered a little nervously how she would carry it off. She came rather
(35) late, one hand still ungloved, and fastening a bracelet about her wrist;
yet she entered without any appearance of haste or embarrassment the
drawing-room in which New York's most chosen company was somewhat
awfully assembled.

In the middle of the room she paused, looking about her with a grave
(40) mouth and smiling eyes; and in that instant Newland Archer rejected the
general verdict on her looks. It was true that her early radiance was gone.
The red cheeks had paled; she was thin, worn, a little older-looking than
her age, which must have been nearly thirty. But there was about her the
mysterious authority of beauty, a sureness in the carriage of the head, the

---

[1]foundling—an abandoned child
[2]Papal title—a title given by the Pope
[3]patronymic—male family name

(45)   movement of the eyes, which, without being in the least theatrical, struck
       him as highly trained and full of a conscious power. At the same time she
       was simpler in manner than most of the ladies present, and many people
       (as he heard afterward from Janey)[4] were disappointed that her appear-
       ance was not more "stylish"—for stylishness was what New York most
(50)   valued. It was, perhaps, Archer reflected, because her early vivacity[5] had
       disappeared; because she was so quiet—quiet in her movements, her voice,
       and the tones of her low-pitched voice. New York had expected something
       a good deal more resonant in a young woman with such a history.

           The dinner was a somewhat formidable business. Dining with the van
(55)   der Luydens was at best no light matter, and dining there with a Duke
       who was their cousin was almost a religious solemnity. It pleased Archer
       to think that only an old New Yorker could perceive the shade of differ-
       ence (to New York) between being merely a Duke and being the van der
       Luydens' Duke. New York took stray noblemen calmly, and even (except
(60)   in the Struthers set) with a certain distrustful *hauteur*;[6] but when they pre-
       sented such credentials as these they were received with an old-fashioned
       cordiality that they would have been greatly mistaken in ascribing solely
       to their standing in Debrett.[7] It was for just such distinctions that the
       young man cherished his old New York even while he smiled at it. ...

(65)   The Countess Olenska was the only young woman at the dinner; yet,
       as Archer scanned the smooth plump elderly faces between their diamond
       necklaces and towering ostrich feathers, they struck him as curiously
       immature compared with hers. It frightened him to think what must have
       gone to the making of her eyes.

(70)   The Duke of St. Austrey, who sat at his hostess's right, was naturally
       the chief figure of the evening. But if the Countess Olenska was less con-
       spicuous than had been hoped, the Duke was almost invisible. Being a
       well-bred man he had not (like another recent ducal[8] visitor) come to the
       dinner in a shooting-jacket; but his evening clothes were so shabby and
(75)   baggy, and he wore them with such an air of their being homespun, that

       ---
       [4]Janey—Newland Archer's sister
       [5]vivacity—liveliness
       [6]hauteur—display of arrogance
       [7]Debrett—British aristocracy reference book
       [8]ducal—relating to a duke

(with his stooping way of sitting, and the vast beard spreading over his shirt-front) he hardly gave the appearance of being in dinner attire. He was short, round-shouldered, sunburnt, with a thick nose, small eyes and a sociable smile; but he seldom spoke, and when he did it was in such low
(80) tones that, despite the frequent silences of expectation about the table, his remarks were lost to all but his neighbours.

When the men joined the ladies after dinner the Duke went straight up to the Countess Olenska, and they sat down in a corner and plunged into animated talk. Neither seemed aware that the Duke should first have
(85) paid his respects to Mrs. Lovell Mingott and Mrs. Headly Chivers, and the Countess have conversed with that amiable hypochondriac, Mr. Urban Dagonet of Washington Square, who, in order to have the pleasure of meeting her, had broken through his fixed rule of not dining out between January and April. The two chatted together for nearly twenty minutes;
(90) then the Countess rose and, walking alone across the wide drawing-room, sat down at Newland Archer's side.

It was not the custom in New York drawing-rooms for a lady to get up and walk away from one gentleman in order to seek the company of another. Etiquette required that she should wait, immovable as an idol,
(95) while the men who wished to converse with her succeeded each other at her side. But the Countess was apparently unaware of having broken any rule; she sat at perfect ease in a corner of the sofa beside Archer, and looked at him with the kindest eyes. ...

—Edith Wharton
excerpted from *The Age of Innocence*, 1920
Windsor Editions, by arrangement with D. Appleton and Company

1 In the context of the entire passage, the tone established by line 1 can best be described as

   (1) indifferent   (3) compassionate
   (2) judgmental   (4) admiring   1____

2 The use of flashback in lines 3 through 30 serves to

   (1) relate Countess Olenska's history
   (2) describe Newland Archer's ancestry
   (3) explain Medora Manson's talents
   (4) identify Thorley Chivers's perspective   2____

3 The meaning of "flout" as used in line 12 is clarified by the word

   (1) "wanderer" (line 7)
   (2) "dusky" (line 10)
   (3) "scandalised" (line 14)
   (4) "relations" (line 20)   3____

4 The description of Ellen in lines 18 through 30 conveys that people viewed her as

   (1) unique   (3) fashionable
   (2) simple   (4) unhealthy   4____

5 The words "disconcerting" (line 21) and "precocious" (line 22) imply that, as a child, the Countess Olenska was

   (1) impatient   (3) timid
   (2) untamed   (4) hesitant   5____

6 Medora Manson, as described in the passage, can best be characterized as

   (1) cautious   (3) intellectual
   (2) overprotective (4) unconventional   6____

7 Based on the text, the reader can infer that Newland
   Archer is

   (1) oblivious to the party's guests
   (2) intimidated by the Duke's presence
   (3) intrigued by the Countess Olenska
   (4) resentful toward the wealthy class   7_____

8 The Duke and the Countess Olenska are similar in
   that they are both

   (1) ignored by almost everyone at dinner
   (2) interested in marriage opportunities
   (3) unconcerned with social expectations
   (4) considered to be of lesser nobility   8_____

9 What effect is created by viewing the Countess at
   the party through Archer's eyes?

   (1) It emphasizes a distinction between the
       Countess and the guests.
   (2) It reveals a conflict between the Countess and
       Medora.
   (3) It clarifies a growing relationship between the
       Countess and the Duke.
   (4) It enhances the differences between the
       Countess and Archer.   9_____

10 The fact that the Countess leaves one gentleman to
   speak with another (lines 89 through 91) shows that
   she

   (1) has an unnatural need for the Duke's attention
   (2) is concerned about her reputation at the party
   (3) is actively avoiding Newland Archer's conversation
   (4) has little regard for customs associated with gender 10_____

Reading Comprehension Passage B

Machines

I hear them grinding, grinding, through the night,
The gaunt machines with arteries of fire,
Muscled with iron, boweled with smoldering light;
I watch them pulsing, swinging, climbing higher,
(5) Derrick[1] on derrick, wheel on rhythmic wheel,
Swift band on whirring band, lever on lever,
Shouting their songs in raucous notes of steel,
Blinding a village with light, damming a river.
I hear them grinding, grinding, hour on hour,
(10) Cleaving the night in twain,[2] shattering the dark
With all the rasping torrents of their power,
Groaning and belching spark on crimson spark.
I cannot hear my voice above their cry
Shaking the earth and thundering to the sky.

(15) Slowly the dawn comes up. No motors stir
The brightening hilltops as the sunrise flows
In yellow tides where daybreak's lavender
Clings to a waiting valley. No derrick throws
The sun into the heavens and no pulley
(20) Unfolds the wildflowers thirsting for the day;
No wheel unravels ferns deep in a gulley; No
engine starts the brook upon its way.
The butterflies drift idly, wing to wing,
Knowing no measured rhythm they must follow;
(25) No turbine drives the white clouds as they swing
Across the cool blue meadows of the swallow.
With all the feathered silence of a swan
They whirr and beat—the engines of the dawn.

—Daniel Whitehead Hicky
from *Bright Harbor*, 1932
Henry Holt and Company

---

[1]derrick—a large machine used for lifting
[2]twain—two

11 The use of figurative language in lines 2 and 3 contributes to the poem's meaning by

   (1) expressing a frustration with the loss of nature
   (2) establishing a parallel between man and machine
   (3) affirming the essential human need for machines
   (4) illustrating the struggle for society's survival   11_____

12 The description of the machines' songs as "raucous" (line 7) conveys that the songs are

   (1) extremely harsh
   (2) largely misunderstood
   (3) deeply inspirational
   (4) highly engaging   12_____

13 The poet's use of "groaning and belching" (line 12) is used to convey

   (1) his affection for most machines
   (2) the importance of inventions
   (3) his desire for progress
   (4) the difficult work of machines   13_____

14 A central idea that is reinforced by lines 27 and 28 is that nature

   (1) contributes to its own destruction
   (2) accomplishes its tasks with ease
   (3) endorses the notion of progress
   (4) reveals the mysteries of life   14_____

Reading Comprehension Passage C

Speech of Patrick Henry, delivered in the House of Delegates of Virginia, in support of his motion to put the colony in a state of defense against the encroachments[1] of Great Britain, March, 1775.

...Mr. President, it is natural to man to indulge in the illusions of hope. We [American colonists] are apt to shut our eyes against a painful truth, and listen to the song of that syren [siren], till she seduces our judgments. Is it the part of wise men, engaged in a great and arduous struggle for liberty?
(5)   Are we disposed to be of the number of those, who having eyes, see not, and having ears, hear not the things which so nearly concern our temporal salvation? For my part, whatever anguish of spirit it might cost, I am willing to know the whole truth; to know the worst, and to provide for it. I have but one lamp by which my feet are guided, and that is the lamp of experience. I
(10) know of no way of judging of the future, but by the past; and, judging by the past, I wish to know what there has been in the conduct of the British ministry for the last ten years, to justify those hopes with which gentlemen have been pleased to solace themselves and the house? Is it that insidious[2] smile with which our petition has been lately received? Trust it not, sir, it
(15) will prove a snare to your feet. Suffer not yourselves to be betrayed with a kiss. Ask yourselves how this gracious reception of our petition, comports[3] with those warlike preparations which cover our waters and darken our land? Are fleets and armies necessary to a work of love and reconciliation? Have we shown ourselves so unwilling to be reconciled, that force must be
(20) called in to win back our love? Let us not deceive ourselves, sir. These are the implements of war and subjugation[4]—the last arguments to which kings resort. I ask gentlemen, sir, what means this martial array, if its purpose be not to force us to submission? Can gentlemen assign any other possible motive for it? Has Great Britain any enemy in this quarter of the world, to
(25) call for all this accumulation of navies and armies? No, sir, she has none: they are meant for us: they can be meant for no other purpose—they are sent over to bind and rivet upon us those chains, which the British ministry

---

[1]encroachments—aggressions
[2]insidious—slyly deceitful
[3]comports—agrees
[4]subjugation—oppression

have been so long forging. And what have we to oppose to them? Shall we try argument? Sir, we have been trying that for the last ten years. Have
(30) we any thing new to offer upon the subject? Nothing. We have held the subject up in every light of which it is capable; but it has been all in vain. Shall we resort to entreaty and humble supplication?[5] What terms shall we find, which have not been already exhausted? Let us not, I beseech you, sir, deceive ourselves longer. Sir, we have done every thing that could be done,
(35) to avert the storm which is now coming on. We have petitioned—we have remonstrated[6] we have supplicated—we have prostrated[7] ourselves before the throne, and have implored its interposition to arrest the tyrannical hands of the ministry and parliament. Our petitions have been slighted; our remonstrances have produced additional violence and insult; our sup-
(40) plications have been disregarded; and we have been spurned, with contempt, from the foot of the throne.

In vain, after these things, may we indulge the fond hope of peace and reconciliation. *There is no longer any room for hope.* If we wish to be free—if we mean to preserve inviolate those inestimable privileges for which we
(45) have been so long contending—if we mean not basely to abandon the noble struggle in which we have been so long engaged, and which we have pledged ourselves never to abandon, until the glorious object of our contest shall be obtained—we must fight!—I repeat it, sir, we must fight—An appeal to arms and to the God of Hosts, is all that is left us!
(50) They tell us, sir, that we are weak—unable to cope with so formidable an adversary. But when shall we be stronger? Will it be the next week, or the next year? Will it be when we are totally disarmed; and when a British guard shall be stationed in our House? Shall we gather strength by irreso-lution and inaction? Shall we acquire the means of effectual resistance, by
(55) lying supinely on our backs, and hugging the delusive phantom of hope, until our enemies shall have bound us, hand and foot? Sir, we are not weak, if we make a proper use of those means which the God of nature hath placed in our power—three millions of people, armed in the holy cause of Liberty, and in such a country as that which we possess; are invincible by any force
(60) which our enemy can send against us.

---

[5]supplication—begging
[6]remonstrated—pleaded in protest
[7]prostrated—laid down in a humble manner

Sir, we shall not fight our battles alone. There is a just God, who presides over the destinies of nations, and will raise up friends to fight our battles for us. The battle, sir, is not to the strong alone; it is to the vigilant, the active, the brave. Besides, sir, we have now no election. If we were base enough to
(65) desire it, it is now too late to retire from the contest. There is no retreat, but in submission and slavery. Our chains are forged:—their clanking may be heard on the plains of Boston! The war is inevitable—and let it come!! I repeat it, sir, let it come!!!

It is in vain, sir, to extenuate the matter. Gentlemen may cry, peace,
(70) peace—but there is no peace! The war is actually begun! The next gale that sweeps from the north, will bring to our ears the clash of resounding arms! Our brethren are already in the field! Why stand we here idle? What is it that gentlemen wish? What would they have? Is life so dear, or peace so sweet, as to be purchased at the price of chains, and slavery? Forbid it, Almighty
(75) God!—I know not what course others may take; but as for me, GIVE ME LIBERTY, OR GIVE ME DEATH!

—Patrick Henry
excerpted and adapted from *The Mental Guide, Being a Compend of the First Principles of Metaphysics, and a System of Attaining an Easy and Correct Mode of Thought and Style in Composition by Transcription; Predicated on the Analysis of the Human Mind*, 1828
Marsh & Capen, and Richardson & Lord

15 Lines 1 through 3 help to frame the speaker's argument by

  (1) addressing human frailties
  (2) exposing outside criticisms
  (3) explaining common misconceptions
  (4) proposing certain compromises   15____

16 Lines 7 and 8 help to express the speaker's desire to

  (1) locate the necessary resources
  (2) rely on outside assistance
  (3) insist on short-term solutions
  (4) confront the unpleasant reality   16____

17 The major effect of the figurative language used in lines 26 through 28 ("they are sent … so long forging") is to emphasize the

  (1) loyalty of subjects
  (2) respect for authority
  (3) penalty for treason
  (4) loss of freedom   17____

18 The overall purpose of the first paragraph (lines 1 through 41) is to

  (1) explain the role of government
  (2) question the importance of reason
  (3) analyze the existing situation
  (4) expose the failings of law   18____

19 In the context of the speech, the purpose of the statement, "They tell us, sir, that we are weak—unable to cope with so formidable an adversary" (lines 50 and 51) is to

  (1) introduce a counterclaim
  (2) address a financial crisis
  (3) explain a confusing concept
  (4) defend a known fact   19____

20 Which phrase clarifies the speaker's view of Britain's
    intentions for the colonies?

    (1) "gracious reception" (line 16)
    (2) "war and subjugation" (line 21)
    (3) "inestimable privileges" (line 44)
    (4) "irresolution and inaction" (lines 53–54)   20_____

21 The purpose of the rhetorical questions in lines 51
    through 56 is to emphasize the consequence of

    (1) selfishness   (3) greed
    (2) arrogance   (4) indecision   21_____

22 What is the main message delivered by the speaker
    to his audience in lines 42 through 49?

    (1) If we fight together we will win.
    (2) The state will supply us with arms.
    (3) The enemy is weaker than first thought.
    (4) We must outlaw slavery forever.   22_____

23 As used in line 64 the word "election" most nearly
    means

    (1) support   (3) enemies
    (2) choice   (4) politics   23_____

24 The speaker's overall tone may best be described as

    (1) contented   (3) passionate
    (2) frightened   (4) satirical   24_____

PART 2—Argument Response

Directions: Closely read each of the **four** texts on pages 181 through 189 and write a source-based argument on the topic below. You may use the margins to take notes as you read and scrap paper to plan your response. Write your argument on a separate sheet of paper.

Topic: Should college athletes be paid?

Your Task: Carefully read each of the **four** texts provided. Then, using evidence from at least **three** of the texts, write a well-developed argument regarding whether or not college athletes should be paid. Clearly establish your claim, distinguish your claim from alternate or opposing claims, and use specific, relevant, and sufficient evidence from at least **three** of the texts to develop your argument. Do *not* simply summarize each text.

Guidelines:

Be sure to

- Establish your claim regarding whether or not college athletes should be paid.
- Distinguish your claim from alternate or opposing claims.
- Use specific, relevant, and sufficient evidence from at least **three** of the texts to develop your argument.
- Identify each source that you reference by text number and line number(s) or graphic (for example: Text 1, line 4 or Text 2, graphic).
- Organize your ideas in a cohesive and coherent manner.
- Maintain a formal style of writing.
- Follow the conventions of standard written English.

Texts:

Text 1—The Case for Paying College Athletes

Text 2—It's Time to Pay College Athletes

Text 3—Sorry Time Magazine: Colleges Have No Reason to Pay Athletes

Text 4—There's No Crying in College: The Case Against Paying College Athletes

Text 1

The Case for Paying College Athletes

The college sports industry generates $11 billion in annual revenues. Fifty colleges report annual revenues that exceed $50 million. Meanwhile, five colleges report annual revenues that exceed $100 million. These rev- enues come from numerous sources, including ticket sales, sponsorship

(5) rights, and the sale of broadcast rights. The National Collegiate Athletic Association [NCAA] recently sold broadcast rights to its annual men's basketball tournament for upwards of $770 million per season. And the Big Ten Conference has launched its own television network that sells air time to sponsors during the broadcast of its football and men's basketball

(10) games.

These college sports revenues are passed along to NCAA executives, athletic directors and coaches in the form of salaries. In 2011, NCAA members paid their association president, Mark Emmert, $1.7 million. Head football coaches at the 44 NCAA Bowl Championship Series schools

(15) received on average $2.1 million in salaries. The highest paid public employee in 40 of the 50 U.S. states is the state university's head football or basketball coach. At the University of Alabama, the head football coach, Nick Saban, recently signed a contract paying him $7 million per year—more than 160 times the average wage of a Tuscaloosa public

(20) school teacher.

Nevertheless, the NCAA member colleges continue to vote to forbid the sharing of revenues with student-athletes. Instead, they hide behind a "veil of amateurism" that maintains the wealth of college sports in the hands of a select few administrators, athletic directors and coaches. This

(25) "veil" not only ensures great wealth for athletic directors and coaches, but it also ensures sustained poverty for many of the athletes who provide their labor. A 2011 report entitled "The Price of Poverty in Big Time College Sport" confirms that 85 percent of college athletes on scholarship live below the poverty line.

(30) Not only are the NCAA rules that prevent colleges from paying student-athletes immoral, but they also are likely illegal. Section 1 of the Sherman Antitrust Act, in pertinent part, states that "every contract, combination ... or conspiracy, in restraint of trade or commerce ... is declared to be illegal." Applying this language, any agreement among

(35) NCAA members to prohibit the pay of student-athletes represents a form of wage fixing that likely violates antitrust law. In addition, the NCAA's no-pay rules seem to constitute an illegal boycott of any college that would otherwise seek to pay its student-athletes.

The NCAA defends its no-pay rules on several dubious grounds. For *(40)* example, it claims that compensating student-athletes would destroy competitive balance in college sports; however, it does not consider the possibility of other less restrictive alternatives to maintain competitive balance. In addition, the NCAA claims that compensating student-athletes would create a Title IX[1] problem; however, the average Division I men's basket-*(45)* ball coach earns nearly twice as much in salary as the average Division I women's basketball coach. NCAA members have not suggested terminating the pay of college basketball coaches to resolve this concern.

The argument in favor of allowing colleges to pay their student-athletes comes down to economic efficiency, distributive justice and a reason-*(50)* able interpretation of antitrust laws. By contrast, the argument against allowing pay to student-athletes arises mainly from greed and self-interest.

—Marc Edelman
excerpted and adapted from "The Case for Paying College Athletes"
http://www.usnews.com, January 6, 2014

---

[1]Title IX—law that prohibits discrimination based on gender in any federally funded education program or activity

Text 2

It's Time to Pay College Athletes

...The historic justification for not paying players is that they are amateur student-athletes and the value of their scholarships—often worth in excess of $100,000 over four years—is payment enough. But a growing number of economists and sports experts are beginning to argue for giv-
(5)   ing athletes a fair share of the take. The numbers are too large to ignore. College athletes are mass-audience performers and need to be rewarded as such. "The rising dollar value of the exploitation of athletes," says Roger Noll, a noted sports economist from Stanford University, "is obscene, is out of control." ...

(10)   Most scholarships are revokable, so if an athlete doesn't perform well on the field, he can, in a sense, be fired from college. But academic work for some athletes is secondary: top men's basketball and football players spend 40 hours per week on their sports, easily. During football season, former Georgia tailback Richard Samuel, who earned an undergraduate
(15)   degree in sports management in 2011, said he was an "athlete-student," not a "student-athlete," as the NCAA wants people to believe. "In the fall, we would spend way more time on sports than academics," says Samuel.

Players are essentially working full-time football jobs while going to school; they deserve to be paid more than a scholarship. Because even
(20)   full-ride athletic scholarships don't cover the full cost of attending school, athletes are often short a few thousand bucks for ancillary expenses on top of tuition, room and board, books and fees: money for gas, shampoo and, yes, maybe a few beers. Some athletes are on only partial scholarship or are walk-ons[1] still paying full tuition.

(25)   While many players scrimp, their head coaches don't. Average salaries for major college football coaches have jumped more than 70% since 2006, to $1.64 million, according to *USA Today*. For major-conference men's hoops coaches who made the 2012 March Madness tournament, pay is up 20%, to $2.25 million, over that of coaches who made the 2010 tour-
(30)   nament, according to the *Journal of Issues in Intercollegiate Athletics*. "It's

---

[1]walk-ons—non-scholarship athletes

nuts," says Michael Martin, chancellor of the Colorado State University system, who was chancellor at Louisiana State University from 2008 to 2012. LSU hired Les Miles to coach its football team in 2005; Miles now earns $4.3 million annually. "It's time for people to step up and say, We (35) think this is the max that a football coach ought to get, and we ought to stick to it," says Martin. ...

The time is right to give schools the option to share their rising sports income with college athletes. Not every school would—or could—participate. Only the 60 or so schools in the power conferences, which have (40) the football and basketball revenues to support such payments, would likely even consider such an option. With conferences and schools set to see record television payouts for the next decade and beyond, the idea of paying players is no longer just fodder for academic debate. It's an ethical imperative. ...

—Sean Gregory
excerpted from "It's Time to Pay College Athletes"
Time, September 16, 2013

Text 3

Sorry Time Magazine: Colleges Have
No Reason to Pay Athletes

...In its current issue that features [Johnny] Manziel on the cover, *Time* argues vehemently for payments to big time college athletes, even calling the issue "an ethical imperative." The magazine cites the usual laundry list—schools enjoying exposure while pulling in millions,
(5)   coaches making big salaries and local bars thriving on game nights. All while the poor players get nothing.

John Rowady, president of sports marketing firm rEvolution, which has worked with many colleges, disagrees. He believes that paying the players as professionals carries a big risk of the public quickly tuning
(10) out. "It would create a massive unknown, you have to wonder if it would change the whole dynamic of what it means to be a student-athlete," he says.

There's also another fundamental issue that never seems to come up. It's called the free marketplace. Why don't schools pay? Because they don't
(15) have to. Recruits jump on the offer of tuition, room and board without hesitation. And let's not call them exploited—they aren't. Slaves were exploited. A scholarship athlete at a university can leave anytime he wants to, free to become a tuition-paying student like anyone else.

When you really think about it, many of us are just way too enamored
(20) with the word "should," as in a college athlete "should" be paid. It's shorthand for trying to impose our own sensibilities onto others, to stick our noses where they don't belong. The issue of compensation for college athletes really comes down to the colleges and the athletes. According to census bureau data, college graduates earn approximately $1 million more
(25) during their lifetimes than people whose highest educational attainment is a high school diploma. Most have to invest $100,000 to $200,000 to get that coveted college degree. A scholarship athlete doesn't.

Rowady sees another form of payment that gets overlooked, at least for the top players: brand building. A top notch football or basketball recruit
(30) isn't just getting the competitive experience he needs for launching a pro career. He's gaining exposure that's bound to pay off in endorsements and a nice contract the moment he turns pro.

"They perform in a high profile environment, and gain access to incredible networks of people," says Rowady. For those who aren't pro
(35) material: study. Your education is free, remember.

Few ever benefitted more from the exposure factor than the man behind an attention-grabbing lawsuit against the NCAA over player media like-nesses, Ed O'Bannon. The former basketball player earned close to $4 million during a brief and disappointing NBA career after he was picked
(40) by the New Jersey Nets in the first round of the 1995 draft.[1] Why was O'Bannon drafted so high? Probably because he had just led UCLA to the 1995 national title in front of a massive March Madness audience. Sure, O'Bannon had talent, but there's little doubt that the big brands of UCLA and March Madness pushed his evaluation a bit out of proportion.

(45)   Add it all up, and the marketplace produces a collegiate athletic population that is generally happy with what it gets—a free education and broad sports exposure. That doesn't mean there's anything wrong adding some cash to college players' current benefits. Or to let Manziel and others make money signing autographs or doing commercials. If they
(50) can get organized and get more for what they do, good for them. ...

—Tom Van Riper
excerpted and adapted from "Sorry Time Magazine:
Colleges Have No Reason to Pay Athletes"
http://www.forbes.com, September 6, 2013

---

[1]draft—process by which teams select eligible athletes

Text 4

There's No Crying in College: The Case
Against Paying College Athletes

...Should college athletes get a piece of the $871.6 million pie the NCAA brings in annually?

The answer is simple: No, absolutely not.

(5) College athletes are already being paid with an athletic scholarship that is worth between $20–$50,000 per year.

Oh, and that does not even begin to factor in the medical and travel expenses, free gear, top-notch coaching, unlimited use of elite athletic facilities and a national stage to audition for a job in the professional ranks.

(10) All of those perks are paid for in full by the universities these athletes choose to attend.

Before attempting to discredit some of the cases for compensating players at the college level, let's take into account all of the things they already receive cost-free.

(15) Athletic scholarships cover just about everything a student-athlete needs to survive for four years at a major university. Campus housing, daily medical care and free meals via training table are all included. Tuition and books are covered as well.

None of those things are cheap. It costs $57,180 to attend Duke
(20) University. The University of Texas charges $35,776 for out-of-state enrollees. Even Butler University charges $31,496 per year.

This means many college athletes are being reimbursed with nearly as much money as the average American makes per year.

Leaving a four-year college with a degree will help former players earn
(25) more money than those who only have a high school diploma, regardless of whether or not they move on to a professional sports career.

Students who attain a Bachelor's degree will make $1.1 million more in their lifetimes than non-graduates.

Traveling around the world is another privilege these student-athletes
(30) are afforded. ...

The Fair Market Value Argument

This is one of the more common stances pay-for-play supporters take. The idea that players are not being paid their "fair market value," however, is a complete myth.

(35) The two sports impacted by this argument the most are football and basketball, because their revenue funds just about every other varsity team at most universities.

These athletes have to be worth millions, right? Wrong. College athletes are not worth a single cent on the open market, at least until they are eligible for the NBA or NFL draft.

(40) Changes to the NBA draft eligibility requirements brought an end to high school athletes heading straight to the professional ranks. Now, NBA hopefuls must be one year removed from high school to enter the draft.

Meanwhile, NFL prospects have to wait three years before they can be drafted.

(45) Every student-athlete knows they cannot get paid in college, but if they do not like it there are other options.

Brandon Jennings was the No. 1-overall basketball prospect in the country in 2008. Instead of attending college, Jennings opted to sign a $1.2 million deal with Lottomatica Roma, a professional team in Italy.

(50) The Compton, CA product was drafted 10th by the Milwaukee Bucks after playing one season overseas.

Much like the foreign basketball associations, the Canadian Football League does not have an age requirement. High school graduates wishing to play pro football can head north and sign a contract right away. ...

(55) Instead of choosing this route, though, NFL and NBA hopefuls take their talents to the NCAA. The media exposure, coaching and training provided by the universities is far better than the athletes will receive in foreign markets. Going to classes is simply the tradeoff for reaping these benefits. ...

Paying College Athletes Will Eliminate Scandals

(60) Contrary to popular belief, the recent scandals involving the Ohio State Buckeyes, Miami (Fla.) Hurricanes and USC Trojans are not exactly anything new to college athletics.

Paying players will not eliminate any of the greed or determination to win at all costs that exists in today's society. Cheating will never stop, and *(65)* it existed at the NCAA level well before the era of modern technology. ...

The NCAA Has More Than Enough Money to Pay Players

Although the NCAA reels in over $800 million per year, 81 percent of which comes from television and marketing-rights fees, the organization continues to be non-profit.

How is this possible? An astounding 96 percent of the revenue the *(70)* NCAA brings in annually is redistributed to its members' institutions.

This is done through donations to academic enhancement, conference grants, sports sponsorships, student assistance funds and grants-in-aid. A percentage of revenue is also added to the basketball fund, which is divided up and distributed to the NCAA tournament field on a yearly *(75)* basis.

The universities themselves are not exactly rolling in wads of cash, either. Last year, only 22 athletic departments were profitable. Football and basketball bring in the dough, and every other college sport survives as a result.

(80) Remember this year's Cinderella story in March Madness, the Florida Gulf Coast Eagles? The university nearly lost money as a result of their run to the Sweet 16.

Two years ago, the Division I Board of Directors approved a $2,000 stipend for college athletes to cover the "full cost of attendance." Less *(85)* than two months later, the NCAA's member institutions repealed the stipend, because they could not afford it.

College athletics may sound like a great business, but in reality only the top-tier programs are churning out a profit.

I do not agree with everything the NCAA does. However, the evidence *(90)* shows it is not the booming business everyone thinks it is. ...

—Zach Dirlam
excerpted from "There's No Crying in College:
The Case Against Paying College Athletes"
http://bleacherreport.com, April 3, 2013

PART 3—Text-Analysis Response

Your Task: Closely read the text on pages 191 through 193 and write a well-developed, text-based response of two to three paragraphs. In your response, identify a central idea in the text and analyze how the author's use of *one* writing strategy (literary element or literary technique or rhetorical device) develops this central idea. Use strong and thorough evidence from the text to support your analysis. Do *not* simply summarize the text. You may use the margins to take notes as you read and scrap paper to plan your response. Write your response on a separate sheet of paper.

Guidelines:

Be sure to

- Identify a central idea in the text.
- Analyze how the author's use of *one* writing strategy (literary element or literary technique or rhetorical device) develops this central idea. Examples include: characterization, conflict, denotation/connotation, metaphor, simile, irony, language use, point-of-view, setting, structure, symbolism, theme, tone, etc.
- Use strong and thorough evidence from the text to support your analysis.
- Organize your ideas in a cohesive and coherent manner.
- Maintain a formal style of writing.
- Follow the conventions of standard written English.

Text

...And so the battle was staged between a crippled, sane boy and a hostile, sane, secretly savage though sometimes merciful world.

Can I climb man-made mountains, questioned Joseph Meehan. Can I climb socially constructed barriers? Can I ask my family to back me when
(5) I know something more than they, I now know the heinous[1] scepticism so kneaded down constantly in my busy sad world. What can a crippled, speechless boy do, asked Joseph, my handicap curtails my collective conscience, obliterates[2] my voice, beckons ridicule of my smile and damns my chances of being accepted as normal. ...

(10) How do I conquer my body, mused the paralysed boy. Paralysed I am labelled, but can a paralytic move? My body rarely stops moving. My arms wage constant battle trying to make me look a fool. My smile which can be most natural, can at times freeze, thereby making me seem sad and uninterested. Two great legs I may have, but put my bodyweight on them and
(15) they collapse under me like a house of cards. How then can I convey to folk that the strength in my legs can be as normal as that of the strongest man? Such were boy Joseph's taunting posers, but he had one more fence that freezed his words while they were yet unspoken.

But fate was listening and fate it was that had frozen his freedom. Now
(20) could fate be wavering in her purpose? Credence[3] was being given to his bowed perceptions—could fate avow him a means of escape?

Writing by hand failed. Typing festered hope. The typewriter was not a plaything. Boy Joseph needed to master it for the good of his sanity, for the good of his soul. Years had taught him the ins and outs of typewrit-
(25) ing, but fate denied him the power to nod and hit the keys with his head-mounted pointer. Destruction secretly destroyed his every attempt to nod his pointer onto the keys. Instead great spasms gripped him rigid and sent his simple nod into a farcical effort which ran to each and every one of his limbs.

(30) Eva Fitzpatrick had done years of duty trying to help Joseph to best his body. She told him everything she knew about brain damage and its

---

[1]heinous—hateful
[2]obliterates—blots out
[3]credence—belief

effects. The boy understood, but all he could do was to look hard into her humble eyes and flick his own heavenwards in affirmation. ...

(35) Eva's room was crested by creative drawings. Her manner was friendly, outgoing, but inwardly she felt for her student as he struggled to typewrite. Her method of working necessitated that her pupil be relaxed so she chatted light-hearted banter as she all the while measured his relaxation. The chatting would continue, but when Joseph saw his teacher wheel the long mirror towards the typing table he knew that they were *(40)* going to play typing gymnastics.

Together they would struggle, the boy blowing like a whale from the huge effort of trying to discipline his bedamned body. Every tip of his pointer to the keys of the typewriter sent his body sprawling backwards. Eva held his chin in her hands and waited for him to relax and tip another *(45)* key. The boy and girl worked mightily, typing sentences which Eva herself gave as a headline to Joseph. Young Boyblue honestly gave himself over to his typing teacher. Gumption[4] was hers as she struggled to find a very voluntary tip coming to the typewriter keys from his yessing head. .

But for Eva Fitzpatrick he would never have broken free. His own *(50)* mother had given up on him and decided that the typewriter was no help at all. She had put the cover on the machine and stored it away. She felt hurt by defeat. Her foolish heart failed to see breathing destructive spasms coming between her son and the typewriter. But how was a mother to know that hidden behind her cross was a Simon[5] ready and willing to *(55)* research areas where she strode as a stranger. How could she know that Eva brought service to a head and that science now was going to join forces with her. Now a new drug was being administered to the spastic boy and even though he was being allowed to take only a small segment of Lioresal[6] tablet, he was beginning already to feel different. The little *(60)* segments of Lioresal tablet seemed harmless, but yet they were the mustard seeds of his and Eva's hours of discovery.

Now he struggled from his certainty that he was going to succeed and with that certainty came a feeling of encouragement. The encouragement was absolute, just as though someone was egging him on. His belief now *(65)* came from himself and he wondered how this came about. He knew that

---

[4]gumption—perseverance, toughness
[5]a Simon—Biblical reference to Simon of Cyrene who helped Jesus carry his cross
[6]Lioresal—a medication to treat skeletal muscle spasms

with years of defeat he should now be experiencing despair, but instead a spirit of enlightenment was telling him you're going to come through with a bow, a bow to break your chain and let out your voice.

(70) At the very same hour fate was also at work on Eva. When it was least expected she sensed that music of which he sampled. She watched Joseph in the mirror as he struggled to find and tip the required keys. Avoiding his teacher's gaze, he struggled on trying to test himself. Glee was gambolling[7] but he had to be sure.

(75) Breathing a little easier, his body a little less trembling, he sat head cupped in Eva's hands. He even noticed the scent of her perfume but he didn't glance in the mirror. Perhaps it won't happen for me today he teased himself but he was wrong, desperately, delightfully wrong. Sweetness of certainty sugared his now. Yes, he could type. He could freely hit the keys and he looked in the mirror and met her eyes. Feebly he smiled

(80) but she continued to study him. Looking back into her face he tried to get her response, but turning his wheelchair she gracefully glided back along the corridor to his classroom. ...

—Christopher Nolan
excerpted from *Under the Eye of the Clock*, 1987
Weidenfeld and Nicolson

---

[7]gambolling—skipping

Regents ELA (Common Core) Answers June 2015
English Language Arts

Answer Key

Part 1

1. 2	9. 1	17. 4
2. 1	10. 4	18. 3
3. 3	11. 2	19. 1
4. 1	12. 1	20. 2
5. 2	13. 4	21. 4
6. 4	14. 2	22. 1
7. 3	15. 1	23. 2
8. 3	16. 4	24. 3

Regents Examination in English Language Arts
(Common Core)—June 2015

Chart for Converting Total Weighted Raw Scores to Final Exam
Scores (Scale Scores) (Use for the June 2015 examination only.)

Weighted Raw Score*	Scale Score	Performance Level	Weighted Raw Score*	Scale Score	Performance Level
56	100	5	27	58	2
55	99	5	26	55	2
54	99	5	25	53	1
53	99	5	24	50	1
52	99	5	23	47	1
51	98	5	22	44	1
50	97	5	21	42	1
49	96	5	20	39	1
48	95	5	19	35	1
47	94	5	18	32	1
46	92	5	17	29	1
45	91	5	16	26	1
44	89	5	15	22	1
43	88	5	14	19	1
42	87	5	13	15	1
41	86	5	12	12	1
40	85	5	11	10	1
39	83	4	10	8	1
38	81	4	9	7	1
37	79	4	8	6	1
36	78	3	7	5	1
35	76	3	6	4	1
34	74	3	5	3	1
33	72	3	4	3	1
32	69	3	3	2	1
31	67	3	2	1	1
30	65	3	1	1	1
29	62	2	0	0	1
28	60	2			

The conversion table is determined independently for each administration of
the exam.

Answers Explained

PART 1—Reading Comprehension

Multiple-Choice Questions

Passage A

(1) **2** "judgmental." The phrase "generally agreed" indicates a form of judgment. In this case, as the rest of the passage reveals, the judgment is one of "old" [late 19th century] society in New York on the return after several years of a young woman whose family was once part of that circle. The phrase "lost her looks" is not indifferent, compassionate, or admiring in tone.

(2) **1** "relate Countess Olenska's history." These paragraphs offer an account of how Ellen Mingott—now the Countess Olenska—grew up in Europe under the guidance of her unconventional aunt. Among other things, we learn that she had had "an expensive but incoherent education." The focus in this passage is on Ellen's past.

(3) **3** "scandalised." The family is shocked and offended (scandalised) when Medora openly contravenes (flouts) the conventions of mourning by wearing a short veil and dressing the child Ellen in colorful clothes. None of the other choices reinforces the concept of defying "unalterable rules."

(4) **1** "unique." This is the best among the choices. This passage reveals that most of the society found Ellen charming and accepted her as "fearless… precocious…and possessed of outlandish arts." None of the other choices is suggested in the passage.

(5) **2** "untamed." This term best captures Ellen's intellectual curiosity and unconventional achievements. She is "untamed" because she has not been formed within the traditional and limited expectations for young women of her society.

(6) **4** "unconventional." Throughout the passage, Medora is represented as "a wanderer…a woman of many peculiarities." Medora is even able to claim for herself a title in Italy. She may also have intellectual qualities, but the details in the passage emphasize that she is original and lives outside many social conventions; she is certainly not cautious or overprotective of Ellen.

(7) **3** "intrigued by the Countess Olenska." We learn first that Archer "wonders a little nervously how she will carry off" her arrival at the van der Luyden's dinner party; he is then struck by her apparent calm and lack of overt "stylishness." Most telling is that, for Archer, "there was about her the mysterious authority of beauty, a sureness in the carriage of the head, the movement of the eyes, which, without being in the least theatrical, struck him as highly trained and full of a conscious power" (lines 43–46). Everything we

learn about Newland Archer in this passage is reflected through his fascinated observations of Countess Olenska.

(8) **3** "unconcerned with social expectations." The Duke seldom speaks at dinner and seems almost out of place. The Duke and Countess Olenska defy a number of conventions as the evening progresses: after dinner, they sit together and engage in "animated talk," when instead the Duke would be expected to pay his respects to other ladies present; then the Countess walks across the room to sit down next to Newland Archer. "It was not the custom in New York drawing-rooms for a lady to get up and walk away from one gentleman in order to seek the company of another. Etiquette required that she should wait" (lines 92–94). None of the other choices describes the manner of these two characters in this scene.

(9) **1** "It emphasizes a distinction between the Countess and the guests." Note that nearly all Archer's observations of Olenska are framed as contrasts to others: she has a calm and "simpler manner than most of the ladies present," and she is less overtly "stylish" than the others. Archer also remarks that, even though "Countess Olenska was the only young woman at the dinner," she had a maturity the others lacked.

(10) **4** "has little regard for customs associated with gender." In the final lines of the passage we observe that, "the Countess was apparently unaware of having broken any rule; she sat at perfect ease…beside Archer." None of the other choices is suggested in the way Countess Olenska acts in this scene.

Passage B

(11) **2** "establishing a parallel between man and machine." Each of the phrases in these lines uses a term from human anatomy: the machines are "*gaunt* with *arteries* of fire/[they are] *Muscled…, boweled.*"

(12) **1** "extremely harsh." *Raucous* means loud, strident, grating, and unpleasant. This is an example of how vocabulary is assessed through meaning in context. None of the other choices is suggested in the imagery and tone of these lines.

(13) **4** "the difficult work of machines." The imagery throughout the first stanza (in sonnet form) is of great power and effort, "grinding, grinding, through the night." The poet's use of "Groaning and belching" is another example of the parallel between man and machine established at the beginning.

(14) **2** "accomplishes its tasks with ease." The contrasts in imagery and tone between the two parts (sonnets) of the poem are striking. In nature there are, "no motors…[there is] no derrick…no wheel…no engine…no turbine." In Nature, dawn comes with ease and grace, "With all the feathered silence of a swan." This choice best expresses a central idea of "Machines."

Passage C

(15) **1** "addressing human frailties." Paine's main line of argument throughout the speech is that the colonists should not be deceived about Great Britain's intentions. In the opening lines, he asserts that it is "natural to man" to have hopeful illusions and "to shut our eyes against a painful truth." He argues that in these times, such illusions are weaknesses and should not be "the part of wise men, engaged in…[the] arduous struggle for liberty." *Frailties* is a stronger term than *misconceptions* and best expresses Paine's appeal to the delegates. None of the other choices is suggested in these lines.

(16) **4** "confront the unpleasant reality." Continuing the line of argument at the beginning, Paine asserts that he is "willing…to know the worst," that Great Britain cannot be trusted and is actually preparing for war.

(17) **4** "loss of freedom." Paine makes several references to the buildup of Great Britain's "navies and armies" in the colonies; he insists that their only purpose is to "bind and rivet us upon [the] chains" of British rule.

(18) **3** "analyze the existing situation." In the course of the first paragraph, Paine traces the "conduct of the British ministry for the last ten years" and then points to the threat in Britain's current military buildup. He insists that "we have done every thing that could be done," only to be "spurned, with contempt." None of the other choices reflects Paine's purpose.

(19) **1** "introduce a counterclaim." Paine will go on to contradict the claim that the colonists are weak and "unable to cope with so formidable an adversary" by declaring: "Sir, we are not weak." Paine is challenging a belief; he is not addressing a financial crisis, known fact, or confusing concept.

(20) **2** "war and subjugation." Paine's view of Britain's intentions for the colonies is summarized in lines 20–21: "Let us not deceive ourselves, sir. These are the implements of war and subjugation—the last arguments to which kings resort." Each of the other choices is contradicted by details in Paine's speech.

(21) **4** "indecision." Paine challenges the idea that the colonists are too weak to resist Great Britain by asking, "when shall we be stronger?" In the rhetorical questions that follow, Paine demonstrates how the colonies would become only weaker and subject to defeat if they are irresolute now.

(22) **1** "If we fight together we will win." Paine insists that if the three million people of the colonies are united and "armed in the holy cause of Liberty," they will overcome any force, "which our enemy can send against us." None of the other choices is suggested in the passage.

(23) **2** "choice." This is the term that most emphatically completes Paine's argument here: "[I]t is now too late to retire [back away].… There is no retreat…. The war is inevitable—and let it come!!"

(24) **3** "passionate." At no point is Paine's tone contented, frightened, or satirical. His passion is heard and felt throughout the speech.

PART 2—Argument Response

Sample Essay Response One

After reviewing both sides of the debate regarding paying college student athletes, the obvious and logical answer is No; they should not be paid! One must first consider the real cost of a college's expenses versus the revenues from sports events. Then one must also understand that this issue involves the true cost of a college education for a student athlete receiving a scholarship.

The primary reason college athletes should not get paid is that they already are well compensated. More often than not, a college athlete walks onto the court or field on a scholarship. Whether it be a partial scholarship or a full ride, these student athletes receive monetary aid sometimes worth up to $50,000 a year (Text 4, line 5). In addition to paid tuition and board, the school pays for its athletes' "medical and travel expenses, free gear, top-notch coaching; unlimited use of elite athletic facilities" (Text 4, lines 6–9).

Not only do these college athletes receive these immediate monetary benefits, they receive the gift of the future. They have a "national stage to audition for a job in the professional ranks" (Text 4, lines 8–9). The athlete "isn't just getting the competitive experience he needs for launching a pro career. He's gaining exposure that's bound to pay off in endorsements and a nice contract when he turns pro." (Text 3, lines 30–32) These are tremendous benefits for a college athlete receiving a paid college education and the possibility of a successful professional sports career.

Some argue that not paying student athletes is immoral and even illegal. They cite Section I of the Sherman Antitrust Law, claiming that not paying student athletes "is a form of wage fixing" (Text 1, lines 35–36). The Sherman Antitrust Law does not apply to schools or their sports teams. The application of this law is an unreasonable objection.

Others claim student athletes should share in the huge revenues that their colleges receive for their sporting events. Although these revenues can be quite high, the profits are not! "An astounding 96 percent of the revenue the NCAA brings in annually is redistributed to its members' institutions… [for] academic enhancement, conference grants, sports sponsorships, student assistance funds and grants-in-aid." (Text 4, lines 69–72) Plus, only 22 athletic departments were even profitable (Text 4, line 77). Colleges do not have the money to pay their student athletes; and, every student athlete knows that there are other alternatives if money becomes an issue. As cited in Text 4, lines 48–49, a student athlete can leave college and play for an international team, often earning a very high salary.

As the evidence clearly shows, college athletes should not get paid over and above their scholarships. They receive full compensation for their skill, effort and hard work by their schools while knowing their future is full of lucrative possibilities.

Analysis

This essay meets the requirements of the task very well. The first paragraph introduces some of the relevant issues regarding pay for student athletes, but it is in the first sentence of the second paragraph that the writer clearly and forcefully establishes the main argument: "The primary reason college athletes should not get paid is that they already are well compensated."

The essay is coherent and well organized; and the language and tone are appropriate for a discussion of this topic. Note that development of the argument is especially effective because the writer acknowledges some of the counter claims at the beginning of key paragraphs: "Some argue that not paying student athletes is immoral and even illegal.... Others claim student athletes should share in the huge revenues." These claims are then refuted with documented references to the texts. The reliance on quotation rather than paraphrase does not diminish the overall quality of the composition. There are no significant errors in the conventions. This essay would merit a high score.

(See pages 80–81 for the scoring guidelines.)

Sample Essay Response Two

A heated debate continues as to whether or not college athletes should be paid. While there are some who may argue against paying these student-athletes because they are already receiving scholarships that cover most of their expenses, in reality, this assumption is not valid. Why is it not valid? One reason is that it does not take into consideration the immense time and effort these student-athletes put into their sport. Secondly is the fact that "85 percent of college athletes on scholarships live below the poverty line" (Text 1, lines 28–29), and still have expenses that need to be met. Last of all is the added fact that the NCAA takes in an excessive amount of revenue thanks to these young athletes.

Oftentimes, "top men's basketball and football players spend 40 hours per week on their sports" (Text 2, lines 12–13) to the extent that, "Georgia tailback Richard Samuel…said he was an 'athlete-student,' not a 'student-athlete'" (Text 2, lines 14–16). The truth is that sports, for many college athletes, become their main priority and their full-time job. Because so much time and effort is dedicated to sports by these students, "it's an ethical imperative" (Text 2, lines 43–44) to pay these students for their labor.

As previously noted, many of these student-athletes are starting out at the poverty level. While it is argued that "Athletic scholarships cover just about everything a student-athlete needs" (Text 4, line 15), this is not entirely true. Although scholarships may cover "campus housing, daily medical care and free meals," as well as tuition and books (Text 4, lines 16–17), there are occasions when "athletes are often short a few thousand bucks for ancillary expenses" (Text 2, line 21), such as money for gas, personal hygiene, and entertainment. However, as mentioned, many student-athletes spend up to forty hours a week on their sport and may not have the time to work at a job as well. Being paid the extra money would assist in covering the added expenses that may not be covered by their scholarships.

As for the final argument, the NCAA is an extremely affluent group. Each year this organization generates about $871.6 million in revenue from college sports (Text 4, line 3). The average salary for a men's college football coach since 2006 is about $1.64 million (Text 2, line 27). However, the salary for the players is zero. As already noted, college athletes dedicate considerable time and effort to their sports. Consequently, they deserve a portion of the profits. It is argued that the reason the NCAA does not allow a school to pay its players is because "[a]lthough it reels in over $800 million per year,…the organization continues to be non-profit" (Text 4, lines 55–56). This argument would be reasonable if coaches did not earn so much each year. For instance, "At the University of Alabama, the head football coach…[is paid] $7 million per year—more than 160 times the average wage of a Tuscaloosa pubic school teacher" (Text 1, lines 17–20). If the bloated salaries of coaches were reduced to reasonable amounts, the NCAA schools would be able to afford to pay their players.

In conclusion, any person who dedicates 40 hours a week towards a sport deserves to be paid. Because they cannot fill the financial gap left by college scholarships, student-athletes deserve and need help. If the NCAA cut the salaries of their top coaches they would be able to pay their players. This would free up money for deserving student-athletes and seems to be the fair course to take.

Analysis

This response to the task is a thoughtful and especially well-documented argument in favor of paying student-athletes. The writer's premise is posed in a rhetorical question and clearly outlined in the first paragraph: "Why is [the assumption that students are already receiving scholarships] not valid?" The essay is then extensively developed with specific information from the texts. The argument moves from a review of the significant revenue in college sports to a specific solution that focuses on how much some coaches are paid. The language and tone are appropriate throughout, and there are no significant errors in the conventions. This essay would merit a high score.

(See pages 80–81 for the scoring guidelines.)

PART 3—Text-Analysis Response

Sample Essay Response

    The author chronicles Joseph's struggles with his near total paralysis and overwhelming muscle spasms. The passage recounts the initial difficulties, culminating in Joseph's triumph over his ailments by beginning to type. In order to emphasize the true importance of Joseph's accomplishment the author must describe in depth the failures of his body. For this work to have its true importance, the reader must be able to comprehend the extent of the damage done to Joseph's body.

    The author is able to describe the condition that Joseph is in through extensive use of imagery. A picture is created of a boy with incurable ailments attempting to make sense of his life. The constant frustration Joseph feels is imparted to the reader by a description of his great legs that, "collapse under me like a house of cards." The author is able to elicit a sense of pity for Joseph by describing how when he nods with his pointer to the keyboard, "great spasms gripped him rigid and sent his simple nod into a farcical effort which ran to each and every one of his limbs." A clear understanding of the willpower it takes to even attempt to type is easy to grasp from the description of his efforts. Without a detailed picture of the state of Joseph's body, the story would lack the depth that is possesses. The use of imagery throughout is essential to developing the narrative and giving a true feel of the monumental accomplishment for Joseph typing a few letters on the keyboard really is.

Analysis

This is a brief but good response to the task. The writer introduces the subject of the text and then establishes the central idea for analysis: "In order to emphasize the true importance of Joseph's accomplishment the author must describe in depth the failures of his body." The discussion of imagery in the second paragraph is focused on how specific images are central to understanding the text: "Without a detailed picture of the state of Joseph's body, the story would lack the depth that is possesses. The use of imagery throughout is essential to developing the narrative." The analysis is coherent, succinct, and convincing; the writing is appropriately formal and free of significant errors in the conventions. This essay would merit a high score.

(See pages 82–83 for the scoring guidelines.)

Regents ELA (Common Core) Examination August 2015

English Language Arts

PART 1—Reading Comprehension

Directions (1–24): Closely read each of the three passages below. After each passage, there are several multiple-choice questions. Select the best suggested answer to each question and write its number in the space provided. You may use the margins to take notes as you read.

Reading Comprehension Passage A

An embittered Gulliver explains English law to someone who has no experience with it.

…I assured his honor that law was a science, in which I had not much conversed, further than by employing advocates in vain, upon some injustice that had been done me: however, I would give him all the satisfaction I was able.

(5) I said there was a society of men among us, bred up from their youth in the art of proving, by words multiplied for the purpose, that white is black, and black is white, according as they are paid. To this society all the rest of the people are slaves. For example, if my neighbor has a mind to my cow, he has a lawyer to prove that he ought to have my cow from

(10) me. I must then hire another to defend my right, it being against all rules of law that any man should be allowed to speak for himself. "Now, in this

case, I, who am the right owner, lie under two great disadvantages: first,
my lawyer, being practiced almost from his cradle in defending falsehood,
is quite out of his element when he would be an advocate for justice, which
(15)   is an unnatural office he always attempts with great awkwardness, if not
with ill-will. The second disadvantage is, that my lawyer must proceed
with great caution, or else he will be reprimanded by the judges, and
abhorred by his brethren, as one that would lessen the practice of the law.
And therefore I have but two methods to preserve my cow. The first is, to
(20)   gain over my adversary's lawyer with a double fee, who will then betray
his client by insinuating that he has justice on his side. The second way is
for my lawyer to make my cause appear as unjust as he can, by allowing
the cow to belong to my adversary; and this, if it be skilfully done, will
certainly bespeak the favor of the bench. Now your honor is to know that
(25)   these judges are persons appointed to decide all controversies of property
as well as for the trial of criminals, and picked out from the most dexter-
ous lawyers, who have grown old or lazy; and having been biased all their
lives against truth and equity, lie under such a fatal necessity of favoring
fraud, perjury, and oppression, that I have known some of them refuse a
(30)   large bribe from the side where justice lay, rather than injure the faculty
by doing anything unbecoming their nature or their office.

"It is a maxim among these lawyers, that whatever has been done
before may legally be done again; and therefore they take special care to
record all the decisions formerly made against common justice and the
(35)   general reason of mankind. These, under the name of precedents, they produce as authorities to justify the most iniquitous[1] opinions; and the judges
never fail of directing accordingly.

"In pleading, they studiously avoid entering into the merits of the
cause; but are loud, violent, and tedious in dwelling upon all circum-
(40)   stances which are not to the purpose. For instance, in the case already
mentioned, they never desire to know what claim or title my adversary has
to my cow, but whether the said cow were red or black, her horns long or
short; whether the field I graze her in be round or square; whether she was
milked at home or abroad; what diseases she is subject to, and the like;
(45)   after which they consult precedents, adjourn the case from time to time,
and in ten, twenty, or thirty years come to an issue.

---

[1]iniquitous—immoral

"It is likewise to be observed that this society has a peculiar cant and jargon[2] of their own that no other mortal can understand, and wherein all their laws are written, which they take special care to multiply; whereby
(50) they have wholly confounded[3] the very essence of truth and falsehood, of right and wrong; so that it will take thirty years to decide whether the field left me by my ancestors for six generations belongs to me or to a stranger three hundred miles off.

"In the trial of persons accused for crimes against the state, the method
(55) is much more short and commendable: the judge first sends to sound the disposition[4] of those in power, after which he can easily hang or save a criminal, strictly preserving all due forms of law."

Here my master, interposing, said it was a pity that creatures endowed with such prodigious[5] abilities of mind as these lawyers, by the descrip-
(60) tion I gave of them, must certainly be, were not rather encouraged to be instructors of others in wisdom and knowledge. In answer to which I assured his honor that in all points out of their own trade they were usually the most ignorant and stupid generation among us; the most despicable in common conversation, avowed enemies to all knowledge and
(65) learning, and equally disposed to pervert the general reason of mankind in every other subject of discourse as in that of their own profession.

—Jonathan Swift
excerpted from *The Works of Jonathan Swift:*
Gulliver's Travels, 1932
Black's Readers Service Company
First published 1726 by Ben J. Motte

---

[2]cant and jargon—a specialized language of a profession
[3]confounded—confused
[4]disposition—inclination
[5]prodigious—enormous

1 The narrator introduces the hypothetical dispute over a cow (lines 7 through 11) in order to show the

    (1) illogical nature of the legal system
    (2) importance of having many lawyers
    (3) ignorance of the common man
    (4) reasonable traditions of dispute resolution   1_____

2 Lines 10 and 11 convey a tone of

    (1) seriousness   (3) empathy
    (2) sarcasm   (4) reluctance   2_____

3 In lines 24 through 31, the narrator observes that the practices of judges are

    (1) respected   (3) indifferent
    (2) constructive   (4) insincere   3_____

4 As used in line 32, the word "maxim" most nearly means

    (1) rule   (3) secret
    (2) question   (4) conflict   4_____

5 The details presented in lines 40 through 46 contribute to a central idea by

    (1) acknowledging a cow's value
    (2) stressing the legal system's irrelevance
    (3) validating the narrator's memory
    (4) recognizing the legal system's history   5_____

6 In lines 47 through 53, the narrator describes lawyers' "peculiar cant and jargon" as being

    (1) primarily ceremonial
    (2) deceptively complex
    (3) deliberately insulting
    (4) consistently objective   6____

7 Lines 54 through 57 suggest that, in crimes against
the state, judges are inclined to

    (1) rely on common sense
    (2) follow the accepted precedent
    (3) impose a lengthy sentence
    (4) submit to higher authority   7____

8 The text supports the narrator's point of view by

    (1) referencing historical examples
    (2) using concrete evidence
    (3) employing exaggerated descriptions
    (4) describing fantastic experiences   8____

9 The text as a whole supports the narrator's opinion
that lawyers and judges are

    (1) stubborn   (3) misunderstood
    (2) corrupt   (4) inexperienced   9____

Reading Comprehension Passage B

Monologue for an Onion

I don't mean to make you cry.
I mean nothing, but this has not kept you
From peeling away my body, layer by layer,

The tears clouding your eyes as the table fills
(5)   With husks, cut flesh, all the debris of pursuit.
Poor deluded human: you seek my heart.

Hunt all you want. Beneath each skin of mine
Lies another skin: I am pure onion—pure union
Of outside and in, surface and secret core.

(10) Look at you, chopping and weeping. Idiot.
Is this the way you go through life, your mind
A stopless knife, driven by your fantasy of truth,

Of lasting union—slashing away skin after skin
From things, ruin and tears your only signs
(15) Of progress? Enough is enough.

You must not grieve that the world is glimpsed
Through veils. How else can it be seen?
How will you rip away the veil of the eye, the veil

That you are, you who want to grasp the heart
(20) Of things, hungry to know where meaning
Lies. Taste what you hold in your hands: onion-juice,

Yellow peels, my stinging shreds. You are the one
In pieces. Whatever you meant to love, in meaning to
You changed yourself: you are not who you are,

(25) Your soul cut moment to moment by a blade
Of fresh desire, the ground sown with abandoned skins.
And at your inmost circle, what? A core that is

Not one. Poor fool, you are divided at the heart,
Lost in its maze of chambers, blood, and love,
(30) A heart that will one day beat you to death.

—Suji Kwock Kim
from *Notes from the Divided Country*, 2003
Louisiana State University Press

10 The phrase "poor deluded human" (line 6) conveys a
sense of

(1) compassion   (3) loneliness
(2) fear   (4) shyness   10_____

11 The search suggested in lines 6 and 7 can best be
described as

(1) boring   (3) futile
(2) simple   (4) brief   11_____

12 The shift in line 10 indicates a transition in tone that
can best be described as

(1) sympathetic to critical
(2) humorous to angry
(3) hopeful to cruel
(4) admiring to fearful   12_____

13 The narrator's references to veils (lines 17 and 18)
remind the reader of the need for

(1) caution   (3) clarity
(2) secrecy   (4) investigation   13_____

14 The phrase "onion-juice" (line 21) contributes to the
narrator's purpose by

(1) demonstrating that self-reflection is satisfying
(2) implying that the search for identity is noble
(3) observing that experimentation is often
    dangerous
(4) suggesting that the quest for truth is harsh   14_____

Reading Comprehension Passage C

The morning chill carried that clean-sheet crispness; that cleansing sort
of air. Actually, for the tip of Long Island in early December, this weather
was a little late in coming. But walking from our house to the shore of the
bay, the new crystal air made me finally look ahead toward winter and turn
(5)   my back to what had been a spectacular, lingering fall.

Every autumn here witnesses two great migrations: one axiomatic and
one nearly unknown. Everybody knows birds fly south for the winter. Here,
the marshes and barrier islands are interstate arteries for heavy traffic of
songbirds, waterfowl, hawks and others. But except for people who fish,
(10)   almost no one realizes the greater migration begins just beyond the beach.

This year, as usual, swarms of fish had arrived from New England in the
last few weeks and departed down the coast in great migrating waves. They
included millions and millions of anchovies and menhaden, pursued to the
surface by armies of bluefish, striped bass, little tuna. Along the seafloor
(15)   battalions of summer flounder, black sea bass, tautog, porgies and others
moved to deeper grounds. Offshore, beyond sight of land on the rolling
blue prairies of the sea, sharks and tunas passed like herds on the Serengeti
(though now, like those herds, much diminished). Herring and mackerel
had arrived mid-November with dolphins on their tails, and the remaining
(20)   schools of striped bass, fattening for their long run to winter grounds, gob-
bled them greedily. Even now, into December, a few boats were still hunting
bass. But we had caught enough, our freezer was stocked for winter and our
smoker racks were busy, and we'd just hauled the boat.

Patricia and I put our footsteps to the gravelly beach and walked to
(25)   the inlet to see who'd recently arrived. Bonaparte's gulls, a few long-tailed
ducks, some black scoters and in the distance the feathered missiles called
gannets were sending geysers skyward as a flock poured into a herring
school. To me, this seasonal sense of place in the path of migrations, this
finger on the pulse of the planet, is the purest joy.

(30)   We were just rounding the inlet entrance when, among the shells and
tide-wrack, my gaze caught something so unexpected—here, and in this
near-frost—it seemed improbable as a fallen angel: a sea turtle.

It was a baby, with a platter-sized shell. Species: Kemp's ridley, most
endangered of all Atlantic turtles. Stunned by the boreal air and 49-degree

(35)   water, the turtle's only sign of life was a mark in the wet sand suggesting a
flipper had moved sometime since high tide had left it and withdrawn.

This nation that sees itself stretching from sea to shining sea conceals
beneath her broad, waving skirts of bordering oceans some of the greatest
wildlife in the world. And because it's so effectively hidden, it's some of the
(40)   least understood.

Though the saltiness of our blood and tears speaks from within of our
parent ocean, for most people oceans seem distant, out of sight and generally out of mind. Even many who love nature, who see our landscape and
imagine herds of bison and skies darkened by passenger pigeons and clouds
(45)   of waterfowl, who escape into the woods or mountains or even the shore,
seem to get their vision stranded on the beach as though wildlife stops at
the high-tide line, where our little stunned turtle reminded us that so much
actually begins.

The water makes a perfect disguise that heightens the mystery, but in
(50)   some ways that's a great pity, because the closest thing we have left to the
thundering herds and great flocks is in the sea. Extending your vision into
the grand swirl and suck of the many-fingered tides and beyond will grant
you a renewed sense of both the abundance and fragility of life.

Whether or not we can see, hear, or feel the ocean from our own home
(55)   territory, the ocean certainly feels all of us. Between a third and half the
world's people now live within 50 miles of a coast (as any traveler can
attest). In China, population density is three times higher in coastal areas
than elsewhere. The collective weight of humanity may rest on land, but we
levy heavy pressure on the sea. Most of us exert our most direct interaction
(60)   with the sea through the seafood we buy. But even air quality affects water
quality because what goes up alights elsewhere, and climate change is challenging ocean habitats by melting sea ice and cooking corals, undermining
food supplies for penguins, polar bears and reef fishes.

People who think of themselves as conservationists carry a concern for
(65)   wildlife, wildlands and habitat quality as part of their sense of right and
wrong. It is time to take these concerns below high tide. Most people would
not question a hawk's place in the sky, nor ask what good is a gazelle, nor
wonder whether the world really needs wild orchids. Yet when told of the
plight of, say, sharks, many still think it quite reasonable to inquire, "What
(70)   good are they; why do we need them?" Fifty million buffalo once roamed
the rolling green prairies of North America. Gunners reduced them to near-

extinction. Now, hunters cut from the same cloth are at work on the rolling blue prairies of the sea and, already, the big fish—including miracles like thousand-pound, warm-blooded bluefin tuna—are 90 percent gone. What
(75) we regret happening on land may again happen in the sea. Those who care about wildlife should get to know about oceans.

We brought the turtle home and warmed it a bit in the sun. It began to shed tears, a sign of ongoing glandular function and, for us, heightened hope. Soon a flipper waved—a certain signal of persistent life. Shortly
(80) thereafter, the aquarium people arrived to bring our little patient into veterinary rehab. Slowly warmed, within a few hours it was conscious and swimming, safe until release next spring.

Whether we help one unlucky creature or wish to save the world, for each of us the challenge and opportunity is to cherish all life as the gift it is, envi-
(85) sion it whole, seek to know it truly, and undertake—with our minds, hearts and hands—to restore its abundance. Where there's life there's hope, and so no place can inspire more hopefulness than the great, life-making sea, home to creatures of mystery and majesty, whose future now depends on human compassion, and our next move.

—Carl Safina
"Comes a Turtle, Comes the World"
http://www.patagonia.com, Winter 2006

15 A purpose of the second paragraph is to draw attention to

    (1)   a popular vacation spot
    (2)   the activities of the fishermen
    (3)   the beauty of the islands
    (4)   a lesser known event   15_____

16 The details in lines 12 through 21 reinforce the idea of

    (1)   diversity   (3)   adaptation
    (2)   discovery   (4)   rehabilitation   16_____

17 The phrase "who'd recently arrived" in line 25 refers to

    (1)   predatory species   (3)   migrating wildlife
    (2)   other observers   (4)   fishing boats   17_____

18 The figurative language in lines 26–27 is used to suggest

    (1)   confusion   (3)   fear
    (2)   speed   (4)   sound   18_____

19 Knowing the turtle's species in lines 33 and 34 serves to make its discovery more

    (1)   serious   (3)   natural
    (2)   mysterious   (4)   controversial   19_____

20 As used in line 34, the word "boreal" most nearly means

    (1)   clean   (3)   salty
    (2)   cold   (4)   hazy   20_____

21 The author's reference to "the saltiness of our blood and tears" (line 41) exposes the irony of our

   (1) disinterest in the ocean
   (2) efforts in conservation
   (3) destructive habits
   (4) current situation   21_____

22 Which lines establish an important cause and effect relationship in the passage?

   (1) lines 6 and 7   (3) lines 58 and 59
   (2) lines 22 and 23   (4) lines 64–69   22_____

23 Which lines best reflect a central claim?

   (1) "Actually, for ... in coming" (lines 2 and 3)
   (2) "This year, as usual ... migrating waves" (lines 11 and 12)
   (3) "Most of us ... we buy" (lines 59 and 60)
   (4) "What we regret ... about oceans" (lines 74 through 76)   23_____

24 The author waits until lines 77 through 82 to reveal the fate of the baby turtle in order to

   (1) present a counterclaim
   (2) inject humor
   (3) introduce irony
   (4) maintain reader interest   24_____

PART 2—Argument Response

Directions: Closely read each of the *four* texts on pages 218 through 226 and write a source-based argument on the topic below. You may use the margins to take notes as you read and scrap paper to plan your response. Write your argument on a separate sheet of paper.

> **Topic:** Should American citizens be required to vote in national elections?

> **Your Task:** Carefully read each of the *four* texts provided. Then, using evidence from at least *three* of the texts, write a well-developed argument regarding whether or not American citizens should be required to vote. Clearly establish your claim, distinguish your claim from alternate or opposing claims, and use specific, relevant, and sufficient evidence from at least *three* of the texts to develop your argument. Do not simply summarize each text.

Guidelines:

Be sure to

- Establish your claim regarding whether or not American citizens should be required to vote.
- Distinguish your claim from alternate or opposing claims.
- Use specific, relevant, and sufficient evidence from at least *three* of the texts to develop your argument.
- Identify each source that you reference by text number and line number(s) or graphic (for example: Text 1, line 4 or Text 2, graphic).
- Organize your ideas in a cohesive and coherent manner.
- Maintain a formal style of writing.
- Follow the conventions of standard written English.

Texts:

Text 1

Telling Americans to Vote, or Else

Jury duty is mandatory; why not voting? The idea seems vaguely un-American. Maybe so, but it's neither unusual nor undemocratic. And it would ease the intense partisan polarization[1] that weakens our capacity for self-government and public trust in our governing institutions.

(5)   Thirty-one countries have some form of mandatory voting, according to the International Institute for Democracy and Electoral Assistance. The list includes nine members of the Organization for Economic Cooperation and Development and two-thirds of the Latin American nations. More than half back up the legal requirement with an enforcement mechanism,

(10)   while the rest are content to rely on the moral force of the law.

Despite the prevalence of mandatory voting in so many democracies, it's easy to dismiss the practice as a form of statism[2] that couldn't work in America's individualistic and libertarian political culture. But consider Australia, whose political culture is closer to that of the United

(15)   States than that of any other English-speaking country. Alarmed by a decline in voter turnout to less than 60 percent in 1922, Australia adopted mandatory voting in 1924, backed by small fines (roughly the size of traffic tickets) for nonvoting, rising with repeated acts of nonparticipation. The law established permissible reasons for not voting,

(20)   like illness and foreign travel, and allows citizens who faced fines for not voting to defend themselves. ...

Proponents offer three reasons in favor of mandatory voting. The first is straightforwardly civic. A democracy can't be strong if its citizenship is weak. And right now American citizenship is attenuated—strong on

(25)   rights, weak on responsibilities. There is less and less that being a citizen requires of us, especially after the abolition of the draft. Requiring people to vote in national elections once every two years would reinforce the principle of reciprocity at the heart of citizenship.

The second argument for mandatory voting is democratic. Ideally, a

(30)   democracy will take into account the interests and views of all citizens. But

---

[1]partisan polarization—one-sidedness
[2]statism—central governmental control of economic and social policy

if some regularly vote while others don't, officials are likely to give greater
weight to participants. This might not matter much if nonparticipants
were evenly distributed through the population. But political scientists
have long known that they aren't. People with lower levels of income
(35) and education are less likely to vote, as are young adults and recent first-
generation immigrants.

Changes in our political system have magnified these disparities.[3]
During the 1950s and '60s, when turnout rates were much higher,
political parties reached out to citizens year-round. At the local level these
(40) parties, which reformers often criticized as "machines," connected even
citizens of modest means and limited education with neighborhood institutions and gave them a sense of participation in national politics as well.
(In its heyday, organized labor reinforced these effects.) But in the absence
of these more organic forms of political mobilization, the second-best
(45) option is a top-down mechanism of universal mobilization.

Mandatory voting would tend to even out disparities stemming from
income, education and age, enhancing our system's inclusiveness. It is true,
as some object, that an enforcement mechanism would impose greater
burdens on those with fewer resources. But this makes it all the more likely
(50) that these citizens would respond by going to the polls, and they would
stand to gain far more than the cost of a traffic ticket.

The third argument for mandatory voting goes to the heart of our current ills. Our low turnout rate pushes American politics toward increased
polarization. The reason is that hard-core partisans are more likely to
(55) dominate lower-turnout elections, while those who are less fervent about
specific issues and less attached to political organizations tend not to participate at levels proportional to their share of the electorate. ...

The United States is not Australia, of course, and there's no guarantee
that the similarity of our political cultures would produce equivalent
(60) political results. For example, reforms of general elections would leave
untouched the distortions generated by party primaries in which small
numbers of voters can shape the choices for the entire electorate. And the
United States Constitution gives the states enormous power over voting procedures. Mandating voting nationwide would go counter to our
(65) traditions (and perhaps our Constitution) and would encounter strong

---

[3]disparities—inequalities

state opposition. Instead, a half-dozen states from parts of the country with different civic traditions should experiment with the practice, and observers—journalists, social scientists, citizens' groups and elected officials— would monitor the consequences.

(70)   We don't know what the outcome would be. But one thing is clear: If we do nothing and allow a politics of passion to define the bounds of the electorate, as it has for much of the last four decades, the prospect for a less polarized, more effective political system that enjoys the trust and confidence of the people is not bright.

—William A. Galston
excerpted from "Telling Americans to Vote, or Else"
http://www.nytimes.com, November 5, 2011

Text 2

Compulsory Voting

All democratic governments consider participating in national elections a right of citizenship and a citizen's civic responsibility. Some consider that participation in elections is also a citizen's duty. In some countries, where voting is considered a duty, voting at elections has been
(5) made compulsory and has been regulated in the national constitutions or electoral laws. Some countries impose sanctions[1] on non-voters.

Compulsory voting is not a new concept. Belgium (1892), Argentina (1914) and Australia (1924) were among the first countries to introduce compulsory voting laws. Countries such as Venezuela and the Netherlands
(10) practised compulsory voting at one time but have since abolished it.

Advocates of compulsory voting argue that decisions made by democratically elected governments are more legitimate when higher proportions of the population participate. They argue further that voting, voluntarily or otherwise, has an educative effect upon the citizens.
(15) Political parties can save money as a result of compulsory voting, since they do not have to spend resources convincing the electorate that it should turn out to vote. Lastly, if democracy is government by the people, presumably this includes all people, so that it is every citizen's responsibility to elect his or her representatives.

(20) The leading argument against compulsory voting is that it is not consistent with the freedom associated with democracy. Voting is not an intrinsic[2] obligation and the enforcement of such a law would be an infringement of the citizen's freedom associated with democratic elections. It may discourage the political education of the electorate because people
(25) forced to participate will react against the perceived source of oppression. Is a government really more legitimate if high voter turnout is achieved against the will of the voters? Many countries with limited financial resources may not be able to justify the expense of maintaining and enforcing compulsory voting laws. It has been proved that forcing the popula-

---

[1]sanctions—penalties
[2]intrinsic—essential

(30)   tion to vote results in an increased number of invalid and blank votes compared to countries that have no compulsory voting laws.

Another consequence of compulsory voting is the possible high number of "random votes". Voters who are voting against their free will may check off a candidate at random, particularly the top candidate on the *(35)* ballot paper. The voter does not care whom they vote for as long as the government is satisfied that they have fulfilled their civic duty. What effect does this immeasurable category of random votes have on the legitimacy of the democratically elected government? ...

—Maria Gratschew
excerpted from "Compulsory Voting"
Voter Turnout Since 1945: A Global Report
International Institute for Democracy and
Electoral Assistance (International IDEA), 2002

Text 3

Does Mandatory Voting Restrict or Expand Democracy?

Does mandatory voting restrict or expand democracy? For many people who have never heard about the idea, mandatory voting sounds very strict: requiring people to go to the polls on Election Day. In the United States, it seems strange to present an action many consider
(5) a right as a required duty. Nevertheless, in many foreign countries, mandatory voting (sometimes referred to as compulsory voting) is an obvious democratic option.

The system in fact is present in more than 30 democracies around the world. However, all policies are not the same. Mandatory voting can be
(10) used to elect all political representatives or it can be restricted to specific elections. For example, in France, mandatory voting is only used for Senatorial elections.

The two most notable examples of compulsory voting occur in Belgium and Australia. Belgium has the oldest tradition of [a] compulsory voting
(15) system. The system was introduced in 1892 for men and 1949 for women. Today, all Belgian citizens age 18 or over have to vote in every electoral event. If an individual fails to vote in at least four elections, he or she lose[s] the right to vote for the next 10 years and as a result face a general social stigma and specific problems like near impossibility in having a job
(20) in the public sector. In Australia, compulsory voting was adopted as a way of integrating the large population of immigrants that the country welcomes and is endorsed through non-voters facing potential fines.

Many people compare voting to taxes. In fact, one of mandatory voting's biggest advocates, former American Political Science Association
(25) president Arend Lijphart, uses this comparison in his writings like Patterns of Democracy. According to him, just as taxes are a way to feed the national economy, voting can be seen as a way to feed the civic economy. Moreover, when compelled to vote, citizens begin to be more involved in political life and in turn are encouraged to take a more active
(30) role in other areas of civic society. And no other change comes close to having as sweeping an impact on rates of voter participation.

Given Lijphart's arguments, would compulsory voting make sense in the United States? Not necessarily—for many Americans the right to vote also implies the right not to vote. In fact, some people might even inter-
(35)   pret mandatory voting as a violation of [the] First Amendment's prohibition of compelled speech. Moreover, mandatory voting opposition argues that a forced electorate would not necessarily be the most politically intelligent electorate.

Some apolitical citizens might choose candidates arbitrarily or for the
(40)   wrong reasons because they do not want to be fined or punished for not doing their hypothetical duty. Finally, voters in fact gain a certain kind [of] influence from their ability not to vote—elected officials can't take their vote for granted.

Whether you are an advocate for or against mandatory voting, the
(45)   concept is a thought provoking idea that should not be overlooked just because it seems so foreign to the United States. But it should never be used to avoid tackling the root of political disengagement.

Democracies don't just need active citizens; they need educated and active citizens, which is why at FairVote we advocate for strong learning
(50)   democracy programs for students. Americans also need faith in the power of elected officials to represent them effectively and the motivation that comes from elections having real choices from across the spectrum. Such changes can't happen overnight, the way passage of compulsory voting could take place. But they are essential building blocks of a successful
(55)   democracy.

—Wael Abdel Hamid
adapted from "Does Mandatory
Voting Restrict or Expand Democracy?"
http://www.fairvote.org, October 18, 2010

Text 4

How Compulsory Voting Subverts Democracy

...Democracy is an achievement that has come about through determination, hard work, struggle, even bloodshed. On these grounds alone, it deserves to be honoured. But democracy can only be honoured if we appreciate the gift we're fortunate enough to possess in the first place. Sadly, a
(5)   considerable number of people do not appreciate it, and have never given the matter a moment's thought. I'd argue that the massive indifference towards politics that now pervades the general populace will only be overcome by removing the compulsion to vote. Politicians would then be forced to argue their cases with more conviction, and to educate their con-
(10)   stituents about the historical struggle that was necessary to achieve what most of us now take for granted.

People have to be persuaded of the importance of voting to the democratic process. Yet compelling people to do so subverts our democratic rights. Democracy is about freedom; it is the antithesis of compulsion.
(15)   Compulsory voting raises a question we shouldn't even be asking: whether voting is a civil right or a civic duty.

The right *not* to vote in an election is as fundamental as the right to vote. Both the Universal Declaration of Human Rights and the UN's International Covenant on Civil and Political Rights refer to
(20)   people's rights to "freely chosen representatives". This right is something we each possess and can each choose to use, but it should never become a dictate. ...

It's certainly true that in countries where voting is voluntary, like the USA and UK, voter apathy is highest among the poor and uneducated.
(25)   It's also hard to dispute the fact that, because these people—in Western countries at least—do not vote, they're ignored, and because they're ignored, they don't bother to vote. But the argument falls down with the claim that, by forcing these people to vote, politicians will be compelled to pay attention to them, and take steps to improve their situation. It's much
(30)   more likely politicians will fight for the welfare of the poor and educated if they have to go out and *seek* their vote. ...

Those who believe countries with compulsory voting are more democratic argue that it legitimises democracy, that the election results in

(35) countries like the USA, where voting isn't compulsory and voter turnout is low, do not accurately reflect the country's political opinion. But I believe that not having an opinion *is* an opinion, that being indifferent to the outcome of an election and disliking all of the options put before one are both opinions. If people don't turn out to vote, they're definitely stat-
(40) ing their opinions, many of which are both strongly held and well thought through. ...

Perhaps the clinching argument as to whether or not compulsory voting is more democratic is that, according to the experts, coercing[1] everyone to the polling booth in fact makes little or no difference to the final
outcome. The experts (academics, pollsters and civil servants) have all cal-
(45) culated that in the last four Australian federal elections the results would
have been the same even had the voting been voluntary. ...

Although falling voting figures around the world may be a worry,
compelling people to vote is not the answer. Too many people feel they're
powerless in the face of both the political system and the huge, undemo-
(50) cratic power of the modern corporation. They also feel that one politician
is little different from another, and that none of them is going to deal in
a meaningful way with any of the big issues. So it takes a politician who
can galvanise[2] the public to get them voting. In the 2008 US Presidential
election, people sensed a new political star in Obama, someone who would
(55) make a difference, and voter turnout was the highest for forty years. ...

Numbers are unimportant. Quality rather than quantity should be the
focus of a healthy democracy. Voting should be carried out by those who
care, by those who want to vote. It isn't too hard to argue that those who
want to vote deserve to be heard more than those who do not. Is it truly
(60) worth listening to someone who has nothing to say or who doesn't want
to say anything? ...

—Peter Barry
excerpted from "How Compulsory
Voting Subverts Democracy"
http://quadrant.org.au, September 1, 2013

---

[1]coercing—forcing
[2]galvanise—excite into action

PART 3—Text-Analysis Response

Your Task: Closely read the text on pages 228 through 230 and write a well-developed, text-based response of two to three paragraphs. In your response, identify a central idea in the text and analyze how the author's use of *one* writing strategy (literary element or literary technique or rhetorical device) develops this central idea. Use strong and thorough evidence from the text to support your analysis. Do *not* simply summarize the text. You may use the margins to take notes as you read and scrap paper to plan your response. Write your response on a separate sheet of paper.

Guidelines:

Be sure to

- Identify a central idea in the text.
- Analyze how the author's use of *one* writing strategy (literary element or literary technique or rhetorical device) develops this central idea. Examples include: characterization, conflict, denotation/connotation, metaphor, simile, irony, language use, point-of-view, setting, structure, symbolism, theme, tone, etc.
- Use strong and thorough evidence from the text to support your analysis.
- Organize your ideas in a cohesive and coherent manner.
- Maintain a formal style of writing.
- Follow the conventions of standard written English.

Text

The following excerpt is a diary entry from the novel Dracula.

When I found that I was a prisoner a sort of wild feeling came over me. I rushed up and down the stairs, trying every door and peering out of every window I could find; but after a little the conviction of my helplessness overpowered all other feelings. When I look back after a few hours
(5) I think I must have been mad for the time, for I behaved much as a rat does in a trap. When, however, the conviction had come to me that I was helpless I sat down quietly—as quietly as I have ever done anything in my life—and began to think over what was best to be done. I am thinking still, and as yet have come to no definite conclusion. Of one thing only am
(10) I certain; that it is no use making my ideas known to the Count. He knows well that I am imprisoned; and as he has done it himself, and has doubtless his own motives for it, he would only deceive me if I trusted him fully with the facts. So far as I can see, my only plan will be to keep my knowledge and my fears to myself, and my eyes open. I am, I know, either being
(15) deceived, like a baby, by my own fears, or else I am in desperate straits;[1] and if the latter be so, I need, and shall need, all my brains to get through.

I had hardly come to this conclusion when I heard the great door below shut, and knew that the Count had returned. He did not come at once to the library, so I went cautiously to my own room and found him making
(20) the bed. This was odd, but only confirmed what I had all along thought—that there were no servants in the house. When later I saw him through the chink of the hinges of the door laying the table in the dining-room, I was assured of it; for if he does himself all these menial offices, surely it is proof that there is no one else to do them. This gave me a fright, for if there is
(25) no one else in the castle, it must have been the Count himself who was the driver of the coach that brought me here. This is a terrible thought; for if so, what does it mean that he could control the wolves, as he did, by only holding up his hand in silence. How was it that all the people at Bistritz and on the coach had some terrible fear for me? What meant the giving of
(30) the crucifix, of the garlic, of the wild rose, of the mountain ash? Bless that good, good woman who hung the crucifix round my neck! for it is a com-

---
[1]straits—difficult situations

fort and a strength to me whenever I touch it. It is odd that a thing which
I have been taught to regard with disfavour and as idolatrous should in a
time of loneliness and trouble be of help. Is it that there is something in the
(35)   essence of the thing itself, or that it is a medium, a tangible help, in con-
veying memories of sympathy and comfort? Some time, if it may be, I must
examine this matter and try to make up my mind about it. In the meantime
I must find out all I can about Count Dracula, as it may help me to understand. To-night he may talk of himself, if I turn the conversation that way.
(40)   I must be very careful, however, not to awake his suspicion. ...

    Later.—I endorse the last words written, but this time there is no
doubt in question. I shall not fear to sleep in any place where he is not. I
have placed the crucifix over the head of my bed—I imagine that my rest is
thus freer from dreams; and there it shall remain.

(45)   When he left me I went to my room. After a little while, not hearing any sound, I came out and went up the stone stair to where I could
look out towards the South. There was some sense of freedom in the vast
expanse, inaccessible though it was to me, as of compared with the narrow
darkness of the courtyard. Looking out of this, I felt that I was indeed
(50)   in prison, and I seemed to want a breath of fresh air, though it were of
the night. I am beginning to feel this nocturnal existence tell on me. It is
destroying my nerve. I start at my own shadow, and am full of all sorts of
horrible imaginings. God knows that there is ground for my terrible fear
in this accursed place! I looked out over the beautiful expanse, bathed in
(55)   soft yellow moonlight till it was almost as light as day. In the soft light
the distant hills became melted, and the shadows in the valleys and gorges
of velvety blackness. The mere beauty seemed to cheer me; there was peace
and comfort in every breath I drew. As I leaned from the window my eye
was caught by something moving a storey below me, and somewhat to my
(60)   left, where I imagined, from the order of the rooms, that the windows of
the Count's own room would look out. The window at which I stood was
tall and deep, stone-mullioned,[2] and though weatherworn, was still complete; but it was evidently many a day since the case had been there. I drew
back behind the stonework, and looked carefully out. ...

---

[2]mullioned—divided into panes

(65)   What manner of man is this, or what manner of creature is it in the semblance of man? I feel the dread of this horrible place overpowering me; I am in fear—in awful fear—and there is no escape for me; I am encompassed about with terrors that I dare not think of. ...

—Bram Stoker
excerpted from *Dracula*, 1897
The Modern Library
Random House, Inc.

Regents ELA (Common Core) Answers August 2015
English Language Arts

Answer Key

Part 1

1. **1**	9. **2**	17. **3**
2. **2**	10. **1**	18. **2**
3. **4**	11. **3**	19. **1**
4. **1**	12. **1**	20. **2**
5. **2**	13. **3**	21. **1**
6. **2**	14. **4**	22. **3**
7. **4**	15. **4**	23. **4**
8. **3**	16. **1**	24. **4**

**Regents Examination in English Language Arts
(Common Core)—August 2015**

Chart for Converting Total Weighted Raw Scores to Final Exam
Scores (Scale Scores) (Use for the August 2015 examination only.)

Weighted Raw Score*	Scale Score	Performance Level	Weighted Raw Score*	Scale Score	Performance Level
56	100	5	27	61	2
55	99	5	26	58	2
54	99	5	25	56	2
53	99	5	24	55	2
52	98	5	23	50	1
51	97	5	22	48	1
50	97	5	21	45	1
49	96	5	20	42	1
48	95	5	19	39	1
47	94	5	18	35	1
46	93	5	17	32	1
45	91	5	16	29	1
44	90	5	15	25	1
43	89	5	14	22	1
42	88	5	13	18	1
41	86	5	12	15	1
40	85	5	11	12	1
39	84	4	10	9	1
38	82	4	9	8	1
37	81	4	8	7	1
36	79	4	7	6	1
35	78	3	6	5	1
34	76	3	5	4	1
33	74	3	4	3	1
32	72	3	3	2	1
31	70	3	2	1	1
30	68	3	1	1	1
29	65	3	0	0	1
28	63	2			

The conversion table is determined independently for each administration of
the exam.

Answers Explained

PART 1—Reading Comprehension

Multiple-Choice Questions

Passage A

(1) **1** "illogical nature of the legal system" Students already familiar with *Gulliver's Travels* will recognize the satirical tone from the beginning of the passage. In these lines, Gulliver explains that it is the role of lawyers to prove that "white is black and black is white"; moreover, it is "against all rules of law that any man should be allowed to speak for himself."

(2) **2** "sarcasm" This is the best choice to describe the tone of mockery and ridicule in Gulliver's explanation.

(3) **4** "insincere" Gulliver describes the judges as "having been biased all their lives against truth and equity . . . favoring fraud, perjury and oppression." None of the other choices expresses the moral corruption of the judges.

(4) **1** "rule" In this brief paragraph, Gulliver explains how precedent, "whatever has been done before," will necessarily direct future opinions. None of the other choices accurately captures the sense of the passage.

(5) **2** "stressing the legal system's irrelevance" Gulliver asserts here that lawyers "never desire to know what claim . . . my adversary has to my cow, but whether said cow were red or black"; instead, they dwell upon completely irrelevant details about the cow, the pasture, her health, and so on. He then says that it may take twenty or thirty years to "come to an issue" [when the cow is most likely dead]. None of the other choices expresses the absurdity of the system Gulliver describes.

(6) **2** "deceptively complex" The sense here is that the specialized language of the legal society is composed so that "no other mortal can understand," and the meanings of truth and falsehood, of right and wrong are "wholly confounded [confused and incomprehensible]." None of the other choices expresses the meaning of *cant* and *jargon*.

(7) **4** "submit to higher authority" Gulliver asserts that the judge "first sends to sound the disposition of those in power" before he renders a decision. That is, the judge first asks those above him what they think and then can find whatever form of law he needs to easily "hang or save a criminal." There is no reference to precedent, common sense, or length of sentence in these lines.

(8) **3** "employing exaggerated descriptions" Fundamental to satire is the use of exaggerated descriptions and examples of actual human behavior in order to criticize society. Exaggeration obliges the reader to look carefully and directly at the author's subject.

(9) **2** "corrupt" The lawyers and judges Gulliver describes are dishonest and immoral, and the legal system is incapable of rendering justice. None of the other choices expresses Gulliver's (Swift's) opinion.

Passage B

(10) **1** "compassion" In the opening line, the narrator expresses regret: "I don't mean to make you cry"; and the phrase "poor deluded human" suggests that the narrator (the onion) has sympathy for the person whose eyes are stinging and tearing. These lines do not suggest fear, loneliness, or shyness.

(11) **3** "futile" In these lines, the narrator declares that the hunt for what the heart of the onion represents will be pointless and unsuccessful (futile). These lines also expand on why the human is "deluded," that is, gullible and misled. These two questions are also examples of how vocabulary may be assessed on the exam.

(12) **1** "sympathetic to critical" This is the best choice to describe the dramatic change in attitude we hear in the voice of the narrator: "Look at you . . . Idiot[!]" We may hear anger here, but the tone in the first two stanzas is sympathetic, not really humorous, hopeful, or admiring. In the lines that follow, the narrator harshly criticizes the human's "fantasy of truth."

(13) **3** "clarity" This is the best answer among the choices. The narrator declares that the knowledge (clarity) the human seeks can only be "glimpsed/Through veils."

(14) **4** "suggesting that the quest for truth is harsh" The images in this stanza are of one who is seeking "to grasp the heart of things, hungry to know where meaning/Lies." The quest is intense, and the result is the harsh taste of onion juice. None of the other choices convincingly expresses the narrator's tone and meaning.

Passage C

(15) **4** "a lesser known event" The author acknowledges that "everyone knows birds fly south for the winter," but then he declares that "almost no one realizes the greater migration begins just beyond the beach." This paragraph introduces the author's main theme: "Those who care about wildlife should get to know about oceans."

(16) **1** "diversity" These lines detail the rich variety (diversity) in migrating swarms of fish. None of the other choices expresses the idea these images convey.

(17) **3** "migrating wildlife" This paragraph continues the author's detailed observations of migrating species and closes with a declaration of the joy he takes in "this seasonal sense of place in the path of migrations." In these lines, there is no reference to fishing boats or other observers; and the gannets feeding on herring are part of the natural food chain.

(18) **2** "speed" This is the best among the choices to describe the images of feeding birds as missiles and the eruption of geysers as they dive. To an

observer, this may appear as confusion and may even suggest fearful noise, but speed is most vividly expressed in the images.

(19) **1** "serious" The author not only recognizes the species of the baby turtle but also knows it is "most endangered of all Atlantic turtles." This passage leads to the author's argument for greater understanding of the oceans and conservation of ocean wildlife. The discovery is serious because the author's general concern is serious.

(20) **2** "cold" The image suggests that the turtle is chilled by the temperature of the air and of the water, which is also very cold. Clean, salty, or hazy air is not likely to have the same effect. This unfamiliar term can be understood in context. "Boreal" refers to northern regions characterized by long winters and short, cool to mild summers.

(21) **1** "disinterest in the ocean" The author refers here to "our parent ocean," as a reminder that much of life has its origins in the sea. The paradox or incongruity (irony) is that even those who love nature and wish to protect wildlife may have their "vision stranded on the beach."

(22) **3** "lines 58 and 59" As the author points out, nearly "half the world's people now live within 50 miles of a coast" (lines 54–55), and in turn we "levy heavy pressure on the sea." These are the only lines among the choices that establish a cause and effect relationship.

(23) **4** "What we regret . . . about oceans" (lines 74 through 76). The sentence that follows is a clear statement of the author's central claim: "Those who care about wildlife should get to know about oceans." The other choices identify passages of description or information only.

(24) **4** "maintain reader interest" At lines 34–35, the narrative shifts to a discussion of the author's main theme, leaving us with the image of a stunned baby sea turtle whose survival is in doubt. The author expects we will want to know what happens, and so he returns at the end to his account of how they save it. For this author, the saving of one "unlucky creature" is a reminder of "the challenge and opportunity . . . to cherish all life . . . to restore its abundance."

PART 2—Argument Response

Sample Essay Response One

The democracy of the United States "has come about through determination, hard work, struggle, even bloodshed." (Text 4, lines 1–2) As a nation, the United States has fought to ensure that its people would be represented in government and that the principles of democracy would be available to all. In a united democracy, all people should be required to vote to assure that the government represents everyone. Responsible and effective citizenship requires that every person of voting age, regardless of class, income, or education, must vote.

A democracy "can't be strong if its citizenship is weak" (Text 1, lines 23–24). It is all citizens' civic duty to voice their opinion to the government. Voting is a natural right and a privilege; voting guarantees that a country does not become oppressive to its citizens. Some people say mandatory voting is wrong because "it is not consistent with the freedom associated with democracy" (Text 2, lines 20–21), but if one describes democracy as the equal opportunity for everyone to participate freely in government, then it naturally follows that everyone must vote. Voters at no time are forced to vote for any one candidate. They have choices, guaranteed by the democracy they live in.

In our nation, where so much inequality exists, voting provides every American with the equal opportunity to cast a ballot, regardless of status or education. Required voting would guarantee that every minority's voice is heard. This is true democracy. The politicians would be forced to listen and change their attitudes if all people were required to vote. Opponents of mandatory voting say that there might be more "random votes" (Text 2, line 33). At least it [a random vote] is a vote, and it helps people get used to going to the polls. Even those voters who vote randomly have participated in their rightful duties. Also, voting equals out tensions between "income, education and age" (Text 1, line 47) and supports the ideals of democracy.

Lastly, every American of voting age should be required to vote because other democracies have found mandatory voting to be successful. "The system in fact is present in more than 30 democracies around the world" (Text 3, lines 8–9). Even though some Americans claim that the right to vote is the right not to vote (Text 3, lines 33–34), what does a non-existent vote say about the willingness of a person to participate in a democracy? If everyone makes an effort to vote in national elections, citizens will "begin to be more involved in political life" (Text 3, lines 28–29). In order to have a true popular mandate, everyone in the United States must vote.

In conclusion, every American must be required to vote. Mandatory voting ensures participation in government and pride in the outcome of elections. Every voting age citizen will be able to voice an opinion and politicians will have to listen.

Analysis

Essay 1 is a very good response because it offers insightful analysis to support a precise and thoughtful argument. This writer develops the analysis with relevant evidence from the texts, using both paraphrase and direct quotes to good effect. The essay achieves coherence through focus on the author's claim that mandatory voting is a requirement of "responsible and effective citizenship." The writing is fluent, the language is forceful, and there is sophisticated variety in sentence structure. This writer also demonstrates mastery of the conventions.

(See pages 80–81 for the scoring guidelines.)

Sample Essay Response Two

In a democracy, a right is an option, not a mandate. This applies to the right to vote. Forcing people to vote is an infringement on their freedoms. Additionally, if citizens don't care enough to vote, they still will not care when they are forced, causing them to vote randomly. Lastly, if politicians have to work to get citizens to vote, they will work even harder to keep those voters. American citizens should not be required to vote in national elections.

No right should ever be forced upon a citizen. Because voting is a right, making it mandatory would be an infringement on the citizen's freedoms (Text 2, line 22–23). The right to vote also constitutes the right to not vote (Text 3, line 33–34), and both are equally important (Text 4, lines 17–18). The right to vote is something a citizen chooses whether he or she wants to act upon, just as with any other right. Forcing someone to vote would be just as foolish as forcing someone to buy a gun or speak out against the government. We have the right to do these things, but exercising our rights needs to be kept an option.

If a citizen doesn't care enough about a vote to show up for it, this same apathy will be present if that citizen is forced to vote. The argument is that we should be focused on finding quality in our votes, not quantity (Text 4, lines 56–57). Similarly, voters need to be educated and active, not just simply active (Text 3, line 48–49). If a voter isn't informed about the politicians running or the current political state of the country, it is impossible for that voter to make an educated vote. "A forced electorate would not necessarily be the most politically intelligent electorate" (Text 3, lines 37–38). Another factor contributing to this [problem] would be citizens voting randomly. Many people will vote for whoever is first on the ballot (Text 2, lines 34–35) or vote for a person for reasons other than politics (Text 2, lines 35–36). In addition, in countries where voting is mandatory, there is a higher number of blank or invalid ballots (Text 2, lines 29–31). While some argue that if all citizens were forced to vote, the government would be more legitimate in representing the country's opinions, these factors clearly show otherwise (Text 2, lines 26–31).

Another argument [against mandatory voting] is that indifference is an opinion. If someone doesn't care who wins an election, not voting is a better indication than choosing a candidate randomly (Text 4, lines 35–40). In order to get people to vote, politicians need to excite them (Text 4, lines 52–53). People don't vote because they don't care for either candidate. If there is a politician that highly appeals to them, they will vote. This forces politicians to work harder to gain votes, creating a better political system (Text 4, lines 27–29).

American citizens should not be forced to vote. This would lessen the need of politicians to appeal to voters and cause a misrepresentation of the country's opinion. If a voter doesn't care about the election, he or she should by no means be forced to vote. Voting is a right that should never be forced upon anyone.

Analysis

Essay 2 is also a very good example of an evidence-based argument. Overall, the writing is less fluent than in Essay 1, but the expression of key points is often sophisticated and convincing: "a right is an option, not a mandate."; "Forcing someone to vote would be just as foolish as forcing someone to buy a gun or speak out against the government"; "indifference is an opinion." The claim that "Voting is a right that should never be forced upon anyone" is developed with thoughtful reasoning and opinions cited from the texts. The essay is coherent and cohesive because it remains focused on the topic and the evidence is relevant. Some awkward expression and minor spelling errors have been corrected, but there are no significant errors in the conventions. Both essays merit a high score.

(See pages 80–81 for the scoring guidelines.)

PART 3—Text-Analysis Response

Sample Essay Response

In the passage, the author uses the eerie setting to explore the idea of fear. Once the narrator realizes that he is a prisoner in Count Dracula's castle, he begins to panic and wonder about the sinister nature of the Count and his home. The author creates a shadowy setting full of doubt and uncertainty to further explore the mystery surrounding the whole affair, a setting designed to feed off of the narrator's fear.

As the narrator begins to suspect a dark undercurrent about the Count, he discovers that he has been essentially imprisoned within the castle. Helpless in his predicament, he begins to ruminate on all the warning signs that he had missed that would reveal the Count's true nature: the supernatural power the Count possessed over the wolves, the lack of servants or other living souls in the castle, and the fright of the villagers. As he begins to panic, the narrator's fear takes over his mind, and he becomes paranoid. He begins to feel there is no escape, even from his own mind as he says, "I am encompassed about with terrors that I dare not think of." Therefore, the Count has trapped him not just inside a castle but also within the fears of his own mind.

The setting is useful in inspiring this fear. The castle is isolated and lonely. The Count seems to be the only one inhabiting it as well. The idea of a huge empty castle with only one other soul in it is enough to inspire terror in the narrator. The fear and hopelessness of escape go to his head, and he begins to imagine sinister shadows in the dark countryside. The entire eerie setting contributes to the passage's ideas of fear and uncertainty.

Analysis

This writer has composed an especially sophisticated analysis of a central idea in the text: "the author uses the eerie setting to explore the idea of fear." The topic is developed with specific and relevant details, leading to the observation that "the Count has not only trapped him inside a castle but also within the fears of his own mind."

The structure of the three brief paragraphs makes the response coherent and cohesive. Note also how the central paragraph is organized to show how the narrator's fear grows, beginning with the narrator's suspicion or unease and ending with his feeling that he cannot escape from the castle or from his own mind. Sentence structure is varied to good effect, and the language is appropriately strong. The writer also demonstrates control of the conventions. This response would merit a high score.

(See pages 82–83 for the scoring guidelines.)

Regents ELA (Common Core) Examination June 2016
English Language Arts

PART 1—Reading Comprehension

Directions (1–24): Closely read each of the three passages below. After each passage, there are several multiple-choice questions. Select the best suggested answer to each question and write its number in the space provided. You may use the margins to take notes as you read.

Reading Comprehension Passage A

...When the short days of winter came dusk fell before we had well eaten our dinners. When we met in the street the houses had grown sombre. The space of sky above us was the colour of ever-changing violet and towards it the lamps of the street lifted their feeble lanterns. The cold air
(5) stung us and we played till our bodies glowed. Our shouts echoed in the silent street. The career of our play brought us through the dark muddy lanes behind the houses where we ran the gauntlet of the rough tribes[1] from the cottages, to the back doors of the dark dripping gardens where odours arose from the ashpits, to the dark odorous stables where a coach-
(10) man smoothed and combed the horse or shook music from the buckled harness. When we returned to the street light from the kitchen windows had filled the areas. If my uncle was seen turning the corner we hid in

---
[1]tribes—gangs

the shadow until we had seen him safely housed. Or if Mangan's sister came out on the doorstep to call her brother in to his tea we watched her (15) from our shadow peer up and down the street. We waited to see whether she would remain or go in and, if she remained, we left our shadow and walked up to Mangan's steps resignedly. She was waiting for us, her figure defined by the light from the half-opened door. Her brother always teased her before he obeyed and I stood by the railings looking at her. Her dress (20) swung as she moved her body and the soft rope of her hair tossed from side to side.

Every morning I lay on the floor in the front parlour watching her door. The blind was pulled down to within an inch of the sash so that I could not be seen. When she came out on the doorstep my heart leaped. I (25) ran to the hall, seized my books and followed her. I kept her brown figure always in my eye and, when we came near the point at which our ways diverged, I quickened my pace and passed her. This happened morning after morning. I had never spoken to her, except for a few casual words, and yet her name was like a summons to all my foolish blood. ...

(30)   At last she spoke to me. When she addressed the first words to me I was so confused that I did not know what to answer. She asked me was I going to *Araby*. I forget whether I answered yes or no. It would be a splendid bazaar,[2] she said she would love to go.

"And why can't you?" I asked.

(35)   While she spoke she turned a silver bracelet round and round her wrist. She could not go, she said, because there would be a retreat[3] that week in her convent.[4] Her brother and two other boys were fighting for their caps and I was alone at the railings. She held one of the spikes, bowing her head towards me. The light from the lamp opposite our door caught the (40) white curve of her neck, lit up her hair that rested there and, falling, lit up the hand upon the railing. It fell over one side of her dress and caught the white border of a petticoat, just visible as she stood at ease.

"It's well for you," she said.

"If I go," I said, "I will bring you something."

(45)   What innumerable follies laid waste my waking and sleeping thoughts after that evening! I wished to annihilate the tedious intervening days. I

---

[2]bazaar—fair
[3]retreat—a time set aside for prayer and reflection
[4]convent—religious school

chafed against the work of school. At night in my bedroom and by day in
the classroom her image came between me and the page I strove to read.
The syllables of the word *Araby* were called to me through the silence in
(50)   which my soul luxuriated and cast an Eastern enchantment over me. I
asked for leave to go to the bazaar on Saturday night. My aunt was surprised and hoped it was not some Freemason[5] affair. I answered few questions in class. I watched my master's face pass from amiability to sternness;
he hoped I was not beginning to idle. I could not call my wandering
(55)   thoughts together. I had hardly any patience with the serious work of life
which, now that it stood between me and my desire, seemed to me child's
play, ugly monotonous child's play.

On Saturday morning I reminded my uncle that I wished to go to the
bazaar in the evening. He was fussing at the hallstand, looking for the hat-
(60)   brush, and answered me curtly:

"Yes, boy, I know." ...

At nine o'clock I heard my uncle's latchkey in the halldoor. I heard him
talking to himself and heard the hallstand rocking when it had received
the weight of his overcoat. I could interpret these signs. When he was
(65)   midway through his dinner I asked him to give me the money to go to the
bazaar. He had forgotten.

"The people are in bed and after their first sleep now," he said.

I did not smile. My aunt said to him energetically: "Can't you give him
the money and let him go? You've kept him late enough as it is."...

(70)   I held a florin[6] tightly in my hand as I strode down Buckingham Street
towards the station. The sight of the streets thronged with buyers and
glaring with gas recalled to me the purpose of my journey. I took my seat
in a third-class carriage of a deserted train. After an intolerable delay the
train moved out of the station slowly. It crept onward among ruinous
(75)   houses and over the twinkling river. At Westland Row Station a crowd
of people pressed to the carriage doors; but the porters moved them back,
saying that it was a special train for the bazaar. I remained alone in the
bare carriage. In a few minutes the train drew up beside an improvised
wooden platform. I passed out on to the road and saw by the lighted dial

---

[5]Freemason—a fraternal organization
[6]florin—coin

(80)   of a clock that it was ten minutes to ten. In front of me was a large building which displayed the magical name. ...

Remembering with difficulty why I had come I went over to one of the
stalls and examined porcelain vases and flowered tea-sets. At the door of
the stall a young lady was talking and laughing with two young gentle-
(85)   men. I remarked their English accents and listened vaguely to their conversation. ...

Observing me the young lady came over and asked me did I wish to buy
anything. The tone of her voice was not encouraging; she seemed to have
spoken to me out of a sense of duty. I looked humbly at the great jars that
(90)   stood like eastern guards at either side of the dark entrance to the stall and
murmured:

"No, thank you."

The young lady changed the position of one of the vases and went back
to the two young men. They began to talk of the same subject. Once or
(95)   twice the young lady glanced at me over her shoulder.

I lingered before her stall, though I knew my stay was useless, to make
my interest in her wares seem the more real. Then I turned away slowly
and walked down the middle of the bazaar. I allowed the two pennies to
fall against the sixpence in my pocket. I heard a voice call from one end
(100) of the gallery that the light was out. The upper part of the hall was now
completely dark.

Gazing up into the darkness I saw myself as a creature driven and
derided by vanity; and my eyes burned with anguish and anger.

—James Joyce
excerpted from "Araby"
Dubliners, 1914
Grant Richards LTD.

1 The description of the neighborhood in lines 1
  through 11 contributes to a mood of

    (1) indifference   (3) anxiety

    (2) gloom   (4) regret   1_____

2 Which quotation from the text best illustrates the
  narrator's attitude toward Mangan's sister?

    (1) "we watched her from our shadow" (lines 14
          and 15)

    (2) "We waited to see whether she would remain
          or go in" (lines 15 and 16)

    (3) "yet her name was like a summons" (line 29)

    (4) "She asked me was I going to *Araby*" (lines 31
          and 32)   2_____

3 Lines 30 through 39 reveal Mangan's sister's

    (1) disinterest   (3) disappointment

    (2) silliness   (4) tension   3_____

4 Lines 45 through 57 help to develop the idea that
  the narrator has

    (1) recognized that his priorities have changed

    (2) determined the academic focus of his studies

    (3) eliminated distractions from his daily routine

    (4) reassessed his relationship with his family   4_____

5 The description of the narrator's train ride (lines 70
  through 79) supports a theme of

    (1) confusion   (3) persecution

    (2) isolation   (4) deception   5_____

6 The description in lines 87 through 97 suggests that
  the bazaar symbolizes

    (1) excessive greed   (3) false promise

    (2) future wealth   (4) lasting love   6_____

7 It can be inferred from the text that the narrator's behavior is most guided by his

   (1) school experience
   (2) family situation
   (3) childhood memories
   (4) romantic feelings   7____

8 As used in line 103, the word "derided" most nearly means

   (1) taunted   (3) rewarded
   (2) restrained   (4) flattered   8____

9 Based on the text as a whole, the narrator's feelings of "anguish and anger" (line 103) are most likely a result of his having

   (1) ignored his opportunities
   (2) defended his family
   (3) realized his limitations
   (4) denied his responsibilities   9____

10 Which quotation best reflects a central theme of the text?

   (1) "Her brother and two other boys were fighting for their caps" (lines 37 and 38)
   (2) " 'Can't you give him the money and let him go?' " (lines 68 and 69)
   (3) "It crept onward among ruinous houses and over the twinkling river" (lines 74 and 75)
   (4) "I lingered before her stall, though I knew my stay was useless" (line 96)   10____

Reading Comprehension Passage B

Assembly Line

In time's assembly line
Night presses against night.
We come off the factory night-shift
In line as we march towards home.
(5) Over our heads in a row
The assembly line of stars
Stretches across the sky.
Beside us, little trees
Stand numb in assembly lines.

(10) The stars must be exhausted
After thousands of years
Of journeys which never change.
The little trees are all sick,
Choked on smog and monotony,
(15) Stripped of their color and shape.
It's not hard to feel for them;
We share the same tempo and rhythm.

Yes, I'm numb to my own existence
As if, like the trees and stars
(20) —perhaps just out of habit
—perhaps just out of sorrow,
I'm unable to show concern
For my own manufactured fate.

—Shu Ting
from *A Splintered Mirror: Chinese Poetry from the
Democracy Movement*, 1991
translated by Carolyn Kizer
North Point Press

11 In the first stanza, a main idea is strengthened through the poet's use of

   (1) repetition   (3) allusion

   (2) simile   (4) understatement   11____

12 Line 17 contributes to a central idea by pointing out a parallel between

   (1) profit and industrialization

   (2) humans and nature

   (3) recreation and production

   (4) sound and motion   12____

13 The structure and language of lines 20 and 21 suggests the narrator's

   (1) bitterness   (3) selfishness

   (2) determination   (4) uncertainty   13____

14 The phrase "manufactured fate" (line 23) emphasizes the narrator's

   (1) resignation to life

   (2) desire for control

   (3) hope for change

   (4) rejection of nature   14____

Reading Comprehension Passage C

...Memory teaches me what I know of these matters. The boy reminds the adult. I was a bilingual child, but of a certain kind: "socially disadvantaged," the son of working-class parents, both Mexican immigrants. ...

(5) In public, my father and mother spoke a hesitant, accented, and not always grammatical English. And then they would have to strain, their bodies tense, to catch the sense of what was rapidly said by *los gringos*. At home, they returned to Spanish. The language of their Mexican past sounded in counterpoint to the English spoken in public. The words would come quickly, with ease. Conveyed through those sounds was the
(10) pleasing, soothing, consoling reminder that one was at home.

During those years when I was first learning to speak, my mother and father addressed me only in Spanish; in Spanish I learned to reply. By contrast, English (*inglés*) was the language I came to associate with gringos, rarely heard in the house. I learned my first words of English overhearing
(15) my parents speaking to strangers. At six years of age, I knew just enough words for my mother to trust me on errands to stores one block away— but no more.

I was then a listening child, careful to hear the very different sounds of Spanish and English. Wide-eyed with hearing, I'd listen to sounds
(20) more than to words. First, there were English (gringo) sounds. So many words still were unknown to me that when the butcher or the lady at the drugstore said something, exotic polysyllabic sounds would bloom in the midst of their sentences. Often the speech of people in public seemed to me very loud, booming with confidence. The man behind the counter would
(25) literally ask, "What can I do for you?" But by being so firm and clear, the sound of his voice said that he was a gringo; he belonged in public society. There were also the high, nasal notes of middle-class American speech— which I rarely am conscious of hearing today because I hear them so often, but could not stop hearing when I was a boy. Crowds at Safeway or at bus
(30) stops were noisy with the birdlike sounds of *los gringos*. I'd move away from them all—all the chirping chatter above me.

My own sounds I was unable to hear, but I knew that I spoke English poorly. My words could not extend to form complete thoughts. And the words I did speak I didn't know well enough to make distinct sounds.
(35) (Listeners would usually lower their heads to hear better what I was trying

to say.) But it was one thing for *me* to speak English with difficulty; it was more troubling to hear my parents speaking in public: their high-whining vowels and guttural[1] consonants; their sentences that got stuck with "eh" and "ah" sounds; the confused syntax; the hesitant rhythm of sounds so
(40) different from the way gringos spoke. I'd notice, moreover, that my parents' voices were softer than those of gringos we would meet.

I am tempted to say now that none of this mattered. (In adulthood I am embarrassed by childhood fears.) And, in a way, it didn't matter very much that my parents could not speak English with ease. Their linguistic
(45) difficulties had no serious consequences. My mother and father made themselves understood at the county hospital clinic and at government offices. And yet, in another way, it mattered very much. It was unsettling to hear my parents struggle with English. Hearing them, I'd grow nervous, and my clutching trust in their protection and power would be weakened. ...

(50) But then there was Spanish: *español*, the language rarely heard away from the house; *español*, the language which seemed to me therefore a private language, my family's language. To hear its sounds was to feel myself specially recognized as one of the family, apart from *los otros*.[2] A simple remark, an inconsequential comment could convey that assurance.
(55) My parents would say something to me and I would feel embraced by the sounds of their words. Those sounds said: *I am speaking with ease in Spanish. I am addressing you in words I never use with* los gringos. *I recognize you as someone special, close, like no one outside. You belong with us. In the family. Ricardo.*

(60) At the age of six, well past the time when most middle-class children no longer notice the difference between sounds uttered at home and words spoken in public, I had a different experience. I lived in a world compounded of sounds. I was a child longer than most. I lived in a magical world, surrounded by sounds both pleasing and fearful. I shared with my
(65) family a language enchantingly private—different from that used in the city around us. ...

If I rehearse here the changes in my private life after my Americanization, it is finally to emphasize a public gain. The loss implies

---

[1]guttural—throaty
[2]los otros—the others

the gain. The house I returned to each afternoon was quiet. Intimate
(70)   sounds no longer greeted me at the door. Inside there were other noises.
The telephone rang. Neighborhood kids ran past the door of the bedroom
where I was reading my schoolbooks—covered with brown shopping-bag
paper. Once I learned the public language, it would never again be easy
for me to hear intimate family voices. More and more of my day was spent
(75)   hearing words, not sounds. But that may only be a way of saying that on
the day I raised my hand in class and spoke loudly to an entire roomful of
faces, my childhood started to end. ...

—Richard Rodriguez
excerpted from "Aria: A Memoir of a Bilingual Childhood"
The American Scholar, Winter 1981
The Phi Beta Kappa Society

15 The phrase "the boy reminds the adult" in the first
paragraph establishes the narrator's

(1) mood   (3) creativity
(2) perspective   (4) disposition   15____

16 The use of the word "counterpoint" in line 8 helps
to develop a central idea by presenting

(1) differing memories
(2) opposing principles
(3) contrasting cultures
(4) conflicting philosophies   16____

17 The use of figurative language in lines 19 and 20
demonstrates the narrator's

(1) eagerness to learn
(2) desire for recognition
(3) frustration with authority
(4) anxiety about adulthood   17____

18 The use of the word "public" in line 26 emphasizes
the narrator's feeling of

(1) accomplishment   (3) satisfaction
(2) disillusionment (4) separation   18____

19 The description of the narrator speaking English in
lines 32 through 36 emphasizes his inability to

(1) communicate effectively
(2) understand the culture
(3) distinguish between languages
(4) express emotions   19____

20 In lines 44 through 49 the narrator's reaction to his parents' "linguistic difficulties" (lines 44 and 45) reveals his

   (1) low expectations   (3) educational concerns

   (2) conflicting feelings   (4) hostile thoughts   20_____

21 Lines 50 through 59 contribute to a central idea in the text by focusing on the

   (1) narrator's sense of security

   (2) family's economic status

   (3) family's traditional beliefs

   (4) narrator's feeling of confusion   21_____

22 Which quotation best reflects the narrator's overall experience with language?

   (1) "The words would come quickly, with ease" (lines 8 and 9)

   (2) "I'd listen to sounds more than to words" (lines 19 and 20)

   (3) "My own sounds I was unable to hear, but I knew that I spoke English poorly" (lines 32 and 33)

   (4) "Hearing them, I'd grow nervous" (line 48)   22_____

23 The phrase "the loss implies the gain" (lines 68 and 69) contributes to a central idea in the text by indicating that when the narrator speaks English comfortably he is

   (1) disconnected from his family

   (2) distressed by hearing English sounds

   (3) uninterested in his school work

   (4) undeterred from making new friends   23_____

24 The narrator's tone in lines 74 through 77 suggests

   (1) distrust   (3) confidence

   (2) respect   (4) intolerance   24_____

PART 2—Argument Response

Directions: Closely read each of the *four* texts on pages 256 through 266 and write a source-based argument on the topic below. You may use the margins to take notes as you read and scrap paper to plan your response. Write your argument on a separate sheet of paper.

> **Topic:** Should celebrities become the voice of humanitarian causes?

> **Your Task:** Carefully read each of the *four* texts provided. Then, using evidence from at least *three* of the texts, write a well-developed argument regarding whether or not celebrities should become the voice of humanitarian causes. Clearly establish your claim, distinguish your claim from alternate or opposing claims, and use specific, relevant, and sufficient evidence from at least *three* of the texts to develop your argument. Do *not* simply summarize each text.

Guidelines:

Be sure to

- Establish your claim regarding whether or not celebrities should become the voice of humanitarian causes.
- Distinguish your claim from alternate or opposing claims.
- Use specific, relevant, and sufficient evidence from at least *three* of the texts to develop your argument.
- Identify each source that you reference by text number and line number(s) or graphic (for example: Text 1, line 4 or Text 2, graphic).
- Organize your ideas in a cohesive and coherent manner
- Maintain a formal style of writing.
- Follow the conventions of standard written English.

Texts:

Text 1

The Celebrity Solution

In 2004, Natalie Portman, then a 22-year-old fresh from college, went to Capitol Hill to talk to Congress on behalf of the Foundation for International Community Assistance, or Finca, a microfinance organization for which she served as "ambassador." She found herself wondering
(5) what she was doing there, but her colleagues assured her: "We got the meetings because of you." For lawmakers, Natalie Portman was not simply a young woman—she was the beautiful Padmé from "Star Wars." "And I was like, 'That seems totally nuts to me,' " Portman told me recently. [*sic*] It's the way it works, I guess. I'm not particularly proud
(10) that in our country I can get a meeting with a representative more easily than the head of a nonprofit can."

Well, who is? But it is the way it works. Stars—movie stars, rock stars, sports stars—exercise a ludicrous influence over the public consciousness. Many are happy to exploit that power; others are wrecked by it. In recent
(15) years, stars have learned that their intense presentness in people's daily lives and their access to the uppermost realms of politics, business and the media offer them a peculiar kind of moral position, should they care to use it. And many of those with the most leverage—Bono and Angelina Jolie and Brad Pitt and George Clooney and, yes, Natalie Portman—have
(20) increasingly chosen to mount that pedestal. Hollywood celebrities have become central players on deeply political issues like development aid, refugees and government-sponsored violence in Darfur.

Activists on these and other issues talk about the political power of stars with a mixture of bewilderment and delight. But a weapon that
(25) powerful is bound to do collateral damage. Some stars, like George Clooney, regard the authority thrust upon them with wariness; others, like Sean Penn or Mia Farrow, an activist on Darfur, seize the bully pulpit with both hands. "There is a tendency," says Donald Steinberg, deputy president of the International Crisis Group, which seeks to prevent con-
(30) flict around the world, "to treat these issues as if it's all good and evil." Sometimes you need the rallying cry, but sometimes you need to accept a complex truth. ...

An entire industry has sprung up around the recruitment of celebrities to good works. Even an old-line philanthropy like the Red Cross employs
(35) a "director of celebrity outreach." Oxfam has a celebrity wrangler in Los Angeles, Lyndsay Cruz, on the lookout for stars who can raise the charity's profile with younger people. In addition to established figures like Colin Firth and Helen Mirren, Oxfam is affiliated with Scarlett Johansson, who has visited South Asia (where the organization promotes girls'
(40) education) and is scheduled to go to Mali. Cruz notes that while "trendy young people" are attracted to the star of "Match Point" and "Lost in Translation," Johansson had "great credibility with an older audience because she's such a great actress." ...

Microfinance is a one-star cause. Though for some reason the subject
(45) appeals to female royalty, including Queen Rania of Jordan and Princess Maxima of the Netherlands, Natalie Portman is the only member of Hollywood royalty who has dedicated herself to it. Perhaps this is because microfinance is a good deal more complicated than supplying fresh water to parched villages, and a good deal less glamorous than confronting the
(50) janjaweed[1] in Darfur. The premise of microfinance is that very poor people should have access to credit, just as the middle class and the rich do. They typically don't have such access because banks that operate in the developing world view the poor as too great a credit risk, and the processing cost of a $50 loan is thought to wipe out much of the potential profit. But
(55) small nonprofit organizations found that tiny loans could not only raise the incomes of the rural and small-town poor but also, unlike aid and other handouts, could help make them self-sufficient. And they found as well that if they harnessed the communities' own social bonds to create group support, repayment rates among the very poor could be higher than
(60) among the more well-off. (Indeed, commercial banks, apparently having recognized their error, have now begun to extend loans to the poor.) The idea of microfinance is thus to introduce the poor to capitalism. This is not, it's true, star material. ...

There's no question that causes do a great deal for the brand identity
(65) of the stars and the sponsors who embrace them. But what, exactly, do stars do for causes? They raise money, of course. But that is often less important than raising consciousness, as Natalie Portman has done. John

---

[1]janjaweed—militia

Prendergast, a longtime activist on African issues and the chairman of Enough, an organization that brings attention to atrocities around the world, says: "Celebrities are master recruiters. If you're trying to expand beyond the already converted, there's no better way to do instant outreach than to have a familiar face where people want to know more about what they're doing in their personal lives." People come to see Natalie Portman, and they go away learning about microfinance. ...

(70)

—James Traub
excerpted from "The Celebrity Solution"
www.nytimes.com, March 9, 2008

Text 2

Ethics of Celebrities and Their Increasing Influence in 21st Century Society

The global influence of celebrities in the 21st century extends far beyond the entertainment sector. During the recent Palestinian presidential elections, the Hollywood actor Richard Gere broadcast a televised message to voters in the region and stated,

(5)   Hi, I'm Richard Gere, and I'm speaking for the entire world. (Richard Gere, actor)

Celebrities in the 21st century have expanded from simple product endorsements to sitting on United Nations committees, regional and global conflict commentators and international diplomacy. The

(10)   Russian parliament is debating whether to send a global celebrity to its International Space Station. The celebrities industry is undergoing, "mission creep", or the expansion of an enterprise beyond its original goals.

There has always been a connection between Hollywood and politics, certainly in the USA. However, global celebrities in the 21st century are

(15)   involved in proselytising[1] about particular religions, such as Scientology, negotiating with the Taliban in Afghanistan and participating in the Iraqi refugee crisis. The Hollywood actor, Jude Law's attempt to negotiate with the Taliban in Afghanistan was not successful; but the mere fact that Jude Law tried, and that it was discussed widely over the global internet, shows

(20)   the expansion of celebrities' domain in today's society. The global entertainment industry, especially based in Hollywood, has vastly exceeded their original mandate in society. …

How is it that celebrities in the 21st century are formulating foreign aid policy, backing political bills or affecting public health debates?

(25)   Traditionally, the economic value or market price of the entertainment industry and its various components was seen as intangible and difficult to measure. Movie stars and films, artists and the quality of art is often seen as difficult to measure in terms of value and price without the role of expert opinions. But global internet-driven 21st century seems to be

---

[1]proselytising—trying to persuade or recruit others

(30)   driven by a general growth of the idea that celebrity can be measured in a
tangible way. ...

The 21st century's internet society seems to thrive on a harmonious
three-way relationship among celebrities, audiences and fame addiction.
The global internet in turns [*sic*] moulds this three-way relationship and
(35)   accelerates its dissemination[2] and communication. This in turn allows
celebrities in the 21st century to "mission creep", or expand and accelerate
their influence into various new areas of society. This interaction of forces
is shown in Figure 1. ...

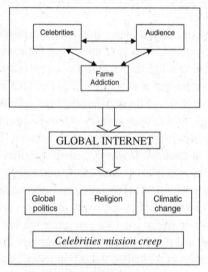

**Figure 1. Celebrities' mission creep
in the 21st century.**

In turn, the global popularity of internet-based social networking
(40)   sites such as MySpace or individual blogspots all show the need to discuss events, but also things that are famous (Choi and Berger, 2009).
Traditionally, celebrities were seen as people that needed to be seen from
afar and while keeping one's distance. In this sense, celebrities were similar
to art pieces, better to be seen from a distance (Halpern, 2008; Hirsch,

---

[2]dissemination—wide distribution

(45) 1972; Maury and Kleiner, 2002). This traditional distance has been reduced due to global technologies in communications. Celebrities, and famous people in turn, help to bring people, including adults, together in conversation and social interaction. The global role of the internet in the 21st century society will further accelerate such social and psychological
(50) trends throughout today's global knowledge-based society. Global internet communications have increased the availability of "fame" and access to the lives of celebrities, which in turn will further accelerate the global influence of celebrities in the 21st century society. ...

—Chong Ju Choi and Ron Berger
excerpted from "Ethics of Celebrities and
Their Increasing Influence in 21st Century Society"
Journal of Business Ethics, 2009
www.idc.ac.il

References

Choi, C.J. and R. Berger: 2009, 'Ethics of Internet, Global Community, Fame Addiction', *Journal of Business Ethics* (forthcoming).

Halpern, J.: 2008, *Fame Junkies* (Houghton Mifflin, New York).

Hirsch, P.: 1972, 'Processing Fads and Fashions: An Organisation Set Analysis of Cultural Industry Systems', *American Journal of Sociology* 77 (1), 45–70.

Maury, M. and D. Kleiner: 2002, 'E-Commerce, Ethical Commerce?', *Journal of Business Ethics* 36 (3), 21–32.

Text 3

Do Celebrity Humanitarians Matter?

...Recent years have seen a growth industry for celebrities engaged in humanitarian activities. The website *Look to the Stars* has calculated that over 2,000 charities have some form of celebrity support. UNICEF has dozens of "Goodwill Ambassadors" and "Advocates" such as Angelina
(5)   Jolie and Mia Farrow. Celebrities have entered forums for global governance to pressure political leaders: George Clooney has spoken before the United Nations while Bob Geldof, Bono, and Sharon Stone have attended summits like DAVOS[1] and the G8[2] to discuss third world debt, poverty, and refugees. In the U.S. policy arena, [Ben] Affleck joins Nicole
(10)   Kidman, Angelina Jolie, and other celebrities who have addressed the U.S. Congress on international issues.[3] The increase in celebrity involvement has spurred debate in academic circles and mainstream media. Celebrity humanitarianism is alternately lauded for drawing media attention and fostering popular engagement and criticized on a number of ethical
(15)   grounds. According to *Mother Jones*, Africa is experiencing a "recolonization" as celebrities from the U.S. and UK lay claim to particular countries as recipients of their star power: South Africa (Oprah), Sudan (Mia Farrow), and Botswana (Russell Simmons). As the involvement of American celebrities in humanitarian causes grows, let us consider the
(20)   activities of Affleck and his Eastern Congo Initiative [ECI].

Celebrity Humanitarians

Affleck can be considered a "celebrity humanitarian," a celebrity figure who has moved beyond his/her day job as an entertainer to delve into the areas of foreign aid, charity, and development. These activities can involve fundraising, hosting concerts and events, media appearances, and engag-

---

[1]DAVOS—an annual meeting of The World Economic Forum, hosted in Davos-Klosters, Switzerland, on global partnership

[2]G8—A group of 8 industrialized nations that hold a yearly meeting to discuss global issues

[3]ProQuest, "Quick Start: Congressional Hearing Digital Collections: Famous (Celebrity) Witnesses," *http://proquest.libguides.com/quick_start_hearings/famouscelebs*

(25) ing in advocacy. Celebrities are distinguished by their unique ability to attract and engage diverse audiences ranging from their fan base and the media to political elites and philanthropists. Celebrity humanitarians often play an important bridging role, introducing Northern publics to issues in the developing world. They also use their star power to gain
(30) access to policy-making circles to effect social and political change. Since 1980, the U.S. Congress has seen the frequency of celebrity witnesses double to around 20 a year with most celebrity appearances taking place before committees addressing domestic issues. Interestingly, fewer than 5 percent of celebrity witnesses testify before committees dealing with
(35) foreign relations, where celebrity humanitarians push the United States to address global concerns.[4]

The rise and influence of celebrity humanitarians activate debates on the consequences of their involvement. For some academics and practitioners, celebrities are welcome figures in humanitarianism: educat-
(40) ing the public on global issues, raising funds, and using their populist appeal to draw attention to policy-making arenas. For others, celebrity humanitarians are highly problematic figures who dilute debates, offer misguided policy proposals, and lack credibility and accountability. Celebrity humanitarianism privileges and invests the celebrity figure
(45) with the responsibility of speaking on behalf of a "distant other" who is unable to give input or consent for their representation. Stakeholders in the developing world unwittingly rely on the celebrity humanitarian as their communicator, advocate, and fundraiser. Finally, celebrities are held to be self-serving, engaging in humanitarian causes to burnish[5] their
(50) careers. ...

Celebrity humanitarians should do their homework to earn credibility while also respecting their bounded roles as celebrity figures. As a celebrity humanitarian, Affleck's proposals are based on serious preparation: spending years to gain an in-depth understanding, consult-
(55) ing with professionals, narrowing his advocacy efforts to a single region, and enduring the scrutiny of the cameras and the blogosphere. Besides this self-education, his credibility is based on ECI's dual mission of

---

[4]See Demaine, L.J., n.d. Navigating Policy by the Stars: The Influence of Celebrity Entertainers on Federal Lawmaking. *Journal of Law & Politics*, 25 (2), 83–143
[5]burnish—improve or enhance

re-granting and policymaking. Since ECI has operations and partnerships in the DRC [Democratic Republic of the Congo], the content of Affleck's
(60) writings and Congressional testimonies are grounded in the realities of the DRC, peppered with first-hand accounts, and supported by statistics and other research. However, there are limits to his knowledge—Affleck is not a development expert or on-the-ground professional; his day job and main career lie elsewhere. And while the decision to found an organization
(65) suggests that Affleck's commitment to the DRC will extend beyond his nascent[6] efforts, rumors that he may seek political office distort this image.

Celebrity humanitarians must find a way to avoid diverting resources and attention. Rather than bring his star power and ample financial support to existing Congolese organizations, ECI furnished a platform for
(70) Affleck's advocacy and leadership that amplifies his voice over those of the Congolese. Nor was ECI crafted inside eastern Congo but in the offices of a strategic advisory firm based in Seattle. ECI is privately funded by a network of financial elites and does not rely on means-tested grant cycles or public support. While Affleck has received multiple awards in the short
(75) period he has been a celebrity humanitarian, his star power also distracts us from the people who work in the field of humanitarianism on a daily basis and rarely receive such recognition.[7] And by concentrating attention and money for Affleck's issue of Eastern Congo, other causes and countries may go unnoticed. ...

—Alexandra Cosima Budabin
excerpted and adapted from "Do Celebrity Humanitarians Matter?"
www.carnegiecouncil.org, December 11, 2014

---

[6]nascent—beginning

[7]Marina Hyde, "Angelina Jolie, Paris Hilton, Lassie and Tony Blair: here to save the world," The Guardian, 27 November 2014 *http://www.theguardian.com/lifeandstyle/ lostinshowbiz/2014/nov/27/angelina-jolie-paris-hilton-tony-blair-lassie-save-the-children- award?CMP=share_btn_fb*

Text 4

The Rise of the Celebrity Humanitarian

...One of the most effective methods of attracting a wide, although perhaps not a deep, following is the use of a celebrity humanitarian: An A-Lister who has delved into areas of foreign aid, charity and international development. The United Nations is the leader in this attention-
(5)   getting ploy, with at least 175 celebrities on the books as goodwill ambassadors[1] for one cause or another. Some celebrities even leverage their star power to promote their very own foundations and philanthropic projects.

It's a mutually beneficial relationship, really. Hollywood's elite get to
(10)   wield their unique ability to engage diverse audiences, and the power of celebrity is put to good use effecting change—whether it's out of the good of their hearts, or because their publicists insist.

There is some downside that comes with publicly linking a campaign to a celebrity. For some, celebrity humanitarians are problematic figures[2]
(15)   who dilute debates, offer misguided policy proposals, and lack credibility and accountability. Take Scarlett Johansson, who became embroiled in a scandal after partnering with soft drink maker SodaStream, which operated a factory in occupied Palestinian territory. This alliance was in direct conflict with her seven-year global ambassador position for Oxfam,
(20)   which opposes all trade with the occupied territories. In the end, she stepped down from her role with Oxfam, stating a fundamental difference of opinion.

Moreover, if the star's popularity takes a hit, it can affect the reception of the cause. For example, when Lance Armstrong's popularity
(25)   plummeted in the wake of doping allegations, it tarnished the brand of the Livestrong Foundation,[3] the nonprofit he founded to support people

---

[1]Bunting, Madeline. "The Issue of Celebrities and Aid Is Deceptively Complex"
http://www.theguardian.com, Dec. 17, 2010
[2]Budabin, Alexandra Cosima. "Do Celebrity Humanitarians Matter?"
http://www.carnegiecouncil.org, December 11, 2014
[3]Gardner, Eriq. "Livestrong Struggles After Lance Armstrong's Fall"
http://www.hollywoodreporter.com, 7/25/2013

affected by cancer. Livestrong does, however, continue today, after cutting ties with Armstrong and undergoing a radical rebranding.

(30)   Even so, the following big names substantiate the idea that celebrity involvement brings massive amounts of attention and money to humanitarian causes and that, usually, this [*sic*] is a good thing. ...

Bono participates in fundraising concerts like Live 8, and has co-founded several philanthropies, like the ONE Campaign and Product (RED). He also created EDUN, a fashion brand that strives to stimulate
(35)   trade in Africa by sourcing production there. He has received three nominations for the Nobel Peace Prize, was knighted by the United Kingdom in 2007, and was named Time's 2005 Person of the Year. ...

Popular singer Akon may not be as famous for his philanthropic work as Angelina Jolie or Bono, but he is in a unique position to help, as he has
(40)   deep roots in the areas in which he works: He was raised in Senegal in a community without electricity, which inspired his latest project, Akon Lighting Africa. He also founded the Konfidence Foundation, raising awareness of conditions in Africa and providing underprivileged African youth access to education and other resources. ...

(45)   In weighing the pros and cons of celebrity activism, perhaps [Ben] Affleck himself summed it up best in an essay reflecting on the constraints and possibilities of his own engagement:

"It makes sense to be skeptical about celebrity activism. There is always suspicion that involvement with a cause may be doing more good for
(50)   the spokesman than he or she is doing for the cause...but I hope you can separate whatever reservations you may have from what is unimpeachably important."

—Jenica Funk
excerpted and adapted from "The Rise of the Celebrity Humanitarian"
www.globalenvision.org, January 29, 2015

PART 3—Text-Analysis Response

Your Task: Closely read the text on pages 268 through 270 and write a well-developed, text-based response of two to three paragraphs. In your response, identify a central idea in the text and analyze how the author's use of **one** writing strategy (literary element or literary technique or rhetorical device) develops this central idea. Use strong and thorough evidence from the text to support your analysis. Do *not* simply summarize the text. You may use the margins to take notes as you read and scrap paper to plan your response. Write your response on a separate sheet of paper.

Guidelines:

Be sure to

- Identify a central idea in the text.
- Analyze how the author's use of **one** writing strategy (literary element or literary technique or rhetorical device) develops this central idea. Examples include: characterization, conflict, denotation/connotation, metaphor, simile, irony, language use, point-of-view, setting, structure, symbolism, theme, tone, etc.
- Use strong and thorough evidence from the text to support your analysis.
- Organize your ideas in a cohesive and coherent manner.
- Maintain a formal style of writing.
- Follow the conventions of standard written English.

Text

It was my father who called the city the Mansion on the River. He was talking about Charleston, South Carolina, and he was a native son, peacock proud of a town so pretty it makes your eyes ache with pleasure just to walk down its spellbinding, narrow streets. Charleston was my father's
(5) ministry, his hobbyhorse, his quiet obsession, and the great love of his life. His bloodstream lit up my own with a passion for the city that I've never lost nor ever will. I'm Charleston-born, and bred. The city's two rivers, the Ashley and the Cooper, have flooded and shaped all the days of my life on this storied[1] peninsula.

(10)   I carry the delicate porcelain beauty of Charleston like the hinged shell of some soft-tissued mollusk. My soul is peninsula-shaped and sun-hardened and river-swollen. The high tides of the city flood my consciousness each day, subject to the whims and harmonies of full moons rising out of the Atlantic. I grow calm when I see the ranks of palmetto trees pulling
(15) guard duty on the banks of Colonial Lake or hear the bells of St. Michael's calling cadence[2] in the cicada-filled trees along Meeting Street. Deep in my bones, I knew early that I was one of those incorrigible[3] creatures known as Charlestonians. It comes to me as a surprising form of knowledge that my time in the city is more vocation than gift; it is my destiny, not my
(20) choice. I consider it a high privilege to be a native of one of the loveliest American cities, not a high-kicking, glossy, or lipsticked city, not a city with bells on its fingers or brightly painted toenails, but a ruffled, low-slung city, understated and tolerant of nothing mismade or ostentatious.[4] Though Charleston feels a seersuckered, tuxedoed view of itself, it
(25) approves of restraint far more than vainglory.[5]

As a boy, in my own backyard I could catch a basket of blue crabs, a string of flounder, a dozen redfish, or a net full of white shrimp. All this I could do in a city enchanting enough to charm cobras out of baskets, one so corniced and filigreed[6] and elaborate that it leaves strangers awed and

---

[1]storied—told of in history
[2]cadence—rhythmic recurrence of sound
[3]incorrigible—cannot be reformed
[4]ostentatious—showy
[5]vainglory—excessive pride
[6]corniced and filigreed—architecturally decorated

(30) natives self-satisfied. In its shadows you can find metalwork as delicate as
      lace and spiral staircases as elaborate as yachts. In the secrecy of its gardens
      you can discover jasmine and camellias and hundreds of other plants that
      look embroidered and stolen from the Garden of Eden for the sheer love of
      richness and the joy of stealing from the gods. In its kitchens, the stoves are
(35) lit up in happiness as the lamb is marinating in red wine sauce, vinaigrette
      is prepared for the salad, crabmeat is anointed with sherry, custards are
      baked in the oven, and buttermilk biscuits cool on the counter.
          Because of its devotional, graceful attraction to food and gardens and
      architecture, Charleston stands for all the principles that make living
(40) well both a civic virtue and a standard. It is a rapturous, defining place
      to grow up. Everything I reveal to you now will be Charleston-shaped
      and Charleston-governed, and sometimes even Charleston-ruined. But
      it is my fault and not the city's that it came close to destroying me. Not
      everyone responds to beauty in the same way. Though Charleston can
(45) do much, it can't always improve on the strangeness of human behavior.
      But Charleston has a high tolerance for eccentricity and bemusement.[7]
      There is a tastefulness in its gentility[8] that comes from the knowledge that
      Charleston is a permanent dimple in the understated skyline, while the rest
      of us are only visitors. ...
(50)   I turned out to be a late bloomer, which I long regretted. My parents
      suffered needlessly because it took me so long to find my way to a place at
      their table. But I sighted the early signs of my recovery long before they
      did. My mother had given up on me at such an early age that a comeback
      was something she no longer even prayed for in her wildest dreams. Yet in
(55) my anonymous and underachieving high school career, I laid the founda-
      tion for a strong finish without my mother noticing that I was, at last, up
      to some good. I had built an impregnable castle of solitude for myself and
      then set out to bring that castle down, no matter how serious the collat-
      eral damage or who might get hurt.
(60)   I was eighteen years old and did not have a friend my own age. There
      wasn't a boy in Charleston who would think about inviting me to a party
      or to come out to spend the weekend at his family's beach house.

---

[7]bemusement—bewilderment
[8]gentility—refinement

I planned for all that to change. I had decided to become the most interesting boy to ever grow up in Charleston, and I revealed this secret to (65) my parents.

Outside my house in the languid[9] summer air of my eighteenth year, I climbed the magnolia tree nearest to the Ashley River with the agility that constant practice had granted me. From its highest branches, I surveyed my city as it lay simmering in the hot-blooded saps of June while the sun (70) began to set, reddening the vest of cirrus clouds that had gathered along the western horizon. In the other direction, I saw the city of rooftops and columns and gables that was my native land. What I had just promised my parents, I wanted very much for them and for myself. Yet I also wanted it for Charleston. I desired to turn myself into a worthy townsman of such a (75) many-storied city.

Charleston has its own heartbeat and fingerprint, its own mug shots and photo ops and police lineups. It is a city of contrivance,[10] of blueprints; devotion to pattern that is like a bent knee to the nature of beauty itself. I could feel my destiny forming in the leaves high above the (80) city. Like Charleston, I had my alleyways that were dead ends and led to nowhere, but mansions were forming like jewels in my bloodstream. Looking down, I studied the layout of my city, the one that had taught me all the lures of attractiveness, yet made me suspicious of the showy or the makeshift. I turned to the stars and was about to make a bad throw of the (85) dice and try to predict the future, but stopped myself in time.

A boy stopped in time, in a city of amber-colored life, that possessed the glamour forbidden to a lesser angel.

—Pat Conroy
excerpted from *South of Broad*, 2009
Nan A. Talese

[9]languid — without energy
[10]contrivance — invention

Regents ELA (Common Core) Answers June 2016
English Language Arts

Answer Key

Part 1

1. **2**	9. **3**	17. **1**
2. **3**	10. **4**	18. **4**
3. **3**	11. **1**	19. **1**
4. **1**	12. **2**	20. **2**
5. **2**	13. **4**	21. **1**
6. **3**	14. **1**	22. **2**
7. **4**	15. **2**	23. **1**
8. **1**	16. **3**	24. **3**

Regents Examination in English Language Arts (Common Core)—June 2016

Chart for Converting Total Weighted Raw Scores to Final Exam Scores (Scale Scores) (Use for the June 2016 examination only.)

Weighted Raw Score*	Scale Score	Performance Level		Weighted Raw Score*	Scale Score	Performance Level
56	100	5		27	60	2
55	99	5		26	57	2
54	98	5		25	55	2
53	97	5		24	51	1
52	96	5		23	47	1
51	95	5		22	44	1
50	94	5		21	40	1
49	93	5		20	37	1
48	93	5		19	33	1
47	92	5		18	29	1
46	91	5		17	25	1
45	90	5		16	22	1
44	89	5		15	18	1
43	88	5		14	15	1
42	87	5		13	11	1
41	86	5		12	9	1
40	85	5		11	8	1
39	83	4		10	7	1
38	82	4		9	6	1
37	81	4		8	5	1
36	79	4		7	4	1
35	78	3		6	3	1
34	76	3		5	3	1
33	74	3		4	2	1
32	72	3		3	2	1
31	70	3		2	1	1
30	67	3		1	1	1
29	65	3		0	0	1
28	62	2				

The conversion table is determined independently for each administration of the exam.

Answers Explained

PART 1—Reading Comprehension

Multiple-Choice Questions

Passage A

(1) **2** "gloom." Of the choices, this is the best answer: the houses are "sombre," the light of the street lamps is "feeble," the air is biting cold, and the street is silent.

(2) **3** "yet her name was like a summons [to all my foolish blood]." This line concludes the narrator's gradual revelation of his silent attraction to Mangan's sister: he watches for her daily, and when she appears, "my heart leaped." None of the other choices suggests the narrator's feelings.

(3) **3** "disappointment." At line 33 Mangan's sister says that "she would love to go" and explains that she must attend a retreat at her school instead. The images of Mangan's sister turning the bracelet on her arm and bowing her head toward the narrator are also subtle indications of her disappointment. This answer best expresses Mangan's sister's feelings.

(4) **1** "recognized that his priorities have changed." In this passage, the narrator reveals that he no longer cares to do well in school and that he "had hardly any patience with the serious work of life." What he had considered priorities before he now regards as "ugly, monotonous child's play."

(5) **2** "isolation." The narrator takes his seat on the "deserted train" and "remained alone in the bare carriage." These details emphasize how alone the narrator feels on his journey to the bazaar.

(6) **3** "false promise." In this passage, the narrator discovers that there is nothing here for him to buy, the young lady at the stand knows he is not a likely customer, and that his stay "was useless." There is no exotic and romantic world to be found in the bazaar; instead, the narrator finds only tea sets and vases he could not possibly afford or even want to buy for Mangan's sister.

(7) **4** "romantic feelings." Romantic here refers both to the narrator's attraction to Mangan's sister and to the idea of *Araby* (the bazaar) as a distant place of exotic attraction and escape from the gloom of the Dublin neighborhood where they live.

(8) **1** "taunted." Other synonyms for "derided" include "ridiculed," "mocked," and "scorned." The narrator feels foolish and ashamed for acting on his romantic notions. None of the other choices expresses the narrator's feelings here.

(9) **3** "realized his limitations." This phrase best expresses the narrator's feelings. This phrase sums up the narrator's recognition of his foolish and naïve behavior cited in the questions above.

(10) **4** "I lingered before her stall, though I knew my stay was useless." This line also best expresses the theme of the story. Note how the details cited in questions 6–9 lead to the answer to this question.

Passage B

(11) **1** "repetition." The opening line reveals the key metaphor in the poem, but the main idea is strengthened through repetition, notably of "night" and "assembly line." There are no examples of simile, allusion, or understatement in the stanza, and metaphor is not offered as a choice.

(12) **2** "humans and nature." The central idea in the second stanza is that "the stars must be exhausted" by years of unchanging work (journeys) and by choking smog and monotony. In line 17, the poet asserts that "We share" the same exhaustion, sickness, and loss of individuality ("their color and shape"). None of the other choices is suggested by the images in this stanza.

(13) **4** "uncertainty." In lines 20–21, repetition of the phrases beginning with "perhaps" establishes the sense of uncertainty in the poet's voice. There is also a strong feeling of bitterness and regret in the poem, but the question focuses on the language in these two lines: "uncertainty" is the best answer among these choices.

(14) **1** "resignation to life." The images in the last stanza reveal the poet's acceptance of a life that is manufactured and fated: he is numb to his existence and "unable to show concern." None of the other choices is suggested in these lines.

Passage C

(15) **2** "perspective." The first sentence establishes Rodriguez's perspective in this passage: the memory of boyhood will "remind the adult" of how through language he grew out of his protected but linguistically limiting childhood.

(16) **3** "contrasting cultures." In this paragraph, Rodriguez recalls how his parents struggled in the public world of English speakers but could recover, at home, the ease and comfort that speaking their native Spanish gave them. The contrast here is in cultures, not in memories, principles, or philosophies.

(17) **1** "eagerness to learn." "Wide-eyed with hearing" is a lovely metaphor to describe how eager Rodriguez was to distinguish first the differences in sound between English and Spanish and to understand how the sounds of a language conveyed meaning even before he knew the words. The image of one who is wide-eyed conveys a sense of wonder and openness to take in something new.

(18) **4** "separation." This paragraph further develops the contrast between the comfort and cultural ease of life at home and the challenges of interactions in the public, English-speaking world. How Rodriguez overcame this "separation" is the key theme of the passage.

(19) **1** "communicate effectively." These lines are a vivid description of what it is like to try to communicate before one has sufficient language skills:

he could not "form complete thoughts ... make distinct [English] sounds"; and listeners struggled to hear what he was trying to say. This is the best answer among the choices.

(20) **2** "conflicting feelings." The narrator claims at first that "it didn't matter much that my parents could not speak English with ease." "And yet ... it mattered very much" because he found it unsettling and became nervous about a loss in their "protection and power."

(21) **1** "narrator's sense of security." In this paragraph, Rodriguez describes the reassurance he would feel in hearing the sounds of the language of their life in private: he feels "recognized as one of the family ... *someone special*." He felt "embraced by the sounds of their words." These are all feelings of security. None of the other choices expresses the feelings in this paragraph.

(22) **2** "I'd listen to sounds more than to words." Throughout the passage, Rodriguez emphasizes the importance of sounds as he grows up and ultimately learns to speak fluent English. It is the sounds of Spanish that console and reassure him; it is the sounds of English in public that signal a different culture. He tells us toward the end of the passage that, " I lived in a world compounded of sounds." This is the best answer to the question.

(23) **1** "disconnected from his family." In the final paragraph, Rodriguez describes the change, the loss, of "intimate sounds" at home: now the sounds are noises from life outside. He is hearing words, the words of public language. The disconnection from his family occurs as "my childhood started to end."

(24) **3** "confidence." The act of raising his hand in class and speaking loudly, "to an entire roomful of faces," is a vivid image of the boy confident in expressing himself in the public world of English. None of the other choices captures the significance of what Rodriguez tells us here.

PART 2—Argument Response

Sample Essay Response

In recent years especially, there has been growing concern for conditions in third-world societies and the welfare of their people. Numerous non-profit organizations have been established to address the humanitarian issues in said societies through fundraising and charity. However, these organizations must grab people's attention to raise what they need to help other people in needy situations. What better way to do that than to use celebrities to promote the cause? There is a debate regarding the ethics of using celebrities to promote non-profit organizations, however. While some may believe that celebrities should not be the voice for humanitarian causes, I emphatically believe that celebrities should become the voice of such causes for two compelling reasons.

First, I believe that celebrities should be the voice of humanitarian causes because they can be actively involved by donating their money and their time. According to "The Celebrity Solution," "the premise of microfinance is that very poor people should have access to credit, just as the middle class and the rich do." (Text 1, lines 50–51) The article states that the support of microfinance projects by the actress Natalie Portman means poor people will benefit immensely.

"People come to see Natalie Portman, and they go away learning about microfinance." (Text 1, lines 73–74) According to the article "Do Celebrity Humanitarians Matter?" "celebrities are welcome figures in humanitarianism: educating the public on global issues, raising funds, and using their populist appeal to draw attention to policy-making arenas." (Text 3, lines 39–41) Basically the article is stating that celebrities can be directly involved in promoting and being dedicated to their causes by educating the public and raising money through concerts or other events.

However, "Do Celebrity Humanitarians Matter?" also claims that "For others, celebrity humanitarians are highly problematic figures who dilute debates, offer misguided policy proposals, and lack credibility and accountability." (Text 3, lines 41–43) I disagree with the previous statement because I believe celebrities can easily become educated themselves about a cause through their own research.

Secondly, celebrities have the ability to use their popularity to draw attention to a humanitarian cause. As "The Rise of the Celebrity Humanitarian" puts it, "Hollywood's elite get to wield their unique ability to engage diverse audiences, and the power of celebrity is put to good use effecting change." (Text 4, lines 9–11) Basically the article states that celebrities can influence change by using their popularity. With the use of social media on the rise, celebrities have a powerful means of connecting with the people to promote a cause. According to "Ethics of Celebrities and Their Increasing Influence in 21st Century Society," "[c]elebrities and famous people in turn, help to bring people, including adults, together in conversation and social interaction." (Text 2, lines 46–48) This means that through the use of the Internet, celebrities can get the pub-

lic involved in their cause. However, Text 4 also argues, "if the star's popularity takes a hit, it can affect the reception of the cause." (Text 4, lines 23–24) Although this has been known to happen, in the case of Lance Armstrong for example, humanitarian causes can recover from their celebrity spokesperson's decline in popularity and find a new voice for the cause.

I emphatically believe that celebrities should be the voice for humanitarian causes. Celebrities have an uncanny ability to draw attention to a cause, which in turn would undoubtedly benefit those in need.

Analysis

This essay offers a good example of the argument supporting the role of celebrities in humanitarian causes. The opening paragraph outlines the issue and clearly establishes the writer's position: first, with a rhetorical question, "What better way … than to use celebrities to promote the cause?" and then with a forceful assertion of the controlling idea: "I emphatically believe that celebrities should become the voice of such causes for two compelling reasons." The reference to a debate over the ethics of using celebrities for humanitarian causes at the beginning establishes that opposing views will be acknowledged.

The argument is organized clearly, with a paragraph devoted to each of the writer's claims. Key points are developed and supported with relevant references to all four texts: some give support to the writer's point of view and some offer opportunities to refute opposing arguments. Development is minimal but adequate; the conclusion is less forcefully expressed than the body of the argument is. The overall strategy of argument is sound, however, and the writer demonstrates control of the conventions. This argument would merit a high score.

(See pages 80–81 for the scoring guidelines.)

PART 3—Text-Analysis Response

Sample Essay Response

In this passage, the author depicts Charleston, South Carolina, as an understated and beautiful place where anything is possible. The author feels that Charleston has the power to shape people and have an ever-lasting influence on their lives. This idea of Charleston's power is developed through the author's use of figurative language.

The author is in awe of Charleston's beauty and subtle power. In lines 27–28, imagery is used when Charleston's gardens are described as containing "plants that look embroidered and stolen from the Garden of Eden." This description emphasizes how delicate and cared for Charleston is because embroidery involves delicate and intricate work. Also, by comparing something in Charleston to the Garden of Eden, it is elevated and placed on a holy level. Additionally, the author uses metaphor on lines 48–49 when he states that "Charleston is a permanent dimple in the understated skyline, while the rest of us are only visitors." This emphasizes Charleston's permanence and subtle power. While people may come and go, Charleston is forever. Lastly, Charleston is personified at line 76 when it is given "its own heartbeat and fingerprint."

By giving Charleston life-like qualities, the author dramatizes the city's power. Charleston is elevated by being compared to a human. The author feels blessed and honored to have grown up in a place like Charleston, and this passage shows its significant and omnipresent force in his life.

Analysis

This richness of language and passionate feelings of the author give students a number of ways to discuss this passage. Point of view is an obvious choice, as are diction, tone, and theme. This writer chose figurative language as a focus for analysis and offers excellent examples of imagery, metaphor, and personification. The essay has a clear plan of development: the opening paragraph expresses the overall theme of the passage and establishes the writer's controlling idea. The second paragraph offers three relevant examples of figurative language, and each is illustrated with an appropriate quote from the passage. Note too that the examples are developed in order of their significance to the overall theme. The final paragraph is a strong statement of how the figurative language supports the author's theme. The writing is clear and demonstrates the writer's control of the conventions. This response would merit a high score.

(See pages 82–83 for the scoring guidelines.)

Regents ELA (Common Core) Examination August 2016
English Language Arts

PART 1—Reading Comprehension

Directions (1–24): Closely read each of the three passages below. After each passage, there are several multiple-choice questions. Select the best suggested answer to each question and write its number in the space provided. You may use the margins to take notes as you read.

Reading Comprehension Passage A

    …Three years in London had not changed Richard, although it had changed the way he perceived the city. Richard had originally imagined London as a gray city, even a black city, from pictures he had seen, and he was surprised to find it filled with color. It was a city of red brick and
(5) white stone, red buses and large black taxis, bright red mailboxes and green grassy parks and cemeteries. …

    Two thousand years before, London had been a little Celtic village on the north shore of the Thames, which the Romans had encountered, then settled in. London had grown, slowly, until, roughly a thousand years
(10) later, it met the tiny Royal City of Westminster immediately to the west, and, once London Bridge had been built, London touched the town of Southwark directly across the river; and it continued to grow, fields and woods and marshland slowly vanishing beneath the flourishing town, and it continued to expand, encountering other little villages and hamlets as

(15)   it grew, like Whitechapel and Deptford to the east, Hammersmith and Shepherd's Bush to the west, Camden and Islington in the north, Battersea and Lambeth across the Thames to the south, absorbing all of them, just as a pool of mercury encounters and incorporates smaller beads of mercury, leaving only their names behind.

(20)   London grew into something huge and contradictory. It was a good place, and a fine city, but there is a price to be paid for all good places, and a price that all good places have to pay.

   After a while, Richard found himself taking London for granted; in time, he began to pride himself on having visited none of the sights of *(25)* London (except for the Tower of London, when his Aunt Maude came down to the city for a weekend, and Richard found himself her reluctant escort).

   But Jessica changed all that. Richard found himself, on otherwise sensible weekends, accompanying her to places like the National Gallery *(30)* and the Tate Gallery, where he learned that walking around museums too long hurts your feet, that the great art treasures of the world all blur into each other after a while, and that it is almost beyond the human capacity for belief to accept how much museum cafeterias will brazenly charge for a slice of cake and a cup of tea. …

(35)   Richard had been awed by Jessica, who was beautiful, and often quite funny, and was certainly going somewhere. And Jessica saw in Richard an enormous amount of potential, which, properly harnessed by the right woman, would have made him the perfect matrimonial accessory. If only he were a little more focused, she would murmur to herself, and so *(40)* she gave him books with titles like *Dress for Success* and *A Hundred and Twenty-Five Habits of Successful Men*, and books on how to run a business like a military campaign, and Richard always said thank you, and always intended to read them. In Harvey Nichols's men's fashion department she would pick out for him the kinds of clothes she thought that he should *(45)* wear—and he wore them, during the week, anyway; and, a year to the day after their first encounter, she told him she thought it was time that they went shopping for an engagement ring.

   "Why do you go out with her?" asked Gary, in Corporate Accounts, eighteen months later. "She's terrifying."

(50)   Richard shook his head. "She's really sweet, once you get to know her."

Gary put down the plastic troll doll he had picked up from Richard's desk. "I'm surprised she still lets you play with these." ...

It was a Friday afternoon. Richard had noticed that events were cow-
(55) ards: they didn't occur singly, but instead they would run in packs and leap out at him all at once. Take this particular Friday, for example. It was, as Jessica had pointed out to him at least a dozen times in the last month, the most important day of his life. So it was unfortunate that, despite the Post-it note Richard had left on his fridge door at home, and
(60) the other Post-it note he had placed on the photograph of Jessica on his desk, he had forgotten about it completely and utterly.

Also, there was the Wandsworth report, which was overdue and tak-ing up most of his head. Richard checked another row of figures; then he noticed that page 17 had vanished, and he set it up to print out again; and
(65) another page down, and he knew that if he were only left alone to finish it...if, miracle of miracles, the phone did not ring....It rang. He thumbed the speakerphone.

"Hello? Richard? The managing director needs to know when he'll have the report."
(70) Richard looked at his watch. "Five minutes, Sylvia. It's almost wrapped up. I just have to attach the P & L projection."

"Thanks, Dick. I'll come down for it." Sylvia was, as she liked to explain, "the MD's PA," [Managing Director's Personal Assistant] and she moved in an atmosphere of crisp efficiency. He thumbed the speaker-
(75) phone off; it rang again, immediately. "Richard," said the speaker, with Jessica's voice, "it's Jessica. You haven't forgotten, have you?"

"Forgotten?" He tried to remember what he could have forgotten. He looked at Jessica's photograph for inspiration and found all the inspira-tion he could have needed in the shape of a yellow Post-it note stuck to her
(80) forehead.

"Richard? Pick up the telephone."

He picked up the phone, reading the Post-it note as he did so. "Sorry, Jess. No, I hadn't forgotten. Seven P.M., at Ma Maison Italiano. Should I meet you there?"
(85) "Jessica, Richard. Not Jess." She paused for a moment. "After what happened last time? I don't think so. You really could get lost in your own backyard, Richard." ...

"I'll meet you at your place," said Jessica. "We can walk down together."

(90)   "Right, Jess. Jessica—sorry."

"You *have* confirmed our reservation, haven't you, Richard."

"Yes," lied Richard earnestly. The other line on his phone had begun to ring. "Jessica, look, I…"

"Good," said Jessica, and she broke the connection. He picked up the
(95) other line.

"Hi Dick. It's me, Gary." Gary sat a few desks down from Richard. He waved. "Are we still on for drinks? You said we could go over the Merstham account."

"Get off the bloody phone, Gary. Of course we are." Richard put down
(100) the phone. There was a telephone number at the bottom of the Post-it note; Richard had written the Post-it note to himself, several weeks earlier. And he *had* made the reservation: he was almost certain of that. But he had not confirmed it. He had kept meaning to, but there had been so much to do and Richard had known that there was plenty of time. But
(105) events run in packs…

Sylvia was now standing next to him. "Dick? The Wandsworth report?"

"Almost ready, Sylvia. Look, just hold on a sec, can you?"

He finished punching in the number, breathed a sigh of relief when
(110) somebody answered. "Ma Maison. Can I help you?"

"Yes," said Richard. "A table for three, for tonight. I think I booked it. And if I did I'm confirming the reservation. And if I didn't, I wondered if I could book it. Please." No, they had no record of a table for tonight in the name of Mayhew. Or Stockton. Or Bartram—Jessica's surname. And
(115) as for booking a table…

They had put down the phone.

"Richard?" said Sylvia. "The MD's waiting."

"Do you think," asked Richard, "they'd give me a table if I phoned back and offered them extra money?" …

—Neil Gaiman
excerpted and adapted from *Neverwhere*, 1997
Avon Books

1 The author most likely includes the description of London in lines 1 through 22 to

- (1) provide reasons for Richard's dislike of the city
- (2) highlight opportunities for Richard's career in the city
- (3) convey a sense of Richard's frustration with the city
- (4) illustrate the nature of Richard's life in the city   1____

2 The figurative language used in lines 17 to 19 reinforces the

- (1) growth of the city
- (2) problems with development
- (3) increase in isolation
- (4) history of the towns   2____

3 The narrator uses lines 28 through 34 to help the reader understand Richard's

- (1) continuous efforts to save money while on dates
- (2) willingness to tolerate undesirable situations to please others
- (3) overall acceptance of cultural experiences in the city
- (4) affection for newfound experiences when shared with others   3____

4 In the context of the text as a whole, which statement regarding lines 48 through 51 is true?

  (1) Gary is jealous of Richard because he has a girlfriend.

  (2) Gary has a moody temperament and hides his feelings.

  (3) Richard has a plan and wishes to keep it a secret.

  (4) Richard is in a state of denial regarding his relationship.   4____

5 How do lines 54 to 56 contribute to the characterization of Richard?

  (1) by portraying him as inefficient at organizing his time

  (2) by indicating that he works well under pressure

  (3) by describing him as likely to succeed

  (4) by suggesting that he is unmotivated in his job   5____

6 The narrator's description of Sylvia as moving "in an atmosphere of crisp efficiency" (line 74) presents a

  (1) shift   (3) contrast

  (2) possibility   (4) solution   6____

7 Lines 81 through 87 contribute to a central idea by highlighting Jessica's

  (1) domineering nature

  (2) compassionate side

  (3) lack of responsibility

  (4) sense of humor   7____

8 The narrator's use of dialogue in lines 81 through 99 enhances a mood of

   (1) satisfaction   (3) confidence

   (2) stress   (4) remorse   8_____

9 Richard's question in lines 118 and 119 reveals his

   (1) subtle refinement

   (2) suppressed hostility

   (3) honest gratitude

   (4) quiet desperation   9_____

10 Which quote best reflects a central theme in the text?

   (1) "London grew into something huge and contradictory ... and a price that all good places have to pay." (lines 20 through 22)

   (2) "Richard checked another row of figures ... and he set it up to print out again;" (lines 63 and 64)

   (3) "Richard looked at his watch. 'Five minutes, Sylvia. It's almost wrapped up. I just have to attach the P & L projection.' " (lines 70 and 71)

   (4) "He finished punching in the number, breathed a sigh of relief when somebody answered. 'Ma Maison. Can I help you?' " (lines 109 and 110)   10_____

Reading Comprehension Passage B

We Are Many

Of the many men whom I am, whom we are,
I cannot settle on a single one.
They are lost to me under the cover of clothing.
They have departed for another city.

(5)   When everything seems to be set
to show me off as a man of intelligence,
the fool I keep concealed on my person
takes over my talk and occupies my mouth.

On other occasions, I am dozing in the midst
(10)   of people of some distinction,
and when I summon my courageous self,
a coward completely unknown to me
swaddles[1] my poor skeleton
in a thousand tiny reservations.

(15)   When a stately home bursts into flames,
instead of the fireman I summon,
an arsonist bursts on the scene,
and he is I. There is nothing I can do.
What must I do to distinguish myself?
(20)   How can I put myself together?

All the books I read
lionize[2] dazzling hero figures,
always brimming with self-assurance.
I die with envy of them;
(25)   and, in films where bullets fly on the wind,
I am left in envy of the cowboys,
left admiring even the horses.

---

[1]swaddles—wraps
[2]lionize—glorify

But when I call upon my dashing being,
out comes the same old lazy self,
(30)   and so I never know just who I am,
nor how many I am, nor who we will be being.
I would like to be able to touch a bell
and call up my real self, the truly me,
because if I really need my proper self,
(35)   I must not allow myself to disappear.

While I am writing, I am far away;
and when I come back, I have already left.
I should like to see if the same thing happens
to other people as it does to me,
(40)   to see if as many people are as I am,
and if they seem the same way to themselves.
When this problem has been thoroughly explored,
I am going to school myself so well in things
that, when I try to explain my problems,
(45)   I shall speak, not of self, but of geography.

—Pablo Neruda
from *We Are Many*, 1970
translated by Alastair Reid
Grossman Publishers

11 The overall purpose of the figurative language in lines 12 through 14 is to show the narrator's

    (1)   contempt for self-reliance
    (2)   desire for adventure
    (3)   lack of self-confidence
    (4)   jealousy of writers   11_____

12 A primary function of the questions in lines 19 and 20 is to

    (1)   introduce the narrator's biases
    (2)   challenge the narrator's beliefs
    (3)   clarify the narrator's dilemma
    (4)   explain the narrator's decision   12_____

13 The contradictions presented throughout the poem serve to illustrate the relationship between

    (1)   society's conflicts and the narrator's reaction
    (2)   the narrator's sensibilities and his determination
    (3)   society's expectations and the narrator's possibilities
    (4)   the narrator's idealism and his reality   13_____

14 The solution proposed in lines 42 through 45 can best be described as

    (1)   balanced
    (2)   universal
    (3)   inappropriate
    (4)   unrealistic   14_____

Reading Comprehension Passage C

...By natural design, dogs' ears have evolved to hear certain kinds of sounds. Happily, that set of sounds overlaps with those we can hear and produce: if we utter it, it will at least hit the eardrum of a nearby dog. Our auditory range is from 20 hertz to 20 kilohertz: from the lowest pitch on
(5) the longest organ pipe to an impossibly squeaky squeak. We spend most of our time straining to understand sounds between 100 hertz and 1 kilohertz, the range of any interesting speech going on in the vicinity. Dogs hear most of what we hear and then some. They can detect sounds up to 45 kilohertz, much higher than the hair cells of our ears bother to bend to.
(10) Hence the power of the dog whistle, a seemingly magical device that makes no apparent sound and yet perks the ears of dogs for blocks around. We call this sound "ultrasonic," since it's beyond our ken,[1] but it is within the sonic range for many animals in our local environment. Don't think for a moment that apart from the occasional dog whistle, the world is quiet for
(15) dogs up at those high registers. Even a typical room is pulsing with high frequencies, detectable by dogs constantly. Think your bedroom is quiet when you rise in the morning? The crystal resonator used in digital alarm clocks emits a never-ending alarm of high-frequency pulses audible to canine ears. Dogs can hear the navigational chirping of rats behind your
(20) walls and the bodily vibrations of termites within your walls. That compact fluorescent light you installed to save energy? You may not hear the hum, but your dog probably can.

The range of pitches we are most intent on are those used in speech. Dogs hear all sounds of speech, and are nearly as good as we are at detect-
(25) ing a change of pitch—relevant, say, for understanding statements, which end in a low pitch, versus questions, which in English end in a raised pitch: "Do you want to go for a walk(?)" With the question mark, this sentence is exciting to a dog with experience going on walks with humans. Without it, it is simply noise. Imagine the confusion generated
(30) by the recent growth of "up-talking," speech that ends every sentence with the sound of a question?

If dogs understand the stress and tones—the *prosody*—of speech, does this hint that they understand language? This is a natural but vexed[2] ques-

---

[1]ken—recognition
[2]vexed—problematic

tion. Since language use is one of the most glaring differences between the
(35) human animal and all other animals, it has been proposed as the ultimate,
incomparable criterion for intelligence. This raises serious hackles[3] in
some animal researchers (not thought of as a hackled species, ironically),
who have set about trying to demonstrate what linguistic ability animals
have. Even those researchers who may agree that language is necessary for
(40) intelligence have nonetheless added reams of results to the growing pile
of evidence of linguistic ability in non-human animals. All parties agree,
though, that there has been no discovery of a humanlike language—a
corpus[4] of infinitely combinable words that often carry many definitions,
with rules for combining words into meaningful sentences—in animals.

(45)   This is not to say that animals might not understand some of our language use, even if they don't produce it themselves. There are, for instance,
many examples of animals taking advantage of the communicative system
of nearby unrelated animal species. Monkeys can make use of nearby birds'
warning calls of a nearby predator to themselves take protective action.
(50) Even an animal who deceives another animal by mimicry—which some
snakes, moths, and even flies can do—is in some way using another species's [*sic*] language.

The research with dogs suggests that they do understand language—to
a limited degree. On the one hand, to say that dogs understand *words* is a
(55) misnomer. Words exist in a language, which itself is product of a culture;
dogs are participants in that culture on a very different level. Their framework for understanding the application of the word is entirely different.
There is, no doubt, more to the words of their world than Gary Larson's
Far Side comics suggest: eat, walk, and fetch. But he is on to something,
(60) insofar as these are organizing elements of their interaction with us: we
circumscribe the dog's world to a small set of activities. Working dogs
seem miraculously responsive and focused compared to city pets. It is not
that they are innately more responsive or focused, but that their owners
have added to their vocabularies types of things to do.

(65)   One component in understanding a word is the ability to discriminate
it from other words. Given their sensitivity to the prosody of speech,
dogs do not always excel at this. Try asking your dog on one morning

---

[3]raises serious hackles—arouses anger
[4]corpus—collection

to *go for a walk*; on the next, ask if your dog wants to *snow forty locks* in
the same voice. If everything else remains the same, you'll probably get
(70) the same, affirmative reaction. The very first sounds of an utterance seem
to be important to dog perception, though, so changing the swallowed
consonants for articulated ones and the long vowels for short ones—*ma
for a polk?*—might prompt the confusion merited by this gibberish. Of
course humans read meaning into prosody, too. English does not give the
(75) prosody of speech syntactical leverage but it is still part of how we interpret "what has just been said."

If we were more sensitive to the *sound* of what we say to dogs, we might
get better responses from them. High-pitched sounds mean something
different than low sounds; rising sounds contrast with falling sounds.
(80) It is not accidental that we find ourselves cooing to an infant in silly,
giddy tones (called *motherese*)—and might greet a wagging dog with
similar baby talk. Infants can hear other speech sounds, but they are more
interested in motherese. Dogs, too, respond with alacrity[5] to baby talk—
partially because it distinguishes speech that is directed *at* them from the
(85) rest of the continuous yammering above their heads. Moreover, they will
come more easily to high-pitched and repeated call requests than to those
at a lower pitch. What is the ecology behind this? High-pitched sounds
are naturally interesting to dogs: they might indicate the excitement of a
tussle or the shrieking of nearby injured prey. If a dog fails to respond to
(90) your reasonable suggestion that he come *right now*, resist the urge to lower
and sharpen your tone. It indicates your frame of mind—and the punish-
ment that might ensue for his prior uncooperativeness. Correspondingly,
it is easier to get a dog to *sit* on command to a longer, descending tone
rather than repeated, rising notes. Such a tone might be more likely to
(95) induce relaxation, or preparation for the next command from their talky
human. ...

—Alexandra Horowitz
excerpted from *Inside of a Dog*, 2010
Scribner

---

[5]alacrity—eagerness

15 Lines 1 through 13 introduce the central idea of the passage by

   (1) explaining how ear structure affects sound
   (2) describing various frequencies dogs hear
   (3) explaining various ways humans hear
   (4) describing how dog whistle tones differ   15____

16 Lines 23 through 27 best support the idea that

   (1) dogs cannot learn to obey human signals
   (2) human actions are difficult for dogs to interpret
   (3) humans can verbally communicate with dogs
   (4) dogs can learn complex human language   16____

17 Based on lines 23 through 31, humans can possibly confuse dogs by

   (1) speaking to dogs in a nonsense language
   (2) giving dogs only direct commands
   (3) making gestures when speaking to dogs
   (4) altering the intonation of familiar words   17____

18 Lines 32 through 36 illustrate that language use is an indicator of

   (1) higher-level thinking
   (2) basic survival instinct
   (3) increased emotional response
   (4) problem-solving skills   18____

19 In lines 41 through 44, the author states there is agreement that non-human animals cannot

   (1) master complicated directions
   (2) duplicate human sound pitches
   (3) create human sentence structures
   (4) interpret foreign languages   19____

20 The primary function of the examples in lines 46 through 52 is to show how some animals can

    (1) imitate behavior and sound
    (2) foster community and diversity
    (3) transform from prey to predator
    (4) compromise freedom for safety   20_____

21 The author uses the term "gibberish" in line 73 to emphasize the

    (1) importance of word order
    (2) complexity of spoken sounds
    (3) relevance of hidden gestures
    (4) necessity of voice and movement   21_____

22 Which sentence best restates a central idea in lines 70 through 79?

    (1) High-pitched sounds often cause dogs to become agitated.
    (2) How we speak to dogs is more important than what we say.
    (3) Dogs must learn to interpret human speech early in life.
    (4) Dogs become distressed when they hear baby talk.   22_____

23 The author's reference to "motherese" (line 81) helps to illustrate a connection between the

    (1) combinations of languages and the effects on listeners
    (2) volume of speech and possible misperception
    (3) importance of word choice and its impact on understanding
    (4) styles of spoken communication and likely responses   23_____

24 The primary purpose of the text is to

   (1)   explain a popular myth regarding dogs' behavior

   (2)   promote a new method for working with dogs

   (3)   educate people about dogs' experience with sound

   (4)   present an alternative to traditional dog training   24____

PART 2—Argument Response

Directions: Closely read each of the *four* texts on pages 297 through 306 and write a source-based argument on the topic below. You may use the margins to take notes as you read and scrap paper to plan your response. Write your argument on a separate sheet of paper.

Topic: Should the United States government create strict sugar regulations?

Your Task: Carefully read each of the *four* texts provided. Then, using evidence from at least *three* of the texts, write a well-developed argument regarding whether or not the United States government should create strict sugar regulations. Clearly establish your claim, distinguish your claim from alternate or opposing claims, and use specific, relevant, and sufficient evidence from at least *three* of the texts to develop your argument. Do *not* simply summarize each text.

Guidelines:

Be sure to

- Establish your claim regarding whether or not the United States government should create strict sugar regulations
- Distinguish your claim from alternate or opposing claims
- Use specific, relevant, and sufficient evidence from at least *three* of the texts to develop your argument
- Identify each source that you reference by text number and line number(s) or graphic (for example: Text 1, line 4 or Text 2, graphic)
- Organize your ideas in a cohesive and coherent manner
- Maintain a formal style of writing
- Follow the conventions of standard written English

Texts:

Text 1—FDA Urged to Regulate Sugar in Drinks

Text 2—Sugar Should Be Regulated As Toxin, Researchers Say

Text 3—The Toxic Truth About Sugar

Text 4—Sugar Taxes Are Unfair and Unhealthy

Text 1

FDA Urged to Regulate Sugar in Drinks

WASHINGTON—The US Food and Drug Administration [FDA] should regulate the amount of added sugars in soda and other sweetened beverages to reverse the obesity epidemic, a Washington-based nutrition activist group urged in a petition signed by Harvard School of Public
(5) Health researchers, the Boston Public Health Commission, and others.

"The FDA considers sugar to be a safe food at the recommended level of consumption, but Americans are consuming two to three times that much," Michael Jacobson, executive director of the Center for Science in the Public Interest, which filed the petition, said at a press briefing on
(10) Wednesday. He added that the average American consumes 78 pounds of added sugars each year, mostly from high fructose corn syrup prevalent in sugary sodas, sports drinks, and fruit punch. ...

Over the past half-century, Americans have dramatically increased their intake of sugary drinks, and research suggests this has contributed to
(15) the obesity epidemic and a rise in related diseases such as type 2 diabetes, heart disease, and a variety of cancers.

"The evidence is very robust that when we eat more sugar we gain weight and when we eat less, we lose weight," said Dr. Walter Willett, chairman of nutrition at the Harvard School of Public Health, who
(20) also spoke at the briefing. "Each 12-ounce serving of soda a person consumes each day raises type 2 diabetes risk by 10 to 15 percent, and many Americans are consuming five or six servings."

While the FDA has the authority to set limits on ingredients on its "generally recognized as safe" list, it has not done so for many of them,
(25) including table sugar and high fructose corn syrup.

Jeffrey Senger, former acting chief counsel of the FDA who is now a partner at the law firm Sidley Austin, said it is unlikely the agency would act to restrict sugar. "Any food, if it's abused, can be unhealthy," he said. "Sugar isn't the same thing as arsenic. It's not a food that's inherently
(30) unsafe." ...

She [FDA spokeswoman, Shelly Burgess] confirmed that the latest petition was received and would be reviewed by FDA officials, but added that the FDA was not aware of any evidence highlighting added safety risks from high fructose corn syrup compared with other sugars such as honey,
(35)   table sugar, or molasses.

That suggests that the agency might have a hard time requiring Coke or Pepsi to limit their products to 10 grams of added sugar per serving—what many public health specialists recommend—without also requiring the same limits on cereal, baked goods, and other processed foods.

(40)   "To limit the amount of added sugars in beverages, the FDA would need to establish that there is enough scientific evidence to justify limiting these ingredients and to go through a rulemaking process that allows for public comment," said Miriam Guggenheim, a partner in the food and beverage practice at Covington & Burling LLP in Washington, D.C.

(45)   Taking a firm position against government regulations to limit added sugars, the American Beverage Association, which represents soft drink manufacturers, pointed out in a statement on its website that companies have already made efforts to reduce sugar in sweetened beverages.

"Today about 45 percent of all non-alcoholic beverages purchased have
(50)   zero calories," the group said, "and the overall average number of calories per beverage serving is down 23 percent since 1998." ...

About half of Americans consume sugary beverages on any given day, according to the latest data from the federal Centers for Disease Control and Prevention, and consumption of sugary beverages has increased
(55)   among children and adults over the past 30 years.

—Deborah Kotz
excerpted and adapted from "FDA Urged to Regulate Sugar in Drinks"
http://www.bostonglobe.com, February 14, 2013

Text 2

Sugar Should Be Regulated As Toxin, Researchers Say

A spoonful of sugar might make the medicine go down. But it also makes blood pressure and cholesterol go up, along with your risk for liver failure, obesity, heart disease and diabetes.

(5) Sugar and other sweeteners are, in fact, so toxic to the human body that they should be regulated as strictly as alcohol by governments worldwide, according to a commentary in the current issue of the journal Nature by researchers at the University of California, San Francisco (UCSF).

(10) The researchers propose regulations such as taxing all foods and drinks that include added sugar, banning sales in or near schools and placing age limits on purchases.

Although the commentary might seem straight out of the Journal of Ideas That Will Never Fly, the researchers cite numerous studies and statistics to make their case that added sugar—or, more specifically, sucrose, (15) an even mix of glucose and fructose found in high-fructose corn syrup and in table sugar made from sugar cane and sugar beets—has been as detrimental to society as alcohol and tobacco.

Sour words about sugar

…Many researchers are seeing sugar as not just "empty calories," but rather a chemical that becomes toxic in excess. At issue is the fact (20) that glucose from complex carbohydrates, such as whole grains, is safely metabolized by cells throughout the body, but the fructose element of sugar is metabolized primarily by the liver. This is where the trouble can begin—taxing the liver, causing fatty liver disease, and ultimately leading to insulin resistance, the underlying causes of obesity and diabetes.

(25) Added sugar, more so than the fructose in fiber-rich fruit, hits the liver more directly and can cause more damage—in laboratory rodents, anyway. Some researchers, however, remained unconvinced of the evidence of sugar's toxic effect on the human body at current consumption levels, as high as they are.

Economists to the rescue

(30)   [Robert] Lustig, a medical doctor in UCSF's Department of Pediatrics, compares added sugar to tobacco and alcohol (coincidentally made from sugar) in that it is addictive, toxic and has a negative impact on society, thus meeting established public health criteria for regulation. Lustig advocates a consumer tax on any product with added sugar.

(35)   Among Lustig's more radical proposals are to ban the sale of sugary drinks to children under age 17 and to tighten zoning laws for the sale of sugary beverages and snacks around schools and in low-income areas plagued by obesity, analogous to alcoholism and alcohol regulation.

     Economists, however, debate as to whether a consumer tax—such as *(40)* a soda tax proposed in many U.S. states—is the most effective means of curbing sugar consumption. Economists at Iowa State University led by John Beghin suggest taxing the sweetener itself at the manufacturer level, not the end product containing sugar.

     This concept, published last year in the journal Contemporary *(45)* Economic Policy, would give companies an incentive to add less sweetener to their products. After all, high-fructose corn syrup is ubiquitous[1] in food in part because it is so cheap and serves as a convenient substitute for more high-quality ingredients, such as fresher vegetables in processed foods.

(50)   Some researchers argue that saturated fat, not sugar, is the root cause of obesity and chronic disease. Others argue that it is highly processed foods with simple carbohydrates. Still others argue that it is a lack of physical exercise. It could, of course, be a matter of all these issues.

—Christopher Wanjek
excerpted and adapted from "Sugar Should Be Regulated As Toxin, Researchers Say"
http://www.livescience.com, February 1, 2012

---

[1]ubiquitous — present everywhere

Text 3

The Toxic Truth About Sugar

...No Ordinary Commodity

In 2003, social psychologist Thomas Babor and his colleagues published a landmark book called *Alcohol: No Ordinary Commodity*, in which they established four criteria, now largely accepted by the public-health community, that justify the regulation of alcohol—unavoidability (or
(5) pervasiveness throughout society), toxicity, potential for abuse and negative impact on society. Sugar meets the same criteria, and we believe that it similarly warrants some form of societal intervention.

First, consider unavoidability. Evolutionarily, sugar as fruit was available to our ancestors for only a few months a year (at harvest time), or
(10) as honey, which was guarded by bees. But in recent years, sugar has been added to virtually every processed food, limiting consumer choice. Nature made sugar hard to get; man made it easy. In many parts of the world, people are consuming an average of more than 500 calories per day from added sugar alone.

(15) Now, let's consider toxicity. A growing body of epidemiological and mechanistic[1] evidence argues that excessive sugar consumption affects human health beyond simply adding calories. Importantly, sugar induces all of the diseases associated with metabolic syndrome. This includes: hypertension (fructose increases uric acid, which raises blood pressure);
(20) high triglycerides and insulin resistance through synthesis of fat in the liver; diabetes from increased liver glucose production combined with insulin resistance; and the ageing process, caused by damage to lipids, proteins and DNA [deoxyribonucleic acid] through non-enzymatic binding of fructose to these molecules. It can also be argued that fructose exerts toxic
(25) effects on the liver similar to those of alcohol. This is no surprise, because alcohol is derived from the fermentation of sugar. Some early studies have also linked sugar consumption to human cancer and cognitive decline.

Sugar also has a clear potential for abuse. Like tobacco and alcohol, it acts on the brain to encourage subsequent intake. There are now numer-

---

[1]epidemiological and mechanistic—evidence based on the study of the causes, incidence, and treatment of diseases

(30)   ous studies examining the dependence-producing properties of sugar in humans. Specifically, sugar dampens the suppression of the hormone ghrelin, which signals hunger to the brain. It also interferes with the normal transport and signalling of the hormone leptin, which helps to produce the feeling of satiety.[2] And it reduces dopamine signalling in the brain's

(35)   reward centre, thereby decreasing the pleasure derived from food and compelling the individual to consume more.

Finally, consider the negative effects of sugar on society. Passive smoking and drink-driving fatalities provided strong arguments for tobacco and alcohol control, respectively. The long-term economic,

(40)   health-care and human costs of metabolic syndrome place sugar overconsumption in the same category. The United States spends $65 billion in lost productivity and $150 billion on health-care resources annually for co-morbidities[3] associated with metabolic syndrome. Seventy-five per cent of all US health-care dollars are now spent on treating these diseases

(45)   and resultant disabilities. Because 75% of military applicants are now rejected for obesity-related reasons, the past three US surgeons general and the chairman of the US Joint Chiefs of Staff have declared obesity a "threat to national security."

How to Intervene

How can we reduce sugar consumption? After all, sugar is natural.

(50)   Sugar is a nutrient. Sugar is pleasure. So is alcohol, but in both cases, too much of a good thing is toxic. It may be helpful to look to the many generations of international experience with alcohol and tobacco to find models that work. So far, evidence shows that individually focused approaches, such as school-based interventions that teach children about

(55)   diet and exercise, demonstrate little efficacy.[4] Conversely, for both alcohol and tobacco, there is robust evidence that gentle 'supply side' control strategies which stop far short of all-out prohibition—taxation, distribution controls, age limits—lower both consumption of the product and accompanying health harms. Successful interventions all share a common

(60)   end-point: curbing availability. ...

---

[2]satiety—fullness

[3]co-morbidities—diseases that occur simultaneously

[4]efficacy—power to produce an effect

DEADLY EFFECT Excessive consumption of fructose can cause many of the same health problems as alcohol.	
Chronic ethanol exposure	**Chronic fructose exposure**
Hematologic disorders	
Electrolyte abnormalities	
Hypertension	Hypertension (uric acid)
Cardiac dilatation	
Cardiomyopathy	Myocardial infarction (dyslipidemia, insulin resistance)
Dyslipidemia	Dyslipidemia (de novo lipogenesis)
Pancreatitis	Pancreatitis (hypertriglyceridemia)
Obesity (insulin resistance)	Obesity (insulin resistance)
Malnutrition	Malnutrition (obesity)
Hepatic dysfunction (alcoholic steatohepatitis)	Hepatic dysfunction (non-alcoholic steatohepatitis)
Fetal alcohol syndrome	
Addiction	Habituation, if not addiction

The Possible Dream

Government-imposed regulations on the marketing of alcohol to young people have been quite effective, but there is no such approach to sugar-laden products. Even so, the city of San Francisco, California, recently instituted a ban on including toys with unhealthy meals such as
(65) some types of fast food. A limit—or, ideally, ban—on television commercials for products with added sugars could further protect children's health. ...

Ultimately, food producers and distributors must reduce the amount of sugar added to foods. But sugar is cheap, sugar tastes good, and sugar
(70) sells, so companies have little incentive to change. Although one institution alone can't turn this juggernaut[5] around, the US Food and Drug Administration could "set the table" for change. To start, it should consider removing fructose from the Generally Regarded as Safe (GRAS) list, which allows food manufacturers to add unlimited amounts to any food.

---

[5]juggernaut—powerful force

(75)   Opponents will argue that other nutrients on the GRAS list, such as iron and vitamins A and D, can also be toxic when over-consumed. However, unlike sugar, these substances have no abuse potential. Removal from the GRAS list would send a powerful signal to the European Food Safety Authority and the rest of the world. ...

—Robert H. Lustig, Laura A. Schmidt, and Claire D. Brindis
excerpted and adapted from "The Toxic Truth About Sugar"
Nature, February 2, 2012

Text 4

Sugar Taxes Are Unfair and Unhealthy

If the regulatory discussion about sugar is going to be based on science, rather than science fiction, it needs to move beyond kicking the soda can.

Conventional wisdom says draconian[1] regulation—specifically, a high tax—on sugary drinks and snacks reduces unhealthy consumption, and
(5) thereby improves public health. There are many reasons, however, why high sugar taxes are at best unsuccessful, and at worst economically and socially harmful.

Research finds that higher prices don't reduce soda consumption, for example. No scientific studies demonstrate a difference either in
(10) aggregate[2] soda consumption or in child and adolescent Body Mass Index [BMI] between the two thirds of states with soda taxes and those without such taxes.

The study that did find taxes might lead to a moderate reduction in soda consumption also found this had no effect on adolescent obesity, as
(15) the reduction was completely offset by increases in consumption of other calorific drinks.

Economic research finds sugar taxes are a futile instrument in influencing the behavior and habits of the overweight and the obese. Why do sugar taxes fail? Those consumers who strongly prefer unhealthy foods
(20) continue to eat and drink according to their individual preferences until such time as it becomes prohibitively expensive to do so.

Demand for food is largely insensitive to price. A 10 percent increase in price reduces consumption by less than 1 percent. Applied to soda, this means that to reduce consumption by 10 percent, the tax rate on sugary
(25) drinks would need to be 100 percent!

A sugar tax also has undesirable social and economic consequences. This tax is economically regressive, as a disproportionate share of the tax is paid by low earners, who pay a higher proportion of their incomes in sales tax and also consume a disproportionate share of sugary snacks and
(30) drinks.

---

[1]draconian—severe
[2]aggregate—total

Such taxes also have perverse, unintended consequences. Taxes on sugary snacks lead many consumers to replace the taxed food with equally unhealthy foods. Poorer consumers react to higher food prices not by changing their diets but by consuming even fewer healthy foods, such as

(35)   fruits and vegetables, and eating more processed foods. For instance, taxes levied specifically on sugar content increase saturated fat consumption.

Sugar taxes have failed where they've been tried, and are unfair and unhealthy. Given that there's no compelling evidence they'll improve public health, we can't justify using the tax code to shape the sweetness of our

(40)   dietary choices.

—Patrick Basham
excerpted and adapted from "Sugar Taxes Are Unfair and Unhealthy"
http://www.usnews.com, March 30, 2012

PART 3—Text-Analysis Response

Your Task: Closely read the text on pages 308 through 310 and write a well-developed, text-based response of two to three paragraphs. In your response, identify a central idea in the text and analyze how the author's use of *one* writing strategy (literary element or literary technique or rhetorical device) develops this central idea. Use strong and thorough evidence from the text to support your analysis. Do *not* simply summarize the text. You may use the margins to take notes as you read and scrap paper to plan your response. Write your response on a separate sheet of paper.

Guidelines:

Be sure to

- Identify a central idea in the text.
- Analyze how the author's use of *one* writing strategy (literary element or literary technique or rhetorical device) develops this central idea. Examples include: characterization, conflict, denotation/connotation, metaphor, simile, irony, language use, point-of-view, setting, structure, symbolism, theme, tone, etc.
- Use strong and thorough evidence from the text to support your analysis.
- Organize your ideas in a cohesive and coherent manner.
- Maintain a formal style of writing.
- Follow the conventions of standard written English.

Text

...In the air now, I feel a new excitement, a slight surge of energy, a new light of a new dawn. This anticipation is like grass in the path of a distant approaching thunderstorm. I feel that the "spirit line" out of our complacencies in art has been drawn. A fresh expression of our passions,

(5)   our joys and pains is in the making. A new generation of interpretations of our legends and stories, strengths and weaknesses as Navajo people are replacing the images of stoic[1] tribalism that so pervaded our recent art history. To paraphrase another artist, "realness instead of redness." I feel as do other young fine artists of the northern reservation, that there is

(10) much potential for individual expression of beauty, of power, of mysteries to be created within the perimeter of our culture in this time. But what inspires us young Navajo artists to create these interpretations of our culture? What force drives us to seek fresher means of expression? We all have our reasons and means to do this. It may be money, it may be recognition

(15) or self-satisfaction. For me, it is a means of confronting myself, my fears and mysteries. A means of coming to terms with childhood phobias and a recognition of my strength and weaknesses in this day. In Navajo society, it is necessary to journey that road to self-discovery. To attain a spiritual growth, we will have to go beyond the world we retreat into. We must

(20) recognize and acknowledge this new high tech world, yet still maintain an identity. We must draw a line beyond which we don't venture. Be able to compromise wisely and know how much to expose of ourselves. Know ourselves and our past, yet still have faith in the future. We are a segment of a society that has been thrust into the 20th century all within 30 years. We

(25) will not allow ourselves to become casualties in this collision of cultures. The art that we represent must be flexible and adaptable, like the nature of our grandfather, if it is to survive, lest we become brittle and blow away like shells of dry piñon nuts. The art that we represent, like the role of the medicine man of today, must help in creating a positive evolution into this

(30) new era for our people and those coming after us. It will scream of tomorrow, yet be dressed in the truth of our past. I believe this to be a collective therapy for us, for our culture and our art. ...

---

[1]stoic—calm and uncomplaining

When I was around four years old, I traveled with my grandmother to the foot of the Sacred Mountain of the West. During this time, she told
(35) me many things. She told me that we are responsible in maintaining and nurturing a good identity with our grandparents every single day. Each day before the sun rises, we should greet the new coming day with pollen and re-affirm our relationship with it. To a young piñon tree, we greet "*Yá'áhtééh shima'sáni*" (Hello, my grandmother); to a young juniper
(40) tree; "*Yá'áhtééh shí'cheii*" (hello, my grandfather). In this manner, we bring new light and life to our world. At this age I learned to feel, see and smell my world. I still associate lots of pieces of past experiences, painful and pleasant, to these subtleties. There are few things more pleasant than waking up in the morning to see dew on blades of grass, or to hear
(45) rolling of the thunder as dark clouds gather on spring days. To smell wet sand and hear the raindrops dancing on parched ground. The cornstalks weeping for joy. Forming figures from clay and feeling like a god. The soft crunching sound in the snow as I make my way home with a rabbit or two on moonlit winters [*sic*] night, or even being momentarily lost in a bliz-
(50) zard. To feel as a tumbleweed rolling across rough landscape, to see the last ray of sunlight hitting the mesa after an autumn day, light reflecting off a distant passing car makes me feel vulnerable and sad at times. These past feelings and experiences, associated with time and places, I regard as a reservoir of my inspiration.
(55) Like most young Navajos my age, we spent many winter nights gathered around our father, listening to stories passed down through generations. We sat in expectation as we journeyed up from the womb of the Mother in creation stories. We sat mesmerized by coyote stories. Laughing at his antics and frightened by his cruelties. We sat in awe as First Man
(60) and First Woman brought forth life upon the Fourth World. We journey back from the west, the home of Changing Woman, into the midst of the Four Sacred Mountains after the creation of our clans. "Slayer of Enemies" and "Born for Water," the hero and savior of the fourth world, came alive for us these nights. I felt the pain of their fathers' testing in the
(65) roaring fire of the hearth. Their war with the Monster Gods raged as the snow storm dusted outside our door, snow sifting through the cracks of the door. Shadows leaping on cribbed wall of the *hooghan*[2] brought to

---

[2]hooghan—traditional dwelling of the Navajo people

life the animal beings as the shoe game was created. As the nights wore on, the youngest ones of us fell asleep where we sat. My mother's spindle
(70) scratching the floor set the tempo of these late night journeys...back. From these sources I draw my inspirations. I am humbled by its beauty and strengthened by its power. With great respect, I relive this in every creation, every all-night Blessingway chant and every vision of glory upon this land. With good intentions, I recreate this in every piece of art: inten-
(75) tions of preserving and passing on, intentions of sharing and inviting all good-willed people for the sake of us as American Indians in general, as Navajos in particular and the beauty of our culture. This culture through art, in whatever form, however expressed, will endure. ...

—Shonto W. Begay
excerpted from "The View From The Mesa: A Source of Navajo Creativity"
Anii Ánáádaalyaa'Ígíí (*Recent ones that are made*), 1988
Wheelright Museum of the American Indian

Regents ELA (Common Core) Answers August 2016
English Language Arts

Answer Key

Part 1

1. 4	9. 4	17. 4
2. 1	10. 1	18. 1
3. 2	11. 3	19. 3
4. 4	12. 3	20. 1
5. 1	13. 4	21. 2
6. 3	14. 2	22. 2
7. 1	15. 2	23. 4
8. 2	16. 3	24. 3

Regents Examination in English Language Arts (Common Core)—August 2016

Chart for Converting Total Weighted Raw Scores to Final Exam Scores (Scale Scores) (Use for the August 2016 examination only.)

Weighted Raw Score*	Scale Score	Performance Level	Weighted Raw Score*	Scale Score	Performance Level
56	100	5	27	55	2
55	99	5	26	52	1
54	99	5	25	49	1
53	98	5	24	45	1
52	97	5	23	42	1
51	96	5	22	38	1
50	96	5	21	35	1
49	95	5	20	31	1
48	94	5	19	27	1
47	93	5	18	24	1
46	92	5	17	20	1
45	91	5	16	17	1
44	90	5	15	13	1
43	89	5	14	10	1
42	88	5	13	9	1
41	87	5	12	8	1
40	85	5	11	7	1
39	84	4	10	6	1
38	82	4	9	5	1
37	81	4	8	4	1
36	79	4	7	4	1
35	77	3	6	3	1
34	74	3	5	2	1
33	72	3	4	2	1
32	69	3	3	1	1
31	67	3	2	1	1
30	65	3	1	1	1
29	61	2	0	0	1
28	58	2			

The conversion table is determined independently for each administration of the exam.

Answers Explained

PART 1—Reading Comprehension

Multiple-Choice Questions

Passage A

(1) **4** "illustrate the nature of Richard's life in the city." The reader is meant to understand from the description of London that Richard perceives the city as colorful, huge, and contradictory, but he is unchanged by it. We learn in the passage that Richard took the city for granted and made no effort to visit the sights. The images of a vibrant city that has grown and changed over time are meant to contrast with Richard's passive and indifferent nature.

(2) **1** "growth of the city." The image in lines 18 and 19, "… a pool of mercury encounters and incorporates smaller beads of mercury …" reinforces the way London expanded by absorbing what had once been separate small villages and towns.

(3) **2** "willingness to tolerate undesirable situations to please others." Richard "learns" from his excursions with Jessica that going to museums means tired feet, boredom, and expensive cafeterias. He tolerates these discomforts because he is "awed by Jessica" and is easily led by her.

(4) **4** "Richard is in a state of denial regarding his relationship." Gary sees how controlling Jessica is and wonders why Richard puts up with her. Gary says to Richard, "She's terrifying." Richard's panic over the dinner reservation suggests that he may indeed be afraid to disappoint Jessica. None of the other choices is suggested in the text.

(5) **1** "by portraying him as inefficient at organizing his time." Richard's feeling that events have a way of piling up and hitting him all at once is a vivid image of what happens to someone who is disorganized and who tends to let things go until the last minute. The text does not suggest that Richard works well under pressure or is likely to succeed. He may be unmotivated by his job, but he seems to be unmotivated by almost everything. These lines best describe Richard's lack of focus and attention to what needs to get done.

(6) **3** "contrast." Sylvia's atmosphere of "crisp efficiency" offers a vivid contrast to all that we know about Richard in the text. This is the best answer among the choices.

(7) **1** "domineering nature." In these lines, we hear Jessica ordering Richard to pick up the phone, insisting that he might have forgotten their date, and correcting him when he calls her "Jess." There is little in this text to suggest compassion, irresponsibility, or a sense of humor in Jessica.

(8) **2** "stress." In this passage, we see Richard juggling two phone lines and being reminded that, not only has he forgotten to make an important din-

ner reservation, but he has made a commitment to have drinks and work with Gary that evening. His manager is also waiting for a report due in the next five minutes. "Stressful" best describes this scene.

(9) **4** "quiet desperation." Richard has run out of ways to meet Jessica's expectations for that evening. He had obviously forgotten to make the reservation weeks before, and he knows he will pay a heavy price for his failure. None of the other choices captures Richard's state of mind here.

(10) **1** "London grew into something huge and contradictory ... ." These lines from the opening of the passage establish the setting and mood of the story. Richard lives in, "... a good place and a fine city," but he is overwhelmed by the variety of forces at work in his life.

Passage B

(11) **3** "lack of self-confidence." The image of the narrator's "courageous self" wrapped in self-doubt and hesitation ("reservations") by a cowardly self is best described as a lack of self-confidence. None of the other choices is suggested by that image.

(12) **3** "clarify the narrator's dilemma." The narrator's predicament or quandary is in determining which of the many selves, or aspects of character, is his "proper self." The narrator is asking the universal question, "Who am I?" This is a dilemma because he cannot seem to find "my real self, the truly me ..." The poem reveals little about the narrator's biases or beliefs, and there is no decision revealed in these lines.

(13) **4** "the narrator's idealism and his reality." Among these choices, this is the best way to describe the contradictions in the narrator's view of himself. He believes that he has courageous, intelligent, and bold selves (his idealism), but, instead of acting as a man of intelligence, he acts the fool. In situations demanding courage, he is cowardly. He envies heroic figures, but when he needs to be confident and daring, "... out comes the same old lazy self (reality)."

(14) **2** "universal." Note that in the preceding lines, the narrator declares that his solution will be, "... to see if the same thing happens/to other people." The narrator plans a thorough exploration of other people's experiences in order to find a way to explain his problems, to find his "real self."

Passage C

(15) **2** "describing various frequencies dogs hear." These lines first outline and compare the range of sounds that can be heard by humans and by dogs. These details support the central idea that, "Dogs hear most of what we hear and then some." These lines are not about *how* dogs and humans hear, but about which range of frequencies each can hear.

(16) **3** "humans can verbally communicate with dogs." What these lines establish is that when they hear humans speak, dogs recognize changes in pitch and tone, not necessarily the meaning of specific words. It is that recognition of patterns in sound that allow humans to communicate verbally with dogs. None of the other choices is supported in the passage.

(17) **4** "altering the intonation of familiar words." This idea is an elaboration on the ideas in the question above. Because dogs recognize intonation, the pattern in a question for example, they could be confused if something they heard sounded like a familiar question, even when the words were expressing no such thing.

(18) **1** "higher-level thinking." These lines include the declaration that language use distinguishes humans from all other animals, and that language use is viewed as an, "… incomparable criterion for intelligence." The passage is asserting that language use implies higher-level thinking.

(19) **3** "create human sentence structures." This passage acknowledges that there is considerable disagreement among researchers about the extent of linguistic ability in non-human animals, but asserts that, "All parties agree …" there is no discovery of the ability in animals to combine "… words into meaningful sentences." None of the other choices applies to these lines.

(20) **1** "imitate behavior and sound." This passage offers examples of how animals can recognize warning signals in bird cries or can trap prey by using deceptive gestures. These forms of communication are, "… in some way using another specie's language."

(21) **2** "complexity of spoken sounds." The key term in this answer is "sounds." This section of the text emphasizes the importance of how dogs understand the sound and pattern of what we say more than recognizing specific words. If an utterance sounds familiar but the actual words (sounds) are meaningless (gibberish), the dog may confuse it with an utterance he has understood in the past. This passage does not refer to word order, hidden gestures, or movement.

(22) **2** "How we speak to dogs is more important than what we say." The first and last paragraphs of the text do point out how dogs respond to high-pitched sounds, but the central idea in lines 57–65 is that dogs are sensitive to how we speak, to the rhythm and tone of voice in what they hear. The other choices are not supported by the text.

(23) **4** "styles of spoken communication and likely responses." The term "motherese" identifies the often babbling, cooing sounds we use in communicating with infants. The author points out that dogs also respond to "baby talk," especially because they perceive that it is actually being directed at them. This passage is further demonstration of the importance of manner and style in spoken communication.

(24) **3** "educate people about dogs' experience with sound." Note that the first sentence of the passage establishes dogs' capacity to hear and respond to sounds as the central idea; the examples that follow are illustrations of how dogs perceive the world and human communication through tone, rhythm, and pitch level.

PART 2—Argument Response

Sample Essay Response

Should the government create strict sugar regulations to protect its citizens from serious health problems? I definitely believe the U.S. government has the responsibility to ensure safe food for its people. It must regulate the production, labeling, and availability of sugary foods and drinks.

Critics of the claim say it's not sugar itself that creates health risks but a person's decision to drink and eat sugar-heavy products. As Jeffrey Senger, a former attorney for the FDA remarked, "Sugar isn't the same thing as arsenic. It's not a food that's inherently unsafe." (Text 1, lines 29–30) In addition, an FDA spokesperson placed sugar and high fructose corn syrup in the same category as honey and molasses. (Text 1, lines 34–35) Opponents of regulation, therefore, place blame and responsibility on the people instead of on the companies that produce these sweetened products. This text explains why it would be difficult for the FDA to set limits on sugar.

However, recent scientific research shows just how dangerous sugar in any form is to a person's health, especially since the average person in America consumes 78 pounds of sugar in one year. (Text 1, lines 10–11) Fructose "is metabolized primarily by the liver, … taxing the liver, causing fatty liver disease, and ultimately leading to insulin resistance." (Text 2, lines 21–24) The graphic from Text 3 further illustrates the very serious damage that excessive fructose intake creates: "hypertension, pancreatitis, obesity, malnutrition, hepatic dysfunction," and even possible addiction. As the number of potential ill effects of sugar consumption rises, the case for government regulation is strengthened. Text 3 compares the effects of sugar consumption to alcohol and tobacco use in its damaging effects on people. Why wouldn't the government take similar steps to regulate sugar?

Besides being a personal health issue, sugar consumption is having effects on the U.S. economy. As the health of individuals becomes compromised, so are employment, health-care costs, and the military in the U.S. Lost time at work due to sugar-related disease is "$65 billion in lost productivity." Add to that the $150 billion spent on health-care resources for obesity every year. (Text 3, lines 41–42) Sugar is even being called "a threat to national security," because "75% of military applicants are now rejected for obesity-related reasons." (Text 3, lines 45–46)

Clearly, the government must take steps to strictly regulate the consumption of sugar. Sugary drinks and foods must be banned from schools and commercials, taxes should be placed on companies that continue to produce and market high-sugar products, and education about the dangers of excess sugar must be emphasized. This issue has gone beyond that of personal responsibility; it is having a negative impact on the country as a whole. The U.S. government must take action to protect its citizens from the deadly consequences of high-sugar products.

Analysis

This response is a good example of an argument developed with evidence from texts. The introduction restates the topic in the form of a rhetorical question, which also suggests the line of reasoning to follow: "Should the government create strict sugar regulations to protect its citizens from serious health problems?" The introduction could be improved if more details to establish the context were included, but the argument that follows is well developed.

The organization is clear. The second paragraph acknowledges one of the key arguments against regulation. The paragraph that follows offers several examples of the health risks of sugar consumption and closes with another effective rhetorical question: "Why wouldn't the government take similar steps to regulate sugar?" The paragraph that follows further develops the argument with examples of economic costs. The conclusion summarizes the argument for regulation, proposes specific regulatory actions, and rejects the opposing view that personal responsibility is a sufficient response. The supporting details come from three of the texts and are accurately cited. This response would merit a high score.

(See pages 80–81 for the scoring guidelines.)

PART 3—Text-Analysis Response

Sample Essay Response

The central idea of this text is that when two cultures collide, a more primitive culture must adapt to the new culture while maintaining its own cultural identity. This text was written in the perspective of an American Indian artist whose artwork displays the culture of the Navajo people. The artist recognizes the difficulty for the Navajo people to transition and adapt to a new and advanced culture, therefore he uses his artwork to help his people cope with the change. The artist understands that if the Navajo culture is not perpetuated in artwork, it will be lost to a new culture.

The artist develops this central idea through the literary technique of figurative language. In lines 26 to 30 the artist states, "The art that we represent, like the role of the medicine man of today, must help in creating a positive evolution in this new era for our people and those coming after us." The artist uses a simile to compare contemporary Navajo artwork to the role of a present day medicine man: art that looks to the future yet is "dressed in the truth of our past ..." is like "a collective therapy." The artwork that is created still incorporates the culture that the Navajo people are accustomed to, making it easier for them to adapt to the new culture while maintaining their own cultural identity. In line 21, the artist states, "We must draw a line beyond which we do not venture." Here, the artist is describing his artwork with a line in the form of a metaphor. This comparison shows a sense of boundary, where the artwork of the Navajo people would show an adaptation to the new culture, but not too much to where they lose their cultural identity. In lines 26 to 28, the artist states, "the art that we represent must be flexible and adaptable ... if it is to survive, lest we become brittle and blow away like shells of dry pinion nuts." Here, the artist uses a simile to show that the culture of the Navajo people will disappear—blow away like dry shells—if it does not remain true to its own cultural identity as it adapts to the new culture.

Analysis

This passage offers several possibilities for a thoughtful response, including vivid imagery in the author's descriptions of his childhood experiences, effective use of tone, voice, and point of view. This writer chose to analyze the author's use of figurative language in developing the central idea of the passage.

The first paragraph gives an excellent paraphrase of the central idea, outlines the context, and clearly establishes the author's point of view. The significance of figurative language is developed in the second paragraph, with relevant quotes and accurate representations of the author's views. The organization of the essay is clear and the style is appropriately formal, with no significant errors in the conventions. This response would merit a high score.

(See pages 82–83 for the scoring guidelines.)

Regents ELA (Common Core) Examination June 2017

English Language Arts

PART 1—Reading Comprehension

Directions (1–24): Closely read each of the three passages below. After each passage, there are several multiple-choice questions. Select the best suggested answer to each question and write its number in the space provided. You may use the margins to take notes as you read.

Reading Comprehension Passage A

I received one morning a letter, written in pale ink on glassy, blue-lined note-paper, and bearing the postmark of a little Nebraska village. This communication, worn and rubbed, looking as if it had been carried for some days in a coat pocket that was none too clean, was from my uncle

(5) Howard, and informed me that his wife had been left a small legacy by a bachelor relative, and that it would be necessary for her to go to Boston to attend to the settling of the estate. He requested me to meet her at the station and render her whatever services might be necessary. On examining the date indicated as that of her arrival, I found it to be no later than

(10) tomorrow. He had characteristically delayed writing until, had I been away from home for a day, I must have missed my aunt altogether. ...

Whatever shock Mrs. Springer [the landlady] experienced at my aunt's appearance, she considerately concealed. As for myself, I saw my aunt's battered figure with that feeling of awe and respect with which we behold

(15) explorers who have left their ears and fingers north of Franz-Joseph-
Land,[1] or their health somewhere along the Upper Congo. My Aunt
Georgiana had been a music teacher at the Boston Conservatory, somewhere back in the latter sixties [1860s]. One summer, while visiting in the
little village among the Green Mountains where her ancestors had dwelt
(20) for generations, she had kindled the callow[2] fancy of my uncle, Howard
Carpenter, then an idle, shiftless boy of twenty-one. When she returned
to her duties in Boston, Howard followed her, and the upshot of this
infatuation was that she eloped with him, eluding the reproaches of her
family and the criticism of her friends by going with him to the Nebraska
(25) frontier. Carpenter, who, of course, had no money, took up a homestead
in Red Willow County, fifty miles from the railroad. There they had measured off their land themselves, driving across the prairie in a wagon, to
the wheel of which they had tied a red cotton handkerchief, and counting
its revolutions. They built a dug-out in the red hillside, one of those cave
(30) dwellings whose inmates so often reverted to primitive conditions. Their
water they got from the lagoons where the buffalo drank, and their slender stock of provisions was always at the mercy of bands of roving Indians.
For thirty years my aunt had not been farther than fifty miles from the
homestead.
(35)   I owed to this woman most of the good that ever came my way in my
boyhood, and had a reverential[3] affection for her. During the years when
I was riding herd for my uncle, my aunt, after cooking the three meals—
the first of which was ready at six o'clock in the morning—and putting
the six children to bed, would often stand until midnight at her ironing-
(40) board, with me at the kitchen table beside her, hearing me recite Latin
declensions and conjugations, gently shaking me when my drowsy head
sank down over a page of irregular verbs. It was to her, at her ironing or
mending, that I read my first Shakspere, and her old text-book on mythology was the first that ever came into my empty hands. She taught me my
(45) scales and exercises on the little parlour organ which her husband had
bought her after fifteen years during which she had not so much as seen
a musical instrument. She would sit beside me by the hour, darning and

---

[1]Franz-Joseph-Land—Russian archipelago of 191 islands in the Arctic Ocean
[2]callow—naive
[3]reverential—with great honor and respect

counting, while I struggled with the "Joyous Farmer." She seldom talked
to me about music, and I understood why. Once when I had been doggedly
(50) beating out some easy passages from an old score of *Euryanthe* I had found
among her music books, she came up to me and, putting her hands over
my eyes, gently drew my head back upon her shoulder, saying tremulously,
"Don't love it so well, Clark, or it may be taken from you."...

At two o'clock the Symphony Orchestra was to give a Wagner pro-
(55) gram, and I intended to take my aunt; though, as I conversed with her,
I grew doubtful about her enjoyment of it. I suggested our visiting the
Conservatory and the Common before lunch, but she seemed altogether
too timid to wish to venture out. She questioned me absently about
various changes in the city, but she was chiefly concerned that she had
(60) forgotten to leave instructions about feeding half-skimmed milk to a certain weakling calf, "old Maggie's calf, you know, Clark," she explained,
evidently having forgotten how long I had been away. She was further
troubled because she had neglected to tell her daughter about the freshly-
opened kit of mackerel[4] in the cellar, which would spoil if it were not used
(65) directly. ...

The first number [of the concert] was the *Tannhauser*[5] overture.
When the horns drew out the first strain of the Pilgrim's chorus, Aunt
Georgiana clutched my coat sleeve. Then it was I first realized that for
her this broke a silence of thirty years. With the battle between the two
(70) motives,[6] with the frenzy of the Venusberg theme and its ripping of
strings, there came to me an overwhelming sense of the waste and wear we
are so powerless to combat; and I saw again the tall, naked house on the
prairie, black and grim as a wooden fortress; the black pond where I had
learned to swim, its margin pitted with sun-dried cattle tracks; the rain
(75) gullied clay banks about the naked house, the four dwarf ash seedlings
where the dish-cloths were always hung to dry before the kitchen door.
The world there was the flat world of the ancients; to the east, a cornfield
that stretched to daybreak; to the west, a corral that reached to sunset;
between, the conquests of peace, dearer-bought than those of war. ...

---

[4]kit of mackerel—container of fish
[5]*Tannhauser*—an opera by Richard Wagner
[6]motives—recurrent musical phrases

(80)   Her lip quivered and she hastily put her handkerchief up to her mouth. From behind it she murmured, "And you have been hearing this ever since you left me, Clark?" Her question was the gentlest and saddest of reproaches. ...

      The deluge of sound poured on and on; I never knew what she found *(85)* in the shining current of it; I never knew how far it bore her, or past what happy islands. From the trembling of her face I could well believe that before the last number she had been carried out where the myriad graves are, into the grey, nameless burying grounds of the sea; or into some world of death vaster yet, where, from the beginning of the world, hope *(90)* has lain down with hope and dream with dream and, renouncing, slept. ...

      I spoke to my aunt. She burst into tears and sobbed pleadingly. "I don't want to go, Clark, I don't want to go!"

      I understood. For her, just outside the concert hall, lay the black pond with the cattle-tracked bluffs; the tall, unpainted house, with weather- *(95)* curled boards, naked as a tower; the crook-backed ash seedlings where the dish-cloths hung to dry; the gaunt, moulting turkeys picking up refuse about the kitchen door.

—Willa Cather
excerpted and adapted from "A Wagner Matinée"
Youth and the Bright Medusa, April 1920

1 A primary function of the first paragraph is to

    (1)   establish the reason for the meeting
    (2)   create an atmosphere of mystery
    (3)   identify preferences of the narrator's aunt
    (4)   reveal flaws in the narrator's character   1____

2 In lines 1 through 11, the commentary about the letter implies that the narrator believes his uncle is

    (1)   uncomfortable with changes
    (2)   careless about details
    (3)   angry with his wife
    (4)   disappointed at his decision   2____

3 The details in lines 16 through 25 suggest that in her youth Aunt Georgiana was

    (1)   courageous yet hesitant
    (2)   compassionate yet critical
    (3)   resourceful yet cautious
    (4)   intelligent yet impulsive   3____

4 Lines 33 and 34, "For thirty years my aunt had not been farther than fifty miles from the homestead" reinforces a sense of

    (1)   discomfort   (3)   isolation
    (2)   happiness   (4)   affection   4____

5 Which statement from the passage best explains the narrator's "reverential affection" (line 36) for his Aunt Georgiana?

   (1) "It was to her, at her ironing or mending, that I read my first Shakspere" (lines 42 and 43)

   (2) " 'Don't love it so well, Clark, or it may be taken from you' " (line 53)

   (3) "Her lip quivered and she hastily put her handkerchief up to her mouth" (line 80)

   (4) "I never knew how far it bore her, or past what happy islands" (lines 85 and 86)   5____

6 Lines 44 through 47 develop a central theme by

   (1) recalling the husband's generosity in supporting the narrator's music lessons

   (2) suggesting that the narrator resented his music lessons

   (3) emphasizing the role of discipline in developing Aunt Georgiana's musical talent

   (4) implying that Aunt Georgiana missed having music in her life   6____

7 In line 49, when the narrator states that he "understood why," he is implying that his Aunt Georgiana

   (1) knew little about current musical trends

   (2) avoided talking about his musical skills

   (3) realized what she has given up

   (4) needed some recognition of her ability   7____

8 Lines 58 through 65 contribute to a central idea by depicting Aunt Georgiana's

   (1) concern for daily responsibilities

   (2) desire for cultural experiences

   (3) fear of future separations

   (4) fixation on painful memories   8____

9 The author's choice of how to end the story (lines 91
   through 97) places emphasis on Aunt Georgiana's

   (1) bleak future   (3) domestic skills
   (2) unusual lifestyle   (4) hostile attitude   9____

10 Which quotation best reflects the narrator's realization resulting from Aunt Georgiana's visit?

   (1) "He requested me to meet her at the station
        and render her whatever services might be
        necessary" (lines 7 and 8)
   (2) "At two o'clock the Symphony Orchestra was to
        give a Wagner program, and I intended to take
        my aunt" (lines 54 and 55)
   (3) "there came to me an overwhelming sense
        of the waste and wear we are so powerless to
        combat" (lines 71 and 72)
   (4) "sound poured on and on; I never knew what
        she found in the shining current of it" (lines 84
        and 85)   10____

Reading Comprehension Passage B

Mi Historia[1]

My red pickup choked on burnt oil
as I drove down Highway 99.[2]
In wind-tattered garbage bags
I had packed my whole life:
(5)   two pairs of jeans, a few T-shirts,
and a pair of work boots.
My truck needed work, and through
the blue smoke rising from under the hood,
I saw almond orchards, plums,
(10)   the raisins spread out on paper trays,
and acres of Mendota cotton my mother picked as a child.

My mother crawled through the furrows
and plucked cotton balls that filled
the burlap sack she dragged,
(15)   shoulder-slung, through dried-up bolls,
husks, weevils, dirt clods,
and dust that filled the air with thirst.
But when she grew tired,
she slept on her mother's burlap,
(20)   stuffed thick as a mattress,
and Grandma dragged her over the land
where time was told by the setting sun....

History cried out to me from the earth,
in the scream of starling flight,
(25)   and pounded at the hulls of seeds to be set free.
History licked the asphalt with rubber,
sighed in the windows of abandoned barns,

---

[1]Mi Historia—Spanish for "my history"
[2]Highway 99—the highway that runs through California's fertile Central Valley where generations of farmworkers have settled and been employed

slumped in the wind-blasted palms,
groaned in the heat, and whispered its soft curses.

(30)   I wanted my own history—not the earth's,
nor the history of blood, nor of memory,
and not the job found for me at Galdini Sausage.
I sought my own—a new bruise to throb hard
as the asphalt that pounded the chassis of my truck.

—David Dominguez
from *Work Done Right*, 2003
The University of Arizona Press

11 The poet's purpose in referencing "Highway 99" in line 2 is most likely to establish

   (1) a connection with the narrator's cultural heritage

   (2) a criticism of the valley's agricultural economy

   (3) an understanding of the narrator's difficult childhood

   (4) an emphasis on the region's diverse landscape   11____

12 The second stanza reveals that the narrator's overall point of view is influenced by

   (1) his experience working on farms

   (2) his nostalgia for farm life

   (3) the labor of his relatives

   (4) the expectations of his family   12____

13 The personification in lines 23 through 29 stresses history's desire to be

   (1) repeated   (3) comforted

   (2) forgotten   (4) heard   13____

14 The figurative language in lines 33 and 34 implies the narrator

   (1) regrets leaving his past behind

   (2) understands that his future will have challenges

   (3) anticipates that his new life will be successful

   (4) thinks he made a wrong decision   14____

Reading Comprehension Passage C

In 1973, a book claiming that plants were sentient[1] beings that feel emotions, prefer classical music to rock and roll, and can respond to the unspoken thoughts of humans hundreds of miles away landed on the New York *Times* best-seller list for nonfiction. "The Secret Life of Plants,"
(5) by Peter Tompkins and Christopher Bird, presented a beguiling mashup of legitimate plant science, quack experiments, and mystical nature worship that captured the public imagination at a time when New Age thinking was seeping into the mainstream. The most memorable passages described the experiments of a former C.I.A. polygraph expert named
(10) Cleve Backster, who, in 1966, on a whim, hooked up a galvanometer to the leaf of a dracaena, a houseplant that he kept in his office. To his astonishment, Backster found that simply by imagining the dracaena being set on fire he could make it rouse the needle of the polygraph machine, registering a surge of electrical activity suggesting that the plant felt stress.
(15) "Could the plant have been reading his mind?" the authors ask. "Backster felt like running into the street and shouting to the world, 'Plants can think!'" ...

In the ensuing years, several legitimate plant scientists tried to reproduce the "Backster effect" without success. Much of the science in "The
(20) Secret Life of Plants" has been discredited. But the book had made its mark on the culture. Americans began talking to their plants and playing Mozart for them, and no doubt many still do. This might seem harmless enough; there will probably always be a strain of romanticism running through our thinking about plants. (Luther Burbank and George
(25) Washington Carver both reputedly talked to, and listened to, the plants they did such brilliant work with.) But in the view of many plant scientists "The Secret Life of Plants" has done lasting damage to their field. According to Daniel Chamovitz, an Israeli biologist who is the author of the recent book "What a Plant Knows," Tompkins and Bird "stymied[2]
(30) important research on plant behavior as scientists became wary[3] of any studies that hinted at parallels between animal senses and plant senses."

---

[1]sentient—conscious
[2]stymied—prevented
[3]wary—cautious

Others contend that "The Secret Life of Plants" led to "self-censorship"
among researchers seeking to explore the "possible homologies[4] between
neurobiology[5] and phytobiology"[6]; that is, the possibility that plants are
(35)   much more intelligent and much more like us than most people think—
capable of cognition,[7] communication, information processing, computation, learning and memory. ...

Indeed, many of the most impressive capabilities of plants can be traced
to their unique existential[8] predicament as beings rooted to the ground
(40)   and therefore unable to pick up and move when they need something or
when conditions turn unfavorable. The "sessile life style," as plant biologists term it, calls for an extensive and nuanced understanding of one's
immediate environment, since the plant has to find everything it needs,
and has to defend itself, while remaining fixed in place. A highly devel-
(45)   oped sensory apparatus is required to locate food and identify threats.
Plants have evolved between fifteen and twenty distinct senses, including
analogues of our five: smell and taste (they sense and respond to chemicals
in the air or on their bodies); sight (they react differently to various wavelengths of light as well as to shadow); touch (a vine or a root "knows"
(50)   when it encounters a solid object); and, it has been discovered, sound. In
a recent experiment, Heidi Appel, a chemical ecologist at the University of
Missouri, found that, when she played a recording of a caterpillar chomping a leaf for a plant that hadn't been touched, the sound primed the
plant's genetic machinery to produce defense chemicals. Another experi-
(55)   ment, done in Mancuso's[9] lab and not yet published, found that plant
roots would seek out a buried pipe through which water was flowing even
if the exterior of the pipe was dry, which suggested that plants somehow
"hear" the sound of flowing water. ...

Scientists have since found that the tips of the plant roots, in addi-
(60)   tion to sensing gravity, moisture, light, pressure, and hardness, can also
sense volume, nitrogen, phosphorus, salt, various toxins, microbes, and
chemical signals from neighboring plants. Roots about to encounter an

---

[4]homologies—similarities
[5]neurobiology—the study of the nervous system
[6]phytobiology—the study of plants
[7]cognition—understanding
[8]existential—relating to existence
[9]Mancuso—Stefano Mancuso, Italian plant physiologist

impenetrable obstacle or a toxic substance change course before they make
contact with it. Roots can tell whether nearby roots are self or other and,
(65)   if other, kin or stranger. Normally, plants compete for root space with
strangers, but, when researchers put four closely related Great Lakes sea-
rocket plants (*Cakile edentula*) in the same pot, the plants restrained their
usual competitive behaviors and shared resources.

Somehow, a plant gathers and integrates all this information about
(70)   its environment, and then "decides"—some scientists deploy the quotation marks, indicating metaphor at work; others drop them—in precisely
what direction to deploy its roots or its leaves. Once the definition of
"behavior" expands to include such things as a shift in the trajectory[10] of
a root, a reallocation of resources, or the emission of a powerful chemical,
(75)   plants begin to look like much more active agents, responding to environmental cues in ways more subtle or adaptive than the word "instinct"
would suggest. "Plants perceive competitors and grow away from them,"
Rick Karban, a plant ecologist at U.C. Davis, explained, when I asked him
for an example of plant decision-making. "They are more leery of actual
(80)   vegetation than they are of inanimate objects, and they respond to potential competitors before actually being shaded by them." These are sophisticated behaviors, but, like most plant behaviors, to an animal they're
either invisible or really, really slow.

The sessile life style also helps account for plants' extraordinary gift for
(85)   biochemistry, which far exceeds that of animals and, arguably, of human
chemists. (Many drugs, from aspirin to opiates, derive from compounds
designed by plants.) Unable to run away, plants deploy a complex molecular vocabulary to signal distress, deter or poison enemies, and recruit
animals to perform various services for them. A recent study in *Science*
(90)   found that the caffeine produced by many plants may function not only as
a defense chemical, as had previously been thought, but in some cases as a
psychoactive drug in their nectar. The caffeine encourages bees to remember a particular plant and return to it, making them more faithful and
effective pollinators.

(95)   One of the most productive areas of plant research in recent years has
been plant signalling. Since the early nineteen-eighties, it has been known
that when a plant's leaves are infected or chewed by insects they emit

---

[10]trajectory—a path

volatile chemicals that signal other leaves to mount a defense. Sometimes this warning signal contains information about the identity of the insect, (100) gleaned from the taste of its saliva. Depending on the plant and the attacker, the defense might involve altering the leaf's flavor or texture, or producing toxins or other compounds that render the plant's flesh less digestible to herbivores. When antelopes browse acacia trees, the leaves produce tannins that make them unappetizing and difficult to digest. (105) When food is scarce and acacias are overbrowsed, it has been reported, the trees produce sufficient amounts of toxin to kill the animals. ...

All species face the same existential challenges—obtaining food, defending themselves, reproducing—but under wildly varying circumstances, and so they have evolved wildly different tools in order to survive. (110) Brains come in handy for creatures that move around a lot; but they're a disadvantage for ones that are rooted in place. Impressive as it is to us, self-consciousness is just another tool for living, good for some jobs, unhelpful for others. That humans would rate this particular adaptation so highly is not surprising, since it has been the shining destination of (115) our long evolutionary journey, along with the epiphenomenon of self-consciousness that we call "free will." ...

—Michael Pollan
excerpted from "The Intelligent Plant"
The New Yorker, December 23 & 30, 2013

15 The first paragraph conveys a sense of

   (1) caution   (3) excitement

   (2) accusation   (4) relief   15____

16 The details in the first paragraph serve mainly to establish the

   (1) relationship between plant science and musical trends

   (2) difference between houseplants and wild plants

   (3) importance of forensic science for theories of plant behavior

   (4) impact of early studies of plant behavior on current research   16____

17 The author uses the word "But" in line 20 to

   (1) express the controversial nature of "The Secret Life of Plants"

   (2) compare "The Secret Life of Plants" with "What a Plant Knows"

   (3) express the similarities between certain types of plants

   (4) compare the learning ability of particular types of plants   17____

18 A primary purpose of the details in lines 46 through 50 is to indicate a connection

   (1) among diverse plant species

   (2) among several independent studies

   (3) between humans and plants

   (4) between predators and prey   18____

19 The use of quotation marks in lines 70 and 73 acknowledges the presence of

   (1) deception   (3) confusion

   (2) debate   (4) resentment   19____

20 Lines 72 through 77 support a central idea suggesting that plants

  (1) resist cooperation   (3) produce sound
  (2) avoid modification   (4) possess intent   20_____

21 The evidence provided in lines 89 through 94 demonstrates that plants may

  (1) develop symbiotic relationships
  (2) attack weaker organisms
  (3) waste essential resources
  (4) produce genetic mutations   21_____

22 The term "plant signalling" (line 96) refers to the
way plants

  (1) reproduce with similar species
  (2) protect themselves from predators
  (3) react to human contact
  (4) adapt themselves to climate   22_____

23 The final paragraph contributes to a central idea by
suggesting that

  (1) humans have acquired superior characteristics
  (2) species develop according to their own needs
  (3) plants would benefit from having self-aware-
       ness
  (4) scientists have dismissed important findings   23_____

24 The text's credibility relies on the author's use of

  (1) order of importance
  (2) extended comparison
  (3) observable evidence
  (4) personal anecdotes   24_____

PART 2—Argument Response

Directions: Closely read each of the **four** texts on pages 338 through 346 and write a source-based argument on the topic below. You may use the margins to take notes as you read and scrap paper to plan your response. Write your argument on a separate sheet of paper.

> **Topic:** Should school recess be structured play?

> **Your Task:** Carefully read each of the **four** texts provided. Then, using evidence from at least **three** of the texts, write a well-developed argument regarding whether or not school recess should be structured play. Clearly establish your claim, distinguish your claim from alternate or opposing claims, and use specific, relevant, and sufficient evidence from at least **three** of the texts to develop your argument. Do *not* simply summarize each text.

Guidelines:

Be sure to

- Establish your claim regarding whether or not school recess should be structured play
- Distinguish your claim from alternate or opposing claims
- Use specific, relevant, and sufficient evidence from at least **three** of the texts to develop your argument
- Identify each source that you reference by text number and line number(s) or graphic (for example: Text 1, line 4 or Text 2, graphic)
- Organize your ideas in a cohesive and coherent manner
- Maintain a formal style of writing
- Follow the conventions of standard written English

Texts:

Text 1

The Crucial Role of Recess in School

...Structured recess is a recess based on structured play, during which games and physical activities are taught and led by a trained adult (teachers, school staff, or volunteers). Proponents[1] for structured recess note that children often need help in developing games and require suggestions

(5) and encouragement to participate in physical activities. Recently, policy makers and funding organizations have called for more opportunities for daily activity as a means to address childhood obesity. These statements have strengthened the argument to maintain or reinstate recess as an integral component of the school day. Although this new dimension to the

(10) recess debate has increased attention on its role, it also has created tension. Some have promoted recess time as a solution for increasing children's physical activity and combating obesity. If recess assumes such a role, then, like physical education, it will need to be planned and directed to ensure that all children are participating in moderately vigorous physical activ-

(15) ity. Pediatric health care providers, parents, and school officials should be cognizant,[2] however, that in designing a structured recess, they will sacrifice the notion of recess as an unstructured but supervised break that belongs to the child; that is, a time for the child to make a personal choice between sedentary, physical, creative, or social options. However, there

(20) are many cited benefits of structured recess to consider, including:

- Older elementary children may benefit from game instruction and encouragement for total class inclusion.
- Children can be coached to develop interpersonal skills for appropriate conflict resolution.

(25)
- More children can actively participate in regular activity, irrespective of skill level.
- Anecdotally,[3] teachers have reported improved behavior and attention in the classroom after vigorous structured recess.

---

[1]proponents—those who support
[2]cognizant—aware
[3]anecdotally—based on casual observation

(30)   To be effective, structured recess requires that school personnel (or volunteers) receive adequate training so that they are able to address and encourage the diverse needs of all students. One aspect of supervision should be to facilitate social relationships among children by encouraging inclusiveness in games. A problem arises when the structured activities of recess are promoted as a replacement for the child's physical education

(35)   requirement. The replacement of physical education by recess threatens students' instruction in and acquisition of new motor skills, exploration of sports and rules, and a concept of lifelong physical fitness.

         There are ways to encourage a physically active recess without necessarily adding structured, planned, adult-led games, such as offering attrac-

(40)   tive, safe playground equipment to stimulate free play; establishing games/boundaries painted on the playground; or instructing children in games, such as four square or hop-scotch. These types of activities can range from fully structured (with the adult directing and requiring participation) to partly unstructured (with adults providing supervision and initial instruc-

(45)   tion) to fully unstructured (supervision and social guidance). In structured, partly structured, or unstructured environments, activity levels vary widely on the basis of school policy, equipment provided, encouragement, age group, gender, and race. Consequently, the potential benefits of mandatory participation of all children in a purely structured recess

(50)   must be weighed against the potential social and emotional trade-off of limiting acquisition of important developmental skills. Whichever style is chosen, recess should be viewed as a supplement to motor skill acquisition in physical education class. ...

—Council on School Health
excerpted from "The Crucial Role of Recess in School," December 31, 2012
http://pediatrics.aapublications.org/

Text 2

Why Children Need More Unstructured Play

The nature of an average child's free time has changed. For the past 25 years kids have been spending decreasing amounts of time outdoors. The time that our kids do spend outdoors is frequently a part of an organized sports activity. Other activities taking up our children's time include

(5) indoor lessons and organized events such as music, art and dance lessons. Another big indoor activity, taking up to 7.5 hours a day of our children's time according to a Kaiser Family Foundation study, is electronic entertainment. Of course some of these activities bring joy and fulfillment to our kids, but, in return, time for unstructured play has decreased.

(10) Unstructured play is that set of activities that children create on their own without adult guidance. Children naturally, when left to their own devices, will take initiative and create activities and stories in the world around them. Sometimes, especially with children past the toddler stage, the most creative play takes place outside of direct adult supervision.

(15) Unstructured free play can happen in many different environments, however, the outdoors may provide more opportunities for free play due to the many movable parts, such as sticks, dirt, leaves and rocks which lend themselves to exploration and creation.

Some parents find it challenging to provide unstructured play time for

(20) their kids. Letting our kids play without constant supervision, especially outside, can be even more difficult. It feels hard to balance reasonable concern, over-vigilance, and the desire to let our kids experience freedom and learn from their own mistakes and experiences. ...

Why might we need to loosen up and get over some of our fears in

(25) order to get our kids outdoor unstructured play time? In the January 2005 *Archives of Pediatric and Adolescent Medicine*, Burdette and Whitaker wrote on the importance of free play. They argue that free play promotes intellectual and cognitive growth, emotional intelligence, and benefits social interactions. They describe how play involves problem

(30) solving which is one of the highest executive functions. ["]Children plan, organize, sequence, and make decisions,["] they explain. In addition, play requires attention to the game and, especially in the case of very young children, frequent physical activity. Unstructured play frequently comes

from or results in exposure to the outdoors. Surveys of parents and teach-
(35) ers report that children's focus and attention are improved after outdoor
physical activity and free play and some small studies suggest that time
spent outdoors improves focus in children with ADHD [Attention Deficit
Hyperactivity Disorder].

Socialization and emotional intelligence benefit through shared inter-
(40) actions and physical movement that take place during play. Children must
work together to decide which game to play, what agreeable rules are, and
how to manage scenarios that invariably involve their differing perspectives. This "work" builds the social qualities that we all wish for our children: empathy, self-awareness, self-regulation, and flexibility. Emotional
(45) development is promoted along with physical health when people spend
time moving. In adults and older children physical activity has been well
documented to decrease stress, anxiety, and depression, and to improve
overall mood. Though the research is sparse in younger children, it seems
likely that our youngest children benefit as well. Free play in toddlers and
(50) young children most frequently involves spurts of gross motor activity
over a period of time with multiple episodes of rest in between. Most children are smiling and laughing when they engage in play, and it is reasonable to assume that their mood is improved during and after play. ...

—Avril Swan, MD
excerpted and adapted from "Why Children Need More
Unstructured Play" *www.kevinmd.com*, July 21, 2011

Text 3

Study Weighs Benefits of Organizing Recess

While an overwhelming number of elementary school principals believe in the power of recess to improve academic achievement and make students more focused in class, most discipline-related problems happen at school when kids cut loose at recess and lunch, according to surveys.

(5)   One of the solutions, according to a study released this week [2012] by the Robert Wood Johnson Foundation: more, and well-trained, staff on the playground.

The study examines an approach to creating more-structured recess time that is provided by Playworks, based in Oakland, Calif. It finds
(10)   that the nonprofit organization's program can smooth the transition between recess and class time—giving teachers more time to spend on instruction—and can cut back on bullying in the schoolyard. Teachers in participating schools also reported that their students felt safer and more included at recess, compared with those at schools without the
(15)   program. ...

The most significant finding shows students who participate in a Playworks-structured recess transition from that to schoolwork more quickly than students in traditional recess, said Susanne James-Burdumy, an associate director of research at Mathematica Policy Research.
(20)   "I think it is an exciting set of findings," Ms. James-Burdumy said. "This is one area where Playworks is aiming to have an impact: specifically trying to improve students' ability to focus on class activities."

The study found that, on average, teachers at participating schools needed about 2.5 fewer minutes of transition time between recess and
(25)   learning time—a difference that researchers termed statistically significant. Over the course of a school year, that can add up to about a day of class time.

Scaling Up

The Robert Wood Johnson Foundation, also based in Princeton, has been funding Playworks since 2005. It helped the program expand from a
(30)   few schools in Oakland to more than 300 schools in 23 cities, said Nancy

Barrand, the foundation's senior adviser for program development. The goal is to expand into 27 cities and 750 schools.

"We're using a process of scaling where we've identified a successful, evidence-based model," Ms. Barrand said. Playworks "is a pretty common-
(35) sense approach. It's really about the school environment and how you create a healthy school environment for the children," she continued. "If children are healthy and happy, they learn better."

Playworks founder and chief executive officer, Jill Vialet, said the idea came from a frustrated principal 15 years ago. The principal had been
(40) dealing with the same three students daily because of scuffles and mischief at recess that spilled over into their classes.

Ms. Vialet wondered whether creating a little structure at recess could quell some of those ongoing woes. She recalled her own days as a child when a municipal parks and recreation worker named Clarence made sure
(45) she—one of the few girls there—was included in the games at a District of Columbia park.

"I wanted to make sure every kid had a Clarence," she said. …

The coaches map the area where students spend recess, setting boundaries for different activities, such as kickball. They help children pick teams
(50) using random measures, such as students' birth months, to circumvent emotionally scarring episodes of being chosen based on skill or popularity. If conflicts arise, coaches teach simple ways to settle disputes and preempt some quibbles by teaching games including rock-paper-scissors.

Forty percent of the surveyed teachers said students used the rock-
(55) paper-scissors game to resolve conflicts or make decisions when they were back in class.

Coaches get involved in the activities, which "makes it possible for kids who don't see themselves as super-sporty to get into the games themselves," Ms. Vialet said. "There's just enough structure for the kids to be
(60) successful."

Solving Own Problems

While adults need to be present and ready to intervene at recess if necessary, said Edward Miller, one of the founding partners of the New York City-based Alliance for Childhood, and Playworks provides that service, children should also have the opportunity for individual and small-group
(65) play. …

The Mathematica study found Playworks has a mixed effect on behaviors related to bullying: Teachers at schools with the program found that there was significantly less bullying and exclusionary behavior during recess than teachers at schools without it, but not a reduction in more
(70) general aggressive behavior. Playworks has no formal curriculum that addresses the problem, Ms. Vialet noted.

"Our coaches are functioning like the older kids in the play yard used to: teaching kids rules to games, intervening if there is conflict, norming[1] behaviors around inclusion," she said.

(75) However, researchers also found that teachers' and students' perception of aggression and bullying on the playground differed. While teachers observed that there was less name-calling, shoving of classmates, and excluding of some students from games because of Playworks, students didn't, Mathematica's Ms. James-Burdumy said. ...

—Nirvi Shah
excerpted and adapted from
"Study Weighs Benefits of Organizing Recess"
www.edweek.org, April 17, 2012

---

[1]norming—setting a standard

Text 4

Forget Goofing Around: Recess Has a New Boss

Newark — At Broadway Elementary School here, there is no more sitting around after lunch. No more goofing off with friends. No more doing nothing.

(5) Instead there is Brandi Parker, a $14-an-hour recess coach with a whistle around her neck, corralling children behind bright orange cones to play organized games. There she was the other day, breaking up a renegade game of hopscotch and overruling stragglers' lame excuses.

They were bored. They had tired feet. They were no good at running.

"I don't like to play," protested Esmeilyn Almendarez, 11.

(10) "Why do I have to go through this every day with you?" replied Ms. Parker, waving her back in line. "There's no choice."

Broadway Elementary brought in Ms. Parker in January out of exasperation with students who, left to their own devices, used to run into one another, squabble over balls and jump-ropes or monopolize the blacktop

(15) while exiling their classmates to the sidelines. Since she started, disciplinary referrals at recess have dropped by three-quarters, to an average of three a week. And injuries are no longer a daily occurrence.

"Before, I was seeing nosebleeds, busted lips, and students being a danger to themselves and others," said Alejandro Echevarria, the principal.

(20) "Now, Coach Brandi does miracles with 20 cones and three handballs."

The school is one of a growing number across the country that are reining in recess to curb bullying and behavior problems, foster social skills and address concerns over obesity. They also hope to show children that there is good old-fashioned fun to be had without iPods and video

(25) games. ...

Although many school officials and parents like the organized activity, its critics say it takes away the only time that children have to unwind. ...

Dr. Romina M. Barros, an assistant clinical professor at Albert Einstein College of Medicine in the Bronx who was an author of a widely

(30) cited study on the benefits of recess, published last year [2009] in the journal *Pediatrics*, says that children still benefit most from recess when they

are let alone to daydream, solve problems, use their imagination to invent their own games and "be free to do what they choose to do."

Structured recess, Dr. Barros said, simply transplants the rules of the
(35) classroom to the playground.

"You still have to pay attention," she said. "You still have to follow rules. You don't have that time for your brain to relax." ...

Ms. Parker, 28, the coach at Broadway Elementary, had worked as a counselor for troubled teenagers in a group home in Burlington, N.C.
(40) Besides her work at recess, she visits each class once a week to play games that teach lessons about cooperation, sportsmanship and respect.

"These are the things that matter in life: who you are as a human being at the core," she said. ...

There are three 15-minute recesses, with more than 100 children at a
(45) time packed into a fenced-in basketball court equipped with nothing more than a pair of netless hoops.

On a chilly morning, Ms. Parker shoveled snow off the blacktop so that the students could go outside after being cooped up in the cafeteria during recess in the previous week. She drew squares in blue and green chalk for
(50) a game called switch, a fast-paced version of musical chairs—without the chairs. (She goes through a box of chalk a week.) Ms. Parker, who greets students with hugs and a cheerful "hello-hello," keeps the rules simple so that they can focus on playing rather than on following directions. "We're trying to get them to exert energy, to get it all out," she said. "They can
(55) be as loud as they want. I never tell them to be quiet unless I'm telling them something." ...

—Winnie Hu
excerpted and adapted from "Forget Goofing Around:
Recess Has a New Boss" *www.nytimes.com*, March 14, 2010

PART 3—Text-Analysis Response

Your Task: Closely read the text on pages 348 through 350 and write a well-developed, text-based response of two to three paragraphs. In your response, identify a central idea in the text and analyze how the author's use of *one* writing strategy (literary element or literary technique or rhetorical device) develops this central idea. Use strong and thorough evidence from the text to support your analysis. Do *not* simply summarize the text. You may use the margins to take notes as you read and scrap paper to plan your response. Write your response on a separate sheet of paper.

Guidelines:

Be sure to

- Identify a central idea in the text.
- Analyze how the author's use of *one* writing strategy (literary element or literary technique or rhetorical device) develops this central idea. Examples include: characterization, conflict, denotation/connotation, metaphor, simile, irony, language use, point-of-view, setting, structure, symbolism, theme, tone, etc.
- Use strong and thorough evidence from the text to support your analysis.
- Organize your ideas in a cohesive and coherent manner.
- Maintain a formal style of writing.
- Follow the conventions of standard written English.

Text

The following excerpt from the memoir of a South Pole explorer includes quotations from his diary.

...Then came a fateful day — Wednesday, October 27. The position was lat. [latitude] 69° 5′ S., long. [longitude] 51° 30′ W. The temperature was −8.5° Fahr. [Fahrenheit], a gentle southerly breeze was blowing and the sun shone in a clear sky. "After long months of ceaseless anxiety and
(5) strain, after times when hope beat high and times when the outlook was black indeed, the end of the *Endurance* has come. But though we have been compelled to abandon the ship, which is crushed beyond all hope of ever being righted, we are alive and well, and we have stores and equipment for the task that lies before us. The task is to reach land with all the members
(10) of the Expedition. It is hard to write what I feel. To a sailor his ship is more than a floating home, and in the *Endurance* I had centred ambitions, hopes, and desires. Now, straining and groaning, her timbers cracking and her wounds gaping, she is slowly giving up her sentient[1] life at the very outset of her career. She is crushed and abandoned after drifting more
(15) than 570 miles in a north-westerly direction during the 281 days since she became locked in the ice. The distance from the point where she became beset[2] to the place where she now rests mortally hurt in the grip of the floes[3] is 573 miles, but the total drift through all observed positions has been 1186 miles, and probably we actually covered more than 1500 miles.
(20) We are now 346 miles from Paulet Island, the nearest point where there is any possibility of finding food and shelter. A small hut built there by the Swedish expedition in 1902 is filled with stores left by the Argentine relief ship. I know all about those stores, for I purchased them in London on behalf of the Argentine Government when they asked me to equip the
(25) relief expedition. The distance to the nearest barrier west of us is about 180 miles, but a party going there would still be about 360 miles from Paulet Island and there would be no means of sustaining life on the barrier. We could not take from here food enough for the whole journey; the weight would be too great.

---

[1]sentient—conscious
[2]beset—hemmed in
[3]floes—ice sheets

(30)   "This morning, our last on the ship, the weather was clear, with a
gentle south-southeasterly to south-south-westerly breeze. From the
crow's-nest there was no sign of land of any sort. The pressure was increasing steadily, and the passing hours brought no relief or respite[4] for the
ship. The attack of the ice reached its climax at 4 p.m. The ship was hove[5]
(35)   stern up by the pressure, and the driving floe, moving laterally across the
stern, split the rudder and tore out the rudder-post and stern-post. Then,
while we watched, the ice loosened and the *Endurance* sank a little. The
decks were breaking upwards and the water was pouring in below. Again
the pressure began, and at 5 p.m. I ordered all hands on to the ice. The
(40)   twisting, grinding floes were working their will at last on the ship. It was
a sickening sensation to feel the decks breaking up under one's feet, the
great beams bending and then snapping with a noise like heavy gunfire.
The water was overmastering the pumps, and so to avoid an explosion
when it reached the boilers I had to give orders for the fires to be drawn[6]
(45)   and the steam let down. The plans for abandoning the ship in case of emergency had been made well in advance, and men and dogs descended to the
floe and made their way to the comparative safety of an unbroken portion
of the floe without a hitch. Just before leaving, I looked down the engine-
room skylight as I stood on the quivering deck, and saw the engines drop-
(50)   ping sideways as the stays and bed-plates gave way. I cannot describe the
impression of relentless destruction that was forced upon me as I looked
down and around. The floes, with the force of millions of tons of moving
ice behind them, were simply annihilating the ship." ...
        "To-night the temperature has dropped to −16° Fahr., and most of
(55)   the men are cold and uncomfortable. After the tents had been pitched I
mustered all hands and explained the position to them briefly and, I hope,
clearly. I have told them the distance to the barrier and the distance to
Paulet Island, and have stated that I propose to try to march with equipment across the ice in the direction of Paulet Island. I thanked the men for
(60)   the steadiness and good *morale* they have shown in these trying circumstances, and told them I had no doubt that, provided they continued to
work their utmost and to trust me, we will all reach safety in the end. Then

[4]respite—rest
[5]hove—heaved
[6]drawn—closed

we had supper, which the cook had prepared at the big blubber stove, and after a watch[7] had been set all hands except the watch turned in."
(65) For myself, I could not sleep. The destruction and abandonment of the ship was no sudden shock. The disaster had been looming ahead for many months, and I had studied my plans for all contingencies[8] a hundred times. But the thoughts that came to me as I walked up and down in the darkness were not particularly cheerful. The task now was to secure the safety of the
(70) party, and to that I must bend my energies and mental power and apply every bit of knowledge that experience of the Antarctic had given me. The task was likely to be long and strenuous, and an ordered mind and a clear programme were essential if we were to come through without loss of life. A man must shape himself to a new mark directly the old one goes to
(75) ground. ...

—Sir Ernest Shackleton
excepted and adapted from *South*, 1920
The MacMillan Company

---

[7]watch — crewman who stays awake on guard all night
[8]contingencies — possibilities

Regents ELA (Common Core) Answers June 2017

English Language Arts

Answer Key

Part 1

1. 1		9. 1		17. 1	
2. 2		10. 3		18. 3	
3. 4		11. 1		19. 2	
4. 3		12. 3		20. 4	
5. 1		13. 4		21. 1	
6. 4		14. 2		22. 2	
7. 3		15. 3		23. 2	
8. 1		16. 4		24. 3	

**Regents Examination in English Language Arts
(Common Core)—June 2017**

Chart for Converting Total Weighted Raw Scores to Final Exam
Scores (Scale Scores) (Use for the June 2017 examination only.)

Weighted Raw Score*	Scale Score	Performance Level		Weighted Raw Score*	Scale Score	Performance Level
56	100	5		27	52	1
55	99	5		26	47	1
54	99	5		25	43	1
53	99	5		24	39	1
52	98	5		23	36	1
51	97	5		22	32	1
50	96	5		21	28	1
49	95	5		20	24	1
48	94	5		19	21	1
47	92	5		18	18	1
46	91	5		17	14	1
45	90	5		16	11	1
44	88	5		15	9	1
43	87	5		14	8	1
42	86	5		13	7	1
41	85	5		12	6	1
40	83	4		11	5	1
39	82	4		10	5	1
38	80	4		9	4	1
37	79	4		8	3	1
36	76	4		7	3	1
35	74	3		6	2	1
34	72	3		5	2	1
33	69	3		4	1	1
32	66	3		3	1	1
31	65	3		2	1	1
30	60	2		1	1	1
29	57	2		0	0	1
28	55	2				

The conversion table is determined independently for each administration of
the exam.

Answers Explained

PART 1—Reading Comprehension

Multiple-Choice Questions

Passage A

(1) **1** "establish the reason for the meeting." In this paragraph, the narrator describes the letter he received from his uncle and the request that he assist his aunt when she comes to Boston to receive a small inheritance. This passage is factual and straightforward in tone and reveals little about the narrator or his aunt.

(2) **2** "careless about details." The narrator tells us that the letter showed signs of being carried in a pocket for several days, and that it arrived only the day before his aunt was to arrive. These details suggest that the uncle neglected to mail the letter in a timely way. None of the other choices is suggested in this paragraph.

(3) **4** "intelligent yet impulsive." We learn in these lines that the narrator's aunt had been an accomplished music teacher in Boston when she met and eloped with the young Howard, "… a young and shiftless [idle, lacking ambition] boy of twenty-one." These lines indicate that both her parents and her friends were deeply opposed to this relationship. Aunt Georgiana's actions suggest that she was not very critical, hesitant, or cautious in her youth.

(4) **3** "isolation." This passage describes a life with no money on a nearly barren prairie homestead of primitive conditions, which is "… fifty miles from the railroad." This detail at line 21 strongly suggests that Aunt Georgiana had been physically and emotionally isolated in the thirty years since she first arrived in Nebraska.

(5) **1** "It was to her, at her ironing or mending, that I read my first Shakespeare." In this section of the story, we learn that Aunt Georgiana gave the narrator his early encounters with classical education, coaching him in Latin, arithmetic, and music. The passage strongly implies that it was because of his aunt that the narrator had a life of possibilities beyond a Nebraska boyhood.

(6) **4** "implying that Aunt Georgiana missed having music in her life." The image in these lines strongly suggests how important music once was in her life as she urges the narrator as a young boy to develop musical ability himself. None of the other choices are suggested in these lines.

(7) **3** "realized what she has given up." Here the narrator indicates that he understood even as a boy how deeply his aunt felt the loss of music in her life. Among the choices, this is the most convincing description of the narrator's understanding.

(8) **1** "concern for daily responsibilities." This passage describes the aunt's reluctance to visit various places in Boston because, before the concert, she is "… chiefly concerned about … a weakling calf …," and a container of fish in the basement at home.

(9) **1** "bleak future." The author closes the story with images of the life Aunt Georgiana will return to: "the tall, unpainted house …," wash-cloths drying on the seedlings of trees, and gaunt turkeys pecking at, "… refuse about the kitchen door."

(10) **3** "there came to me an overwhelming sense of the waste and wear we are so powerless to combat." The first two choices are simple statements of fact, and the fourth is a statement about what the narrator does not fully understand. What he does feel is the sense of loss—of "waste and wear"—in his aunt's life.

Passage B

(11) **1** "a connection with the cultural heritage." The footnote identifies Highway 99 as the main route through California's Central Valley, where for generations migrant farm workers—historically from Mexico—have picked the crops. The poem ends with the poet's assertion that he will seek his own, and a different, life history. Note here how the title, "Mi Historia," contributes to the meaning of the poem.

(12) **3** "the labor of his relatives." The second stanza of the poem offers vivid images of what that life was like for his mother and grandmother. Close reading reveals that his mother was picking cotton as a young child, who, "… when she grew tired/… slept on her mother's burlap." The grandmother is also in the field picking cotton. It is this "history" that the poet is determined not to live.

(13) **4** "heard." The images in these lines are of the sounds the poet hears when, "History cried out to me … and pounded … sighed in the windows … groaned in the heat, and whispered its soft curses." None of the other choices describes the effect of the personification in these lines.

(14) **2** "understands that his future will have challenges." The poet says his new life, will be a "…bruise to throb hard as the asphalt … ." His new "history" may be a life as hard as the one of his ancestors, but it will be of his own choice. The tone of voice in the last five lines does not suggest that the poet feels regret at leaving or that he has made a wrong decision, nor does he express confidence that he will necessarily be successful.

Passage C

(15) **3** "excitement." This paragraph, about a once popular belief that plants had thoughts and emotions, closes with a description of Clive Backster's thrilling belief that he had proved, "Plants can think!" He is so excited, "… he felt like running into the street and shouting to the world … ."

(16) **4** "impact of early studies of plant behavior on current research." The author describes the claims of a popular book on "The Secret Life of

Plants" as "... a mashup of legitimate plant science, quack experiments, and mystical nature worship ... ." Because this kind of thinking, "was seeping into the mainstream ...," many legitimate scientists later tried to reproduce Backster's experiment, but without success.

(17) **1** "express the controversial nature of 'the Secret Life of Plants.'" Because "'The Secret Life of Plants', had made its mark on the culture ..., and people were talking to their plants and playing Mozart for them ...," many plant scientists later believed that the book had "... done lasting damage to their field." Because the science in Tompkins and Bird's work was formally discredited, later researchers were reluctant to explore "... any parallels between animal senses and plant senses."

(18) **3** "between humans and plants." This passage outlines the scientific view that plants have evolved, "... between fifteen and twenty distinct senses, ... which are analogues of our five ... ." None of the other choices accurately describes the purpose of this passage.

(19) **2** "debate." The terms "decides" and "behavior" are in quotes because they attribute human intentional acts to plants. This passage indicates that some scientists prefer to use these terms as metaphors, while others drop the quotation marks and describe plants as "active agents" in their behavior.

(20) **4** "possess intent." In the preceding paragraphs, the author outlines a number of ways in which plants actively respond to their environment: they can emit chemicals to defend from insects or to make themselves "... unappetizing and indigestible ..."; they can "... somehow 'hear' the sound of flowing water ..." and they will, "... share or compete for resources ...," with neighboring plants.

(21) **1** "develop symbiotic relationships." This item is an example of how the Regents Exam indirectly assesses vocabulary. The term "symbiotic" refers to a mutually beneficial relationship between or among plants and animals. These lines describe, for example, how the caffeine produced by many plants as a defense mechanism also "... encourages bees to remember [them] ..., making [the bees] more faithful and effective pollinators."

(22) **2** "protect themselves from predators." This paragraph presents examples of how, "when chewed or infected," plants can "... emit volatile chemicals that signal other leaves to mount a defense." Some plants or trees can produce, "toxins or other compounds that render [them] ... less digestible," even poisonous. None of the other choices accurately refers to the term "plant signalling."

(23) **2** "species develop according to their own needs." This paragraph concludes with the observation that, "All species face the same existential challenges ..., but under wildly varying circumstances, and so they have evolved wildly different tools in order to survive." This is the best choice to describe a central idea of the article, which is about the evolutionary adaptability of plants, not about the importance of brains and self-consciousness in humans.

(24) **3** "observable evidence." The author cites "several legitimate plant scientists" and reliable, published research to support each illustration of the plant world's "impressive capabilities."

PART 2—Argument Response

Sample Essay Response

Elementary school is a pivotal time for the development of children. A child's brain, emotions, and skills are very rapidly developing. With all of the structure and classroom education forced into children at that age, a time to unwind and grow interpersonally is crucial. Recess is a very important part of child development and should be a time for free, unlimited expression—not structured play.

Anyone who watches children play freely can see that they are completely capable of creating games and physical activities on their own. Students have shown that during this free playing time, "intellectual and cognitive growth, emotional intelligence, and social interactions" are all benefited and promoted (Text 2, lines 21–24). At a time when the brain is most delicate and moldable, these experiences are crucial. On the other hand, structured play forces a burden onto children who may not enjoy or feel comfortable in group sports and games. At one school practicing structured recess, the children would claim they, "were bored … had tired feet … were no good at running" (Text 4, line 7). In these programs, children are told they have "no choice" and are thus apt to develop negative attitudes toward physical activity and group play if they are forced to participate. Unstructured recess allows children a period of time to make their own choices and freely express themselves in a safe environment, while structured play takes away from this freedom and restricts the developing minds of young children.

Although structured recess shows potential benefits, there is contradictory and negative evidence. Supporters of structured recess claim that "significantly less bullying and exclusionary behavior" occurs during recess with structured play programs. However, there is no shown reduction in more general aggressive behavior (Text 3 lines 55–57). The lower aggression levels solely during recess will remain only during that period of time. Children will still find a way to bully and hurt others. Therefore, a simple reduction in immediate bullying is not worth further taking away from the freedom and creative expression of children. Reducing child obesity is another objective on the minds of supporters (Text 1, lines 4–5). However, children in elementary school are already offered a physical education class, which they regularly attend. The option to pursue more physical activities should then be left up to the students, and not miserably forced upon them.

Structured recess is an unnecessary stressor on young children. This form of play takes away from children's creative expression and initial exposure to freedom. Children should be allowed freedom at recess time, and schools should not force structured play upon them.

Analysis

This is a good response to the task. The writer establishes a clear and thoughtful position in the opening paragraph: "Recess is a very important part of child development and should be a time for free, unlimited expression—not structured play." The argument is then briefly, but adequately, developed in the body of the essay and supported with relevant references to the texts. The argument is logical, coherent, and generally well written. The final sentence of the second paragraph is an especially strong assertion of the writer's argument: "Unstructured recess allows children a period of time to make their own choices and freely express themselves in a safe environment, while structured play takes away from this freedom and restricts the developing minds of young children."

An even stronger response to this part of the exam would offer a more extensive discussion, with additional examples and citations from the wide range of evidence in the texts. This response, however, reflects understanding of the main issue and offers a strong argument on one side of the issue. This response would merit a high score.

(See pages 80–81 for the scoring guidelines.)

PART 3—Text-Analysis Response

Sample Essay Response

 The South Pole explorer develops an important and central theme throughout this memoir, excerpted from his diary. The explorer conveys that the destruction of the Endurance, the ship that was more than just his "floating home," was heartbreaking. The explorer states that it was in the ship that he had "centered ambitions, hopes, and desires." At several points, the explorer declares that he finds it difficult to put into words his true feelings about the demise of the Endurance. He explains that even though he had planned for the possible disaster and that the end of the ship was "looming ahead for many months," he was profoundly disturbed by the loss. The explorer recounts this devastating loss in vivid language and images.

 The South Pole explorer, Edwin Shackleton, develops this central theme through the use of figurative language, primarily personification. He gives the ship human qualities to illustrate the importance of the Endurance in his life and heart. The most vivid example of personification is, "Now straining and groaning ... her wounds gaping, she is slowly giving up her sentient life ..." This personification shows how Shackleton feels the pain of his ship "dying." He also personifies the cause of destruction, the floes in which the ship is breaking up, "mortally hurt," as "the attack of the ice." The explorer also uses a simile in describing the breaking up of the Endurance, which was "snapping with a noise like heavy gunfire." For Shackleton, it was as if a loved one was being gunned down. This South Pole explorer successfully conveys his profound loss to the reader in beautiful and moving figurative language.

Analysis

This writer recognizes the author's powerful use of figurative language to describe a central incident in this passage, an account that is otherwise composed in the language of factual detail and scientific observation. The first paragraph explains the significance of the event to the author and establishes the central idea of the response. In the second paragraph, this writer illustrates, with relevant quotes, how Shackleton conveys the heartbreak of the loss of his ship. The significance of the examples is presented clearly and convincingly, with skillful use of complex sentence structures. There are no significant errors in the conventions. This response would merit a high score.

(See pages 82–83 for the scoring guidelines.)

Regents ELA (Common Core) Examination August 2017

English Language Arts

PART 1—Reading Comprehension

Directions (1–24): Closely read each of the three passages below. After each passage, there are several multiple-choice questions. Select the best suggested answer to each question and write its number in the space provided. You may use the margins to take notes as you read.

Reading Comprehension Passage A

In this passage, Dora-Rouge, a Native American Indian elder, is traveling back to her homeland by canoe with a small group of women.

 ...As we traveled, we entered time and began to trouble it, to pester it apart or into some kind of change. On the short nights we sat by firelight and looked at the moon's long face on water. Dora-Rouge would lie on the beaver blankets and tell us what place we would pass on the next day.
(5) She'd look at the stars in the shortening night and say, "the Meeting Place," or "God Island." True to her word, the next day we reached those places. ...
 Now, looking back, I understand how easily we lost track of things. The time we'd been teasing apart, unraveled. And now it began to unravel
(10) us as we entered a kind of timelessness. Wednesday was the last day we called by name, and truly, we no longer needed time. We were lost from

it, and lost in this way, I came alive. It was as if I'd slept for years, and was now awake. The others felt it, too. Cell by cell, all of us were taken in by water and by land, swallowed a little at a time. What we'd thought of as
(15) our lives and being on earth was gone, and now the world was made up of pathways of its own invention. We were only one of the many dreams of earth. And I knew we were just a small dream.

But there was a place inside the human that spoke with land, that entered dreaming, in the way that people in the north found direction in
(20) their dreams. They dreamed charts of land and currents of water. They dreamed where food animals lived. These dreams they called hunger maps and when they followed those maps, they found their prey. It was the language animals and humans had in common. People found their cures in the same way. ...

(25) For my own part in this dreaming, as soon as I left time, when Thursday and Friday slipped away, plants began to cross my restless sleep in abundance. A tendril reached through darkness, a first sharp leaf came up from the rich ground of my sleeping, opened upward from the place in my body that knew absolute truth. It wasn't a seed that had been planted
(30) there, not a cultivated growing, but a wild one, one that had been there all along, waiting. I saw vines creeping forward. Inside the thin lid of an eye, petals opened, and there was pollen at the center of each flower. Field, forest, swamp. I knew how they breathed at night, and that they were linked to us in that breath. It was the oldest bond of survival. I was devoted to
(35) woods the wind walked through, to mosses and lichens. Somewhere in my past, I had lost the knowing of this opening light of life, the taking up of minerals from dark ground, the magnitude of thickets and brush. Now I found it once again. Sleep changed me. I remembered things I'd forgotten, how a hundred years ago, leaves reached toward sunlight, plants bent into
(40) currents of water. Something persistent nudged me and it had morning rain on its leaves.

Maybe the roots of dreaming are in the soil of dailiness, or in the heart, or in another place without words, but when they come together and grow, they are like the seeds of hydrogen and the seeds of oxygen that
(45) together create ocean, lake, and ice. In this way, the plants and I joined each other. They entangled me in their stems and vines and it was a beautiful entanglement. ...

Some mornings as we packed our things, set out across water, the
world was the color of copper, a flood of sun arrived from the east, and a
(50) thick mist rose up from black earth. Other mornings, heating water over
the fire, we'd see the world covered with fog, and the birdsongs sounded
forlorn and far away. There were days when we traveled as many as thirty
miles. Others we traveled no more than ten. There were times when I
resented the work, and days I worked so hard even Agnes' liniment and
(55) aspirin would not relax my aching shoulders and I would crave ice, even a
single chip of it, cold and shining. On other days I felt a deep contentment
as I poled[1] inside shallow currents or glided across a new wide lake.

We were in the hands of nature. In these places things turned about
and were other than what they seemed. In silence, I pulled through the
(60) water and saw how a river appeared through rolling fog and emptied
into the lake. One day, a full-tailed fox moved inside the shadows of trees,
then stepped into a cloud. New senses came to me. I was equal to the other
animals, hearing as they heard, moving as they moved, seeing as they saw.

One night we stayed on an island close to the decaying, moss-covered
(65) pieces of a boat. Its remains looked like the ribs of a large animal. In the
morning, sun was a dim light reaching down through the branches of
trees. Pollen floated across the dark water and gathered, yellow and life-
giving, along the place where water met land. ...

One evening it seemed cooler. The air had a different feel, rarefied,
(70) clean, and thin. Wolves in the distance were singing and their voices made
a sound that seemed to lie upon the land, like a cloud covering the world
from one edge of the horizon to the other. We sat around the fire and listened, the light on our faces, our eyes soft. Agnes warmed her hands over
the flames.

(75) There was a shorter time of darkness every night, but how beautiful the
brief nights, with the stars and the wolves. ...

Sometimes I felt there were eyes around us, peering through trees and
fog. Maybe it was the eyes of land and creatures regarding us, taking our
measure. And listening to the night, I knew there was another horizon,
(80) beyond the one we could see. And all of it was storied land, land where
deities[2] walked, where people traveled, desiring to be one with infinite
space.

---

[1]poled—propelled a boat with a pole
[2]deities—gods

We were full and powerful, wearing the face of the world, floating in silence. Dora-Rouge said, "Yes, I believe we've always been lost," as we
(85) traveled through thick-grown rushes, marsh, and water so shallow our paddles touched bottom.

The four of us became like one animal. We heard inside each other in a tribal way. I understood this at once and was easy with it. With my grand-mothers, there was no such thing as loneliness. Before, my life had been
(90) without all its ears, eyes, without all its knowings. Now we, the four of us, all had the same eyes, and when Dora-Rouge pointed a bony finger and said, "This way," we instinctively followed that crooked finger.

I never felt lost. I felt newly found, opening, like the tiny eggs we found in a pond one day, fertile and transparent. I bent over them. The life was
(95) already moving inside them, like an eye or heartbeat. One day we passed alongside cliff walls that bore red, ancient drawings of moose and bear. These were said to have been painted not by humans, but by spirits. ...

—Linda Hogan
excerpted from "Solar Storms," 1995
Scribner

1 In lines 3 through 7, the narrator portrays Dora-Rouge as

   (1) compassionate   (3) knowledgeable
   (2) detached   (4) misguided   1____

2 In lines 16 and 17, the narrator compares people's lives to dreams in order to illustrate the idea of

   (1) resourcefulness   (3) vulnerability
   (2) individuality   (4) insignificance   2____

3 Which phrase from the text best illustrates the meaning of "tendril" as used in line 27?

   (1) "I saw vines creeping forward" (line 31)
   (2) "there was pollen at the center" (line 32)
   (3) "Field, forest, swamp" (lines 32 and 33)
   (4) "woods the wind walked through" (line 35)   3____

4 The imagery in lines 31 through 35 can best be described as

   (1) amusing   (3) confusing
   (2) threatening   (4) enlightening   4____

5 The description in lines 58 through 63 creates a sense of

   (1) transformation   (3) division
   (2) isolation   (4) vindication   5____

6 The phrase, "We were full and powerful, wearing the face of the world," (line 83) suggests that the group

   (1) believed they were something they were not
   (2) developed a kinship with the environment
   (3) became outwardly proud and aggressive
   (4) adopted a casual attitude toward nature   6____

7 The language use in lines 93 through 97 serves to

   (1) link the past with the future
   (2) continue an ongoing struggle
   (3) present a cultural dilemma
   (4) clarify the need for cooperation   7____

8 The passage is primarily developed through the use of

   (1) rhetorical questions
   (2) comparison and contrast
   (3) parallel structure
   (4) personal narrative   8____

9 The passage as a whole supports the theme that with

   (1) approval of society comes cultural freedom
   (2) clarity of mind comes connection of spirit
   (3) support of others comes environmental change
   (4) passage of time comes acceptance of nature   9____

10 Which quotation best supports a central idea of the passage?

   (1)   "Maybe the roots of dreaming are in the soil of dailiness" (line 42)

   (2)   "On other days I felt a deep contentment as I poled inside shallow currents or glided across a new wide lake" (lines 56 and 57)

   (3)   "The air had a different feel, rarefied, clean, and thin" (lines 69 and 70)

   (4)   "And listening to the night, I knew there was another horizon, beyond the one we could see" (lines 79 and 80)   10____

Reading Comprehension Passage B

I Am Vertical

But I would rather be horizontal.
I am not a tree with my root in the soil
Sucking up minerals and motherly love
So that each March I may gleam into leaf,
(5)   Nor am I the beauty of a garden bed
Attracting my share of Ahs and spectacularly painted,
Unknowing I must soon unpetal.
Compared with me, a tree is immortal
And a flower-head not tall, but more startling,
(10)   And I want the one's longevity and the other's daring.

Tonight, in the infinitesimal[1] light of the stars,
The trees and flowers have been strewing their cool odors.
I walk among them, but none of them are noticing.
Sometimes I think that when I am sleeping
(15)   I must most perfectly resemble them—
Thoughts gone dim.
It is more natural to me, lying down.
Then the sky and I are in open conversation,
And I shall be useful when I lie down finally:
(20)   Then the trees may touch me for once, and the flowers
                  have time for me.

—Sylvia Plath
from *Uncollected Poems*, 1965
Turret Books

---

[1]infinitesimal—very small

11 The word "unpetal" in line 7 suggests

    (1)   inspiration   (3)   isolation

    (2)   invisibility   (4)   impermanence   11_____

12 Lines 11 through 13 reveal the narrator's awareness of

    (1)   the limited time people exist on earth

    (2)   the unexpected changes that affect one's life

    (3)   her anxiety over the shifting of seasons

    (4)   her insignificance in the eyes of nature   12_____

13 In lines 14 through 16, the narrator suggests that

    (1)   consciousness is a barrier to connecting with nature

    (2)   nature's ability to impress surpasses human's imagination

    (3)   the future depends on natural forces beyond human control

    (4)   nature's cruelty causes one to feel helpless   13_____

14 Throughout the poem, the tone can best be described as

    (1)   envious   (3)   hostile

    (2)   skeptical   (4)   indignant   14_____

Reading Comprehension Passage C

(5)

(10)

(15)

(20)

(25)

(30)

Jian Lin was 14 years old in 1973, when the Chinese government under Mao Zedong recruited him for a student science team called "the earthquake watchers." After a series of earthquakes that had killed thousands in northern China, the country's seismologists[1] thought that if they augmented[2] their own research by having observers keep an eye out for anomalies like snakes bolting early from their winter dens and erratic[3] well-water levels, they might be able to do what no scientific body had managed before: issue an earthquake warning that would save thousands of lives.

In the winter of 1974, the earthquake watchers were picking up some suspicious signals near the city of Haicheng. Panicked chickens were squalling and trying to escape their pens; water levels were falling in wells. Seismologists had also begun noticing a telltale pattern of small quakes. "They were like popcorn kernels," Lin tells me, "popping up all over the general area." Then, suddenly, the popping stopped, just as it had before a catastrophic earthquake in 1966 that killed more than 8,000. "Like 'the calm before the storm,'" Lin says. "We have that exact same phrase in Chinese." On the morning of February 4, 1975, the seismology bureau issued a warning: Haicheng should expect a big earthquake, and people should move outdoors.

At 7:36 p.m., a magnitude 7.0 quake struck. The city was nearly leveled, but only about 2,000 people were killed. Without the warning, easily 150,000 would have died. "And so you finally had an earthquake forecast that did indeed save lives," Lin recalls. "People were excited. Or, you could say, uplifted. *Uplifted* is a great word for it." But uplift turned to heartbreak the very next year, when a 7.5 quake shattered the city of Tangshan without so much as a magnitude 4 to introduce it. When the quake hit the city of 1.6 million at 3:42 a.m., it killed nearly 250,000 people, most of whom were asleep. "If there was any moment in my life when I was scared of earthquakes, that was it," Lin says. "You think, what if it happened to you? And it could. I decided that if I could do

---

[1]seismologists—people who study earthquakes
[2]augmented—added to
[3]erratic—unpredictable

anything—*anything*—to save lives lost to earthquakes, it would be worth the effort."

(35)   Lin is now a senior scientist of geophysics at Woods Hole Oceanographic Institution, in Massachusetts, where he spends his time studying not the scurrying of small animals and fluctuating electrical current between trees (another fabled warning sign), but seismometer readings, GPS coordinates, and global earthquake-notification reports. He and his (40) longtime collaborator, Ross Stein of the U.S. Geological Survey, are champions of a theory that could enable scientists to forecast earthquakes with more precision and speed.

Some established geophysicists[4] insist that all earthquakes are random, yet everyone agrees that aftershocks are not. Instead, they follow certain empirical laws. Stein, Lin, and their collaborators hypothesized that many (45) earthquakes classified as main shocks are actually aftershocks, and they went looking for the forces that cause faults to fail.

Their work was in some ways heretical:[5] For a long time, earthquakes were thought to release only the stress immediately around them; an earthquake that happened in one place would decrease the possibility of (50) another happening nearby. But that didn't explain earthquake sequences like the one that rumbled through the desert and mountains east of Los Angeles in 1992. The series began on April 23 with a 6.2 near the town of Joshua Tree; two months later, on June 28, a 7.3 struck less than 15 miles away in the desert town of Landers. Three and a half hours after (55) that, a 6.5 hit the town of Big Bear, in the mountains overlooking the Mojave. The Big Bear quake was timed like an aftershock, except it was too far off the Landers earthquake's fault rupture. When Lin, Stein, and Geoffrey King of the Paris Geophysical Institute got together to analyze it, they decided to ignore the distance rule and treat it just as a different (60) kind of aftershock. Their ensuing report, "Static Stress Changes and the Triggering of Earthquakes," became one of the decade's most-cited earthquake research papers.

Rocks can be subject to two kinds of stresses: the "clamping" stress that pushes them together, and the "shear" stress they undergo as they

---

[4]geophysicists—people who study the physics of the earth and its environment, including seismology
[5]heretical—against the opinion of authorities

(65) slide past each other. Together, these stresses are known as Coulomb stress, named for Charles-Augustin de Coulomb, an 18th-century French physicist. Coulomb calculations had been used for years in engineering, to find the failure points of various building materials, but they'd never been applied properly to faults. It turned out, though, that faults in the ground

(70) behave much like rocks in the laboratory: they come unglued when shear stress exceeds the friction and pressure (the clamping stress) holding them together. When Stein, Lin, and King applied the Coulomb model to the California sequence, they found that most of the earthquakes had occurred in areas where the shifting of the ground had caused increased stress.

(75) In 1997, Stein and two other geologists using the model found that there was a 12 percent chance that a magnitude 7 or greater would hit near Izmit, Turkey, within 30 years; two years later, on August 17, 1999, a magnitude 7.4 destroyed the city, which wasn't designed to withstand such a tremor. A Turkish geologist named Aykut Barka quickly wrote up

(80) a paper warning that Coulomb stress from the Izmit quake could trigger a similar rupture near Düzce, a town roughly 60 miles east. His work persuaded authorities there to close school buildings damaged during the Izmit shaking. On November 12, a segment of the North Anatolian Fault gave way, in a magnitude 7.2. The empty school buildings collapsed.

(85) Lin and Stein both admit that Coulomb stress doesn't explain all earthquakes. Indeed, some geophysicists, like Karen Felzer, of the U.S. Geological Survey, think their hypothesis gives short shrift[6] to the impact that dynamic stress—the actual rattling of a quake in motion—has on neighboring faults.

(90) In the aftermath of the disastrous March 11 Tōhoku quake, both camps are looking at its well-monitored aftershocks (including several within 100 miles of Tokyo) for answers. Intriguingly, it was *preceded* by a flurry of earthquakes, one as large as magnitude 7.2, that may have been foreshocks, although no one thought so at the time; the researchers are

(95) trying to determine what those early quakes meant.

When I ask Lin whether California, where I live, is next, he laughs. "I understand that the public now thinks that we've entered a global earthquake cluster. Even my own mother in China thinks that. But there's no scientific evidence whatsoever to suggest that the earthquake in New

---

[6]short shrift—little consideration

(100) Zealand triggered the earthquake in Japan, or Japan will trigger one in California." Still, Lin and his colleagues do wonder whether Tōhoku has pushed neighboring faults closer to rupture. "I am particularly interested in how this earthquake might have changed the potential of future earthquakes to the south, even closer to Tokyo," Lin tells me. "There,
(105) even a much smaller earthquake could be devastating."

—Judith Lewis Mernit
"Is San Francisco Next?"
The Atlantic, June 2011

15 As used in line 6, the word "anomalies" most nearly
means

   (1) seasonal changes
   (2) odd occurrences
   (3) dangerous incidents
   (4) scheduled events   15____

16 The first paragraph contributes to a central idea in
the text by

   (1) contributing historical facts
   (2) contrasting early theories
   (3) comparing two philosophies
   (4) challenging cultural beliefs   16____

17 The figurative language in lines 14 and 15 conveys a
sense of

   (1) disbelief   (3) disappointment
   (2) apathy   (4) urgency   17____

18 The contrast drawn between the Haicheng and
Tangshan earthquakes (lines 10 through 33) contributes to a central idea that earthquakes are

   (1) preceded by reliable signs
   (2) controlled by observable factors
   (3) not always predictable
   (4) not often studied   18____

19 The purpose of lines 34 through 38 is to emphasize
that Jian Lin

   (1) relied on his past experience to identify earthquakes
   (2) modified his methods of observing earthquakes
   (3) changed his understanding about the causes of
earthquakes
   (4) disagreed with his co-researcher on the measure-
ment of earthquakes   19____

20 The word "champions" as used in line 40 most nearly means

   (1) advisers   (3) adaptors

   (2) supporters   (4) survivors   20____

21 Which statement reflects a long-held belief disproved by Lin, Stein, and King?

   (1) "many earthquakes classified as main shocks are actually aftershocks" (lines 44 and 45)

   (2) "an earthquake that happened in one place would decrease the possibility of another happening nearby" (lines 48 through 50)

   (3) "Rocks can be subject to two kinds of stresses" (line 63)

   (4) "faults in the ground behave much like rocks in the laboratory" (lines 69 and 70)   21____

22 According to lines 63 through 74, seismologists realized that the California sequence of earthquakes happened because

   (1) shear stress forced rocks to fuse together

   (2) clamping stress caused rocks to move apart

   (3) shear stress was greater than clamping stress

   (4) clamping stress balanced the shear stress   22____

23 Throughout the text, the author portrays Jian Lin as

   (1) satisfied   (3) cautious

   (2) superstitious   (4) dedicated   23____

24 Jian Lin's research regarding earthquakes can best be described as

   (1) flawed by inconsistent methodology

   (2) concurrent with prior theories

   (3) challenged by conflicting findings

   (4) important to future studies   24____

PART 2—Argument Response

Directions: Closely read each of the *four* texts on pages 377 through 386 and write a source-based argument on the topic below. You may use the margins to take notes as you read and scrap paper to plan your response. Write your argument on a separate sheet of paper.

Topic: Should self-driving cars replace human drivers?

Your Task: Carefully read each of the *four* texts provided. Then, using evidence from at least *three* of the texts, write a well-developed argument regarding whether or not self-driving cars should replace human drivers. Clearly establish your claim, distinguish your claim from alternate or opposing claims, and use specific, relevant, and sufficient evidence from at least *three* of the texts to develop your argument. Do *not* simply summarize each text.

Guidelines:

Be sure to

- Establish your claim regarding whether or not self-driving cars should replace human drivers.
- Distinguish your claim from alternate or opposing claims.
- Use specific, relevant, and sufficient evidence from at least *three* of the texts to develop your argument.
- Identify each source that you reference by text number and line number(s) or graphic (for example: Text 1, line 4 or Text 2, graphic).
- Organize your ideas in a cohesive and coherent manner.
- Maintain a formal style of writing.
- Follow the conventions of standard written English.

Texts:

Text 1—How Google's Self-Driving Car Will Change Everything

Text 2—Google's Driverless Cars Run Into Problem: Cars With Drivers

Text 3—Autonomous Vehicles Will Replace Taxi Drivers, But That's Just the Beginning

Text 4—Along for the Ride

Text 1

How Google's Self-Driving Car Will Change Everything

Imagine getting in your car, typing or speaking a location into your vehicle's interface, then letting it drive you to your destination while you read a book, surf the web or nap. Self-driving vehicles—the stuff of science fiction since the first roads were paved—are coming, and they're
(5) going to radically change what it's like to get from point A to point B.

Basic Technology Already In Use
...The first big leap to fully autonomous[1] vehicles is due in 2017, when Google Inc. (GOOG) said it would have an integrated system ready to market. Every major automotive manufacturer is likely to follow by the early 2020s, though their systems could wind up being more sensor-based,
(10) and rely less on networking and access to map information. Google probably wont [*sic*] manufacture cars. More likely, it'll license the software and systems.

A Drastic Change
As with the adoption of any new revolutionary technology, there will be problems for businesses that don't adjust fast enough. Futurists esti-
(15) mate that hundreds of billions of dollars (if not trillions) will be lost by automakers, suppliers, dealers, insurers, parking companies, and many other car-related enterprises. And think of the lost revenue for governments via licensing fees, taxes and tolls, and by personal injury lawyers and health insurers.
(20) Who needs a car made with heavier-gauge steel and eight airbags (not to mention a body shop) if accidents are so rare? Who needs a parking spot close to work if your car can drive you there, park itself miles away, only to pick you up later? Who needs to buy a flight from Boston to Cleveland when you can leave in the evening, sleep much of the way, and arrive in the
(25) morning?
Indeed, Google's goal is to increase car utilization from 5–10% to 75% or more by facilitating sharing. That means fewer cars on the road. Fewer cars period, in fact. Who needs to own a car when you can just order a

---
[1]autonomous—self-directed

shared one and it'll drive up minutes later, ready to take you wherever
(30)   you want? ...

Changing Oil Demand

If you're in the business of finding, extracting, refining and marketing
hydrocarbons,[2] such as Exxon Mobil Corp. (EOX), Chevron Corp. (CVX)
or BP plc (BP), you could see your business fluctuate as use changes.

"These vehicles should practice very efficient eco-driving practices,
(35)   which is typically about 20% better than the average driver," said [Robin]
Chase[3] [*sic*] "On the other hand, if these cars are owned by individuals, I
see a huge rise in the number of trips, and vehicle miles traveled. People
will send out their car to run errands they would never do if they had to
be in the car and waste their own time. If the autonomous cars are shared
(40)   vehicles and people pay for each trip, I think this will reduce demand, and
thus (vehicle miles traveled)."

Safety Dividend

..."Over 90% of accidents today are caused by driver error," said
Professor Robert W. Peterson of the Center for Insurance Law and
Regulation at Santa Clara University School of Law. "There is every rea-
(45)   son to believe that self-driving cars will reduce frequency and severity of
accidents, so insurance costs should fall, perhaps dramatically."

"Cars can still get flooded, damaged or stolen," notes Michael Barry,
the v.p. [vice president] of media relations at the Insurance Information
Institute. "But this technology will have a dramatic impact on underwrit-
(50)   ing.[4] A lot of traditional underwriting criteria will be upended."

Barry said it's too early to quantify exactly how self-driving vehicles
will affect rates, but added that injured parties in a crash involving a self-
driving car may choose to sue the vehicle's manufacturer, or the software
company that designed the autonomous capability. ...

Risks, Hurdles and the Unknown

(55)   There are regulatory and legislative obstacles to widespread use of self-
driving cars, and substantial concerns about privacy (who will have access

---

[2]hydrocarbons—organic compounds that are chief components of petroleum
and natural gas
[3]Robin Chase—founder and CEO of Buzzcar
[4]underwriting—risk determination

to any driving information these vehicles store?). There's also the question of security, as hackers could theoretically take control of these vehicles, and are not known for their restraint or civic-mindedness.

The Bottom Line

(60)   However it plays out, these vehicles are coming—and fast. Their full adoption will take decades, but their convenience, cost, safety and other factors will make them ubiquitous[5] and indispensable. Such as with any technological revolution, the companies that plan ahead, adjust the fastest and imagine the biggest will survive and thrive. And companies invested in
(65) old technology and practices will need to evolve or risk dying.

—Joseph A. Dallegro
excerpted and adapted from "How Google's
Self-Driving Car Will Change Everything"
www.investopedia.com, 2015

---

[5]ubiquitous—everywhere

Text 2

Google's Driverless Cars Run Into Problem: Cars With Drivers

Google, a leader in efforts to create driverless cars, has run into an odd safety conundrum:[1] humans.

Last month, as one of Google's self-driving cars approached a crosswalk, it did what it was supposed to do when it slowed to allow a pedes-
(5) trian to cross, prompting its "safety driver" to apply the brakes. The pedestrian was fine, but not so much Google's car, which was hit from behind by a human-driven sedan.

Google's fleet of autonomous test cars is programmed to follow the letter of the law. But it can be tough to get around if you are a stickler for
(10) the rules. One Google car, in a test in 2009, couldn't get through a four-way stop because its sensors kept waiting for other (human) drivers to stop completely and let it go. The human drivers kept inching forward, looking for the advantage—paralyzing Google's robot.

It is not just a Google issue. Researchers in the fledgling[2] field of auton-
(15) omous vehicles say that one of the biggest challenges facing automated cars is blending them into a world in which humans don't behave by the book. "The real problem is that the car is too safe," said Donald Norman, director of the Design Lab at the University of California, San Diego, who studies autonomous vehicles. ...

(20) Traffic wrecks and deaths could well plummet in a world without any drivers, as some researchers predict. But wide use of self-driving cars is still many years away, and testers are still sorting out hypothetical risks—like hackers—and real world challenges, like what happens when an autonomous car breaks down on the highway.

(25) For now, there is the nearer-term problem of blending robots and humans. Already, cars from several automakers have technology that can warn or even take over for a driver, whether through advanced cruise control or brakes that apply themselves. Uber is working on the self-driving car technology, and Google expanded its tests in July to Austin, Tex[as].

---
[1]conundrum—difficult problem
[2]fledgling—new and inexperienced

(30)   Google cars regularly take quick, evasive maneuvers or exercise caution in ways that are at once the most cautious approach, but also out of step with the other vehicles on the road. ...

Since 2009, Google cars have been in 16 crashes, mostly fender-benders, and in every single case, the company says, a human was at fault.
(35)   This includes the rear-ender crash on Aug. 20, and reported Tuesday by Google. The Google car slowed for a pedestrian, then the Google employee manually applied the brakes. The car was hit from behind, sending the employee to the emergency room for mild whiplash.

Google's report on the incident adds another twist: While the safety
(40)   driver did the right thing by applying the brakes, if the autonomous car had been left alone, it might have braked less hard and traveled closer to the crosswalk, giving the car behind a little more room to stop. Would that have prevented the collision? Google says it's impossible to say.

There was a single case in which Google says the company was respon-
(45)   sible for a crash. It happened in August 2011, when one of its Google cars collided with another moving vehicle. But, remarkably, the Google car was being piloted at the time by an employee. Another human at fault. ...

On a recent outing with *New York Times* journalists, the Google driverless car took two evasive maneuvers that simultaneously displayed how
(50)   the car errs on the cautious side, but also how jarring that experience can be. In one maneuver, it swerved sharply in a residential neighborhood to avoid a car that was poorly parked, so much so that the Google sensors couldn't tell if it might pull into traffic.

More jarring for human passengers was a maneuver that the Google
(55)   car took as it approached a red light in moderate traffic. The laser system mounted on top of the driverless car sensed that a vehicle coming the other direction was approaching the red light at higher-than-safe speed. The Google car immediately jerked to the right in case it had to avoid a collision. In the end, the oncoming car was just doing what human drivers so
(60)   often do: not approach a red light cautiously enough, though the driver did stop well in time.

Courtney Hohne, a spokeswoman for the Google project, said current testing was devoted to "smoothing out" the relationship between the car's software and humans. For instance, at four-way stops, the program lets
(65)   the car inch forward, as the rest of us might, asserting its turn while looking for signs that it is being allowed to go.

The way humans often deal with these situations is that "they make eye contact. On the fly, they make agreements about who has the right of way," said John Lee, a professor of industrial and systems engineering and expert in driver safety and automation at the University of Wisconsin.

(70)

"Where are the eyes in an autonomous vehicle?" he added. ...

—Matt Richtel and Conor Dougherty
excerpted and adapted from
"Google's Driverless Cars Run Into Problem: Cars With Drivers"
www.nytimes.com, Sept. 1, 2015

Text 3

Autonomous Vehicles Will Replace
Taxi Drivers, But That's Just the Beginning

...According to the Bureau of Labor Statistics [BLS] there are about 178,000 people employed as taxi drivers or chauffeurs in the United States. But once driverless technology advances to the point that vehicles can be fully autonomous—without the need for any human behind the
(5) wheel in case of emergencies—professional drivers will become a thing of the past. Bus drivers, whether they're for schools, cities, or long-distance travel, would be made obsolete. Once cars drive themselves, food deliveries will be a matter of restaurants filling a car with orders and sending it off, eliminating the need for a delivery driver. Each of these professions
(10) employ more people and are better paid than taxi drivers, as shown in the table below.

Occupation	Average annual wage	Number of jobs	Total annual wages
Taxi drivers & chauffeurs	$25,690	178,260	$4,579,499,400
Bus drivers – transit & intercity	$39,410	158,050	$6,228,750,500
Driver / sales workers (delivering food, newspapers)	$27,720	405,810	$11,249,053,200
Bus drivers – school or special client	$29,910	499,440	$14,938,250,400
Postal service mail carriers	$51,790	307,490	$15,924,907,100
Light truck or delivery services drivers (UPS, FedEx)	$33,870	797,010	$26,994,728,700
Heavy and tractor-trailer truck drivers	$41,930	1,625,290	$68,148,409,700
TOTAL	**$35,760.00**	**3,971,350**	**$148,063,599,000.00**

Source: Bureau of Labor Statistics

Some of these may be a bit surprising, like postal carriers. But once fully autonomous vehicles are commonplace it would make sense for the Postal Service to make use of the technology to deliver mail, especially

(15) in areas where curbside mailboxes are standard and it would be rather simple for a mechanical arm to deposit and retrieve mail directly. Drivers of delivery trucks for companies like UPS and FedEx may also face extinction, if they're not replaced by Amazon's delivery drones first—or perhaps they'll develop a combined system where self-driving trucks bring
(20) packages from the warehouse to their destination, and a drone delivers them the last few yards from curbside to doorstep.

Despite their importance for the economy, each of these professions pale [*sic*] in comparison to heavy and tractor-trailer truck drivers. This field employs the most by far—nine times as many people work as truck-
(25) ers than as taxi drivers, and it's the most common job in a whopping 29 states—and is also better paid than most, with an average salary of about $42,000. When considering the total amount of wages paid to each of the seven occupations in the table above, truck drivers make up nearly half, while taxi drivers & chauffeurs only account for 3%. The development of
(30) self-driving tractor-trailers won't be far behind automated taxi cabs, with companies like Daimler already testing out partially-automated trucks in Nevada.

While there may be other driving-focused jobs not included in these BLS statistics, there are certainly many more industries that will be
(35) impacted by the replacement of humans with self-driving vehicles. If this technology leads to a sharp decline in car ownership like many predict, insurance companies will have far fewer customers and may not need as many employees to service them. The same goes for mechanics and auto part manufacturers, who could face a massive drop in demand. Fewer
(40) human truckers on the road means fewer motel stays and rest stop visits, and cheaper trucking could take business away from freight trains or even oil pipelines. Vehicles programmed to obey traffic laws won't need nearly as much policing, which also means fewer traffic tickets and less revenue for municipalities. The full scale of these economic shifts will be impossible
(45) to understand until they're upon us, but the one thing we can know for sure is that they'll touch almost every aspect of society. ...

—Sam Tracy
excerpted and adapted from "Autonomous Vehicles Will
Replace Taxi Drivers, But That's Just the Beginning"
www.huffingtonpost.com, June 11, 2015

Text 4

Along for the Ride

...Automotive designers have a good incentive to get human drivers out from behind the wheel: public safety. In 2012, according to the most recent figures from the National Highway Traffic Safety Administration (NHTSA), 33,561 people were killed in car crashes in the United States,
(5)   and an estimated 2.36 million were injured. According to NHTSA, a number of major crash studies have found that human error caused more than 90 percent of those crashes. In a perfect world, technology would take driver error out of the equation. ...

But before society can reap those benefits, experts caution there are
(10) important problems to solve. Namely, since people interact with technology in unexpected ways, how will each individual driver engage with an automated car?

For some people, automation might lead to complacency,[1] says Nicholas Ward, PhD, a human factors psychologist in the department
(15) of mechanical and industrial engineering at Montana State University. Drivers who put too much trust in automation may become overly reliant on it, overestimating what the system can do for them. ...

Information overload may be another concern, says Neville Stanton, PhD, a psychologist at the University of Southampton in the United
(20) Kingdom, who studies human performance in technological systems. While automated systems are designed to take pressures off the driver, he's found that they may add complexity in some cases. In an automated system, drivers may feel compelled to monitor the behavior of the system as well as keep an eye on the driving environment. That extra pressure might
(25) increase stress and error. ...

Given a nearly infinite combination of driver personalities, road conditions and vehicle technologies, the answer is anything but straightforward. In a study using a driving simulator, for example, Stanton found that adaptive cruise control—in which a car maintains a safe following
(30) distance from the vehicle ahead of it—can reduce a driver's mental workload and stress levels. However, that technology also caused a reduction in

---

[1]complacency—a feeling of security, often while unaware of potential dangers

drivers' situational awareness. And while a lower mental workload may be a good thing in tricky traffic jams, it could cause problems if drivers totally tune out.

(35)   Indeed, driver disengagement is a serious concern for automated-car designers. Users in such vehicles are expected to tune out. After all, the appeal of such cars is that they can transport us to and fro without our having to do the hard work. But that presents a problem for our busy brains. ...

(40)   Detached from the activity of driving, most people soon begin to experience "passive fatigue," says Gerald Matthews, PhD, a psychologist at the Applied Cognition and Training in Immersive Virtual Environments Lab at the University of Central Florida. That cognitive muddling can be a big problem, Matthews says, if the driver has to take back control of the

(45)   vehicle (when leaving a highway "platoon" of automated cars to re-enter city streets, for instance—or, in a worst-case scenario, if automated systems fail). ...

Like it or not, though, carmakers are pressing forward with automated systems, and psychologists can play a role in making them as safe

(50)   as possible. One important issue, says Pradhan,[2] is how drivers of different ages, personalities, experience levels and cognitive abilities will deal with such systems. "There is no average driver. The field is so new, we're still asking a lot of fundamental questions—and there are very few people looking at driver characteristics," he says. "Automation has to be

(55)   designed for everybody." ...

—Kirsten Weir
excerpted from "Along for the Ride"
www.apa.org, January 2015

---

[2]Anuj K. Pradhan, PhD—a research scientist who studies driver behavior and injury prevention at the University of Michigan Transportation Research Institute

PART 3—Text-Analysis Response

Your Task: Closely read the text on pages 388 through 390 and write a well-developed, text-based response of two to three paragraphs. In your response, identify a central idea in the text and analyze how the author's use of *one* writing strategy (literary element or literary technique or rhetorical device) develops this central idea. Use strong and thorough evidence from the text to support your analysis. Do *not* simply summarize the text. You may use the margins to take notes as you read and scrap paper to plan your response. Write your response on a separate sheet of paper.

- **Guidelines:**

    Be sure to

    - Identify a central idea in the text.
    - Analyze how the author's use of *one* writing strategy (literary element or literary technique or rhetorical device) develops this central idea. Examples include: characterization, conflict, denotation/connotation, metaphor, simile, irony, language use, point-of-view, setting, structure, symbolism, theme, tone, etc.
    - Use strong and thorough evidence from the text to support your analysis.
    - Organize your ideas in a cohesive and coherent manner.
    - Maintain a formal style of writing.
    - Follow the conventions of standard written English.

Text

The following excerpt is taken from a novel set in France during the World War II era.

Sixteen paces to the water fountain, sixteen back. Forty-two to the stairwell, forty-two back. Marie-Laure draws maps in her head, unreels a hundred yards of imaginary twine, and then turns and reels it back in. Botany smells like glue and blotter paper and pressed flowers.
(5) Paleontology smells like rock dust, bone dust. Biology smells like formalin and old fruit; it is loaded with heavy cool jars in which float things she has only had described for her: the pale coiled ropes of rattlesnakes, the severed hands of gorillas. Entomology smells like mothballs and oil: a preservative that, Dr. Geffard explains, is called naphthalene. Offices smell of
(10) carbon paper, or cigar smoke, or brandy, or perfume. Or all four.

She follows cables and pipes, railings and ropes, hedges and sidewalks. She startles people. She never knows if the lights are on.

The children she meets brim with questions: Does it hurt? Do you shut your eyes to sleep? How do you know what time it is?
(15) It doesn't hurt, she explains. And there is no darkness, not the kind they imagine. Everything is composed of webs and lattices and upheavals of sound and texture. She walks a circle around the Grand Gallery, navigating between squeaking floorboards; she hears feet tramp up and down museum staircases, a toddler squeal, the groan of a weary grandmother
(20) lowering herself onto a bench.

Color—that's another thing people don't expect. In her imagination, in her dreams, everything has color. The museum buildings are beige, chestnut, hazel. Its scientists are lilac and lemon yellow and fox brown. Piano chords loll in the speaker of the wireless in the guard station, pro-
(25) jecting rich blacks and complicated blues down the hall toward the key pound.[1] Church bells send arcs of bronze careening off the windows. Bees are silver; pigeons are ginger and auburn and occasionally golden. The huge cypress trees she and her father pass on their morning walk are shimmering kaleidoscopes, each needle a polygon of light.
(30) She has no memories of her mother but imagines her as white, a soundless brilliance. Her father radiates a thousand colors, opal, strawberry

---

[1]key pound—the office of her father, the museum locksmith

red, deep russet, wild green; a smell like oil and metal, the feel of a lock
tumbler sliding home, the sound of his key rings chiming as he walks. He
is an olive green when he talks to a department head, an escalating series
(35) of oranges when he speaks to Mademoiselle Fleury from the greenhouses,
a bright red when he tries to cook. He glows sapphire when he sits over his
workbench in the evenings, humming almost inaudibly as he works, the
tip of his cigarette gleaming a prismatic blue.

She gets lost. Secretaries or botanists, and once the director's assis-
(40) tant, bring her back to the key pound. She is curious; she wants to know
the difference between an alga and a lichen, a *Diplodon charruanus* and a
Diplodon delodontus. Famous men take her by the elbow and escort her
through the gardens or guide her up stairwells. "I have a daughter too,"
they'll say. Or "I found her among the hummingbirds."

(45) "*Toutes mes excuses*,"[2] her father says. He lights a cigarette; he plucks
key after key out of her pockets. "What," he whispers, "am I going to do
with you?"

On her ninth birthday, when she wakes, she finds two gifts. The first
is a wooden box with no opening she can detect. She turns it this way
(50) and that. It takes her a little while to realize one side is spring-loaded;
she presses it and the box flips open. Inside waits a single cube of creamy
Camembert that she pops directly into in [*sic*] her mouth.

"Too easy!" her father says, laughing.

The second gift is heavy, wrapped in paper and twine. Inside is a mas-
(55) sive spiral-bound book. In Braille.

"They said it's for boys. Or very adventurous girls." She can hear him
smiling.

She slides her fingertips across the embossed[3] title page. *Around. The.
World. In. Eighty. Days.* "Papa, it's too expensive."

(60) "That's for me to worry about."

That morning Marie-Laure crawls beneath the counter of the key
pound and lies on her stomach and sets all ten fingertips in a line on
a page. The French feels old-fashioned, the dots printed much closer
together than she is used to. But after a week, it becomes easy. She finds

---
[2]toutes mes excuses—my apologies
[3]embossed—a stamped, molded or carved design

(65) the ribbon she uses as a bookmark, opens the book, and the museum falls
away.

Mysterious Mr. Fogg lives his life like a machine. Jean Passepartout
becomes his obedient valet. When, after two months, she reaches the
novel's last line, she flips back to the first page and starts again. At night
(70) she runs her fingertips over her father's model: the bell tower, the display
windows. She imagines Jules Verne's characters walking along the streets,
chatting in shops; a half-inch-tall baker slides speck-sized loaves in and
out of his ovens; three minuscule burglars hatch plans as they drive slowly
past the jeweler's; little grumbling cars throng the rue[4] de Mirbel, wip-
(75) ers sliding back and forth. Behind a fourth-floor window on the rue des
Patriarches, a miniature version of her father sits at a miniature workbench in their miniature apartment, just as he does in real life, sanding
away at some infinitesimal[5] piece of wood; across the room is a miniature
girl, skinny, quick-witted, an open book in her lap; inside her chest pulses
(80) something huge, something full of longing, something unafraid.

—Anthony Doerr
excerpted from *All the Light We Cannot See*, 2014
Scribner

[4]rue—street
[5]infinitesimal—very small

Regents ELA (Common Core) Answers August 2017
English Language Arts

Answer Key

Part 1

1. 3	9. 2	17. 4
2. 4	10. 4	18. 3
3. 1	11. 4	19. 2
4. 4	12. 4	20. 2
5. 1	13. 1	21. 2
6. 2	14. 1	22. 3
7. 1	15. 2	23. 4
8. 4	16. 1	24. 4

Regents Examination in English Language Arts (Common Core)—August 2017

Chart for Converting Total Weighted Raw Scores to Final Exam Scores (Scale Scores) (Use for the August 2017 examination only.)

Weighted Raw Score*	Scale Score	Performance Level	Weighted Raw Score*	Scale Score	Performance Level
56	100	5	27	52	1
55	99	5	26	48	1
54	99	5	25	45	1
53	99	5	24	41	1
52	99	5	23	38	1
51	98	5	22	34	1
50	98	5	21	31	1
49	97	5	20	27	1
48	96	5	19	24	1
47	94	5	18	21	1
46	92	5	17	17	1
45	91	5	16	14	1
44	89	5	15	12	1
43	88	5	14	10	1
42	87	5	13	8	1
41	85	5	12	8	1
40	84	4	11	7	1
39	82	4	10	6	1
38	80	4	9	5	1
37	79	4	8	4	1
36	76	3	7	4	1
35	74	3	6	3	1
34	72	3	5	2	1
33	69	3	4	2	1
32	67	3	3	1	1
31	65	3	2	1	1
30	61	2	1	1	1
29	58	2	0	0	1
28	55	2			

The conversion table is determined independently for each administration of the exam.

Answers Explained

PART 1—Reading Comprehension

Multiple-Choice Questions

Passage A

(1) **3** "knowledgeable." In this introductory scene, the character of Dora-Rouge would look at the stars and, "… tell us what place we would pass on the next day." The narrator tells us that the next day they did reach those places.

(2) **4** "insignificance." In this passage, the narrator illustrates how the characters enter a sense of timelessness and leave behind their lives on earth; they become, "… just a small dream among the … many dreams of earth." "Insignificance" best describes these feelings.

(3) **1** "I saw vines creeping forward." A tendril is a vine or stem. The meaning of the word is revealed in the images of a leaf and flowers reaching up through darkness to reveal a truth, "… that had been there all along … ." None of the other choices expresses the feeling in these images.

(4) **4** "enlightening." In this passage, the narrator describes how she recovers a lost knowledge, "the oldest bond of survival … this opening light of life … ." This passage does not suggest feelings of confusion, amusement, or threat.

(5) **1** "transformation." Here the narrator tells us that, "New senses came to me." In becoming equal to other animals (transformed), she moves, "… as they moved, seeing as they saw."

(6) **2** "developed a kinship with the environment." For the women in this story, the experience of their journey is one of recovering an ancestral relationship with the natural world. Among the choices, this answer best expresses the meaning of their experience.

(7) **1** "link the past with the future." Toward the end of the passage, the narrator tells us that she, "… felt newly found … ." Before recovering a lost relationship with nature and her ancestral past, she felt her life had been, "… without all its knowings." Looking forward, she says, "Now, we, the four of us, had the same eyes … ."

(8) **4** "personal narrative." This passage, from a novel, is a vivid example of a first-person narrative of a significant experience.

(9) **2** "[with] clarity of mind comes connection of spirit." This statement best describes the spiritual journey of the narrator and her companions. The other choices express themes that might reliably fit other contexts but are not central to this passage.

(10) **4** "And listening to the night, I knew there was another horizon, beyond the one we could see." This quote best supports the central idea of rediscovery and spiritual enlightenment in the passage. It recalls both the experience of the journey and suggests its meaning for the women in the future.

Passage B

(11) **4** "impermanence." The poet creates her own verb to describe what happens as flowers wither and die: they lose their petals. None of the other choices is suggested in this stanza.

(12) **4** "her insignificance in the eyes of nature." In these lines, the poet remarks that, "… none of [The trees and flowers] are noticing [her]" as she walks among them. This best describes what the narrator is feeling in these lines.

(13) **1** "consciousness is a barrier to connecting with nature." The narrator expresses the feeling that she, "… most perfectly resembles" the trees and flowers, "… when I am sleeping … ." The poet and the sky are, "… in open conversation," only with, "Thoughts gone dim." None of the other choices expresses these ideas in this poem.

(14) **1** "envious." In the first stanza, the narrator tells us that she does not, "gleam into leaf …" like a tree, or dazzle with beauty like a flower. She wishes she had (envies) the tree's longevity and the flower's daring.

Passage C

(15) **2** "odd occurrences." The meaning of "anomalies" is clarified in the examples that follow: snakes that leave their winter dens early and erratic (unpredictable) well-water levels are best described as odd occurrences.

(16) **1** "contributing historical facts." The article begins with a reference to a decision by the Chinese government, after a series of devastating earthquakes in 1973, to recruit young students to be "earthquake watchers." The article is developed and uses historical and scientific facts throughout.

(17) **4** "urgency." The sense of urgency is felt when, suddenly, "… the popping stopped just as it had before a catastrophic earthquake in 1966 that killed more than 8,000."

(18) **3** "not always predictable." The contrast between the two earthquakes in this passage are (1) the warnings were effective and saved many lives, and (2) the quake hit without warning and "… killed nearly 250,000 people, most of whom were asleep." None of the other choices is an accurate statement about earthquakes.

(19) **2** "modified his methods of observing earthquakes." This paragraph reports on how as a scientist Jian Lin no longer observes odd behavior in snakes but, instead, uses sophisticated scientific methods to observe earthquakes. This section of the article focuses on how his methods of study changed.

(20) **2** "supporters." The meaning of "champions" as supporters and advocates is clarified in the context of the sentence and in the subsequent information about how the scientists presented their theories to other scientists.

(21) **2** "an earthquake that happened in one place would decrease the possibility of another happening nearby." This long-held belief about earthquakes failed to explain a sequence of quakes in Los Angeles in 1992; further analysis by Lin, Stein and King ignored this belief and showed them to be a series of aftershocks. Their work became "one of the decade's most-cited earthquake research papers." Review of the text will show that each of the other choices is reported as reliable.

(22) **3** "shear stress was greater than clamping stress." Determining the answer to this question requires careful reading of the paragraph to understand the two kinds of stress and how they account for earthquakes. The seismologists determined that, "… most of the earthquakes [in the Los Angeles series] had occurred in areas where the shifting of the ground had caused increased stress." None of the other choices is consistent with the information in the passage.

(23) **4** "dedicated." As a young man, Jian Lin experienced a devastating earthquake in China: "… I was scared of earthquakes … . I decided that if I could do anything—*anything*—to save lives lost to earthquakes, it would be worth the effort." None of the other choices adequately describes his character and determination.

(24) **4** "important to future studies." Throughout the article, there are references to the ways in which Lin's work has supported further research. At the end, we understand that Lin and other seismologists continue their research to find ways to reliably predict earthquakes and to save lives.

PART 2—Argument Response

Sample Essay Response

As technology advances, innovations are introduced to society on a regular basis. One of these innovations, which humans may see in the near future, is a self-driving car. Although this idea may seem promising, many disadvantages come along with it. Self-driving cars should not replace human drivers, despite how beneficial they sound.

A primary reason to oppose self-driving cars is that many people would lose their jobs. At present, autonomous cars usually have a person in the driver's seat in case of a problem. However, once the cars can function safely without human intervention, professional drivers will no longer be needed. Heavy truck and tractor-trailer drivers have "the most common job in a whopping 29 states." (Text 3, lines 25–26) In addition to the 1,625,290 heavy and tractor-trailer drivers who would lose their jobs, other workers, such as taxi drivers, bus drivers, and mail carriers, might face unemployment. (Text 3, graphic)

Another concern about self-driving cars is the risk of confusion that can occur between drivers and robots. This is not a good idea, "blending [self-driving cars] into a world in which humans don't behave by the book." (Text 2, lines 16–17) One example of this confusion is when a Google car, "sensed that a vehicle coming the other direction was approaching the red light at a higher-than-safe speed." (Text 2, lines 56–57) In response, the Google car immediately veered to the side in anticipation of a crash; however, the driver of the other car stopped in plenty of time. Although challenging driving situations may occur on a regular basis, "the way humans often deal with these situations is that, "they make eye contact." (Text 2, lines 67–68) This interaction is not possible between a self-driving car and a human. An automated reaction could result in otherwise avoidable crashes.

A third issue with self-driven cars is privacy. Just as home computers and other technology can be hacked, the same applies for the software in a self-driving car. For example, "who will have access to any driving information these vehicles store?" (Text 1, lines 56–57) If the vehicle stores a person's payment information or a record of places the person usually goes, a hacker might have access to significant personal and financial information of someone who rides in a self-driving car.

Supporters of self-driving cars argue that self-driving cars are safer. They explain that, "Over 90% of accidents today are caused by driver error." (Text 1, line 42) However, that does not prove that self-driving cars will be safer. Humans make errors, but technology can malfunction. Errors and accidents can still occur, whether they are caused by a human or by a computer.

The idea of self-driving cars is exciting, but the truth is that technology is never 100% reliable. Self-driving cars, once they become part of everyday life, could bring about a loss of jobs, confusion between human and automated drivers, and concerns about privacy. Although the immediate attraction is *that self-driving cars are safer than human drivers, the reality is this world is not ideal or perfect. These two worlds—realistic and idealistic—will never mesh. Too many risks are at stake here, with little to no benefits.*

Analysis

This argument represents a good response to the task. The first paragraph identifies the context and establishes a claim that is distinguished from opposing claims. The argument is clearly organized, and each section begins with an appropriate transition: "A primary reason ... Another concern ... A third issue ... ." The writer's claim is supported by relevant evidence in the texts. Development is adequate, but the argument would be stronger if the fifth paragraph, refuting the claim that self-driving cars are safer, were more fully developed with evidence from Text 4. The conclusion appropriately acknowledges the appeal of self-driving cars but forcefully urges the need for caution. The writing is clear and free of significant errors in the conventions. This response would merit a high score.

(See pages 80–81 for the scoring guidelines.)

PART 3—Text-Analysis Response

Sample Essay Response

The story centers around a young girl who, after losing her sense of sight, compensates for it by heightening the strength of her imagination and other senses. Through the vivid, colorful things that she imagines on a morning walk, such as the image of "huge cypress trees" that "are shimmering kaleidoscopes, with each needle a polygon of light," the character, Marie-Laure, is able to construct her own vision of the world without letting her blindness cripple her. The author intends to express to the reader that there are no limitations to what a human can do. A person with a disability such as Marie-Laure's can function nearly as well as anyone, and can even go beyond seeing and feeling what people normally can. For their loss of a sense, these people develop a creativity that cannot be mimicked and is entirely unique to themselves.

The author uses imagery to convey the point of the story. He answers questions such as, "How does Marie-Laure feel being blind?" and, "How exactly is she able to live in the world without sight?" We understand that Marie-Laure must have had vision at one time: "In her imagination, in her dreams, everything has color." When other children are curious and ask her what it is like, she assures them that it does not hurt, and it is not all darkness. She says, "… everything is composed of webs and lattices and upheavals of sound and texture."

The author chose to use images to create a visual in the reader's mind, where Marie has color in her imagination, where "museum buildings are beige, chestnut, hazel," and its scientists are "lilac and lemon yellow and fox-brown." She describes bees as silver and "pigeons are ginger and auburn and occasionally gold." The author's use of vivid imagery gives the reader a clear sense of the girl's experiences and her imaginative way of seeing her world.

Analysis

This response (edited for clarity) is especially good in the way the central idea is expressed as answers to a series of questions: "How does Marie-Laure feel being blind?" and, "How exactly is she able to live in the world without sight?" The analysis is supported through extensive use of relevant quotes and skillful use of the language of vision, seeing, and imagery. The response is brief but clearly organized in two paragraphs. The writing is appropriately formal and demonstrates control of complex sentence structures and the conventions. This response would merit a high score.

(See pages 82–83 for the scoring guidelines.)

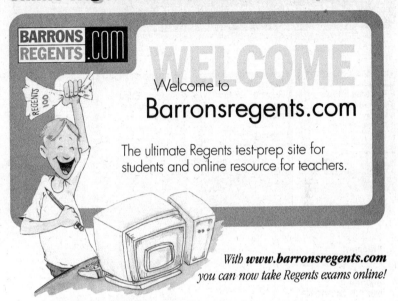

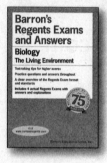
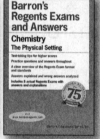
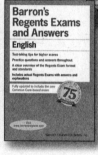

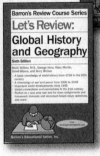

NOTES

FREE

Barron's Regents Exams and Answers

English

Latest Examination

- **A full-length New York State Regents Examination**
- **Complete Answers**

Barron's Educational Series, Inc.

CHECK OUR WEBSITE FOR THE LATEST REGENTS EXAM IN ENGLISH

To ensure that you are always up-to-date we will post a PDF of the most current Regents exam with answers and explanations on our website:

http://barronsregents.com/supps/mnx527.html

(#247)   (R7/17)

Barron's Review Course Series

Let's Review:

English

5th Edition

Carol Chaitkin, M.S.

Former Director of American Studies
Lycée Français de New York
New York, New York

Former English Department Head
Great Neck North High School
Great Neck, New York

BARRON'S

Acknowledgments

Page 75: "The Pitcher" from *The Orb Weaver* by Robert Francis © 1960, by Robert Francis and reprinted by permission of Wesleyan University Press.

Page 79: "Old Photograph of the Future" by Robert Penn Warren © 1985. Reprinted by permission of Random House, Inc.

Page 81: "Child on Top of a Greenhouse," copyright © 1946 by Editorial Publications, Inc.; from COLLECTED POEMS by Theodore Roethke. Used by permission of Doubleday, an imprint of Knopf Doubleday Publishing Group, a division of Random House LLC. All rights reserved.

Page 81: "The Sleeping Giant" from OLD AND NEW POEMS by Donald Hall. Copyright © 1990 by Donald Hall. Reprinted by permission of Houghton Mifflin Harcourt Publishing Company. All rights reserved.

All inquiries should be addressed to:
Barron's Educational Series, Inc.
250 Wireless Boulevard
Hauppauge, NY 11788
www.barronseduc.com

Library of Congress Control Number: 2015943734
ISBN: 978-1-4380-0626-0

PRINTED IN CANADA
9 8 7 6 5 4 3 2

TABLE OF CONTENTS

REGENTS ELA (COMMON CORE) EXAMINATIONS

INDEX 293

INTRODUCTION

Let's Review is designed as a handbook for high school English courses, including those aligned with the new Common Core Standards, and as a review book for students preparing to take the Regents Exam in English Language Arts (Common Core). Because the English Regents Exam is not a test of specific curriculum but an assessment of skills in reading comprehension, literary analysis, and composition, *Let's Review* offers a comprehensive guide to essential language, literature, and critical reading and writing skills all high school students should seek to demonstrate as they prepare for college and the workplace.

A GUIDE TO THE NEW YORK STATE STANDARDS IN LITERACY (ELA)

Most middle school and high school students in New York State should already be familiar with some key shifts in curriculum and instruction in their English courses. These shifts in emphasis include the following:

- Students will read more informational texts and perhaps fewer literary texts than in the past. Alignment with the Common Core requires a balancing of the two.
- In all academic subjects, students will be expected to build their knowledge primarily through engaging directly with text.
- Throughout secondary school, students will read texts of increasing complexity and will be expected to develop skills in **close reading** in all academic subjects.
- Students will be expected to engage in rich and rigorous **evidence-based** conversations/class discussions about text.
- Student writing will emphasize **use of evidence** from sources to express their understanding and to form and develop argument.
- Students will acquire the **academic vocabulary** they need to comprehend and respond to grade level complex texts. This vocabulary is often relevant to more than one subject.

TERMS TO HELP YOU UNDERSTAND THE STATE STANDARDS

- **ELA/LITERACY**—**English Language Arts** refers to skills in reading, writing, speaking, and listening. Courses and exams once identified as English may also be identified as ELA. **Literacy** refers to the ability to read and write and to use language proficiently. The term also identifies the quality of being knowledgeable in a particular subject or field. For example, we often refer to "digital" or "computer literacy."

- **COMMON CORE LEARNING STANDARDS (CCLS)***—These are the learning standards in ELA and math, also known as **CCSS** (Common Core State Standards), developed and adopted by a consortium of over 40 states. New York State adopted the CCLS in 2010 and continues to implement them in curriculum and assessments (testing).

- **CCR**—The phrase **"college and career ready"** is widely used in discussion of new curriculum and assessments. This refers to the fundamental principle of the Common Core Standards: to reflect the knowledge and skills that all students need for success in college and careers.

- **ASSESSMENT**—You may hear teachers and other educators using the term **assessment** instead of test or examination. An **assessment** is more than a simple test (in vocabulary, say) because it seeks to measure a number of skills at one time. Although we continue to refer to the English Regents as an exam or test, its goal is to be a valid **assessment** of a broad range of reading, thinking, language, and writing skills outlined in the Standards.

- **TEXT**—Broadly, the term text refers to any written material. The Common Core standards use the term to refer to the great variety of material students are expected to be able to read, understand, analyze, and write about. Texts may include **literary** works of fiction, drama, and poetry; and **informational**, or nonfiction, including essays, memoirs, speeches, and scientific and historical documents. The Common Core also emphasizes the use of **authentic texts;** that is, students will read actual historical documents or scientific essays rather than simply read articles about them.

- **CLOSE READING**—Skill in close, analytic reading is fundamental to the CCLS and to the new Regents exam. The Common Core curriculum focuses student attention on the text itself in order to understand not only what the text says and means but also how that meaning is constructed and revealed. Close reading enables students to understand central ideas and key supporting details. It also enables students to reflect on the meanings of individual words and sentences, the order in which sentences unfold, and the development of ideas over the course of the text, which ultimately leads students to arrive at an understanding of the text as a whole.

- **ARGUMENT**—What is an argument? In academic writing, an argument is usually a central idea, often called a **claim** or **thesis statement,** which is backed up with evidence that supports the idea. Much of the writing high school students do in their English courses constitutes essays of argument, in addition to personal essays, descriptive pieces, and works of imagination.
- **SOURCE-BASED/EVIDENCE-BASED**—The ability to compose sound arguments using relevant and specific evidence from a given text is central to the expectations of the Common Core Standards.
- **WRITING STRATEGY**—This is the general term for a literary element, literary technique, or rhetorical device. Examples include characterization, conflict, denotation/connotation, metaphor, simile, irony, language use, point of view, setting, structure, symbolism, theme, and tone. In class discussions and on examinations, students are expected to understand and explain how literary elements and writing strategies contribute to the meaning of a text.

*The Anchor (Common Core) Standards for Grades 11–12 Reading, Writing, and Language are found in the Appendices, pages 223–227.

THE REGENTS ELA (COMMON CORE) EXAM

This 3-hour examination requires students to read, analyze, and write about both literary and informational texts.

PART I—READING COMPREHENSION

This part requires close reading of three texts and will contain at least one literature text, one poem, and one informational text, followed by 24 multiple-choice questions.

PART II—WRITING FROM SOURCES: ARGUMENT

This part includes close reading of four informational texts and may contain some information in graphics; students will compose an essay of argument with a claim based on the sources.

PART III—TEXT ANALYSIS: EXPOSITION

Students will perform a close reading of one informational or one literature text and write a two to three paragraph expository response that identifies a central idea in the text and analyzes how the author's use of one writing strategy develops that central idea.

Note: The ACT and the new SAT (2015) include similar assessments of close reading, text analysis, the rhetoric of arguments, and the use of academic vocabulary.

WAYS TO USE *LET'S REVIEW: ENGLISH*

As a handbook for literature study in high school and college courses, see especially

Chapter 4—Reading Prose
Chapter 5—Reading Poetry
Chapter 6—Writing About Literature: A General Review

As a handbook for reading comprehension and language skills, see especially

Chapter 1—Reading Comprehension
Chapter 3—Reading and Writing to Analyze Text
Chapter 4—Reading Prose
Chapter 5—Reading Poetry
Chapter 8—Vocabulary

As a handbook for writing and proofreading, see especially

Chapter 2—Writing from Sources
Chapter 3—Reading and Writing to Analyze Text
Chapter 6—Writing About Literature: A General Review
Chapter 9—Grammar and Usage for the Careful Writer
Chapter 10—Punctuation: Guidelines and Reminders

As a review text for the ELA (Common Core) Regents exam, the SAT, and the ACT, see especially

Chapter 1—Reading Comprehension
Chapter 2—Writing from Sources
Chapter 3—Reading and Writing to Analyze Text
Chapter 8—Vocabulary
Appendices—The New York State Common Core Learning Standards
    for English Language Arts

Chapter 1

READING COMPREHENSION

Throughout your schooling, you have been developing skills in the ability to read and comprehend works of literature as well as informational texts in nearly every subject, including history and social studies, science, and technical studies. Because the ability to understand, interpret, and make use of a wide range of texts is central to learning, it is a skill students are regularly asked to demonstrate. Assessment of students' reading comprehension skills may be informal or indirect, as in a class discussion or short quiz, or through formal testing.

Students at Regents level—11th and 12th grades—are expected to have the ability to understand and interpret both literary and informational texts of significant complexity: that is, Regents-level students understand literary texts with multiple levels of meaning, with structures that may be complex or unconventional, and with elements of figurative or deliberately ambiguous language that are integral to its meaning. The expectations for reading informational texts include the ability to interpret and analyze personal essays, speeches, opinion pieces, and memoir and autobiographical works as well as official documents and historical, scientific, and technical material for subject courses other than English. This increased emphasis on a wide range of informational texts is one of the key shifts in high school curriculum and should already be familiar to most students. It is also helpful to know that both the ACT and new SAT (2015) exams include a similar variety of texts and primary source documents.

CLOSE READING

One useful way to think about what we mean by "close reading" is to think about what you are doing when you can annotate something you are reading; that is, what do you underline? circle? check in the margins? You are probably checking off main ideas and conclusions, underlining the most important details, and circling significant or unfamiliar words. Whether or not you actually mark up a text, that process of checking, underlining, and circling is the thinking process of close reading.

In-class discussions of literary works are often exercises in what is meant by close reading—Where are we? Which details give us an image of the setting? What just happened? What is this character thinking now? What does the story lead us to expect? What is surprising? How were we prepared? How does the author/narrator guide our understanding of characters and their actions? Why is this incident important in the plot? What does this character's remark really mean? Was the ending convincing?

The most satisfying "close reading," however, is what we are doing when our imaginations are fully engaged in a story, a play, a poem, or a film(!) Then it is not an academic exercise or assessment but the pleasure of experiencing a good story.

Reading for information in history, social studies, or science requires careful attention to the sequence of ideas, to how general statements are supported with relevant details. This kind of reading may also require familiarity with specialized language. (See Academic Language in Chapter 8 — Vocabulary.)

On exams, you will exercise this same kind of thinking and engagement with the text on your own. The multiple-choice questions are designed to assess your close reading skills and the depth of your understanding.

QUESTIONS TO KEEP IN MIND AS YOU READ

If you are reading a literary passage, ask yourself

What is this piece about? What is the narrative point of view?
What do we understand about the setting?
What do we understand about the narrator? Other characters?

In reading a poem, consider

What experience, memory, or dramatic situation is the poem about?
Who and where is the narrator/speaker?
How does the organization of lines and stanzas affect the meaning?
How are language and imagery used?

In passages of memoir and personal essay, ask

What experience is meant to be shared and understood?
What does the author say? Describe? Suggest? Reveal?

If you are reading an informational text, ask yourself

What is the subject? What do I already know about this subject?
What main idea or theme is being developed? What phrases or terms
    signal that?
What is the purpose? To inform? To persuade? To celebrate? To guide? To
    show a process? To introduce a new or unfamiliar subject?

READING COMPREHENSION PASSAGES AND QUESTIONS FOR REVIEW

The following passages and questions are from actual tasks on Regents ELA exams.

PASSAGE ONE—LITERATURE

This passage is from a classic Sherlock Holmes story by Sir Arthur Conan Doyle. Many of the expressions are unfamiliar but can be understood in context. High school students may already be familiar with the character of Sherlock Holmes, both through reading of the original stories and through modern retelling in popular American and British television series. On the Regents ELA exam, you are expected to read and analyze texts from works of American literature as well as works from British and world literatures.

It was upon the 4th of March, as I have good reason to remember, that I rose somewhat earlier than usual, and found that Sherlock Holmes had not yet finished his breakfast. The landlady had become so accustomed to my late habits that my place had not been laid nor my coffee prepared. With the unreasonable petulance[1] of
(5) mankind I rang the bell and gave a curt intimation that I was ready. Then I picked up a magazine from the table and attempted to while away the time with it, while my companion munched silently at his toast. One of the articles had a pencil-mark at the heading, and I naturally began to run my eye through it. ...

"From a drop of water," said the writer, "a logician could infer the possibility
(10) of an Atlantic or a Niagara without having seen or heard of one or the other. So all life is a great chain, the nature of which is known whenever we are shown a single link of it. Like all other arts, the Science of Deduction and Analysis is one which can only be acquired by long and patient study, nor is life long enough to allow any mortal to attain the highest possible perfection in it. Before turning to those
(15) moral and mental aspects of the matter which present the greatest difficulties, let the inquirer begin by mastering more elementary problems. Let him, on meeting a fellow-mortal, learn at a glance to distinguish the history of the man and the trade or profession to which he belongs. Puerile[2] as such an exercise may seem, it sharpens the faculties of observation and teaches one where to look and what to look for. By
(20) a man's fingernails, by his coat-sleeve, by his boot, by his trouser-knees, by the callosities of his forefinger and thumb, by his expression, by his shirt-cuffs—by each of these things a man's calling is plainly revealed. That all united should fail to enlighten the competent inquirer in any case is almost inconceivable."

---

[1]petulance — a quality or state of being rude
[2]puerile — childish

(25)   "What ineffable twaddle!" I cried, slapping the magazine down on the table; "I never read such rubbish in my life."

     "What is it?" asked Sherlock Holmes.

     "Why, this article," I said, pointing at it with my egg-spoon as I sat down to my breakfast. "I see that you have read it, since you have marked it. I don't deny that it is smartly written. It irritates me, though. It is evidently the theory of some arm-
(30) chair lounger who evolves all these neat little paradoxes in the seclusion of his own study. It is not practical. I should like to see him clapped down in a third-class carriage on the Underground and asked to give the trades of all his fellow-travellers. I would lay a thousand to one against him."

     "You would lose your money," Sherlock Holmes remarked, calmly. "As for the
(35) article, I wrote it myself."

     "You?"

     "Yes, I have a turn both for observation and for deduction. The theories which I have expressed there, and which appear to you to be so chimerical, are really extremely practical—so practical that I depend upon them for my bread-and-
(40) cheese."

     "And how?" I asked, involuntarily.

     "Well, I have a trade of my own. I suppose I am the only one in the world. I'm a consulting detective, if you can understand what that is. Here in London we have lots of government detectives and lots of private ones. When these fellows are at
(45) fault they come to me, and I manage to put them on the right scent. They lay all the evidence before me, and I am generally able, by the help of my knowledge of the history of crime, to set them straight. There is a strong family resemblance about misdeeds, and if you have all the details of a thousand at your finger-ends, it is odd if you can't unravel the thousand and first. Lestrade is a well-known detective. He
(50) got himself into a fog recently over a forgery case, and that was what brought him here."

     "And these other people?"

     "They are mostly sent out by private inquiry agencies. They are all people who are in trouble about something, and want a little enlightening. I listen to their story,
(55) they listen to my comments, and then I pocket my fee."

     "But do you mean to say," I said, "that without leaving your room you can unravel some knot which other men can make nothing of, although they have seen every detail for themselves?"

     "Quite so. I have a kind of intuition that way. Now and again a case turns up
(60) which is a little more complex. Then I have to bustle about and see things with my own eyes. You see, I have a lot of special knowledge which I apply to the problem, and which facilitates matters wonderfully. Those rules of deduction laid down in that article which aroused your scorn are invaluable to me in practical work. Obser-

(65) vation with me is second nature. You appeared to be surprised when I told you, on our first meeting, that you had come from Afghanistan."

"You were told, no doubt."

"Nothing of the sort. I *knew* you came from Afghanistan. From long habit the train of thought ran so swiftly through my mind that I arrived at the conclusion without being conscious of intermediate steps. There were such steps, however. The
(70) train of reasoning ran: 'Here is a gentleman of a medical type, but with the air of a military man. Clearly an army doctor, then. He has just come from the tropics, for his face is dark, and that is not the natural tint of his skin, for his wrists are fair. He has undergone hardship and sickness, as his haggard face says clearly. His left arm has been injured. He holds it in a stiff and unnatural manner. Where in the tropics
(75) could an English army doctor have seen much hardship and got his arm wounded? Clearly in Afghanistan.' The whole train of thought did not occupy a second. I then remarked that you came from Afghanistan, and you were astonished." …

I was still annoyed at his bumptious style of conversation. I thought it best to change the topic.
(80) "I wonder what that fellow is looking for?" I asked, pointing to a stalwart, plainly dressed individual who was walking slowly down the other side of the street, looking anxiously at the numbers. He had a large, blue envelope in his hand, and was evidently the bearer of a message.

"You mean the retired sergeant of marines," said Sherlock Holmes.
(85) "Brag and bounce!" thought I to myself. "He knows that I cannot verify his guess." The thought had hardly passed through my mind when the man whom we were watching caught sight of the number on our door, and ran rapidly across the roadway. We heard a loud knock, a deep voice below, and heavy steps ascending the stair.
(90) "For Mr. Sherlock Holmes," he said, stepping into the room and handing my friend the letter.

Here was an opportunity of taking the conceit out of him. He little thought of this when he made that random shot. "May I ask, my lad," I said, blandly, "what your trade may be?"
(95) "Commissionnaire, sir," he said, gruffly. "Uniform away for repairs."

"And you were?" I asked, with a slightly malicious glance at my companion. "A sergeant, sir, Royal Marine Light Infantry, sir. No answer? Right, sir." He clicked his heels together, raised his hand in a salute, and was gone.

—A. Conan Doyle
excerpted from *A Study in Scarlet*, 1904
Harper & Brothers Publishers

Questions for Comprehension

This passage, narrated by the character of Dr. Watson, reveals the differences in character and personality of the two men. The discussion of the magazine article leads to a dramatic demonstration of Holmes's powers of observation and deduction. At the end, Watson's doubts are erased, and he is left speechless.

1 The phrase "with the unreasonable petulance of mankind" (lines 4–5) emphasizes the narrator's

  (1) frustration with himself for missing sleep
  (2) irritation about not finding his breakfast ready
  (3) concern regarding the pencil-mark on the newspaper
  (4) impatience with Sherlock Holmes's silence   1____

2 How do the words "logician" (line 9), "deduction" (lines 12, 37, and 62), and "analysis" (line 12) advance the author's purpose?

  (1) by indicating the relationship between science and art
  (2) by suggesting the reasons why private inquiry agencies seek outside help
  (3) by highlighting the complexity of the crimes encountered by Sherlock Holmes
  (4) by emphasizing the systematic nature of Sherlock Holmes's approach to solving crimes   2____

3 What is the effect of withholding the identity of Sherlock Holmes as the author of the article (lines 9 through 35)?

  (1) It creates a somber mood.
  (2) It foreshadows an unwelcome turn of events.
  (3) It allows the reader to learn the narrator's true feelings.
  (4) It leads the reader to misunderstand who the writer is.   3____

4 In this passage, the conversation between Holmes and the narrator (lines 24 through 40) serves to

(1) reinforce the narrator's appreciation for deduction
(2) establish a friendship between the narrator and Holmes
(3) reveal how Holmes makes his living
(4) expose some of Holmes's misdeeds   4____

5 As used in line 38, the word "chimerical" most nearly means

(1) unfair   (3) aggravating
(2) unrealistic   (4) contradictory   5____

6 Which analysis is best supported by the details in lines 45 through 58 of the text?

(1) Private detectives base their analyses on an understanding of human nature.
(2) Sherlock Holmes's association with other well-known detectives improves his crime-solving abilities.
(3) Government detectives are mostly ineffective at solving complicated crimes.
(4) Sherlock Holmes's intuition relies on his ability to detect similarities among various crimes.   6____

Looking at the Questions and the Standards

- Questions 1, 2, and 5 ask you to determine the meaning of words and phrases as they are used in context and to understand how they contribute to the meaning of the text.
- Question 3 asks you to recognize how the author uses one element or detail to structure the plot. Holmes deliberately allows Watson to think someone else wrote the article, which then creates the situation in which he can show how skilled and clever he is.
- Questions 4 and 6 ask you to recognize how specific details contribute to character development and plot structure.

Answers

(1) **2**   (2) **4**   (3) **3**   (4) **3**   (5) **2**   (6) **4**

(See Chapter 4—Reading Prose for a detailed review of the elements of fiction.)

PASSAGE TWO—POEM

Money Musk

Listen, you upstate hillsides (nothing
Like the herb-strewn fields of Provence[1])
Which I have loved
So loyally, your wood lots
(5)   And trailers and old farmhouses,
Your satellite dishes—

Haven't I driven
Past the strip malls and country airports,
The National Guard armories and even
(10)   That abandoned missile depot
Clutched in the lake's fingers
Past the tattered billboards.
The barns spray-painted with praise,

---

[1]Provence—a region of southern France

Past the farm tools, fiddles,
(15) And fishing lures, the sprung bellows
Of accordions on the tables of flea markets,
Just to catch a glimpse of you as you once were,
Like the brass showing, raw and dull,
Where the silver plate has worn off
(20) The frame around this mirror, and the silver
Gone too, the only reflection as faint

As light on dusty glass,
And beyond it, tarnished, dim, the rafters
And beams of the attic where I climbed
(25) To take out my grandmother's mandolin
And play on the three or four unbroken strings
With a penny for a pick.
                              Listen,
Wasn't that offering enough, a life
(30) Of playing half-badly on an antique instrument,
Trying to catch a tune you'd long ago
Forgotten even the name of, *Money Musk*
Or *Petronella*.[2] Wasn't it enough
To take my vows of poverty of spirit
(35) Before the plain geometry of a 19th-century
Farmhouse, and praise no other goods
Than this rectitude,[3] this stillness,
This clarity you have spurned now, oh
Landscape I have sung
(40) Despite my voice, despite the stubborn
Silence behind your tawdry,[4] best intentions.

—Jordan Smith
from *The Cortland Review*
Issue Eight, August 1999

[2]Money Musk or Petronella—classic old American dances
[3]rectitude—honesty
[4]tawdry—cheap

Questions for Comprehension

The opening line establishes the dramatic situation and the speaker in this poem: we hear the voice of someone who once lived in the area he is now driving through and who now regrets the changes he sees. The poem is a song to the landscape he has loved and been loyal to.

1 The details presented in lines 4 through 13 emphasize the landscape's

   (1) historical significance
   (2) beauty
   (3) economic possibilities
   (4) transformation   1____

2 What shift in focus occurs from lines 7 through 27?

   (1) from social conflict to personal conflict
   (2) from external description to childhood memory
   (3) from the narrator's feelings to his family's feelings
   (4) from the narrator's thoughts to the narrator's actions   2____

3 What is the effect of the simile used in lines 21 and 22?

   (1) It suggests how the narrator has changed.
   (2) It conveys the narrator's lack of awareness.
   (3) It indicates the darkness of the setting.
   (4) It emphasizes the diminishing of the past.   3____

4 Which word best describes the narrator's tone in lines 28 through 38 of the poem?

   (1) frustrated   (3) contentment
   (2) embarrassed   (4) respectful   4____

14

5 Lines 33 through 37 contribute to a central theme in the poem by describing the narrator's

  (1) wish to live in a suburban setting
  (2) obligation to continue a past tradition
  (2) commitment to the values of a past era
  (4) reluctance to accept different points of view   5____

Looking at the Questions and the Standards

- Questions 1 and 3 focus on the significance of key details. The importance of the landscape to the narrator is the central theme of the poem. The simile in these lines reflects the changes in the landscape the narrator so regrets.
- Question 4 asks you to recognize how the meaning of a word or phrase establishes tone, that is, the attitude of the narrator is revealed throughout the poem.
- Questions 2 and 5 ask you to recognize key elements in the structure of the poem, through a shift in focus and in the narrator's final address to the landscape.

Answers

(1) **4**   (2) **2**   (3) **4**   (4) **1**   (5) **3**

(See Chapter 5—Reading Poetry for a detailed review of the elements of poetry.)

PASSAGE THREE—INFORMATIONAL

This passage is an engaging and effective presentation for a general reader of a challenging question in modern physics and cosmology: Is there "a theory of everything"? Readers familiar with the highly successful film *The Theory of Everything* (2014) will recognize some of the ideas explored in the article.

A few years ago the City Council of Monza, Italy, barred pet owners from keeping goldfish in curved fishbowls. The sponsors of the measure explained that it is cruel to keep a fish in a bowl because the curved sides give the fish a distorted view of reality. Aside from the measure's significance to the poor goldfish, the story raises
(5) an interesting philosophical question: How do we know that the reality we perceive is true?

The goldfish is seeing a version of reality that is different from ours, but can we be sure it is any less real? For all we know, we, too, may spend our entire lives staring out at the world through a distorting lens.
(10) In physics, the question is not academic. Indeed, physicists and cosmologists are finding themselves in a similar predicament to the goldfish's. For decades we have strived to come up with an ultimate theory of everything—one complete and consistent set of fundamental laws of nature that explain every aspect of reality. It now appears that this quest may yield not a single theory but a family of intercon-
(15) nected theories, each describing its own version of reality, as if it viewed the universe through its own fishbowl.

This notion may be difficult for many people, including some working scientists, to accept. Most people believe that there is an objective reality out there and that our senses and our science directly convey information about the material world.
(20) Classical science is based on the belief that an external world exists whose properties are definite and independent of the observer who perceives them. In philosophy, that belief is called realism.

Do Not Attempt to Adjust the Picture

The idea of alternative realities is a mainstay of today's popular culture. For example, in the science-fiction film *The Matrix* the human race is unknowingly liv-
(25) ing in a simulated virtual reality created by intelligent computers to keep them pacified and content while the computers suck their bioelectrical energy (whatever that is). How do we know we are not just computer-generated characters living in a Matrix-like world? If we lived in a synthetic, imaginary world, events would not necessarily have any logic or consistency or obey any laws. The aliens in control
(30) might find it more interesting or amusing to see our reactions, for example, if everyone in the world suddenly decided that chocolate was repulsive or that war was not

(35) an option, but that has never happened. If the aliens did enforce consistent laws, we would have no way to tell that another reality stood behind the simulated one. It is easy to call the world the aliens live in the "real" one and the computer-generated world a false one. But if—like us—the beings in the simulated world could not gaze into their universe from the outside, they would have no reason to doubt their own pictures of reality.

(40) The goldfish are in a similar situation. Their view is not the same as ours from outside their curved bowl, but they could still formulate scientific laws governing the motion of the objects they observe on the outside. For instance, because light bends as it travels from air to water, a freely moving object that we would observe to move in a straight line would be observed by the goldfish to move along a curved path. The goldfish could formulate scientific laws from their distorted frame of reference that would always hold true and that would enable them to make predictions

(45) about the future motion of objects outside the bowl. Their laws would be more complicated than the laws in our frame, but simplicity is a matter of taste. If the goldfish formulated such a theory, we would have to admit the goldfish's view as a valid picture of reality.

Glimpses of the Deep Theory

(50) In the quest to discover the ultimate laws of physics, no approach has raised higher hopes—or more controversy—than string theory. String theory was first proposed in the 1970s as an attempt to unify all the forces of nature into one coherent framework and, in particular, to bring the force of gravity into the domain of quantum[1] physics. By the early 1990s, however, physicists discovered that string theory suffers from an awkward issue: there are five different string theories. For

(55) those advocating that string theory was the unique theory of everything, this was quite an embarrassment. In the mid-1990s researchers started discovering that these different theories—and yet another theory called supergravity—actually describe the same phenomena, giving them some hope that they would amount eventually to a unified theory. The theories are indeed related by what physicists call dualities,

(60) which are a kind of mathematical dictionaries for translating concepts back and forth. But, alas, each theory is a good description of phenomena only under a certain range of conditions—for example at low energies. None can describe every aspect of the universe.

String theorists are now convinced that the five different string theories are just

(65) different approximations to a more fundamental theory called M-theory. (No one seems to know what the "M" stands for. It may be "master," "miracle" or "mystery," or all three.) People are still trying to decipher the nature of M-theory, but it seems that the traditional expectation of a single theory of nature may be untenable[2]

---

[1]quantum—a small, indivisible unit of energy
[2]untenable—indefensible

and that to describe the universe we must employ different theories in different situ-
(70) ations. Thus, M-theory is not a theory in the usual sense but a network of theories. It
is a bit like a map. To faithfully represent the entire Earth on a flat surface, one has
to use a collection of maps, each of which covers a limited region. The maps overlap
one another, and where they do, they show the same landscape. Similarly, the different theories in the M-theory family may look very different, but they can all be
(75) regarded as versions of the same underlying theory, and they all predict the same
phenomena where they overlap, but none works well in all situations.

Whenever we develop a model of the world and find it to be successful, we tend
to attribute to the model the quality of reality or absolute truth. But M-theory,
like the goldfish example, shows that the same physical situation can be modeled
(80) in different ways, each employing different fundamental elements and concepts. It
might be that to describe the universe we have to employ different theories in different situations. Each theory may have its own version of reality, but according to
model-dependent realism, that diversity is acceptable, and none of the versions can
be said to be more real than any other. It is not the physicist's traditional expecta-
(85) tion for a theory of nature, nor does it correspond to our everyday idea of reality.
But it might be the way of the universe.

—Stephen Hawking and Leonard Mlodinow
excerpted from "The (Elusive) Theory of Everything,"
Scientific American, October 2010

Questions for Comprehension

The topic is highly complex, but the narrative of description and explanation is composed in language that is highly readable and developed through
a series of vivid images and analogies, beginning with the anecdote about
goldfish in curved bowls.

1 The authors' anecdote about pet owners in Monza, Italy,
serves to introduce a

(1) proof of a universal world view
(2) measure that is objectionable to scientists
(3) central question about the way we see
(4) philosophical question about what we value   1____

2 The primary purpose of lines 10 through 16 is to clarify the

   (1) need for a single theory
   (2) role of the senses in understanding
   (3) possibility of other life in the universe
   (4) origin of alternative theories   2_____

3 How do lines 17 through 22 develop a claim?

   (1) by providing details about a philosophical challenge faced by scientists
   (2) by showing how scientists should handle alternate realities
   (3) by arguing for an approach that scientists have always followed
   (4) by explaining how scientists should view a philosophical approach   3_____

4 The reference to *The Matrix* in lines 24 through 28 is used to emphasize the questioning of our

   (1) virtues
   (2) perception
   (3) education
   (4) ideals   4_____

5 The references to goldfish in lines 39 through 49 contribute to the authors' purpose by suggesting that

   (1) people's theories are influenced by their viewpoints
   (2) nature's mysteries are best left undiscovered
   (3) reality can only be determined by an outside perspective
   (4) light must be viewed under similar circumstances   5_____

6 As used in lines 51 and 52 of the text, what does the word "coherent" mean?

   (1) balanced
   (2) indisputable
   (3) popular
   (4) understandable   6_____

7 The authors' reference to "a collection of maps" (line 72)
is used to help clarify

(1) a complex theory
(2) a historical concept
(3) the representation of space
(4) the limitations of previous theories   7____

8 The function of lines 77 through 84 is to

(1) argue for a specific theory
(2) suggest that theories relate to expectations
(3) describe the way differing theories should co-exist
(4) evaluate theories based on specific needs   8____

9 With which statement would the authors most likely
agree?

(1) The perception of the universe can never be questioned.
(2) There is a single, agreed upon theory of reality.
(3) There are multiple realities that are possible to prove.
(4) The understanding of the universe continues to
change.   9____

10 The authors attempt to engage the audience through the
use of

(1) absolute statements
(2) real-world examples
(3) detailed descriptions
(4) simple questions   10____

Looking at the Questions and the Standards

- Questions 1 and 10 call your attention to how rhetorical elements are part of the structure.
  The anecdote at the beginning and the real-world examples used throughout the article help the reader understand key ideas.
- Question 6 is an example of determining the meaning of a term in context, and question 7 calls attention to how a specific image clarifies the meaning of a central idea.
- Questions 2–5 and 7–9 focus on the need to determine the central ideas and analyze how they are developed over the course of a text.

Answers

(1) **3**	(4) **2**	(7) **1**	(10) **2**
(2) **4**	(5) **1**	(8) **3**	
(3) **1**	(6) **4**	(9) **4**	

(See Chapter 4—Reading Prose for a detailed review of elements of nonfiction.)

Chapter 2

WRITING FROM SOURCES

Most high school students already have experienced writing essays of opinion and personal experience; these are likely to have been on topics the writer was interested in. The shift in the new standards is to source-based argument, where the writer must first do research to understand a topic before trying to develop an opinion.

In the second part of the Regents ELA exam, you will demonstrate your ability to comprehend and analyze several documents on a substantive, even controversial topic. The topics raise questions that have a variety of legitimate answers or present problems with alternative solutions. You then must take a position on that topic and develop a coherent essay of argument, which is supported by specific evidence in the texts; the final essay must include references to at least three of the sources. These are, in fact, the skills you use when you do any kind of research and writing project.

Close reading in this part means first reading to understand the issue and then to analyze the information in the texts to see how they support various points of view. As you read the following documents, keep in mind the process of annotation: note central ideas and themes, key details, and important terms and phrases. On an actual exam, you are permitted to take notes in the margins, and you will have scrap paper to plan your essay.

STEP ONE—READING FOR INFORMATION AND UNDERSTANDING

Here are the texts from a recent Regents ELA Exam.

Topic: Should companies be allowed to track consumers' shopping or other preferences without their permission?

Text 1

Cell Phone Carrier Marketing Techniques:
An Invasion of Privacy?

BOSTON (CBS) – Your cell phone may be spying on you.

Every time you download an app, search for a website, send a text, snap a QR code or drive by a store with your GPS on, you are being tracked by your cell phone company.

(5)   "They know you were playing Angry Birds. They know that you drove by Sears. They know you drove by Domino's Pizza. They can take that and take a very unique algorithm[1] that can focus on your behavior," explained marketing expert Mark Johnson. "It's very impactful."

According to Johnson, your data trail is worth big money to the cell phone com-
(10) panies.

Details about your habits, your age and gender are compiled and can be sold to third parties. The information is predominantly used as a marketing tool so advertisers can target you with products or services that you are more likely to use or want.

(15)   The idea does not sit well with smartphone user Harrine Freeman. "It does seem creepy that companies are collecting all this information about consumers," she said.

Freeman is so uneasy; she turns off her GPS when she is not using it. She also clears her browser history.

(20)   "I think it is an invasion of privacy," she said.

All of the major cell phone carriers admit to collecting information about its customers. Some in the industry argue it benefits consumers because they get ads that are relevant to them. Cell phone companies do notify customers about the data they collect, but critics say the notices are often hard to understand and written in
(25) fine print.

Rainey Reitman of the Electronic Frontier Foundation doesn't like the fact that those who don't want to be tracked have to go out of their way to get the company to stop.

"This is something that consumers are automatically opted into," Reitman said.
(30)   To find out how your cell phone company might be monitoring you, be sure to carefully read the privacy policy.

---

[1]algorithm — process or set of rules followed in calculations

Also, make sure you read all of the updates your carrier might send you because this tracking technology keeps changing.

—Paula Ebben
http://boston.cbslocal.com, January 16, 2012

Text 2

EyeSee You and the Internet of Things: Watching You While You Shop

...Even the store mannequins have gotten in on the gig. According to the *Washington Post*, mannequins in some high-end boutiques are now being outfitted with cameras that utilize facial recognition technology. A small camera embedded in the eye of an otherwise normal looking mannequin allows storekeepers to keep
(5) track of the age, gender and race of all their customers. This information is then used to personally tailor the shopping experience to those coming in and out of their stores. As the *Washington Post* report notes, "a clothier introduced a children's line after the dummy showed that kids made up more than half its mid-afternoon traffic... Another store found that a third of visitors using one of its
(10) doors after 4 p.m. were Asian, prompting it to place Chinese-speaking staff members by the entrance."

At $5,072 a pop, these EyeSee mannequins come with a steep price tag, but for store owners who want to know more—*a lot more*—about their customers, they're the perfect tool, able to sit innocently at store entrances and windows, leaving
(15) shoppers oblivious to their hidden cameras. Itaian mannequin maker Almax SpA, manufacturer of the EyeSee mannequins, is currently working on adding ears to the mannequins, allowing them to record people's comments in order to further tailor the shopping experience. ...

It's astounding the amount of information—from the trivial to the highly per-
(20) sonal—about individual consumers being passed around from corporation to corporation, all in an effort to market and corral potential customers. Data mining companies collect this wealth of information and sell it to retailers who use it to gauge your interests and tailor marketing to your perceived desires.

All of the websites you visit collect some amount of information about you,
(25) whether it is your name or what other sites you have visited recently. Most of the time, we're being tracked without knowing it. For example, most websites now include Facebook and Twitter buttons so you can "like" the page you are viewing or "Tweet" about it. Whether or not you click the buttons, however, the companies can still determine which pages you've visited and file that information away for
(30) later use. ...

25

As the EyeSee mannequins show, you no longer even have to be in front of your computer to have your consumer data accessed, uploaded, stored and tracked. In August 2012, for example, data mining agency Redpepper began testing a service known as Facedeals in the Nashville, Tennessee area. Facial recognition cameras set
(35)   at the entrances of businesses snap photos of people walking in, and if you've signed up to have a Facedeals account via your Facebook, you receive instant coupons sent to your smartphone. Similarly, a small coffee chain in San Francisco, Philz Coffee, has installed sensors at the front door of their stores in order to capture the Wi-Fi signal of any smartphone within 60 yards. Jacob Jaber, president of Philz Coffee,
(40)   uses the information gleaned from these sensors to structure his stores according to the in-store behavior of customers. …

Not even politicians are immune to the lure of data mining. In the run-up to the 2012 presidential election, the Romney and Obama campaigns followed voters across the web by installing cookies on their computers and observing the
(45)   websites they visited in an attempt to gather information on their personal views. CampaignGrid, a Republican affiliated firm, and Precision Network, a Democratic affiliated firm, both worked to collect data on 150 million American Internet users, or 80% of the registered voting population. …

—John W. Whitehead
excerpted *https://www.rutherford.org*, December 17, 2012

Text 3

Where Will Consumers Find Privacy Protection from RFIDs?: A Case for Federal Legislation

What Are RFIDs? How Do RFIDs Work?

…RFID [Radio Frequency Information Device] technology is an automatic identification system that identifies objects, collects data, and transmits information about the object through a "tag." A device called a reader extracts and processes the information on the tag. Experts characterize RFIDs as devices "that can be sensed
(5)   at a distance by radio frequencies with few problems of obstruction or misorientation."[1] In essence, RFIDs are wireless barcodes. However, unlike typical barcodes, which are identical for all common products, each RFID has a unique identification. Therefore, every individually tagged item has a different barcode sequence.

[1] KATHERINE ALBRECHT & LIZ MCINTRYE, SPYCHIPS 13 (Nelson Current 2005) quoting Raghu Das, *RFID Explained: An Introduction to RFID and Tagging Technologies*, ID TECHEX (2003).
[2] *Id.*

Typical barcodes also require unobstructed paths for scanning, whereas RFIDs can (10) be scanned through solid objects.[2] RFIDs have communication signals that facilitate data storage on RFID tags and enable the stored information to be gathered electronically—hypothetically permitting, for example, Coca-Cola to have a database storing information about the life cycle of a Coke can. The database would contain tracking details from the moment the can is manufactured through its processing at a (15) garbage dump—since RFID readers can be attached to garbage trucks. Between the birth and death of a customer's Coke can, the RFID tags would tell the Coca-Cola Company where and when the Coke was purchased, what credit card the Coke was purchased with, and, in turn, the identity of the purchaser. Even if the customer did not purchase the Coke with a credit card, state issued ID cards equipped with RFID (20) technology could relay the customer's identity to RFID readers as he or she leaves the store. Coca-Cola's final product of the RFIDs' communications is a database of the life cycles of individual cans of Coke and personal information about their purchasers. With this myriad of information, Coca-Cola has the ability to individually market to each of the 1.3 billion daily Coca-Cola consumers. ...

How Are RFIDs Used?

(25)   RFIDs are currently used in many ways, including, "livestock management[,] 24 hour patient monitoring[,] authentication of pharmaceuticals[,] tracking consignments in a supply chain[,] remote monitoring of critical components in aircraft [, and] monitoring the safety of perishable food."[3] Advocates of RFID technology, including retailers and manufacturers, praise the increased functionality and effi- (30) ciency that will likely ensue from using RFIDs. Once all products are individually tagged, shoppers are expected to be able to purchase items without checking-out. This should be possible since RFID readers will be able to scan every item as the customer exits the store and charge an RFID credit card, thereby simultaneously increasing efficiency and possibly reducing shoplifting. Other RFID uses include (35) easy monitoring of product recalls, tracking lobsters for conservation purposes, and purchasing products with transaction-free payment systems.[4] Additionally, in October 2003, the Department of Defense set standards mandating suppliers to place RFID tags on all packaging for the Department of Defense.[5] Thus, RFIDs can be used to increase efficiency and safety. ...

---

[2]*Id.*

[3]Viviane Reding, Member of the European Commission responsible for Information Society and Media, Address at EU RFID 2006 Conference: Heading for the Future, RFID: WHY WE NEED A EUROPEAN POLICY, 1,3 (Oct. 16, 2006).

[4]David Flint, *Everything with Chips!*, BUS. L. REV., Mar. 2006, 73, 73.

[5]PRESS RELEASE, US DEP. OF DEFENSE, DOD ANNOUNCES RADIO FREQUENCY IDENTIFICATION POLICY, UNITED STATES DEPARTMENT OF DEFENSE NEWS RELEASE (Oct. 23, 2003).

Do Consumers Have a Right to Privacy
from RFIDs under Tort Law?[6]

(40)   ...In the context of RFIDs, there are some situations where gathering information from RFID tags violates consumers' privacy expectations. For example, a consumer does not have a reasonable expectation of privacy when carrying RFID equipped items in a transparent shopping cart. However, once the items are placed in an opaque bag, a right to privacy immediately arises. If a business or third-party
(45) gathers data about the items once the items are no longer visible to the naked eye, there is an objective invasion of privacy. Gathering information stored in the RFID tag in a winter jacket worn in public is also not an invasion of privacy, yet pulling data off undergarments is intrusive. However, since the home is always considered a private place, once an active RFID tag enters the home, any information gathered,
(50) including information from the winter jacket, immediately offends the principles of privacy. Protecting consumers from unreasonably intrusive actions of businesses requires that RFID tags become unreadable once they enter private places. However, the fundamental nature of the technology does not harmonize with this privacy goal because RFID readers do not scrutinize whether the information is
(55) considered private before it gathers data from the tag. ...

     With new technologies come new methods of consumer tracking and changing parameters for what may be considered highly offensive. These new methods of tracking are not considered intrusive simply because the nature of the technology requires consumer purchases to be recorded. If individuals make active decisions to
(60) use a credit card instead of cash—a voluntary act—their purchases can be tracked. Similarly, the gathering of information stored on RFID technology in consumer goods may not be deemed highly offensive depending on changing consumer expectations. ...

—Serena G. Stein excerpted and adapted
Duke Law & Technology Review, 2007, No.3

_____

[6]Tort Law — covers civil wrongs resulting in an injury or harm constituting the basis for
a claim by the injured person

Text 4

RFID Consumer Applications and Benefits

...One of the first consumer applications of RFID was automated toll collection systems, which were introduced in the late 1980s and caught on in the 1990s. An active transponder is typically placed on a car's or truck's windshield. When the car reaches the tollbooth, a reader at the booth sends out a signal that wakes up the
(5) transponder on the windshield, which then reflects back a unique ID to the reader at the booth. The ID is associated with an account opened by the car owner, who is billed by the toll authority. Consumers spend less time fumbling for change or waiting on lines to pay their toll fee.

In the late 1990s, ExxonMobil (then just Mobil) introduced Speedpass, an RFID
(10) system that allows drivers who have opened an account to pay for gas automatically. Drivers are given a small, passive 13.56 MHz transponder in a small wand or fob that can be put on a key chain. To pay for gas, they just wave the key fob by a reader built into the gas pump. Seven million people in the United States use the system, and it has increased the number of cars each gas station can serve during
(15) rush periods. ...

RFID has other consumer applications, besides being a convenient payment system. One is the recovery of lost or stolen items. A company called Snagg in Palo Alto, Calif., has created an electronic registry for musical instruments. It provides an RFID tag that can be affixed to a classic guitar or priceless violin and keeps a
(20) record of the serial number in the tag. If the instrument is recovered by the police after being lost or stolen, they can call Snagg, which can look up the rightful owner. ...

Merloni Elettrodomestici, an Italian appliance maker, has created a smart washing machine. When you drop your clothes in the machine, an RFID reader in the
(25) appliance can read the tags in the clothes (if your clothes have tags) and wash the clothes based on instructions written to the tag.

Whether smart appliances with RFID readers catch on depends on how long it takes for RFID tags to become cheap enough to be put into packaging for items. It also depends on whether consumers find RFID-enabled products convenient
(30) enough to accept the potential invasion of privacy that comes with having RFID tags in products. But RFID will certainly have a positive impact on people's lives in less direct ways.

One area of importance is product recalls. Today, companies often need to recall all tires, meat or drugs if there is a problem to ensure people's safety. But
(35) they can never be sure they recovered all the bad goods that were released into the supply chain. With RFID, companies will be able to know exactly which items are bad and trace those through to stores. Customers that register their products

could be contacted individually to ensure they know something they bought has been recalled. …

(40)   And RFID should enable consumers to get more information about the products they want to purchase, such as when the items were made, where, whether they are under warrantee and so on. When RFID tags are eventually put on the packaging of individual products, consumers will be able to read the tag with a reader embedded in a cell phone or connected to a computer and download data

(45)   from a Web site. They'll be able to learn, for example, whether the steak they are about to buy is from an animal that was raised organically in the United States. Some companies will be reluctant to share this information, but smart companies will provide it to their customers to build trust and loyalty.

RFID could also have an [sic] positive impact on our environment by greatly

(50)   reducing waste. The main reason many companies want to use RFID is to better match supply and demand and to make sure that products are where they are supposed to be. If successful, there should be fewer products that are thrown away because no one wants to buy them or they pass their sell-by date (it's estimated that 50 percent of all food harvested in the United States is never eaten).

(55)   RFID tags could also help improve our environment by identifying hazardous materials that should not be dumped in landfills. One day, robots at landfills might be equipped with RFID tags, and they might be able to quickly sort through garbage to locate batteries and other items that contain toxic materials. …

—Bob Violino
excerpted *http://www.rfidjournal.com*, January 16, 2005

LOOKING AT THE TEXTS

Text 1—*Cell Phone Carrier Marketing Techniques: An Invasion of Privacy?*

This document opens with a dramatic assertion: "Your cell phone may be spying on you." The rest of the short article, from a television news report, gives a general description of data collection by cell phone companies and provides a useful introduction to the issue.

Text 2—*EyeSee You and the Internet of Things: Watching You While You Shop*

This article, from a website devoted to issues of civil liberties, presents several detailed examples of how retailers, Internet providers, and political campaigns make use of data mining. This text is an excellent source of material to support an argument opposed to tracking consumers' behavior without their permission.

Text 3—*Where Will Consumers Find Privacy Protection from RFIDs?: A Case for Federal Legislation*

This article, from a university law review, is the most challenging: The article offers a detailed technical description of what RFIDs are and how they operate. It also offers an analysis of the complex legal issues they raise. Finally, the last paragraph seems to suggest that if consumers are aware of this new technology, its use might not be considered intrusive.

Text 4—*RFID Consumer Applications and Benefits*

The title of this document, from a journal that promotes development and use of RFIDs, is a clear statement of the content and point of view. What follows is a list of various applications of RFID technology in language that is technical but readily understood, and the examples are presented as only beneficial for consumers.

STEP TWO—COMPOSING A SOURCE-BASED ARGUMENT

Because the issues presented for argument will be relevant and may already be familiar to high school students, you should be able to choose a position (claim) that you can make convincing. Here are the Guidelines for Part 2 of the Regents ELA (Common Core) Exam:

BE SURE TO:

- Establish your claim regarding companies being allowed to track consumers' shopping or other preferences without their permission
- Distinguish your claim from alternate or opposing claims
- Use specific, relevant, and sufficient evidence from at least **three** of the texts to develop your argument
- Identify each source that you reference by text number and line number(s) or graphic (for example: Text 1, line 4 or Text 2, graphic)
- Organize your ideas in a cohesive and coherent manner
- Maintain a formal style of writing
- Follow the conventions of standard written English

PLANNING THE ESSAY

First, consider **who your audience is**. You should assume a reader who is interested in the subject but who has not yet formed a strong opinion about the issue. Your reader is interested in what you have to say and can be convinced by a sound and well-documented argument.

Establishing a claim and distinguishing it from an alternate or opposing claim means that you are taking a particular position on the issue, you are not just offering a description or explanation of the subject. In each of the following examples, there is a reference to at least one of the issues the topic raises, and there is an indication of how the writer's argument is going to be developed.

Supporting the claim with specific and relevant evidence is part of any effective argument; supporting the claim with **sufficient** evidence means the writer has included not only several examples from different sources but has also used analysis of the texts to determine which evidence **best supports** the argument. Remember, too, that showing faulty or weak reasoning in examples from documents with opposing views is one of the most effective strategies in argument. Identifying references is, of course, part of any source-based writing.

The organization (structure) of the essay should be determined by the logic of the argument. An effective essay moves from establishing the claim through a series of examples (evidence) to a persuasive conclusion. In a **coherent** essay, the reader should understand how each new section extends the ideas that have come before and leads to the ideas that follow and to a convincing conclusion. **Cohesive** writing means that the connection of your ideas within each sentence and at the paragraph level is clear and that the writing follows the conventions of standard written English.

LOOKING AT A VARIETY OF EFFECTIVE CLAIMS

Here are several examples of how students established effective claims for arguments on the topic of data mining and consumer privacy:

> *Technology is changing, allowing companies and other interests . . . to track our location any given time and collect information about what we buy, all without our consent. There should be a limit to what these entities can gather on us . . .*

Companies should be permitted to have access to consumers' spending habits without their permission. The companies may seem like they are invading our privacy, but they are simply finding better and more efficient ways to help their customers and profit their businesses.

Under most circumstances, consumers should not be tracked without permission for sole benefit of companies. However, if the consumer does authorize its use by way of contract, companies should have right to track them.

Companies should not be permitted to track consumers' shopping and other activities without their consent. Without informing people of new tracking devices and methods and letting them decide, companies invade people's personal privacy . . .

Technology has made major improvements all over the world; however, these improvements have made it much easier for companies to track consumers without their permission. I support the view that the tracking of a customer's habits and preferences is an invasion of privacy.

New innovations in technology have enabled companies to monitor cell phone usage, the goods bought by consumers, or the places that people travel. In some cases, this is seen as an invasion of privacy. However, for the majority of the time, this new technology should be seen as a benefit to both consumers and the companies involved.

(See also Chapter 7—Writing on Demand for more discussion.)

READING AND WRITING TO ANALYZE TEXT

TEXT ANALYSIS: EXPOSITION

Text analysis requires first doing a close reading of a passage to identify a central idea and then analyzing how the author develops that central idea. This means understanding the author's purpose and seeing how the author's choice of literary techniques or a specific rhetorical strategy serves that purpose. In this part of the Regents ELA exam, you may read a literary passage of autobiography or memoir, a speech of historical significance, or a personal essay on a historical or scientific subject or on a philosophical idea.

SAMPLE TEXT AND EXPOSITORY RESPONSE

...It turned out to be true. The face of the water [Mississippi River], in time, became a wonderful book—a book that was a dead language to the uneducated passenger, but which told its mind to me without reserve, delivering its most cherished secrets as clearly as if it uttered them with a voice. And it was not a book to be

(5) read once and thrown aside, for it had a new story to tell every day. Throughout the long twelve hundred miles there was never a page that was void of interest, never one that you could leave unread without loss, never one that you would want to skip, thinking you could find higher enjoyment in some other thing. There never was so wonderful a book written by man; never one whose interest was

(10) so absorbing, so unflagging, so sparklingly renewed with every reperusal. The passenger who could not read it was charmed with a peculiar sort of faint dimple on its surface (on the rare occasions when he did not overlook it altogether); but to the pilot that was an *italicized* passage; indeed, it was more than that, it was a legend of the largest capitals, with a string of shouting exclamation points at

(15) the end of it, for it meant that a wreck or a rock was buried there that could tear the life out of the strongest vessel that ever floated. It is the faintest and simplest expression the water ever makes, and the most hideous to a pilot's eye. In truth, the passenger who could not read this book saw nothing but all manner of pretty pictures in it, painted by the sun and shaded by the clouds, whereas to the trained

(20) eye these were not pictures at all, but the grimmest and most dead-earnest of reading matter.

Now when I had mastered the language of this water, and had come to know every trifling feature that bordered the great river as familiarly as I knew the letters of the alphabet, I had made a valuable acquisition. But I had lost something, too. I
(25) had lost something which could never be restored to me while I lived. All the grace, the beauty, the poetry, had gone out of the majestic river! I still kept in mind a certain wonderful sunset which I witnessed when steamboating was new to me. A broad expanse of the river was turned to blood; in the middle distance the red hue brightened into gold, through which a solitary log came floating, black and
(30) conspicuous; one place a long, slanting mark lay sparkling upon the water; in another the surface was broken by boiling, tumbling rings, that were as many-tinted as an opal; where the ruddy flush was faintest, was a smooth spot that was covered with graceful circles and radiating lines, ever so delicately traced; the shore on our left was densely wooded, and the sombre shadow that fell from this forest
(35) was broken in one place by a long, ruffled trail that shone like silver; and high above the forest wall a clean-stemmed dead tree waved a single leafy bough that glowed like a flame in the unobstructed splendor that was flowing from the sun. There were graceful curves, reflected images, woody heights, soft distances; and over the whole scene, far and near, the dissolving lights drifted steadily, enriching it every passing
(40) moment with new marvels of coloring.

I stood like one bewitched. I drank it in, in a speechless rapture. The world was new to me, and I had never seen any thing like this at home. But as I have said, a day came when I began to cease from noting the glories and the charms which the moon and the sun and the twilight wrought upon the river's face; another
(45) day came when I ceased altogether to note them. Then, if that sunset scene had been repeated, I should have looked upon it without rapture, and should have commented upon it, inwardly, after this fashion: "This sun means that we are going to have wind to-morrow; that floating log means that the river is rising, small thanks to it; that slanting mark on the water refers to a bluff reef which is going to
(50) kill somebody's steamboat one of these nights, if it keeps on stretching out like that; those tumbling 'boils' show a dissolving bar and a changing channel there; the lines and circles in the slick water over yonder are a warning that that troublesome place is shoaling up dangerously; that silver streak in the shadow of the forest is the 'break' from a new snag, and he has located himself in the very best place he could
(55) have found to fish for steamboats; that tall dead tree, with a single living branch, is not going to last long, and then how is a body ever going to get through this blind place at night without the friendly old landmark?"

No, the romance and the beauty were all gone from the river. All the value any feature of it had for me now was the amount of usefulness it could furnish toward
(60) compassing the safe piloting of a steamboat. Since those days, I have pitied doc-

tors from my heart. What does the lovely flush in a beauty's cheek mean to a doctor but a "break" that ripples above some deadly disease? Are not all her visible charms sown thick with what are to him the signs and symbols of hidden decay? Does he ever see her beauty at all, or doesn't he simply view her professionally, and comment (65) upon her unwholesome condition all to himself? And doesn't he sometimes wonder whether he has gained most or lost most by learning his trade?

—Mark Twain
excerpted and adapted from *Life on the Mississippi*, 1901
Harper & Brothers Publishers

RESPONSE

In this excerpt, Twain introduces the central idea as a metaphor: "The face of the water {Mississippi River}...became a wonderful book."

Throughout the passage he uses vivid imagery to convey the beauty of the river and to convey how the acquisition of knowledge means losing that beauty. Before the author learned to see the signs of danger in navigating the river, he saw only beauty. When Twain was new to steam boating, he witnessed a particularly magnificent sunset. The sky was red, which reflected on the water and slowly transitioned to gold. He noticed delicate rings growing from a spot in the water. He noticed a dead tree rising above the wall of forest, with a bough of leaves that shone with brightness of flames. He was in a state of "speechless rapture."

Later on, the beauty faded as he learned the signals behind what he saw. Twain tells us that the river was a "wonderful book"; but it was also "the grimmest and most dead-earnest of reading matter." That beautiful red hue in his surroundings would mean wind the next day. The growing ripples marked a dangerous obstacle that could kill a steamboat. The dead tree, whose leaves were like fire, was a "friendly landmark" and would be lost after it fell. In learning to read the book of the river, Twain loses forever the ability to see the beauty and grace of the Mississippi and regrets what he has lost in learning his trade: "No, the romance and beauty were all gone from the river... all it had for me now was the amount of usefulness it could furnish. . . ."

This is an excellent example of an expository response: In the opening sentence, this writer expresses the central idea of the passage and identifies Twain's use of vivid imagery as key to understanding its meaning. The analysis is developed in two paragraphs, each of which cites several specific and relevant examples from the text. In the first paragraph, the images recall Twain's delight in the beauty of the river; in the second, these images become examples of how the knowledge Twain acquires destroys his ability to see beauty in them. This organization in parallel details is both sophisticated and effective. The incorporation of quoted phrases enhances development of the central idea and meets the requirement for an evidence-based analysis.

ADDITIONAL TEXTS FOR ANALYSIS AND REVIEW

PASSAGE ONE

This passage is an excerpt from a speech given by Red Jacket, Chief of the Seneca Nation, to the United States acting secretary of war in Washington, D.C., on February 10, 1801.

...Brother, the business on which we are now come is to restore the friendship that has existed between the United States and the Six Nations, agreeably to the direction of the commissioner from the fifteen fires[1] of the United States. He assured us that whensoever, by any grievances, the chain of friendship should
(5) become rusty, we might have it brightened by calling on you. We dispense with the usual formality of having your speech again read, as we fully comprehended it yesterday, and it would therefore be useless to waste time in a repetition of it.

Brother, yesterday you wiped the tears from our eyes, that we might see clearly; you unstopped our ears that we might hear; and removed the obstructions
(10) from our throats that we might speak distinctly. You offered to join with us in tearing up the largest pine-tree in our forests, and under it to bury the tomahawk. We gladly join with you, brother, in this work, and let us heap rocks and stones on the root of this tree that the tomahawk may never again be found. ...

---

[1]fires—fires refers to states

38

Brother, we observe that the men now in office are new men, and, we fear, not
(15)   fully informed of all that has befallen us. In 1791 a treaty was held by the commissioners of Congress with us at Tioga Point, on a similar occasion. We have lost
seven of our warriors, murdered in cold blood by white men, since the conclusion
of the war. We are tired of this mighty grievance and wish some general arrangement to prevent it in future. The first of these was murdered on the banks of
(20)   the Ohio, near Fort Pitt. Shortly after two men belonging to our first families
were murdered at Pine Creek; then one at Fort Franklin; another at Tioga Point;
and now the two that occasion this visit, on the Big Beaver. These last two had
families. The one was a Seneca; the other a Tuscarora. Their families are now destitute of support, and we think that the United States should do something toward
(25)   their support, as it is to the United States they owe the loss of their heads.

Brother, these offences are always committed in one place on the frontier
of Pennsylvania. In the Genesee country we live happy and no one molests
us. I must therefore beg that the President will exert all his influence with
all officers, civil and military, in that quarter, to remedy this grievance, and
(30)   trust that he will thus prevent a repetition of it and save our blood from being
spilled in future.

Brother, let me call to mind the treaty between the United States and the Six
Nations, concluded at Canandaigua. At that treaty Colonel Pickering, who was
commissioner on behalf of the United States, agreed that the United States should
(35)   pay to the Six Nations four thousand five hundred dollars per annum, and that this
should pass through the hands of the superintendent of the United States, to be
appointed for that purpose. This treaty was made in the name of the President of
the United States, who was then General Washington; and, as he is now no more,
perhaps the present President would wish to renew the treaty. But if he should
(40)   think the old one valid and is willing to let it remain in force we are also willing.
The sum above mentioned we wish to have part of in money, to expend in more
agricultural tools and in purchasing a team, as we have some horses that will do
for the purpose. We also wish to build a sawmill on the Buffalo creek. If the President, however, thinks proper to have it continue as heretofore, we shall not be very
(45)   uneasy. Whatever he may do we agree to; we only suggest this for his consideration.

Brother, I hand you the above-mentioned treaty, made by Colonel Pickering,
in the name of General Washington, and the belt that accompanied it; as he is now
dead we know not if it is still valid. If not, we wish it renewed—if it is, we wish it
copied on clean parchment. Our money got loose in our trunk and tore it. We also
(50)   show you the belt which is the path of peace between our Six Nations and the
United States. ...

Brother, the business that has caused this our long journey was occasioned by
some of your bad men; the expense of it has been heavy on us. We beg that as so

39

great a breach has been made on your part, the President will judge it proper that
(55)   the United States should bear our expenses to and from home and whilst here.

Brother, three horses belonging to the Tuscarora Nation were killed by some men
under the command of Major Rivardi, on the plains of Niagara. They have made
application to the superintendent and to Major Rivardi, but get no redress. You
make us pay for our breaches of the peace, why should you not pay also? A white
(60)   man has told us the horses were killed by Major Rivardi's orders, who said they
should not be permitted to come there, although it was an open common on
which they were killed. Mr. Chapin has the papers respecting these horses, which
we request you to take into consideration.

—Red Jacket
excerpted from *Orations from Homer to William McKinley*,
Vol. VII, 1902
P. F. Collier and Son

Looking at the Text

The repetition of "Brother, . . ." at the beginning of each point is the most
obvious rhetorical element in this speech. Careful analysis will show how
that not only establishes the speaker's attitude toward his audience (the tone
of the speech) but also structures the various examples as reminders of past
history and treaty obligations and establishes the legitimacy of the Chief's
demands for compensation and justice.

PASSAGE TWO

Here is an example of a classic essay form, in which a specific aspect
of human nature or conduct is explored. First made popular by the French
writer Michel de Montaigne in the 16th century, this kind of essay is relatively brief, offers intellectual insight, and often includes anecdotes or analogies as illustrations. In "Of Suspicion," Sir Francis Bacon, a contemporary of
Shakespeare, first offers his observations on how suspicion clouds the mind
and then suggests ways to avoid its corrosive effects.

Of Suspicion

SUSPICIONS amongst thoughts are like bats amongst birds, they ever fly by twilight. Certainly they are to be repressed, or at least well guarded: for they cloud the mind; they leese [lose] friends; and they check with [hinder, restrain] business, whereby business cannot go on currently and constantly. They dispose [lead]
(5) kings to tyranny, husbands to jealousy, wise men to irresolution [indecisiveness] and melancholy. They are defects, not in the heart, but in the brain; for they take place in the stoutest [bravest] natures; as in the example of Henry the Seventh of England. There was not a more suspicious man, nor a more stout. And in such a composition they do small hurt. For commonly they are not admitted, but [unless]
(10) with examination, whether they be likely or no. But in fearful natures they gain ground too fast. There is nothing makes a man suspect much, more than to know little; and therefore men should remedy suspicion by procuring to know more, and not to keep their suspicions in smother [suppressed]. What would men have? Do they think those they employ and deal with are saints? Do they not think they will
(15) have their own ends, and be truer to themselves than to them? Therefore there is no better way to moderate suspicions, than to account upon such suspicions as true and yet to bridle them as false. For so far a man ought to make use of suspicions, as to provide, as if that should be true that he suspects, yet it may do him no hurt. Suspicions that the mind of itself gathers are but buzzes; but suspicions that are
(20) artificially nourished, and put into men's heads by the tales and whisperings of others, have stings. Certainly, the best mean [strategy] to clear the way in this same wood of suspicions is frankly to communicate them with the party that he suspects; for thereby he shall be sure to know more of the truth of them than he did before; and withal shall make that party more circumspect not to give further cause of sus-
(25) picion. But this would not be done to men of base [dishonorable, corrupt] natures; for they, if they find themselves once suspected, will never be true. . . . (c 1625)

Looking at the Text

This is a passage that requires careful, slow reading. The essay begins with a simile that establishes the tone of what is to follow: suspicions are creatures of twilight; they are elusive, ambiguous, and potentially dangerous. Bacon then insists that suspicions must be kept under control and offers guidance on how best to "clear the way in...the wood of suspicions." Note how condensed the development of ideas is and how each sentence balances two or three assertions. The meanings of some unfamiliar terms have been inserted here, but the language of Bacon is also the language of Shakespeare and should be accessible to high school students at Regents level.

(There is a list of Archaic and Unfamiliar terms in Chapter 8 — Vocabulary.)

PASSAGE THREE

In 1858, Abraham Lincoln and Stephen Douglas were campaigning in Illinois for the U.S. Senate seat then held by Douglas. They held a series of debates throughout the state, which were widely and often raucously attended. Douglas argued that it was an absolute right of self-government for residents of a territory to permit or to prohibit slavery. Here is a passage from an eyewitness account of the seventh and final of the Lincoln-Douglas debates.

. . . Douglas had been theatrical and scholarly, but this tall, homely man [Lincoln] was creating by his very looks what the brilliant lawyer and experienced Senator had failed to make people see and feel. The Little Giant [Douglas] had assumed striking attitudes, played tricks with his flowing white hair, mimicking
(5) the airs of authority, with patronizing allusions; but these affectations, usually so effective when he addressed an audience alone, went for nothing when brought face to face with realities. Lincoln had no genius for gesture and no desire to produce a sensation. The failure of Senator Douglas to bring conviction to critical minds was caused by three things: a lack of logical sequence in argument, a lack of
(10) intuitional judgment, and a vanity that was caused by too much intellect and too little heart. Douglas had been arrogant and vehement, Lincoln was now logical and penetrating. . . .

The enthusiasm created by Douglas was wrought out of smart epigram thrusts and a facile, superficial eloquence. . . . His weight in the political balance was
(15) purely materialistic; his scales of justice tipped to the side of cotton, slavery, and popular passions, while the man who faced him now brought to the assembly cold logic in place of wit, frankness in place of cunning, reasoned will and judgment in place of chicanery and sophistry. . . . His looks, his words, his voice, his attitude, were like a magical essence dropped into the seething cauldron of politics, reacting
(20) against the foam, calming the surface and letting the people see to the bottom. It did not take him long:

"Is it not a false statesmanship," he asked, "that undertakes to build
up a system of policy upon the basis of caring nothing about the very
thing that everybody does care the most about? Judge Douglas may say
(25) *he cares not whether slavery is voted up or down, but he must have a*
choice between a right thing and a wrong thing. He contends that what-
ever community wants slaves has a right to have them. So they have, if
it is not a wrong; but if it is a wrong he cannot say people have a right
to do wrong. He says that upon the score of equality slaves should be
(30) *allowed to go into a new Territory like other property. This is strictly logi-*

cal if there is no difference between it [slaves] and other property. If it and other property are equal his argument is entirely logical; but if you insist that one is wrong and the other right there is no use to institute a comparison between right and wrong."

(35)   This was the broadside. The great duel on the high seas of politics was over.
The Douglas ship of State Sovereignty was sinking. The debate was a triumph that would send Lincoln to Washington as President in a little more than two years from that date.

—Francis Grierson, *The Valley of Shadows*

Looking at the Text

In this passage, we can see how the observer uses various rhetorical elements to recreate the experience of hearing the two famous men, and within this account, we see how Lincoln himself revealed the morally flawed logic in Douglas's position on slavery.

The observer sets the stage with a series of balanced and contrasting images: Douglas is theatrical and vain, a man of "too much intellect and too little heart." Lincoln "had no genius for gesture" or sensational language; Lincoln was ". . . now logical and penetrating." He introduces Lincoln's words with a vivid image of an alchemist calming intense passions—the seething cauldron of politics—with the "magical essence" of clear, moral argument.

Lincoln attacks Douglas for "caring nothing about" slavery, that is, for being neutral on the issue, when it is the issue the nation most cares about. Douglas contends that slavery is an issue of property and rights of States, but Lincoln says that is a logical fallacy: the issue is not about property, it is about right and wrong; " . . . *he cannot say people have a right to do wrong.*" The passage ends with another strong metaphor: Douglas's ship of State Sovereignty has been sunk in a battle on the [political] high seas by the cannon shot of Lincoln's words.

(The Lincoln-Douglas Debates, Twain's memoir, and Red Jacket's speech are examples of what is meant by "seminal U.S. texts" in the State Standards. Analyzing and evaluating the reasoning in these and other "foundational U.S. documents of historical and literary significance" can be expected on the Regents ELA exam and on the new SAT (2015). See the Appendices, pages 223–227, to review the standards.)

Chapter 4

READING PROSE

One of the characters in Moliere's satire *Le Bourgeois Gentilhomme* (*The Bourgeois Gentleman*) makes an astonishing discovery: "For over forty years I have been speaking prose without knowing it!" Prose writing is composed in the rhythms and patterns of spoken discourse. When we read novels and short stories, essays and reports, journals and letters, we are usually reading prose. In our daily lives and as students, we read prose that varies widely in purpose, in method of development, and in tone. Prose serves the purposes of personal expression, persuasion, literary effect, and information.

WHAT WRITERS DO: A LIST OF USEFUL TERMS

A group of high school juniors recently was asked to list all the verbs they could think of to denote what writers *do*. Here is the list they came up with:

address	declare	imply	refine
affirm	defend	infer	reflect
alert	define	influence	refute
amuse	delineate	inform	remind
analyze	depict	inspire	reveal
appraise	describe	interpret	revise
argue	discern	invent	scrutinize
assert	discover	judge	see
assess	dramatize	note	select
capture	edit	observe	shock
caution	emphasize	offer	show
censure	enhance	persuade	suggest
cite	enrich	play	summarize
clarify	establish	ponder	support
classify	evaluate	portray	symbolize
comment	examine	present	teach
conclude	explain	probe	theorize
condemn	explore	produce	uncover
conjecture	expose	propose	view
convey	expound	provoke	work(!)
create	forewarn	question	
create images	formulate	reassure	
criticize	illustrate	recreate	

45

As you consider these terms, you will note that they are not separated by categories; many of them denote both purpose and tone, and many suggest a method of development as well. While this list may not include everything writers "do," it is a useful reminder of the great variety in written expression. (Because command of this vocabulary will also help you to express your understanding and appreciation of what you read, you will find examples showing how many of these words are applied to discussions of nonfiction and, in Chapter 6, writing about literature. Note also that most of these terms are part of the vocabulary that is considered Academic Language. (See Chapter 8 — Vocabulary.)

To read well you must be listening actively to the narrator's voice, thinking with the author. If you are reading a piece for information or direction, ask questions; expect them to be answered. If you are reading a work of argument or persuasion, question it; actively agree or disagree; follow how the argument is developed. If you are reading a piece of personal expression, try to imagine, even share, the experience. If you are reading a piece of vivid description, recreate the images and feelings for yourself. Reading well offers us the entire range of human history and experience expressed in language.

Works of fiction are usually narrative in form. They tell us stories of what *happened* in the lives of the characters and, more important, *why it happened*. Nonfiction takes many forms, and its subjects touch on nearly everything in the human and natural worlds.

READING FICTION

When we speak of fiction, we are generally referring to narrative works — works in which events are recounted, are *told,* and have been imagined and structured by the author. (Although not narrative in form, drama shares many of the essential characteristics of fiction.) The subjects of fiction, however, are no less real than those of history or of what we call the actual or real world. In *Aspects of the Novel*, E. M. Forster shows how "fiction is truer than history." He reminds us that only in narrative fiction and drama can we truly know what is in a character's heart or mind; that is, only in a novel, short story, or play can we fully understand the motives, desires, and reasons for characters' actions. The historian draws conclusions from records of the past; the psychologist interprets interviews and tests; a jury weighs evidence and testimony; and our experience indicates that these are highly reliable ways to understand people and their lives. But only the author of a fictional work can offer an absolutely reliable account of what a character feels, believes, and desires, of why things happen as they do.

Plot and Story

The primary pleasure for most readers of narrative fiction is the story. The reason we become involved in a novel or short story is that we want to know how it turns out; we want to know what is going to happen to those characters. An author creates a **plot*** when he or she gives order and structure to the action: in a plot, the incidents, or episodes, of the story have meaningful relationships to one another. A story becomes a plot when we understand not only *what happened* but also *why*. In good fiction we are *convinced* of the causal relationship among incidents, and we are convinced by the relationship of characters' motives and feelings to the action.

For most readers of fiction, the first response is to keep track of the plot. We do this spontaneously. If you are preparing a novel or story for class discussion, one of the first things your instructor will expect you to know is, "What happens in . . . ?" This is not a trivial question, because you cannot fully understand the significance of character, theme, or structure if you do not first understand the action as it is presented. Understanding plot, of course, requires memory, and remembering the major incidents of a plot is usually a natural and relatively easy response. The more extensively you read, however, the more skilled you become in remembering and relating the key incidents in a complex plot and in recalling details when their full significance becomes evident—sometimes well after the incidents themselves occur. Keeping notes on the development of a complex plot is very useful, especially for students whose reading of a novel is broken up over days or weeks.

For a class, or as part of your preparation for the Regents exam questions on literature, practice summarizing the plots of works you know or are reading. Be able to tell the story of a novel or play to someone who does not know it in a narrative of your own words, including all the major incidents and their consequences. Be able to tell the story in the same way you would retell a familiar children's story or narrate a significant experience of your own.

Plot and Conflict

At the end of any meaningful story, something has *happened;* something is significantly different in the world and lives of the characters from what it was at the beginning. **Conflict** in the most general sense refers to the forces that move the action in a plot. Conflict in plot may be generated from a search or pursuit, from a discovery, from a deception or misunderstanding, from opportunities to make significant choices, or from unexpected consequences of an action. Although the term *conflict* connotes an active struggle

---

*Terms in bold are featured in A Glossary of Literary Terms and Techniques at the end of the chapter.

between opposing or hostile forces, conflict in fiction may refer to any progression, change, or discovery. The resolution of conflict in a plot may be subtle and confined to the inner life of a character or it may be dramatic and involve irreversible change, violent destruction, or death.

This term may identify an actual struggle between characters, anything from dominance or revenge to simple recognition or understanding. A plot may also focus on conflict between characters and the forces of nature or society. These are essentially **external conflicts**. A work may also center on **internal conflicts**, characters' struggle to know or change themselves and their lives. Most works of fiction and drama contain more than one aspect of conflict.

In Shakespeare's *Romeo and Juliet*, the most dramatic conflicts are external, vivid, and literal: the street brawls between followers of the rival Capulets and Montagues, the fatal fight with Tybalt that leads to Romeo's banishment, and the tragic deaths of the young lovers. In *Macbeth,* however, the primary interest is in the internal conflict between Macbeth's ambitious desires and his understanding of the moral consequences of the actions he takes to achieve those desires. The action in Edith Wharton's most famous story, "Roman Fever," is ironically serene and pleasant: two middle-aged women, longtime friends now both widowed, sit on a terrace overlooking the splendors of Rome and reflect on their common experiences and lifelong friendship. At the end of the conversation—and the story—their actual feelings of rivalry have surfaced, and one of the two learns something that reveals how little she truly knew her husband or understood her marriage or the life of her friend. The conflict between the two women emerges almost imperceptibly, and its meaning is fully understood only in the completely unexpected revelation of the last line.

Plot and Chronology

Narrative is not necessarily presented in chronological order, but it does have a chronology. In other words, incidents may be presented out of the order in which they actually occurred, but by the end of the work the reader understands their order and relationship and appreciates why the story was structured as it was. Plots that are narrated in flashback or from different points of view are common examples.

The Great Gatsby, by F. Scott Fitzgerald, and *Ethan Frome,* by Edith Wharton, are novels in which the narrators first introduce themselves and their interest in the story, then tell the story in a narrative flashback whose full significance to the narrator (and reader) is revealed only at the end. Tennessee Williams's play *The Glass Menagerie* has a similar structure, in which the character of Tom serves both as a narrator in the present and as a principal character in the series of memory scenes that make up the drama. The memory scenes in Arthur Miller's play *Death of a Salesman,* however, are not flashbacks in the same way. Willy Loman relives incidents from the past while the other characters and the action of the play continue in the present. As the play progresses, the shifts in time occur only within Willy's mind.

Shakespeare's tragedies are dramas in which normal chronology is preserved, as it is in such familiar novels as William Golding's *Lord of the Flies* and Mark Twain's *Huckleberry Finn*.

Plot and Time

Related to understanding of chronology is appreciation of how an author creates understanding of *elapsed time*. In the several hours required to read a novel, the two to three hours for a full-length play, and the half-hour to an hour for a one-act play or short story, how much time in the lives of the characters has been accounted for? In one-act plays and many short stories, the time covered by the action is equal to the time to read them. In Wharton's "Roman Fever," for example, the action of the story is contained in a few hours of one afternoon—little more time than it takes to read the story. That conversation, however, completely transforms the women's, and the reader's, understanding of their lives over twenty-five years. The time required for the action in Shirley Jackson's widely read story "The Lottery" is also roughly equal to the time required to read it, yet the plot accounts indirectly for events that have taken place for longer than anyone in the story can even remember. Miller's play *Death of a Salesman* takes place over a period of only twenty-four hours, but the plot and Willy's memories tell us the story of an entire lifetime. Awareness of how an author uses and accounts for time adds considerably to the reader's appreciation of a work.

Narrative Point of View

The **narrator** of a work is the character or author's **persona** that tells a story. **Point of view** is the standpoint, perspective, and degree of understanding from which the narrator speaks. For many students and scholars, how a story is told is one of the most interesting questions. What is the narrative point of view? Is the narration **omniscient**, essentially the point of view of the author? If not, who is the narrator? What is the narrator's relationship to the story? What is the narrator's understanding of the story? How much does the narrator really know? Appreciating how, or by whom, a story is told is often essential to understanding its meaning.

One of the most easily discerned narrative points of view is the first person (*I*), in which either the central character or another directly involved in the action tells the story. J. D. Salinger's novel *The Catcher in the Rye* is a vivid and popular example of such narration. Fitzgerald's *The Great Gatsby* is also told in the first person. In each of these works, the fundamental meaning of the novel becomes apparent only when the reader understands the character of the narrator. In each of these works, what the narrator experiences and what he learns about himself and the world are the novel's most important themes.

In first-person narration, the incidents of the plot are limited to those that the narrator himself experiences. First-person narrators can, however, report what they learn from others. In Wharton's *Ethan Frome,* the engineer who narrates tells us that he has "pieced together the story" from the little he has been able to learn in the town of Starkfield, from his limited conversations with Frome himself, and from his brief visit to the Frome house. Wharton's method, of course, dramatizes Frome's inability to express or fulfill the desires of his heart and reveals the reluctance of the people of Starkfield to fully understand the lives of those around them.

Authors may also use first-person narration to achieve an ironic or satiric effect. In Ring Lardner's well-known story "Haircut," a barber in a small midwestern town narrates a story about a local fellow who kept the town entertained with his practical jokes on people. As the story progresses, the reader understands how cruel and destructive the fellow's pranks were, but the barber does not. The narrative method in this story reveals, indirectly, a story of painful ignorance and insensitivity in the "decent" citizens of a small town. Mark Twain's masterpiece, *Huckleberry Finn*, is told by Huck himself. Through the morally naive observations of Huck, Twain satirizes the evils of slavery, fraud, hypocrisy, and virtually every other kind of corrupt human behavior. Edgar Allan Poe's story "The Tell-Tale Heart" is the confession of a cunning madman.

In third-person narration (*he, she, it, they*) a story is reported. The narrative voice may be *omniscient* and, therefore, able to report everything from everywhere in the story; this voice can also report on the innermost thoughts and feelings of the characters themselves. In many novels of the eighteenth and nineteenth centuries, the omniscient narrator even speaks directly to the reader, as if taking him or her into the storyteller's confidence. In Nathaniel Hawthorne's *The Scarlet Letter,* the narrator pauses from time to time to share personal feelings with the reader, as does Nick Carraway, the narrator of *The Great Gatsby*.

A widely used narrative method is the **limited omniscient** point of view. The narrative is in the third person but is focused on and even may represent the point of view of a central character. The actions and feelings of other characters are presented from the perspective of that character. Hawthorne's short story "Young Goodman Brown" is an excellent example.

Some third-person narration is dramatically **objective** and detached; it simply reports the incidents of the plot as they unfold. This narrative method, too, can be used for intensely **ironic** effect. Jackson's "The Lottery" is one of the best examples. The real horror of the story is achieved through the utterly detached, nonjudgmental unfolding of the plot.

In some plays, too, there is a character who serves a narrative role: the Chorus in Shakespeare's *Henry V*, the character of Tom in Williams's *The Glass Menagerie,* and the Stage Manager in Thornton Wilder's *Our Town* are familiar examples.

In each of the works discussed here, the narrative method is not simply a literary device; it is an intrinsic part of the meaning of the work.

Setting

The setting of a work includes the time and places in which the action is played out; setting may also include a significant historical context. In drama, setting may be presented directly in the set, costumes, and lighting. In narrative fiction, it is usually presented directly through description. In some works, the physical setting is central to the plot and developed in great detail; in other works, only those details necessary to anchor the plot in a time or place will be developed. Regardless of detail, responsive readers recreate images of setting as they read.

In addition to the physical and natural details of the fictional world, setting also includes mood and **atmosphere**. In some works, social or political realities constitute part of the setting. *The Scarlet Letter* is not only set in Puritan Boston, it is also *about* that society; and *The Great Gatsby* presents a vivid picture of life in New York during Prohibition and the roaring twenties.

For some works, the author may create specific details of setting to highlight a theme. In Golding's novel *Lord of the Flies*, the island on which the story takes place has everything essential for basic survival: food and water are available, and the climate is temperate. In order to explore the moral questions of the boys' regression into savagery, Golding carefully establishes a setting in which survival itself is not a primary issue. In *Ethan Frome,* details of the harsh winter and of the isolation of a town "bypassed by the railroad" intensify the story of a man's desperately cold and isolated life.

Character

We understand characters in fiction and drama, as we do the people in our own lives, by what they say and do and by what others say about them. Because characters are imagined and created by an author, we can even understand them more reliably and fully than we can many of the people around us. Many students find their greatest satisfaction in reading works about characters to whom they can relate, characters whose struggles are recognizable and whose feelings are familiar.

Understanding character in fiction means understanding a person's values and **motivation**, beliefs and principles, moral qualities, strengths and weaknesses, and degree of self-knowledge and understanding. To fully appreciate a work, the reader must understand what characters are searching for and devoting their lives to.

Literature also seeks to account for the forces outside individuals that influence the directions and outcomes of their lives. These "forces" range from those of nature and history to the demands of family, community, and society. The response of characters to inner and outer forces is what literature depicts and makes comprehensible.

Any meaningful or convincing plot stems from human thought, motive, and action. Depending on the narrative point of view (see page 49), a character's thoughts and feelings may be presented directly through omniscient narrative or first-person commentary. In "Young Goodman Brown," the narrator tells us directly what the title character is thinking and feeling; in "Roman Fever," the reader discovers the most important revelations of character simultaneously with the two central characters. Character in drama is revealed directly in dialogue and action, but it may be expanded through soliloquies and asides. In Shakespeare's *Othello,* for example, the full extent of Iago's evil is revealed through the variety of methods Iago uses to manipulate different characters and through his **soliloquies**.

In some works, the author's primary purpose is to reveal character gradually through plot; in others, the author establishes understanding of character from the beginning in order to account for what happens. In the opening pages of *The Great Gatsby,* the narrator, Nick, who is also a character in the novel, introduces himself and declares his judgment of the moral quality of the people and events he is about to narrate. With Nick's own character and motives clearly established, the reader then shares his *gradual* discovery of the truth about Gatsby and his life.

Theme

The subjects of literature may come from any aspect of human experience: love, friendship, growing up, ambition, family relationships, conflicts with society, survival, war, evil, death, and so on. **Theme** in a work of literature is the understanding, insight, observation, and presentation of such subjects. Theme is what a work *says about* a subject. Themes are the central ideas of literary works.

One way to think about theme is to consider it roughly analogous to the topic or thesis of an expository essay. If the author of a novel, story, or play had chosen to examine the subjects of the work in an essay, what might be the topic assertions of such an essay? The student is cautioned, however, not to overinterpret the analogy. Themes in literature are rarely "morals," such as those found at the end of a fable, but neither are they "hidden meanings." Although scholars and critics often express thematic ideas in phrases, students are often required to state themes in full sentences. In the next paragraph are some examples of statements about theme.

Macbeth is a play about the temptation to embrace evil forces and about the power of ambition to corrupt; Macbeth himself makes one of the most important statements of theme in the play when he says, "I do all that becomes a man/who does more is none." *Ethan Frome* and Lardner's "Haircut" both illustrate that people in small towns do not truly understand the innermost needs and desires of other people they *think* they know. William Golding's novel *Lord of the Flies* illustrates the bleak view that human beings' savage nature will prevail without external forces of authority, that human beings are not civilized in their fundamental natures. In contrast, in *Adventures of Huckleberry Finn,* Twain presents civilization as the source of corruption and finds truly moral behavior only in the runaway slave, Jim, and the ignorant boy, Huck.

In Chapter 6 you will find an extensive list of literature topics, many of which are expressed in terms of theme.

READING NONFICTION

Fiction and nonfiction share many common elements; they also make similar demands and offer comparable rewards to the thoughtful reader. In broad contrast to fiction, where characters and plot are imaginative creations of the author, nonfiction is about actual persons, experiences, and phenomena. The texts reviewed in Chapter 3 are good examples of how nonfiction speculates on abstract and philosophical questions of history and politics, ethics and religion, culture and society, as well as the natural world. In biography and autobiography, the writer focuses on what is meaningful and interesting in the life of an individual. The purpose of this section is to review some of the distinctive features of formal and informal essays and to illustrate some of the methods authors use to develop arguments in persuasive writing. The glossary at the end of the chapter also features extended definitions and examples of many important terms.

Questions for the Critical Reader

Here again are the questions you are urged to keep in mind as you prepare for the reading comprehension and text analysis sections of the Regents ELA exam:

What is the purpose of this piece? Its tone or mood? Its overall effect?

What does the author say? believe? recall? value? assert?

What does the author mean? imply? suggest? agree with? disagree with?

How are language and imagery used?

What conclusions or inferences is the reader led to?

What experience is meant to be shared and understood?

Purpose

In speaking of fiction, the central ideas of a work are identified as its themes. In essays, purpose refers both to the central ideas and to their intended effect on the reader. For example, many authors of essays develop a thesis with a view to influencing opinion or urging action. We encounter such writing daily on the editorial and Op-Ed pages of a newspaper. Many of the verbs on the list of "what writers do" (page 45) identify such purposes: *affirm, alert, argue, assert, caution, censure, condemn, criticize, declare, defend, evaluate, expose, forewarn, imply, inspire, judge, persuade, propose, provoke, reveal, scrutinize, support*.

Much nonfiction, of course, has as its purpose to explain and inform. The verbs used to identify informative writing include *analyze, assess, clarify, define, describe, explore, formulate, illustrate, interpret, recreate, summarize*.

Other purposes may be likened to conversations between the author and the reader; these "conversations" may be about anything from the most personal experiences to reflections on the nature of life and the universe. Some useful verbs here might be *address, amuse, capture, comment, conjecture, depict, discover, enhance, enrich, examine, explore, invent, observe, offer, ponder, probe, propose, question, recreate, reflect, shock*.

Methods of Development and Patterns of Organization

The ability to use a variety of methods to organize and express ideas is one of the most important skills a student writer learns, and the thoughtful reader should also be able to appreciate how a writer develops material. Informational texts are part of the reading comprehension and text analysis parts of the Regents ELA exam and the new SAT (2015); reviewing the following methods of organization is also useful preparation for composing essays of argument.

From Abstract to Concrete/from General to Specific

Going from the general to the specific is the most common and natural pattern for explanation, illustration, and reasoning. A passage by author and playwright Sandy Asher is an especially good example:

> **As a child, I sensed there was something I desperately needed from books. As a writer for young readers, I've tried to figure out what that something was. It turned out to be a combination of three things: companionship, a sense of control, and magic.**

In her essay, Asher goes on to develop a paragraph about each of the three things that make up the "something" she is explaining.

Here is how journalist Ernie Pyle begins his explanation of what "The awful waste and destruction of war" really means:

> **I walked for a mile and a half along the water's edge of our many-miled invasion beach. I walked slowly, for the detail on the beach was infinite.**
>
> **The wreckage was vast and startling. The awful waste and destruction of war, even aside from the loss of human life, has always been one of its outstanding features to those who are in it. Anything and everything is expendable. And we did expend on our beachhead in Normandy during those first few hours.**
>
> **For a mile out from the beach there were scores of tanks and trucks and boats that were not visible, for they were at the bottom of the water—swamped by overloading, or hit by shells, or sunk by mines.**

His description of a Normandy beach following the D-Day invasion in 1944 is developed in a series of vivid images and poignant details that make the waste and destruction of war comprehensible to those who have not experienced it.

From Concrete to Abstract/from Specific to General

Reversing the more common pattern, going from the specific to the general can also be a very effective way to develop understanding of a general concept. This is the pattern author William Kittredge uses in the **anecdote** about his boyhood encounter with a sage grouse. The passage recounts a specific experience, which leads to the closing general observation:

> **For that childhood moment I believed the world to be absolutely inhabited by an otherness which was utterly demonic and natural, not of my own making. But soon as that bird was enclosed in a story which defined it as a common-place prairie chicken, I was no longer frightened. It is a skill we learn early, the art of inventing stories to explain away the fearful sacred strangeness of the world. Storytelling and make-believe, like war and agriculture, are among the arts of self-defense, and all of them are ways of enclosing otherness and claiming ownership.**

Here is how the passage by Stephen Hawking in Chapter 1 (page 16) begins:

> **A few years ago the City Council of Monza, Italy, barred pet owners from keeping goldfish in curved fishbowls. The sponsors of the measure explained that it is cruel to keep a fish in a bowl because the curved sides give the fish a distorted view of reality. Aside from the measure's significance to the poor goldfish, the story raises an interesting philosophical question: How do we know that the reality we perceive is true?**
>
> **The goldfish is seeing a version of reality that is different from ours, but can we be sure it is any less real? For all we know, we, too, may spend our entire lives staring out at the world through a distorting lens.**

FROM QUESTION TO ANSWER

Another method of developing **argument** and explanation is to pose a question, which the paragraph or essay then answers. Here is an example from the conclusion of Thoreau's *Walden:*

> **Why should we be in such desperate haste to succeed, in such desperate enterprises? If a man does not keep pace with his companions, perhaps it is because**

he hears a different drummer. Let him step to the music which he hears, however measured or far away.

And here is a passage from "The Almost Perfect State," an essay by Don Marquis:

> You have seen the tall towers of Manhattan, wonderful under the stars. How did it come about that such growths come from such soil—that a breed lawless and prosaic has written such a mighty hieroglyphic against the sky? How is it that this hideous, half-brute city is also beautiful and a fit habitation for demi-gods? How come? . . . It comes about because the wise and subtle deities permit nothing worthy to be lost. It was with no thought of beauty that the builders labored . . . the baffled dreams and broken visions and the ruined hopes and the secret desires of each one labored with him . . . the rejected beauty, the strangled appreciation, the inchoate art, the submerged spirit—these groped and found each other and gathered themselves together and worked themselves into the tiles and mortar of the edifice and made a town that is a worthy fellow of the sunrise and the sea winds.

This passage by Sandy Asher is also an example of this method; the final paragraph reveals that the essay is an answer to the question, "Why do I write for children?"

> Magic, companionship, a sense of control. The wonder of ourselves, of each other, and of life—this is the true subject matter of all novels. The best children's literature speaks not only to children but to the human condition. Writing for children simply means writing for human beings in the beginning, when you can still take part in creation, before habit, cynicism and despair have set in, and while there is still hope and energy, a willingness to learn, and a healthy sense of humor. These qualities I find irresistible in the young people I write about and for, quali-

ties I want to hang onto and to cultivate in myself. So I write for children, not just for their sakes — but for my own.

CHRONOLOGICAL ORDER/NARRATION

Although narration is the primary mode of development for fiction, it is also widely used in **exposition** and argument. The historian uses narration and chronology in recounting significant events; the scientific writer may use narration to explain a process. Narration is also an essential part of biography and the personal essay. The passage from *Life on the Mississippi* (page 60) is a classic example of personal narrative. Here, author Annie Dillard, in a passage that appeared on a past Regents exam, uses narration to explain what she means by the "unwrapped gifts and free surprises" of Nature.

I walked up to a tree, an Osage orange, and a hundred birds flew away. They simply materialized out of the tree. I saw a tree, then a whisk of color, then a tree again. I walked closer and another hundred blackbirds took flight. Not a branch, not a twig budged: the birds were apparently weightless as well as invisible. Or, it was as if the leaves of the Osage orange had been freed from a spell in the form of red-winged blackbirds; they flew from the tree, caught my eye in the sky, and vanished. When I looked again at the tree, the leaves had reassembled as if nothing had happened. Finally I walked directly to the trunk of the tree and a final hundred, the real diehards, appeared, spread, and vanished. How could so many hide in the tree without my seeing them? The Osage orange, unruffled, looked just as it had looked from the house, when three hundred red-winged blackbirds cried from its crown. I looked upstream where they flew, and they were gone. Searching, I couldn't spot one. I wandered upstream to force them to play their hand, but they'd crossed the creek and scattered. One show to customer. These appearances catch at my throat; they are the free gifts, the bright coppers at the roots of trees.

CAUSE AND EFFECT

Formal development of cause and effect arguments is essential to the historian, the scientist, and the lawyer. It also serves as a basic method for much of the expository writing students do. This paragraph from a speech by former governor Madeleine Kunin offers a good example of explanation through cause and effect:

> **In my own case, most essential to my political evo-lution was a strong desire to have an effect on events around me, whether that was a flashing red light at the railroad crossing in my neighborhood, to protect my children on their way to school, or whether it was a new environmental law for the state of Vermont. The fact that I succeeded in obtaining the flashing red light, as a private citizen, enabled me to change the environmental laws as governor. Each step builds a new self-image, enabling us to move from the pas-sive to the active voice.**

Here is a brief example from the Text on RFID technology (page 26) in Chapter 2:

> **All of the websites you visit collect some amount of information about you, whether it is your name or what other sites you have visited recently. Most of the time, we're being tracked without knowing it. For example, most websites now include Facebook and Twitter buttons so you can "like" the page you are viewing or "Tweet" about it. Whether or not you click the buttons, however, the companies can still determine which pages you've visited and file that information away for later use. . . .**

COMPARISON AND CONTRAST

In these paragraphs, historian Bruce Catton in "Lee and Grant: A Study in Constrasts," brings to a close his extended discussion of the contrasts between Ulysses S. Grant and Robert E. Lee and introduces the discussion of how the two men were alike:

So Grant and Lee were in complete contrast, representing two diametrically opposed elements in American life. Grant was the modern man emerging; beyond him, ready to come on the stage, was the great age of steel and machinery, of crowded cities and a restless burgeoning vitality. Lee might have ridden down from the old age of chivalry, lance in hand, silken banner fluttering over his head. Each man was the perfect champion of his cause, drawing both his strengths and his weaknesses from the people he led.

Yet it was not all contrast, after all. Different as they were—in background, in personality, in underlying aspiration—these two great soldiers had much in common. Under everything else, they were marvelous fighters. Furthermore, their fighting qualities were really very much alike.

Here, from *Life on the Mississippi* (1883), is Mark Twain's comparison of how the North and South treated the Civil War as a topic of conversation, years after it ended:

In the North one hears the war mentioned, in social conversations, once a month; sometimes as often as once a week; but as a distinct subject for talk, it has long ago been relieved of duty. There are sufficient reasons for this. Given a dinner company of six gentlemen to-day, it can easily happen that four of them—and possibly five—were not in the field at all. So the chances are four to two, or five to one, that the war will at no time during the evening become the topic of conversation; and the chances are still greater that if it becomes the topic it will remain so but a little while. If you add six ladies to the company, you have added six people who saw so little of the dread realities of the war that they ran out of talk concerning them years ago, and now would soon weary of the topic if you brought it up.

The case is very different in the South. There, every man you meet was in the war; and every lady you meet saw the war. The war is the great chief topic

of conversation. The interest in it is vivid and constant; the interest in other topics is fleeting. Mention
of the war will wake up a dull company and set their
tongues going, when nearly any other topic would
fail. In the South, the war is what A.D. is elsewhere:
they date from it . . . . It shows how intimately every
individual was visited, in his own person, by the tremendous episode. It gives the inexperienced stranger a better idea of what a vast and comprehensive
calamity invasion is than he can ever get by reading
books at the fireside.

DEVELOPMENT THROUGH EXTENDED METAPHOR

An extended metaphor or **analogy** is a very effective way to develop an
argument or illustrate a concept. It uses the known and familiar to explain
the unfamiliar. The excerpt from *Life on the Mississippi* is also a vivid
example of how a writer relates an experience through extended metaphor.
Here is the introduction to an essay written by a student on the topic "All
the World's a Stage."

All the world is indeed a stage. And we are the
performers. Everything we do in life is a production,
and we must constantly perform our best because,
in life, there are no rehearsals. Each of us performs
on a separate stage, some for a larger audience than
others. But each performance, regardless of the size
of the audience, is of equal importance, and each performer must meet the standard of life's most important critic—himself.

Here is a passage from Stephen Crane's novel *The Red Badge of Courage:*

The ground was cluttered with vines and bushes,
and the trees grew close and spread out like bou-
quets. The creepers, catching against his legs, cried
out harshly as their sprays were torn from the barks
of trees. The swishing saplings tried to make known
his presence to the world. He could not conciliate the
forest. As he made his way, it was always calling out

protestations. When he separated embraces of trees
and vines the disturbed foliage waved their arms and
turned their face leaves toward him.

Here is an illustrative passage from *The Education of Henry Adams*, published in 1918:

For convenience as an image, the [dynamic theory
of history] may liken man to a spider in its web,
watching for chance prey. Forces of nature dance
like flies before the net, and the spider pounces on
them when it can; but it makes many fatal mistakes,
though its theory of force is sound. The spider-mind
acquires a faculty of memory, and, with it, a singular
skill of analysis and synthesis, taking apart and putting together in different relations the meshes of its
trap. Man had in the beginning no power of analysis
or synthesis approaching that of the spider, or even of
the honey-bee; he had acute sensibility to the higher
forces. Fire taught him secrets that no other animal
could learn; running water probably taught him even
more, especially in his first lessons of mechanics; the
animals helped to educate him, trusting themselves
into his hands merely for the sake of their food, and
carrying his burdens or supplying his clothing; the
grasses and grains were academies of study. With
little or no effort on his part, all these forces formed
his thought, induced his action, and even shaped his
figure.

DEFINITION OR CLASSIFICATION

In this paragraph from a speech by Madeleine Kunin, she develops a key term by classifying its component parts:

Political courage stems from a number of sources:
anger, pain, love, hate. There is no lack of political
motivation within women. We feel it all. Anger at a
world which rushes toward saber-rattling displays of
power. Pain at a world which ignores the suffering of
its homeless, its elderly, its children. Hatred toward

the injustice which occurs daily as the strong over-power the weak. And love for the dream of peace on earth.

Here is a brief passage from *The Federalist #10* by James Madison:

... The two great points of difference between a democracy and a republic are: first, the delegation of the government, in the latter, to a small number of citizens elected by the rest; secondly, the greater number of citizens, and greater sphere of country, over which the latter may be extended.

The effect of the first difference is, on the one hand, to refine and enlarge the public views, by passing them through the medium of a chosen body of citi-zens, whose wisdom may best discern the true inter-est of their country, and whose patriotism and love of justice will be least likely to sacrifice it to temporary or partial considerations. Under such a regulation, it may well happen that the public voice, pronounced by the representatives of the people, will be more con-sonant to the public good than if pronounced by the people themselves, convened for the purpose.

EXAMPLES IN ORDER OF IMPORTANCE

The most persuasive arguments are those in which the reasoning has a cumulative effect. The skilled writer does not present the supporting details of a thesis in random order; rather, the skilled writer presents details in an order that stresses importance and significance. Here is how Abraham Lincoln concluded his speech marking the celebration of Independence Day in 1858:

... So I say in relation to the principle that all men are created equal, let it be as nearly reached as we can. If we cannot give freedom to every creature, let us do nothing that will impose slavery upon any other creature. Let us then turn this government back into the channel in which the framers of the Constitution originally placed it.

... Let us discard all this quibbling about this man and the other man—this race and that race and the other race being inferior, and therefore they must be placed in an inferior position—discarding our standard that we have left us. Let us discard all these things, and unite as one people throughout this land, until we shall once more stand up declaring that all men are created equal.

This excerpt is from one of the best-known speeches in Shakespeare's *Hamlet*. The character of Polonius is advising his son on how to conduct himself honorably as a university student in Paris:

... Give thy thoughts no tongue,
Nor any unproportioned thought his act.
Be thou familiar, but by no means vulgar.
Those friends thou hast, and their adoption tried,
Grapple them to thy soul with hoops of steel;
But do not dull thy palm with entertainment
Of each new-hatch'd, unfledged comrade. Beware
Of entrance to a quarrel, but being in,
Bear't that the opposed may beware of thee.
Give every man thy ear, but few thy voice;
Take each man's censure, but reserve thy
    judgment.
Costly thy habit as thy purse can buy,
But not express'd in fancy; rich, not gaudy;
For the apparel oft proclaims the man,
And they in France of the best rank and station
Are of a most select and generous chief in that.
Neither a borrower nor a lender be;
For loan oft loses both itself and friend,
And borrowing dulls the edge of husbandry.
This above all: to thine ownself be true,
And it must follow, as the night the day,
Thou canst not then be false to any man.
Farewell: my blessing season this in thee!

These models offer examples of only some of the ways in which writers develop ideas. As you read more widely, you will appreciate the extent to which every writer, especially the writer of essays, creates a form best suited to the subject and purpose. When you find a piece of writing you especially admire or find convincing, note how the author developed the ideas.

Tone

When we speak of **tone** in writing we are referring to the attitude of the writer toward the subject and/or toward the reader. It is closely related to what we mean when we refer to someone's "tone of voice." Tone may range from *harsh* and *insistent* to *gentle* and *reflective*. There is as much variety of tone in writing as there is in human feeling. Some pieces—essays of opinion, for example—usually have a very distinct tone; other works, especially in fiction or personal expression, may have a more subtle and indirect tone.

Here is a list of adjectives to help you identify the tone or mood of a prose passage. Many have been gathered by students in their reading of Op-Ed page essays. These terms are part of the academic language you are expected to comprehend in reading and to use appropriately in discussing works of nonfiction. Each reflects a distinctive feeling; be sure to look up in a dictionary any that you are not sure about.

admiring	cautious	informed	provocative
advisory	challenging	inquiring	questioning
affectionate	concerned	instructive	reasoned
alarmed	credible	intense	reflective
amused	critical	ironic	sad
anguished	curious	knowledgeable	sarcastic
appalled	cynical	melancholy	satirical
apprehensive	defensive	mocking	sentimental
argumentative	disappointed	mysterious	skeptical
arrogant	dismayed	nonchalant	surprised
assured	eerie	nostalgic	thoughtful
(with) awe	frank	objective	troubled
bewildered	grateful	offended	understanding
bitter	haughty	optimistic	whimsical
boastful	humorous	outraged	wondering
candid	indifferent	peaceful	
cautionary	indignant	probing	

The Op-Ed pages of most newspapers offer daily examples of essays on current topics, representing widely varied methods of argument, style, and tone. *Harper's Magazine*, *The Atlantic Monthly*, and *The New Yorker* include excellent selections of essays and other examples of literary non-fiction. National magazines such as *Time* and *Sports Illustrated* also offer examples of feature writing and reporting on current issues. The list of Recommended Reading on page 215 also offers titles of books of nonfiction available in paperback.

A GLOSSARY OF LITERARY TERMS AND TECHNIQUES

abstract In contrast to the *concrete,* abstract language expresses general ideas and concepts apart from specific examples or instances. Very formal writing is characterized by abstract expression. An *abstract* (n.) is a brief summary of the key ideas in a scientific, legal, or scholarly piece of writing.

analogy An expression of the similarities between things that are not wholly alike or related. (See, for example, the student essay on page 61.) See *metaphor* in A Glossary of Poetic Terms and Techniques, Chapter 5.

anecdote A very brief, usually vivid, story or episode. Often humorous, anecdotes offer examples of typical behavior or illustrate the personality of a character. Writers of biography and autobiography make extensive use of anecdote to reveal the lives of their subjects.

antithesis In formal argument, a statement that opposes or contrasts with a *thesis* statement. Informally, we use the term to refer to any expression or point of view completely opposed to another. In literature, even an experience or feeling may be expressed as the *antithesis* of another. See also *thesis.*

argument In persuasive writing or speaking, the development of reasons to support the writer's position; also the method of reasoning used to persuade. Informally, we may use the term to describe the development of a topic in any piece of exposition. Historically, it has also denoted a summary of a literary work's plot or main ideas.

atmosphere Closely related to *tone* or mood, it refers to a pervasive feeling in a work. Atmosphere often stems from setting and from distinctive characters or actions. For example, the atmosphere in many of Poe's stories is mysterious, troubling, even sinister, and Hawthorne's "Young Goodman Brown" reflects the threatening and ambiguous world of its Puritan setting.

autobiography A formally composed account of a person's life, written by that person. While we must trust, or be skeptical of, the reliability of the account, we often appreciate the firsthand narration of experience. Autobiography is also a rich source of information and insight into an historical period or into literary or artistic worlds. Autobiography, like the novel, has *narrative* and chronology. (See also *journal.*) We describe literary works that are closely based on the author's life as "auto-biographical." Eugene O'Neill's *Long Day's Journey into Night* and Tennessee Williams's *The Glass Menagerie* are plays that reflect many details of their authors' lives.

biography A narrative, historical account of the life, character, and significance of its subject. Contemporary biography is usually researched in detail and may not always paint an admiring portrait of its subject. A critical biography of a literary figure includes discussion of the writer's works to show the writer's artistic development and career. Biographies of figures significant in history or public affairs also offer commentary on periods and events of historical importance.

character Characters are the imagined persons, created figures, who inhabit the worlds of fiction and drama. E. M. Forster distinguished between *flat* and *round* characters: Flat are those, like stereotypes, who represent a single and exaggerated human characteristic; round are those whose aspects are complex and convincing, and who change or develop in the course of a work. In good fiction, plot must develop out of character. The desires, values, and motives of characters account for the action and conflict in a plot.

characterization The method by which an author establishes character; the means by which personality, manner, and appearance are created. It is achieved directly through description and dialogue and indirectly through observations and reactions of other characters.

concrete Refers to the particular, the specific, in expression and imagery. That which is concrete can be perceived by the senses. Concrete also refers to that which is tangible, real, or actual, in contrast to the *abstract,* which is intangible and conceptual.

conflict In the most general sense, it identifies the forces that give rise to a plot. This term may identify an actual struggle between characters, anything from revenge to simple recognition or understanding. A plot may focus on conflict between characters and the forces of nature or society. These are essentially **external conflicts**. A work may also center on **internal conflicts**, characters' struggles to know or change themselves and their lives. Most works of fiction and drama contain more than one aspect of conflict. (See the discussion on page 47.)

denouement A French term meaning "untying a knot," it refers to the way the complications or conflict of a plot are finally resolved. It also refers to what is called the "falling action" in a drama, that part of the play that follows the dramatic climax and reveals the consequences of the main action for minor characters; it also accounts briefly for what happens in the world of the play after the principal drama is resolved. In Arthur Miller's *Death of a Salesman*, the "Requiem" may be considered a denouement; it accounts for the response to Willy's death by his wife, sons, and only friend. In Shakespeare's *Macbeth,* the climax is in the scene following the death of Lady Macbeth in which Macbeth understands that he has destroyed all capacity for feeling and has rendered his life meaningless; the denouement includes the battle in which Macbeth comprehends the treachery of the witches and is killed by MacDuff, thus restoring the throne to the rightful heir, Malcolm.

determinism The philosophical view that human existence is determined by forces over which humans have little or no control. The concept that fate predestines the course of a character's life or a tragic figure's downfall is a form of determinism.

episode A series of actions or incidents that make up a self-contained part of a larger narrative. Some novels are structured so that each chapter is a significant episode. Fitzgerald's *The Great Gatsby* and Mark Twain's *Huckleberry Finn* are good examples of this structure. A *scene* in a play is often analogous to an episode in a narrative. Many television series are presented in weekly episodes.

essay A general term (from French *essai,* meaning an attempt, a trying out of something) to denote an extended composition, usually expository, devoted to a single topic. Essays may be composed to persuade, to reflect on philosophical questions, to analyze a subject, to express an opinion, or to entertain. As a literary form, the essay dates from the sixteenth century and remains a popular and widely practiced form. The essay by Francis Bacon on page 41 is a classic example. See *formal/ informal* essay.

exposition Writing whose purpose is to inform, illustrate, and explain. In literature, exposition refers to those passages or speeches in which setting, offstage or prior action, or a character's background is revealed. In *The Great Gatsby,* Nick Carraway pauses in the narrative to give the reader additional information about Gatsby's background. The prologue to Shakespeare's *Romeo and Juliet* is an example of exposition.

flashback A presentation of incidents or episodes that occurred prior to the beginning of the narrative itself. When an author or filmmaker uses flashback, the "present" or forward motion of the plot is suspended. Flashback may be introduced through the device of a character's memory or through the narrative voice itself. William Faulkner's "Barn Burning" and *Light in August* include vivid passages of memory and narrative flashback. Jack Burden's recounting of the Cass Mastern story in Robert Penn Warren's *All the King's Men* is also a form of flashback.

foreshadowing A technique in which an author establishes details or mood that will become more significant as the plot of a work progresses. Thoughtful readers usually sense such details and accumulate them in their memories. In one of the opening scenes of *Ethan Frome*, Ethan and Mattie talk about the dangers of sledding down Starkfield's steepest hill; and, in the second paragraph of "The Lottery," the boys are stuffing their pockets with stones or making piles of them on the edge of the square.

form The organization, shape, and structure of a work. Concretely, form may refer to *genre* (see below), for example, the sonnet form, the tragic form. More abstractly, form also refers to the way we sense inherent structure and shape.

formal/informal essay The formal essay emphasizes organization, logic, and explanation of ideas, whereas the informal essay emphasizes the voice and perspective of the writer. In the latter, also called a *personal essay*, the reader is aware of the author's *persona* and is asked to share the author's interest in the subject.

genre A type or form of literature. Examples include *novel, short story, epic poem, essay, sonnet, tragedy.*

image Although the term suggests something that is visualized, an image is an evocation through language of *any* experience perceived directly through the senses. See also A Glossary of Poetic Terms and Techniques, Chapter 5.

irony In general, a tone or figure of speech in which there is a discrepancy (a striking difference or contradiction) between what is expressed and what is meant or expected. Irony achieves its powerful effect indirectly: in satire, for example, which often uses *understatement* or *hyperbole* to express serious criticism of human behavior and social institutions. We also speak of *dramatic irony* when the narrator or reader understands more than the characters do.

journal A diary or notebook of personal observations. Many writers use journals to compose personal reflection and to collect ideas for their works; the journals of many writers have been published. Students are often urged to keep journals as a way to reflect on their reading, compose personal pieces, and practice writing free of concern for evaluation.

melodrama A plot in which incidents are sensational and designed to provoke immediate emotional responses. In such a plot, the "good" characters are pure and innocent and victims of the "bad" ones, who are thoroughly evil. The term refers to a particular kind of drama popular in the late nineteenth century and, later, in silent films and early Westerns. A work becomes melodramatic when it relies on improbable incidents and unconvincing characters for strong emotional effect.

memoir A form of autobiographical writing that reflects on the significant events the writer has observed and on the interesting and important personalities the writer has known.

monologue In a play, an extended expression or speech by a single speaker that is uninterrupted by response from other characters. A monologue is addressed to a particular person or persons, who may or may not actually hear it. Ring Lardner's short story "Haircut" is an example of monologue as a method of narration. In it, a barber tells the story to a customer (the reader) who is present but does not respond. See also *dramatic monologue* in A Glossary of Poetic Terms and Techniques, Chapter 5.

motivation The desires, values, needs, or impulses that move characters to act as they do. In good fiction the reader understands, appreciates, and is convinced that a character's motivation accounts for the significant incidents and the outcome of a plot.

narrative point of view The standpoint, perspective, and degree of understanding from which a work of narrative fiction is told. See *omniscient point of view, objective point of view*.

narrator The character or author's *persona* that tells a story. It is through the perspective and understanding of the narrator that the reader experiences the work. In some works, the narrator may inhabit the world of the story or be a character in it. In other works, the narrator is a detached but knowledgeable observer.

naturalism Closely related to *determinism,* naturalism depicts characters who are driven not by personal will or moral principles but by natural forces that they do not fully understand or control. In contrast to other views of human experience, the naturalistic view makes no moral judgments on the lives of the characters. Their lives, often bleak or defeating, simply *are* as they are, determined by social, environmental, instinctive, and hereditary forces. Naturalism was in part a reaction by writers against the nineteenth century Romantic view of man as master of his own fate. It is important to note, however, that none of the Naturalistic writers in America (Crane, Dreiser, London, Anderson, and Norris chief among them) presented a genuinely deterministic vision. Several of these authors began their careers in journalism and were drawn to the Naturalistic view of life as a result of their own experience and observation of life in the United States. See also *realism.*

objective point of view In fiction or nonfiction, this voice presents a story or information, respectively, without expressed judgment or qualification. A fundamental principle of journalism is that news *reports* should be objective. Ernest Hemingway's short story "The Killers" is an example of fiction rendered in a completely detached, objective point of view.

omniscient point of view Spoken in third person (*she, he, it, they*), this is the broadest narrative perspective. The omniscient narrator speaks from outside the story and sees and knows everything about the characters and incidents. Omniscient narration is not limited by time or place. In **limited omniscient** point of view, the author may choose to reveal the story through full understanding of only one character and limit the action to those incidents in which this character is present.

persona A term from the Greek meaning "mask," it refers in literature to a narrative voice created by an author and through which the author speaks. A narrative persona usually has a perceptible, even distinctive, personality that contributes to our understanding of the story. In Nathaniel Hawthorne's *The Scarlet Letter,* the omniscient narrator has a

distinctive persona whose attitudes toward Puritan society and the characters' lives are revealed throughout the novel.

plot The incidents and experiences of characters selected and arranged by
the author to create a meaningful narrative. A good plot is convincing in
terms of what happens and why.

poetic justice The concept that life's rewards and punishments should
be perfectly appropriate and distributed in just proportions. In Ring
Lardner's short story "Haircut," Jim Kendall's ironic fate is an example
of poetic justice: He is a victim of one of his own crude and insensitive
practical jokes.

point of view In nonfiction, this denotes the attitudes or opinions of the
writer. In narrative fiction, it refers to how and by whom a story is told:
the perspective of the narrator and the narrator's relationship to the story.
Point of view may be *omniscient,* where the narrator knows everything
about the characters and their lives; or it may be *limited* to the understanding of a particular character or speaker. Point of view may also be
described as *objective* or *subjective. Third-person* narrative refers to characters as "he, she, it, they." *First-person* narrative is from the "I" point of
view. J. D. Salinger's *The Catcher in the Rye* and Twain's *Huckleberry
Finn* are told in the first person. *Second-person* narrative, the "you" form,
is rare but is found in sermons addressed to a congregation or in essays of
opinion addressed directly to a leader or public figure: "You, Mr. Mayor
(Madame President), should do the following . . ." Thomas Friedman and
Gail Collins occasionally write pieces in the second-person voice for the
Op-Ed page of *The New York Times*.

prologue An introductory statement of the dramatic situation of a play or
story. Shakespeare's *Romeo and Juliet* begins with a brief prologue. The
first two pages of Fitzgerald's *The Great Gatsby* are a prologue to the
story Nick Carraway will tell.

prose Most of what we write is prose, the expression in sentences and
phrases that reflect the natural rhythms of speech. Prose is organized
by paragraphs and is characterized by variety in sentence length and
rhythm.

protagonist A term from Ancient Greek drama, it refers to the central
character, the hero or heroine, in a literary work.

realism The literary period in the United States following the Civil War is
usually called the Age of Realism. Realism depicts the directly observable in everyday life. Realistic writers seek to *present* characters and
situations as they would appear to a careful observer, not as they are
imagined or created by the author. After 1865, American writers became
increasingly interested in the sources of power and force, and in the
means to survival and success, in an increasingly materialistic society.
For writers of this period, realism was a literary mode to express a *naturalistic* philosophy. See also *naturalism, verisimilitude.*

rhetoric From Ancient Greece, the art of persuasion in speech or writing achieved through logical thought and skillful use of language.

rhetorical question A question posed in the course of an *argument* to provoke thought or to introduce a line of reasoning.

romance A novel or tale that includes elements of the supernatural, heroic adventure, or romantic passion. Hawthorne's *The Scarlet Letter* is a romance, not because it is a love story but because it goes beyond *verisimilitude* in dramatizing elements of demonic and mystical forces in the characters and their lives.

satire A form or style that uses elements of irony, ridicule, exaggeration, understatement, sarcasm, humor, or absurdity to criticize human behavior or a society. All satire is **ironic** (see above) in that meaning or theme is conveyed in the discrepancy between what is said and what is meant, between what is and what should be, between what appears and what truly is. While satire is often entertaining, its purpose is serious and meant to provoke thought or judgment. The verses of Alexander Pope are often extended satire, and many poems by e. e. cummings are satiric. In prose, much of the writing of Mark Twain is satire; *Huckleberry Finn* is the most striking example. Other American writers of satire include Sinclair Lewis, Dorothy Parker, Edith Wharton, Joseph Heller, and Tom Wolfe. On television, *Saturday Night Live*, and *The Simpsons* are good examples of contemporary satire, as was *The Colbert Report*.

short story This form is distinguished from most novels not simply by length but by its focus on few characters and on a central, revealing incident. In short stories, however, there is as much variety in narrative point of view, subject, and technique as there is in novels. Edgar Allan Poe characterized the short story as "a short prose narrative, requiring from a half-hour to one or two hours in its perusal."

soliloquy A form of *monologue* in which a character expresses thoughts and feelings aloud but does not address them to anyone else or intend other characters in the work to hear them. In essence, the audience for a play is secretly listening in on a character's innermost thoughts. Macbeth's reflection on "Tomorrow, and tomorrow, and tomorrow . . . " is the best-known soliloquy in the play.

speaker The narrative voice in a literary work (see *persona*). Also, the character who speaks in a *dramatic monologue*.

symbol Most generally, anything that stands for or suggests something else. Language itself is symbolic; sounds and abstract written forms may be arranged to stand for virtually any human thought or experience. In literature, symbols are not Easter eggs or mushrooms—they are not "hidden meanings." Symbols are real objects and *concrete* images that lead us to *think about* what is suggested. They organize a wide variety of ideas into single acts of understanding. They embody not single "meanings" but suggest whole areas of meaning.

theme Roughly analogous to thesis in an essay, this is an observation about human experience or an idea central to a work of literature. The *subject* of a work is in the specific setting, characters, and plot. Theme in a work of fiction is what is meaningful and significant to human experience generally; themes are the ideas and truths that transcend the specific characters and plot. Shakespeare's *Macbeth* is about an ambitious nobleman who, encouraged by his equally ambitious wife, murders the king of Scotland in order to become king himself. The themes in *Macbeth* include the power of ambition to corrupt even those who are worthy and the mortal consequences of denying what is fundamental to one's nature.

thesis The central point, a statement of position in a formal or logical argument. Also used to refer to the topic, or controlling, idea of an essay. Use of the term *thesis* implies elaboration by reasons and examples. See *antithesis*.

tone The attitude of the writer toward the subject and the reader. See also A Glossary of Poetic Terms and Techniques, Chapter 5.

transition A transition is a link between ideas or sections in a work. In prose arguments, single words such as *first, second . . . moreover,* and *therefore* or phrases such as *in addition, on the other hand,* and *in conclusion* serve as transitions. In fiction, a brief passage or chapter may serve as a transition. In *The Great Gatsby,* the narrator pauses from time to time to "fill in" the reader and to account for the passage of time between the dramatic episodes that make up the novel's main plot.

turning point In drama and fiction, the moment or episode in a plot when the action is moved toward its inevitable conclusion.

verisimilitude A quality in fiction and drama of being "true to life," of representing that which is real or actual. Verisimilitude in fiction is often achieved through specific, vivid description and dialogue; first-person narration also creates the effect of verisimilitude. In drama it may be enhanced through means of set, costumes, and lighting that are realistic in all their details.

(See also, in Chapter 5—A Glossary of Poetic Terms and Techniques.)

Chapter 5

READING POETRY

INTRODUCTION

How to Read a Poem

How should you read a poem? Aloud. Several times. And never quickly. Here is a short poem about baseball. As you read, pay attention first to what the poem by Robert Francis says.

Pitcher

His art is eccentricity, his aim
How not to hit the mark he seems to aim at,
His passion how to avoid the obvious,
His technique how to vary the avoidance.
The others throw to be comprehended. He
Throws to be a moment misunderstood.
Yet not too much. Not errant, arrant, wild,
But every seeming aberration willed.
Not to, yet still, still to communicate
Making the batter understand too late.

Now, read the poem again, with particular attention to the varied length of the statements; read from comma to comma or period to period as you would in prose. When you reach the end of the first and fifth lines, for example, pause very slightly—but do not stop. After several readings, you will not only appreciate what Robert Francis undertands about the art of pitching but also feel the way in which the rhythm of the poem is also the rhythm of pitching.

In poetry we are meant to sense a structure and to feel the rhythm. (See **meter*** and **rhythm**.) The structure and rhythm of poetry may be formal, informal, even "free." Poetry is also characterized by its directness of effect and by its concentration—ideas and feelings are expressed in relatively few words. Karl Shapiro says, "Poems are what ideas *feel like*." Robert Francis's poem is about what good pitching *feels like*.

---

*Terms in bold type are defined in A Glossary of Poetic Terms and Techniques at the end of the chapter.

This poem, by Emily Dickinson (1830–1886), recalls the feeling of mourning:

> **After great pain, a formal feeling comes—**
> **The nerves sit ceremonious, like Tombs—**
> **The stiff Heart questions was it He, that bore,**
> **and Yesterday, or Centuries before?**
>
> **The Feet, mechanical, go round—**
> **Of Ground, or Air or Ought—**
> **A Wooden way**
> **Regardless grown,**
> **A Quartz contentment, like a stone—**
>
> **This is the Hour of Lead—**
> **Remembered, if outlived,**
> **As Freezing persons, recollect the Snow—**
> **First—Chill—then Stupor—then the letting go—**

In this poem, Dickinson recreates what it feels like suddenly to encounter a snake in the grass:

> **A narrow Fellow in the Grass**
> **Occasionally rides—**
> **You may have met Him—did you not**
> **His notice sudden is—**
> **The Grass divides as with a Comb—**
> **A spotted shaft is seen—**
> **And then it closes at your feet**
> **And opens further on—**
>
> **He likes a Boggy Acre**
> **A Floor too cool for corn—**
> **Yet when a boy, and Barefoot—**
> **I more than once at Noon**
> **Have passed, I thought, a Whip lash**
> **Unbraiding in the Sun**
> **When stooping to secure it**
> **It wrinkled, and was gone—**

Several of Nature's People
I know, and they know me—
I feel for them a transport
Of cordiality—

But never met this Fellow
Attended, or alone
Without a tighter breathing
And Zero at the Bone—

Where the writer of prose may seek immediate clarity of meaning above all, the poet often seeks **ambiguity**, not to create "confusion," but to offer multiplicity of meaning, in single words, in images, in the meaning of the poem itself. Look again at "Pitcher." Might this poem also be a reflection on the art of poetry itself? It is because of such richness in meaning that poems often require several readings.

The experience of poetry is conveyed in vivid **imagery**, which appeals to the mind and to the senses. It is often expressed in **figurative language**, that is, words and comparions that are not literal but that imaginatively create original, vivid, and often unexpected images and associations. (See **metaphor** and **simile**.) Finally, in poetry there is particular significance in the way words and lines sound. The story or experience is enhanced through musical effects. A poem must be felt and heard!

In this poem by Laurence Binyon, a boy kept home from school with a fever, is dazzled by the light of the sun as it comes out after rain, and he no longer regrets being "…a captive/Apart from his schoolfellows."

The rain was ending, and light

THE rain was ending, and light
Lifting the leaden skies.
It shone upon ceiling and floor
And dazzled a child's eyes.

Pale after fever, a captive
Apart from his schoolfellows,
He stood at the high room's window
With face to the pane pressed close,

And beheld an immense glory
Flooding with fire the drops
Spilled on miraculous leaves
Of the fresh green lime-tree tops.

Washed gravel glittered red
To a wall, and beyond it nine
Tall limes in the old inn yard
Rose over the tall inn sign.

And voices arose from beneath
Of boys from school set free,
Racing and chasing each other
With laughter and games and glee.

To the boy at the high room-window,
Gazing alone and apart,
There came a wish without reason,
A thought that shone through his heart.

I'll choose this moment and keep it,
He said to himself, for a vow,
To remember for ever and ever
 As if it were always now.

A note on reading this poem: do not read to emphasize regular meter and rhyming pattern; remember, read from comma to comma, period to period. For example, the second and third stanzas should be read with only slight pauses at the commas and through the third stanza, where there is no end punctuation, in as few breaths as possible. The fourth stanza completes the vivid image of the "immense glory" the boy sees as he looks out the window.

STRUCTURE AND LANGUAGE IN POETRY

All the traditional poetic forms stem from an oral tradition, in which poetry was sung or recited. The **epic** and the **ballad** are the oldest forms of **narrative poetry**, but modern poets also tell stories in narrative verse. (Robert Frost's "Out, Out—" is a well-known example.) Most of the poetry we read today, however, is **lyric** poetry.

Think of the lyric poem as a song; in the Ancient Greek tradition, the lyric poem was meant to be sung to the accompaniment of a lyre, a small harplike instrument. Indeed, we speak of the words for a song as its lyrics. The ancient form is evident in the songs for Shakespeare's plays, in the tradition of the nineteenth-century art song, and in the twentieth-century ballads and songs. The ancient form is evident in the songs for Shakespeare's plays, in the tradition of the nineteenth-century art song, and in the twentieth-century ballads and songs we associate, for example, with Rodgers and Hart, Cole Porter, and Stephen Sondheim and sung by Frank Sinatra, Barbra Streisand, among many others, including Tony Bennett in his duets with Lady Gaga.

Lyric poems are relatively brief and are expressed in the voice (that is, from the point of view) of a single speaker. They express a powerful emotion, usually captured in a significant experience or dramatic situation. A lyric poem, like a song, often tells a story, but it does so in nonnarrative form. The **speaker** (or "poet") may recall an experience, or render it directly, in order to understand its meaning and then reveal it to the reader. Thus, many lyric poems are *meditations, reflections,* or *recollections* of experience that lead to a *discovery,* to an emotionally powerful *recognition* of the meaning of the experiences. The effect of the poem is to convey that meaning directly, to engage readers in such a way that they share the experience, feel the emotion, with the speaker. The poems by Robert Francis, Emily Dickinson, and Laurence Binyon on the previous pages are examples of lyrics.

This poem by Robert Penn Warren appeared on a past Regents ELA exam.

Old Photograph of the Future

That center of attention—an infantile face
That long years ago showed, no doubt, pink and white—
Now faded, and in the photograph only a trace
Of grays, not much expression in sight.

(5) That center of attention, swathed in a sort of white dress,
Is precious to the woman who, pretty and young,
Leans with a look of surprised blessedness
At the mysterious miracle forth-sprung.

In the background somewhat, the masculine figure
(10) Looms, face agleam with achievement and pride.
In black coat, derby at breast, he is quick to assure
You the world's in good hands—lay your worries aside.

The picture is badly faded. Why not?
Most things show wear around seventy-five,
(15) And that's the age this picture has got.
The man and woman no longer, of course, live.

> **They lie side by side in whatever love survives**
> **Under green turf, or snow, and that child, years later,**
>   **stands there**
> **While old landscapes blur and he in guilt grieves**
> *(20)* **Over nameless promises unkept, in undefinable despair.**

In this poem, the speaker expresses the profound feelings of guilt and despair he feels in looking at an old photograph of himself and his parents when he was an infant. The **tone** of the poem is reflective, that of an elegy. The mood at the end is one of regret and loss as the speaker recalls his dead parents, confronts his own age, "the age this picture has got," and grieves at the "nameless promises unkept." Although the narrator speaks of "that child, years later" who "stands there . . . and . . . in guilt grieves," the intensity and privacy of feeling at the end indicate that the speaker is that child. The narrative voice and the lack of specific identification of the characters serve to emphasize the passage of time and underscore the fact that looking at the photograph leads the "child," now old, to reflect on his entire life.

The structure is simple and easy to observe: five **quatrains** with alternating **rhyme**; each quatrain is self-contained—ends with a period—and tells a part of the story. The first fifteen lines of the poem describe the picture and the "characters" in it. Note that the final section of the poem begins with the last line of the fourth quatrain, the description having concluded in line 15. Line 16 both ends the narrator's rendering of the photograph and also begins the "conclusion," which is the significance of the experience of looking at the photograph.

The rhythm within lines is varied and often broken by dashes or other pauses; this rhythm allows us to share the speaker's questions and reflections. The rhythm of the fourth stanza slows as each line completes a thought. In contrast, the final stanza should be heard as a single, long gesture of recognition and regret.

The experience of looking at the picture—in which he is the "center of attention"—leads the speaker to reflect on whether he has satisfied the "promises" that the "mysterious miracle" of his birth meant to his awed and proud parents. The photograph also leads the speaker to reflect on the unfulfilled promises of his own life.

There is little in the way of figurative language in this poem. The imagery, however, reveals more than a description of a photograph, and the paradox in the title reveals one of the poem's central **themes**, the cycle of birth, life, and death. On rereading Warren's poem, with our appreciation of the poet's experience in mind, we see how the third and fourth lines are more than a description of the photograph—they also suggest the speaker's age. He sees himself (in the photo and metaphorically) as "faded . . . only a trace of grays, not much expression in sight." The repetition of the fact that he was the "center of attention" (in the photograph and in his parents' lives) makes more poignant the grief over "promises unkept" at the end.

The poet offers only a few details of the photograph, but they are the details we all recognize from our own photographs of grandparents and great-grandparents: the father "In the background somewhat" and in formal pose—"in black coat, derby at breast"—the child (girl or boy) in "a sort of white dress." It is, of course, such widely shared experience that is both the poem's form and its theme.

In this poem by Theodore Roethke, the speaker recalls a significant experience from childhood:

Child on Top of a Greenhouse

The wind billowing out of the seat of my britches,
My feet crackling splinters of glass and dried putty,
The half-grown chrysanthemums staring up like accusers,
Up through the streaked glass, flashing with sunlight,
A few white clouds all rushing eastward,
A line of elms plunging and tossing like horses,
And everyone, everyone pointing up and shouting!

Try repeating just the verbs of this poem, feeling their dramatic energy. The repetition of "-ing" forms also creates what is called **internal rhyme**, while the words "like," "sunlight," "white," "line" form the pattern of sound called **assonance**.

In this poem by Donald Hall the speaker also recalls an important childhood experience:

The Sleeping Giant
(A Hill, So Named, in Hamden, Connecticut)

The whole day long, under the walking sun
That poised an eye on me from its high floor,
Holding my toy beside the clapboard house
I looked for him, the summer I was four.

I was afraid the waking arm would break
From the loose earth and rub against his eyes
A fist of trees, and the whole country tremble
In the exultant labor of his rise;

Then he with giant steps in the small streets
Would stagger, cutting off the sky, to seize
The roofs from house and home because we had
Covered his shape with dirt and planted trees;

And then kneel down and rip with fingernails
A trench to pour the enemy Atlantic
Into our basin, and the water rush,
With the streets full and the voices frantic.

That was the summer I expected him.
Later the high and watchful sun instead
Walked low behind the house, and school began,
And winter pulled a sheet over his head.

In this poem, a child's fearful and vivid imagination is sparked by **personification** of the hill near his house. This poem is particularly effective because it recalls for us the fact that small children are literal and that they tend to give names and human character to inanimate things. This child actually sees—and fears—the sleeping giant. Note too how the images of the sun in the first and last stanzas both unify the poem and denote the passage of time. Finally, there is a gentle **irony** in the final line that suggests that the child, no longer fearful, can now "play" with the metaphor of the sleeping giant, as "winter pulled a sheet over his head."

Shakespeare's Sonnet 30 illustrates several of the formal aspects of verse:

When to the sessions of sweet silent thought

When to the sessions of sweet silent thought
I summon up remembrance of things past
I sigh the lack of many a thing I sought
And with old woes new wail my dear time's waste:

(5) Then can I drown an eye, unused to flow,
For precious friends hid in death's dateless night,
And weep afresh love's long-since-canceled woe,
And moan th'expense of many a vanished sight;

Then can I grieve at grievances forgone,
(10) And heavily from woe to woe tell o'er
The sad account of fore-bemoaned moan,
Which I new pay as if not paid before.
 But if the while I think on thee, dear friend,
 All losses are restored and sorrows end.

The structure of the Shakespearean **sonnet** is three **quatrains** and a closing **couplet**. The **rhyme scheme** is *abab/cdcd/efef/gg*. This pattern allows us
to hear the structure of the poem, to hear the development of the ideas. The
couplet, with its similar end rhyme and self-contained thought, contrasts the
feelings expressed in the previous 12 lines and concludes the poem.

We find in this Shakespearean sonnet, as well, examples of **alliteration**
and assonance: In the first quatrain, we hear alliteration in the many words
that begin with "s." In lines 7 through 12 we hear assonance in the repetition of "oh" sounds, which are also examples of **onomatopoeia**—that is,
the sounds reflect the meanings of the words. Lines 4 and 10 also illustrate
what is called internal rhyme.

THEME IN POETRY

Some lyric poems may assert a belief. Others may be a comment on the
nature of human experience—love, death, loss or triumph, mystery and
confusion, conflict and peace, on the humorous and the ironic, on the imagined and the unexpected in all its forms. Some poems reflect on the nature
of time, of existence. Many lyrics are about poetry itself. These aspects of
human experience are what we refer to as the themes of poetry.

In this well-known sonnet, Number 55, Shakespeare asserts that poetry
confers immortality, that it can prevail over the most powerful forces of
time. Note how the central idea is developed in the three quatrains and how
the couplet—in its thought and its rhyme—concludes the development of
that idea.

Not marble, nor the gilded monuments

Not marble, nor the gilded monuments
Of princes, shall outlive this pow'rful rhyme;
But you shall shine more bright in these contents
Than unswept stone besmeared with sluttish time.

When wasteful war shall statues overturn,
And broils root out the work of masonry,
Nor Mars his sword nor war's quick fire shall burn
The living record of your memory.

'Gainst death and all-oblivious enmity
Shall you pace forth; your praise shall still find room
Even in the eyes of all posterity
That wear this world out to the ending doom.
  So, till the judgment that yourself arise,
  You live in this, and dwell in lovers' eyes.

In this lyric by Carl Sandburg, the poet suggests that poetry is "about" the meaning in life itself.

Last Answers

I WROTE a poem on the mist
And a woman asked me what I meant by it.
I had thought till then only of the beauty of the mist,
    how pearl and gray of it mix and reel,
And change the drab shanties with lighted lamps
    at evening into points of mystery quivering with
    color.
  I answered:
The whole world was mist once long ago and some
    day it will all go back to mist,
Our skulls and lungs are more water than bone and
    tissue
And all poets love dust and mist because all the last
    answers
Go running back to dust and mist.

The best-known lyrics, however, are probably love poems—Sonnet 116 of Shakespeare, for example:

Let me not to the marriage of true minds

Let me not to the marriage of true minds
Admit impediments. Love is not love
which alters when it alteration finds,
Or bends with the remover to remove.

O, no, it is an ever-fixed mark
That looks on tempests and is never shaken;
It is the star to every wand'ring bark,
Whose worth's unknown, although his height be taken.

Love's not Time's fool, though rosy lips and cheeks
Within his bending sickle's compass come;
Love alters not with his brief hours and weeks,
But bears it out even to the edge of doom.
  If this be error and upon me proved,
  I never writ, nor no man ever loved.

In this lyric by Claude McKay, the poet is overcome with longing for his homeland on the island of Jamaica.

The Tropics in New York

Bananas ripe and green, and ginger-root,
  Cocoa in pods and alligator pears,
And tangerines and mangoes and grape fruit,
  Fit for the highest prize at parish fairs,

Set in the window, bringing memories
  Of fruit-trees laden by low-singing rills,
And dewy dawns, and mystical blue skies
  In benediction over nun-like hills.

My eyes grew dim, and I could no more gaze;
  A wave of longing through my body swept,
And, hungry for the old, familiar ways,
  I turned aside and bowed my head.

85

TONE

Tone in poetry, as in prose and all forms of human communication, expresses the *attitude* of the speaker toward the reader or listener and toward the subject. Tone in literature is as varied as the range of human experience and feeling it reflects. When we speak of the *mood* of a piece of writing, we are also speaking of tone, of an overall feeling generated by the work.

Here are some terms to help you recognize and articulate tone or mood:

ambiguous*	insistent	reconciled
amused	ironic*	reflective
angry	melancholy	regretful
bitter	mournful	reminiscent
celebratory	mysterious	satiric*
elegiac (from elegy*)	nostalgic	sorrowful
grateful	optimistic	thoughtful
harsh	paradoxical*	understated*
humorous	questioning	

WRITING ABOUT POETRY/EXPLICATION

When you are asked to *explicate* a poem, you are being asked to look closely at it and "unfold" its meaning, line by line, idea by idea. Explication combines paraphrase with close reading of form. You are explaining both the content *and* the form: the ideas and meaning as well as the structure and poetic elements.

To begin an explication, read the poem several times to discover what it says. Who is the speaker? What is the subject? the dramatic situation? What theme or experience is central to the poem? What is the tone or mood? Try to summarize or paraphrase the poem as a whole. Then note the formal details: What is the pattern of organization? What is the movement of ideas and feeling? of images and metaphors? How do stanzas or arrangement of lines reveal that? How do rhyme, meter, and rhythm contribute to the experience, to the meaning of the poem? (The commentary that follows Robert Penn Warren's "Old Photograph of the Future" on page 79 is an example of explication.)

---

*These terms are defined in A Glossary of Poetic Terms and Techniques at the end of the chapter.

POETRY ON EXAMINATIONS

On examinations, such as the Regents ELA exam and the AP Literature and Composition exam, the multiple-choice questions are designed to measure your skill at close reading and *explication*. You are expected to recognize and identify the elements of poetry. (See A Glossary of Poetic Terms and Techniques.) In addition, you are usually required to compose an essay/explication of a poem on the AP Literature and Composition exam, and such essays are commonly assigned in high school and college literature courses. *Analysis,* which requires detailed examination of particular elements of a poem or passage, is usually reserved for course assignments. The thoughtful student will, of course, develop skill in both explication and analysis.

A HANDFUL OF POEMS FOR FURTHER READING

In this excerpt from an extended essay in verse, Alexander Pope reflects on how poets express meaning through sound and rhythm.

An Essay on Criticism

True ease in writing comes from art, not chance,
As those move easiest who have learned to dance.
'Tis not enough no harshness gives offense,
The sound must seem an echo to the sense:
Soft is the strain when Zephyr gently blows,
And the smooth stream in smoother numbers flows;
But when loud surges lash the sounding shore,
The hoarse, rough verse should like the torrent roar.

The horror and loss of war are often expressed through irony. Here is Stephen Crane's reflection on war:

Do Not Weep, Maiden, for War Is Kind

Do not weep, maiden, for war is kind.
Because your lover threw wild hands against the sky
And the affrighted steed ran on alone,
Do not weep.
War is kind.

>Hoarse, booming drums of the regiment
>Little souls who thirst for fight
>These men were born to drill and die.
>The unexplained glory flies above them,
>Great is the battle-god, great, and his kingdom—
>A field where a thousand corpses lie.

Do not weep, babe, for war is kind.
Because your father tumbled in the yellow trenches,
Raged at his breast, gulped and died,
Do not weep.
War is kind.

>Swift blazing flag of the regiment,
>Eagle with crest of red and gold,
>These men were born to drill and die.
>Point for them the virtue of slaughter,
>Make plain to them the excellence of killing
>And a field where a thousand corpses lie.

Mother whose heart hung humble as a button
On the bright splendid shroud of your son,
Do not weep.
War is kind.

In this poem, by Walt Whitman (1819–1892), the speaker moves from the observation of a spider to a reflection on the soul's search to understand all existence.

A Noiseless Patient Spider

A noiseless patient spider,
I mark'd where on a little promontory it stood isolated,
Mark'd how to explore the vacant vast surrounding,
It launch'd forth filament, filament, filament, out of itself,
Ever unreeling them, ever tirelessly speeding them.

And you O my soul where you stand,
Surrounded, detached, in measureless oceans of space,
Ceaselessly musing, venturing, throwing, seeking the
  spheres to connect them,
Till the bridge you will need be form'd, till the ductile
  anchor hold,
Till the gossamer thread you fling catch somewhere,
  O my soul.

In this brief poem by Alfred, Lord Tennyson (1809–1892) the language and imagery convey the experience of both the observer and of the eagle itself.

The Eagle

He clasps the crag with crooked hands;
Close to the sun in lonely lands,
Ringed with the azure world, he stands.

The wrinkled sea beneath him crawls;
He watches from his mountain walls,
And like a thunderbolt he falls.

Here, in free verse, is Whitman's vision of eagles:

The Dalliance of Eagles

Skirting the river road, (my forenoon walk, my rest,)
Skyward in air a sudden muffled sound, the dalliance
    of the eagles,
The rushing amorous contact high in space together,
The clinching interlocking claws, a living, fierce,
    gyrating wheel,
Four beating wings, two beaks, a swirling mass tight
    grappling,
In tumbling turning clustering loops, straight downward
    falling.
Till o'er the river pois'd, the twain yet one, a moment's
    lull,
A motionless still balance in the air, then parting, talons
    loosing,
Upward again on slow-firm pinions slanting, their
    separate diverse flight,
She hers, he his, pursuing.

And here is a poet, Katharine Lee Bates, who takes delight in playing with the names and characters of various fish; the result is a collection of puns, wordplay, and forms of internal and external rhyme.

Don't You See?

THE day was hotter than words can tell,
So hot the jelly-fish wouldn't jell.
The halibut went all to butter,
And the catfish had only force to utter
A faint sea-mew—aye, though some have doubted,
The carp he capered and the horn-pout pouted.
The sardonic sardine had his sly heart's wish
When the angelfish fought with the paradise fish.
'T was a sight gave the bluefish the blues to see,
But the seal concealed a wicked glee—
The day it went from bad to worse,
Till the pickerel picked the purse-crab's purse.

And the crab felt crabedder yet no doubt,
Because the oyster wouldn't shell out.
The sculpin would sculp, but hadn't a model,
And the coddlefish begged for something to coddle.
But to both the dolphin refused its doll,
Till the whale was obliged to whale them all.

In the first of these two poems by Robert Browning (1812–1889) the rich and varied imagery recreates the journey of a lover to his beloved and, in the second, his return to the "world of men."

Meeting at Night

The grey sea and the long black land;
And the yellow half-moon large and low;
And the startled little waves that leap
In fiery ringlets from their sleep,
As I gain the cove with pushing prow,
And quench its speed i' the slushy sand.

Then a mile of warm sea-scented beach;
Three fields to cross till a farm appears;
A tap at the pane, the quick sharp scratch
And spurt of a lighted match,
And a voice less loud, through its joys and fears,
Than the two hearts beating each to each.

Parting at Morning

Round the cape of a sudden came the sea,
And the sun looked over the mountain's rim:
And straight was a path of gold for him,
And the need of a world of men for me.

In this sonnet, George Meredith (1828–1909) imagines the desire of this fallen angel, now Satan, to return to the heavens he once inhabited.

Lucifer in Starlight

On a starred night Prince Lucifer uprose.
Tired of his dark dominion swung the fiend
Above the rolling ball in cloud part screened,
Where sinners hugged their spectre of repose.
Poor prey to his hot fit of pride were those.
And now upon his western wing he leaned,
Now his huge bulk o'er Afric's sands careened,
Now the black planet shadowed Arctic snows.
Soaring through wider zones that pricked his scars
With memory of the old revolt from Awe,
He reached a middle height, and at the stars,
Which are the brain of heaven, he looked, and sank.
Around the ancient track marched, rank on rank,
The army of unalterable law.

In this well-known sonnet by Percy Bysshe Shelley (1792–1822) we experience the ironic fate of a once proud and arrogant king.

Ozymandias

I met a traveler from an antique land
Who said: Two vast and trunkless legs of stone
Stand in the desert. Near them, on the sand,
Half sunk a shattered visage lies, whose frown,
And wrinkled lip, and sneer of cold command,
Tell that its sculptor well those passions read
Which yet survive, stamped on these lifeless things,
The hand that mocked them and the heart that fed;
And on the pedestal these words appear:
"My name is Ozymandias, king of kings:
Look on my works, ye Mighty, and despair!"
Nothing beside remains. Round the decay
Of that colossal wreck, boundless and bare,
The lone and level sands stretch far away.

Romantic poets and painters were fond of celebrating sunsets. Here is an excerpt from "Enough Has Been Said of Sunset," by Iris Barry.

> **LIGHT—imperceptible as**
> **One thin veil drawn across blackness:**
> **Is it dawn? . . .**
> **Comes the twitter-whistle of sleepy birds**
> **Crescendo . . .**
> **Now bright grayness creeping**
> **Drowns the dark; and waves of sea-wind**
> **Rock the thin leaves . . .**
> **A door bangs; sharp barks from dogs released,**
> **scampering.**
> **After some silence, footsteps.**
> **And the rising bustle of people**
> **Roused by the day-break.**

Here is what dawn "feels like" to William Carlos Williams:

Metric Figure

> **THERE is a bird in the poplars—**
> **It is the sun!**
> **The leaves are little yellow fish**
> **Swimming in the river;**
> **The bird skims above them—**
> **Day is on his wings.**
> **Phoenix!**
> **It is he that is making**
> **The great gleam among the poplars.**
> **It is his singing**
> **Outshines the noise**
> **Of leaves clashing in the wind.**

These poems represent only a few examples of the great variety of expression in verse. Your own textbooks and anthologies offer many more examples; and the list of Recommended Reading at the end of the book includes titles of collections readily available in paperback. You will also find the addresses of some excellent websites devoted to poetry. You should read as widely as possible, and always read aloud!

A GLOSSARY OF POETIC TERMS AND TECHNIQUES

allegory A narrative, in prose or verse, in which abstract ideas, principles, human values or states of mind, are *personified*. The purpose of the allegory is to illustrate the signficance of the ideas by dramatizing them. *Parable* and *fable* are particular kinds of allegory, in which a moral is illustrated in the form of a story.

alliteration The repetition of initial consonant sounds in words and syllables. This is one of the first patterns of sound a child creates (for instance "ma-ma," "pa-pa"). The children's stories of Dr. Seuss use alliteration and assonance. Poets use alliteration for its rich musical effect: "Fish, flesh, and fowl commend all summer long/Whatever is begotten, born, and dies" (Yeats); for humor: "Where at, with blade, with bloody, blameful blade/He bravely broached his boiling bloody breast" (Shakespeare); and to echo the sense of the lines: "The iron tongue of midnight hath told twelve" (Shakespeare).

allusion A reference to a historical event, to Biblical, mythological, or literary characters and incidents with which the reader is assumed to be familiar. Allusion may, with few words, enrich or extend the meaning of a phrase, idea, or image. Allusion may also be used for ironic effect. In his poem "Out, out . . ." Robert Frost expects the reader to recall from Macbeth's final soliloquy the line, "Out, out brief candle!" Such expressions as "a Herculean task" or "Achilles heel" are also forms of allusion.

ambiguity Denotes uncertainty of meaning. In literature, however, especially in poetry, we speak of *intentional* ambiguity, the use of language and images to suggest more than one meaning at the same time.

assonance The repetition of vowel sounds among words that begin or end with different consonants. Sonnet 30 of Shakespeare (page 82) and "Child on Top of a Greenhouse" by Theodore Roethke (page 81), for example, are rich in assonance. Some poets may vary end rhymes with assonance; for example, Emily Dickinson (page 76) does it here: "The Feet, mechanical, go round—Of Ground, or Air, or Ought—."

ballad Narrative poem, sometimes sung, that tells a dramatic story.

blank verse Unrhymed *iambic pentameter,* usually in "paragraphs" of verse instead of stanzas. Shakespeare's plays are composed primarily in blank verse. For example, from *Macbeth* (Act I, Scene 5):

> Your face, my Thane, is as a book where men
> May read strange matters. To beguile the time,
> Look like the time; bear welcome in your eye,
> Your hand, your tongue; look like the innocent flower,
> But be the serpent under't . . .

connotation The feelings, attitudes, images, and associations of a word or expression. Connotations are usually said to be "positive" or "negative." See also discussion on page 148 in Chapter 8—Vocabulary.

couplet Two lines of verse with similar meter and end rhyme. Couplets generally have self-contained ideas as well, so they may function as stanzas within a poem. In the English (Shakespearean) *sonnet,* the couplet concludes the poem. (See the sonnets on pages 82–84.) Also many scenes in Shakespeare's plays end with rhymed couplets: "Away, and mock the time with fairest show/False face must hide what the false heart doth know" (*Macbeth* Act I, Scene 7).

denotation That which a word actually names, identifies, or "points to." Denotation is sometimes referred to as "the dictionary definition" of a word.

dramatic monologue A poem in which a fictional character, at a critical or dramatic point in life, addresses a particular "audience," which is identifiable but silent. In the course of the monologue, we learn a great deal, often ironically, about the character, who is speaking and the circumstances that have led to the speech. Robert Browning is the best-known nineteenth-century poet to compose dramatic monologues; "My Last Duchess" is a famous example. In the twentieth century, such poets as Kenneth Fearing, E. A. Robinson, T. S. Eliot ("The Love Song of J. Alfred Prufrock"), Robert Frost, and Amy Lowell have composed well-known dramatic monologues.

elegy A meditative poem mourning the death of an individual.

epic A long narrative poem often centering on a heroic figure who represents the fate of a great nation or people. *The Iliad* and *The Odyssey* of Homer, *The Aeneid* of Vergil, and the Anglo-Saxon *Beowulf* are well-known epics. Milton's *Paradise Lost* and Dante's *The Divine Comedy* are examples of epic narratives in which subjects of great human significance are dramatized. *Omeros,* by Derek Walcott, is a contemporary example of an epic poem.

figurative language The intentional and imaginative use of words and comparisons that are not literal but that create original, vivid, and often unexpected images and associations. Figurative language is also called *metaphorical language*. See *metaphor* and *simile*.

free verse A poem written in free verse develops images and ideas in patterns of lines without specific metrical arrangements or formal rhyme. Free verse is distinguished from prose, however, because it retains such poetic elements as assonance, alliteration, and figurative language. The poetry of Walt Whitman offers striking examples.

hyperbole An exaggerated expression (also called overstatement) for a particular effect, which may be humorous, satirical, or intensely emotional. Hyperbole is the expression of folk tales and legends and, of course, of lovers: Romeo says to Juliet, "there lies more peril in thine eye/Than twenty of their swords." Hyperbole is often the expression of any overwhelming feeling. After he murders King Duncan, Macbeth looks with horror at his bloody hands: "Will all great Neptune's ocean wash this blood/Clean from my hand . . . ?" In her sleepwalking scene, Lady Macbeth despairs that "All the perfumes of Arabia will not sweeten this little hand." And every one of us has felt, "I have mountains of work to do!"

iambic pentameter The basic meter of English speech: "I think I know exactly what you need/and yet at times I know that I do not." Formally, it identifies verse of ten syllables to the line, with the second, fourth, sixth, eight, and tenth syllables accented. There is, however, variation in the stresses within lines to reflect natural speech — and to avoid a "sing-song" or nursery rhyme effect. Most of the dialogue in Shakespeare's plays is composed in this meter. See *blank verse*.

image Images and imagery are the heart of poetry. Although the term suggests only something that is visualized, an image is the recreation through language of *any* experience perceived directly through the senses. For example, Tennyson's "The Eagle" (page 89) is composed of striking visual images. The feelings of fear and of mourning in Emily Dickinson's poems are also images. In "Pitcher" (page 75) we feel the motion of pitching.

internal rhyme A pattern in which a word or words within a line rhyme with the word that ends it. Poets may also employ internal rhyme at irregular intervals over many lines. The verbs in Theodore Roethke's poem "Child on Top of a Greenhouse" (page 81) create the effect of internal rhyme.

irony In general, a tone or figure of speech in which there is a discrepancy — (a striking difference or contradiction) — between what is expressed and what is meant or expected. Irony may be used to achieve a powerful effect indirectly. In satire, for example, it may be used to ridicule or criticize. Stephen Crane's poem "Do Not Weep, Maiden, for War Is Kind" (page 88) is intensely ironic, both in the stanzas apparently seeking to comfort those whose lovers, fathers, and sons have died and in the contrasting stanzas of apparent celebration of the glories of war. We also speak of *dramatic irony* in fiction in which the reader understands more than the characters do. Ring Lardner's short story "Haircut" is an excellent example.

lyric A general term used to describe poems that are relatively brief and expressed in the voice of a single *speaker* (narrative voice). Lyric poems express a powerful emotion revealed in a significant experience or observation. (See discussion on page 78.)

metaphor A form of analogy. Through metaphor, a poet discovers and expresses a similarity between dissimilar things. The poet use metaphors to imaginatively find common qualities between things we would not normally or literally compare. As a figure of speech, metaphor is said to be implicit or indirect. This contrasts to *simile* (see page 98), where the comparison is expressed directly. In his final soliloquy, Macbeth uses a series of metaphors to express the meaninglessness of his own life: "Life's but a walking shadow, a poor player . . . it is a tale told by an idiot . . . ."

meter and **rhythm** Rhythm refers to the pattern of movement in a poem. As music has rhythm, so does poetry. Meter refers to specific patterns of stressed and unstressed syllables. See *iambic pentameter*.

ode A meditation or celebration of a specific subject. Traditional odes addressed "elevated" ideas and were composed in elaborate stanza forms. Keats's "Ode to a Nightingale" and "Ode to Autumn" are particularly fine examples. Modern odes may address subjects either serious or personal. One well-known contemporary ode is Pablo Neruda's "Ode to My Socks."

onomatopoeia The use of words whose sound reflects their sense. "Buzz," "hiss," and "moan" are common examples. Shakespeare's Sonnet 30 shows how the sounds and rhythm of whole lines may be onomatopoetic.

oxymoron Closely related to *paradox,* oxymoron is a figure of speech in which two contradictory or sharply contrasting terms are paired for emphasis or ironic effect. Among students' favorite examples are "jumbo shrimp" and "army intelligence." Poets have written of the "wise fool," a "joyful sadness," or an "eloquent silence."

paradox An expression, concept, or situation whose literal statement is contradictory, yet which makes a truthful and meaningful observation. Consider the widely used expression "less is more," for example. Shakespeare's play *Macbeth* opens with a series of paradoxes to establish the moral atmosphere in which "foul is fair." John Donne's famous poem "Death Be Not Proud" ends with the paradox "Death thou shalt die," and the title of Robert Penn Warren's poem "Old Photograph of the Future" is a paradox.

personification A form of metaphor or simile in which nonhuman things—objects, plants and animals, forces of nature, abstract ideas—are given human qualities; for example, "The half-grown chrysanthemums staring up like accusers" (Roethke, page 81), "the walking sun/that poised an eye on me from its high floor" (Hall, page 81), "Time . . . the thief of youth" (Milton), and "Blow winds, and crack your cheeks! Blow! Rage!" (Shakespeare).

prose poem This form appears on the page in the sentences and paragraphs of prose yet its effect is achieved through rhythm, images, and patterns of sound associated with poetry.

quatrain Stanza of four lines. The quatrain is the most commonly used stanza form in English poetry. Quatrains may be rhymed, *abab, aabb, abba,* for example, or they may be unrhymed. The sonnets of Shakespeare (pages 82–83), the poem by Laurence Binyon (page 77), "Old Photograph of the Future" (page 79), and "The Sleeping Giant" (page 81) are also composed in quatrains.

rhyme In general, any repetition of identical or similar sounds among words that are close enough together to form an audible pattern. Rhyme is most evident when it occurs at the ends of lines of metrical verse. The *quatrains* of Shakespeare's Sonnet 55 (pages 83–84) have alternating rhyme as do those of Robert Penn Warren's poem "Old Photograph of the Future" (page 79).

rhyme scheme A regular pattern of end rhyme in a poem. The rhyme scheme in Shakespeare's sonnets, for example, is *abab/cdcd/efef/gg*.

satire A form or style that uses elements of irony, ridicule, exaggeration, understatement, sarcasm, humor, or absurdity to criticize human behavior or a society. All satire is *ironic* (see page 96) in that meaning or theme is conveyed in the discrepancy between what is said and what is meant, between what is and what should be, between what appears and what truly is. While satire is often entertaining, its purpose is serious and meant to provoke thought or judgment. The verse of Alexander Pope is often extended satire, and many poems by e. e. cummings are satiric.

simile An expression that is a direct comparison of two things. It uses such words as *like, as, as if, seems, appears*. For instance: "A line of elms plunging and tossing like horses" (Theodore Roethke); "Mind in its purest play is like some bat" (Richard Wilbur); "I wandered lonely as a cloud" (William Wordsworth).

soliloquy A form of monologue found most often in drama. It differs from a dramatic monologue in that the speaker is alone, revealing thoughts and feelings to or for oneself that are intentionally unheard by other characters. In Shakespeare's plays, for example, the principal characters' reflections on how to act or questions of conscience are revealed in their soliloquies. Hamlet's "To be, or not to be . . ." is probably the most famous dramatic soliloquy in English.

sonnet A poem of fourteen lines in *iambic pentameter* that may be composed of different patterns of stanzas and rhyme schemes. The most common forms are the English, or Shakespearean, sonnet, which consists of three quatrains and a closing couplet, and the Italian sonnet, which consists of an *octave* of eight lines and a *sestet* of six lines.

speaker The narrative voice in a poem. Also, the character who speaks in a *dramatic monologue*. The poems "The Sleeping Giant" and "Old Photograph of the Future" have distinctive speakers who are also the central characters in the dramatic experience of the poem.

stanza The grouping of lines within a poem. A stanza provides the basic organization and development of ideas, much as a paragraph does in an essay. Many stanza patterns have a fixed number of lines and a regular pattern of rhyme; the poems of Robert Penn Warren (page 79) and Donald Hall (page 81) are good examples. Poets, however, often create stanzas of varying length and form within a single poem. A stanza that ends with a period, completing an idea or image, is considered "closed," while a stanza that ends with a comma or with no punctuation, is called "open," indicating that there should be very little pause in the movement from one stanza to another. Roethke's poem "Child on Top of a Greenhouse" (page 81) is an example of a poem composed in a single stanza.

symbol Most generally, anything that stands for or suggests something else. Language itself is symbolic; sounds and abstract written forms may stand for almost any human thought or experience. Symbols are real objects and *concrete* images that lead us to think about what is suggested. Symbols organize a wide variety of ideas into single acts of understanding. They embody not single "meanings" but suggest whole areas of meaning.

tone The attitude or feeling of the speaker toward the subject. Tone may also refer to the dominant mood of a poem. (See discussion of *tone* on page 86.)

understatement Expression in which something is presented as less important or significant than it really is. The first and third stanzas of Stephen Crane's "Do Not Weep, Maiden" (page 88) ironically understate the horror of death in battle and the loss for those who mourn. Understatement is often used for humorous, *satiric,* or *ironic* effect. Much of the satire in *Huckleberry Finn* stems from Huck's naive and understated observations. One particular form of understatement, actually a double negative, includes such expressions as "I was not uninterested," which really means "I was interested," or "He was not without imagination," which really means "He had some imagination."

Chapter 6

WRITING ABOUT LITERATURE: A GENERAL REVIEW

For most students, writing papers and responding to essay questions on exams are the most challenging aspects of their course work. Writing requires that you articulate and focus your understanding of what you read. Like all good writing, writing about literature not only demonstrates to others what you understand and think but also obliges you to clarify *for yourself* what you truly know. That process is sometimes hard, but it is worthwhile. Writing is essential to developing your critical reading and thinking skills.

TOPICS FOR LITERARY ESSAYS

Much of your writing about literature is done in response to assignments and exam questions. Students are also urged to maintain notes and journals. For essays, instructors may assign very specific topics, or they may offer general subjects that require you to develop your own topic and controlling idea.

In your literature courses and exams you will find that the majority of the questions focus on **character**. Because essay topics may apply to many works of nonfiction you read—personal essay, memoir, and autobiography in particular—the term *character* should be understood to refer to any persons, not exclusively to those of fiction and drama.

As you think about characters in the literature you read, keep the following questions in mind: What are a character's values and motives? beliefs and principles? moral qualities? strengths and weaknesses? illusions or delusions? For what is a character searching? striving? devoting his or her life? What significant decisions and actions does a character take? What are the consequences of those decisions and actions? To what extent does a character "succeed" or "fail"? understand or fail to understand?

Literature also seeks to account for the forces outside individuals, that is, the external forces that influence the direction and outcome of their lives. These "forces" range from those of nature and history to the demands of family, community, and society. The response of individuals to inner and outer forces is what literature considers and dramatizes. (See Chapters 4 and 5 for discussions of reading literature and for glossaries of important terms and techniques.)

TOPIC AND FOCUS

As any essay must, your paper must have a clear purpose, a controlling idea; moreover, the development of the purpose must be convincing to the reader. *Focus* means in writing, as it does in a photograph, that the subject is clear! We can see it, even recognize it. And, if the photographer/writer has "framed" the material properly, we see the relationship of the background details to the principal subject. When you take a picture of your best friend at camp, or of the place you most want to remember from a vacation trip, you keep the lens of your camera directed at what is most important—not at the tree next to your friend, not at the bus that took you to Niagara Falls.

SELECTION OF SIGNIFICANT DETAILS

One of the most widely observed characteristics of short stories is that they are very selective in detail. The author of a short story includes only those elements of setting, character, and plot that reveal the significance of the central incident. In "The Lottery," for example, we do not know when the story takes place, we do not even know the name of the town or where it is located, and we know little about the lives of individual characters. Those details are not *significant*—they do not matter—to the story Shirley Jackson tells; comparable details *are* significant in "Haircut," and, therefore, Ring Lardner includes them.

To achieve focus in your essays about works of literature, you must exercise the same rigorous process of selection. However interesting you may find a particular incident or aspect of a character, do not include those details if they do not directly explain or clarify your topic.

DEVELOPING THE TOPIC

Many of the common methods of developing arguments are discussed in Chapter 4—Reading Prose. Here are some of those methods as they might be used to develop essays on works of literature:

Comparison/Contrast

Although *compare* means to identify similarities, and *contrast* means to identify differences, the term *comparison* is often used for a discussion that examines both similarities and differences among the items being compared. This is one of the most useful approaches, and one of the most commonly used, because the process of comparing helps sharpen thought. To compose a meaningful comparison, the writer must understand the objects of comparison in detail.

Any literary aspect found in two or more works may serve as a basis for comparison. For example, one could compare the effective use of first-person narration in *The Great Gatsby* and *Ethan Frome,* or in *The Catcher in the Rye* and *Huckleberry Finn.* Although the circumstances of their lives are vastly different, the fact that both Ethan Frome and Jay Gatsby fail to achieve what they most desire—a life with the women they love—offers a rich possibility for comparison and contrast. "Haircut" and "The Lottery" share common elements of setting and irony. *Othello* and *Romeo and Juliet* have a common theme—the tragic destruction of great love.

Comparison may, of course, focus on much narrower topics and be confined to a single work. The best way to develop notes for a comparison is first to list the aspects common to the items under comparison, then to list for each all the specific details that differentiate them. Finally, as you do in preparation for any essay, you select those that are most significant.

Analysis

Analysis requires detailed examination of a particular aspect of a literary work. The purpose of an analytic paper is to show the significance of that aspect to the meaning of the work as a whole. Examples of analytic topics include the use of time in Miller's *Death of a Salesman,* the imagery of light and dark in *Othello,* and the extended metaphor in Emily Dickinson's poem "I Taste a Liquor Never Brewed."

Classification

Classification organizes objects, people, and other living things into categories; it is a process of identifying and relating. In discussions of literature, classification may be an important part of an essay, or it may constitute a topic in its own right. An essay in which the writer shows how a particular work exemplifies a **genre** is considered classification: *The Scarlet Letter* as a **romance**; Shakespeare's *Macbeth* as Elizabethan **tragedy**; Dreiser's *Sister Carrie* as **naturalism**.

Cause and Effect

Many of the topics for writing and discussion of literature may be developed by showing how circumstances or actions have direct and observable consequences. Demonstrating actual cause and effect, however, requires careful thinking and attention to detail. Cause and effect are more easily demonstrated in logic and chemistry than in human experience.

Literary topics that focus on **plot** often lend themselves to cause and effect development because essentially any plot is built on cause and effect: specific circumstances, actions, or decisions lead to others and have consequences in the lives of the characters. Plot summary alone does *not* establish cause and effect; it simply relates "what happened." Cause-and-effect argument requires the writer to show how and why incidents are related.

Exemplification

Whenever you cite specific details to support a thesis, and when you choose the works you will use to answer the literature question in Part B of Session Two, you are using exemplification. *To exemplify* means to illustrate the meaning of a general concept through use of specific examples. This method is fundamental to the development of nearly any essay or literary topic.

LOOKING AT KEY TERMS IN LITERATURE QUESTIONS

identify   To name and also to characterize and to place in context; sometimes you may be required to state the significance of what you are identifying. Often identification includes linking characters to the theme or experience that serves as the topic.

describe   To give the essential characteristics of a person, object, or experience. If you are asked to describe, your choice of details or characteristics must reveal your understanding of a larger question. Why are these details relevant to the topic? Description alone will not be the focus of a literature topic.

explain/show/discuss   These terms indicate the most important parts of a question, which will be developed in the body of an essay. Once you have identified and described your subject, you must interpret and demonstrate the significance of your examples and details; you must offer evidence, using specific references, to support your argument.

USING FLUENT AND PRECISE LANGUAGE

Effective writing is characterized by interesting and vivid language, and "use of precise and engaging language" is among the criteria for evaluation of Regents essays. From the list of what writers *do,* here are some terms to help you articulate your observations about creation of plot:

> *convey, create, delineate, depict, describe, dramatize, foreshadow,*
> *illustrate, invent, portray, present, recreate, reveal, select, shock,*
> *show, symbolize*

The following terms offer precision and variety in discussing details of a plot:

> *affair, circumstance, climax, development, episode, event, experience,*
> *incident, instance, juncture, moment, occasion, occurrence, opportunity,*
> *scene, situation*

Terms useful in referring to *character* include:

> *disposition, identity, individuality, makeup, mettle, nature, persona,*
> *personality, self, spirit, temperament*

Finally, here is a list of adjectives collected by students to describe some of the many relationships and attitudes among characters in literature (and in our own lives!):

> *admiring, affectionate, bitter, cautious, compassionate, curious, deceitful,*
> *disapproving, disdainful, dishonest, distant, envious, false, fearful,*
> *generous, hostile, indifferent, loving, optimistic, reluctant, resentful,*
> *reserved, respectful, scornful, sincere, skeptical, stern, suspicious,*
> *sympathetic, treacherous, watchful*

(See also Using Synonymies to Enhance Your Writing in Chapter 7.)

CHOOSING YOUR OWN TOPIC: REPRESENTATIVE LITERARY SUBJECTS AND THEMES

In many high school and college literature courses, students must select their own topics for writing. The subjects of literature are as varied as human experience itself, and below are some of the many themes authors dramatize. You will encounter these as topics in class discussion and as topics for essays and examination questions. These topics may, of course, serve for discussion of more than one work in an essay.

Topics That Focus on Character

- In many works of literature, an important theme is an **individual's achievement of self-knowledge as a result of undergoing an ordeal**. This self-knowledge may be a recognition of the individual's own strengths, weaknesses, values, prejudices, aspirations, or fears. Identify the individual and the self-knowledge he or she achieves. Using specific references from the work, explain how the ordeal led the individual to the self-knowledge.
- **Nature** can have different effects on different people. It can defeat someone with its power; it can inspire someone with its beauty. Identify the character; using specific references, show how he or she was either defeated or inspired by nature.
- It has been said that to live with **fear** and not be overcome by it is the final **test of maturity**. Explain what fear a character lives with; show how the character "passes" or "fails" the test of maturity on the basis of his or her response to that fear.
- A commonly held belief is that **suffering strengthens an individual's character**. The suffering can be physical, mental, or emotional. Identify the individual; describe the nature of the suffering; explain how the suffering did or did not strengthen the individual's character.
- Sometimes a person **struggles to achieve a goal** only to discover that, once the goal is achieved, the results are not what was expected.
- In many works of literature there are characters who are **troubled by injustice** in society, such as poverty, discrimination, or lawlessness, and **who try to correct** the injustice. Identify the character and the injustice, explain what actions the character takes; discuss whether or not the efforts are successful.
- In many works, characters who love one another or share a special friendship often face **obstacles to their relationship**. Sometimes characters overcome the obstacle; sometimes they are defeated by it. Identify the characters and the obstacle; explain how the characters overcome or are defeated by the obstacle; discuss the effect this outcome (the success or failure, not the obstacle) has on the relationship.
- In many works of literature, **a character sacrifices something of value** in order to achieve something of greater value.
- Sometimes a character faces a **conflict between his or her conscience** and the standards of behavior expected by others. Identify the character; explain the specific nature of the conflict; discuss how the character was affected by this conflict.
- In many works of literature, a character reaches a **major turning point** in his or her life. From that point onward, the character undergoes a significant change.
- Characters in works of literature frequently **learn about life or themselves** by taking risks.

106

- The phrase **"rite of passage"** describes a situation in which a young person is faced with an experience that results in his or her becoming mature. Explain the experience; discuss how the young person matures as a result of the way in which he or she deals with the experience.
- In many works of literature, characters are **challenged by unfamiliar environments**. Show how the character was or was not successful in meeting the challenge.
- Some individuals in literature **try to do what they believe is right**, even though they face opposition.
- In some works of literature, an important character **makes a mistake that advances the reader's understanding of that individual**.
- Confusion, danger, or tragedy sometimes results when **one character misunderstands the words or actions of another character**.
- In many works of literature, a character **struggles against circumstances that seem to be beyond his or her control**. Sometimes the character is victorious, sometimes not.

Topics That Focus on Literary Elements and Techniques

While topics that focus on character may be the most common in literature courses or on exams, various literary elements also provide topics for essays. The AP literature exam, for example, often features a question based on a literary element or technique.

- Some authors are especially successful at creating **a memorable visual image** that contributes to the reader's understanding of a work. Identify the image and its importance; show how the image contributes to the meaning of the work.
- In many works of literature, the **setting** contributes to the reader's understanding of the central conflict in the plot. Describe the setting; show how it contributes to the reader's understanding of the conflict on which the plot hinges.
- Authors often create a **predominant mood** in a work of literature. Using specific references, discuss incidents that convey that mood and explain the importance of mood to the work.
- Authors sometimes use **foreshadowing** to help develop the plot of a work. Foreshadowing usually takes the form of incidents that seem to be unimportant at first, but take on added significance later. Discuss examples of foreshadowing and show how they contribute to the overall effect and meaning of the work.
- A work of literature may be defined as **a classic** because it promotes deep insight into human behavior, presents a universal theme, or uses

language in an exceptional way. Show how a particular work meets the above definition of the term *classic*.

- Through their work, some **authors reveal their acceptance or rejection of values** held by society. Identify the value; state whether the author accepts or rejects it; using specific references, show how the author reveals his or her attitude toward that value.
- In literature, **symbols** are used to reinforce the central idea or to represent characters. Using specific references, explain how the symbol in a particular work enriches the reader's understanding of either the central idea or a character.
- The **narrative point of view** is significant to the effect and meaning of a literary work. Illustrate the truth of this statement by specific references to a work of literature.

AUDIENCE AND LITERATURE ESSAYS

Most teachers mention audience in the assignments they give; if it is not clear for whom you are writing, it is a good idea to ask before you complete an assignment. For most outside examinations, including the Regents, assume that you are writing for a reader who is familiar with the works of literature but who has not considered the topic; background discussion and *detailed* explanation of plot are not needed.

A NOTE ON CONCLUSIONS

No essay, however brief, should simply stop. Even if you run out of time or things to say, try not to telegraph that information to the reader. A conclusion must come back to the topic, must complete the discussion, in a way that leaves the reader feeling convinced by what you have written. On examinations, most students close with a brief, summative conclusion that highlights the relationship of the literary work or works to the topic or restates the thesis of the essay. Even if the reader of a short essay does not really *need* the conclusion to appreciate your argument, the obligation to compose a conclusion keeps you focused on the topic.

Student writers are urged to avoid the following in their conclusions: the expression "what this paper has shown . . ." or "As you can see . . ."; a reminder that Shakespeare was a great playwright or that Mark Twain was an important figure in American literature; a confession that the reader *really* liked or did not like a particular work. Above all, the conclusion is not the place to introduce a new topic or tack on an idea that properly belongs in the body of the essay.

Chapter 7

WRITING ON DEMAND

Writing has always been an important part of a student's education as well as an essential skill for a successful professional life. The National Commission on Writing is only one of the more recent initiatives in American education to emphasize the importance of good writing among our students. American colleges and universities also seek independent assessment of students' writing skills as part of the admissions process. In this chapter you will find some guidelines for effective writing on demand.

WRITING TO INFORM OR PERSUADE

A General Review

Much of the work you do in high school or college requires writing to demonstrate your ability to understand, analyze, and organize information and ideas. On exams and essays for science and social studies courses, as well as in English and writing courses, you are expected to do many of the following:

- Tell your audience (readers) what they need to know
- Use specific, accurate, and relevant information
- Use a tone and level of language appropriate for the task and audience
- Organize your ideas in a logical and coherent manner
- Follow the conventions of standard written English

These guidelines are also reminders of what your teachers mean when they direct you to compose a "well-written essay" on a given topic.

Personal Narrative

Here is an example of an informal essay written in response to a specific task. It is a good example of what is meant by **tone and level of language** appropriate for the audience. The essay is also organized in a logical and coherent manner.

Task: A representative of a middle school in your district has invited you to speak at the middle school graduation ceremonies on the topic "Getting Off to a Good Start in High School." Write a brief speech that you would give to the students, stating your recommendations for a successful start in high school. Use specific reasons, examples, or details to support your recommendations.

Sample Student Response

Not so long ago, I too was sitting where you are now, thinking and worrying about what my life in high school would be like. Will I stand out? Will I make friends? How should I approach people? Will my classes be too difficult? Will I be able to cope with the stress? These questions kept badgering me throughout the summer before ninth grade. I was especially nervous about starting school because I had just moved to a new neighborhood and did not know a single person.

By the end of the summer, the thought that especially frustrated me was that I would have no one to eat lunch with on the first day of school. This does not seem like such a big deal but it bothered me a lot. I knew that at the high school people went out to eat with a group of friends. I had no one to go out with. I told myself that I still had a week before school started and did not need to worry.

The first day of school finally arrived. As I neared the high school, I felt helpless and lonely. I wanted to plead with my mom to turn the car around and go back home. But I reluctantly got out of the car and slowly approached the front entrance of the school.

Luckily, I found my first class and quickly took a seat in the front. I felt as if all eyes were on me. The new kid. The freak. While everyone was talking and laughing about their summer, I sat in my seat trying to look as though I was busy fiddling with my notebook. I couldn't wait to get out of the classroom. I wanted to run home and hide, for this was one of the most difficult experiences of my life.

Things started to look better around fifth period. I got up the courage and started talking to people. I even went out to lunch with a few girls and had a comfortable time. I was not totally relaxed but knew that I would adapt and soon make more friends.

I have just finished my junior year in high school. I have many friends and am very happy in my school. I will be a senior this coming September and expect to experience new ideas and challenges. I am now starting to think about what I want to do with my life and what colleges I might want to attend. Soon I will be leaving high school and will again feel the nervousness and anxiety that all of you are going through in preparing for high school. I guess what we are experiencing is not trepidation but life, and what to expect in the future. You may be scared now, but be confident that you will overcome those fears and the experiences will only make you stronger.

Analysis

Although this speech is more a personal narrative than a list of recommendations, the writer/speaker clearly understands the purpose of the task and understands her audience:

"Not so long ago, I too was sitting where you are now. . . ." The diction is informal, the tone is conversational, and first-person narrative is highly appropriate for the occasion.

The theme is established in the opening sentence, but the speaker's main point is not stated until the very end: "You may be scared now, but . . . you will overcome those fears . . . and [be] stronger." She leads her audience to this conclusion by narrating her own feelings and experiences, starting with a series of "fears" she knows her listeners have.

The narrative covers a period of many weeks, but it is made coherent by specific references to time: "throughout the summer . . . by the end of summer . . . on the first day of school . . . my first class . . . around fifth period . . . lunch." She also uses a reference to time to come back to the present and bring the speech to a close: "I have just finished my junior year. . . ."

The ideas are well expressed; and the paragraph in which the writer describes what it was like to sit in her first class—"The new kid." "The freak."—pretending to be busy with her notebook is especially vivid and convincing. We also trust the speaker when she tells us that she had "a comfortable time" at lunch but that she "was not totally relaxed" either. If she had claimed that after lunch all her fears had disappeared, we would not believe her. This is also a good example of what is meant by honesty in writing: it rings true in our ears. This piece would be even better if the writer had included more specific examples of how she overcame her fears.

Persuasive Writing

Here are two examples of what is called persuasive writing, pieces that develop and support an opinion on a particular topic. In contrast to the essay of argument in Part 2 of the Regents ELA exam, which must be based on evidence from given sources, these essays are developed with the writer's own reasoning and examples. Note what makes each a successful argument.

Task: The students in your science class have been invited to submit essays on topics of current interest or controversy for possible publication on the Op-Ed page of the school newspaper.

Sample Student Response

Using Animals for Scientific Research

The question of whether or not to use animals as subjects for scientific research is a difficult one. Those in opposition claim that using animals in research is inhumane, while those holding a diametrically opposing view maintain that it is a necessary evil whose long-term benefits far outweigh the sacrifice of a handful of animals. I am an ardent supporter of the latter view. I feel that the use of animals is justified by the benefits that are reaped by all of mankind, and that halting the use of animals as subjects would greatly impede advancements in the field of medicine.

One example of the tremendous benefits that animal research can bring about is the case of the discovery of insulin by Dr. William Banting and his assistant, Charles Best. Before this amazing discovery, diabetes mellitus was a devastating and inevitably fatal disease. The extent of treatment that doctors could offer afflicted patients was a starvation diet, which prolonged life only for a short time and caused the obviously detrimental and painful effects of virtual starvation.

When Dr. Banting came up with a unique idea that linked the cause of the disease to a hormonal secretion of the pancreas, a potential way to control this deadly disease arose. But the idea had to be tested and proven successful before it could be offered to human patients. Dr. Banting proceeded with his experiments, using fifteen dogs as his subjects. Although several of the dogs did die as a result of the experiment, the benefits that society gained because of the tests are infinitely greater. If those opposed to utilizing animals in testing had their way, the concept would have died prematurely because there would have been no way to test the idea. Fortunately for the field of science and for the millions of diabetics that have lived in the past few decades, Dr. Banting was able to find this treatment.

As a diabetic, I am greatly indebted to the work of Dr. Banting and the studies he conducted using animals as subjects. Today, I am not only alive, but healthy and active. I cannot help but be a supporter of animal testing because I owe my life to it. I understand how one may object to senseless cruelty to animals and the wasting of their lives worthlessly. But using animals strictly for scientific use is not "senseless cruelty" and it is clearly justified.

Analysis

This is a good example of a short essay of opinion because the student has chosen a subject that he could develop with expertise and compelling personal experience; it also demonstrates his skill in organizing and presenting an argument.

One of the most effective ways to approach a controversial topic is to "acknowledge the opposition." Indicate that you recognize, and even respect, the opposing view. This writer agrees that the question "is a difficult one," but goes on to say he is "an ardent supporter" of animal testing. Note that he skillfully saves his personal reasons for the end, first developing a factual but dramatic example of the benefits of testing for millions of people. Introducing his personal reasons earlier would have made the argument less persuasive because he would have appeared less objective. The conclusion is emotionally effective when he says, "I cannot help but be a supporter of animal testing because I owe my life to it." More importantly, the writer demonstrates skillful argument when he says, "I understand how one may object. . ." and closes with a distinction between scientific experiment and "senseless cruelty." This essay would be a good contribution to an Op-Ed page.

Task: The editor of your local newspaper has proposed that businesses that hire high school graduates pay them salaries in proportion to their grades from the last two years of high school; that is, the higher a graduate's grades for the last two years of high school, the higher the salary. Write a letter to the editor in which you state your opinion of the proposal. Use specific reasons, examples, or details.

Sample Student Response

I vehemently oppose the proposal that graduates be paid salaries in proportion to their grades for the last two years of high school.

First, grades should not affect the equal opportunity of all workers to receive the same paycheck for the same work. It must be taken into account that there are many factors that influence a student's grades in high school. For example, one student may have a harder course load than another student with higher grades. It is unfair to compare grades from different level classes. Perhaps a student does not do well on tests, but is an excellent student in class. Participation and the ability to speak one's mind are very beneficial in a career, yet that is not reflected by grades. Furthermore, if a student has an inborn proficiency in a subject (and gets good grades), it is unfair to assume that that student works hard to achieve his or her scores. An average student works harder and may still not get the same scores. Hard work and dedication are important factors in choosing an employee, but these factors cannot always be relayed by a report card.

There are other factors besides grades that play a role in whether a student is right for a job. The applicant may have experience in the field of interest, but the proposed system would not take this into account. Perhaps a student has been a volunteer or has been active in clubs and organizations outside of school. By looking at his or her track record with reference to involvement in organizations, the student's ability to follow through would be noted. This is an important factor to take into account when hiring a worker.

Also, grades do not indicate strength of personal character, an important determinant in the selection of an employee. One must not make the generalization that a student with good grades is also a good person, and that a student with poor grades is not a good person. Only a personal interview can give the employer some sense of personal character of the worker. Positive interactions with other workers are vital to the success of a business.

Finally, by locking in different salaries and pay rates based on high school grades, the employer is creating unnecessary competition and tension in the workplace. A worker with a lower salary may not work as hard, as a result. The worker with the lower salary might be treated differently, or unfairly, by the employer by not being encouraged to work up to potential.

114

Thank you for your attention to this matter. Perhaps now an employee will be viewed as a person, and not as a report card. Everyone deserves a fair chance.

Analysis

This essay would receive a relatively good evaluation because it expresses a clear and thoughtful opinion, it is well organized, and it is excellent in its development; on the other hand, the essay is not always focused on the specific topic. The letter begins well, with a clear statement of position, and the first section makes several important points about the limited significance of grades. Note, however, that the argument shifts from a discussion of how workers should be paid to how they should be hired in the first place. The second section makes several good points, but it too refers to *hiring* workers. The writer comes back to the topic of differentiated pay only in the third full paragraph.

If the writer had followed her statement of opinion with a *because* statement and a summary of her main points, she could have established the focus needed. This writer clearly took time to gather good examples and reasons, but she did not always show how they related to the topic. The task directed the student to write a letter to an editor and to write *the body of the letter only*, but such letters are really essays of argument and must have focus and coherence to be effective. Composing "letters" of this kind is a very good way to practice writing persuasive essays.

WRITING FROM A PROMPT

On many examinations and in high school or college courses, you will encounter the term *prompt*. This term is used to refer in general to any set of directions for a writing task. In the theater, the prompter is the one who gives an actor or singer in danger of forgetting his or her lines the phrase that he or she needs to remember to continue the performance. In writing, a prompt serves to recall ideas or stimulate discussion. A prompt is also meant to inspire, or even provoke. A prompt may be in the form of a task and directions, as in the examples above, or it may be in the form of a quote or even a photograph—anything that offers the writer a subject and a reason to produce a piece of writing.

Here are two examples of persuasive writing where the prompt was in the form of a quote only; the writers had to establish controlling ideas and develop the examples on their own.

"All the World's a Stage"

William Shakespeare once wrote, "all the world's a stage and all the people players . . ." This well-known phrase has stuck in people's minds through time because theater is a prominent medium in society; whether it's an amphitheater in ancient Rome or Broadway in New York City, crowds of people are drawn to the theater every day.

The theater appeals to people for many different reasons. Some attend the theater to escape from the harsh realities of life for a little while. While sitting in a dark auditorium and watching trials and disputes played by live actors in front of you, it is very easy to forget your own problems. Other people find the theater simply entertaining. Plays and musicals involve audiences because they stimulate the senses and the mind. And some people go to the theater as a social event.

But theater is not only something to be watched. For many people, theater is their life. Every day, more and more people are becoming actors and actresses in hopes of becoming rich and famous. And for some people, that dream actually comes true. Many actors join the world of theater for their love of expressing themselves through their bodies, the tools of the trade. Nothing can compare to that adrenaline rush an actor gets just before he or she steps on stage in front of hundreds of people who all have their eyes focused on him or her, and the applause of an audience is all the gratitude some actors need to feel appreciated.

Many people don't realize that theater goes beyond the actors though, and that is where they are deceived. Sometimes the technical aspect of a production is more interesting than the acting is. A Broadway production can have a set with more complicated plans than a skyscraper building. Shows like "Phantom of the Opera" can have over twenty major trap doors and more than ninety minor ones. There are dozens of people in charge of sound, lighting, props, and costumes that no one ever sees or thinks about when sitting in the audience. There is just that wonderful feeling that these things just magically happen; no one seems to be responsible.

The theater is an art that will live on for a long time to come, as long as people take the time to support it. The magic of a show that enthralls most viewers, though, is a culmination of the hard work, time, and dedication of many people who never get credit for their actions. But Shakespeare was right because, for many people in the theater, all the world is a stage.

"All the World's a Stage"

All the world is indeed a stage. And we are the performers. Everything we do in life is a production, and we must constantly perform our best because, in life, there are no rehearsals. Each of us performs on a separate stage, some for a larger audience than others. But each performance, regardless of the size of the audience, is of equal importance, and each performer must meet the standard of life's most important critic—himself.

As a high school student, I often find that there exists much pressure to perform: pressure to perform academically, pressure to perform in sports, pressure to perform in social situations, and countless others. Furthermore, there are many individuals for whom I constantly must perform. At this juncture in life, parents, teachers, friends, and others comprise what I often perceive as an overwhelmingly large audience, which is sometimes overly critical.

As I grow older, I am learning to accept new responsibilities, and I find that my role in life is changing. Often in life, we cannot constantly adhere to a routine performance; sometimes we must improvise. The improvisation, or adjustment to new responsibility, is often difficult though of critical importance to a successful production. In life, I have come to expect the unexpected and have done my best to deal with new situations. As performers, we must not allow tragedy, depression, and self-doubt to unnerve us. Instead, we must cope, adjust, and continue to perform.

Throughout my performance I have received evaluation from many critics, some of which I have taken better than others. No matter how many critics we have, we should remind ourselves that we are our most important critics, for of life's performance we will make the ultimate evaluation. Even though all the world's a stage, each of us need be concerned with only one performance.

Analysis

The first essay stumbles at the beginning: The introduction has a central idea, but it is not well expressed and there is no coherence in the reference to ancient Rome. This essay reads like a first draft, and perhaps the writer was pressed for time. It would be improved not only in revision of the opening paragraph but also in the transitions. This writer begins too many sentences with *and* or *but*, and the language is not always fluent or precise. The writer, however, does establish organization and some unity in the opening of the second paragraph: "The theater appeals to people for many different reasons."

The writer also shows skill in development by moving from the role of theater for audiences to its importance for participants. The concluding sentence also works well because it relates the major part of the essay to a fresh meaning of the quote. In this case, a good conclusion rescues an essay with a weak introduction.

The second essay is effective because of the exceptional way in which the writer developed the topic as an extended metaphor. The essay is brief, but it is absolutely focused; every detail supports the central idea, the comparison of one's life to a dramatic performance. The writer has maintained a consistent point of view and has developed the topic in a creative way.

EVALUATING COMPOSITION

Every student has seen on a paper or an essay test the comment "develop this point more." The Regents rubric on page 229 is a reminder that one of the most important criteria in evaluating essays for class or for an exam is the extent to which <u>the topic has been developed</u> to achieve the writer's purpose. Simply to announce a subject and say that you have thoughts on that subject is not enough.

For any topic, the student must show skill in establishing a central idea and in creating an effective way to develop it. All compositions must be unified and expressed in fluent and precise language, and they must follow the conventions of standard written English. (See Guide to Standard Written English beginning on page 161.)

PREPARING FOR ESSAY EXAMS

Nearly all the writing you have done, both personal and for school, serves as preparation. Just as an athlete or musician practices regularly in order to have the skills to draw on in a performance, high school students are developing their skills whenever they compose written responses. Reflect on what you know your strengths and weaknesses are. To review, go over the essays and exams you have written in high school; note what is consistently strong and what needs revision; review carefully your teachers' comments.

Good writers are also readers. Read good writing, observe what makes it effective, emulate it, and imitate for practice what you admire. In serious magazines and in the editorial pages, letters to the editor, and Op-Ed sections of newspapers you can often find good essays of argument on current topics. (See also Recommended Reading on page 215 for suggested works and authors of nonfiction.)

To succeed in any assigned task, you need to know what is expected and how you will be evaluated. Review the Regents exam scoring guides, which describe the criteria for scoring the written responses.

WRITING ON TIMED EXAMINATIONS

If you are writing an essay for an examination, you do not have time for extensive preparation, but you can learn to condense the kind of thinking and notetaking you do for course assignments into a process for planning an examination response. How to begin?

Gather Your Ideas

First, be sure you understand the task or the meaning of the topic. One way to do that is to rephrase the question into a topic assertion. This may not be original, but if a restatement of the question serves as a topic sentence for your introduction and gets you started—use it! You may not use such statements in your final essay, but the fact that you can express them for yourself means you understand what the question expects or that you have something to say about the topic

If you are creating your own topic, be sure you know what you want to say about it. This may seem obvious, but only when you sketch or outline can you be sure you have sufficient material for an essay. Use the brainstorming techniques you have learned in class or workshops. For example, if you have practiced "freewriting" in the past or have written journal entries as a way of developing ideas, take a few minutes to address the topic in that way, without regard to organization or "getting it absolutely right." Similarly, you can just note down in words or phrases everything the prompt brings to mind. It is better to note more ideas than you can use than to discover after twenty-five minutes that you have too few.

Organize

Second, take a few minutes to make a plan or outline. All essay writing requires this step. Do not leave it out, even on the SAT, in which you have only 25 minutes for the essay. The outline may consist of only phrases or a brief list to remind you of the points you want to make. Consider possible lines of argument. That is, answer for yourself the questions "How can I prove that? What information in the text (if given) can I quote or paraphrase as evidence? How can I show or persuade someone who is interested in what I have to say? What do I know or believe that will make my discussion convincing?" Finally, decide on the order that is best: chronological? sequence of cause and effect? order of importance or intensity? (Common methods of developing ideas in essays are reviewed, with examples, in Reading Nonfiction, Chapter 4.)

Compose

The essays you write for the Regents exam and for the SAT are, of course, "tests." You are not being asked to demonstrate acquired knowledge so much as you are to demonstrate how well you can communicate in standard written English what you understand about the given subjects and texts or what you think about a particular issue. What is being assessed is your ability to articulate a controlling idea and support it with reasons and appropriate examples. On the Regents exam, you must also be able to work from given texts and write for clearly defined purposes and audiences.

Concentrate on good development—not a finished product. An essay that reveals critical thinking and coherence and effectively develops several appropriate examples or reasons with command of sentence variety and language will receive a high score even if it remains somewhat unfinished or lacks a formal conclusion. Remember, on the SAT optional essay you are writing what will be evaluated as a first draft. Regents essays are viewed as somewhat more "finished," but those too are understood to have been written in only one sitting.

Edit as You Go

The time you take in planning is also well spent because on-demand writing requires you to edit and revise as you compose your response. If you still make spelling errors in commonly used words, make a deliberate effort to look for those errors and correct them on the exams. A few neatly corrected spelling or usage errors are not only acceptable, they reveal the writer's ability to edit his or her own work. (See Chapter 9 on Grammar and Usage and Chapter 10 on Punctuation.)

USING SYNONYMIES TO ENHANCE YOUR WRITING

Included in the expectations for any well-written essay is use of language that is vivid and appropriate; the rubrics for scoring Regents essays include "use of original, fluent, and precise language." The term *synonymy* refers to words that can be grouped according to general meaning; that is, they all denote or describe a specific instance of a general concept. Reviewing and creating synonymies will help you develop the vivid and precise language characteristic of good writing. Below are some examples of synonymies for commonly used but often vague or overused expressions.

to cause

bring about	generate	originate	raise
create	give rise to	persuade	spawn
effect	incite	produce	
engender	invent	promote	
excite	lead to	provoke	

to change

adapt	develop	grow	revise
adjust	deviate	mature	rework
alter	differ	metamorphose	transform
amend	digress	modify	turn (into)
become	diverge	modulate	vary
convert	diversify	mutate	
correct	edit	progress	
depart	evolve	remake	

to look upon someone/something

analyze	discern	judge	scrutinize
appraise	dismiss	observe	stereotype
censure	distinguish	perceive	summarize
classify	esteem	ponder	typecast
conclude	evaluate	reckon	value
condemn	honor	regard	view
consider	hypothesize	review	watch
deem	infer	ruminate	

121

to look down upon someone/something

belittle	diminish	frown upon	ridicule
censure	discredit	have disdain for	scorn
condescend	disfavor	hold inferior	shame
condemn	disgrace	humiliate	shun
degrade	disparage	ignore	taunt
demote	disregard	jeer	vilify
depreciate	show disrespect	mock	
deride	embarrass	rebuke	
devalue	find fault with	reject	

bad

abhorrent	detrimental	inequitable	scandalous
atrocious	devilish	infamous	scurrilous
awful	dirty	inferior	shameless
base	disquieting	loathsome	sinful
belittling	evil	malevolent	sinister
blemished	false	malign	slanderous
calumnious	fiendish	marred	sour
catastrophic	foul	mean	spiteful
contemptible	fraudulent	merciless	spoiled
corrupt	grotesque	monstrous	squalid
counterfeit	hateful	nefarious	tasteless
criminal	heinous	negative	terrible
cruel	hellish	notorious	unethical
damaged	hideous	odious	unscrupulous
deceptive	horrible	ominous	vile
defective	horrid	perverse	villainous
defiled	horrific	putrid	wicked
delinquent	immoral	rotten	
depraved	imperfect	ruthless	
despicable	impish	scabrous	

effective

capable	dazzling	forceful	persuasive
cogent	dramatic	impressive	potent
commanding	effectual	influential	powerful
compelling	efficacious	lively	strong
convincing	emotional	moving	telling

caring

affectionate	devoted	giving	selfless
benevolent	doting	goodhearted	sympathetic
bountiful	empathetic	humane	tender
compassionate	empathic	kind	thoughtful
concerned	fond	loving	warm
courteous	generous	philanthropic	warmhearted

due to

as a consequence of	because of	from	on account of
as a result of	by reason of	in light of	resulting from
because	caused by	in view of	
	following from	induced by	

hard/difficult

arduous	fatiguing	intricate	strong
bitter	galling	labyrinthine	tiresome
challenging	grievous	mighty	toilsome
complex	grim	oppressive	tough
daunting	harsh	relentless	unattainable
demanding	Herculean	resistant	unbending
enigmatic	impenetrable	rigorous	uncompromising
esoteric	impossible	serious	unyielding
exacting	impregnable	severe	wearisome
exhausting	inflexible	sharp	
exigent	insurmountable	strenuous	

sad/depressing (depressed)

abject	dejected	forsaken	somber
aching	desolate	gloomy	sorrowful
aggrieved	despairing	joyless	tormenting
bereaved	disconsolate	lugubrious	tragic
bereft	discontent	melancholy	unhappy
bleak	distraught	miserable	upset
blue	distressing	morose	wretched
cheerless	down	painful	
dark	forlorn	saddening	

same

akin	compatible	generic	parallel
alike	conformable	homogeneous	photocopy
allied	conforming	identical	related
analogous	congruent	imitation	replica
associated	consonant	indiscernible	same
clone	copy	inseparable	shared
cognate	correspondent	interchangeable	similar
collective	corresponding	joint	synonymous
common	duplicate	like	tantamount
comparable	equal	matching	twin
comparative	equivalent	mutual	

A GLOSSARY OF TERMS FOR WRITING*

anecdote   A brief story or account of a single experience, often biographical, which illustrates something typical or striking about a person. Anecdotes, like parables, are effective as vivid, specific examples of a general observation or quality.

argument   The development of reasons, examples to support a thesis; narrowly, to outline a position on an issue or problem with the intent to clarify or persuade. Argument is also used in a broad sense to refer to the way a writer develops any topic.

audience   For the writer this term refers to the intended reader. Awareness of an audience determines, for example, what the writer may assume a reader already knows, level of diction, and tone.

coherence   A piece of writing has coherence when the logical relationship of ideas is evident and convincing. In a coherent discussion, statements and sections follow one another in a natural, even inevitable way. A coherent discussion hangs together; an incoherent one is scattered and disorganized.

cohesion   This refers to the grammatical and usage aspects of writing. **Cohesive** writing means that the connection of ideas within each sentence and at the paragraph level is clear and that the writing follows the conventions of standard written English.

controlling idea   This refers to the writer's thesis or main idea. It asserts what the writer has to say <u>about</u> the topic or question.

conventions   These are the "rules" or common guidelines for punctuation, spelling, and usage.

description   The expression in words of what is experienced by the senses. Good description recreates what is felt, seen, heard—sensed in

---

*Many of the terms in this glossary are also discussed in Chapter 4, Reading Prose.

any way. We also use the term describe to mean *identify, classify, characterize,* even for abstract ideas. Description permits readers to recreate the subject in their own imaginations.

development   This refers to the choice and elaboration of examples, reasons, or other details that support an argument or illustrate a controlling idea. (See also the rubric for scoring Regents essays in Appendix D.)

diction   This refers to word choice. Diction may be formal or informal, complex or simple, elegant or modest, depending on the occasion and the audience. The language we use in casual conversation is different from the language we use in formal writing. The good writer uses language that is varied, precise, and vivid; the good writer has resources of language to suit a wide range of purposes.

exposition   The development of a topic through examples, reasons, details, which explain, clarify, show, instruct—the primary purpose of exposition is to convey information. Much of the writing assigned to students is referred to as expository writing: Through exposition you can demonstrate what you have learned, discovered, understood, appreciated.

focus   This refers to the way a writer contains and directs all the information, examples, ideas, reasons in an essay on the specific topic.

narrative   Because it tells a story, narrative has chronological order. Narrative method is commonly used in exposition when examples are offered in a chronological development.

position paper   A form of persuasive writing, a position paper is meant to generate support for an issue or cause; the essay is based on specific evidence that can be cited to support the writer's argument. A position paper may also evaluate solutions or suggest courses of action.

prompt   This refers to a set of directions for a writing task; may also be a quote or passage meant to stimulate a piece of writing.

tone   In writing, tone refers to the attitude of the writer toward the subject and/or toward the reader. Tone may range from *harsh and insistent* to *gentle and reflective.* There is as much variety of tone in writing as there is in human feeling. Some pieces, essays of opinion, for example, usually have a very distinct tone; other works, especially in fiction or personal expression, may have a more subtle and indirect tone. (See discussion of Tone on page 65 in Reading Prose and on page 86 in Reading Poetry.)

transition   Words or phrases used to link ideas and sections in a piece of writing. Common transitions include *first, second . . . in addition . . . finally; on the other hand, moreover, consequently, therefore.* Transitions make the development of an argument clear.

unity   In the narrowest sense, unity refers to focus: The ideas and examples are clearly related to the topic and to one another. In the largest sense, unity refers to a feature of our best writing: All elements—ideas, form, language, and tone—work together to achieve the effect of a complete and well-made piece.

Chapter 8

VOCABULARY

Formal vocabulary study may begin as early as kindergarten; associating meaning with different sounds begins virtually at birth. As all students have discovered, however, there always seem to be new words to learn. Every novel, essay, or newspaper article we read is likely to include some new expressions or unfamiliar words. Deliberately studying new words and preparing for tests on them is certainly one way to expand our vocabularies, and every serious student has developed a method for such study. But if you do not continue to use those new words—that is, read, speak, and write with them—they may be forgotten soon after the test.

The thousands of words you *know* were acquired through repeated use over time and through association with their contexts, that is, through reading and listening. As you study vocabulary words associated with a course in English, social studies, or science, you are learning them in a context, and you are also expanding your reading and writing vocabularies. Every word you study should create some kind of image for you: try to associate it with a phrase, an experience or feeling, an object or person, an action or incident. If you have no image, you do not truly know the word yet.

The vocabulary you are expected to know and use, and that will be assessed on the Regents ELA, the SAT, and the ACT exams, is the language of literary authors, essayists, historians, and scientists. On the Regents ELA exam, this means that your mastery of relevant vocabulary will be assessed through questions about the meanings of words within the extended reading comprehension passages. You will also be expected to understand how particular words or expressons establish tone and clarify an author's meaning in the texts for analysis. This shift in how vocabulary is assessed represents a shared goal of the Common Core aligned state exams (Regents, PARCC, SBAC) and the SAT and ACT. For high school students, this means less need to study exotic and unfamiliar vocabulary in isolation; rather, students will need to be able to understand—and use—what is called academic language.

In the next section, you will find examples of what is meant by academic language. At the end of the chapter, you will find three collections of words to review as well. The first represents words that have been tested on Regents exams over several years. The second is a list compiled by high school students from their reading of the Op-Ed pages of *The New York Times* and other sources. The third, from published book reviews, was also compiled by students. Each list offers the thoughtful reader and writer a rich source of vocabulary in current use.

ACADEMIC LANGUAGE

Academic language is the language you use to express understanding of texts in class discussion, lecture, and writing. It is the language of interpretation, analysis, evaluation, and explanation. This term also refers to the language of a particular subject or discipline: literature, history, biology, economics, art, and so on. Reviewing the glossaries of literary and poetic terms and the terms for writing is another way of strengthening your command of academic language.

Here is a list of **verbs**, followed by their noun and adjective forms, commonly used to express how nonfiction texts are written and how arguments are developed. You will recognize many of these terms from the list of What Writers Do at the beginning of Chapter 4.

allege	allegation	alleged, allegedly
analyze	analysis	analytic, analytically
apply	application	
argue	argument	argumentative
arrange	arrangement	
articulate		
assemble		
assert	assertion	assertive
assess	assessment	
associate	association	
assume	assumption	
categorize	category	categorical
cite	citation	
characterize	characterization	
claim	(a/the) claim	
clarify	clarification	
classify	classification	
compare	comparison	
compile	compilation	
complement	(a/the) complement	complementary
compose	composition	
comprehend	comprehension	comprehensive
conclude	conclusion	conclusive
construct	construct, construction	
contend	contention	contentious
contradict	contradiction	contradictory
contrast	contrast	contrasting
correlate	correlation	correlative
criticize	criticism	critical, critically
critique	(a/the) critique	

debate	(a/the) debate	debatable
deduce	deduction	deductive, deductively
defend	defense	defensive
define	definition	definitive
demonstrate	demonstration	demonstrative
derive	derivation	derivative
design	(a/the) design	
develop	development	
differentiate	differentiation	
discern	discernment	discerning
discover	discovery	
discuss	discussion	
distinguish	distinction	distinguished
elaborate	elaboration	elaborate, elaborately
emphasize	emphasis	
estimate	estimation	
evaluate	evaluation	
exaggerate	exaggeration	
examine	examination	
exclude	exclusion	
explain	explanation	
explore	exploration	exploratory
focus	(a/the) focus	
form	(a/the) form	formal, formally
formulate	formulation	
frame		
generalize	generalization	
highlight	highlight	
hypothesize	hypothesis	hyhpothetical
identify	identification	
illustrate	illustration	
imply	implication	
include	inclusion	inclusive
infer	inference	inferential, inferentially
influence	influence	influential
inquire	inquiry	
integrate	integration	
interpret	interpretation	interpretive
introduce	introduction	
investigate	investigation	
judge	judgment	judgmental, judgmentally
mean	meaning	meaningful
modify	modification	
observe	observation	
oppose	opposition	

organize	organization	
originate	origin	original
outline	(a/the) outline	
paraphrase	paraphrase	
persuade	persuasion	persuasive
predict	prediction	predictive
presume	presumption	presumptive
project	projection	
propose	proposition	
recall	recollection	
refer	reference	referential
report	report	
represent	representation	
respond	response	responsive
review	review	
select	(a/the) selection	selective, selectively
sequence	(a/the) sequence	sequential, sequentially
specify	specification	
speculate	speculation	speculative
state	statement	
structure	(a/the) structure	structural, structurally
suggest	suggestion	suggestive
summarize	summary	summarily
support	support	supportive
suppose	supposition	supposed, supposedly
symbolize	symbol	symbolic
synthesize	synthesis	
translate	translation	
utilize	utilization	
vary	variation	
verify	verification	

Note: The -ed (past participle) forms of all these verbs are also used as modifiers: *assembled, classified, identified*, and so on. The adjective/adverb forms listed previously are widely used as separate forms and some have differences in meaning from the verb and noun forms.

Here is a list of **nouns and adjectives** used to identify and describe rhetorical methods as well as a writer's tone and purpose:

abstraction	abstract
analogy	analogous
approach	
	appropriate
	approximate

argument	argumentative
aspect	
audience	
authenticity	authentic
background	
chronology	chronological
coherence	coherent
concision	concise
	concrete
consequence	consequentially
consistency	consistent, consistently
constancy	constant
context	contextually
credibility	credible
criterion/criteria	
detail	
diction	
dimension	
direction	direct
effect	effective
element	elemental
equivalence	equivalent
	essential
evidence	evident
example	
excerpt	
exercise	
expository	exposition
extract	extraction
fact	factual
factor	
feature	
	figurative, figuratively
fragment	
frequence	frequent
general	generally
graph	graphic
highlight	
image	
inclination	
indirection	indirect
intention	intentional
irony	ironic
irrelevance	irrelevant

131

literalness	literal, literally
logic	logical, logically
metaphor	metaphorical
method	*methodical
motivation	motivating
narration	narrative
narrator	
objectivity	objective
opinion	opinionated
order	ordered
origin	original
pattern	
perspective	
plagiarism	plagiarized
plan	
plausibility	plausible
point of view	
possibility	possible
primary	
priority	*prior
probability	probable
process	
profile	
prompt	
proposition	
purpose	purposeful
relevance	relevant
revision	revised
sequence	sequential
series	
signal	
significance	significant
source	
speaker	
specificity	specific
strategy	strategic
structure	
style	stylistic
subject	*subjective
subsequence	subsequent
substitution	substitute
succinctness	succinct
summary	
survey	

technique	technical
theme	
thesis	
tone	
topic	*topical
transition	
uniqueness	unique
validity	valid
variation, variety	varied
viewpoint	
voice	

*Note: As in the list of verbs, some nouns and adjectives with a common derivation may have differences in meaning.

Throughout *Let's Review*, you will find sources of what is meant by academic language, along with glossaries of terms for fiction, nonfiction, poetry, and writing. Your ability to recognize examples of various literary and rhetorical elements strengthens your comprehension; you will also be expected to use them appropriately when you write essays of argument and text analysis.

UNFAMILIAR AND ARCHAIC LANGUAGE

Here is some of the vocabulary you will encounter as you read and discuss what are considered authentic or historically significant texts. Some of the words are familiar in their current use; but, the meanings offered here are from texts as early as the 16th century, including works of Shakespeare, and are also found in 18th, 19th , and early 20th century writings in English.

Verbs

address	to consider, think about, speak to
apprise	to give verbal or written notice
behold	to observe with care, witness
breach	to break through
discover	to learn, to disclose
dispose	to be inclined
divine	to guess, figure out, foresee
endeavor	to try, attempt a task or challenge
fashion	to form or make something

forbear	to pause, delay, avoid voluntarily or decline to do something
have	to prefer, think, believe, consider, think about
peruse	to read or examine with care
relish	to enjoy, take delight in
smart	to cause pain
suffer	to put up with, tolerate
thirst	to have an intense desire for something
thwart	to oppose, frustrate or defeat
want	to fail, be deficient or lacking
witness	to see by personal presence, observe directly
wreak	to revenge, throw or dash with violence

Nouns

appendages	arms and legs
appetite	desire, interest
ardor	passion
aught, naught	anything, nothing
conveyance	vehicle
countenance	look, appearance
dominion	area of authority, knowledge or power
eloquence	artful, expressive speech
faculties	senses, aptitudes, abilities
fashion	a distinctive or habitual manner
forebearance	patience, tolerance
grievance	suffering, distress; grudge, resentment
humor	temperament
idleness	unimportance, uselessness, emptiness
infirmity	weakness, disorder; personal failing
justice	accuracy, wisdom
labors	efforts
nature	disposition, inherent quality
perusal	reading, consideration
petulance	irritability, contrariness
rapture	extreme joy or pleasure; passionate intensity
sensibility	acuteness of perception; capacity to feel or perceive
temper	disposition of mind
vanity	emptiness, untruth, unfruitful labor
virtue	strength of character, bravery, valor; moral excellence

Adjectives

base	corrupt, vile
bumptious	arrogant, brash
clever	intelligent, skilled
familiar	agreeable in conversation, not formal or distant
idle	unimportant, trivial
imbued	tinged, affected with
infirm	weak of mind, body, or will
petulant	pert, wanton, sour in temper
prevailing	having effect; persuading, succeeding
puerile	childish, trifling, weak
rough	coarse in manners, uncivil; terrible, dreadful
sensible	having perception by the mind or the senses
sober	serious, calm, subdued
stout	bold, intrepid, brave
sublime	high in excellence, lofty, grand
wholesome	contributing to health of mind, conducive to good

STUDYING NEW WORDS

Learning in Context

Even the most diligent student cannot reasonably expect simply to memorize—out of context—the hundreds, even thousands, of words on Regents and SAT lists. Recent studies also confirm that vocabulary study confined to lists of words without a context or pattern of association—as with a particular work of literature, for example—does not result in long-term retention. Moreover, the practice of recording dictionary definitions alone gives only general and sometimes misleading information about the meaning and correct use of words. Learning words means learning their precise meanings, connotations, and appropriate context.

Unless you are working with an unabridged dictionary, which often includes illustrative examples in sentences or phrases, you are likely to find in a desk dictionary only brief definitions, general in nature, and possibly a list of synonyms. This limited information is valuable as a *reference,* especially if you are reading a passage and need to know a word's meaning in order to understand the passage. Learning the full meaning of unfamiliar words, however, requires more active study. In the sections below you will find recommendations for ways to prepare and organize your vocabulary study.

ROOTS AND PREFIXES FROM LATIN AND GREEK

Although English is certainly not derived from Greek and Latin only, familiarity with the Greek or Latin forms in English words is often useful to students taking vocabulary tests. Recognition of root meanings in particular may help you determine the correct answer for a word you may not be sure of. Even more important, however, is the value of knowing the Latin and Greek origins of English when you are first studying new words. When you are aware of the meanings of the individual parts of a word you often can form an image for it. Think of the Latin root *spect*, for example. This root means *look into, observe, behold* and, with variations in spelling *spec* and *spic,* is the base of many English words: *inspect, introspect, expect, respect, speculate, spectacle, spectacular, conspicuous*—and many others. Even the word *spy* is related to this Latin root.

When you are looking up words in the dictionary, do not skip over the etymology—the section that shows you in abbreviated form the origin and history of a word. Grouping words by related origin can be a very useful way to organize when you are studying large groups of new words; by using their common origin, you will learn to associate a new word with others you already know. It is the process of forming associations in meaning, forming images, and knowing contexts that permits you to learn efficiently—and to remember—the words you study. (Familiarity with roots and prefixes is also very helpful in understanding spelling patterns, as you will see in Chapter 11.)

Listed below, with examples, are many of the Latin and Greek roots found in English. (As you review the meanings of these roots, provide additional examples from your own knowledge; you should also guess about possible examples—then look them up in a dictionary to confirm your guess.) This process is a demonstration of what is meant by *active* vocabulary study. It means you are thinking about a word and associating it with others you know.

As you examine the list of Greek and Latin roots common in English, you should be struck by how familiar many of these forms are. You should also note that all these roots denote specific actions or ideas. Knowing the meanings of these elements as you study new words, or review familiar ones, will give you specific images or experiences to associate with them. This in turn will make the meaning of many words more vivid and easier to remember than will an abstract definition or list of synonyms alone.

LATIN ROOTS

Forms	Meaning	Examples
alter	other	altercation, alternative
ami (amicus)	friend	amiable, amicable, amity
amor	love	amorous, enamored
anima	breath, mind, spirit	animation, unanimous, inanimate, animosity
bell (bellum)	war	bellicose, belligerent, antebellum
cad (cadere), cid	to fall	decay, decadence, deciduous
cap, cip	contain	captivate, capacity, capable
capit (caput)	head	capital, capitol, recapitulate
cede, ceed, cess (cedere)	to move, yield	proceed, accede, exceed, precede, excess, success, procession
cept (capere)	to take, seize, hold	intercept, reception, accept
cid, cis (caedere)	to cut, kill	precise, incisive, homicide
clam, claim (clamare)	to cry, call out	exclaim, proclaim, clamor
clud, clus (claudere)	to shut, close	include, exclusion, recluse
cred (credere)	to believe, loan, trust	creditable, incredible, credulous
culp (culpa)	fault, guilt	culpable, exculpate
cur, curs (currere)	to run	course, cursor, current, incur, precursor, recur
dict (dicere)	to say, tell	dictator, diction, edict, predict
doc (docere)	to teach	doctor, docile, indoctrinate
duc, duct (ducere)	to lead	deduce, induction, conduct
err (errare)	to go, lead astray	error, erroneous, erratum
err (errer)	to travel, wander	errand, arrant, erratic
fac, fact, fect, fic (facere)	to make, do	affect, defect, effect, facsimile, factor, artificial, deficit
fer (ferre)	to bear, carry	inference, offer, reference
fid (fidelitas)	faith, loyalty	infidel, perfidious, diffident
flect, flex (flectere)	to bend	reflex, reflection, flexibility
flu, fluct, flux (fluere)	to flow	affluent, fluctuation, fluent, influence, influx
fund (fundare) (fundus)	to base, bottom	(to) found, fundamental, profundity
fus (fundere)	pour	effusive, foundry, fusion
gen (genus) (genare)	kind, sort, birth, to beget	genre, heterogenous, genetic, generate, progenitor, genocide
grad, gress (gradus)	to walk, go, stage or step	digress, graduate, progress, grade, gradient, retrograde
greg (gregis)	flock, herd, group	egregious, gregarious, integrate
her, hes (haerere)	to cling, stick	adhesive, coherence, inherently
ject, jet (jacere)	to throw	inject, projection, jettison
jud, jur, jus (jus)	to judge; to swear just, right; law	abjure, adjudicate, prejudge, jury, justification, perjury
lat (latus)	borne, carried	correlative, related, superlative
leg (legis, lex)	law	legality, legislative
locus	place	location, locale, locomotive

137

locu, loqu (loqui)	to speak	eloquent, loquacious, soliloquy,
locutor	speaker	interlocutor, locution, obloquy
lude (ludere)	to play	interlude, ludicrous, prelude
mit, mitt, mis,	to dispatch, send,	emit, permit, remit, submissive,
miss (mittere)	to let go	commission, missile, permission
mob, mot (movere)	to move	demote, motivate, promote,
		commotion, mobility
mor, mort (mortis)	death	immortal, mortality, mortified
ped (pedis)	foot	expeditious, impede, pedestrian
pel, puls (pellere)	to drive, push	compel, dispel, impulse,
		repel, compulsive, repellent
pend, pens	to hang, weigh, pay	append, compensate, dependent,
(pendere)		impending, pension, pensive
ple, plet (plere)	to fill	complete, complement, deplete
plen (plenus)	full	plentiful, replete
pon, pos, posit	to place, put	component, depose, propose,
(ponere)		juxtapostion, impose, opponent
port (portare)	to carry	comport, deportment,
		purport, portable, portfolio
pot, poten,	to be able	impossibility, omnipotent,
poss (posse)		potential
rad (radius)	root, spoke (wheel)	eradicate, radical, radiation
rect, reg (regula)	right, straight	direction, rectified, regal
(regire)	to guide, rule	regimen, regime
rupt (rumpere)	to break, burst	disrupt, corrupt, interruption
sat (satis)	enough	dissatisfy, insatiable, saturated
sci (scire)	to know	conscience, omniscient,
		prescience, scientific
scrib, script (scribere)	to write	describe, inscription, scripture
sect (sectare)	to cut	dissect, intersection
secu, sequ (sequi)	to follow	consequence, obsequious,
		sectarian, sequel
sed, sid, sess	to sit	dissidence, possess, residual,
(sedere)		sedation, sedentary
sent, sens (sentire)	to feel	consensus, insensitive, sentient
son (sonus)	sound	consonant, dissonance, sonic,
		sonogram, sonority, unison
spec, spect, spic	to look at, observe	auspicious, conspicuous, expect,
(spectare)		inspect, respect, spectacular
spir, spirit	to breathe	inspiration, respiratory, spirit
sta, state, stit (stare)	to stand	constitute, instability, obstacle,
		stability, status
strict, string	to draw tight	constrict, restriction, stringent
(stringere)		
sume, sump	to take	assume, consume, presumption
(sumere)		
tact, tang, ting,	to touch	contact, contiguous, intangible,
tig (tangere)		tactile, tangential

ten, tain (tenere)	to hold, keep	abstain, pertain, restrain, tenacious, untenable
tend, tens (tendere)	to reach, stretch	contend, intensity, portent, pretentious, tendency
tort (torque)	to twist	contortion, extort, tortuous
tract (trahere)	to draw, pull	distract, intractible, protracted, retraction
ver (veritas)	truth	aver, veracity, verification
vers, vert (vertere)	to turn	adverse, aversion, diversity, inadvertent, reversion, subvert, version, versification
vid, vis (videre) (video)	to see	evident, improvident, supervise, revision, visage, visionary
vit, viv (vivere) (viva)	to live; life	revival, survive, vivacious, unviable
vinc, vict (vincere)	to conquer	conviction, eviction, invincible
voc, voke (vocare)	to call	advocate, equivocal, invocation, provocative, revoke, vocation
volv, volu (volvere)	to roll, turn	convoluted, evolution, revolving

GREEK ROOTS

Forms	Meaning	Examples
anthrop	man, humankind	anthropocentric, misanthropist, philanthropy
arch	rule, ruler	anarchy, patriarchal
astr, astron	star	astronomical, disastrous
bio	life, living things	biography, microbiology
chron	time	anachronistic, chronic
cosm (kosmos)	order, universe	cosmic, microcosm
demo	among the people	democratic, demography
gen	birth, race	genesis, progeny
gno, gnosis	know	agnostic, diagnosis, gnomic
gram, graph	write, writing	epigrammatic, biography
log, logue	word, reason	analogy, illogical, prologue
lect, lex	language, speak	dialect, lexical
lysis	dissolution, destruction	catalyst, paralysis
metr	measure	diametric, metrical
morph	form, shape	amorphous, metamorphose
mne, mnes	memory, remember	amnesty, mnemonic
onym	a name	eponymous, synonym
opti, optic	eye, sight	optical, synopsis
path (pathos)	feeling, suffering	apathy, empathetic, pathetic
ped	child	pediatrician, pedagogy, pedantic
phon	sound	euphony, phonetic, symphonic

Prefixes are units of one or two syllables that are not words in themselves but that have distinct meanings. The addition of a prefix to the beginning of an existing word (what is called a *stem* or *root)* creates a word with an additional meaning. The spelling variations for many of the prefixes listed below are reminders that in English the spelling of a prefix will be altered to match the root to which it is attached. For example, *ad,* which means *to* or *toward*, is attached to many words in English; the *d* often changes to the first letter of the word to which it is added, making the resulting new forms easier to pronounce. (See the examples below as well as those in Chapter 11 — Spelling.)

LATIN PREFIXES

Forms	Meaning	Examples*
a, ab, abs	away, from	abdicate, absence, abstraction
a, ad (ac, af, al, etc.)	to, toward	absent, acclimate, adherent, alliteration, assign, attribution
ambi	both, around	ambiance, ambiguous, ambidextrous, ambivalent
ante	before	antebellum, antecedent
bene, ben	good, well	beneficial, beneficent, benign
circum	around	circumnavigate, circumstances, circumlocution
co (col, com, cor)	together	coincidence, collaboration, commiserate, correspondence
contra, contro, counter	against, opposite	contradiction, controversy, counterfeit, counteract
de	away, down, from	deduction, deterrence, deviate
dis (di, dif)	apart, away; not; separate	disavow, disdain, disappear, disregard, disperse, discern
en (var. of in)	make, put into	enable, enhance, encourage
equ, equi	equal, even	equable, equanimity, equivalence, equivocate
ex (e, ef)	away from, out	efface, effective, ejection, exodus, expiration
in (il, im, ir)	in, within	immersion, impending, innate
in (il, im, ir)	not, without	illegible, imprudent, incognito
inter	among, between	intercede, intermediary, interim
magn	great	magnificence, magnanimous
mal	bad, evil	malevolent, malice, malefactor, malign, malignant
ob (oc, of, op)	to, toward; against; over; totally	objection; obdurate, obnoxious; obfuscate; obsolete, obliterate
omni	all	omnipotent, omniscient
per	completely; through	perceive, perdurable, pervasive
post	after	posterity, posthumous

pre	before, in advance	pre-empt, preclude, premonition
pro	before, forward	proclivity, prodigy, profane
re	again	reiterate, reverberate, retort, revise, remember
retro	backward	retrogression, retroactive
se	apart, aside	secession, sedition, select
sub (suf, sup, sus)	from below, under	subsidize, substandard, suffuse, suppress, sustenance
super	above, over	supercilious, superfluous, supervise, supersede
tra, trans	across, beyond	transgression, transcend

GREEK PREFIXES

Forms	Meaning	Examples
a, an	not, without	agnostic, anarchy, apathetic
ana	back, backward according to; through	anagram, anachronistic, anapest analogy, analysis
ant, anti	against, opposite	antipathy, antithesis, antipodes
auto	self	autonomous, autocracy
cata	down	cataclysm, catalyst, catastrophe
dia	through, between	dialect, dialogue, diameter
dys	bad, ill, difficult	dysfunctional, dyspeptic
epi	upon	epicenter, epigram, epilogue
eu	good, well	euphemism, euphoria, eugenics
hetero	different	heterodox, heterogeneous
homo	alike, same	homogeneous, homonym
macro	large, long duration	macrocosm, macroscopic
meta, met	after, beyond; changed	metaphor, metaphysical, metamorphosis
micro	small	microscope, microbe
mon, mono	one, single	monotheism, monolith
pan	all, complete	panacea, pandemonium
pro	before; favorable	prophecy; propitiate
proto	first, primary	protagonist, prototype
sym, syn	together, with	symmetry, synergy, synopsis

* When you review the lists for study at the end of the chapter you will readily see how many words in English are formed with these prefixes. Use those lists to add to the examples offered here.

Here is the first group of vocabulary words from the Regents exams list on page 149. Note how many are formed from the Greek or Latin prefixes reviewed on the previous pages.

abdicate	**ad**monish	amorphous	**as**pire
aberrant	**ad**versity	**ana**chronistic	assay
abhorrent	**af**flict	**an**ecdotes	astute
abridgment	agrarian	animation	**as**ylum
absolve	allot	**ap**pease	atrocious
acclaim	allure	**ap**prehend	audacity
accost	ally	arbitrator	**auto**nomous
accredit	**alter**cation	archaic	avarice
acme	amass	ardent	**a**verse
acquiesce	**ambi**ance	armistice	**a**version
acquittal	**ambi**dextrous	**ar**ray	avidly
adage	**ambi**guous	**ar**rogantly	azure
adhere	**ambi**valent	ascendancy	
adjunct	amnesty	ashen	

In many of these examples, the meaning of the original prefix has been absorbed into the meaning of the entire word, in **adage** and **allot**, for example. The highlighted prefixes illustrate, however, how extensively Greek and Latin forms are found in English.

A NOTE ON SYNONYMS AND USING A THESAURUS

As thoughtful students and careful writers know, synonyms are rarely equivalents. Synonyms are words closely related in meaning to a given word, but they should not be considered equally interchangeable with it.

Here is a list of synonyms for **acquiesce** that you might gather from a thesaurus:

accede	capitulate	concur	permit
accept	come to terms	conform	submit
agree to	with	consent	surrender
allow	comply with	give in	yield
assent	concede	grant	

This list is very helpful in enriching your understanding of the word, especially because it includes several terms that emphasize that there is a sense of giving in, of reluctance, in **acquiesce**. The closest synonyms in this list are *accede, come to terms with, conform, give in, yield. Capitulate, submit,* and *surrender* accurately reflect the connotation of the word, but they denote a more forceful sense of defeat than does *acquiesce*. The others, *accept, agree to, concur, consent, permit*, are less precise because they reflect only the general meaning and do not denote the sense of reluctance and the lack of enthusiam inherent in **acquiesce**.

Learning to distinguish among variations in meaning and context is an important part of developing your vocabulary. It is also essential to the craft of good writing. In Chapter 6, Writing About Literature, and Chapter 7, Writing on Demand, you will find several *synonymies,* which are words grouped by general meaning or connotation. The purpose of the *synonymies* is to help you develop precision and variety in your own writing. You should review those as part of your vocabulary study as well.

ORGANIZING VOCABULARY STUDY

Another way to work with lists such as the ones at the end of this chapter is to *sort* them, much as you would sort playing cards. Depending on the card game you are playing, you might sort a hand by suit, by numerical sequence, or by kind. You can sort a group of words in various ways as well: by part of speech, by connotation, by human or abstract qualities, and so on. Many students create their own flash cards for the words they study, which makes sorting in various ways easy.

Here are some suggestions for how you might sort the first group of words from the Regents list (page 149). First, sort by part of speech. In the list below, the *verbs* are printed in bold type:

VERBS

abdicate	adversity	anecdote	asylum
aberrant	**afflict**	animation	atrocious
abhorrent	agrarian	**appease**	audacity
abridgment	**allot**	**apprehend**	autonomous
absolve	allure	arbitrator	avarice
acclaim	**ally**	archaic	averse
accost	altercation	ardent	aversion
accredit	**amass**	armistice	avidly
acme	ambiance	**array**	azure
acquiesce	ambidextrous	arrogantly	
acquittal	ambiguous	ascendancy	
adage	ambivalent	ashen	
adhere	amnesty	**aspire**	
adjunct	amorphous	**assay**	
admonish	anachronistic	astute	

143

Then classify the group of verbs further as either *transitive* or *intransitive;* that is, according to the nature of the action they denote and the nature of the objects, if any, they take. When you look up these words in a dictionary, they will be identified as *v.i.* or *v.t. Transitive verbs* (*v.t.*) take a direct object; the action is directed from the subject to an object. For example, "She *admonished* (scolded, warned) the unruly child" and "King Midas *amassed* (accumulated) a fortune in gold." *Direct objects,* of course, may be persons and living creatures, or they may be things, even abstractions: "She quickly *apprehended* the danger she was in."

Intransitive verbs (*v.i.*) denote actions that are contained within the subject or that signify what we call states of being: "He *adhered* strictly to his ethical principles." *Adhere* connotes a state of mind, an attitude.

The distinction between transitive and intransitive action is not always easily made, but one way to demonstrate the difference is to make an active statement passive. For example, we can reverse the statement "She admonished the child" and turn it into "The child was admonished by her." The statement above about King Midas can be expressed in the passive as "A fortune in gold was amassed by King Midas." Although transitive actions may be reversed in this way, intransitive actions do not reverse. For example, the sentence "The principles were adhered by him" has no meaning. Some verbs may function both as transitive and intransitive. A simple example is the verb *to sink*: "The small sailboat sank during the heavy storm" (*v.i.*), but "The submarine fired a torpedo that sank the enemy battleship." (*v.t.*).

Most verbs in this first group are transitive, so it would be useful to sort them by the kinds of objects they take; that is, whether they denote actions directed at persons or at things and abstractions. You would, of course, note this information as you look up each unfamiliar word in a dictionary. Here is the list of verbs further sorted:

ACTIONS DIRECTED AT PERSONS

to **absolve** (free from, relieve) someone of guilt or responsibility

to **acclaim** (praise, honor) a person's performance, action, or work

to **accost** (approach, confront) someone

to **admonish** (caution, scold) someone for misbehavior or inaction

to **afflict** (burden, attack) someone with suffering or illness

to **appease** (conciliate) a person, a nation, or a government

to **apprehend** (catch, capture) a suspect or a criminal

ACTIONS DIRECTED AT THINGS OR ABSTRACTIONS

to **abdicate** (relinquish, abandon) a throne, a responsibility

to **accredit** (certify, recognize) a school or university, the value of an idea

to **allot** (distribute, assign) funds, resources

to **amass** (gather, accumulate) a fortune, an army

to **append** (add, match) a section, passage, body of information

to **apprehend** (understand, comprehend, capture) an idea, a concept

to **articulate** (verbalize, clarify, explain) ideas, feelings, understanding

to **array** (arrange) a display, a number of objects

to **assay** (measure, evaluate) a task, a situation

to **assert** (declare, claim, affirm, profess) ideas, an opinion, a judgment

INTRANSITIVE ACTIONS

to **acquiesce** (give in to, agree reluctantly) in demands of others

to **adhere** (hold, cling to, comply) to demands or to principles

to **ally** (join, support) with another person, group, or nation

to **aspire** (strive, seek) to a goal, an achievement

For purposes of study, these verbs could be shuffled, and then resorted, by *connotation*. Which are generally positive in feeling and association, and which are negative? There are many words for which this is not a useful distinction, but appreciation of connotation is often essential to fully understanding the meaning of a word.

POSITIVE

absolve	accredit	ally
acclaim	adhere	aspire

NEGATIVE

abdicate	acquiesce	afflict
accost	admonish	appease

As you make your notes or compose your flash cards, be sure to include connotation if it is relevant. A dictionary usually does not define a word by its connotation; you must infer it from the meanings and examples offered.

NOUNS

The *nouns* are in bold type:

abdicate	**adversary**	anachronistic	aspire
aberrant	**adversity**	**anecdote**	**assay**
abhorrent	afflict	**animation**	assert
abridgment	affluent	appease	astute
absolve	agrarian	append	**asylum**
acclaim	allot	apprehend	atrocious
accost	**allure**	apprehensive	**audacity**
accredit	**ally**	**arbitrator**	autonomous
acme	**altercation**	archaic	**avarice**
acquiesce	amass	ardent	averse
acquittal	**ambiance**	**armistice**	**aversion**
adage	ambidextrous	**array**	avidly
adamant	ambiguous	arrogant	azure
adhere	ambivalent	articulate	
adjunct	**amnesty**	**ascendancy**	
admonish	amorphous	ashen	

As you look at a collection of nouns, try to group them in various ways based on the kinds of things or persons they name. Note that in this group only two, **adversary** and **arbitrator,** name persons. This list, however, includes several political or legal terms that would form a useful group for study:

acquittal	**arbitrator** (arbitration)
adversary (adversarial)	**armistice**
ally	**ascendancy**
amnesty	**asylum**

A small group of terms is related to literature:

abridgment	**adage**	**anecdote**

Other terms name attitudes or feelings. (Note the contrast in connotation here.)

POSITIVE

acclaim   **animation**

NEGATIVE

audacity   **aversion**   **avarice**

Finally, there are nouns that name forces, situations, conditions, and other concepts.

acme   **ambiance**   **allure**   **array**

ADJECTIVES

The *adjectives* are in bold type:

abdicate	adversary	**anachronistic**	aspire
aberrant	adversity	anecdote	assay
abhorrent	afflict	animation	assert
abridgment	**affluent**	appease	**astute**
absolve	**agrarian**	append	asylum
acclaim	allot	apprehend	**atrocious**
accost	allure	**apprehensive**	audacity
accredit	ally	arbitrator	autonomous
acme	altercation	**archaic**	avarice
acquiesce	amass	**ardent**	**averse**
acquittal	ambiance	armistice	aversion
adage	**ambidextrous**	array	avidly
adamant	**ambiguous**	**arrogant**	**azure**
adhere	**ambivalent**	articulate	
adjunct	amnesty	ascendancy	
admonish	**amorphous**	**ashen**	

Because adjectives modify—that is, qualify, limit, or describe—nouns, a useful way to group them is by the nature of what they describe. For example, some of the adjectives in the list above describe human behavior or *actions*:

aberrant   **abhorrent**   **atrocious**

(all strongly negative in connotation)

Several adjectives describe human *attitudes, feelings, aspects of character:*

NEGATIVE

adamant   ambivalent   arrogant

POSITIVE

ardent   astute   avid

Still others characterize *the way people appear or express themselves:*

ambiguous   ambivalent   apprehensive   averse

Language may be:

ambiguous   anachronistic   archaic

Two adjectives relate to color:

ashen   azure

One term, **ambidextrous,** describes a physical characteristic.

This particular group contains no adverb forms, but for many of the adjectives in the list, the adverb is formed by adding *-ly.* For example:

aberrantly	apprehensively	avidly
adamantly	astutely	
ambiguously	atrociously	

Reminder: If you prepare your own note cards for study, be sure to include all forms of the word. For example, your notes for **ambivalent** (adj.) would also include **ambivalence** (n.). This is how the lists of academic vocabulary on page 128 are organized.

These groups overlap and should be combined in different ways as you work through larger numbers of words. The process of sorting, or reshuffling, as new categories and associations occur to you is a very effective way to learn new words. Each time you sort, you are actively thinking about a word in a particular context and are associating it with other words; this process is essential to making a word a permanent part of your reading and writing vocabulary.

VOCABULARY FOR STUDY

Below are lists of words that have been collected from past Regents exams, Op-Ed pages, and book reviews. You will recognize many of them from the section on academic language.

Vocabulary from Regents Exams

abdicate	admonish	amorphous	aspire
aberrant	adversity	anachronistic	assay
abhorrent	afflict	anecdotes	astute
abridgment	agrarian	animation	asylum
absolve	allot	appease	atrocious
acclaim	allure	apprehend	audacity
accost	ally	arbitrator	autonomous
accredit	altercation	archaic	avarice
acme	amass	ardent	averse
acquiesce	ambiance	armistice	aversion
acquittal	ambidextrous	array	avid
adage	ambiguous	arrogantly	azure
adhere	ambivalent	ascendancy	
adjunct	amnesty	ashen	
badger	belied	blatant	breach
barrage	bemused	bleary	brevity
bask	benevolent	boisterous	
beguile	berate	brazen	
cache	charisma	commencement	converse
carnage	chasm	commiserate	convivial
celebrated	clandestine	conception	craven
chafe	clique	congeal	credence
chagrin	coalition	consecrate	crestfallen
charade	collate	constrict	cringe
dauntless	deified	desist	discreet
de facto	deluge	desolate	dissidence
debonair	delve	deter	dissuade
decrepit	demeaning	detest	divulge
deduce	denizen	diffuse	domain
deferred	depict	dilemma	dredge
deflect	deride	diminutive	dynamic
defunct	derogatory	discord	

eccentric	encore	envoy	euphoric
edify	endorse	equanimity	eviction
eject	endow	equilibrium	exemplary
elicit	enfeeble	equitable	exodus
elude	enhance	equivocal	exonerate
elusive	ensnare	eradicate	expedite
embroil	entail	erratic	exploitation
eminence	entreaty	escapade	exulted
facet	feasible	flail	fortitude
fallible	fiasco	fleeting	fortuitous
fanatic	fidelity	forage	fracas
fanfare	finesse	foreboding	frugal
farcical	finite	formidable	futility
garish	genuine	grate	guise
garrulous	geriatric	gratuity	guttural
gaudy	gesticulate	grievously	
genial	grapple	grisly	
hallowed	harrowing	heretical	homage
harangue	heinous	hinder	humid
idiosyncrasies	impertinent	indisputably	insomnia
ignoble	imprudent	induce	insubordinate
illuminate	inadvertent	infernal	insurgent
immutable	inaugural	infringe	inundated
impartial	incensed	ingenuity	invoked
impending	incessant	inherent	irate
imperative	incognito	inimitable	irksome
imperceptible	incompetent	innocuous	irrational
imperiled	incorrigible	insatiable	itinerant
imperious	indignant	insolent	
jeer	jovial	jut	
jocular	juncture		
lacerated	latent	lesion	lucrative
lackluster	lateral	lineage	lugubrious
lament	lavish	liquidate	lull
languorously	laxity	loquacious	

madcap	marauding	meticulous	mollify
maim	martial	militant	morose
malefactor	meager	misconstrue	mortify
malice	mediate	misgivings	mundane
malleable	melancholy	mitigate	muzzle
nefarious	niche	nostalgia	nuptial
negligible	nimble	notorious	nurture
nepotism	nonentity	nullification	
obliquely	omnipotent	optimum	override
obliterate	omniscient	oscillate	
obstinate	onslaught	oust	
oligarchy	opportune	ouster	
pacifism	perplexity	poise	profoundly
palatable	philanthropic	precariously	proponent
pandemonium	piety	precipice	protrude
parable	pinnacle	precludes	prowess
paraphrase	placid	prestige	proxy
penchant	plague	prevail	putrid
perjury	plausible	procrastinate	
perpetual	plight	prodigious	
qualms	quandary		
ramification	recalcitrant	reparation	revulsion
rampant	reciprocal	repercussion	roster
ramshackle	recoil	repress	rouse
rancid	recrimination	resolute	rue
rant	rectify	retort	ruinous
rapport	refute	revamped	russet
ravenous	reminiscent	reverberate	
sacrosanct	sheen	squalor	substantiate
salve	shortcomings	stalwart	subtlety
sanction	shrewd	stark	sullen
sanctity	singularly	stealthily	sumptuous
saunter	skeptical	strew	superfluous
scandalous	skulk	strut	suppress
scathing	sleek	subliminal	surcease
scrupulous	slipshod	submissive	surreptitious
scrutiny	smolder	subside	swagger
seedy	sporadic	subsidize	synopsis

tainted	throng	transient	trudge
tally	token	trauma	tumult
tawny	topple	traverse	
tenacity	transcend	trifling	
unassuming	unnerve	unpalatable	utilitarian
uncanny	unobtrusive	unscrupulous	
vanquish	verbatim	viable	
variance	verbose	vigilance	
vehement	veritable	virtually	
waive	whack	wrangle	
warily	wield	wrath	
weather (vb.)	wily	writhe	
yield			
zenith			

Vocabulary from Op-Ed Pages

a priori	ad hoc	amiss	arcane
abdicate	adamant	amorphous	archetype
aberration	addled	androgyny	archive
abrogation	aegis	annals	ardent
abysmal	affidavit	annotate	artifice
abyss	affront	anoint	ascribe
accede	aggrieved	antidote	assessment
acclimate	agnostics	antipathy	assimilate
accolade	albeit	apathy	assuage
accrue	alleviate	append	asylum
acrimonious	allude (to)	arbiter	au courant
actuary	amalgamation	arbitrage	audit
acumen	ambivalence	arbitrary	autonomous
barrage	berth	blighted	bureaucrats
beguile	besmirch	blunder	burgeoning
beleaguered	bias	brass (slang def.)	
benighted	bipartisan	brute (vb.)	
bereft	blatant	budgetary	

152

cacophony	civics	concubine	convocation
cajole	clandestine	condone	covet
callous	clerical	confrere	crafty
canard	coda	conspiratorial	craven
candor	coffer	constituent	credibility
canonical/canon	collusion	contemporaries	cul-de-sac
capitulate	compliant	contend	cupidity
cataclysmic	complicit	contender	curtail
caveat	compound (vb.)	contingent	cushy
censure	compulsion	conundrum	cynical
chasm	concede	convene	cynicism
chimera	conciliate	conversant	
circumspect	conciliatory	conversely	
daunting	demur	despot	dispirit
debase	demystify	deter	disposition
decadence	denounce	detract	disquieting
decibel	denuded	didactic	dissemble
decree	denunciation	disavow	disseminate
decry	deplorable	discernible	dissident
deferment	depredation	discourse	dissipate
defrocked	deprivation	discretion	diversity
defunct	derail	discretionary	don (vb.)
deluded	derangement	disenchantment	doting
demagogue	deregulation	disingenuous	Draconian
demise	deride	disjointed	
demonize	derisive	dispel	
earmark	enclave	equivocate	exorbitant
egregious	enfranchise	eradicate	expenditure
electorate	enmesh	erode	expostulate
elixir	ennobling	ethos	expunge
eminence	ennui	eugenics	exude
empathetic	envoy	eviscerate	
empathy	epitomize	exhort	
encapsulate	equanimity	exonerate	
fallacious	firebrand	forlorn	frothing
farcical	fiscal	formidable	furor
fedora	flounder (vb.)	formulate	fusillade (fig.)
feint	flummoxed	fray (n.)	futility
fiasco	fodder (fig.)*	frenetic	
finagle	folly	fritter (vb.)	

---

*In this case, consider the figurative meaning of the words.

gaffe	gaudy	gouging	gubernatorial
gag rule	gauge	grapple	guffaw
galvanize	gerrymander	grim	
garner	glut	grotesque	

habeus corpus	hapless	hectoring	hubris
hackneyed	harbor (vb.)	heresy	hyperbole
hamlet	heckle	hoosegow (slang)	

iconography	importune	indignity	insular
ideological	impunity	ineptitude	integrity
idiosyncratic	incendiary	infiltrate	interlocking
idyllic	incessant	infirmity	intransigence
ignominious	incipient	inflationary	inure
ilk	incite	infuse	invaluable
impede	incontrovertible	inherent	inviolate
imperil	incumbent	innuendo	irk
implement (vb.)	indefatigable	inquisitorial	irredentism
implicit	indigenous	insignia	

lacerate	largess	leery	lout
laconic	latent	leitmotif	lucid
lambaste	laureate	levitate	
languish	lebensraum	litany	

malady	maudlin	molder	mortar
malaise	megalomaniac	monolith	murky
malign	meritorious	morass	myopic
manifestation	meticulous	moratorium	
mantra	milieu	moribund	
martyr	mimesis	morose	

nadir	nexus	nuance	
nascent	nomadic		

obfuscate	odious	oppression	overweening
obsolescence	ominous	outlay	
obstreperous	omnipresent	overhaul	
oddity	oncology	overt	

palliative
panacea
pandering
paradox
paramount
parochial
parsimonious
partisan (adj.)
passel
pathology
patrician
pedantic
peevish
pejorative
penchant

perennial
peripheral
pernicious
peroration
perpetuate
perquisite
perversion
pillage
pinnacle
pious
pique
placable/placate
plaudits
plight
plummet

plunder
pogrom
polarization
polemic
polyglot
portend
pragmatism
prattle
preeminent
preempt
preclude
presage
probity
profound
progeny

prohibitive
proliferate
proliferation
propensity
protocol
provocation
prurience
psyche
pugnacity
pundit
purport
purvey/purveyor
pusillanimous
pyrotechnics

quagmire
qualm

quaver
quibble

quintessential

rabid (fig.)
rakish
rancor
rapacious
rapprochement
raucous
realpolitik

recidivism
reconcile
rectitude
rejoinder
relegate
reparations
replete

resolute
resonance
restorative
retributive
reverberate
reverence
revile

rhetoric
rifle (vb.)
rogue
rudimentary
ruse

salve (vb.)
sartorial
sashay
scion
scoff
scourge
seamy
self-effacing
sham
shaman
shore up
shudder

siphon
snare
snide
sobriquet
sophomoric
sordid
sorghum
sovereignty
spate
speculative
staggering
stagnation

staid
stark
staunch
steely eyed
stint
stipend
strident
stringent
stymie
subsidize
substantive
subterfuge

sullen
summarily
sumptuary
sunder
supersede
supplant
surfeit
swindle
sword of
  Damocles
sycophant
synergy

temporal
temporize
tenacity
tendentious

throng
thwart
torpor
totter

tout
transgression
transitory
treacherous

troupe
tsunami
turbulent

155

undergird   unduly   unilateral   unrelenting
undermine   unencumbered   universality   unscrupulous
undiluted   unfettered   unprecedented   usurp

vagaries   vestige   vigilante   volatile
venality   vexing   vilify   voyeurs
veracity   viable   visceral
verdant   victimize   vituperation

waffling   welter   writ
wallow   wheedling   writhe
wastrels   winnow   wrongheaded

xenophobia

zeal   zeitgeist

Vocabulary from Book Reviews

accolade   adumbrate   animus   arduous
accretion   adversity   annotate   arsenal
accrue   aesthetic   antipodes   ascetic
acerbic   albeit   aphrodisiac   asinine
acolyte   alluring   aplomb   aspire
acrimonious   amatory   apotheosis   attenuate
acumen   amiable   arbiter   austere
adage   amok   arbitrary   authorial
adduce   anapest   archaic
adherent   ancillary   ardor

banal   bemused   blight   boulevardier
barren   bestiality   blithe   bowdlerize
bathetic   bevy   bohemian   Byzantine
bedraggled   bifurcation   boorish

cache   chic   compendium   credo
cadence   clandestine   complicity   cribbed
canny   cleric   congenial   crotchety
catharsis   cloying   consign   cupidity
caveat   coffer   contend   curmudgeon
chafe   cohere   contrivance   cursory
charisma   coherence   copious
chastening   colloquial   counterpoise
chastise   compendious   covert

156

dash
daunting
debunk
deft
delineate
delude

demigod
denouement
deploy
despotic
detritus
devolve

dichotomy
didactic
discursive
dispense
dispossess
dither

divagation
divergence
droll
duplicity
dysfunctional
dystopia

eccentric
eclectic
edify
egregious
elegy
elocution
elucidate
enclave
encomium

ensconce
entreaty
envisage
epigraph
epitomize
equanimity
eradicate
Eros
eschew

esoteric
espouse
esthetic
ethereal
ethos
evangelical
evocative
exacerbate
exhort

exigency
existential
expansive
expatriate
expurgate
exultant

fabulist
facsimile
faction

farce
fervid
florid

foray
forbearance
formulaic

fruition
furtive

galvanize
gamut

gorgon
grapple

guile
gustatory

hackneyed
hagiography

harrowing
hedonism

hewn (details)

iconoclast
iconography
idiosyncratic
idyll/idyllic
ignite (fig.)
imminent
imperative
impetus

implacable
impresario
incoherent
incongruous
incur
indelible
indeterminate
indigenous

ineffable
ineffectual
inept
inextricably
insidious
insinuation
insouciance
intelligentsia

intercede
intractable
inured
invidious
irreverent
itinerant

jarring

jettison

jostle

Joycean

kamikaze

lacuna
lament
languish
lapidary

largess
libertine
lilting
litigious

loquacious
Lothario
lucid
lucrative

lyricism

macabre	mawkish	minutiae	mosaic
malaise	melodrama	misogyny	muddle
malevolent	mendacious	mogul	murky
malign	mercurial	moldering	musing
manifold (adj.)	mien	mordant	muster
matrix	milieu	moribund	myopia

naiveté	natter	nonpareil	nuance
narcissistic	nihilism	non sequitur	
nascent	nimble	noxious	

obfuscation	opprobrium	ostensible	ostracize

palatable	penumbra	portent	prevaricate
pantheon	perdurable	portentous	prodigious
paradigm	peregrination	practitioner	prosaic
pathos	perennial	pragmatic	protean
paucity	petulance	prattle	punitive
pedagogical	piety	precocious	purport
pelt (vb.)	placebo	premonition	
penchant	plodding	prescient	

querulous	quintessential	quotidian
query	quixotic	

rancor	recalcitrant	reverence	riveting
rapacious	recapitulate	revile	rudimentary
rapture	relegate	rhetorical	ruminate
rancor	repatriation	ricochet	
raucous	replete	riff	
reap	repository	risible	

sagacity	sedentary	stanch	sunder
salacious	self-effacement	standoffish	supercilious
sally forth	sepulchral	staunch	surreptitious
sap (vb.)	shaman	stilted	surrogate
savor	shenanigans	stultifying	symbiosis
scatological	snippet	sublimate	symmetry
scourge	solicitous	sublime	synoptic
scuttlebutt	spurn	subterfuge	
searing	squander	succumb	

taut	titillating	transient	trenchant
teeter	torpid	transitory	trilogy
temporal	tortuous	transmogrify	truism
thrall	traffic (vb.)	travail	tweak
throng	transcendent	treatise	
unabashed	uncanny	unfathomable	unflinching
vacillate	venality	vignette	vitriol
valediction	verisimilitude	vindictiveness	voluminous
vapid	vernacular	virtuosity	vortex
venal	vicissitude	vis à vis	votary
waft	wend	withal	
welter	whimsy		

Chapter 9

GRAMMAR AND USAGE FOR THE CAREFUL WRITER: A GUIDE TO STANDARD WRITTEN ENGLISH

The grammar of a language is its logic. We observe the conventions of standard usage in order to write and speak clearly, in order to communicate precisely what we mean. This section reviews those aspects of grammar and usage you are expected to know and to apply.

On the Regents ELA exam, your command of the conventions—standard written English—is evaluated by how well you write the essay of argument and the text analysis. On the SAT, your command of the grammar and usage is assessed in the writing and language section and on the optional essay; the ACT exam includes a specific section on grammar and usage, sentence structure, and mechanics (see Chapter 10 for Punctuation Guidelines and Reminders).

None of these exams requires you to identify errors in usage by name, but a review of the essential terms and structures will help you to recognize errors and to understand how to correct them. What are the essentials?

REVIEWING THE FUNDAMENTALS

The Parts of Speech

Below are the parts of speech that you should review. These include the noun, pronoun, adjective, verb, and adverb, as well as conjunction, preposition, and interjection.

Noun

Names or identifies persons, creatures, objects, ideas. The articles *the, a, an* usually precede and signal a noun. For example:

book	education	history
child	English	politics
climate	happiness	woman

Pronoun

Replaces or "stands in for" nouns or other pronouns already stated; the noun or pronoun referred to (replaced) is the **antecedent**.

Subject Forms:	I, you, he/she/it, we, you, they
Object Forms:	me, you, him/her/it, us, you, them
Possessive Forms:	mine, yours, his/hers/its, ours, yours, theirs
Relatives:	that, which, who, whom, whose, whoever, whomever

Adjective

Modifies nouns, that is, it describes, limits, specifies, what a noun names. For instance:

tall woman	*young* child	*illustrated* book
temperate climate	*American* history	*public* education

Verb

Denotes any *action*: run, talk, think, intend, suggest, play, strike, have, do; or *state of being*: appear, seem, be, feel. The principal parts of a verb are as follows:

Infinitive:	to run, to talk, to think, to intend, to appear, to seem
Simple past:	ran, talked, thought, intended, appeared, seemed
Present participle:	running, talking, thinking, intending, appearing, seeming
Past participle:	(has) run, (has) talked, (has) thought, intended, appeared, seemed

ADVERB

Modifies verbs; it indicates the manner, quality, or degree of an *action*.

run *swiftly*	talk *loudly*	think *clearly*
play *well*	strike *suddenly*	

Adverbs also function as *intensifiers*; that is, they indicate the degree or intensity of modifiers, both adjectives and adverbs.

rather tall woman	*very* young child
talk *too* loudly	*nearly* complete project

CONJUNCTION

A word that connects two or more words or groups of words.

Coordinating conjunctions: and, but, yet, so, for

Subordinating conjunctions: because, although, since, while, if, until, when, unless, before, after

There are a tall woman *and* a young child.

We will stay home *if* it rains.

Because he trains regularly, he plays well.

PREPOSITION

Expresses relationships of time, space, or position.

above	behind	in	under
across	beside	into	within
after	between	on	without
at	except	over	
before	for	to	

INTERJECTION

An expression that begins or interrupts a sentence to express a particular feeling.

Ouch!, that hurts.	*Oh,* how interesting!	*Bravo!*

Phrases, Clauses, and Sentences

While we may express feelings and give commands with single words, our most useful expression is in words grouped in phrases, clauses, and sentences.

PHRASE

A meaningful group of words. There are many kinds of phrases in English. Here are some common examples:

A noun and its modifiers:

the large brick building   the tall young woman

A verb and its auxiliaries (to show different tenses):

has run   will arrive
should have been done

A preposition and its object:

across the room   in the final chapter
down the hill   on the roof

A participle and its object or modifiers:

opening the door carefully   sensing danger
returning after many years*   walking slowly

CLAUSE

A meaningful group of words that contains a verb and its subject.
Clauses are *dependent* when they form only part of a complex sentence of more than one clause:

Because he was late, . . .   If it rains tomorrow, . . .
. . . when the plane arrives   . . . that you requested

Each of these expressions contains a verb and *its* subject, but you can see that the sentence will not be complete—that is, the assertion will not be fully expressed or understood—until at least one additional clause is added.

---

* Note that prepositional phrases, which are modifiers because they function as adjectives and adverbs do, may be part of a larger participial phrase.

In these examples, one *independent* clause has been added to form a *complete sentence:*

> [Because he was late], his appointment was canceled.
>
> I will call you [when the plane arrives].
>
> The book [that you requested] is now available.

A *sentence,* then, may be made up of a few words—a subject, and a predicate verb that establishes the action or state of being of the subject, and modifiers:

> She ran.
>
> The dog barked.
>
> He was late.
>
> The crowd cheered enthusiastically.

Or a sentence may be made up of more than one clause and contain several phrases as modifiers.

> Because he was late, his appointment was canceled and had to be rescheduled for the following week.
>
> The large crowd in the bleachers cheered enthusiastically as the home team took the field in the last inning.

Tests of standard usage are tests of how well you understand and can compose the many relationships of words, phrases, clauses, and sentences that make up standard written English.

Most of the problems in grammar and usage you are expected to recognize and be able to correct are considered "errors" because they result in a lack of clarity, even confusion, in the writer's expression.

Although writing that contains minor errors in standard usage may still be understood, careful writers seek expression that is precise and clear—even elegant—and that demonstrates their ability to use variety in language and structure. It is only through mastery of a wide range of expression that students may fully reveal their ideas, insights, and feelings.

AVOIDING COMMON ERRORS IN WRITING

When we refer to errors in writing, we are referring to expressions that are illogical, inconsistent, vague, or imprecise. The elements of usage reviewed here are those that high school students should be able to recognize.

Agreement of Subject and Verb

Agreement is a form of consistency and is one of the most basic elements of grammar. When you learn to conjugate verbs, for example, you are applying the concept of agreement. Singular subjects take singular verbs; plural subjects take plural verbs.

He speaks/they speak; One is/many are

Errors in agreement commonly occur in sentences where the subject follows the verb:

On the desk *are* my notebook, a few pencils, and the assignments for tomorrow.

"Desk" is not the subject of the verb; "notebook, pencils, assignments" is the subject, *they* are on the desk. In such inverted word order, the writer must hear and think ahead to choose the correct form of the verb. Similarly:

There *seems* to be only *one answer*.

There *seem* to be *several ideas* worth considering.

Here *are* the *pieces* you have been looking for.

Agreement errors may also occur when a subject followed by a phrase precedes the verb:

New York with its many historical sites and tourist attractions *is* a fascinating city to visit.

His *many talents* in sports, academics, and student leadership *make* him a popular candidate.

Subjects may be expanded by such prepositional phrases as *along with, in addition to, as well as, together with*. These phrases, however, do not form part of the *grammatical* subject; they modify the subject:

English, as well as math, science, and social studies, *is* a required subject for most high school students.

Evan, along with several of his friends, *is* planning to visit colleges in the fall.

In some sentences, the subject may be modified by one or more clauses before the predicate verb is stated. In such sentences the writer must "remember" the actual subject before composing the correct form of the verb:

The *fact* that Americans must now compete in a global economy and must recognize the necessity for higher standards in our schools *has led* to educational reform in many states.

Many common pronouns are singular and must take a singular verb:

Each one of these books *is* worth reading.

Every one of us *is* prepared to contribute.

None of these solutions *is* acceptable. (No *one* is)

Note how agreement with correlatives *either/or, neither/nor* is achieved:

Either Susan or her brother *is* home now.

(Either Susan is . . . or her brother is)

Neither rain, nor sleet, nor snow *deters* us . . . .

When the correlative contains both a singular and plural expression, the verb agrees with the one closest:

Neither Susan nor her sisters *are* at home.

Either the members of the legislature or the governor *is* authorized to submit a budget.

Do not be confused when the predicate is completed with a plural expression:

His most reliable *source* of encouragement *is* friends and family.

To avoid the correct but awkward-sounding expression above, rewrite as follows:

His *friends and family are* his most reliable source of encouragement.

Collective nouns take singular verbs because all the "members" are understood to act as a single unit:

The *jury was* unanimous in its decision to acquit.

A school *board has* extensive responsibilities.

Our *family has agreed* on plans for the vacation.

The *team practices* for two hours every day.

When there is not such unity of action, you may use a plural verb:

> The *jury are* not in unanimous agreement.

> The *family are* expected to arrive at different times.

It is better, however, to avoid such awkward-sounding expressions by rewriting to make the plural idea clear:

> The *members of the jury are* not in agreement.

> *Players on the team are required* to keep their uniforms and equipment in good order.

> *Family members are* expected to arrive at different times.

Agreement of Pronoun and Antecedent

Because pronouns replace nouns or other pronouns, they must agree with their singular or plural antecedents.

> *Evelyn* is very grateful to *her parents* for *their* constant support and encouragement.

Most pronoun/antecedent errors arise when we use the indefinite pronouns *anyone, anybody, everyone, everybody, someone, somebody, no one,* and so on. These pronouns are singular because they refer to *individuals:*

> *Everybody* is responsible for *his* own work.

> *Someone* has left *her* books on the floor.

> If *anyone* calls while I am out, please tell *him* or *her* I will call back after lunch.

The common practice of replacing *him/her* with *them,* or *her/his* with *their,* solves the problem of choosing gender, but it is ungrammatical and illogical. The careful writer (and speaker) avoids these errors or rewrites:

> Please tell *anyone who calls* that I will return at noon.

> *Someone's books* have been left on the floor.

> *Everyone* has individual responsibility for the assignments.

Form of Pronouns

Use the subject forms when pronouns are *subjects* of verbs or identify the subject after a linking verb:

> *He and I* received the information we needed.
>
> *She* is the favorite candidate of the party.
>
> *He* is the head baseball coach.
>
> The head baseball coach is *he*.
>
> (Think of the verb *is* as an = sign.)

It is easy to avoid the awkward sound of the last sentence by choosing the preceding expression, which uses the pronoun first.

Pronouns as *objects* of verbs or prepositions must be in the object form:

> Please give *him* the information.
>
> Give the information to *them*.
>
> *Whom* did you see yesterday?

Errors often occur when we have pronouns preceded by a noun; the writer no longer "hears" the preposition and is reluctant to use the object form. But,

> Please give the information to Ellen and *him*. (to Ellen . . . to him)
>
> The host was very gracious to Ellen and *me*.
> (to Ellen . . . to me; *not* to Ellen and I)
>
> Just between you and me, this is simple.

We also use the object form with infinitives:

> We understand *her to be* the favorite candidate.
>
> We understand the favorite candidate *to be her*.

Remember to use the possessive form with *gerunds* ("-ing" verb forms that function as nouns):

> I do not approve of *your staying* out so late.
> (of your "late hours")
>
> She was concerned about *his working* too hard.
> (about his excessive work)

Note the following:

Mark's mother saw *him* [*running* after the bus].

Mark's mother encouraged [*his running* on the cross-country team].

In the first example, *running* is a participle describing *him,* which is the object of the verb *saw.* In the second example, *running* is a noun; it is the object of the verb *encouraged.*

Parallelism

Parallelism is used for consistency and clarity. Parallel ideas and expressions in a series should be composed in the same form:

He wants to spend the summer *reading, sleeping, and traveling.*

He plans *to read, to sleep, and to travel.*

Use parallel phrases and clauses:

She is known *for* her talent and *for* her generosity.

We expect our presidents to be skilled *not only in* domestic affairs *but also in* foreign policy.

Our state senator was reelected *because* she is honest, *because* she works hard for the district, *and because* she has an important leadership position in the senate.

Use parallel construction when you use correlatives: *either, or; not only, but also:*

Either you will complete the work now, *or* he will complete it in the morning.

We will *either take* a train this afternoon *or take* a plane this evening.

Consistency of active and passive voice is also a form of parallelism:

The research team *formulated* its ideas and *developed* its proposal.

Ideas *were formulated* and a proposal *was developed* by the research team.

Verbs: Using the Correct Tense

Use the simple past tense for actions completed in the past:

> The train *arrived* at 6:30.
>
> He *retired* in 1993.
>
> The Nobel prizes *were announced* in January.

Use the present perfect tense to establish facts, to assert that something *has occurred, has happened, has been done*, without reference to a specific time.

> *Have you done* your homework yet?
>
> The renovation of our house *has been completed.*
>
> I *have read Macbeth* several times.

Note the correct *sequence of tenses* in the following:

> The novelist *completed* the book in 1993, two years after he *had begun* it.
>
> She *recorded* the names of everyone who *had called* the day before.

> In the Middle Ages, most people *believed* that the earth *is* round.
>
> Copernicus *demonstrated* that the earth *orbits* the sun.

> If I *were* you, I *would accept* the offer.
>
> If the congressman *were indicted,* he *would* lose the support of many constituents.

> If we *had taken* more time to plan, our trip *would have been* more pleasant.
>
> If you *had trained* harder, you *would have* made the team.

If you would have called earlier is sometimes heard but this is not an acceptable construction in standard English.

Finally, you are generally expected to write about works of literature in the *present tense.*

> Macbeth *is driven* by ambition.
>
> Jay Gatsby *believes* he can recreate the past.
>
> Willy Loman *dies* believing his son will achieve great success.

Aspects of character, themes, plot, and setting remain constant—they *are* what they are—regardless of how the plot concludes or when we finish reading the work.

Logical Comparisons

My sister is *taller* than I [am].

She is *more* clever than he [is].

Josh is the *tallest* member of the team.

Among all of Miller's plays, *Death of a Salesman* is the *best* known.

Avoid incomplete comparisons in your writing:

Dreiser's novels are *more* popular now [than they were when they were first published].

Shakespeare's plays are *harder* to read [than modern works are].

The passages in brackets should be fully stated.
In informal speech we may use *so* as an intensifier:

I was *so* tired. He was *so* angry.

In writing, however, be sure every *so* is followed by a *that,* every *more* by a *than.*
Comparisons must be parallel and logical:

The paintings of Monet are more popular than Goya **should read**:

The paintings of Monet are more popular than *the paintings* of Goya.

You must compare paintings to paintings, not inadvertently compare paintings to a man.
And,

Anne is a better player than anyone on her team. **should read**:

Anne is a *better* player *than any other* [player] on her team.

or,

Anne is the *best player* on the team.

It is illogical to suggest Anne is better than she herself is.

Clear and Logical Modification

The careful writer must also be aware of errors in modification and in the logical relationships of ideas. Many such errors are corrected simply, with commas; others may require revision or reorganization of sentences.

Introductory subordinate (dependent) clauses must be set off by a comma:

> *After the lights had come back on,* the children were no longer frightened by the thunderstorm.
>
> *When it rains,* cats and dogs prefer not to go outside.

Without the comma, such sentences would be ambiguous.
Nonrestrictive (nonessential) phrases and clauses are set off by commas:

> My aunt, *who lives in Milwaukee,* will be flying in for a weekend visit to New York.
>
> Several stranded passengers, *feeling restless and impatient,* demanded flights on another airline.

When such phrases or clauses are restrictive* (essential to the meaning of the sentence), do not set them off with commas:

> Passengers *traveling with small children* will be permitted to board the plane first.
>
> My cousin *who lives in Milwaukee* will have to fly, but the cousins *who live in the New York area* will be able to drive to my brother's wedding.

A common error occurs when we begin a sentence with a participial phrase:

> Feeling restless and impatient, seats were demanded on other airlines' flights [by many travelers].
> (The seats are not restless . . .)
>
> *Barking loudly,* we were afraid the dog would wake our neighbors.
> (We are not barking, the dog is . . .)
>
> *Tired and hungry,* even cold leftovers looked good to us.
> (The leftovers are not hungry, we are . . .)

---

*For additional examples, see *which/that/who* on page 181.

173

The *subject* of the participle must also be stated as the subject of the clause that follows:

> *Feeling restless and impatient, many stranded travelers* sought seats on other airlines' flights.
>
> *Barking loudly, the dog* wakened our neighbors.
>
> *Tired and hungry, we* were satisfied with the cold leftovers.

You may also recompose sentences to make the modification clear:

> We were afraid our dog, *barking loudly,* would wake the neighbors.
>
> *Because we were tired and hungry,* even cold leftovers looked good to us.

EXPRESSIONS OFTEN CONFUSED, MISUSED, AND OVERUSED*

accept/except

> To **accept** is to receive, take willingly, agree to:
>
> I **accept** your offer, apology, invitation
>
> To **except** is to exclude, to separate out:
>
> I will **except** you from the requirement.
>
> **Except** is also a preposition:
>
> Everyone **except** him will be leaving on Tuesday.

affect/effect

> To **affect** (vb.) means to move, influence, or change. It also means to put on an artificial quality of personality or character; such an exaggerated or artificial person may be called **affected**.
>
> An **effect** (n.) is a consequence or result.
>
> To **effect** (vb.) means to put into action, to complete—a plan or a change, for example.

---

*See also Words Commonly Confused/Misspelled in Chapter 11, Spelling.

aggravate

To **aggravate** means to make worse. Do not use it when you really mean to irritate or annoy.

allusion/illusion

An **allusion** is a reference (see Glossary of Poetic Terms and Techniques, Chapter 5); an **illusion** is a false or deceptive idea or vision.

among/between

Use **between** for two, **among** for three or more:

between you and me

among all the members of the family

amount/number

One has an **amount** of something (the quantity as a whole) and a **number** of things (that can be counted):

an **amount** of time/a **number** of hours, days

a large **amount** of work/a **number** of tasks

See also **fewer/less** for the same distinction.

as far as . . . is/are concerned

The expression **as far as** used by itself creates an incomplete and illogical statement; it must be completed with **is/are concerned.** The expression as **far as . . . goes/go** is also widely used and correct as completed.

Faulty: **As far as** plans for school construction in the future, we expect the legislature to take action in the next session.

As far as the weather, it will be sunny and pleasant tomorrow.

Correct: **As far as** plans for school construction in the future are concerned, we expect the legislature to take action in the next session

As far as the weather goes, it will be sunny and pleasant.

bad/badly, good/well

Use **bad** and **good** (adjectives) to describe how one feels; use **badly** and **well** (adverbs) to describe how one does something.

He felt **bad** (sorry, regretful) because he caused the team to lose.

The team lost the game because he played so **badly**.

She feels **good** (in good spirits, positive) when her work is going **well**.

She is feeling **well** (no longer ill) now after a long bout with the flu.

The team lost because he did not play **well**.

being as, being that

These expressions are not standard speech. Use *because* or *since* instead.

compare to, compare with

Use **compare to** when you are expressing an analogy or similarity; use **compare with** when you are showing similarities and differences between two things.

He compared his small room **to** a closet.

The critics compared the movie **with** the book.

could of/ should of

Do not make this unfortunate confusion in the way words sound! You mean **could have/should have**.

different from (not **than**)

You should use the preposition **from** with **different** because you are making a distinction, a separation. Use **than** for comparisons, to show degrees of the same quality:

She is only slightly older **than** her sister, but her personality is very different **from** her sister's.

due to

This expression is popularly used for almost any cause and effect relationship. Avoid its overuse in your writing:

Absence **due to** illness is excused.

Delays **due to** bad weather are common in winter.

It is more precise to say:

The road was closed **because of** an accident.

The defendant was acquitted **by reason of** insanity.

There were many landslides **caused by** the heavy rains.

everybody, somebody, someone, nobody

> These are *singular* forms; they may refer to many people, but they refer to *each one individually*. Singular antecedents take singular pronouns:
>
> **Everybody** has *his/her* books, lunch, opinions.
>
> **Someone, a person** has *his/her* opinions.

farther/further

> In general, you may use **farther** or **further** for actual or figurative distance:
>
> The nearest town is ten miles **farther** from here.
>
> The latest agreements move us **further** toward a full peace.
>
> Use **further** when you mean more:
>
> We have nothing **further** to discuss.
>
> A final agreement requires **further** negotiations.

fewer/less

> One has **fewer** things and **less** something.
>
> **fewer** hours/**less** time
>
> **fewer** dollars/**less** money
>
> **fewer** ideas/**less** content

first, second, . . .

> To show transition and to enumerate examples, use these terms instead of *firstly, secondly, . . .*

hang/hanged/hung

> When we use this verb in the past tense to denote an execution, we use **hanged**; for such things as clothes and pictures, we use **hung**.
>
> The condemned man was **hanged** at dawn.
>
> We **hung** our winter coats in the hall closet.

hopefully

> This expression is popularly used to mean we hope, it is hoped, and so on. The careful writer should use it only as an adverb:
>
> The cat looked **hopefully** at the leftover chicken.

But:

We **hope** the situation will improve.

It is hoped that research will lead to a cure.

however

Along with its cousins *therefore, moreover,* and *consequently,* **however** should be placed *within the sentence*, close to the verb it modifies; think of it as a conjunction, not as a transition at the beginning of a sentence.

if/whether

Use **if** to introduce conditional expressions; use **whether** (or not) for choices, decisions, questions:

If it rains, our game will be postponed.

If you work hard, you will succeed.

I do not know **whether** we will play or not.

infer/imply

To **infer** is to conclude, to draw an inference from evidence; to **imply** is to suggest or hint.

We can **infer** from his comments that he is pleased.

She **implied** in her speech that she is planning to run for public office.

its/it's

it's = a contraction* for it is.

its = a possessive form; do not add an apostrophe.

if . . . were/if . . . was

Use the **if . . . were** construction for *hypothetical* conditions and situations:

If you were president, what would you do?

If I were you, I would accept the offer.

---

*Contractions should be avoided in formal writing, unless you are quoting someone. Contractions are features of spoken language.

Use **if . . . was** for situations that *were possible*:

> **If** that really **was** Linda who called yesterday, she should have left a message.

incredible/incredulous

Incredible means unbelievable, beyond belief or understanding. In formal writing, avoid using it as *hyperbole*. Use instead such terms as *astonishing* or *extraordinary*.

A person is **incredulous** when he/she utterly cannot believe what is being said.

kind of/sort of/type of

Avoid using *a* or *an* with these expressions:

> **That type of** character is popular in children's books.

> **Those types of** characters are . . .

> **This kind of** fabric is best for the new sofa.

Also avoid using **kind of** or **sort of** when you mean *a little, rather, somewhat*.

lie/lay

These verbs are often confused. Note their principal parts and distinctions in meaning: to **lie (down)** means to recline, be situated, rest:

> You **lie** on your bed to take a nap.

> The mail **has lain** on your desk since yesterday.

> Last winter the snow **lay** on the ground for weeks.

Note that to **lay** means to put or place something. (It is a transitive verb and always takes a direct object.):

> You can **lay** your hat and gloves on the hall table.

> Masons **lay bricks** and hens **lay eggs**.

> He cannot remember where he **laid** his car keys.

like/as/as if

Use **like** as a preposition, use **as** and **as if** as conjunctions:

> He looks just **like** his father.

> A talent **like** hers is rare.

It looks **as if** it will rain this afternoon.

You should do the assignments **as** you were instructed to.

"Do **as** I say, not **as** I do!"

only/just

These modifiers should be placed as close as possible to the expressions they actually limit:

I have **only** two dollars for lunch.

He has time for **only** a brief conversation.

I have **just** one thing to say.

presently

This should be used to denote the immediate future; it means right *away* or in *a little while:*

I will answer your question **presently**.

He is expected to arrive **presently**.

The meeting will begin **presently**.

For current time, use **at present** or **currently**:

He is **currently** a junior at North High.

At present, she is working on her master's degree.

purposely/purposefully

Use **purposely** to mean intentionally, knowingly, deliberately, that is, to describe an action done "on purpose" and not by accident.

purposefully is best used to mean decisively, firmly, resolutely, with determination, and with a specific purpose or goal in mind.

so

Try to avoid the casual use of "so" just to introduce an idea or an explanation. You will hear "so" widely used in informal speech to begin the answer to almost any question, but that should be avoided in your formal writing. Use *so* as a conjunction to show a consequence:

We were hungry, **so** we went to lunch early.

Our plane was delayed, **so** we spent several hours waiting at the airport.

toward/towards

Either is acceptable; **toward** is more formal.

when/where

These are terms of time and place; do not use them to introduce definitions.

which/that/who

These relative *pronouns* introduce *clauses* that describe or define. Use **that** for clauses that are *restrictive* (defining, limiting):

The books **that** you ordered will arrive tomorrow; the ones **that** Sam ordered will come next week. (those particular books . . .)

He likes the car **that** he bought last year better than any other he has owned. (that particular car)

Basketball is the game **that** he plays best.

Use **which** for clauses that are *nonrestrictive* (descriptive):

The house on the corner, **which** was built in the 1880s, will be restored to its original design.

Shakespeare's plays, **which** were written nearly 400 years ago, remain popular in theaters and movies as well as in English courses.

Use **who** for people. (**That** is sometimes used when the identification is distant or impersonal.) Do not use **which** for people:

Lady Macbeth is a character **that** (**who**) remains fascinating to many students.

Use **whom** when the pronoun is an object:

To **whom** should I give the information? (obj. of prep.)

Whom did you ask? (obj. of verb)

who/whom/whoever/whomever

When these *pronouns* introduce *clauses,* their form is determined *solely* by their function in the clause:

The new coach, **who** led the team to a county title, gave all the credit to her players.
(**Who** is the subject of the verb *led;* therefore, it is in the subject form.)

Please give the information to (**whoever** needs it.)

(**Whoever** is the subject in the clause; the *entire* clause is the object of *give to*.)

Please give the award to (**whomever** you choose.)
(**Whomever** is the object of the verb *choose;* the *entire* clause is the object of *give to*.)

Careful attention to the conventions of usage and style outlined in this chapter will enhance your ability to express ideas and discuss information clearly and persuasively. When you have command of the language you use, you have command of the relationship between thought and expression.

Chapter 10

PUNCTUATION: GUIDELINES AND REMINDERS

When is the semicolon or colon used? Are there any rules for commas? Do I underline titles of books and poems or put them in quotation marks? Where do I put the period when a sentence ends with quotation marks? Even experienced writers need to consult a usage handbook for the answers to some of these questions.

In conversation we use pauses, stresses, and tone of voice to make our meaning clear. The printed page, however, does not readily show what voice and gesture can reveal, so the writer uses punctuation to achieve absolute clarity. Below, you will find a review of the elements of punctuation high school students should know and use in their own writing. Featured are answers to those questions most often raised about how to punctuate. (Many of the examples from the writing of specific authors come from the passages reprinted elsewhere in the book.)

END PUNCTUATION

The period, exclamation mark, and question mark bring statements and expressions to a close; they signal a full stop.

The Period

Use a **period** to indicate the end of a sentence or of a group of words having the emphasis of a sentence.

Declarative sentences (make a statement):

Good writers are also good readers.

"The guns squatted in a row like savage chiefs." (Stephen Crane, *The Red Badge of Courage*)

Imperative sentences (give an order or direction):

Be sure to proofread.

Come to practice on time or leave the team.

Tell me how much I owe you.

Fragments for emphasis:

"No doubt my younger brother and sister were in the house and warm. *Eating cookies.*" (William Kittredge)

"Much of their [whales'] behavior seems to be recreational: they sing, they play. *And so on.*" (Robert Finch)

The Exclamation Mark

Use an **exclamation mark** to show intensity and emphasis in sentences or fragments.

Come to practice!

Be sure to proofread!

Look out!

Congratulations!

CAUTION: *Do not overuse the **exclamation mark** in expository writing; use effective language and sentence structure to achieve emphasis.*

The Question Mark

Use a **question mark** to signal interrogative forms in complete sentences, fragments, or series.

Can you explain how to do this?

Do you understand what he said?

Can you recommend a good restaurant in the theater district?

What was that all about? a joke? a mistake?

Where should we meet? at home? at school?

Ask questions as you read an essay: What is the author's purpose? tone? conclusion? Do you agree? disagree? feel convinced?

Question marks may also be used with single words or phrases as needed:

When?

Leave the team?

You did?

What homework?

SPECIAL CONSIDERATIONS

Periods are used in many abbreviations. For example:

U.S. government	Dipl.	B.A.	M.A.	Ph.D.
U.N. Security Council	D.D.S.	M.D.	Esq.	
N.Y.S. Board of Regents	A.M.	P.M.		

Some abbreviations take no periods:

CIA	mph
MTV	rpm
WCBS	

A sentence may end with more than one kind of punctuation. If it ends with an abbreviation using a period, do not add a second period.

Please report to my office promptly at 10:00 A.M.

In order to apply for a teaching position, you must have completed your M.A.

If it ends with a quotation or expression in quotation marks, place the final period *inside* the quotation marks.

Most high school students have read Poe's short story "The Cask of Amontillado."

When told his wife is dead, Macbeth remarks, "She should have died hereafter."

If the **entire sentence** requires a question mark, place it outside the quotation marks:

Have you read Poe's story "The Cask of Amontillado"?

Why does Macbeth say, "She should have died hereafter"?

If the quotation at the end of a sentence requires a question mark, keep it within the quotes. (Do not add an additional period.)

> The title of a recent editorial in *The New York Times* was "Where do we go from here?"

If a statement within the quotes is a question, the question mark within the quote is sufficient.

> Did you read the editorial entitled "Where do we go from here?"

Similarly, if an exclamation point is part of a quoted expression, place it within the quote. An additional period is not required.

> One of my favorite pieces by James Thurber is called "Excelsior!"

To make the above into a question, however:

> Have you read Thurber's story "Excelsior!"?

If a sentence ends with a passage in parentheses, put the period outside the closing parenthesis:

> We did not leave on time because Sally was late (as usual).

Even if the expression is a complete sentence, do not punctuate within the parentheses:

> We did not leave on time because Sally was late (she always is).

If, however, the expression within the parentheses requires quotation marks, a question mark, or an exclamation point, include them:

> We did not leave on time because Sally was late (isn't she always?).

In such cases, a better solution would be to separate the parenthetical statement:

> We did not leave because Sally was late. (Isn't she always?)

What is the logic to all this? When sentences or passages are made up of a variety of elements, punctuation should make the structure of each element clear. If the end of a sentence becomes cluttered by the need to bring several individual pieces to a close at the same time, punctuate from the inside out—smaller pieces first, then larger. But do not double the end punctuation unless it is required for accuracy. If you have a question within a question, one question mark will do. If a closing quotation ends with a "strong" piece of punctuation, don't add a modest and redundant period to the whole sentence. Close with the strength of the quote.

INTERNAL PUNCTUATION

Internal punctuation includes the comma, the semicolon, the colon, and the dash. The single purpose of internal punctuation is to prevent confusion, to achieve clarity. The comma indicates brief pauses between separate elements in a sentence; the semicolon establishes a direct connection between two independent statements to form a single sentence; the colon serves to introduce things; and the dash permits you to digress or emphasize.

The Comma

Use the comma in compound sentences with coordinating conjunctions *and, but, yet, so, or, for*. A compound sentence joins two or more independent clauses that could be expressed separately as simple sentences. *Note that the comma precedes the conjunction:*

> "I walked slowly, *for* the detail on the beach was infinite." (Ernie Pyle)
>
> "The luncheon hour was long past; *and* the two had their end of the vast terrace to themselves." (Edith Wharton, "Roman Fever")
>
> "I was not going to talk about Whitewater today, *but* then I thought that if I didn't you'd think I know something about it, *and* the only way for me to prove that I don't is to talk about it at length, *so* I will." (Garrison Keillor)

In sentences where the clauses are short and the meaning is clear, you may omit a comma:

> The team tied the score in the last seconds of the game and the crowd cheered wildly.

If there is any possibility of misreading, you must use a comma:

> I went to the movies with Roger and Sally stayed home.
> I went to the movies with Roger, and Sally stayed home.

WHAT IS A COMMA SPLICE?

One of the most common errors in writing is the use of a comma alone to join independent clauses. This is the error familiar to students as the "run-on" sentence.

Run on:	The crowd cheered wildly, the game was tied in the last few seconds.
	I went to the movies with Roger, Sally stayed home.
	The novel was riveting, I did not want it to end.
Correct:	The crowd cheered wildly when the game was tied in the final seconds.
	I went to the movies with Roger, and Sally stayed home.
	The novel was riveting, so I did not want it to end.

DO I USE A COMMA BEFORE THE LAST ITEM IN A SERIES?

Some editors and instructors insist that all items in a series be set off by a comma; others prefer that you omit the last one, especially in a series of single words:

You can find models of style in books, newspapers, and magazines.

You can find models of style in books, newspapers and magazines.

SUGGESTION: For sentences like the one above, the second comma needlessly slows down the sentence and makes no contribution to clarity. In a series of longer expressions, however, or in a series without a conjunction, set off each with a comma.

For class you are expected to bring a notebook, a pen or pencil, and the text we are reading.

"He was white-headed as a mountain, bowed in the shoulders, and faded in general aspect." (Thomas Hardy)

Writing has many purposes: personal expression, persuasion, literary effect, information.

USE A COMMA AFTER INTRODUCTORY CLAUSES

As the crowd cheered them on, the home team scored the winning touchdown.

If you are hungry, please help yourself to a sandwich.

"As the bell sounded the hour, there came a knocking at the street door." (Edgar Allan Poe)

Do not use a comma if the main clause is followed by a dependent clause:

Please help yourself to a sandwich whenever you get hungry.

The home team scored the winning touchdown as the crowd cheered them on.

USE A COMMA AFTER AN INTRODUCTORY PHRASE ONLY WHEN NEEDED

At last, the rain began to ease, and the sun came through breaks in the clouds.

The son of a tanner, Grant was everything Lee was not.

After the Labor Day recess, Congress will reconvene.

Feeling ill and confused, he left the dinner table without speaking.

These sentences require no comma:

On the desk you will find your final check and a letter of recommendation.

"For a long time they continued to sit side by side without speaking." (Edith Wharton)

USE COMMAS TO SET OFF DESCRIPTIVE AND NONESSENTIAL CLAUSES OR PHRASES WITHIN SENTENCES

"They were two strong men, these oddly different generals, and they represented the strengths of two conflicting currents that, through them, had come into final collision." (Bruce Catton)

The house on the corner, which was built in the 1880s, will be restored to its original design.

Shakespeare's plays, written nearly four hundred years ago, remain popular in theaters and movies as well as in English courses.

USE COMMAS WITH SOME SINGLE WORDS AND EXPRESSIONS

"Well, Jim's habits and his jokes didn't appeal to Julie . . ." (Ring Lardner, "Haircut")

"Now, I'll read the names—heads of families first." (Shirley Jackson, "The Lottery")

USE COMMAS WITH PARENTHETIC AND TRANSITIONAL EXPRESSIONS

Use commas to set off such expressions as *however, moreover, therefore, nevertheless, after all, by the way, of course, on the other hand, I think.*

"Yet it was not all contrast, after all . . . Furthermore, their fighting qualities were really very much alike." (Bruce Catton)

After all, what you learn is what really matters.

You must, of course, always proofread a paper before handing it in.

COMMAS IN DATES

For expressions of day, month, and year:

July 4, 1776, marks the beginning of the American Revolution.

Registration will take place on September 9, 1994, for the fall semester and on January 12, 1995, for the spring semester.

Do not use commas for expressions of month and year only.

Joan completed graduate school in June 1987, began her legal work in September 1987, and joined our firm in January 1993.

COMMAS WITH ADJECTIVES IN A SERIES

Use a comma when it means *and:*

The little room in Appomattox was "the scene of one of the poignant, dramatic contrasts in American history." (Bruce Catton)

The Regents examinations require you to write thoughtful, well-organized essays.

Do not use a comma if the adjective is part of the meaning of the noun:

She greeted her guests in the large sitting room.

USE COMMAS TO SET OFF QUOTES

"I always used to think," Mrs. Slade continued, "that our mothers had a much more difficult job than our grandmothers." (Edith Wharton, "Roman Fever")

"It isn't fair, it isn't right," Mrs. Hutchinson screamed, and then they were upon her. (Shirley Jackson, "The Lottery")

ADDITIONAL ILLUSTRATIONS OF COMMA USE

If you must sing, sing quietly.
These incidents took place a long, long time ago.

That's not what you meant, is it?
You have everything you need, don't you?

First come, first served.
Now you see it, now you don't.

Shakespeare's tragedy, *Macbeth*, is one of his best-known plays.
Verdi's only comic opera, *Falstaff,* is the last work he composed.

My sister Anne lives in Seattle; my sister Julia lives in New York.
My only sister, Anne, lives in Seattle.

COMMON ERRORS IN COMMA USE

Do not separate compound elements or isolate essential elements with commas.

Correct: "They greeted one another and exchanged bits of gossip as they went to join their husbands." (Shirley Jackson, "The Lottery")

Faulty: They greeted one another, and exchanged bits of gossip as they went to join their husbands.

Alternative: *They greeted* one another, and *they exchanged* bits of gossip as they went to join their husbands.

Correct: "Whales possess a highly complex language and have developed sophisticated communications systems that transmit over long distances." (Robert Finch)

Faulty: Whales possess a highly complex language, and have developed sophisticated communications systems, that transmit over long distances.

Alternative: *Whales possess* a highly complex language, *and they have developed* sophisticated communications systems that transmit over long distances.

In the faulty examples, the first comma may *look* necessary, but it improperly separates the subject from the second verb; the final clause in each case is essential description and should not be separated from the rest of the sentence. The alternative versions are accurately punctuated and show how the original, correct sentences could be revised into compound sentences.

SUGGESTION: In all the examples and explanations above, the commas serve one purpose: to make the expression clear on first reading. Insert commas in your own writing as you compose, as you hear the need for them. When you revise, do not be tempted to add commas simply because they look right—chances are, they do not belong.

The Semicolon

A comma indicates a brief pause between separate elements in a sentence, whereas a semicolon indicates a longer pause between independent statements that form a single sentence. The semicolon may replace *and* or *but* in compound sentences. Here are some of the examples used earlier now revised with semicolons.

I walked slowly; the detail on the beach was infinite.

The luncheon hour was long past; the two had their end of the vast terrace to themselves.

I was not going to talk about Whitewater today; then I thought that if I didn't, you'd think I know something about it; the only way for me to prove that I don't is to talk about it at length; so I will.

In each of these revisions, you can see that the effect of the semicolon is to indicate a cause and effect relationship or to show consequence without stating it directly. This results in forceful and emphatic sentences. The semicolon also has a formal quality; it creates a feeling of balance and equivalence among statements.

> ". . . with a semicolon . . . you get a pleasant little feeling of expectancy; there is more to come; read on; it will get clearer." (Lewis Thomas)

The Colon

Use the colon to introduce something: a list, the body of a letter, a quotation, or an explanation.

> "Political courage stems from a number of sources: anger, pain, love, hate." (Madeleine Kunin)

> "Mrs. Slade began again: 'I suppose I did it as a sort of joke'—" (Edith Wharton)

> "The purpose of life is to be useful. It is, above all, to *matter:* to have it make some difference that you lived at all." (Leo Rosten)

The Dash

The dash permits you to pause without notice and insert an idea too interesting to delay and too important to put in parentheses—but don't overdo it!

> "At some gut level, the art of politics—combative, competitive, self-asserting—is sometimes difficult to integrate with our feminine selves." (Madeleine Kunin)

> "Different as they were—in background, in personality, in underlying aspiration—these two great soldiers had much in common." (Bruce Catton)

> "The wonder of ourselves, of each other, and of life—this is the true subject matter of all novels." (Sandy Asher)

The Ellipsis

The ellipsis is used in quoted passages to show that something has been omitted.

> "The purpose of life is to be useful . . . above all, to *matter.*" (Rosten)

When an ellipsis comes at the end of a sentence, the final period must be retained; that is, you will use four periods, not three. The following example shows the use of three ellipses: one in the middle of a sentence and two, each with a fourth period added, at the ends of sentences:

> Mark Van Doren asserts that "Iago's cynicism consists of believing that . . . the passions of men are toys for him to play with . . . . He likes nothing better than to make plans which other men's emotions will execute . . . ."

The Bracket

Brackets indicate where the writer has added a word or phrase to a quoted passage. Such additions are sometimes necessary to make connections in extended quotes where you have used ellipsis.

> "The persons of the tale were long since types [to Hawthorne], as were their souls' predicaments. The broken law, the hidden guilt, the hunger for confession, the studious, cold heart that watches and does not feel . . ." (Mark Van Doren)

> Men's passions should lead them to "more and better feeling . . . ," but Iago's knowledge of men's hearts transforms those passions into destructive forces, into "toys . . . tools to use." Iago contrives malign "plans which other men's [benign] emotions will execute."

The Apostrophe

The apostrophe has many important uses: to form contractions, to show possession, and to form the plural of numbers, symbols, and letters. Apostrophes are also easily misused. Below are examples of the most common uses.

CONTRACTIONS

The apostrophe takes the place of a missing letter or letters in a contraction:

> It's very warm today. = It is very warm today.

> You don't have to return the book right now. = You do not . . .

Remember that contractions are characteristic of spoken language and are not generally used in formal writing.

The apostrophe is also used to abbreviate dates:

June '82

The Class of '98

POSSESSIVE FORMS OF NOUNS AND PROPER NAMES

You form the possessive of a singular noun or name by adding an apostrophe and an *s*:

The novel's major themes (= The major themes of the novel)

My neighbor's house

Charles's notebook

Dickens's novels

In general, you form the possessive of a plural noun by adding the apostrophe alone:

My neighbors' yards

the jurors' verdict

the witnesses' statements

The Smiths' house

the Davises' horse

NOTE: Be sure to avoid the common error of confusing the possessive form with the plural.

Mark Twain wrote several novels; he did not write "novel's."

The local nursery sells plants; it does not sell "plant's."

SOME PLURALS

Use the apostrophe to form the plurals of letters and some abbreviations:

There were sixteen A's on the last exam.

"Dot your *i*'s and cross your *t*'s."

Mark has earned two Ph.D.'s, each in a different discipline.

TITLES OF WORKS OF LITERATURE

Titles of books and other full-length, separately published works should be set in italics. If you are composing on a typewriter or writing by hand, *underline* such titles. Movies and plays are also set in italics.

The Great Gatsby   *Death of a Salesman*

Huckleberry Finn   *The Glass Menagerie*

To Kill a Mockingbird   *Macbeth*

The names of newspapers and magazines should also be in italics.

The New York Times   *Harper's*   *Newsweek*

Titles of poems, essays, and short stories are set off in quotes.

"The Tell-Tale Heart"   "The Sleeping Giant"

"Roman Fever"   "The Road Not Taken"

"The Lottery"   "Old Photograph of the Future"

A title should not be underlined *and* set in quotes; this is redundant and confusing.

Your own title for an essay or paper should not be underlined; use quotes only for names or phrases actually quoted within the title.

A FINAL NOTE ON PUNCTUATION

The topics reviewed here are meant to offer fundamental guidelines and to illustrate how accurate punctuation helps make writing clear. Review some of the prose passages in other parts of the book for vivid examples of how different authors use punctuation to make their meaning and tone clear.

Chapter 11

SPELLING

We know how to spell many words because we recognize them from our reading and because we have, from childhood or as English language learners, developed awareness of the conventions of English spelling. Even though English spelling may seem confusing at times, most of the troublesome sounds or patterns reflect the history of English pronunciation and the fact that the English language developed after the forces of William the Conqueror, a Frenchman from Normandy, had invaded and settled in what is now the island of Great Britain. The resulting language is a fusion of Anglo-Saxon, French, and Latin.

SPELLING ON WRITING EXAMS

Does spelling count? The rubrics for the essays on the English Regents ELA exam include the "conventions" as a quality to be assessed. These are defined as ". . . conventional spelling, punctuation, paragraphing, capitalization, grammar and usage"; and on the SAT essay, frequent errors in grammar, usage, and mechanics are considered significant weaknesses in a student's writing.

If you know you have difficulties in spelling, use this chapter to review the common patterns of English spelling and to study the list of words commonly misspelled.

A word misspelled is a word misused, and egregious spelling errors may affect the scoring of your essay. You would also be expected to observe conventional spelling in preparing a college essay, a resume, or cover letter, and would avoid the spelling "shortcuts" we sometimes find useful in composing e-mail or text messages.

SPELLING RULES AND PATTERNS

As you review spelling rules and patterns, you need to be familiar with the following terms:

vowels The letters *a, e, i o, u,* and occasionally *y* signal the vowel, or sustained, sounds in English. The variations in these vowel sounds are spelled as combinations of more than one letter or as combinations with consonants.

197

consonants In English, the consonant letters and sounds are composed by the following: *b, c, d, f, g, h, j, k, l, m, n, p, q, r, s, t, v, w, x, z.* In contrast to vowels, consonant sounds do not sustain.

syllable A vowel sound or a combination of a vowel and consonant sounds that makes up a single impulse, or "beat," in a word. Words of one syllable: *think, read, act.* Words of two syllables: *reflect, insist, review.* We regularly use words of six or more syllables: *unintentionally, coincidentally.*

endings Single letters or syllables that indicate grammatical forms, such as noun plurals or verb conjugations. English, in contrast to other languages high school students may study, has relatively few "endings." Among them are *-s* or *-es* to form plural nouns or to indicate third-person *singular* verb forms, and the verb endings *-ing* and *-ed.*

suffixes Endings used to form new words and different parts of speech: *love, lovely, loveliness; occur, occurrence.* The addition of endings and suffixes to words often alters their spelling. (See next page.)

prefixes Units of one or two syllables that, like suffixes, are not "words" in themselves but have distinct meanings. They are placed at the beginning of existing words, or of what are called *stems* or *roots.* (See the section "Roots and Prefixes from Latin and Greek," Chapter 8, for many examples in English of Latin and Greek roots.) Words formed in this way are spelled to show their meanings: *illogical, overreact, misspell.*

Although most spelling "rules" have exceptions, there are many common patterns for spelling in English. The first group (pages 198–202) involves adding endings or suffixes.

Words That End in Silent *e*

➤ Drop the *e* before adding a suffix or ending that begins with a vowel:

dare + -ing	→ = daring	→ + -ed = dared
hope + -ing	→ = hoping	→ + -ed = hoped
amuse + -ing	→ = amusing	→ + -ed = amused
revise + -ion	→ = revision	→ + -ed = revised
advise + -able	→ = advisable,	→ + -ed = advised
reverse + -ible	→ = reversible	→ + -ed = reversed

➤ When adding *s* or a suffix that begins with a consonant, retain the *e*:

amuse	→ amuses	→ amusement
arrange	→ arranges	→ arrangement
hope	→ hopes	→ hopeless
huge	→ hugeness	→ hugely
place	→ places	→ placement
spite	→ spiteful	
sure	→ surely	

➤   When the word ends in *ce* or in *ge,* retain the *e* when adding *able* or *ous:*

change   ➤   changeable
peace   ➤   peaceable
service   ➤   serviceable
advantage   ➤   advantageous
courage   ➤   courageous
outrage   ➤   outrageous

➤   But drop the silent *e* before adding *ing:*

change   ➤   changing
rage   ➤   raging
service   ➤   servicing
trace   ➤   tracing

➤   Note the following **exceptions:**

argue   ➤   argument
true   ➤   truly
judge   ➤   judgment
nine   ➤   ninety
whole   ➤   wholly

Words That End in y

➤   For words preceded by a consonant, change the *y* to an *i* before adding a suffix:

accompany   ➤   accompaniment
busy   ➤   business   ➤   busily
easy   ➤   easily
funny   ➤   funnier   ➤   funniest
happy   ➤   happiness   ➤   happily
lonely   ➤   loneliness
silly   ➤   silliness   ➤   sillier   ➤   silliest

➤   The same pattern applies when we add *s* to form plural nouns or third-person-singular verb forms:

army   ➤   armies
baby   ➤   babies
city   ➤   cities
marry   ➤   marries
try   ➤   tries
worry   ➤   worries

➤ But retain the *y* before adding *ing, ism, ish*:

baby	➤	babyish	➤ babying
copy	➤	copying	
crony	➤	cronyism	
marry	➤	marrying	
try	➤	trying	
worry	➤	worrying	

➤ For words that end in *y* preceded by a vowel, retain *y:*

annoy	➤ annoys	➤ annoyance	➤ annoyed	➤ annoying
boy	➤ boys	➤ boyish		
day	➤ days			
destroy	➤ destroys	➤ destroyed	➤ destroying	
monkey	➤ monkeys			
play	➤ plays	➤ played	➤ playing	➤ player ➤ playful
valley	➤ valleys			

➤ However:

say	➤	says	➤ **said**
pay	➤	pays	➤ **paid**

Double Letters

In writing, we must often stop to think whether to double letters in adding suffixes to words. Here are guidelines to follow.

➤ For one-syllable words that end in a single consonant preceded by a single vowel, *double* the final consonant before a suffix beginning with a vowel:

bat	➤	batter	➤	batting	
big	➤	bigger	➤	biggest	
fit	➤	fitted	➤	fitting	➤ fittest
sit	➤	sitter	➤	sitting	
spot	➤	spotty	➤	spotted	

As you look at the examples, you will see that the effect of the double consonant is to retain the pronunciation of the base word.

➤ Words formed by adding prefixes to one-syllable words follow the same pattern:

outfit	➤	outfitted	➤	outfitter
unwrap	➤	unwrapped		

➤ For one-syllable words that have double vowels or that end in more than one consonant, do *not* double the final consonant:

beat	➤	beating		
neat	➤	neatest		
mail	➤	mailing	➤	mailed
read	➤	reading	➤	reader
fail	➤	failure		
list	➤	listed		
faint	➤	fainted		

➤ However:

quit	➤	quitting

Because *u* must follow the *q*, *-ui* is considered a single vowel.

➤ Do not double the final consonant for words ending in *w, x,* or *y:*

draw	➤	drawing		
mix	➤	mixing		
play	➤	playing	➤	player

It is when we add endings to words of more than one syllable that spelling errors commonly occur.

➤ For words of more than one syllable ending in one vowel and one consonant, double the final consonant before an ending that begins with a vowel *if the last syllable of the base word is accented*:

confer	➤	conferred
infer	➤	inferred
refer	➤	referred
begin	➤	beginning
deter	➤	deterrence
omit	➤	omitted
commit	➤	committed
occur	➤	occurrence
equip	➤	equipped

➤ If the accent is *not* on the syllable to which the ending is added, *do not* double the final consonant:

benefit	➤	benefited		
credit	➤	credited		
open	➤	opening		
happen	➤	happening		
develop	➤	developing	➤	developed
deliver	➤	delivered	➤	delivering

➤ Note how the shift in accent determines spelling:

confer	➤	conference
infer	➤	inference
prefer	➤	preference
refer	➤	reference

Note the following exceptions:

➤ The following words double the final consonant:

program	➤	programmed	➤	programmer
question	➤	questionnaire		
excel	➤	excellence	➤	excellent

➤ Either form is considered acceptable for the following, but the first form, with a single *-l*, is preferred:

canceled	➤	cancelled
traveled	➤	travelled
traveling	➤	travelling

Adding Prefixes and Suffixes

With the exception of the patterns reviewed on the previous pages, which reflect how we pronounce the words, most words formed by adding prefixes and suffixes retain the spelling of each separate part. As a result, the full meaning of the word is reflected in its spelling:

mis + spell + ed	➤	= misspelled (both *s*'s are required)
mis + understand + ing	➤	= misunderstanding
dis + agree + able	➤	= disagreeable
dis + taste + ful	➤	= distasteful
dis + appear + ance	➤	= disappearance
dis + satisfaction	➤	= dissatisfaction

un + necessary	➤	= unnecessary
un + ending	➤	= unending
cool + ly	➤	= coolly
moral + ly	➤	= morally
co + operate	➤	= cooperate
de + emphasize	➤	= de-emphasize
re + entry	➤	= reentry
mean + ness	➤	= meanness
amuse + ment	➤	= amusement

➤   Note that words ending in *c* add a *k* as follows:

panic, panics	➤	panicky, panicked, panicking
mimic, mimics	➤	mimicked, mimicking
picnic, picnics	➤	picnicking, picnickers

Words That Include *ie* or *ei*

➤   Is it *i* before *e* or *e* before *i*? This is the spelling pattern everyone remembers.

i before *e*:

| chief | thief | relief | yield |

➤   Except after *c*:

| receive | ceiling | conceit |

➤   Or, when *ei* sounds long *a*:

| sleigh | neighbor | weigh | veil |

There are, however, several **exceptions** to this pattern. They must be memorized:

caffeine	foreign	plebeian	sovereign
counterfeit	forfeit	protein	surfeit
either	leisure	seize	weird
financier	neither	sheik	

Noun Plurals

➤ Noun *plurals* are generally formed by adding *s*:

cat	➤	cats
house	➤	houses
delay	➤	delays
piano	➤	pianos

➤ Nouns ending in *s, sh, ch, x,* and *z,* add *es* to form the plural:

watch	➤	watches
brush	➤	brushes
waltz	➤	waltzes

➤ Nouns ending in the consonant *y*: drop the *y* and add *ies*:

spy	➤	spies
lady	➤	ladies
quantity	➤	quantities

➤ However, do *not* alter the spelling of proper names:

There are two "Sallys" in the junior class.

Shakespeare wrote plays about the "Henrys" of England.

➤ Some words ending in *o* add *es* to form the plural:

echo	➤	echoes
tomato	➤	tomatoes
potato	➤	potatoes
hero	➤	heroes
veto	➤	vetoes

➤ Some nouns ending in *f* or *fe* form the plural with *ves*:

calf	➤	calves
elf	➤	elves
knife	➤	knives
life	➤	lives
self	➤	selves
thief	➤	thieves
wife	➤	wives

➤ Other nouns change their form internally:

man   →   men
woman → women
child → children
mouse → mice

➤ In compound expressions, the principal noun is made plural:

sisters-in-law

passers-by

spoonsful

Homophones

Many spelling problems occur because words have syllables whose sounds are alike but could be spelled in more than one way: for example, *cede, ceed, sede*. These are called homophones.

➤ The most common form is *cede:*

precede   antecede
concede   intercede

➤ A few forms are spelled *ceed:*

exceed   proceed   succeed

➤ Only one form is spelled *sede:*

supersede

➤ For *able, ible,* the more common form is *able:*

curable   lovable   peaceable
imaginable   movable

➤ Though fewer in number, there are many common words ending in *ible*:

admissible   horrible   possible
compatible   intelligible   visible
credible   legible
eligible   perceptible

➤ There are also words ending in *ance, ant,* or *ence, ent:*

assistant	extravagant	ignorance
attendant	fragrant	relevance
dominant	hesitance	resistance

➤ Note, however:

adolescent	current	permanence
competent	frequent	vehemence
correspondent	negligence	

➤ Many nouns end in *-er:*

consumer	interpreter	philosopher
defender	organizer	

➤ Note, however:

actor	counselor	professor
creator	governor	tailor

NOTE: *The careful writer must memorize the most common spellings. We cannot always use a dictionary or a spellcheck program!*

On the following pages you will find a list of words often confused and an extensive list of words commonly misspelled.

WORDS COMMONLY CONFUSED

Many words in English sound or look very similar to one another. Such words are often "misspelled" as a result of the writer's confusion about them. Here are some of the most commonly confused words; *all are correctly spelled*. Be sure you know their respective meanings.

accept/except	breath/breathe
access/excess	choose/chose/chosen
adapt/adopt	cite/sight/site
advice/advise	cloths/clothes
affect/effect	coarse/course
allusion/illusion	complement/compliment
already/all ready	desert/dessert
altogether/all together	device/devise

discreet/discrete
dyeing/dying
elicit/illicit
elude/allude
envelop/envelope
formally/formerly
fourth/forth
hear/here
holy/wholly
hoping/hopping
idle/idol
imminent/eminent/emanate
its/it's
loath/loathe
local/locale
loose/lose
medal/meddle/metal/mettle
moral/morale
night/knight

principal/principle
quite/quiet
rain/reign/rein
right/rite
shone/shown
sight/site
stationary/stationery
than/then
their/there/they're
thorough/through
though/thought
threw/through
throne/thrown
to/too/two
vain/vane/vein
weather/whether
which/witch
who's/whose
your/you're

WORDS COMMONLY MISSPELLED

You will recognize the most familiar and the most notorious spelling demons in this list.

absence	acquire	against	analysis
absolutely	across	aggravate	analyze
academic	actually	aggravation	ancient
accept	address	aggressive	angrily
acceptance	adequately	alleviate	announcement
accessory	adherence	alliance	annually
accidentally	adjournment	ally	antagonist
accommodate	adjustment	almanac	antibiotic
accompanying	admittance	already	anticipation
accomplish	adolescent	altitude	antique
accuracy	advantage	amateur	anxious
achievement	advantageous	ambassador	apologetically
acknowledge	advertisement	amendment	apologies
acquaintance	advising	among	apologize

apology
apostrophe
apparently
appreciate
appropriate
approximate
aptitude
architecture
Arctic
argue

argument
arising
arrangement
article
artistically
ascend
ascent
assassin
assent
assistance

assumption
assurance
atheist
athlete
athletic
attempt
attendance
attractive
audience
authoritative

authority
auxiliary
availability
avalanche
average
awfully
awkward

bachelor
baggage
banana
bankruptcy
bargain
barrel
basement
basically
beautify
becoming

before
beginning
belief
believing
beneficial
benefit
benefited
bibliography
bicycle
biscuit

boring
boundary
breakfast
breath
breathe
bribery
brief
brilliant
Britain
brittle

bruise
budget
buoy
buoyant
bureau
burglar
burglarize
business
businesslike
busy

cafeteria
caffeine
calculator
calendar
calorie
campaign
candidate
cannibal
canoe
capable
capacity
captain
career
carrying
cashier
catastrophe
category
caucus
carefully
cease
ceiling
cellar

cemetery
censor
censure
century
certainly
challenge
changeable
changing
channel
characterize
chauffeur
chief
chimney
chivalry
chloride
cholera
choose
choosing
choral
chose
chuckle
cite

client
closet
clustered
coalition
coherence
collar
college
colonel
column
combustible
comfortable
coming
commencement
commercial
commission
commit
committee
communal
community
companies
comparative
comparison

compatible
compel
compelled
competitive
competitor
comprehensible
conceivable
conceive
concentrate
conception
condemn
condescend
conference
conferred
confidence
confidential
connotation
connote
conqueror
conscience
conscious
consequence

consequently
considerable
considerably
consistency
consistent
conspicuous
contemporary
contempt
contemptible
contemptuous
continual
continuous
contribution

controlled
controlling
controversial
convenience
convenient
convertible
convocation
cool
coolly
cooperate
corollary
corps
correlate

corrode
corrupt
counterfeit
courteous
courtesy
cousin
credible
creditor
credulous
crisis
critical
criticism
criticize

cruel
cruelly
cupola
curiosity
curious
current
curriculum
curtain
customary
customer
cyclical
cylinder

dangerous
debris
debt
debtor
deceit
deceitful
deceived
decency
decent
deception
decide
decision
default
defendant
defense
defer
deference
deferred
define
definitely
definition
deity
delegate

deliberately
deodorant
dependable
dependent
depth
deputy
descend
descendant
descent
desert
desirable
despair
despite
dessert
destroy
detriment
devastate
developed
development
deviate
device
devise
dexterity

diameter
different
difficult
dilemma
diligent
dining
disappearance
disappointment
disapprove
disaster
disastrous
discern
disciple
disciplinary
discipline
discomfort
discriminate
discriminatory
disease
disillusion
dispatch
disposal
disregard

dissatisfied
dissent
dissimilar
dissipate
divinity
divisible
division
doesn't
dominant
dominate
dormitory
dough
dramatize
drunkenness
due
dully
duly
during
dye
dyeing
dying

earnest
easily
economically
economy
ecstasy
edge

edgy
edition
editor
effect
efficiency
efficient

eight
eighth
eighty
electoral
elicit
eligible

eliminate
eloquent
elude
emanate
embarrass
embassy

emigrant	entirely	evidently	existence
emigrate	envelop	exaggerate	expedite
emphasis	envelope	exaggeration	expedition
emphasize	environment	exceed	experience
emphatic	equality	excellence	experiment
empirical	equally	exceptional	explanation
employee	equipment	excessive	explanatory
encouragement	equipped	excitable	exploit
encouraging	equivalent	excitement	explore
endeavor	erroneous	exclusive	extension
enough	escapade	exclusively	extraordinary
entangle	especially	excursion	extravagant
enterprise	essential	exhibit	extremely
entertain	everything	exhibition	
facility	feminine	forbidden	frequently
fallacious	feminist	forehead	fried
fallacy	feud	foreign	friendless
familiar	fictitious	forewarn	friendliness
fantasy	fidelity	forgetting	friendly
fascinate	fiend	formally	friendship
fashion	fiery	formerly	fulfill
fatality	filial	forth	fulfillment
faulty	finally	forty	fundamental
favorable	financial	fourth	furious
favorite	financier	fraternity	furthermore
February	flair	freight	
felicity	fluent	frequency	
gaiety	genetics	governor	grievous
gallant	genius	gradually	grocery
gardener	genuine	grammar	guarantee
gaseous	global	grandeur	guidance
gasoline	glorious	graphics	guilt
generally	glossary	grief	gymnasium
generation	goddess	grievance	
generic	government	grieve	
hammer	headache	hereditary	hopeful
handkerchief	heard	heroes	hopeless
handsome	heathen	heroic	hoping
happiness	heavily	heroine	hopping
harassment	height	hindrance	humidity
harpoon	heir	honorable	humor

humorous	hybrid	hypnotize	hysteria
hundredth	hygiene	hypocrisy	
hungrily	hypnosis	hypocrite	
hurrying	hypnotism	hypothesis	
icicle	incidentally	infancy	interaction
ignorant	incompetent	inferiority	intercede
illegal	inconvenience	infinite	interrelated
illicit	incredible	ingenious	interrupt
illusion	indebted	ingenuity	intimate
illusory	indecisive	ingenuous	introduce
imaginary	indefinite	inhabitant	invisible
imagine	independence	initiative	ironic
immaculate	indispensable	innocence	irony
immediately	indivisible	inquiry	irrelevant
immense	indulge	insistent	irresistible
immigrant	interference	inspiration	irritable
immoderate	inertia	intelligence	island
impressionable	inevitable	intentionally	isle
jealousy	journey	junction	
jewelry	judge	justifiable	
journal	judgment	justify	
kerosene	knight	kowtow	
kindergarten	knowledge		
laboratory	leisure	limb	losing
laborer	leisurely	literary	lottery
launch	lenient	literature	lovable
lawyer	library	liveliness	loveless
league	license	loathe	luncheon
legacy	lighten	loneliness	luscious
legible	lightning	lonely	luxurious
legislator	likelihood	loose	lying
legitimate	likely	lose	
macaroni	management	meanness	memorable
machinery	managing	medical	merchandise
magazine	maneuver	medicinal	merchant
magnificent	marriage	medicine	merger
maintenance	massacre	medieval	meteor
malaria	mathematics	medley	mettle
manageable	maximum	melancholy	miniature

minimum	misdemeanor	monogram	mosquitoes
minister	misfit	monopoly	mountain
miracle	missile	moral	movable
mirror	missionary	morale	muffle
mischief	misspell	mortgage	muscle
mischievous	monarch	mortified	mysterious
naturally	neighborly	ninth	nuisance
necessary	nickel	noticeable	
necessity	niece	notorious	
negligent	ninety	nuclear	
obedience	occasionally	opinion	originally
oblige	occur	opportunity	outrageous
obnoxious	occurred	opposite	overrated
obscure	occurrence	optimism	owing
observant	official	orchard	
obstacle	omission	ordinarily	
obtuse	omitted	organize	
package	pennant	pierce	predominant
pageant	perceive	pigeon	preference
paid	percentage	pillar	preferred
pamphlet	perception	planned	prejudice
parachute	perilous	plausible	preoccupied
paradox	permanence	playwright	preparation
paradoxical	permanent	pleasant	presence
paragraph	permissible	pledge	presidency
parallel	perplex	plentiful	prestige
paralysis	persistence	politeness	prevail
parcel	persistent	politician	prevalence
parenthesis	personally	popularity	priest
parliament	personnel	portable	primitive
partial	persuade	possess	principal
particle	persuasion	possession	principles
particularly	persuasive	possibility	priority
pastime	pertinent	possibly	privilege
patient	philosophy	potatoes	probability
patriotic	physical	practicality	probable
patriotism	physician	prairie	procedural
patron	pianos	prayer	procedure
peaceable	picnic	precede	proceed
peasant	picnicking	precedent	professional
peculiar	piece	precious	professor

prohibitive
prologue
promenade
prominent
promising
pronunciation

propel
propeller
prophecy
proprietor
psychiatrist
psychoanalysis

psychologist
psychosomatic
publicity
punctuation
purchase
purchasing

purgatory
purity
pursue
pursuit

qualified
qualitative

quandary
quantity

query
questionable

quiet
quite

radiant
ratify
realize
really
recede
receipt
receive
recessive
recognizable
recollect
recommend

recruit
recur
reference
referred
reign
rein
reliable
relieve
reluctance
remembrance
reminisce

repetitious
requirement
requisition
residence
resistance
resolving
resourceful
responsible
restaurant
reveille
rewrite

rhapsody
rhetoric
rheumatism
rhyme
rhythm
ridiculous
rigidity
routine

sacrifice
safety
salary
satellite
satisfactory
savage
scandal
scarcely
scary
scenery
scent
schedule
schism
scissors
scold
sculptor
secede
secrecy
secretary
seize
seniority
senseless

sensible
sensitive
separate
sergeant
several
shadowy
shady
shepherd
sheriff
shield
shining
shoulder
siege
sieve
significant
simile
simultaneous
sincerely
singular
siphon
skillful
society

solemn
solicit
soliloquy
solos
sophomore
source
sovereign
spaghetti
specimen
spectacles
spectacular
spirited
sponsor
squirrel
statue
stifle
stomach
straight
strategy
strength
strenuous
stressful

studying
submission
subsidy
substantial
substitute
subtle
succeed
successful
successive
sufficient
suffix
summary
superb
surgeon
surprise
susceptible
suspense
suspicion
suspicious
sustained
syllable
syllabus

symbol
symmetrical

sympathize
symphonic

symptom
synonym

tableau
tailor
technique
temperament
temperature
temporary
tendency
terrific
terrifying
territory
testimony

thematic
theoretical
therefore
thorough
tireless
tobacco
tolerance
tomato
tomatoes
tomorrow
tournament

traction
traffic
trafficked
tragedy
tragic
transfer
transferred
transistor
transitive
transparent
traveler

treachery
treason
treasury
truant
truly
turmoil
twelfth
twilight
typical
tyranny
tyrant

umbrella
unanimous
unconscious
undoubtedly

unison
unnecessary
unprecedented
unveil

urban
urgent
usually
utensil

utterance

vacuum
valleys
valuable
variety
various

varying
vegetable
vehicle
vengeance
vengeful

vicinity
victim
village
villain
villainous

vinegar
volcano
volunteer

warrant
warrior
wary
weapon
weather

weird
whereabouts
whimsical
whistle
wholesome

wholly
woolen
wrangle
wrestle
write

writing
written

yacht

yield

RECOMMENDED READING

The titles listed below, readily available in paperback, represent many of the classic and contemporary works most widely read and studied in comprehensive high school English courses; the emphasis is on works written in English, primarily by American writers. These titles are recommended to the student seeking to supplement regular course assignments or to prepare independently for the Regents exam. All would be suitable choices for an essay on the AP English Literature and Composition exam. These works also represent valuable additions to a student's personal library.

NOVELS

1984	George Orwell
A Death in the Family	James Agee
A Farewell to Arms	Ernest Hemingway
A Separate Peace	John Knowles
A Star Called Henry	Roddy Doyle
A Tale of Two Cities	Charles Dickens
All the King's Men	Robert Penn Warren
Americanah	Chimamanda Ngozi Adichie
Arrowsmith	Sinclair Lewis
Babbitt	Sinclair Lewis
Beloved	Toni Morrison
Billy Budd	Herman Melville
Brave New World	Aldous Huxley
Catch-22	Joseph Heller
Catcher in the Rye	J. D. Salinger
Cold Mountain	Charles Frazier
Daisy Miller	Henry James
Deliverance	James Dickey
Ethan Frome	Edith Wharton
Farenheit 451	Ray Bradbury
Felicia's Journey	William Trevor
Great Expectations	Charles Dickens
Huckleberry Finn	Mark Twain
Invisible Man	Ralph Ellison
Light in August	William Faulkner
Lord of the Flies	William Golding
Main Street	Sinclair Lewis

Native Son	Richard Wright
Netherland	Joseph O'Neill
Oliver Twist	Charles Dickens
One Hundred Years of Solitude	Gabriel Garcia Marquez
Ordinary People	Judith Guest
Rabbit, Run	John Updike
Ragtime	E. L. Doctorow
Rebecca	Daphne DuMaurier
Red Badge of Courage	Stephen Crane
Rumors of Peace	Ella Leffland
Sister Carrie	Theodore Dreiser
Slaughterhouse Five	Kurt Vonnegut
So Long, See You Tomorrow	William Maxwell
Summer	Edith Wharton
That Night	Alice McDermott
The Age of Innocence	Edith Wharton
The Assistant	Bernard Malamud
The Awakening	Kate Chopin
The Bean Trees	Barbara Kingsolver
The Bonfire of the Vanities	Tom Wolfe
The Caine Mutiny	Herman Wouk
The Centaur	John Updike
The Color Purple	Alice Walker
The Crying of Lot 49	Thomas Pynchon
The Grapes of Wrath	John Steinbeck
The Great Fire	Shirley Hazzard
The Great Gatsby	F. Scott Fitzgerald
The Heart Is a Lonely Hunter	Carson McCullers
The Human Stain	Philip Roth
The Joy Luck Club	Amy Tan
The Known World	Edward P. Jones
The Natural	Bernard Malamud
The Old Man and the Sea	Ernest Hemingway
The Secret Agent	Joseph Conrad
The Scarlet Letter	Nathaniel Hawthorne
The Time Machine	H. G. Wells
Things Fall Apart	Chinua Achebe
Things Invisible to See	Nancy Willard
To Kill a Mockingbird	Harper Lee
Underworld	Don DeLillo
Washington Square	Henry James
White Teeth	Zadie Smith
Wolf Hall	Hilary Mantel
World's Fair	E. L. Doctorow

AUTOBIOGRAPHY, ESSAYS, AND OTHER NONFICTION

A Civil Action	Jonathan Harr
A Hole in the Sky	Robert Finch
An American Childhood	Annie Dillard
Angela's Ashes	Frank McCourt
Black Boy	Richard Wright
Blood Dark Track	Joseph O'Neill
Cities on a Hill	Francis Fitzgerald
Dreams from My Father	Barack Obama
Growing Up	Russell Baker
Hiroshima	John Hersey
Hunger of Memory	Richard Rodriguez
I Know Why the Caged Bird Sings	Maya Angelou
Into Thin Air	Jon Krakauer
Iron and Silk	Mark Salzman
King of the World	David Remnick
Late Innings	Roger Angell
Nickel and Dimed	Barbara Ehrenreich
Night	Elie Wiesel
Notes of a Native Son	James Baldwin
Out of Africa	Isak Dinesen
Pilgrim at Tinker Creek	Annie Dillard
Stop-Time	Frank Conroy
Such, Such Were the Joys	George Orwell
The Art of Fiction	David Lodge
The Color of Water	James McBride
The Courage of Turtles	Edward Hoagland
The Crack-Up	F. Scott Fitzgerald
The Devils of Loudon	Aldous Huxley
The Duke of Deception	Geoffrey Wolff
The Last Cowboy	Jane Kramer
The Lives of a Cell	Lewis Thomas
The Mismeasure of Man	Stephen Jay Gould
The Solace of Open Spaces	Gretel Ehrlich
The Way to Rainy Mountain	N. Scott Momaday
The Warmth of Other Suns	Isabel Wilkerson
The White Album	Joan Didion
This Boy's Life	Tobias Wolff
This House of Sky	Ivan Doig
Travels with Charley	John Steinbeck
Up from Slavery	Booker T. Washington
Walden	Henry David Thoreau

There are many excellent collections of essays and literary nonfiction available. Here are some recommended classic and contemporary authors whose works are available in paperback editions:

Roger Angell	Stephen Jay Gould	Cynthia Ozick
Joan Didion	Garrison Keillor	David Remnick
Ralph Waldo	Tracy Kidder	Richard Rodriguez
Emerson	Verlyn Klinkenborg	Roger Rosenblatt
M. F. K. Fisher	Jane Kramer	Gore Vidal
Ian Frazier	Peter Mathiesson	Eudora Welty
Atul Gawande	Jane Mayer	E. B. White
Malcolm Gladwell	John McPhee	
Adam Gopnik	H. L. Mencken	

Recommended anthologies include:

The Art of the Personal Essay, by Philip Lopate; Anchor Books
The Best American Essays of the Century, Joyce Carol Oates, ed.;
    Houghton Mifflin Co.
The Best American Essays, compiled from essays written for magazines
    and journals and published annually by Houghton Mifflin Co.

Other volumes in the Best American Series, also published annually, include:

The Best American Sports Writing
The Best American Travel Writing
The Best American Science and Nature Writing
The Best American Nonrequired Reading

POETRY

Readers are urged to seek out collections of work by poets whom they encounter in class readings and whom they especially admire. *Dover Publications* offers nicely produced and very inexpensive paperback collections of poetry, including works of Shakespeare and other major British poets, as well as major American poets of the nineteenth and twentieth centuries. They are available from Dover online and in bookstores. Among the many poets introduced to high school students and whose work is widely available in paperback collections are the following:

W. H. Auden	Donald Hall	Adrienne Rich
Elizabeth Bishop	Langston Hughes	Theodore Roethke
Louise Bogan	Denise Levertov	Carl Sandburg
Gwendolyn Brooks	W. S. Merwin	Vijay Seshadri
Billy Collins	Edna St. Vincent	Charles Simic
e. e. cummings	Millay	*May Swenson
Emily Dickinson	Marianne Moore	William Stafford
*Rita Dove	Howard Nemerov	Richard Wilbur
T. S. Eliot	*Sharon Olds	Nancy Willard
Carolyn Forché	*Marge Piercy	William Carlos
Robert Frost	Robert Pinsky	Williams
Louise Glück	Sylvia Plath	

* denotes a poet whose work has appeared on a New York State English
   Regents exam

Some currently available paperback anthologies of poetry include:

Poetry 180, An Anthology of Contemporary Poems, Billy Collins, ed.;
   Random House
Good Poems, selected and introduced by Garrison Keillor; Penguin Books
Poetry Daily, 366 Poems, selected from the Poetry Daily website;
   Sourcebooks Inc.
The Best American Poetry, annual series, David Lehman, ed.; Scribner
Contemporary American Poetry, Donald Hall, ed.; Viking
The Mentor Book of Major American Poets, Oscar Williams and Edwin
   Honig, eds.; New American Library
The Vintage Book of Contemporary American Poetry, J. D. McClatchy, ed.

   Websites for the interested reader:

Poetry Daily: *www.poems.com*
Poetry Foundation: *www.poetryfoundation.org*
Academy of American Poets: *www.poets.org*
Poet's House: *www.poetshouse.org*
www.poemhunter.com

SHORT STORIES

Some recommended authors whose stories are available in paperback:

Sherwood Anderson	Nathaniel Hawthorne	Edgar Allan Poe
John Barth	Ernest Hemingway	Isaac Bashevis Singer
Ambrose Bierce	Bernard Malamud	William Trevor
Willa Cather	Bharati Mukherjee	John Updike
Isak Dinesen	Alice Munro	Kurt Vonnegut
William Faulkner	Joyce Carol Oates	Edith Wharton
F. Scott Fitzgerald	Tim O'Brien	Eudora Welty
Mavis Gallant	Flannery O'Connor	John Edgar Wideman

Collections available in paperback include:

Annual publications:
The O. Henry Prize Stories
The Best American Short Stories
The Pushcart Prize: Best of the Small Presses

Anthologies:
American Short Story Masterpieces, Raymond Carver and Tom Jenks, eds.
The Norton Anthology of Short Fiction, R. V. Cassill, ed.
The Oxford Book of American Short Stories, Joyce Carol Oates, ed.
The Oxford Book of Short Stories, V. S. Pritchett, ed.
   (includes British and American writers)
The Vintage Book of Contemporary American Short Stories, Tobias Wolff, ed.

PLAYS

Shakespeare	*Macbeth, Julius Caesar, Othello, As You Like It, Hamlet, King Lear, Much Ado About Nothing, The Tempest, Henry V*
Paddy Chayevsky	*Marty*
Anton Chekov	*Three Sisters, The Cherry Orchard, Uncle Vanya*
Henrik Ibsen	*A Doll's House, The Master Builder*
Edward Albee	*Who's Afraid of Virginia Woolf?, Zoo Story*
David Auburn	*Proof*
Samuel Beckett	*Waiting for Godot*
Robert Bolt	*A Man for All Seasons*
Noel Coward	*Blithe Spirit, Private Lives*
Mart Crowley	*The Boys in the Band*

Horton Foote	*Dividing the Estate, The Trip to Bountiful, The Young Man from Atlanta*
William Gibson	*The Miracle Worker*
Susan Glaspell	*Trifles*
John Guare	*Six Degrees of Separation*
A. R. Gurney	*The Dining Room*
Lorraine Hansberry	*A Raisin in the Sun*
Lillian Hellman	*The Little Foxes*
Beth Henley	*Crimes of the Heart*
William Inge	*Come Back, Little Sheba; Picnic; Bus Stop*
Eugene Ionesco	*The Lesson, The Bald Soprano, Rhinoceros*
George S. Kaufman/Moss Hart	*You Can't Take It With You, The Man Who Came to Dinner*
Jerome Lawrence/ Robert Lee	*Inherit the Wind*
Terrence McNally	*Master Class*
Arthur Miller	*All My Sons, Death of a Salesman, The Crucible, The Price, A View From the Bridge*
Clifford Odets	*Waiting for Lefty, The Country Girl*
Eugene O'Neill	*Long Day's Journey into Night*
Harold Pinter	*The Caretaker*
Terrence Rattigan	*The Winslow Boy, The Browning Version*
Yasmina Reza	*Art*
Rod Serling	*Requiem for a Heavyweight*
Peter Shaffer	*Equus, Black Comedy, The Royal Hunt of the Sun, Amadeus*
George Bernard Shaw	*Pygmalion*
Neil Simon	*The Odd Couple, Brighton Beach Memoirs*
Tom Stoppard	*Rosenkrantz and Guildenstern Are Dead, Arcadia, The Real Thing, Jumpers, The Coast of Utopia*
Alfred Uhry	*Driving Miss Daisy*
Wendy Wasserstein	*The Heidi Chronicles*
Oscar Wilde	*The Importance of Being Earnest*
Thornton Wilder	*Our Town, The Matchmaker, The Skin of Our Teeth*
Tennessee Williams	*The Glass Menagerie, A Streetcar Named Desire, Cat on a Hot Tin Roof, Sweet Bird of Youth*
August Wilson	*Fences, The Piano Lesson, Ma Rainey's Black Bottom, Jitney, Joe Turner's Come and Gone*

Appendices

The New York State Common Core Learning Standards for English Language Arts

The following 11/12 grade-specific standards define end-of-year expectations and a cumulative progression designed to enable students to meet college and career readiness (CCR) expectations no later than the end of high school. The new ELA/Common Core Regents Exam is designed to assess many (but not all) of the standards in each of the categories: Reading Literature, Reading Informational Texts, Writing, and Language.

READING STANDARDS FOR LITERATURE GRADES 11/12 (RL)

1. Cite strong and thorough textual evidence to support analysis of what the text says explicitly as well as inferences drawn from the text, including determining where the text leaves matters uncertain.

2. Determine two or more themes or central ideas of a text and analyze their development over the course of the text, including how they interact and build on one another to produce a complex account; provide an objective summary of the text.

3. Analyze the impact of the author's choices regarding how to develop and relate elements of a story or drama (e.g., where a story is set, how the action is ordered, how the characters are introduced and developed).

4. Determine the meaning of words and phrases as they are used in the text, including figurative and connotative meanings; analyze the impact of specific word choices on meaning and tone, including words with

multiple meanings or language that is particularly fresh, engaging, or beautiful. (Include Shakespeare as well as other authors.)

5. Analyze how an author's choices concerning how to structure specific parts of a text (e.g., the choice of where to begin or end a story, the choice to provide a comedic or tragic resolution) contribute to its overall structure and meaning as well as its aesthetic impact.

6. Analyze a case in which grasping a point of view requires distinguishing what is directly stated in a text from what is really meant (e.g., satire, sarcasm, irony, or understatement).

7. Analyze multiple interpretations of a story, drama, or poem (e.g., recorded or live production of a play or recorded novel or poetry), evaluating how each version interprets the source text. (Include at least one play by Shakespeare and one play by an American dramatist.)

*8. Delineate and evaluate the argument and specific claims in a text, including the validity of the reasoning as well as the relevance and sufficiency of the evidence.

9. Demonstrate knowledge of eighteenth-, nineteenth-, and early-twentieth-century foundational works of American literature, including how two or more texts from the same period treat similar themes or topics.

10. By the end of grade 11, read and comprehend literature, including stories, dramas, and poems, in the grades 11–CCR text complexity band proficiently, with scaffolding as needed at the high end of the range.

11. By the end of grade 12, read and comprehend literature, including stories, dramas, and poems, at the high end of the grades 11–CCR text complexity band independently and proficiently.

*This anchor standard does not apply to literature.

READING STANDARDS FOR INFORMATIONAL TEXT GRADES 11/12 (RI)

1. Cite strong and thorough textual evidence to support analysis of what the text says explicitly as well as inferences drawn from the text, including determining where the text leaves matters uncertain.

2. Determine two or more central ideas of a text and analyze their development over the course of the text, including how they interact and build on one another to provide a complex analysis; provide an objective summary of the text.

3. Analyze a complex set of ideas or sequence of events and explain how specific individuals, ideas, or events interact and develop over the course of the text.

4. Determine the meaning of words and phrases as they are used in a text, including figurative, connotative, and technical meanings; analyze how an author uses and refines the meaning of a key term or terms over the course of a text.

5. Analyze and evaluate the effectiveness of the structure an author uses in his or her exposition or argument, including whether the structure makes points clear, convincing, and engaging.

6. Determine an author's point of view or purpose in a text in which the rhetoric is particularly effective, analyzing how style and content contribute to the power, persuasiveness, or beauty of the text.

7. Integrate and evaluate multiple sources of information presented in different media or formats (e.g., visually, quantitatively) as well as in words in order to address a question or solve a problem.

8. Delineate and evaluate the reasoning in seminal U.S. texts, including the application of constitutional principles and use of legal reasoning (e.g., in U.S. Supreme Court majority opinions and dissents) and the premises, purposes, and arguments in works of public advocacy (e.g., The Federalist, presidential addresses).

9. Analyze seventeenth-, eighteenth-, and nineteenth-century foundational U.S. documents of historical and literary significance (including The Declaration of Independence, the Preamble to the Constitution, the Bill of Rights, and Lincoln's Second Inaugural Address) for their themes, purposes, and rhetorical features.

10. By the end of grade 11, read and comprehend literary nonfiction in the grade 11–CCR text complexity band proficiently, with scaffolding as needed at the high end of the range. By the end of grade 12, read and comprehend literary nonfiction at the high end of the grade 11–CCR text complexity band independently and proficiently.

WRITING STANDARDS
GRADES 11/12   (W)

1. Write arguments to support claims in an analysis of substantive topics or texts, using valid reasoning and relevant and sufficient evidence.

2. Write informative/explanatory texts to examine and convey complex ideas and information clearly and accurately through the effective selection, organization, and analysis of content.

3. Write narratives to develop real or imagined experiences or events using effective technique, well-chosen details, and well-structured event sequences.

4. Produce clear and coherent writing in which the development, organization, and style are appropriate to task, purpose, and audience.

5. Develop and strengthen writing as needed by planning, revising, editing, rewriting, or trying a new approach.

6. Use technology, including the Internet, to produce and publish writing and to interact and collaborate with others.

7. Conduct short as well as more sustained research projects based on focused questions, demonstrating understanding of the subject under investigation.

8. Gather relevant information from multiple print and digital sources, assess the credibility and accuracy of each source, and integrate the information while avoiding plagiarism.

9. Draw evidence from literary or informational texts to support analysis, reflection, and research.

10. Write routinely over extended time frames (time for research, reflection, and revision) and shorter time frames (a single sitting or a day or two) for a range of tasks, purposes, and audiences.

11. Develop personal, cultural, textual, and thematic connections within and across genres as they respond to texts through written, digital, and oral presentations, employing a variety of media and genres.

LANGUAGE STANDARDS
GRADES 11/12   (L)

Conventions of Standard English

1. Demonstrate command of the conventions of standard English grammar and usage when writing or speaking.

2. Demonstrate command of the conventions of standard English capitalization, punctuation, and spelling when writing.

Knowledge of Language

3. Apply knowledge of language to understand how language functions in different contexts, to make effective choices for meaning or style, and to comprehend more fully when reading or listening.

Vocabulary Acquisition and Use

4. Determine or clarify the meaning of unknown and multiple meaning words and phrases by using context clues, analyzing meaningful word parts, and consulting general and specialized reference materials, as appropriate.

5. Demonstrate understanding of figurative language, word relationships, and nuances in word meanings.

6. Acquire and use accurately a range of general academic and domain-specific words and phrases sufficient for reading, writing, speaking, and listening at the college and career readiness level; demonstrate independence in gathering vocabulary knowledge when considering a word or phrase important to comprehension or expression.

HOW IS THE REGENTS ELA
(COMMON CORE) EXAM SCORED?

WEIGHTING OF PARTS

Each of the three parts of the Regents Examination in English Language Arts (Common Core) has a number of raw score credits associated with the questions/tasks within that part. In order to ensure an appropriate distribution of credits across the test, each part is weighted.

For Part 1, each multiple-choice question is worth one point. The Part 2 essay is scored on a 6-point rubric and then weighted $\times$ 4. The Part 3 Text Analysis is scored on a 4-point rubric and then weighted $\times$ 2.

As you can see, the Part 2 Argument Essay is the most heavily weighted section.

The table below shows the raw score credits, weighting factor, and weighted score credits for each part of the test. This information will be used to determine each student's scale score (final exam score) through the use of a conversion chart provided by NYSED.

Part	Maximum Raw Score Credits	Weighting Factor	Maximum Weighted Score Credits
Part 1	24	1	24
Part 2	6	4	24
Part 3	4	2	8
			Total 56

The conversion table is determined independently for each administration of the exam. You can find the conversion tables for both forms of the Regents English Exams at *http://www.nysedregents.org*.

SCORING RUBRICS FOR THE REGENTS ELA (COMMON CORE) EXAM

Parts 2 and 3 of the Regents Examination in English Language Arts (Common Core) will be scored using new holistic rubrics. Part 2 will be scored using a 6-credit rubric, and Part 3 will be scored using a 4-credit rubric. Both rubrics reflect the new demands called for by the Common Core Learning Standards for English Language Arts and Literacy through the end of Grade 11.

New York State Regents Examination in English Language Arts (Common Core)
Part 2 Rubric
Writing from Sources: Argument

Criteria	6 Essays at this Level	5 Essays at this Level	4 Essays at this Level	3 Essays at this Level	2 Essays at this Level	1 Essays at this Level
Content and Analysis: the extent to which the essay conveys complex ideas and information clearly and accurately in order to support claims in an analysis of the texts	-introduce a precise and insightful claim, as directed by the task -demonstrate in-depth and insightful analysis of the texts, as necessary to support the claim and to distinguish the claim from alternate or opposing claims	-introduce a precise and thoughtful claim, as directed by the task -demonstrate thorough analysis of the texts, as necessary to support the claim and to distinguish the claim from alternate or opposing claims	-introduce a precise claim, as directed by the task -demonstrate appropriate and accurate analysis of the texts, as necessary to support the claim and to distinguish the claim from alternate or opposing claims	-introduce a reasonable claim, as directed by the task -demonstrate some analysis of the texts, but insufficiently distinguish the claim from alternate or opposing claims	-introduce a claim -demonstrate confused or unclear analysis of the texts, failing to distinguish the claim from alternate or opposing claims	-do not introduce a claim -do not demonstrate analysis of the texts
Command of Evidence: the extent to which the essay presents evidence from the provided texts to support analysis	-present ideas fully and thoughtfully, making highly effective use of a wide range of specific and relevant evidence to support analysis -demonstrate proper citation of sources to avoid plagiarism when dealing with direct quotes and paraphrased material	-present ideas clearly and accurately, making effective use of specific and relevant evidence to support analysis -demonstrate proper citation of sources to avoid plagiarism when dealing with direct quotes and paraphrased material	-present ideas sufficiently, making adequate use of specific and relevant evidence to support analysis -demonstrate proper citation of sources to avoid plagiarism when dealing with direct quotes and paraphrased material	-present ideas briefly, making use of some specific and relevant evidence to support analysis -demonstrate inconsistent citation of sources to avoid plagiarism when dealing with direct quotes and paraphrased material	-present ideas inconsistently and/or inaccurately, in an attempt to support analysis, making use of some evidence that may be irrelevant -demonstrate little use of citations to avoid plagiarism when dealing with direct quotes and paraphrased material	-present little or no evidence from the texts -do not make use of citations

Coherence, Organization, and Style: the extent to which the essay logically organizes complex ideas, concepts, and information using formal style and precise language	-exhibit skillful organization of ideas and information to create a cohesive and coherent essay -establish and maintain a formal style, using sophisticated language and structure	-exhibit logical organization of ideas and information to create a cohesive and coherent essay -establish and maintain a formal style, using fluent and precise language and sound structure	-exhibit acceptable organization of ideas and information to create a coherent essay -establish and maintain a formal style, using precise and appropriate language and structure	-exhibit some organization of ideas and information to create a mostly coherent essay -establish but fail to maintain a formal style, using primarily basic language and structure	-exhibit inconsistent organization of ideas and information, failing to create a coherent essay -lack a formal style, using some language that is inappropriate or imprecise	-exhibit little organization of ideas and information -are minimal, making assessment unreliable -use language that is predominantly incoherent, inappropriate, or copied directly from the task or texts
Control of Conventions: the extent to which the essay demonstrates command of conventions of standard English grammar, usage, capitalization, punctuation, and spelling	-demonstrate control of conventions with essentially no errors, even with sophisticated language	-demonstrate control of the conventions, exhibiting occasional errors only when using sophisticated language	-demonstrate partial control, exhibiting occasional errors that do not hinder comprehension	-demonstrate emerging control, exhibiting occasional errors that hinder comprehension	-demonstrate a lack of control, exhibiting frequent errors that make comprehension difficult	-are minimal, making assessment of conventions unreliable

- An essay that addresses fewer texts than required by the task can be scored no higher than a 3.
- An essay that is a personal response and makes little or no reference to the task or texts can be scored no higher than a 1.
- An essay that is totally copied from the task and/or texts with no original student writing must be scored a 0.
- An essay that is totally unrelated to the task, illegible, incoherent, blank, or unrecognizable as English must be scored as a 0.

New York State Regents Examination in English Language Arts (Common Core)
Part 3 Rubric
Text Analysis: Exposition

Criteria	4 Responses at this Level	3 Responses at this Level	2 Responses at this Level	1 Responses at this Level
Content and Analysis: the extent to which the response conveys complex ideas and information clearly and accurately in order to respond to the task and support an analysis of the text	-introduce a well-reasoned central idea and a writing strategy that clearly establish the criteria for analysis -demonstrate a thoughtful analysis of the author's use of the writing strategy to develop the central idea	-introduce a clear central idea and a writing strategy that establish the criteria for analysis -demonstrate an appropriate analysis of the author's use of the writing strategy to develop the central idea	-introduce a central idea and/or a writing strategy -demonstrate a superficial analysis of the author's use of the writing strategy to develop the central idea	-introduce a confused or incomplete central idea or writing strategy and/or -demonstrate a minimal analysis of the author's use of the writing strategy to develop the central idea
Command of Evidence: the extent to which the response presents evidence from the provided text to support analysis	-present ideas clearly and consistently, making effective use of specific and relevant evidence to support analysis	-present ideas sufficiently, making adequate use of relevant evidence to support analysis	-present ideas inconsistently, inadequately, and/or inaccurately in an attempt to support analysis, making use of some evidence that may be irrelevant	-present little or no evidence from the text
Coherence, Organization, and Style: the extent to which the response logically organizes complex ideas, concepts, and information using formal style and precise language	-exhibit logical organization of ideas and information to create a cohesive and coherent response -establish and maintain a formal style, using precise language and sound structure	-exhibit acceptable organization of ideas and information to create a coherent response -establish and maintain a formal style, using appropriate language and structure	-exhibit inconsistent organization of ideas and information, failing to create a coherent response -lack a formal style, using language that is basic, inappropriate, or imprecise	-exhibit little organization of ideas and information -use language that is predominantly incoherent, inappropriate, or copied directly from the task or text -are minimal, making assessment unreliable

231

Control of Conventions: the extent to which the response demonstrates command of conventions of standard English grammar, usage, capitalization, punctuation, and spelling	-demonstrate control of the conventions with infrequent errors	-demonstrate partial control of conventions with occasional errors that do not hinder comprehension	-demonstrate emerging control of conventions with some errors that hinder comprehension	-demonstrate a lack of control of conventions with frequent errors that make comprehension difficult -are minimal, making assessment of conventions unreliable

- A response that is a personal response and makes little or no reference to the task or text can be scored no higher than a 1.
- A response that is totally copied from the text with no original writing must be given a 0.
- A response that is totally unrelated to the task, illegible, incoherent, blank, or unrecognizable as English must be scored as a 0.

Regents ELA (Common Core) Examination June 2016

English Language Arts

PART 1—Reading Comprehension

Directions (1–24): Closely read each of the three passages below. After each passage, there are several multiple-choice questions. Select the best suggested answer to each question and write its number in the space provided. You may use the margins to take notes as you read.

Reading Comprehension Passage A

...When the short days of winter came dusk fell before we had well
eaten our dinners. When we met in the street the houses had grown sombre. The space of sky above us was the colour of ever-changing violet and
towards it the lamps of the street lifted their feeble lanterns. The cold air
(5) stung us and we played till our bodies glowed. Our shouts echoed in the
silent street. The career of our play brought us through the dark muddy
lanes behind the houses where we ran the gauntlet of the rough tribes[1]
from the cottages, to the back doors of the dark dripping gardens where
odours arose from the ashpits, to the dark odorous stables where a coach-
(10) man smoothed and combed the horse or shook music from the buckled
harness. When we returned to the street light from the kitchen windows
had filled the areas. If my uncle was seen turning the corner we hid in
the shadow until we had seen him safely housed. Or if Mangan's sister
came out on the doorstep to call her brother in to his tea we watched her

---

[1]tribes—gangs

233

(15) from our shadow peer up and down the street. We waited to see whether she would remain or go in and, if she remained, we left our shadow and walked up to Mangan's steps resignedly. She was waiting for us, her figure defined by the light from the half-opened door. Her brother always teased her before he obeyed and I stood by the railings looking at her. Her
(20) dress swung as she moved her body and the soft rope of her hair tossed from side to side.

Every morning I lay on the floor in the front parlour watching her door. The blind was pulled down to within an inch of the sash so that I could not be seen. When she came out on the doorstep my heart leaped. I
(25) ran to the hall, seized my books and followed her. I kept her brown figure always in my eye and, when we came near the point at which our ways diverged, I quickened my pace and passed her. This happened morning after morning. I had never spoken to her, except for a few casual words, and yet her name was like a summons to all my foolish blood. ...

(30) At last she spoke to me. When she addressed the first words to me I was so confused that I did not know what to answer. She asked me was I going to *Araby*. I forget whether I answered yes or no. It would be a splendid bazaar,[2] she said she would love to go.

"And why can't you?" I asked.

(35) While she spoke she turned a silver bracelet round and round her wrist. She could not go, she said, because there would be a retreat[3] that week in her convent.[4] Her brother and two other boys were fighting for their caps and I was alone at the railings. She held one of the spikes, bowing her head towards me. The light from the lamp opposite our door caught the
(40) white curve of her neck, lit up her hair that rested there and, falling, lit up the hand upon the railing. It fell over one side of her dress and caught the white border of a petticoat, just visible as she stood at ease.

"It's well for you," she said.

"If I go," I said, "I will bring you something."

(45) What innumerable follies laid waste my waking and sleeping thoughts after that evening! I wished to annihilate the tedious intervening days. I chafed against the work of school. At night in my bedroom and by day in the classroom her image came between me and the page I strove to read. The syllables of the word *Araby* were called to me through the silence in
(50) which my soul luxuriated and cast an Eastern enchantment over me. I asked for leave to go to the bazaar on Saturday night. My aunt was sur-

---

[2]bazaar—fair
[3]retreat—a time set aside for prayer and reflection
[4]convent—religious school

prised and hoped it was not some Freemason[5] affair. I answered few questions in class. I watched my master's face pass from amiability to sternness;
he hoped I was not beginning to idle. I could not call my wandering
(55)   thoughts together. I had hardly any patience with the serious work of life
which, now that it stood between me and my desire, seemed to me child's
play, ugly monotonous child's play.

On Saturday morning I reminded my uncle that I wished to go to the
bazaar in the evening. He was fussing at the hallstand, looking for the hat-
(60)   brush, and answered me curtly:

"Yes, boy, I know." ...

At nine o'clock I heard my uncle's latchkey in the halldoor. I heard him
talking to himself and heard the hallstand rocking when it had received
the weight of his overcoat. I could interpret these signs. When he was
(65)   midway through his dinner I asked him to give me the money to go to the
bazaar. He had forgotten.

"The people are in bed and after their first sleep now," he said.

I did not smile. My aunt said to him energetically: "Can't you give him
the money and let him go? You've kept him late enough as it is." ...

(70)   I held a florin[6] tightly in my hand as I strode down Buckingham Street
towards the station. The sight of the streets thronged with buyers and
glaring with gas recalled to me the purpose of my journey. I took my seat
in a third-class carriage of a deserted train. After an intolerable delay the
train moved out of the station slowly. It crept onward among ruinous
(75)   houses and over the twinkling river. At Westland Row Station a crowd
of people pressed to the carriage doors; but the porters moved them back,
saying that it was a special train for the bazaar. I remained alone in the
bare carriage. In a few minutes the train drew up beside an improvised
wooden platform. I passed out on to the road and saw by the lighted dial
(80)   of a clock that it was ten minutes to ten. In front of me was a large building which displayed the magical name. ...

Remembering with difficulty why I had come I went over to one of the
stalls and examined porcelain vases and flowered tea-sets. At the door of
the stall a young lady was talking and laughing with two young gentle-
(85)   men. I remarked their English accents and listened vaguely to their
conversation. ...

Observing me the young lady came over and asked me did I wish to buy
anything. The tone of her voice was not encouraging; she seemed to have
spoken to me out of a sense of duty. I looked humbly at the great jars that

[5]Freemason—a fraternal organization
[6]florin—coin

235

(90) stood like eastern guards at either side of the dark entrance to the stall and
murmured:

"No, thank you."

The young lady changed the position of one of the vases and went back
to the two young men. They began to talk of the same subject. Once or
(95) twice the young lady glanced at me over her shoulder.

I lingered before her stall, though I knew my stay was useless, to make
my interest in her wares seem the more real. Then I turned away slowly
and walked down the middle of the bazaar. I allowed the two pennies to
fall against the sixpence in my pocket. I heard a voice call from one end
(100) of the gallery that the light was out. The upper part of the hall was now
completely dark.

Gazing up into the darkness I saw myself as a creature driven and
derided by vanity; and my eyes burned with anguish and anger.

—James Joyce
excerpted from "Araby"
Dubliners, 1914
Grant Richards LTD.

1 The description of the neighborhood in lines 1 through 11 contributes to a mood of

   (1) indifference   (3) anxiety
   (2) gloom   (4) regret   1____

2 Which quotation from the text best illustrates the narrator's attitude toward Mangan's sister?

   (1) "we watched her from our shadow" (lines 14 and 15)
   (2) "We waited to see whether she would remain or go in" (lines 15 and 16)
   (3) "yet her name was like a summons" (line 29)
   (4) "She asked me was I going to *Araby*" (lines 31 and 32)   2____

3 Lines 30 through 39 reveal Mangan's sister's

   (1) disinterest   (3) disappointment
   (2) silliness   (4) tension   3____

4 Lines 45 through 57 help to develop the idea that the narrator has

   (1) recognized that his priorities have changed
   (2) determined the academic focus of his studies
   (3) eliminated distractions from his daily routine
   (4) reassessed his relationship with his family   4____

5 The description of the narrator's train ride (lines 70 through 79) supports a theme of

   (1) confusion   (3) persecution
   (2) isolation   (4) deception   5____

6 The description in lines 87 through 97 suggests that the bazaar symbolizes

   (1) excessive greed   (3) false promise
   (2) future wealth   (4) lasting love   6____

7 It can be inferred from the text that the narrator's behavior is most guided by his

   (1)   school experience
   (2)   family situation
   (3)   childhood memories
   (4)   romantic feelings   7____

8 As used in line 103, the word "derided" most nearly means

   (1)   taunted   (3)   rewarded
   (2)   restrained   (4)   flattered   8____

9 Based on the text as a whole, the narrator's feelings of "anguish and anger" (line 103) are most likely a result of his having

   (1)   ignored his opportunities
   (2)   defended his family
   (3)   realized his limitations
   (4)   denied his responsibilities   9____

10 Which quotation best reflects a central theme of the text?

   (1)   "Her brother and two other boys were fighting for their caps" (lines 37 and 38)
   (2)   " 'Can't you give him the money and let him go?' " (lines 68 and 69)
   (3)   "It crept onward among ruinous houses and over the twinkling river" (lines 74 and 75)
   (4)   "I lingered before her stall, though I knew my stay was useless" (line 96)   10____

Reading Comprehension Passage B

Assembly Line

In time's assembly line
Night presses against night.
We come off the factory night-shift
In line as we march towards home.
(5) Over our heads in a row
The assembly line of stars
Stretches across the sky.
Beside us, little trees
Stand numb in assembly lines.

(10) The stars must be exhausted
After thousands of years
Of journeys which never change.
The little trees are all sick,
Choked on smog and monotony,
Stripped of their color and shape.
(15) It's not hard to feel for them;
We share the same tempo and rhythm.

Yes, I'm numb to my own existence
As if, like the trees and stars
(20) —perhaps just out of habit
—perhaps just out of sorrow,
I'm unable to show concern
For my own manufactured fate.

—Shu Ting
from *A Splintered Mirror: Chinese Poetry from the
Democracy Movement*, 1991
translated by Carolyn Kizer
North Point Press

11 In the first stanza, a main idea is strengthened through the poet's use of

   (1) repetition   (3) allusion

   (2) simile   (4) understatement   11_____

12 Line 17 contributes to a central idea by pointing out a parallel between

   (1) profit and industrialization

   (2) humans and nature

   (3) recreation and production

   (4) sound and motion   12_____

13 The structure and language of lines 20 and 21 suggests the narrator's

   (1) bitterness   (3) selfishness

   (2) determination   (4) uncertainty   13_____

14 The phrase "manufactured fate" (line 23) emphasizes the narrator's

   (1) resignation to life

   (2) desire for control

   (3) hope for change

   (4) rejection of nature   14_____

Reading Comprehension Passage C

...Memory teaches me what I know of these matters. The boy reminds the adult. I was a bilingual child, but of a certain kind: "socially disadvantaged," the son of working-class parents, both Mexican immigrants. ...

(5) In public, my father and mother spoke a hesitant, accented, and not always grammatical English. And then they would have to strain, their bodies tense, to catch the sense of what was rapidly said by *los gringos*. At home, they returned to Spanish. The language of their Mexican past sounded in counterpoint to the English spoken in public. The words would come quickly, with ease. Conveyed through those sounds was the

(10) pleasing, soothing, consoling reminder that one was at home.

During those years when I was first learning to speak, my mother and father addressed me only in Spanish; in Spanish I learned to reply. By contrast, English (*inglés*) was the language I came to associate with gringos, rarely heard in the house. I learned my first words of English overhearing

(15) my parents speaking to strangers. At six years of age, I knew just enough words for my mother to trust me on errands to stores one block away— but no more.

I was then a listening child, careful to hear the very different sounds of Spanish and English. Wide-eyed with hearing, I'd listen to sounds

(20) more than to words. First, there were English (gringo) sounds. So many words still were unknown to me that when the butcher or the lady at the drugstore said something, exotic polysyllabic sounds would bloom in the midst of their sentences. Often the speech of people in public seemed to me very loud, booming with confidence. The man behind the counter would

(25) literally ask, "What can I do for you?" But by being so firm and clear, the sound of his voice said that he was a gringo; he belonged in public society. There were also the high, nasal notes of middle-class American speech— which I rarely am conscious of hearing today because I hear them so often, but could not stop hearing when I was a boy. Crowds at Safeway or at bus

(30) stops were noisy with the birdlike sounds of *los gringos*. I'd move away from them all—all the chirping chatter above me.

My own sounds I was unable to hear, but I knew that I spoke English poorly. My words could not extend to form complete thoughts. And the words I did speak I didn't know well enough to make distinct sounds.

(35) (Listeners would usually lower their heads to hear better what I was trying

241

to say.) But it was one thing for *me* to speak English with difficulty; it was more troubling to hear my parents speaking in public: their high-whining vowels and guttural[1] consonants; their sentences that got stuck with "eh" and "ah" sounds; the confused syntax; the hesitant rhythm of sounds so
(40) different from the way gringos spoke. I'd notice, moreover, that my parents' voices were softer than those of gringos we would meet.

I am tempted to say now that none of this mattered. (In adulthood I am embarrassed by childhood fears.) And, in a way, it didn't matter very much that my parents could not speak English with ease. Their linguistic
(45) difficulties had no serious consequences. My mother and father made themselves understood at the county hospital clinic and at government offices. And yet, in another way, it mattered very much. It was unsettling to hear my parents struggle with English. Hearing them, I'd grow nervous, and my clutching trust in their protection and power would be weakened. ...

(50) But then there was Spanish: *español*, the language rarely heard away from the house; *español*, the language which seemed to me therefore a private language, my family's language. To hear its sounds was to feel myself specially recognized as one of the family, apart from *los otros*.[2] A simple remark, an inconsequential comment could convey that assurance.
(55) My parents would say something to me and I would feel embraced by the sounds of their words. Those sounds said: *I am speaking with ease in Spanish. I am addressing you in words I never use with* los gringos. *I recognize you as someone special, close, like no one outside. You belong with us. In the family. Ricardo.*

(60) At the age of six, well past the time when most middle-class children no longer notice the difference between sounds uttered at home and words spoken in public, I had a different experience. I lived in a world compounded of sounds. I was a child longer than most. I lived in a magical world, surrounded by sounds both pleasing and fearful. I shared with my
(65) family a language enchantingly private—different from that used in the city around us. ...

If I rehearse here the changes in my private life after my Americanization, it is finally to emphasize a public gain. The loss implies the gain. The house I returned to each afternoon was quiet. Intimate
(70) sounds no longer greeted me at the door. Inside there were other noises.

---

[1]guttural—throaty
[2]los otros—the others

The telephone rang. Neighborhood kids ran past the door of the bedroom where I was reading my schoolbooks—covered with brown shopping-bag paper. Once I learned the public language, it would never again be easy for me to hear intimate family voices. More and more of my day was spent (75) hearing words, not sounds. But that may only be a way of saying that on the day I raised my hand in class and spoke loudly to an entire roomful of faces, my childhood started to end. ...

—Richard Rodriguez
excerpted from "Aria: A Memoir of a Bilingual Childhood"
The American Scholar, Winter 1981
The Phi Beta Kappa Society

15 The phrase "the boy reminds the adult" in the first paragraph establishes the narrator's

    (1) mood   (3) creativity

    (2) perspective   (4) disposition   15_____

16 The use of the word "counterpoint" in line 8 helps to develop a central idea by presenting

    (1) differing memories

    (2) opposing principles

    (3) contrasting cultures

    (4) conflicting philosophies   16_____

17 The use of figurative language in lines 19 and 20 demonstrates the narrator's

    (1) eagerness to learn

    (2) desire for recognition

    (3) frustration with authority

    (4) anxiety about adulthood   17_____

18 The use of the word "public" in line 26 emphasizes the narrator's feeling of

    (1) accomplishment   (3) satisfaction

    (2) disillusionment   (4) separation   18_____

19 The description of the narrator speaking English in lines 32 through 36 emphasizes his inability to

    (1) communicate effectively

    (2) understand the culture

    (3) distinguish between languages

    (4) express emotions   19_____

20 In lines 44 through 49 the narrator's reaction to his parents' "linguistic difficulties" (lines 44 and 45) reveals his

  (1) low expectations   (3) educational concerns

  (2) conflicting feelings   (4) hostile thoughts   20____

21 Lines 50 through 59 contribute to a central idea in the text by focusing on the

  (1) narrator's sense of security

  (2) family's economic status

  (3) family's traditional beliefs

  (4) narrator's feeling of confusion   21____

22 Which quotation best reflects the narrator's overall experience with language?

  (1) "The words would come quickly, with ease" (lines 8 and 9)

  (2) "I'd listen to sounds more than to words" (lines 19 and 20)

  (3) "My own sounds I was unable to hear, but I knew that I spoke English poorly" (lines 32 and 33)

  (4) "Hearing them, I'd grow nervous" (line 48)   22____

23 The phrase "the loss implies the gain" (lines 68 and 69) contributes to a central idea in the text by indicating that when the narrator speaks English comfortably he is

  (1) disconnected from his family

  (2) distressed by hearing English sounds

  (3) uninterested in his school work

  (4) undeterred from making new friends   23____

24 The narrator's tone in lines 74 through 77 suggests

  (1) distrust   (3) confidence

  (2) respect   (4) intolerance   24____

PART 2—Argument Response

Directions: Closely read each of the *four* texts on pages 247 through 257 and write a source-based argument on the topic below. You may use the margins to take notes as you read and scrap paper to plan your response. Write your argument on a separate sheet of paper.

Topic: Should celebrities become the voice of humanitarian causes?

Your Task: Carefully read each of the *four* texts provided. Then, using evidence from at least *three* of the texts, write a well-developed argument regarding whether or not celebrities should become the voice of humanitarian causes. Clearly establish your claim, distinguish your claim from alternate or opposing claims, and use specific, relevant, and sufficient evidence from at least *three* of the texts to develop your argument. Do *not* simply summarize each text.

Guidelines:

Be sure to

- Establish your claim regarding whether or not celebrities should become the voice of humanitarian causes.
- Distinguish your claim from alternate or opposing claims.
- Use specific, relevant, and sufficient evidence from at least *three* of the texts to develop your argument.
- Identify each source that you reference by text number and line number(s) or graphic (for example: Text 1, line 4 or Text 2, graphic).
- Organize your ideas in a cohesive and coherent manner
- Maintain a formal style of writing.
- Follow the conventions of standard written English.

Texts:

Text 1—The Celebrity Solution

Text 2—Ethics of Celebrities and Their Increasing Influence in 21st Century Society

Text 3—Do Celebrity Humanitarians Matter?

Text 4—The Rise of the Celebrity Humanitarian

Text 1

The Celebrity Solution

   In 2004, Natalie Portman, then a 22-year-old fresh from college, went to Capitol Hill to talk to Congress on behalf of the Foundation for International Community Assistance, or Finca, a microfinance organization for which she served as "ambassador." She found herself wondering
(5) what she was doing there, but her colleagues assured her: "We got the meetings because of you." For lawmakers, Natalie Portman was not simply a young woman—she was the beautiful Padmé from "Star Wars." "And I was like, 'That seems totally nuts to me,' " Portman told me recently. [sic] It's the way it works, I guess. I'm not particularly proud
(10) that in our country I can get a meeting with a representative more easily than the head of a nonprofit can."
   Well, who is? But it is the way it works. Stars—movie stars, rock stars, sports stars—exercise a ludicrous influence over the public consciousness. Many are happy to exploit that power; others are wrecked by it. In recent
(15) years, stars have learned that their intense presentness in people's daily lives and their access to the uppermost realms of politics, business and the media offer them a peculiar kind of moral position, should they care to use it. And many of those with the most leverage—Bono and Angelina Jolie and Brad Pitt and George Clooney and, yes, Natalie Portman—have
(20) increasingly chosen to mount that pedestal. Hollywood celebrities have become central players on deeply political issues like development aid, refugees and government-sponsored violence in Darfur.
   Activists on these and other issues talk about the political power of stars with a mixture of bewilderment and delight. But a weapon that
(25) powerful is bound to do collateral damage. Some stars, like George Clooney, regard the authority thrust upon them with wariness; others, like Sean Penn or Mia Farrow, an activist on Darfur, seize the bully pulpit with both hands. "There is a tendency," says Donald Steinberg, deputy president of the International Crisis Group, which seeks to prevent con-
(30) flict around the world, "to treat these issues as if it's all good and evil." Sometimes you need the rallying cry, but sometimes you need to accept a complex truth. ...
   An entire industry has sprung up around the recruitment of celebrities to good works. Even an old-line philanthropy like the Red Cross employs
(35) a "director of celebrity outreach." Oxfam has a celebrity wrangler in Los Angeles, Lyndsay Cruz, on the lookout for stars who can raise the charity's profile with younger people. In addition to established figures like

Colin Firth and Helen Mirren, Oxfam is affiliated with Scarlett Johansson, who has visited South Asia (where the organization promotes girls' (40) education) and is scheduled to go to Mali. Cruz notes that while "trendy young people" are attracted to the star of "Match Point" and "Lost in Translation," Johansson had "great credibility with an older audience because she's such a great actress." …

Microfinance is a one-star cause. Though for some reason the subject (45) appeals to female royalty, including Queen Rania of Jordan and Princess Maxima of the Netherlands, Natalie Portman is the only member of Hollywood royalty who has dedicated herself to it. Perhaps this is because microfinance is a good deal more complicated than supplying fresh water to parched villages, and a good deal less glamorous than confronting (50) the janjaweed[1] in Darfur. The premise of microfinance is that very poor people should have access to credit, just as the middle class and the rich do. They typically don't have such access because banks that operate in the developing world view the poor as too great a credit risk, and the processing cost of a $50 loan is thought to wipe out much of the potential profit. (55) But small nonprofit organizations found that tiny loans could not only raise the incomes of the rural and small-town poor but also, unlike aid and other handouts, could help make them self-sufficient. And they found as well that if they harnessed the communities' own social bonds to create group support, repayment rates among the very poor could be higher than (60) among the more well-off. (Indeed, commercial banks, apparently having recognized their error, have now begun to extend loans to the poor.) The idea of microfinance is thus to introduce the poor to capitalism. This is not, it's true, star material. …

There's no question that causes do a great deal for the brand identity (65) of the stars and the sponsors who embrace them. But what, exactly, do stars do for causes? They raise money, of course. But that is often less important than raising consciousness, as Natalie Portman has done. John Prendergast, a longtime activist on African issues and the chairman of Enough, an organization that brings attention to atrocities around the (70) world, says: "Celebrities are master recruiters. If you're trying to expand beyond the already converted, there's no better way to do instant outreach than to have a familiar face where people want to know more about what they're doing in their personal lives." People come to see Natalie Portman, and they go away learning about microfinance. …

—James Traub
excerpted from "The Celebrity Solution"
www.nytimes.com, March 9, 2008

---

[1]janjaweed—militia

Text 2

Ethics of Celebrities and Their Increasing
Influence in 21st Century Society

The global influence of celebrities in the 21st century extends far
beyond the entertainment sector. During the recent Palestinian presidential elections, the Hollywood actor Richard Gere broadcast a televised
message to voters in the region and stated,

(5)   Hi, I'm Richard Gere, and I'm speaking for the entire world. (Richard
Gere, actor)

Celebrities in the 21st century have expanded from simple product endorsements to sitting on United Nations committees, regional
and global conflict commentators and international diplomacy. The

(10)   Russian parliament is debating whether to send a global celebrity to its
International Space Station. The celebrities industry is undergoing, "mission creep", or the expansion of an enterprise beyond its original goals.

There has always been a connection between Hollywood and politics,
certainly in the USA. However, global celebrities in the 21st century are

(15)   involved in proselytising[1] about particular religions, such as Scientology,
negotiating with the Taliban in Afghanistan and participating in the Iraqi
refugee crisis. The Hollywood actor, Jude Law's attempt to negotiate with
the Taliban in Afghanistan was not successful; but the mere fact that Jude
Law tried, and that it was discussed widely over the global internet, shows

(20)   the expansion of celebrities' domain in today's society. The global entertainment industry, especially based in Hollywood, has vastly exceeded
their original mandate in society. ...

How is it that celebrities in the 21st century are formulating foreign
aid policy, backing political bills or affecting public health debates?

(25)   Traditionally, the economic value or market price of the entertainment
industry and its various components was seen as intangible and difficult
to measure. Movie stars and films, artists and the quality of art is often
seen as difficult to measure in terms of value and price without the role
of expert opinions. But global internet-driven 21st century seems to be

(30)   driven by a general growth of the idea that celebrity can be measured in a
tangible way. ...

---

[1]proselytising—trying to persuade or recruit others

The 21st century's internet society seems to thrive on a harmonious three-way relationship among celebrities, audiences and fame addiction. The global internet in turns [*sic*] moulds this three-way relationship and

(35) accelerates its dissemination[2] and communication. This in turn allows celebrities in the 21st century to "mission creep", or expand and accelerate their influence into various new areas of society. This interaction of forces is shown in Figure 1. ...

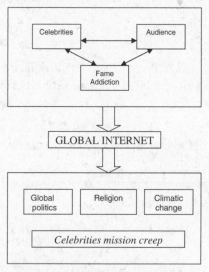

**Figure 1. Celebrities' mission creep
in the 21st century.**

In turn, the global popularity of internet-based social networking

(40) sites such as MySpace or individual blogspots all show the need to discuss events, but also things that are famous (Choi and Berger, 2009). Traditionally, celebrities were seen as people that needed to be seen from afar and while keeping one's distance. In this sense, celebrities were similar to art pieces, better to be seen from a distance (Halpern, 2008; Hirsch,

(45) 1972; Maury and Kleiner, 2002). This traditional distance has been reduced due to global technologies in communications. Celebrities, and famous people in turn, help to bring people, including adults, together in conversation and social interaction. The global role of the internet in the 21st century society will further accelerate such social and psychological

(50) trends throughout today's global knowledge-based society. Global inter-

---

[2]dissemination—wide distribution

net communications have increased the availability of "fame" and access to the lives of celebrities, which in turn will further accelerate the global influence of celebrities in the 21st century society. ...

—Chong Ju Choi and Ron Berger
excerpted from "Ethics of Celebrities and
Their Increasing Influence in 21st Century Society"
Journal of Business Ethics, 2009
www.idc.ac.il

References

Choi, C.J. and R. Berger: 2009, 'Ethics of Internet, Global Community, Fame Addiction', *Journal of Business Ethics* (forthcoming).

Halpern, J.: 2008, *Fame Junkies* (Houghton Mifflin, New York).

Hirsch, P.: 1972, 'Processing Fads and Fashions: An Organisation Set Analysis of Cultural Industry Systems', *American Journal of Sociology* 77 (1), 45–70.

Maury, M. and D. Kleiner: 2002, 'E-Commerce, Ethical Commerce?', *Journal of Business Ethics* 36 (3), 21–32.

Text 3

Do Celebrity Humanitarians Matter?

...Recent years have seen a growth industry for celebrities engaged in humanitarian activities. The website *Look to the Stars* has calculated that over 2,000 charities have some form of celebrity support. UNICEF has dozens of "Goodwill Ambassadors" and "Advocates" such as Angelina
(5) Jolie and Mia Farrow. Celebrities have entered forums for global governance to pressure political leaders: George Clooney has spoken before the United Nations while Bob Geldof, Bono, and Sharon Stone have attended summits like DAVOS[1] and the G8[2] to discuss third world debt, poverty, and refugees. In the U.S. policy arena, [Ben] Affleck joins Nicole
(10) Kidman, Angelina Jolie, and other celebrities who have addressed the U.S. Congress on international issues.[3] The increase in celebrity involvement has spurred debate in academic circles and mainstream media. Celebrity humanitarianism is alternately lauded for drawing media attention and fostering popular engagement and criticized on a number
(15) of ethical grounds. According to *Mother Jones*, Africa is experiencing a "recolonization" as celebrities from the U.S. and UK lay claim to particular countries as recipients of their star power: South Africa (Oprah), Sudan (Mia Farrow), and Botswana (Russell Simmons). As the involvement of American celebrities in humanitarian causes grows, let us consider
(20) the activities of Affleck and his Eastern Congo Initiative [ECI].

Celebrity Humanitarians

Affleck can be considered a "celebrity humanitarian," a celebrity figure who has moved beyond his/her day job as an entertainer to delve into the areas of foreign aid, charity, and development. These activities can involve fundraising, hosting concerts and events, media appearances, and engag-
(25) ing in advocacy. Celebrities are distinguished by their unique ability to attract and engage diverse audiences ranging from their fan base and the media to political elites and philanthropists. Celebrity humanitarians often play an important bridging role, introducing Northern publics

---

[1]DAVOS—an annual meeting of The World Economic Forum, hosted in Davos-Klosters, Switzerland, on global partnership
[2]G8—A group of 8 industrialized nations that hold a yearly meeting to discuss global issues
[3]ProQuest, "Quick Start: Congressional Hearing Digital Collections: Famous (Celebrity) Witnesses," *http://proquest.libguides.com/quick_start_hearings/famouscelebs*

to issues in the developing world. They also use their star power to gain
(30)   access to policy-making circles to effect social and political change. Since
1980, the U.S. Congress has seen the frequency of celebrity witnesses
double to around 20 a year with most celebrity appearances taking place
before committees addressing domestic issues. Interestingly, fewer than 5
percent of celebrity witnesses testify before committees dealing with for-
(35)   eign relations, where celebrity humanitarians push the United States to
address global concerns.[4]

The rise and influence of celebrity humanitarians activate debates on
the consequences of their involvement. For some academics and practitioners, celebrities are welcome figures in humanitarianism: educat-
(40)   ing the public on global issues, raising funds, and using their populist
appeal to draw attention to policy-making arenas. For others, celebrity
humanitarians are highly problematic figures who dilute debates, offer
misguided policy proposals, and lack credibility and accountability.
Celebrity humanitarianism privileges and invests the celebrity figure
(45)   with the responsibility of speaking on behalf of a "distant other" who
is unable to give input or consent for their representation. Stakeholders
in the developing world unwittingly rely on the celebrity humanitarian
as their communicator, advocate, and fundraiser. Finally, celebrities are
held to be self-serving, engaging in humanitarian causes to burnish[5] their
(50)   careers. ...

Celebrity humanitarians should do their homework to earn credibility while also respecting their bounded roles as celebrity figures.
As a celebrity humanitarian, Affleck's proposals are based on serious
preparation: spending years to gain an in-depth understanding, con-
(55)   sulting with professionals, narrowing his advocacy efforts to a single
region, and enduring the scrutiny of the cameras and the blogosphere.
Besides this self-education, his credibility is based on ECI's dual mission of
re-granting and policymaking. Since ECI has operations and partnerships
in the DRC [Democratic Republic of the Congo], the content of Affleck's
(60)   writings and Congressional testimonies are grounded in the realities of
the DRC, peppered with first-hand accounts, and supported by statistics
and other research. However, there are limits to his knowledge—Affleck
is not a development expert or on-the-ground professional; his day job and
main career lie elsewhere. And while the decision to found an organization

---

[4]See Demaine, L.J., n.d. Navigating Policy by the Stars: The Influence of Celebrity
Entertainers on Federal Lawmaking. *Journal of Law & Politics*, 25 (2), 83–143
[5]burnish—improve or enhance

(65)   suggests that Affleck's commitment to the DRC will extend beyond his nascent[6] efforts, rumors that he may seek political office distort this image.

     Celebrity humanitarians must find a way to avoid diverting resources and attention. Rather than bring his star power and ample financial support to existing Congolese organizations, ECI furnished a platform for
(70)   Affleck's advocacy and leadership that amplifies his voice over those of the Congolese. Nor was ECI crafted inside eastern Congo but in the offices of a strategic advisory firm based in Seattle. ECI is privately funded by a network of financial elites and does not rely on means-tested grant cycles or public support. While Affleck has received multiple awards in the short
(75)   period he has been a celebrity humanitarian, his star power also distracts us from the people who work in the field of humanitarianism on a daily basis and rarely receive such recognition.[7] And by concentrating attention and money for Affleck's issue of Eastern Congo, other causes and countries may go unnoticed. ...

—Alexandra Cosima Budabin
excerpted and adapted from "Do Celebrity Humanitarians Matter?"
www.carnegiecouncil.org, December 11, 2014

---

[6]nascent—beginning
[7]Marina Hyde, "Angelina Jolie, Paris Hilton, Lassie and Tony Blair: here to save the world," The Guardian, 27 November 2014 *http://www.theguardian.com/lifeandstyle/lostinshowbiz/2014/nov/27/angelina-jolie-paris-hilton-tony-blair-lassie-save-the-children-award?CMP=share_btn_fb*

Text 4

The Rise of the Celebrity Humanitarian

...One of the most effective methods of attracting a wide, although perhaps not a deep, following is the use of a celebrity humanitarian: An A-Lister who has delved into areas of foreign aid, charity and international development. The United Nations is the leader in this attention-

(5) getting ploy, with at least 175 celebrities on the books as goodwill ambassadors[1] for one cause or another. Some celebrities even leverage their star power to promote their very own foundations and philanthropic projects.

It's a mutually beneficial relationship, really. Hollywood's elite get

(10) to wield their unique ability to engage diverse audiences, and the power of celebrity is put to good use effecting change—whether it's out of the good of their hearts, or because their publicists insist.

There is some downside that comes with publicly linking a campaign to a celebrity. For some, celebrity humanitarians are problem-

(15) atic figures[2] who dilute debates, offer misguided policy proposals, and lack credibility and accountability. Take Scarlett Johansson, who became embroiled in a scandal after partnering with soft drink maker SodaStream, which operated a factory in occupied Palestinian territory. This alliance was in direct conflict with her seven-year global ambas-

(20) sador position for Oxfam, which opposes all trade with the occupied territories. In the end, she stepped down from her role with Oxfam, stating a fundamental difference of opinion.

Moreover, if the star's popularity takes a hit, it can affect the reception of the cause. For example, when Lance Armstrong's popularity

(25) plummeted in the wake of doping allegations, it tarnished the brand of the Livestrong Foundation,[3] the nonprofit he founded to support people affected by cancer. Livestrong does, however, continue today, after cutting ties with Armstrong and undergoing a radical rebranding.

Even so, the following big names substantiate the idea that celebrity

(30) involvement brings massive amounts of attention and money to humanitarian causes and that, usually, this [*sic*] is a good thing. ...

[1]Bunting, Madeline. "The Issue of Celebrities and Aid Is Deceptively Complex"
http://www.theguardian.com, Dec. 17, 2010
[2]Budabin, Alexandra Cosima. "Do Celebrity Humanitarians Matter?"
http://www.carnegiecouncil.org, December 11, 2014
[3]Gardner, Eriq. "Livestrong Struggles After Lance Armstrong's Fall"
http://www.hollywoodreporter.com, 7/25/2013

Bono participates in fundraising concerts like Live 8, and has co-founded several philanthropies, like the ONE Campaign and Product (RED). He also created EDUN, a fashion brand that strives to stimulate
(35) trade in Africa by sourcing production there. He has received three nominations for the Nobel Peace Prize, was knighted by the United Kingdom in 2007, and was named Time's 2005 Person of the Year. ...

Popular singer Akon may not be as famous for his philanthropic work as Angelina Jolie or Bono, but he is in a unique position to help, as he has
(40) deep roots in the areas in which he works: He was raised in Senegal in a community without electricity, which inspired his latest project, Akon Lighting Africa. He also founded the Konfidence Foundation, raising awareness of conditions in Africa and providing underprivileged African youth access to education and other resources. ...

(45) In weighing the pros and cons of celebrity activism, perhaps [Ben] Affleck himself summed it up best in an essay reflecting on the constraints and possibilities of his own engagement:

"It makes sense to be skeptical about celebrity activism. There is always suspicion that involvement with a cause may be doing more good for the
(50) spokesman than he or she is doing for the cause...but I hope you can separate whatever reservations you may have from what is unimpeachably important."

—Jenica Funk
excerpted and adapted from "The Rise of the Celebrity Humanitarian"
www.globalenvision.org, January 29, 2015

PART 3—Text-Analysis Response

Your Task: Closely read the text on pages 259 through 261 and write a well-developed, text-based response of two to three paragraphs. In your response, identify a central idea in the text and analyze how the author's use of *one* writing strategy (literary element or literary technique or rhetorical device) develops this central idea. Use strong and thorough evidence from the text to support your analysis. Do *not* simply summarize the text. You may use the margins to take notes as you read and scrap paper to plan your response. Write your response on a separate sheet of paper.

Guidelines:

Be sure to

- Identify a central idea in the text.
- Analyze how the author's use of *one* writing strategy (literary element or literary technique or rhetorical device) develops this central idea. Examples include: characterization, conflict, denotation/connotation, metaphor, simile, irony, language use, point-of-view, setting, structure, symbolism, theme, tone, etc.
- Use strong and thorough evidence from the text to support your analysis.
- Organize your ideas in a cohesive and coherent manner.
- Maintain a formal style of writing.
- Follow the conventions of standard written English.

Text

It was my father who called the city the Mansion on the River. He was talking about Charleston, South Carolina, and he was a native son, peacock proud of a town so pretty it makes your eyes ache with pleasure just to walk down its spellbinding, narrow streets. Charleston was my father's
(5) ministry, his hobbyhorse, his quiet obsession, and the great love of his life. His bloodstream lit up my own with a passion for the city that I've never lost nor ever will. I'm Charleston-born, and bred. The city's two rivers, the Ashley and the Cooper, have flooded and shaped all the days of my life on this storied[1] peninsula.
(10) I carry the delicate porcelain beauty of Charleston like the hinged shell of some soft-tissued mollusk. My soul is peninsula-shaped and sun-hardened and river-swollen. The high tides of the city flood my consciousness each day, subject to the whims and harmonies of full moons rising out of the Atlantic. I grow calm when I see the ranks of palmetto trees pulling
(15) guard duty on the banks of Colonial Lake or hear the bells of St. Michael's calling cadence[2] in the cicada-filled trees along Meeting Street. Deep in my bones, I knew early that I was one of those incorrigible[3] creatures known as Charlestonians. It comes to me as a surprising form of knowledge that my time in the city is more vocation than gift; it is my destiny, not my
(20) choice. I consider it a high privilege to be a native of one of the loveliest American cities, not a high-kicking, glossy, or lipsticked city, not a city with bells on its fingers or brightly painted toenails, but a ruffled, low-slung city, understated and tolerant of nothing mismade or ostentatious.[4] Though Charleston feels a seersuckered, tuxedoed view of itself, it
(25) approves of restraint far more than vainglory.[5]

As a boy, in my own backyard I could catch a basket of blue crabs, a string of flounder, a dozen redfish, or a net full of white shrimp. All this I could do in a city enchanting enough to charm cobras out of baskets, one so corniced and filigreed[6] and elaborate that it leaves strangers awed and
(30) natives self-satisfied. In its shadows you can find metalwork as delicate as lace and spiral staircases as elaborate as yachts. In the secrecy of its gardens you can discover jasmine and camellias and hundreds of other plants that

---

[1]storied—told of in history
[2]cadence—rhythmic recurrence of sound
[3]incorrigible—cannot be reformed
[4]ostentatious—showy
[5]vainglory—excessive pride
[6]corniced and filigreed—architecturally decorated

look embroidered and stolen from the Garden of Eden for the sheer love of richness and the joy of stealing from the gods. In its kitchens, the stoves are

(35) lit up in happiness as the lamb is marinating in red wine sauce, vinaigrette is prepared for the salad, crabmeat is anointed with sherry, custards are baked in the oven, and buttermilk biscuits cool on the counter.

Because of its devotional, graceful attraction to food and gardens and architecture, Charleston stands for all the principles that make living

(40) well both a civic virtue and a standard. It is a rapturous, defining place to grow up. Everything I reveal to you now will be Charleston-shaped and Charleston-governed, and sometimes even Charleston-ruined. But it is my fault and not the city's that it came close to destroying me. Not everyone responds to beauty in the same way. Though Charleston can

(45) do much, it can't always improve on the strangeness of human behavior. But Charleston has a high tolerance for eccentricity and bemusement.[7] There is a tastefulness in its gentility[8] that comes from the knowledge that Charleston is a permanent dimple in the understated skyline, while the rest of us are only visitors. …

(50) I turned out to be a late bloomer, which I long regretted. My parents suffered needlessly because it took me so long to find my way to a place at their table. But I sighted the early signs of my recovery long before they did. My mother had given up on me at such an early age that a comeback was something she no longer even prayed for in her wildest dreams. Yet in

(55) my anonymous and underachieving high school career, I laid the foundation for a strong finish without my mother noticing that I was, at last, up to some good. I had built an impregnable castle of solitude for myself and then set out to bring that castle down, no matter how serious the collateral damage or who might get hurt.

(60) I was eighteen years old and did not have a friend my own age. There wasn't a boy in Charleston who would think about inviting me to a party or to come out to spend the weekend at his family's beach house.

I planned for all that to change. I had decided to become the most interesting boy to ever grow up in Charleston, and I revealed this secret to

(65) my parents.

Outside my house in the languid[9] summer air of my eighteenth year, I climbed the magnolia tree nearest to the Ashley River with the agility that constant practice had granted me. From its highest branches, I surveyed

---

[7]bemusement—bewilderment
[8]gentility—refinement
[9]languid—without energy

(70) my city as it lay simmering in the hot-blooded saps of June while the sun began to set, reddening the vest of cirrus clouds that had gathered along the western horizon. In the other direction, I saw the city of rooftops and columns and gables that was my native land. What I had just promised my parents, I wanted very much for them and for myself. Yet I also wanted it for Charleston. I desired to turn myself into a worthy townsman of such a (75) many-storied city.

Charleston has its own heartbeat and fingerprint, its own mug shots and photo ops and police lineups. It is a city of contrivance,[10] of blue-prints; devotion to pattern that is like a bent knee to the nature of beauty itself. I could feel my destiny forming in the leaves high above the (80) city. Like Charleston, I had my alleyways that were dead ends and led to nowhere, but mansions were forming like jewels in my bloodstream. Looking down, I studied the layout of my city, the one that had taught me all the lures of attractiveness, yet made me suspicious of the showy or the makeshift. I turned to the stars and was about to make a bad throw of the (85) dice and try to predict the future, but stopped myself in time.

A boy stopped in time, in a city of amber-colored life, that possessed the glamour forbidden to a lesser angel.

—Pat Conroy
excerpted from *South of Broad*, 2009
Nan A. Talese

[10]contrivance—invention

Regents ELA (Common Core) Answers June 2016
English Language Arts

Answer Key

Part 1

1. 2	9. 3	17. 1
2. 3	10. 4	18. 4
3. 3	11. 1	19. 1
4. 1	12. 2	20. 2
5. 2	13. 4	21. 1
6. 3	14. 1	22. 2
7. 4	15. 2	23. 1
8. 1	16. 3	24. 3

Regents ELA (Common Core) Examination June 2017

English Language Arts

PART 1—Reading Comprehension

Directions (1–24): Closely read each of the three passages below. After each passage, there are several multiple-choice questions. Select the best suggested answer to each question and write its number in the space provided. You may use the margins to take notes as you read.

Reading Comprehension Passage A

I received one morning a letter, written in pale ink on glassy, blue-lined note-paper, and bearing the postmark of a little Nebraska village. This communication, worn and rubbed, looking as if it had been carried for some days in a coat pocket that was none too clean, was from my uncle
(5) Howard, and informed me that his wife had been left a small legacy by a bachelor relative, and that it would be necessary for her to go to Boston to attend to the settling of the estate. He requested me to meet her at the station and render her whatever services might be necessary. On examining the date indicated as that of her arrival, I found it to be no later than
(10) tomorrow. He had characteristically delayed writing until, had I been away from home for a day, I must have missed my aunt altogether. ...

Whatever shock Mrs. Springer [the landlady] experienced at my aunt's appearance, she considerately concealed. As for myself, I saw my aunt's battered figure with that feeling of awe and respect with which we behold

(15) explorers who have left their ears and fingers north of Franz-Joseph-Land,[1] or their health somewhere along the Upper Congo. My Aunt Georgiana had been a music teacher at the Boston Conservatory, somewhere back in the latter sixties [1860s]. One summer, while visiting in the little village among the Green Mountains where her ancestors had dwelt *(20)* for generations, she had kindled the callow[2] fancy of my uncle, Howard Carpenter, then an idle, shiftless boy of twenty-one. When she returned to her duties in Boston, Howard followed her, and the upshot of this infatuation was that she eloped with him, eluding the reproaches of her family and the criticism of her friends by going with him to the Nebraska *(25)* frontier. Carpenter, who, of course, had no money, took up a homestead in Red Willow County, fifty miles from the railroad. There they had measured off their land themselves, driving across the prairie in a wagon, to the wheel of which they had tied a red cotton handkerchief, and counting its revolutions. They built a dug-out in the red hillside, one of those *(30)* cave dwellings whose inmates so often reverted to primitive conditions. Their water they got from the lagoons where the buffalo drank, and their slender stock of provisions was always at the mercy of bands of roving Indians. For thirty years my aunt had not been farther than fifty miles from the homestead.

(35) I owed to this woman most of the good that ever came my way in my boyhood, and had a reverential[3] affection for her. During the years when I was riding herd for my uncle, my aunt, after cooking the three meals— the first of which was ready at six o'clock in the morning—and putting the six children to bed, would often stand until midnight at her ironing- *(40)* board, with me at the kitchen table beside her, hearing me recite Latin declensions and conjugations, gently shaking me when my drowsy head sank down over a page of irregular verbs. It was to her, at her ironing or mending, that I read my first Shakspere, and her old text-book on mythology was the first that ever came into my empty hands. She taught me my *(45)* scales and exercises on the little parlour organ which her husband had bought her after fifteen years during which she had not so much as seen a musical instrument. She would sit beside me by the hour, darning and counting, while I struggled with the "Joyous Farmer." She seldom talked to me about music, and I understood why. Once when I had been doggedly *(50)* beating out some easy passages from an old score of *Euryanthe* I had found among her music books, she came up to me and, putting her hands over

---

[1]Franz-Joseph-Land—Russian archipelago of 191 islands in the Arctic Ocean
[2]callow—naive
[3]reverential—with great honor and respect

my eyes, gently drew my head back upon her shoulder, saying tremulously, "Don't love it so well, Clark, or it may be taken from you.". . .

(55) At two o'clock the Symphony Orchestra was to give a Wagner program, and I intended to take my aunt; though, as I conversed with her, I grew doubtful about her enjoyment of it. I suggested our visiting the Conservatory and the Common before lunch, but she seemed altogether too timid to wish to venture out. She questioned me absently about various changes in the city, but she was chiefly concerned that she had

(60) forgotten to leave instructions about feeding half-skimmed milk to a certain weakling calf, "old Maggie's calf, you know, Clark," she explained, evidently having forgotten how long I had been away. She was further troubled because she had neglected to tell her daughter about the freshly-opened kit of mackerel[4] in the cellar, which would spoil if it were not used

(65) directly. . . .

The first number [of the concert] was the *Tannhauser*[5] overture. When the horns drew out the first strain of the Pilgrim's chorus, Aunt Georgiana clutched my coat sleeve. Then it was I first realized that for her this broke a silence of thirty years. With the battle between the two

(70) motives,[6] with the frenzy of the Venusberg theme and its ripping of strings, there came to me an overwhelming sense of the waste and wear we are so powerless to combat; and I saw again the tall, naked house on the prairie, black and grim as a wooden fortress; the black pond where I had learned to swim, its margin pitted with sun-dried cattle tracks; the rain

(75) gullied clay banks about the naked house, the four dwarf ash seedlings where the dish-cloths were always hung to dry before the kitchen door. The world there was the flat world of the ancients; to the east, a cornfield that stretched to daybreak; to the west, a corral that reached to sunset; between, the conquests of peace, dearer-bought than those of war. . . .

(80) Her lip quivered and she hastily put her handkerchief up to her mouth. From behind it she murmured, "And you have been hearing this ever since you left me, Clark?" Her question was the gentlest and saddest of reproaches. . . .

The deluge of sound poured on and on; I never knew what she found

(85) in the shining current of it; I never knew how far it bore her, or past what happy islands. From the trembling of her face I could well believe that before the last number she had been carried out where the myriad graves are, into the grey, nameless burying grounds of the sea; or into some

---

[4]kit of mackerel—container of fish

[5]*Tannhauser*—an opera by Richard Wagner

[6]motives—recurrent musical phrases

world of death vaster yet, where, from the beginning of the world, hope
(90) has lain down with hope and dream with dream and, renouncing, slept. ...

I spoke to my aunt. She burst into tears and sobbed pleadingly. "I
don't want to go, Clark, I don't want to go!"

I understood. For her, just outside the concert hall, lay the black pond
with the cattle-tracked bluffs; the tall, unpainted house, with weather-
(95) curled boards, naked as a tower; the crook-backed ash seedlings where the
dish-cloths hung to dry; the gaunt, moulting turkeys picking up refuse
about the kitchen door.

—Willa Cather
excerpted and adapted from "A Wagner Matinée"
Youth and the Bright Medusa, April 1920

1 A primary function of the first paragraph is to

   (1) establish the reason for the meeting
   (2) create an atmosphere of mystery
   (3) identify preferences of the narrator's aunt
   (4) reveal flaws in the narrator's character   1_____

2 In lines 1 through 11, the commentary about the letter implies that the narrator believes his uncle is

   (1) uncomfortable with changes
   (2) careless about details
   (3) angry with his wife
   (4) disappointed at his decision   2_____

3 The details in lines 16 through 25 suggest that in her youth Aunt Georgiana was

   (1) courageous yet hesitant
   (2) compassionate yet critical
   (3) resourceful yet cautious
   (4) intelligent yet impulsive   3_____

4 Lines 33 and 34, "For thirty years my aunt had not been farther than fifty miles from the homestead" reinforces a sense of

   (1) discomfort   (3) isolation
   (2) happiness   (4) affection   4_____

5 Which statement from the passage best explains the narrator's "reverential affection" (line 36) for his Aunt Georgiana?

   (1) "It was to her, at her ironing or mending, that I read my first Shakspere" (lines 42 and 43)

   (2) " 'Don't love it so well, Clark, or it may be taken from you' " (line 53)

   (3) "Her lip quivered and she hastily put her hand-kerchief up to her mouth" (line 80)

   (4) "I never knew how far it bore her, or past what happy islands" (lines 85 and 86)   5____

6 Lines 44 through 47 develop a central theme by

   (1) recalling the husband's generosity in support-ing the narrator's music lessons

   (2) suggesting that the narrator resented his music lessons

   (3) emphasizing the role of discipline in develop-ing Aunt Georgiana's musical talent

   (4) implying that Aunt Georgiana missed having music in her life   6____

7 In line 49, when the narrator states that he "under-stood why," he is implying that his Aunt Georgiana

   (1) knew little about current musical trends

   (2) avoided talking about his musical skills

   (3) realized what she has given up

   (4) needed some recognition of her ability   7____

8 Lines 58 through 65 contribute to a central idea by depicting Aunt Georgiana's

   (1) concern for daily responsibilities

   (2) desire for cultural experiences

   (3) fear of future separations

   (4) fixation on painful memories   8____

9 The author's choice of how to end the story (lines 91 through 97) places emphasis on Aunt Georgiana's

   (1) bleak future   (3) domestic skills

   (2) unusual lifestyle   (4) hostile attitude   9____

10 Which quotation best reflects the narrator's realization resulting from Aunt Georgiana's visit?

   (1) "He requested me to meet her at the station and render her whatever services might be necessary" (lines 7 and 8)

   (2) "At two o'clock the Symphony Orchestra was to give a Wagner program, and I intended to take my aunt" (lines 54 and 55)

   (3) "there came to me an overwhelming sense of the waste and wear we are so powerless to combat" (lines 71 and 72)

   (4) "sound poured on and on; I never knew what she found in the shining current of it" (lines 84 and 85)   10____

Reading Comprehension Passage B

Mi Historia[1]

My red pickup choked on burnt oil
as I drove down Highway 99.[2]
In wind-tattered garbage bags
I had packed my whole life:
(5)   two pairs of jeans, a few T-shirts,
and a pair of work boots.
My truck needed work, and through
the blue smoke rising from under the hood,
I saw almond orchards, plums,
(10)   the raisins spread out on paper trays,
and acres of Mendota cotton my mother picked as a child.

My mother crawled through the furrows
and plucked cotton balls that filled
the burlap sack she dragged,
(15)   shoulder-slung, through dried-up bolls,
husks, weevils, dirt clods,
and dust that filled the air with thirst.
But when she grew tired,
she slept on her mother's burlap,
(20)   stuffed thick as a mattress,
and Grandma dragged her over the land
where time was told by the setting sun....

History cried out to me from the earth,
in the scream of starling flight,
(25)   and pounded at the hulls of seeds to be set free.
History licked the asphalt with rubber,
sighed in the windows of abandoned barns,
slumped in the wind-blasted palms,
groaned in the heat, and whispered its soft curses.

---

[1]Mi Historia—Spanish for "my history"
[2]Highway 99—the highway that runs through California's fertile Central Valley
where generations of farmworkers have settled and been employed

(30)   I wanted my own history—not the earth's,
nor the history of blood, nor of memory,
and not the job found for me at Galdini Sausage.
I sought my own—a new bruise to throb hard
as the asphalt that pounded the chassis of my truck.

—David Dominguez
from *Work Done Right*, 2003
The University of Arizona Press

11 The poet's purpose in referencing "Highway 99" in line 2 is most likely to establish

(1) a connection with the narrator's cultural heritage
(2) a criticism of the valley's agricultural economy
(3) an understanding of the narrator's difficult childhood
(4) an emphasis on the region's diverse landscape   11____

12 The second stanza reveals that the narrator's overall point of view is influenced by

(1) his experience working on farms
(2) his nostalgia for farm life
(3) the labor of his relatives
(4) the expectations of his family   12____

13 The personification in lines 23 through 29 stresses history's desire to be

(1) repeated   (3) comforted
(2) forgotten   (4) heard   13____

14 The figurative language in lines 33 and 34 implies the narrator

(1) regrets leaving his past behind
(2) understands that his future will have challenges
(3) anticipates that his new life will be successful
(4) thinks he made a wrong decision   14____

Reading Comprehension Passage C

In 1973, a book claiming that plants were sentient[1] beings that feel emotions, prefer classical music to rock and roll, and can respond to the unspoken thoughts of humans hundreds of miles away landed on the New York *Times* best-seller list for nonfiction. "The Secret Life of Plants,"
(5)   by Peter Tompkins and Christopher Bird, presented a beguiling mashup of legitimate plant science, quack experiments, and mystical nature worship that captured the public imagination at a time when New Age thinking was seeping into the mainstream. The most memorable passages described the experiments of a former C.I.A. polygraph expert named
(10)   Cleve Backster, who, in 1966, on a whim, hooked up a galvanometer to the leaf of a dracaena, a houseplant that he kept in his office. To his astonishment, Backster found that simply by imagining the dracaena being set on fire he could make it rouse the needle of the polygraph machine, registering a surge of electrical activity suggesting that the plant felt stress.
(15)   "Could the plant have been reading his mind?" the authors ask. "Backster felt like running into the street and shouting to the world, 'Plants can think!' " ...

In the ensuing years, several legitimate plant scientists tried to reproduce the "Backster effect" without success. Much of the science in "The
(20)   Secret Life of Plants" has been discredited. But the book had made its mark on the culture. Americans began talking to their plants and playing Mozart for them, and no doubt many still do. This might seem harmless enough; there will probably always be a strain of romanticism running through our thinking about plants. (Luther Burbank and George
(25)   Washington Carver both reputedly talked to, and listened to, the plants they did such brilliant work with.) But in the view of many plant scientists "The Secret Life of Plants" has done lasting damage to their field. According to Daniel Chamovitz, an Israeli biologist who is the author of the recent book "What a Plant Knows," Tompkins and Bird "stymied[2]
(30)   important research on plant behavior as scientists became wary[3] of any studies that hinted at parallels between animal senses and plant senses." Others contend that "The Secret Life of Plants" led to "self-censorship" among researchers seeking to explore the "possible homologies[4] between

---

[1]sentient—conscious
[2]stymied—prevented
[3]wary—cautious
[4]homologies—similarities

(35) neurobiology[5] and phytobiology"[6]; that is, the possibility that plants are much more intelligent and much more like us than most people think—capable of cognition,[7] communication, information processing, computation, learning and memory. ...

Indeed, many of the most impressive capabilities of plants can be traced to their unique existential[8] predicament as beings rooted to the ground (40) and therefore unable to pick up and move when they need something or when conditions turn unfavorable. The "sessile life style," as plant biologists term it, calls for an extensive and nuanced understanding of one's immediate environment, since the plant has to find everything it needs, and has to defend itself, while remaining fixed in place. A highly devel-(45) oped sensory apparatus is required to locate food and identify threats. Plants have evolved between fifteen and twenty distinct senses, including analogues of our five: smell and taste (they sense and respond to chemicals in the air or on their bodies); sight (they react differently to various wavelengths of light as well as to shadow); touch (a vine or a root "knows" (50) when it encounters a solid object); and, it has been discovered, sound. In a recent experiment, Heidi Appel, a chemical ecologist at the University of Missouri, found that, when she played a recording of a caterpillar chomping a leaf for a plant that hadn't been touched, the sound primed the plant's genetic machinery to produce defense chemicals. Another experi-(55) ment, done in Mancuso's[9] lab and not yet published, found that plant roots would seek out a buried pipe through which water was flowing even if the exterior of the pipe was dry, which suggested that plants somehow "hear" the sound of flowing water. ...

Scientists have since found that the tips of the plant roots, in addi-(60) tion to sensing gravity, moisture, light, pressure, and hardness, can also sense volume, nitrogen, phosphorus, salt, various toxins, microbes, and chemical signals from neighboring plants. Roots about to encounter an impenetrable obstacle or a toxic substance change course before they make contact with it. Roots can tell whether nearby roots are self or other and, (65) if other, kin or stranger. Normally, plants compete for root space with strangers, but, when researchers put four closely related Great Lakes sea-rocket plants (*Cakile edentula*) in the same pot, the plants restrained their usual competitive behaviors and shared resources.

---

[5]neurobiology—the study of the nervous system
[6]phytobiology—the study of plants
[7]cognition—understanding
[8]existential—relating to existence
[9]Mancuso—Stefano Mancuso, Italian plant physiologist

(70) Somehow, a plant gathers and integrates all this information about its environment, and then "decides"—some scientists deploy the quotation marks, indicating metaphor at work; others drop them—in precisely what direction to deploy its roots or its leaves. Once the definition of "behavior" expands to include such things as a shift in the trajectory[10] of a root, a reallocation of resources, or the emission of a powerful chemical,

(75) plants begin to look like much more active agents, responding to environmental cues in ways more subtle or adaptive than the word "instinct" would suggest. "Plants perceive competitors and grow away from them," Rick Karban, a plant ecologist at U.C. Davis, explained, when I asked him for an example of plant decision-making. "They are more leery of actual

(80) vegetation than they are of inanimate objects, and they respond to potential competitors before actually being shaded by them." These are sophisticated behaviors, but, like most plant behaviors, to an animal they're either invisible or really, really slow.

The sessile life style also helps account for plants' extraordinary gift for

(85) biochemistry, which far exceeds that of animals and, arguably, of human chemists. (Many drugs, from aspirin to opiates, derive from compounds designed by plants.) Unable to run away, plants deploy a complex molecular vocabulary to signal distress, deter or poison enemies, and recruit animals to perform various services for them. A recent study in *Science*

(90) found that the caffeine produced by many plants may function not only as a defense chemical, as had previously been thought, but in some cases as a psychoactive drug in their nectar. The caffeine encourages bees to remember a particular plant and return to it, making them more faithful and effective pollinators.

(95) One of the most productive areas of plant research in recent years has been plant signalling. Since the early nineteen-eighties, it has been known that when a plant's leaves are infected or chewed by insects they emit volatile chemicals that signal other leaves to mount a defense. Sometimes this warning signal contains information about the identity of the insect,

(100) gleaned from the taste of its saliva. Depending on the plant and the attacker, the defense might involve altering the leaf's flavor or texture, or producing toxins or other compounds that render the plant's flesh less digestible to herbivores. When antelopes browse acacia trees, the leaves produce tannins that make them unappetizing and difficult to digest.

(105) When food is scarce and acacias are overbrowsed, it has been reported, the trees produce sufficient amounts of toxin to kill the animals. ...

---

[10]trajectory—a path

All species face the same existential challenges—obtaining food, defending themselves, reproducing—but under wildly varying circumstances, and so they have evolved wildly different tools in order to survive.
(110) Brains come in handy for creatures that move around a lot; but they're a disadvantage for ones that are rooted in place. Impressive as it is to us, self-consciousness is just another tool for living, good for some jobs, unhelpful for others. That humans would rate this particular adaptation so highly is not surprising, since it has been the shining destination of
(115) our long evolutionary journey, along with the epiphenomenon of self-consciousness that we call "free will." ...

—Michael Pollan
excerpted from "The Intelligent Plant"
The New Yorker, December 23 & 30, 2013

15 The first paragraph conveys a sense of

   (1)   caution   (3)   excitement

   (2)   accusation   (4)   relief   15_____

16 The details in the first paragraph serve mainly to establish the

   (1)   relationship between plant science and musical trends

   (2)   difference between houseplants and wild plants

   (3)   importance of forensic science for theories of plant behavior

   (4)   impact of early studies of plant behavior on current research   16_____

17 The author uses the word "But" in line 20 to

   (1)   express the controversial nature of "The Secret Life of Plants"

   (2)   compare "The Secret Life of Plants" with "What a Plant Knows"

   (3)   express the similarities between certain types of plants

   (4)   compare the learning ability of particular types of plants   17_____

18 A primary purpose of the details in lines 46 through 50 is to indicate a connection

   (1)   among diverse plant species

   (2)   among several independent studies

   (3)   between humans and plants

   (4)   between predators and prey   18_____

19 The use of quotation marks in lines 70 and 73 acknowledges the presence of

   (1)   deception   (3)   confusion

   (2)   debate   (4)   resentment   19_____

20 Lines 72 through 77 support a central idea suggesting that plants

    (1) resist cooperation   (3) produce sound
    (2) avoid modification   (4) possess intent   20_____

21 The evidence provided in lines 89 through 94 demonstrates that plants may

    (1) develop symbiotic relationships
    (2) attack weaker organisms
    (3) waste essential resources
    (4) produce genetic mutations   21_____

22 The term "plant signalling" (line 96) refers to the way plants

    (1) reproduce with similar species
    (2) protect themselves from predators
    (3) react to human contact
    (4) adapt themselves to climate   22_____

23 The final paragraph contributes to a central idea by suggesting that

    (1) humans have acquired superior characteristics
    (2) species develop according to their own needs
    (3) plants would benefit from having self-awareness
    (4) scientists have dismissed important findings   23_____

24 The text's credibility relies on the author's use of

    (1) order of importance
    (2) extended comparison
    (3) observable evidence
    (4) personal anecdotes   24_____

PART 2—Argument Response

Directions: Closely read each of the *four* texts on pages 279 through 287 and write a source-based argument on the topic below. You may use the margins to take notes as you read and scrap paper to plan your response. Write your argument on a separate sheet of paper.

Topic: Should school recess be structured play?

Your Task: Carefully read each of the *four* texts provided. Then, using evidence from at least *three* of the texts, write a well-developed argument regarding whether or not school recess should be structured play. Clearly establish your claim, distinguish your claim from alternate or opposing claims, and use specific, relevant, and sufficient evidence from at least *three* of the texts to develop your argument. Do *not* simply summarize each text.

Guidelines:

Be sure to

- Establish your claim regarding whether or not school recess should be structured play
- Distinguish your claim from alternate or opposing claims
- Use specific, relevant, and sufficient evidence from at least *three* of the texts to develop your argument
- Identify each source that you reference by text number and line number(s) or graphic (for example: Text 1, line 4 or Text 2, graphic)
- Organize your ideas in a cohesive and coherent manner
- Maintain a formal style of writing
- Follow the conventions of standard written English

Texts:

Text 1—The Crucial Role of Recess in School

Text 2—Why Children Need More Unstructured Play

Text 3—Study Weighs Benefits of Organizing Recess

Text 4—Forget Goofing Around: Recess Has a New Boss

Text 1

The Crucial Role of Recess in School

...Structured recess is a recess based on structured play, during which games and physical activities are taught and led by a trained adult (teachers, school staff, or volunteers). Proponents[1] for structured recess note that children often need help in developing games and require suggestions
(5) and encouragement to participate in physical activities. Recently, policy makers and funding organizations have called for more opportunities for daily activity as a means to address childhood obesity. These statements have strengthened the argument to maintain or reinstate recess as an integral component of the school day. Although this new dimension to the
(10) recess debate has increased attention on its role, it also has created tension. Some have promoted recess time as a solution for increasing children's physical activity and combating obesity. If recess assumes such a role, then, like physical education, it will need to be planned and directed to ensure that all children are participating in moderately vigorous physical activ-
(15) ity. Pediatric health care providers, parents, and school officials should be cognizant,[2] however, that in designing a structured recess, they will sacrifice the notion of recess as an unstructured but supervised break that belongs to the child; that is, a time for the child to make a personal choice between sedentary, physical, creative, or social options. However, there
(20) are many cited benefits of structured recess to consider, including:

- Older elementary children may benefit from game instruction and encouragement for total class inclusion.
- Children can be coached to develop interpersonal skills for appropriate conflict resolution.
(25) - More children can actively participate in regular activity, irrespective of skill level.
- Anecdotally,[3] teachers have reported improved behavior and attention in the classroom after vigorous structured recess.

To be effective, structured recess requires that school personnel (or
(30) volunteers) receive adequate training so that they are able to address and encourage the diverse needs of all students. One aspect of supervision should be to facilitate social relationships among children by encouraging

---

[1]proponents—those who support
[2]cognizant—aware
[3]anecdotally—based on casual observation

inclusiveness in games. A problem arises when the structured activities of recess are promoted as a replacement for the child's physical education

(35) requirement. The replacement of physical education by recess threatens students' instruction in and acquisition of new motor skills, exploration of sports and rules, and a concept of lifelong physical fitness.

There are ways to encourage a physically active recess without necessarily adding structured, planned, adult-led games, such as offering attrac-

(40) tive, safe playground equipment to stimulate free play; establishing games/ boundaries painted on the playground; or instructing children in games, such as four square or hop-scotch. These types of activities can range from fully structured (with the adult directing and requiring participation) to partly unstructured (with adults providing supervision and initial instruc-

(45) tion) to fully unstructured (supervision and social guidance). In structured, partly structured, or unstructured environments, activity levels vary widely on the basis of school policy, equipment provided, encouragement, age group, gender, and race. Consequently, the potential benefits of mandatory participation of all children in a purely structured recess

(50) must be weighed against the potential social and emotional trade-off of limiting acquisition of important developmental skills. Whichever style is chosen, recess should be viewed as a supplement to motor skill acquisition in physical education class. ...

—Council on School Health
excerpted from "The Crucial Role of Recess in School," December 31, 2012
http://pediatrics.aapublications.org/

Text 2

Why Children Need More Unstructured Play

The nature of an average child's free time has changed. For the past 25 years kids have been spending decreasing amounts of time outdoors. The time that our kids do spend outdoors is frequently a part of an organized sports activity. Other activities taking up our children's time include
(5) indoor lessons and organized events such as music, art and dance lessons. Another big indoor activity, taking up to 7.5 hours a day of our children's time according to a Kaiser Family Foundation study, is electronic entertainment. Of course some of these activities bring joy and fulfillment to our kids, but, in return, time for unstructured play has decreased.

(10) Unstructured play is that set of activities that children create on their own without adult guidance. Children naturally, when left to their own devices, will take initiative and create activities and stories in the world around them. Sometimes, especially with children past the toddler stage, the most creative play takes place outside of direct adult supervision.
(15) Unstructured free play can happen in many different environments, however, the outdoors may provide more opportunities for free play due to the many movable parts, such as sticks, dirt, leaves and rocks which lend themselves to exploration and creation.

Some parents find it challenging to provide unstructured play time for
(20) their kids. Letting our kids play without constant supervision, especially outside, can be even more difficult. It feels hard to balance reasonable concern, over-vigilance, and the desire to let our kids experience freedom and learn from their own mistakes and experiences. ...

Why might we need to loosen up and get over some of our fears in
(25) order to get our kids outdoor unstructured play time? In the January 2005 *Archives of Pediatric and Adolescent Medicine*, Burdette and Whitaker wrote on the importance of free play. They argue that free play promotes intellectual and cognitive growth, emotional intelligence, and benefits social interactions. They describe how play involves problem
(30) solving which is one of the highest executive functions. ["]Children plan, organize, sequence, and make decisions,["] they explain. In addition, play requires attention to the game and, especially in the case of very young children, frequent physical activity. Unstructured play frequently comes from or results in exposure to the outdoors. Surveys of parents and teach-
(35) ers report that children's focus and attention are improved after outdoor

physical activity and free play and some small studies suggest that time spent outdoors improves focus in children with ADHD [Attention Deficit Hyperactivity Disorder].

(40)   Socialization and emotional intelligence benefit through shared interactions and physical movement that take place during play. Children must work together to decide which game to play, what agreeable rules are, and how to manage scenarios that invariably involve their differing perspectives. This "work" builds the social qualities that we all wish for our children: empathy, self-awareness, self-regulation, and flexibility. Emotional

(45)   development is promoted along with physical health when people spend time moving. In adults and older children physical activity has been well documented to decrease stress, anxiety, and depression, and to improve overall mood. Though the research is sparse in younger children, it seems likely that our youngest children benefit as well. Free play in toddlers and

(50)   young children most frequently involves spurts of gross motor activity over a period of time with multiple episodes of rest in between. Most children are smiling and laughing when they engage in play, and it is reasonable to assume that their mood is improved during and after play. ...

—Avril Swan, MD
excerpted and adapted from "Why Children Need More
Unstructured Play" *www.kevinmd.com*, July 21, 2011

Text 3

Study Weighs Benefits of Organizing Recess

While an overwhelming number of elementary school principals believe in the power of recess to improve academic achievement and make students more focused in class, most discipline-related problems happen at school when kids cut loose at recess and lunch, according to surveys.

(5) One of the solutions, according to a study released this week [2012] by the Robert Wood Johnson Foundation: more, and well-trained, staff on the playground.

The study examines an approach to creating more-structured recess time that is provided by Playworks, based in Oakland, Calif. It finds
(10) that the nonprofit organization's program can smooth the transition between recess and class time—giving teachers more time to spend on instruction—and can cut back on bullying in the schoolyard. Teachers in participating schools also reported that their students felt safer and more included at recess, compared with those at schools without the
(15) program. ...

The most significant finding shows students who participate in a Playworks-structured recess transition from that to schoolwork more quickly than students in traditional recess, said Susanne James-Burdumy, an associate director of research at Mathematica Policy Research.
(20) "I think it is an exciting set of findings," Ms. James-Burdumy said. "This is one area where Playworks is aiming to have an impact: specifically trying to improve students' ability to focus on class activities."

The study found that, on average, teachers at participating schools needed about 2.5 fewer minutes of transition time between recess and
(25) learning time—a difference that researchers termed statistically significant. Over the course of a school year, that can add up to about a day of class time.

Scaling Up

The Robert Wood Johnson Foundation, also based in Princeton, has been funding Playworks since 2005. It helped the program expand from a
(30) few schools in Oakland to more than 300 schools in 23 cities, said Nancy Barrand, the foundation's senior adviser for program development. The goal is to expand into 27 cities and 750 schools.

"We're using a process of scaling where we've identified a successful, evidence-based model," Ms. Barrand said. Playworks "is a pretty common-

(35)   sense approach. It's really about the school environment and how you create a healthy school environment for the children," she continued. "If children are healthy and happy, they learn better."

Playworks founder and chief executive officer, Jill Vialet, said the idea came from a frustrated principal 15 years ago. The principal had been (40) dealing with the same three students daily because of scuffles and mischief at recess that spilled over into their classes.

Ms. Vialet wondered whether creating a little structure at recess could quell some of those ongoing woes. She recalled her own days as a child when a municipal parks and recreation worker named Clarence made sure (45) she—one of the few girls there—was included in the games at a District of Columbia park.

"I wanted to make sure every kid had a Clarence," she said. ...

The coaches map the area where students spend recess, setting boundaries for different activities, such as kickball. They help children pick (50) teams using random measures, such as students' birth months, to circumvent emotionally scarring episodes of being chosen based on skill or popularity. If conflicts arise, coaches teach simple ways to settle disputes and preempt some quibbles by teaching games including rock-paper-scissors.

Forty percent of the surveyed teachers said students used the rock-(55) paper-scissors game to resolve conflicts or make decisions when they were back in class.

Coaches get involved in the activities, which "makes it possible for kids who don't see themselves as super-sporty to get into the games themselves," Ms. Vialet said. "There's just enough structure for the kids to be (60) successful."

Solving Own Problems

While adults need to be present and ready to intervene at recess if necessary, said Edward Miller, one of the founding partners of the New York City-based Alliance for Childhood, and Playworks provides that service, children should also have the opportunity for individual and small-group (65) play. ...

The Mathematica study found Playworks has a mixed effect on behaviors related to bullying: Teachers at schools with the program found that there was significantly less bullying and exclusionary behavior during recess than teachers at schools without it, but not a reduction in more (70) general aggressive behavior. Playworks has no formal curriculum that addresses the problem, Ms. Vialet noted.

"Our coaches are functioning like the older kids in the play yard used to: teaching kids rules to games, intervening if there is conflict, norming[1] behaviors around inclusion," she said.

(75)   However, researchers also found that teachers' and students' perception of aggression and bullying on the playground differed. While teachers observed that there was less name-calling, shoving of classmates, and excluding of some students from games because of Playworks, students didn't, Mathematica's Ms. James-Burdumy said. ...

—Nirvi Shah
excerpted and adapted from
"Study Weighs Benefits of Organizing Recess"
www.edweek.org, April 17, 2012

---

[1]norming—setting a standard

Text 4

Forget Goofing Around: Recess Has a New Boss

Newark — At Broadway Elementary School here, there is no more sitting around after lunch. No more goofing off with friends. No more doing nothing.

Instead there is Brandi Parker, a $14-an-hour recess coach with a
(5)   whistle around her neck, corralling children behind bright orange cones to play organized games. There she was the other day, breaking up a renegade game of hopscotch and overruling stragglers' lame excuses.

They were bored. They had tired feet. They were no good at running.

"I don't like to play," protested Esmeilyn Almendarez, 11.
(10) "Why do I have to go through this every day with you?" replied Ms. Parker, waving her back in line. "There's no choice."

Broadway Elementary brought in Ms. Parker in January out of exasperation with students who, left to their own devices, used to run into one another, squabble over balls and jump-ropes or monopolize the blacktop
(15) while exiling their classmates to the sidelines. Since she started, disciplinary referrals at recess have dropped by three-quarters, to an average of three a week. And injuries are no longer a daily occurrence.

"Before, I was seeing nosebleeds, busted lips, and students being a danger to themselves and others," said Alejandro Echevarria, the principal.
(20) "Now, Coach Brandi does miracles with 20 cones and three handballs."

The school is one of a growing number across the country that are reining in recess to curb bullying and behavior problems, foster social skills and address concerns over obesity. They also hope to show children that there is good old-fashioned fun to be had without iPods and video
(25) games. ...

Although many school officials and parents like the organized activity, its critics say it takes away the only time that children have to unwind. ...

Dr. Romina M. Barros, an assistant clinical professor at Albert Einstein College of Medicine in the Bronx who was an author of a widely
(30) cited study on the benefits of recess, published last year [2009] in the journal *Pediatrics*, says that children still benefit most from recess when they are let alone to daydream, solve problems, use their imagination to invent their own games and "be free to do what they choose to do."

Structured recess, Dr. Barros said, simply transplants the rules of the
(35) classroom to the playground.

"You still have to pay attention," she said. "You still have to follow rules. You don't have that time for your brain to relax." ...

Ms. Parker, 28, the coach at Broadway Elementary, had worked as a counselor for troubled teenagers in a group home in Burlington, N.C.
(40) Besides her work at recess, she visits each class once a week to play games that teach lessons about cooperation, sportsmanship and respect.

"These are the things that matter in life: who you are as a human being at the core," she said. ...

There are three 15-minute recesses, with more than 100 children at a
(45) time packed into a fenced-in basketball court equipped with nothing more than a pair of netless hoops.

On a chilly morning, Ms. Parker shoveled snow off the blacktop so that the students could go outside after being cooped up in the cafeteria during recess in the previous week. She drew squares in blue and green chalk for
(50) a game called switch, a fast-paced version of musical chairs—without the chairs. (She goes through a box of chalk a week.) Ms. Parker, who greets students with hugs and a cheerful "hello-hello," keeps the rules simple so that they can focus on playing rather than on following directions. "We're trying to get them to exert energy, to get it all out," she said. "They can
(55) be as loud as they want. I never tell them to be quiet unless I'm telling them something." ...

—Winnie Hu
excerpted and adapted from "Forget Goofing Around:
Recess Has a New Boss" *www.nytimes.com*, March 14, 2010

287

PART 3—Text-Analysis Response

Your Task: Closely read the text on pages 289 through 291 and write a well-developed, text-based response of two to three paragraphs. In your response, identify a central idea in the text and analyze how the author's use of **one** writing strategy (literary element or literary technique or rhetorical device) develops this central idea. Use strong and thorough evidence from the text to support your analysis. Do *not* simply summarize the text. You may use the margins to take notes as you read and scrap paper to plan your response. Write your response on a separate sheet of paper.

Guidelines:

Be sure to

- Identify a central idea in the text.
- Analyze how the author's use of **one** writing strategy (literary element or literary technique or rhetorical device) develops this central idea. Examples include: characterization, conflict, denotation/connotation, metaphor, simile, irony, language use, point-of-view, setting, structure, symbolism, theme, tone, etc.
- Use strong and thorough evidence from the text to support your analysis.
- Organize your ideas in a cohesive and coherent manner.
- Maintain a formal style of writing.
- Follow the conventions of standard written English.

Text

The following excerpt from the memoir of a South Pole explorer includes quotations from his diary.

...Then came a fateful day — Wednesday, October 27. The position was lat. [latitude] 69° 5′ S., long. [longitude] 51° 30′ W. The temperature was –8.5° Fahr. [Fahrenheit], a gentle southerly breeze was blowing and the sun shone in a clear sky. "After long months of ceaseless anxiety and
(5) strain, after times when hope beat high and times when the outlook was black indeed, the end of the *Endurance* has come. But though we have been compelled to abandon the ship, which is crushed beyond all hope of ever being righted, we are alive and well, and we have stores and equipment for the task that lies before us. The task is to reach land with all the members
(10) of the Expedition. It is hard to write what I feel. To a sailor his ship is more than a floating home, and in the *Endurance* I had centred ambitions, hopes, and desires. Now, straining and groaning, her timbers cracking and her wounds gaping, she is slowly giving up her sentient[1] life at the very outset of her career. She is crushed and abandoned after drifting more
(15) than 570 miles in a north-westerly direction during the 281 days since she became locked in the ice. The distance from the point where she became beset[2] to the place where she now rests mortally hurt in the grip of the floes[3] is 573 miles, but the total drift through all observed positions has been 1186 miles, and probably we actually covered more than 1500 miles.
(20) We are now 346 miles from Paulet Island, the nearest point where there is any possibility of finding food and shelter. A small hut built there by the Swedish expedition in 1902 is filled with stores left by the Argentine relief ship. I know all about those stores, for I purchased them in London on behalf of the Argentine Government when they asked me to equip the
(25) relief expedition. The distance to the nearest barrier west of us is about 180 miles, but a party going there would still be about 360 miles from Paulet Island and there would be no means of sustaining life on the barrier. We could not take from here food enough for the whole journey; the weight would be too great.
(30)   "This morning, our last on the ship, the weather was clear, with a gentle south-southeasterly to south-south-westerly breeze. From the crow's-nest there was no sign of land of any sort. The pressure was increas-

[1]sentient—conscious
[2]beset—hemmed in
[3]floes—ice sheets

ing steadily, and the passing hours brought no relief or respite[4] for the ship. The attack of the ice reached its climax at 4 p.m. The ship was hove[5]
(35) stern up by the pressure, and the driving floe, moving laterally across the stern, split the rudder and tore out the rudder-post and stern-post. Then, while we watched, the ice loosened and the *Endurance* sank a little. The decks were breaking upwards and the water was pouring in below. Again the pressure began, and at 5 p.m. I ordered all hands on to the ice. The
(40) twisting, grinding floes were working their will at last on the ship. It was a sickening sensation to feel the decks breaking up under one's feet, the great beams bending and then snapping with a noise like heavy gunfire. The water was overmastering the pumps, and so to avoid an explosion when it reached the boilers I had to give orders for the fires to be drawn[6]
(45) and the steam let down. The plans for abandoning the ship in case of emergency had been made well in advance, and men and dogs descended to the floe and made their way to the comparative safety of an unbroken portion of the floe without a hitch. Just before leaving, I looked down the engine-room skylight as I stood on the quivering deck, and saw the engines drop-
(50) ping sideways as the stays and bed-plates gave way. I cannot describe the impression of relentless destruction that was forced upon me as I looked down and around. The floes, with the force of millions of tons of moving ice behind them, were simply annihilating the ship." ...

"To-night the temperature has dropped to −16° Fahr., and most of
(55) the men are cold and uncomfortable. After the tents had been pitched I mustered all hands and explained the position to them briefly and, I hope, clearly. I have told them the distance to the barrier and the distance to Paulet Island, and have stated that I propose to try to march with equipment across the ice in the direction of Paulet Island. I thanked the men for
(60) the steadiness and good *morale* they have shown in these trying circumstances, and told them I had no doubt that, provided they continued to work their utmost and to trust me, we will all reach safety in the end. Then we had supper, which the cook had prepared at the big blubber stove, and after a watch[7] had been set all hands except the watch turned in."
(65) For myself, I could not sleep. The destruction and abandonment of the ship was no sudden shock. The disaster had been looming ahead for many months, and I had studied my plans for all contingencies[8] a hundred times.

---

[4]respite—rest
[5]hove—heaved
[6]drawn—closed
[7]watch — crewman who stays awake on guard all night
[8]contingencies — possibilities

But the thoughts that came to me as I walked up and down in the darkness
were not particularly cheerful. The task now was to secure the safety of the
(70)   party, and to that I must bend my energies and mental power and apply
every bit of knowledge that experience of the Antarctic had given me. The
task was likely to be long and strenuous, and an ordered mind and a clear
programme were essential if we were to come through without loss of
life. A man must shape himself to a new mark directly the old one goes to
(75)   ground. ...

—Sir Ernest Shackleton
excepted and adapted from *South*, 1920
The MacMillan Company

Regents ELA (Common Core) Answers June 2017
English Language Arts

Answer Key

Part 1

1. 1	9. 1	17. 1
2. 2	10. 3	18. 3
3. 4	11. 1	19. 2
4. 3	12. 3	20. 4
5. 1	13. 4	21. 1
6. 4	14. 2	22. 2
7. 3	15. 3	23. 2
8. 1	16. 4	24. 3

INDEX